The
Copyeditor's
Handbook

# The Copyeditor's Handbook

A Guide for Book Publishing
and Corporate Communications

*Fourth Edition*
REVISED, UPDATED, AND EXPANDED

AMY EINSOHN AND
MARILYN SCHWARTZ

UNIVERSITY OF CALIFORNIA PRESS

University of California Press, one of the most distinguished university presses in the United States, enriches lives around the world by advancing scholarship in the humanities, social sciences, and natural sciences. Its activities are supported by the UC Press Foundation and by philanthropic contributions from individuals and institutions. For more information, visit www.ucpress.edu.

University of California Press
Oakland, California

Library of Congress Cataloging-in-Publication Data

Names: Einsohn, Amy, author. | Schwartz, Marilyn, author.
Title: The copyeditor's handbook : a guide for book publishing and corporate communications / Amy Einsohn and Marilyn Schwartz.
Description: Fourth edition, revised, updated, and expanded. | Oakland, California : University of California Press, [2019] | Includes bibliographical references and index.
Identifiers: LCCN 2018042184 | ISBN 9780520286726 (pbk. : alk. paper) | ISBN 9780520972278 (pdf)
Subjects: LCSH: Copy editing—Handbooks, manuals, etc. | Editing—Handbooks, manuals, etc. | Journalism, Commercial—Editing—Handbooks, manuals, etc.
Classification: LCC PN4784.C75 E37 2019 | DDC 808.02/7—dc23
LC record available at https://lccn.loc.gov/2018042184

Manufactured in the United States of America

27  26  25  24  23  22  21  20  19
10  9  8  7  6  5  4  3  2

*For Amy*

# Contents

# Preface to the Fourth Edition

*The Copyeditor's Handbook* began, like numerous books, in a conversation many years ago. At the time, Amy Einsohn was running a freelance editing business; I was supervising a staff of production editors at the University of California Press. We both also moonlighted as instructors of copyediting for UC Berkeley Extension's program and the local freelance cooperative Editcetera. Whenever our paths crossed, we would stop to chat about our work and to commiserate over the dearth of instructional material for our students. Someone, we agreed, should write a book for aspiring copyeditors. Eventually, Amy wrote that book, and in 2000 UC Press published her now-indispensable introduction to professional editing. As Amy's editor, I steered the *Handbook* through its initial publication and the production of two subsequent editions.

Amy's book was unstuffy, hip, and often funny—traits not normally associated with copyediting. It demolished zombie rules of grammar and usage (those undead hordes of proscriptions against split infinitives and other imaginary faults) by advocating the counsel of professional linguists and lexicographers. It described the emerging procedures for on-screen editing at the end of the era when many editors still marked copy with No. 1 Ticonderoga pencils and queried authors on seas of yellow Post-its affixed to the margins of a manuscript. It offered technical tips, introduced new digital resources for editors, and adjudicated transformations in language and in the formal conventions for written English that were being accelerated by the internet, email, and social media.

With each fresh edition, Amy refined, amplified, and updated content to keep pace with changes in editorial practice, but she was constrained, despite her genius at copyfitting, by the need to shoehorn revisions into the original pages, which served as camera-ready copy for the printer. In time, we started to plan a more substantial revision of the *Handbook,* along with the creation of a new *Copyeditor's Workbook,* a complementary volume of student exercises, in both print and digital form, that would greatly expand upon the fifteen assignments originally bound into the *Handbook.*

Regrettably, Amy's declining health prevented her from completing these projects. But she bequeathed extensive notes for retooling and expanding her entire *Handbook* in this fourth edition, a task I undertook at the bidding of UC Press and with the gracious permission of her husband, Chris Raisner. In revising the *Handbook,* I have followed Amy's own tracks—more than one hundred thousand words of stenographic "marginalia" and scores of articles, blog posts, email exchanges, and links saved in her computer files—and have also incorporated the latest advice from editing professionals, language authorities, usage guides, and new editions of major style manuals, including *The Chicago Manual of Style.*

Tectonic shifts in the publishing industry have affected twenty-first-century copyediting in ways that Amy could not have foreseen when she first wrote the *Handbook,* and I have tried to address these changes as well. No longer do editors merely groom manuscripts for print production as books and corporate reports: they often prepare text for several formats, including e-book publication, print-on-demand (POD) distribution, PDF output, digital sampling, and a concurrent existence or an afterlife on the web. Editors are also using, sometimes improvising, new tools, such as PDF markup, collaborative writing software, videoconferencing, and institutional clients' proprietary production systems. They are expected to know how to emend text for global audiences; to conform manuscripts to governmental mandates for "plain language" (which is actually a thing); to edit the writing of nonnative English speakers; and sometimes to comply with accessibility requirements.

With the disappearance of many staff copyediting positions, more editors are plying their trade as freelancers. The new *Handbook* anticipates the demands of their increasingly diversified clientele, which includes soaring numbers of independent (self-publishing) authors, international scholars writing in English as a foreign language, and the intermediaries that have sprung up to serve such constituencies. In this new Wild West of publishing, I argue, editors must forge a professional code of ethics, establish independent standards, and undertake continuous self-education. And they must be prepared to negotiate the inevitable mission creep—the expectation that "copyediting" encompasses the full suite of services once provided by an entire team of specialists or the staff of a traditional publishing house—while never abandoning the copyeditor's prime directive: Remember that words matter.

---

I will always be grateful to Amy for her editorial wisdom and her friendship. When I was still a green and overzealous editor, she inspired me to relax some priggish rules of grammar I embraced after years of parochial school and graduate education. I am indebted as well to my many former colleagues in UC Press's Editing Department, who gently prompted me to become a better leader and a more technically adept editor, and whose unflagging support (and excellent humor) sustained me in my long career at the press.

I am deeply appreciative of the help provided by UC Press at every stage of this project. Eric Schmidt, my acquiring editor, has graciously finessed the relationship with this headstrong managing-editor-turned-author. Considering my occasional impatience with wayward authors during my former role at the press, I'm especially thankful for the consideration he has shown me. (I've learned a few things by walking a mile in an author's shoes.) Despite my all-too-predictable delays and missteps in completing authorial tasks by the specified deadlines, Archna Patel guided me through final manuscript preparation with admirable forbearance and professionalism.

Steven Baker, Alice Falk, and Barbara Fuller provided thorough—and sometimes chastening—peer reviews of the draft manuscript. Thanks to their diligence and long lists of corrections and suggestions, I've avoided numerous pratfalls. This book has profited immeasurably from their rigorous evaluations.

The imperturbable Dore Brown once told me that she considered part of her project editor's role as that of balancing the somewhat unequal relationship between author and publisher. How fortunate I am to have, as ballast, her tranquil influence and empathy, as well as her patient attention to the many demands of making this the best book possible!

I am particularly grateful to Juliana Froggatt, my copyeditor, who bravely faced the challenge of schooling an old-school editor. She pruned my excesses, emended my departures from editorial style (except where I resisted), and delicately queried my many faults and errors. As an author once said to me, it is most flattering to have someone read your manuscript even more closely than you have.

Claudia Smelser designed the cover and provided in-house artistic direction for this book, and Barbara Haines—who long ago designed the original edition from my rococo list of handwritten markup codes—crafted the interior and composed the pages of this new edition. Two ace proofreaders, Anne Canright and Barbara Armentrout, pored over the typeset proofs. And the redoubtable Do Mi Stauber prepared the index.

Many individuals offered advice, read excerpts, supplied information, and gave moral support during my revisions to this book. Mark Allen kindly shared his knowledge of dictionary editions with me. Bonnie Britt counseled me on Associated Press style and described her workflow for self-publishing authors. Erika Búky vetted descriptions of Unicode and other technical passages and, incidentally, taught me how to type the Hungarian long $u$ in her surname. Beth Jusino generously shared the syllabus from her workshop for independent authors. Scott Norton answered my questions about accessibility requirements for publishers and tolerated my excited monologues about esoterica discovered during my research for this book. David Peattie served as a ready resource for production questions.

Thanks are also due to the *literally* thousands of colleagues who continue to contribute to my education through editorial email lists and online discussion boards. As a long-time lurker (I should say, *reader*), I have benefited immensely over the years from the information, advice, conversations, and opinions of many publishing professionals in the vast online editorial community. I salute the hive mind!

With the considerable help of all these friends and associates, I've tried to remove every trace of error from this book. I alone am responsible for any remaining blemishes. Authors and editors aspire to perfection, but, under Muphry's Law (a little-known corollary of Murphy's Law), a copyeditor writing about copyediting is bound to err. I ask only that discerning readers remember Amy Einsohn's own tolerance for writers' frailties.

Finally, I acknowledge my personal entourage: Harvey Schwartz, who still believes I'm a "fantastic editor" after fifty years of marriage and his own experience as a much-published professional historian; and our son, David, who once crowned me the Grammar Queen and still sometimes brightens my inbox with grammar cartoons.

Marilyn Schwartz
2019

# Preface to the Third Edition

This handbook is addressed to new and aspiring copyeditors who will be working on nonfiction books, journal articles, newsletters, and corporate publications. Many of the topics will also be of interest to copyeditors working for newspapers and magazines, although I do not discuss the editorial conventions peculiar to journalism.

One of the first things a new copyeditor learns is that there are two general-purpose style manuals (*The Chicago Manual of Style* and *Words into Type*), two widely used scientific style manuals (*Publication Manual of the American Psychological Association* and *Scientific Style and Format: The CSE Manual*), and a variety of specialized style manuals. (All the manuals are discussed in chapter 3.) This guide is intended as a supplement to, not a substitute for, an editorial style manual.

Given that each of those manuals runs hundreds of pages, you might wonder why a copyeditor would need this handbook in addition. One reason is that although all the manuals are filled with rules, preferences, exceptions, and examples, they assume that their readers already understand what copyeditors do, why the rules matter, and how and when to apply, bend, or break the rules. Second, because the manuals are addressed to both copyeditors and authors, they do not discuss the procedures peculiar to copyediting, nor the kinds of minute-by-minute decisions that copyeditors make.

Here's the example I used in the second edition of this book. In 2005 I was editing a memo intended to help employees manage their email. The manuscript read: "You'll find it easier to locate a particular message if you folderize your emails." "Folderize your emails" piqued my curiosity: Was *folderize* a widely recognized word? If so, was this writer using it correctly? Would the company's employees understand it? Might some, recalling their schoolroom Strunk and White, snicker?[1] What was it that readers were to

---

NOTE: Amy Einsohn's preface to the previous edition of *The Copyeditor's Handbook* is here reproduced in its original form, with two exceptions: portions of "Tips for Using This Book" have been updated to reflect revisions in this new edition; the abbreviations and conventions used in the book have been revised and moved to a separate front matter section.

1. After labeling *customize, prioritize,* and *finalize* as "abominations," Strunk and White lay down the law: "Never tack *-ize* onto a noun to create a verb. Usually you will discover that a useful verb already exists. Why say 'moisturize' when there is the simple, unpretentious word *moisten*?" (*Elements of Style,* pp. 50–51). Because, dear sirs, the remedy for dry skin is not to moisten it (make it slightly wet) but to moisturize it (rub in a small amount of an emollient that is to be absorbed). And even if these words were closer in meaning, can writers and speakers ever have too many synonyms?

Fortunately, dozens of verbs made their way into the language before Strunk and White's edict: agonize, alphabetize, apologize, categorize, demonize, deputize, digitize, emphasize, hospitalize, idolize, itemize, lionize, monopolize, patronize, philosophize, satirize, serialize, sermonize, stigmatize, symbolize, terrorize, unionize, vandalize, winterize.

folderize: their emails (count noun) or their email (mass noun)? Did the company's style guide recommend *email* or *e-mail?*

I was working on a tight deadline, and the schedule called for me to edit roughly 1,500 words an hour. The most practical, most efficient way to handle the sentence was to propose that the writer revise it, and I wrote him a quick note: "*Folderize* too techie for your readers? How about: You'll find it easier to locate a particular message if you save your messages in folders—one for each of your projects or clients."

A week later, after I was off the clock, I sought to satisfy my curiosity. I began with *folderize:* Nothing in any of my print dictionaries, nothing at www.onelook.com, and nothing when I typed "definition:folderize" in the Google search box. At that time Google displayed only ninety-five hits for the term. Many of these were from blogs and e-bulletinboards, but a handful were from edited publications, for example:

> Sure, you can categorize and folderize all of your links for easy finding, but a really savvy and cool way to access all of the sites you regularly visit is to create what's called a Start page, or in my case, a Super Kickstart page. (Alexandra Krasne, GeekTech column, PC World website, April 27, 2004)

At least one computer-literate employee wondered about the term: "I've also heard 'folderize' at my work, and I'm still trying to figure out exactly what is meant by it! Is that like 'filing'?" (www.ezboard.com, undated). Another used scare quotes: "I need to be able to 'folderize' emails on arrival, so I can keep jobs separate" (www.mobileminds .com, undated). One writer pounced on the term to characterize the speaker: "'It's better to spend one hour getting organized than to spend 10 hours being frustrated,' says the woman who uses verbs like 'folderize'" (www.wright.edu/news_events, November 1998).

A patent application (March 2004) doubled my pleasure by introducing a normalizer to do the folderizing: "A normalizer adaptively tailors and folderizes markup based information content. . . . The user of the electronic device can then further explore the folders of interest as desired."

I concluded that *folderize* was for now the property of the techies. Even among the in crowd, various meanings of *folderize* seemed to radiate from the core notion of sorting digital information into folders. And though I don't blink at *prioritize* or *moisturize,* I was taught to be suspicious of newfangled terms ending in *-ize.*[2] Delicate sensibilities aside, *folderize* seems to fill a semantic need, and I suspect it will move into general circulation someday soon.

---

2. Two usage notes in *Merriam-Webster's Collegiate Dictionary* (11th ed., 2003) attest to the ubiquity of this prejudice in certain circles:

The suffix *-ize* has been productive in English since the time of Thomas Nashe (1567–1601). . . . Nashe noted in 1591 that his *-ize* coinages were being criticized, and to this day new words ending in *-ize* . . . are sure to draw critical fire.

*Finalize* has been frequently castigated as an unnecessary neologism or as United States government gobbledygook. It appears to have first gained currency in Australia (where it has been acceptable all along) in the early 1920s. . . . Currently, it is most frequently used in government and business dealings; it usually is not found in belles-lettres.

My research into *email* was easier: both *e-mail* and *email* are in current use. In conversation, I have heard *e-mail* used as a count noun ("He sent me six e-mails on this topic alone!") and as a mass noun ("We received a lot of e-mail on this topic"), and the examples in *Merriam-Webster's Collegiate* showed both usages.

Of course, working copyeditors usually cannot devote hours to researching a word or two. Instead, as they go about their job of advising authors and mending manuscripts, copyeditors develop judgment about when to leave something alone, when to ask the author to recast, and when to propose a revision. Some problems are easily solved: there is only one correct way to spell *accordion*. But many questions do not have a single correct answer, and these require the copyeditor to consult more than one reference book, to identify and weigh conflicting opinions, and to make an informed decision about when to apply, adapt, or ignore various conventions and rules. This guide is intended to help you make just those sorts of informed decisions.

## TIPS FOR USING THIS BOOK

1. The sequence of chapters in this book follows the order I use in teaching copyediting courses. We explore the general tasks, procedures, and processes (part 1) before scrutinizing the mechanical conventions (part 2), and then we look at grammar, organization, and other "big picture" topics (part 3). You may, however, prefer to read part 3 before part 2.

2. If you are perplexed by a term, consult the Glossary of Copyediting Terms and the Glossary of Grammar Terms at the back of the book. You could also check the index to see if the term is discussed elsewhere in the book.

3. Most of the recommendations in part 2 follow those stated in *The Chicago Manual of Style,* but widely used alternatives are also discussed. To locate the precise point in one of these style manuals, consult that manual's index.

4. Cross-references within the text are by first-level head and chapter number; all first-level heads are listed in the table of contents. (If you're wondering why the cross-references are not to page numbers, see the discussion of cross-referencing under "Organization" in chapter 15.)

5. Because *The Chicago Manual of Style* is the style manual used by the University of California Press, this book was copyedited to conform to that manual. Eagle-eyed readers, however, will notice a few spots in which the editorial style here diverges from *Chicago*, especially on some matters of hyphenation (see "One Word or Two?" in chapter 5). Kindly construe all errors in the text as opportunities for you to exercise your editorial acumen.

## ACKNOWLEDGMENTS

Since the mid-1980s I have taught copyediting classes to hundreds of students, both in Berkeley, California, and through correspondence study. I want to thank all these students for their inquisitiveness and high spirits as we explored the picayune aspects of the copyeditor's life.

I am also grateful to the two people most responsible for my editorial career: Gracia Alkema, the first managing editor to hire me as a freelancer (at Jossey-Bass in San Francisco), and Marilyn Schwartz, managing editor of the University of California Press, who has always given wise answers to my questions. She also guided this book from acquisition through production with meticulous care and unflagging enthusiasm. Barbara Ras—first at the University of California Press, then at North Point Press, and later at Trinity University Press—has been extremely helpful and generous. Many other editors at California—Rose Vekony and Mary Lamprech, in particular—and dozens of my colleagues in Editcetera (a Bay Area editors' co-op) have offered valuable professional advice over the years.

Suzanne Knott did a first-rate job on the editorial equivalent of deciphering a lithograph by Escher (copyediting a manuscript about copyediting written by a copyeditor). All the remaining mechanical inconsistencies and errors are mine and represent instances when I failed to heed her advice.

Barbara Jellow designed this book, Anne Canright and Desne Border did the proofreading, Zippie Collins reviewed the Answer Keys, and Elinor Lindheimer wrote the first draft of the index. I thank and salute all of them for their skills and assistance.

The support of long-time friends Carolyn Tipton, Ellen Frankel, Laura Rivkin, and Evan Frances Agnew has made all the difference. Above all, I thank my husband, Chris Raisner, for sweetly nudging me to finish this book.

Amy Einsohn
2011

# Abbreviations and Conventions

The following abbreviations and short titles are used for works frequently cited in the text. Online dictionaries that differ from their similarly titled print counterparts are further identified as "online" when they are specifically referenced. Some locators are given as numbered paragraphs (e.g., *Chicago* 7.89) or as alphabetical entries *sub verbo*, "under the word" (e.g., s.v. "hopefully"), rather than as page numbers.

| | |
|---|---|
| *AHD* | *American Heritage Dictionary of the English Language*, 5th ed. |
| *AP Stylebook* | *The Associated Press Stylebook and Briefing on Media Law 2018* |
| *APA* | *Publication Manual of the American Psychological Association*, 6th ed. |
| *Butcher's* | Judith Butcher, Caroline Drake, and Maureen Leach, *Butcher's Copy-editing*, 4th ed. |
| *Chicago* | *The Chicago Manual of Style*, 17th ed. |
| *CSE* | *Scientific Style and Format: The CSE Manual for Authors, Editors, and Publishers*, 8th ed. |
| *DEU* | *Merriam-Webster's Dictionary of English Usage* |
| *Fowler's* | *Fowler's Dictionary of Modern English Usage*, 4th ed., ed. Jeremy Butterfield |
| *Garner's* | *Garner's Modern English Usage*, 4th ed. |
| *GPO* | *GPO Style Manual: An Official Guide to the Form and Style of Federal Government Publishing*, 31st ed. |
| *Gregg* | *The Gregg Reference Manual*, 11th ed. |
| *MAU* | Wilson Follett, *Modern American Usage: A Guide*, rev. ed. |
| *M-W Collegiate* | *Merriam-Webster's Collegiate Dictionary*, 11th ed. |
| *M-W Unabridged* | *Merriam-Webster Unabridged* (online) |
| *WIT* | *Words into Type*, 3rd ed. |

Complete bibliographical details for these and other cited works are provided in the Selected Bibliography or in notes.

Frequently used technical terms are italicized and explained at or near the first occurrence in the text; key concepts are defined in the Glossary of Copyediting Terms or the Glossary of Grammar Terms.

Indisputably incorrect sample sentences are preceded by the symbol ✗. An explanation, a corrected version, or both follow. Sample sentences that are unsatisfactory but not incorrect are preceded by a label such as *Weak* or *Tangled*.

# PART 1

# ❡ The ABCs of Copyediting

THE THREE CHAPTERS in this part introduce the craft of copyediting. Chapter 1 outlines the copyeditor's responsibilities and principal tasks. Chapter 2 shows how copyeditors hand-mark manuscripts and edit on-screen. Chapter 3 describes a variety of reference works and online resources for copyeditors.

# ¶ What Copyeditors Do

Copyeditors always serve the needs of three constituencies:

> the author(s)—the person (or people) who wrote or compiled the manuscript
> the publisher—the individual or company that is paying the cost of producing
>     and distributing the material
> the readers—the people for whom the material is being produced

All these parties share one basic desire: an error-free publication. To that end, the copy-editor acts as the author's second pair of eyes, pointing out—and usually correcting—mechanical errors and inconsistencies; errors or infelicities of grammar, usage, and syntax; and errors or inconsistencies in content. If you like alliterative mnemonic devices, you can conceive of a copyeditor's chief concerns as comprising the "4 Cs"—clarity, coherency, consistency, and correctness—in service of the "Cardinal C": communication.

Certain projects require the copyeditor to serve as more than a second set of eyes. Heavier intervention may be needed, for example, when the author does not have native or near-native fluency in English, when the author is a professional or a technical expert writing for a lay audience, when the author is addressing a readership with limited English proficiency, or when the author has not been careful in preparing the manuscript.

Sometimes, too, copyeditors find themselves juggling the conflicting needs and desires of their constituencies. For example, the author may feel that the manuscript requires no more than a quick read-through to correct a handful of typographical errors, while the publisher, believing that a firmer hand would benefit the final product, instructs the copyeditor to prune verbose passages. Or a budget-conscious publisher may ask the copyeditor to attend to only the most egregious errors, while the author is hoping for a conscientious sentence-by-sentence polishing of the text.

Different publishing environments tend to favor different constituencies. Self-publishing authors—sometimes called independent, or *indie,* authors—may hire an editor directly; as both author and publisher, indie authors control all decisions about their manuscripts. Companies that serve indie clients or that publish writers with special subject expertise or artistic license usually cater to authors as well, whereas commercial and corporate publishers may elevate financial goals or the needs of end users over their authors' prerogatives. Regardless of the culture and politics of a particular working environment, copyeditors always serve other constituencies, not their own vanity, and must therefore exercise a degree of self-effacement. The mantra of professional copyeditors everywhere is this: "It's not my manuscript."

Traditional book and journal publishers and some of the large production services often make an initial determination of a manuscript's editorial needs and do some preliminary manuscript preparation before transmitting the job. Copyeditors who work for such clients are thus usually given general instructions, and sometimes even an edited sample, specifying how light or heavy a hand to apply; manuscript files may already be cleaned up and prepared for editing, permissions secured, and the illustration program set. But no one looks over the copyeditor's shoulder, giving detailed advice about how much or how little to do line by line. Publishing professionals use the term *editorial judgment* to denote a copyeditor's intuition and instincts about when to intervene, when to leave well enough alone, and when to ask the author to rework a sentence or a paragraph. In addition to having a good eye and ear for language, copyeditors must develop a sixth sense about how much effort, and what kind of effort, to put into each project that crosses their desk.

In the pre-computer era, copyeditors used pencils or pens and marked their changes and questions on a typewritten manuscript. Today few copyeditors still work on hard copy; most use a computer and key in their work—a process variously called *on-screen editing, electronic manuscript (EMS) editing,* or *online editing.* This last term can be misleading, since editing on a computer does not necessarily involve a connection to the internet or to a local area network. But in practice, on-screen editors need an internet connection to access online resources—online reference works, file storage and exchange services, and backup utilities—as they work. A few on-screen editing and production systems are in fact entirely web-based.

Some on-screen editors make do with the limited functionality of open-source word processors, such as Apache OpenOffice or LibreOffice, or of the proprietary Pages (Apple) or InCopy (Adobe). But many editors currently use Microsoft Word and must, at minimum, develop sufficient skill in this software to edit efficiently. Editors in an office or other environment where multiple individuals work on a document together may employ a collaborative writing application, such as Google Docs, following a carefully defined work process to ensure version control (see "Computer Skills" in chapter 2). Or editors may—somewhat reluctantly—undertake the laborious editing of PDF files using a stylus or the markup and comment tools of free or purchased PDF readers, such as Adobe Acrobat Reader or Adobe Acrobat Pro. Clients may sometimes expect an editor to correct material prepared in other applications (even if marking changes is cumbersome), such as Excel, PowerPoint, or InDesign, or to use the client's own proprietary software or production platform. Indeed, some of these current applications may be superseded by entirely new tools before the information in this paragraph is even published. But here is the point: given the range of possible requirements for on-screen work and the continuous evolution of technology, editors must cultivate proficiency in several major applications, systematically follow new technological developments affecting their work, and regularly update their hardware, software, and technical skills.

Regardless of the medium and the editing tools, a copyeditor must read a document letter by letter, word by word, with excruciating care and attentiveness. In many ways, being a copyeditor is like sitting for an English exam that never ends: at every moment, your knowledge of spelling, grammar, punctuation, usage, syntax, and diction is being tested.

You're not expected to be perfect, though. Every copyeditor misses errors here and there. According to one study of human error rates, 95 percent accuracy is the best a human can do. To pass the certification test administered by Editors Canada, an applicant must score approximately 80 percent or higher.[1] And, as experienced editors know, accuracy declines in an error-riddled manuscript. Software tools such as the ones listed in the Selected Bibliography can reduce the number of distracting, low-level faults before an editor even begins reading in earnest. Many traditional editorial processes also winnow errors by requiring multiple reviews of a text by different sets of eyes—peer evaluators or beta readers, editors, authors, proofreaders—at successive stages of production. Still, despite every care, fugitive faults are inevitable. In the published text they will twinkle like tiny fairy lights, probably visible only to the mortified copyeditor and a few exceptionally discriminating readers.

Don't beat yourself up over such tiny oversights; learn from them. And always respect the four commandments of copyediting:

1. Thou shalt not lose or damage the manuscript or muddle versions of the files.
2. Thou shalt not introduce an error into a text that is correct. As in other areas of life, in copyediting an act of commission is more serious than an act of omission.
3. Thou shalt not change the author's meaning. In the hierarchy of editorial errors, replacing the author's wording with language the copyeditor simply likes better is a transgression, but changing the author's meaning is a mortal offense.
4. Thou shalt not miss a critical deadline.

## PRINCIPAL TASKS

Copyediting is one step in the iterative process by which a manuscript is turned into a final published product (e.g., a book, an annual corporate report, a newsletter, a web document). Here, we will quickly survey the copyeditor's six principal tasks; the procedures and conventions for executing these tasks are described in the chapters that follow.

---

1. Adrienne Montgomerie, "Error Rates in Editing," *Copyediting,* Aug. 7, 2013, https://www .copyediting.com/error-rates-in-editing/. Is there a difference in error rates between hard-copy editing and on-screen editing? There are too many variables for a scientifically valid comparison, but most editors have adapted to both the benefits and the limitations of on-screen work. Besides using the powerful tools available in word processing applications to reduce much time-consuming drudgery, they typically make adjustments to the digital medium—e.g., eliminating on-screen distractions from incoming messages, magnifying text to suppress the habit of scanning rather than reading digital content closely, changing background colors on the monitor, reducing the brightness of the backlit screen, and taking frequent short breaks to avoid eyestrain.

## 1. MECHANICAL EDITING

The heart of copyediting consists of making a manuscript conform to an *editorial style,* also called *house style*—a term deriving from the practices of a given "publishing house" or a company's "house of business." Editorial style includes

> spelling
> hyphenation
> capitalization
> punctuation
> treatment of numbers and numerals
> treatment of quotations
> use of initialisms, acronyms, and other abbreviations
> use of italics and bold type
> treatment of special elements (e.g., headings, lists, tables, charts, graphs)
> format of footnotes or endnotes and other documentation

*Mechanical editing* comprises all editorial interventions made to ensure conformity to house style. There is nothing mechanical, however, about mechanical editing; it requires a sharp eye, a solid grasp of a wide range of conventions, and good judgment. The mistake most frequently made by novice copyeditors is to rewrite portions of a text (for better or for worse, depending on the copyeditor's writing skills) and to ignore such "minor details" as capitalization, punctuation, and hyphenation. Wrong! Whatever else you are asked to do, you are expected to repair any mechanical inconsistencies in the manuscript.

For an example of the differences purely mechanical editing can make in the look and feel—but not the meaning—of a document, compare these selections from articles that appeared on the same day in the *New York Times* and the *San Francisco Examiner.*

---

*New York Times*
February 22, 1987
**TARGET QADDAFI**
By Seymour M. Hersh

Eighteen American warplanes set out from Lakenheath Air Base in England last April 14 to begin a 14-hour, 5,400-mile round-trip flight to Tripoli, Libya. It is now clear that nine of those Air Force F-111's had an unprecedented peacetime mission. Their targets: Col. Muammar el-Qaddafi and his family. . . .

Since early 1981, the Central Intelligence Agency had been encouraging and abetting Libyan exile groups and foreign governments, especially those of Egypt and France, in their efforts to stage a coup d'état. . . . Now the supersonic Air Force F-111's were ordered to accomplish what the C.I.A. could not.

*San Francisco Examiner*
February 22, 1987
**TARGET GADHAFI**
By Seymour M. Hersh

Eighteen U.S. warplanes set out from Lakenheath Air Base in England last April 14 to begin a 14-hour, 5,400-mile round-trip flight to Tripoli, Libya. It is now clear that nine of those Air Force F-111s had an unprecedented peacetime mission. Their targets: Col. Moammar Gadhafi and his family. . . .

Since early 1981, the CIA had been encouraging and abetting Libyan exile groups and foreign governments, especially those of Egypt and France, in their efforts to stage a coup d'etat. . . . Now the supersonic Air Force F-111s were ordered to accomplish what the CIA could not.

---

Which is correct? (Or which is "more correct"?): American warplanes or U.S. warplanes? Col. Muammar el-Qaddafi or Col. Moammar Gadhafi? F-111's or F-111s? coup d'état or coup d'etat? C.I.A. or CIA? In each case, the choice is not a matter of correctness per se but of preference, and the sum total of such preferences constitutes an editorial style. A copyeditor's job is to ensure that the manuscript conforms to the publisher's editorial style; if the publisher does not have a house style, the copyeditor must make sure that the author has been consistent in selecting among acceptable variants.

At book publishing firms, scholarly journals, newspapers, and magazines, a house style is generated by having all copyeditors use the same dictionary and the same style manual (e.g., *The Chicago Manual of Style, Words into Type, The Associated Press Stylebook, Publication Manual of the American Psychological Association*). In contrast, companies that produce documents, reports, brochures, catalogs, or newsletters but do not consider themselves to be bona fide publishers often rely on in-house style guides, on general lists of do's and don'ts, or on the judgments and preferences of copyeditors and *editorial coordinators.*[2] Besides a few guidelines for the mechanics listed above (and possibly some idiosyncratic preferences reflecting the particular business culture), a company's house style guide is likely to contain specific instructions for handling its corporate and product names, trademarks, and logos.

The purpose of a house style is to ensure consistency within multiauthor publications (magazines, journals, reports, collaborative books), within a series of publications, and across similar publications. Rigorous consistency is needed, for example, in the form of source citations to support online searches for bibliographical information in a database of journal issues. A house style may also be mandated for purposes of corporate branding. Or it may simply be required for the sake of expediency: editors usually find it easier to enforce a house style than to extrapolate each individual author's preferences and apply them consistently in that author's manuscript. But even when a house style exists, it may sometimes yield to an author's own style choices—at the copyeditor's discretion and with authorization from the editorial coordinator—owing to special manuscript content, an author's strongly held preferences, or simple convenience. Case in point: The University of Chicago Press itself, home of the authoritative *Chicago Manual of Style,* allows exceptions to its house style when, for example, an author has consistently followed a justifiable alternative style and Chicago's editor judges that no value is added by undertaking the substantial work of changing it.

## 2. CORRELATING PARTS

Unless the manuscript is very short and simple, the copyeditor must devote special attention to correlating its parts. Such tasks include

---

2. I use the term *editorial coordinator* to denote the person who is supervising an in-house copyeditor or who is assigning work to a freelance copyeditor. In book publishing, this person's title may be *managing editor, chief copyeditor, production editor,* or *project editor.* In other industries, the title begins with a modifier like *communications, pubs* (short for "publications"), or *documentation* and concludes with one of the following nouns: *manager, editor, specialist.*

verifying any cross-references that appear in the text

checking the numbering of footnotes, endnotes, tables, and illustrations

specifying the placement of (callouts for) tables and illustrations

checking the content of the illustrations against the captions and against the text

reading the list of illustrations against the captions and comparing the entries in
the list to the illustrations themselves

reading the table of contents against the headings in the manuscript

reading the footnotes or endnotes against the bibliography

Some types of texts require special cross-checking. For example, in cookbooks the list of ingredients that precedes a recipe must be read against the recipe: Is every ingredient in the initial list used in the recipe? Does every ingredient used in the recipe appear in the list of ingredients? Similarly, when copyediting other kinds of how-to texts, one may need to check whether the list of equipment or parts matches the instructions.

## 3. LANGUAGE EDITING: GRAMMAR, USAGE, AND DICTION

Copyeditors also correct—or ask the author to correct—errors or lapses in grammar, usage, and diction.[3] Ideally, copyeditors set right whatever is incorrect, unidiomatic, confusing, ambiguous, or inappropriate without attempting to impose their stylistic preferences or prejudices on the author.

The "rules" for language editing are far more subjective than those for mechanical editing. Most copyeditors come to trust a small set of usage books and then to rely on their own judgment when the books offer conflicting recommendations or fail to illuminate a particular issue. Indeed, the "correct" usage choice may vary from manuscript to manuscript, depending on the publisher's house style, the conventions in the author's field, and the expectations of the intended audience.

A small example: Many copyeditors who work for academic presses and scholarly journals have been taught to treat *data* as a plural noun, a convention long upheld by grammatical purists and still observed in economics and in some scientific writing (e.g., The data for 1999 are not available). But copyeditors in corporate communications departments are often expected to treat *data* as a singular noun (The data for 1999 is not available).[4] Moreover, a corporate copyeditor is likely to accept *1999* as an adjective and

---

3. *The Chicago Manual of Style* defines *grammar* as "the set of rules governing how words are put together in sentences to communicate ideas"; native speakers learn and usually apply these rules unconsciously (5.1). Grammar includes *syntax* (the construction of phrases, clauses, and sentences) and *morphology* (the forms of words). But "the great mass of linguistic issues that writers and editors wrestle with don't really concern grammar at all"; rather, they concern *usage*, "the collective habits of a language's native speakers" (5.249)—especially the habits of educated speakers and the conventions of what is called Standard Written English. *Diction* simply means word choice.

4. The origin of the controversy lies in the etymology of *data*, which is the plural form of *datum* in Latin but functions differently in English: "*Data* occurs in two constructions: as a plural noun (like *earnings*), taking a plural verb and certain plural modifiers (such as *these, many, a few of*) but not cardinal numbers, and serving as a referent for plural pronouns (such as *they, them*); and as an abstract mass

to favor contractions (The 1999 data isn't available). Whether a copyeditor uses *data* as a plural noun with a plural verb or as a mass noun with a singular verb, someone may object. A judicious editor must consult the publisher's style guide and follow the custom of the specific subject matter—or substitute a less vexed word, such as *information, statistics, facts, reports,* or *figures.*

A second example: Between the 1960s and the late 1980s, many prominent usage experts denounced the use of *hopefully* as a sentence adverb, and copyeditors were instructed to revise "Hopefully, the crisis will end soon" to read "It is to be hoped that the crisis will end soon." Almost all members of the anti-*hopefully* faction have since recanted, though some people, unaware that the battle has ended, continue what they believe to be the good fight.[5]

In navigating such controversies, what should a copyeditor do? The answer in a given situation requires editorial judgment, the thoughtful consideration of such factors as the desired level of formality or informality (the *register*), the author's preferences, the publisher's brand, and the likely reactions of readers.

"Words do not live in dictionaries," Virginia Woolf observed; "they live in the mind."[6] The history of *hopefully* serves as a reminder that there are fads and fashions, crotchets and crazes, in that cultural creation known as usage. For copyeditors who work on corporate publications, a solid grasp of current fashion is usually sufficient. But an understanding of current conventions alone will not do for copyeditors who work on manuscripts written by scholars, professional writers, and other creative and literary authors. To succeed on these types of projects, the copyeditor needs to learn something about the history of usage controversies:

> [A copyeditor] should know the old and outmoded usages as well as those that are current, for not all authors have current ideas—some, indeed, seem bent upon perpetuating the most unreasonable regulations that were obsolescent fifty years ago. Yet too great stress upon rules—upon "correctness"—is perilous. If the worst disease in copyediting is arrogance [toward authors], the second worst is rigidity.[7]

In all contested matters of language, then, copyeditors must aim to strike a balance between permissiveness and pedantry. They are expected to correct (or ask the author to correct) locutions that are likely to confuse, distract, or disturb readers, but they are not

---

noun (like *information*), taking a singular verb and singular modifiers (such as *this, much, little*), and being referred to by a singular pronoun (*it*). Both of these constructions are standard" (*DEU,* s.v. "data").

5. For a history of the debate and its resolution in the United States, see *DEU,* s.v. "hopefully"; on the controversy in the United Kingdom, see the 2015 *Fowler's,* s.v. "sentence adverb." Surprisingly, after years of opposition the Associated Press at last accepted *hopefully* as a sentence modifier meaning "it is hoped," as noted in the 2015 edition of the *AP Stylebook.*

6. "Craftsmanship," in *Virginia Woolf: Selected Essays,* ed. David Bradshaw (Oxford: Oxford University Press, 2008), p. 89.

7. William Bridgwater, "Copyediting," in *Editors on Editing: An Inside View of What Editors Really Do,* rev. ed., ed. Gerald Gross (New York: Harper & Row, 1985), p. 87. (This essay was dropped from the 1993 edition of *Editors on Editing* listed in the Selected Bibliography.)

hired for the purpose of "defending the language" against all innovations, nor of impos-ing their own taste and sense of style on the author. Novice editors sometimes change an author's wording to obey a spurious or long-outmoded rule or, worse, simply because "it looks funny" (ILF) or "it sounds funny" (ISF). But when reading a manuscript, the copyeditor must ask, "Is this sentence acceptable as the author has written it?" The issue is *not* "Would William Strunk have approved of this sentence?"[8] or "If I were the writer, would I have written it some other way?"

## 4. CONTENT EDITING

Many publishers discourage an excess of developmental initiative during copyediting. But sometimes a copyeditor must call the author's (or editorial coordinator's) attention to serious internal inconsistencies, major organizational problems, or the need for addi-tional apparatus, such as tables, maps, or glossary. If so, use discretion: an interruption in the production schedule to address fundamental deficiencies is rarely welcome. Still, self-publishing authors and inexperienced clients, who may not have used a peer-review or beta-reading process to winnow such faults from the manuscript, often depend on the copyeditor's judgment to flag previously undetected substantive problems. On some projects you may be asked to fix these kinds of problems by doing heavy editing, rewrit-ing, or preparing supplementary content (tasks beyond a copyeditor's normal responsi-bilities). More often, though, you will be instructed to point out the difficulty and ask the author to resolve it.

Some editors spot-check a few facts in a manuscript to test for possible inaccura-cies, alerting the author or publisher if these random checks suggest the presence of per-vasive errors. Copyeditors working in book publishing and corporate communications are not normally responsible for the factual correctness of a manuscript.[9] But they are expected to offer a polite query about any factual statements that are clearly incorrect.

*Manuscript:* The documents arrived on February 29, 1985.

*Copyeditor's query:* Please check date—1985 not a leap year.

---

*Manuscript:* Along the Kentucky-Alabama border . . .

*Copyeditor's query:* Please fix—Kentucky and Alabama are not contiguous.

---

8. The first edition of William Strunk and E. B. White's perennially popular *Elements of Style,* pub-lished in 1959, was based on Strunk's original 1918 book. Although successive editions of this esteemed classic have guided generations of undergraduate writers, and it is still fondly quoted, many of its idio-syncratic precepts are oversimplified, outdated, or just plain wrong. When judging a sentence, con-temporary editors must take into account as much as a century of subsequent language change and linguistic data.

9. In the very different culture of journalism (i.e., newspaper and magazine publishing), copyedi-tors may be expected to do fact-checking, or the editorial process may include a separate fact-checking function. To be sure, with the advent of digital news media, both copyediting and fact-checking are sometimes abridged—or even omitted—in the rush to publish.

*Manuscript:* During the Vietnam War, the most divisive in American history, . . .

*Copyeditor's query:* Accurate to imply that Vietnam was more divisive than the Civil War?

If you have some knowledge of the subject matter, you may be able to catch an error that would go unquestioned by a copyeditor who is unfamiliar with the subject. Such catches will be greatly appreciated by the author, but only if you can identify the errors without posing dozens of extraneous questions about items that are correct. And while your familiarity with a subject may be an asset in identifying the author's lapses, you must beware the dangers of illusory knowledge—what you think you know but don't. When making factual corrections, as when making other editorial emendations, novices are strongly cautioned: before correcting a presumed error, look it up! But don't dive down that rabbit hole of Googling *every* statement of fact, which will waste time and undermine your efficiency. Instead, query internal inconsistencies and suspected errors and ask the author to undertake the necessary research to answer your questions.

Another misdeed you must guard against is inadvertently changing the author's meaning while you are repairing a grammatical error or tightening a verbose passage. And it is never acceptable to alter the author's meaning simply because you disagree with the author or believe that the author could not have meant what he or she said. Whenever the content is unclear or confusing, the copyeditor's recourse is to point out the difficulty and ask the author to resolve it.

Most publishers also expect their copyeditors to help authors avoid inadvertent sexism and other forms of biased language. In addition, copyeditors call the author's attention to any material (text or illustrations) that might form the basis for a lawsuit alleging libel, invasion of privacy, or obscenity.

Validating the originality of an author's work is beyond a copyeditor's scope of duties. But sometimes an editor recognizes or accidentally discovers that an author has appropriated another's content without attribution. If you uncover irrefutable evidence of plagiarism, you have an obligation to advise the publisher of the problem. Sometimes plagiarism is simply the result of carelessness or naiveté ("If it's on the internet, it's free"). But whether an unacknowledged borrowing is inadvertent or intentional, you should point out the problem and politely recommend that proper credit be given.

## 5. PERMISSIONS

If the manuscript contains lengthy excerpts from a published work that is still under copyright, the copyeditor may be expected to remind the author to obtain permission to reprint them unless the publisher has performed a thorough permissions review prior to copyediting. Permission may also be needed to reprint tables, charts, graphs, and illustrations that have appeared in print. Copyright law and permissions rules also apply to works on the internet. Special rules pertain to the reproduction of unpublished materials (e.g., diaries, letters). Regardless of whether formal permission is required for borrowed content, the copyeditor should ensure that proper source and credit lines are supplied.

## 6. MARKUP

Copyeditors may be asked to provide *markup* (also called *tagging, styling,* or *typecoding*) on the manuscript, that is, to identify those specially configured features of the manuscript other than regular running text. These *elements* of a manuscript include part and chapter numbers, titles, and subtitles; headings and subheadings; lists, extracts, and displayed equations; table numbers, titles, source lines, and footnotes; and figure numbers and figure captions. In addition, copyeditors may be expected to identify, to list, and sometimes to code unusual *entities*—characters with diacritics (accents used in languages other than English), non-Latin characters and alphabets, symbols, and glyphs that are not available on a standard QWERTY keyboard.

In the days of pencil editing, this task was often referred to as typecoding, a term that persists in some production workflows. Copyeditors working on hard copy used to identify elements by writing mnemonic codes in the left margin of the manuscript; they listed entities in a special section of the style sheet for the designer's and typesetter's attention. Editors working on-screen today either verify and correct the publisher's provisional markup of elements in the files as they work or identify the elements themselves by inserting generic codes or applying styles defined in the word processor's template. They may also be expected to code entities or to rekey them correctly in *Unicode,* an international character encoding standard, in addition to listing them on the style sheet for the production staff.

## WHAT COPYEDITORS DO NOT DO

Given that there is no consensus about how to spell *copyediting,*[10] it is not surprising that the meaning of the term is somewhat unsettled. In traditional print production, copyediting, the last editorial step before typesetting, once clearly referred to the set of responsibilities outlined above. It was usually differentiated from *line editing,* improvements in literary style at the sentence and paragraph levels. (The organization Editors Canada still differentiates such crafting, which it calls *stylistic editing.*) But many US publishers today conflate mechanical and line editing under the rubric of copyediting.

*The Chicago Manual of Style* prefers the term *manuscript editing.* As described by *Chicago,* manuscript editing encompasses any or all of the tasks along a continuum from simple mechanical corrections (*mechanical editing*) through sentence-level interventions (line, or stylistic, editing) to substantial remedial work on literary style and clarity, disorganized passages, baggy prose, muddled tables and figures, and the like (*substantive editing*). Several professional associations of editors further describe this continuum of manuscript editing in terms of *levels of editing* and characterize the degrees of intervention as light, medium, and heavy copyediting (see the next section, "Levels of Copyediting").

10. The closed forms *copyedit, copyeditor,* and *copyediting* are used in *The Chicago Manual of Style* and in most book publishing, but newspapers are apt to employ *copy editors* who *copy edit. WIT* prefers *copy editor* (recognizing *copyeditor* as a variant) and *copy-edit. M-W Collegiate* shows *copy editor* and *copyedit,* whereas *AHD* recognizes the open and closed noun and verb forms as equal variants.

In the world beyond traditional book and journal publishing, the term *copyediting* is sometimes applied to an even more expansive range of tasks, or the work is incorrectly referred to as *proofreading* by authors despite their lofty expectations of the services to be provided. This is particularly the case among self-publishing authors who hire editorial professionals but who may be unfamiliar with the functional distinctions among types of editing and different editorial tasks. Besides performing the conventional copyediting duties described in this book, an editor in these nontraditional publishing environments may be expected to assess the suitability of a manuscript for publication (usually the role of an acquisitions editor or literary agent); to midwife content, evaluate and reshape a manuscript, or overhaul organization and literary style (the work of a developmental or substantive editor); or to provide other additional services, such as

- fact-checking (verifying factual details)
- art editing (finding or developing illustrations to accompany the text)
- permissions editing (researching and securing rights to use copyrighted content)
- project or production editing (managing the production process: hiring and supervising production specialists, scheduling and tracking progress, overseeing the production budget, maintaining quality standards, and facilitating communication among the members of a production team)
- design (determining the document's physical appearance)
- formatting (preparing files for print and e-book production)
- proofreading (ensuring that the approved final copy is correctly rendered in type)
- indexing
- distributing and marketing the final product

In addition to copyediting, editorial freelancers may supply some of these (and other) services that were once offered by traditional publishers, especially if their clientele includes indie authors. But all these tasks involve discrete skills and command different pay rates; none are included in a copyeditor's duties. Staff manuscript editors, too, often shoulder additional responsibilities and may have to develop editorial and production skills beyond those required for conventional copyediting.

For clarity's sake, therefore, the following distinctions are worth preserving:

*Copyeditors are not proofreaders.* Although many copyeditors are good proofreaders, and all copyeditors are expected to catch typographical errors, copyediting and proofreading are two different functions. Copyeditors work on an author's manuscript and are concerned with imposing mechanical consistency; correlating parts; correcting infelicities of grammar, usage, and diction; querying internal inconsistencies and structural or organizational problems; flagging content requiring permission; and tagging or styling elements. Proofreaders, in contrast, are charged with correcting errors introduced during the typesetting, formatting, or file conversion of the final document; with emending deficient page layout; and with identifying any serious errors that were not caught during copyediting.[11]

*Copyeditors are not rewriters or ghostwriters.* Although copyeditors are generally expected to make simple revisions to smooth awkward passages, they do not have license to rewrite a text line by line, nor do they prepare material on an author's behalf. Making wholesale revisions is sometimes called *substantive editing* (the "heavy" end of the manuscript editing continuum defined by *Chicago*) or, if the work involves significant engagement with the subject matter, *content editing.* Creating original content to be published under another person's name is called *ghostwriting.*

*Copyeditors are not developmental editors.* Copyeditors are expected to query structural and organizational problems, but they are not expected to fix these problems. Helping an author develop an idea into a publishable manuscript, overhauling a rough draft, identifying gaps in subject coverage, devising strategies for more effective communication of the content, and creating features to enhance the final product and make it more competitive in the marketplace—these tasks describe *developmental editing.*

*Copyeditors are not publication designers.* Copyeditors are expected to point out any item in the manuscript that may cause difficulties during production, for example, a table that seems too wide to fit on a typeset page or an entity that may not display properly in a digital environment. But they are not responsible for making decisions about the physical appearance of the publication. All physical specifications—typefaces, layout, the formatting of tables, the typographical treatment of titles and headings, and so on— are set by the publication's designer or by someone wearing the designer's (not the copyeditor's) hat.

## LEVELS OF COPYEDITING

If time and money were not issues, copyeditors could linger over each sentence and paragraph in a manuscript until they were wholly satisfied with its clarity, coherency, consistency, and correctness—even with its beauty and elegance. But since time and money are always considerations, many book and corporate publishers let copyeditors know how to focus and prioritize their efforts by using a *levels-of-edit* scheme. In determining how much and what kind of copyediting to request for a given project, the publisher generally weighs such criteria as

> the quality of the author's writing
> the intended audience

11. Some publishers skip formal copyediting, typeset the raw manuscript, and hire a "proofreader" to correct the most egregious errors and inconsistencies in proofs. But this is just deferred copyediting at a lower pay rate. Other publishers skip the conventional word-by-word proofreading stage when a manuscript has been typeset directly from copyedited files. The author is usually sent a set of proofs and encouraged to read them carefully, but at the publishing firm the proofs are simply spot-checked for gross formatting errors.

the schedule and budget for editing and publication

the author's reputation, attitude toward editing, and work schedule

the size of the print run or the public visibility of the electronic document

the importance of the publication to the publisher's core mission

the publisher's standards

In the best of all possible worlds, decisions about the level of copyediting would be based solely on an assessment of the quality of the writing and the needs of the intended audience. But in many cases, financial considerations and deadline pressures win out: "This manuscript is poorly written, but our budget allows for only light copyediting" or "This manuscript would benefit from a heavier hand, but the author has many pressing commitments and won't have time to read through a heavily edited manuscript, so let's go for light editing."

Many book and corporate publishers use a light-medium-heavy grid to describe the kinds of problems the editor should resolve, those the editor may ignore, and those the editor should prompt the author to address. There are no universal definitions for light, medium, and heavy copyediting, but you won't be too far off target if you follow the guidelines presented in table 1. You could even show these guidelines to your editorial coordinator and ask which statements best match the expectations for your work.

Some corporate publishers use an FIQ checklist, which itemizes problems to fix (F), ignore (I), or query (Q) and is keyed to either the audience or the type of publication. The sample entries in table 2 apply this scheme to corporate reports prepared with four different target audiences in mind: in-house readers, low-visibility clients, high-visibility clients, and the general public. Still another levels-of-edit scheme (table 3) prioritizes the copyeditor's efforts on the basis of the stage of a corporate document's editorial review: early draft, final draft, and final copy.[12]

In determining the desired level of editing, you should also assess the overall project by considering the following issues:

*Audience*

- Who is the primary audience for this text? How will this audience affect your choices regarding tone, level of diction, and sentence length? (Today, for example, copyeditors must sometimes accommodate a *global* audience, one that may include readers with limited English proficiency, lack of familiarity with Anglo-American references, and particular cultural sensitivities.)
- How much are readers expected to know about the subject?
- Will readers use the publication for pleasure or for professional development? Is it a reference guide or a skim-once-and-throw-away document? Will most users read the piece straight through, from start to finish, or will they consult sections of it from time to time?

12. The schemes described in tables 2 and 3 are based on Amy Einsohn, "Levels of Edit: Scalpel, Weed-Whacker, or Machete?," unpublished manuscript; a version of this essay was published without these tables in *Editorial Eye* 27, no. 4 (April 2004), pp. 5–6.

TABLE 1. Levels of Copyediting: Light-Medium-Heavy Grid

| | Light Copyediting | Medium Copyediting | Heavy Copyediting |
|---|---|---|---|
| Mechanical editing | Ensure consistency in all mechanical matters—spelling, capitalization, punctuation, hyphenation, abbreviations, format of lists, etc. Optional guideline: Allow deviations from house style if the author consistently uses acceptable variants. | | |
| Correlating parts | Check contents page against chapters; check numbering of footnotes or endnotes, tables, and figures. Check alphabetization of bibliography or reference list; read footnote, endnote, or in-text citations against bibliography or reference list. | | |
| Language editing | Correct all indisputable errors in grammar, syntax, and usage, but ignore any locution that is not an outright error. | Correct all errors in grammar, syntax, and usage. Point out or revise any infelicities. | Correct all errors and infelicities in grammar, syntax, and usage. |
| | Point out paragraphs that seem egregiously wordy or convoluted, but do not revise. Ignore minor patches of wordiness, imprecise wording, and jargon. | Point out any patches that seem wordy or convoluted, and supply suggested revisions. | Rewrite any wordy or convoluted patches. |
| | Ask for clarification of terms likely to be new to readers. | Ask for or supply definitions of terms likely to be new to readers. | Ask for or supply definitions of terms likely to be new to readers. |
| Content editing | Query factual inconsistencies and any statements that seem incorrect. | Query any facts that seem incorrect. Use standard online and printed references to verify content. Query faulty organization and gaps in logic. | Verify and revise any facts that are incorrect. Query or fix faulty organization and gaps in logic. |
| Permissions | Note any text, tables, or illustrations that may require permission to reprint. | | |
| Markup | Mark up all elements. | | |

TABLE 2.  Levels of Copyediting: FIQ Checklist

|  | In-house | Low Viz Client | High Viz Client | Public |
|---|---|---|---|---|
| Contact information | F | F | F | F |
| Gender-specific language | I | I | Q | Q |
| Grammar errors, glaring | F | F | F | F |
| Grammar errors, minor | I | I | F | F |
| Passive voice, overuse of | I | I | Q | Q |
| Pricing data | F | F | F | F |
| Wordiness | I | I | Q | F |

*Note:* F = fix; I = ignore; Q = query

TABLE 3.  Levels of Copyediting: Stages of Editorial Review

|  | Early Drafts (content edit) | Final Draft (deep edit) | Final Copy (proof-edit) |
|---|---|---|---|
| Audience, suitability for | ■ | □ |  |
| Organization and coherence | ■ | □ |  |
| Pacing | □ | ■ |  |
| Wordiness, diction |  | ■ |  |
| Punctuation |  | ■ | □ |
| Grammar and spelling |  | ■ | ■ |
| Executive summary |  | ■ | ■ |

■ = principal emphasis    □ = secondary emphasis    (blank) = ignore

*Text*
- How difficult is the text? Is it a simple narrative? genre or young adult fiction? academic, scientific, technical, or professional writing with scholarly apparatus? text written by a nonnative speaker of English?
- How long is the text? Length is now generally expressed as a total word count, including any notes and nontext apparatus, but it was once based on a count of double-spaced 8½-by-11-inch manuscript pages typed in 12-point Courier with one-inch margins all around. Some editors still convert the total word count into equivalent manuscript pages of 250 words for

purposes of estimating required editing time and fees. Regardless of how many words an author has crammed on to each page, what matters in determining length is the word count, which cannot be manipulated by changing the font or line spacing.

- What physical form is the text in?

    *For hard-copy editing:* Although editors rarely mark paper manuscripts these days, some exceptions persist, such as photocopies of old magazine articles assembled for a book-length collection of essays, or tear sheets from a work being revised for a new edition. If you must work on hard copy, consider the following: Is the space between lines of text generous enough to accommodate interlinear markings? (Single-spaced typing and tightly spaced lines of print are difficult to copyedit unless only a sprinkling of commas is required.) How many words are on a page? How legible is the font? Are all four margins at least one inch?[13]

    *For on-screen editing:* What word processing or other computer program did the author use? Has any additional file preparation been done? Has the publisher performed any setup or *file cleanup* routines, or is the copyeditor expected to

    > convert the author's files into another program or format
    > pull apart (or combine) the author's original document files
    > remove embedded tables and illustrations from the text and place them in separate files
    > convert foot-of-page notes to end-of-document notes (or vice versa)
    > provide markup or styling of manuscript elements, such as headings, lists, and block quotations
    > remove multiple tabs, extra line and word spaces, and other aberrant formatting
    > clean up nonstandard keyboarding of special typographic characters (e.g., non-Latin alphabets and ideograms, diacritics, symbols, quotation marks, dashes, and ellipses)
    > execute other preliminary search-and-replace operations

- How will the copyedited manuscript be processed?

    *For hard-copy editing:* Will the entire document be rekeyed, or will someone be keying only the changes into existing production files? (If the latter, the copyeditor must use a brightly colored pencil or pen for marking, so that the inputter can easily spot all the changes.)

---

13. Some publishers may rekey the hard copy or scan the printed text, using *optical character recognition* (OCR) technology, to create a digital file *prior* to editing so the copyeditor can work on-screen. This intermediate step is likely to produce a less costly and more accurate publication in the end.

*For on-screen editing:* Is the copyeditor to supply *redlined files* (i.e., files that show insertions and deletions), clean files (i.e., files that contain only the final edited version of the text), or both? Is the copyeditor expected to code elements or special characters (e.g., letters that carry diacritic marks, non-Latin alphabets)? perform other file cleanup operations?

- Does the manuscript contain material other than straightforward running text (e.g., tables, footnotes or endnotes, bibliography, photos, graphs)? how much of each kind?
- Are there legible reference copies of all art, supplied as low-resolution digital images, thumbnails, or photocopies?

*Type of editing*

- Has the person assigning the job read the entire manuscript or skimmed only parts of it?
- How many hours or dollars have been budgeted for the copyediting?
- Is the copyeditor expected to substantially cut the text?
- Is the copyeditor expected to check the math in the tables? to verify direct quotations or bibliographical citations? to test URLs?
- Are there any important design constraints or preferences: limits on the amount of art, size of tables, number of heading levels? use of special characters (non-Latin alphabets, math symbols, musical notation)? footnotes or endnotes?

*Editorial style*

- What is the preferred style manual? the preferred dictionary?
- Is there an in-house style guide, tipsheet, or checklist of editorial preferences? (A sample Checklist of Editorial Preferences is provided in an appendix to this book.)
- Are there earlier editions or comparable texts that should be consulted? Is this piece part of a series?

*Author*

- Who is the author? Is the author a novice or a veteran writer?
- Has the author seen a sample edit?
- Has the author been told what kind of (or level of) editing to expect?

*Administrative details*

- Is the copyeditor to work directly with the author, designer, or typesetter? Or will these relationships be mediated by an editorial coordinator?
- To whom should the copyeditor direct questions that arise during editing?
- What is the deadline for completion of the editing? How firm is it?

## THE EDITORIAL PROCESS

Once you have a sense of the assignment, the next steps are to inventory the materials you have been given, confirm that they are complete or track down any missing items immediately, and prepare the project for editing.

If you will be copyediting on paper, make sure you have

all the pages (numbered in sequence)
copies of any tables, charts, or illustrations
captions for the illustrations
text for any footnotes or endnotes
the bibliography or reference list (for an article or book that includes references)
any supplementary materials (e.g., appendixes or glossaries)

Prepare—or make sure that the publisher has retained—a backup hard copy before beginning work. (Hard-copy manuscripts, especially ones without backup files, are rare these days, but they still exist, for example, in the form of tear sheets from the previous edition of a book, photocopies of assorted journal articles assembled for an edited collection, a laboriously hand-typed memoir by a self-publishing prison inmate without access to digital writing tools, or the faded typescript of a naturalist who has spent thirty years perched in a forest canopy in Costa Rica, recording observations of birds on an old Smith-Corona.) Handling and navigating a large paper manuscript can be facilitated by some old-school techniques, such as inserting colored dividers or tabs between major sections, removing nontext elements to the ends of their sections or to the back of the manuscript, and, if the pages are not already through-numbered, stamping them with a numbering machine—preferably before spilling the manuscript on the floor. As you turn through the pages, you can also assess the overall formatting and features of the manuscript by doing preliminary tagging of major elements.

If you will be editing on-screen—by far the more common procedure—you need to set up and inspect the project files and process them for editing before you begin. Editors develop individual routines for preparing electronic manuscripts and modify these routines based on a publisher's own preliminary file preparation, but all editors must develop protocols for consistently naming files and folders, saving and differentiating successive manuscript versions generated during the editing process, and backing up their work at each major stage.

Here are typical steps for setting up an on-screen editing project prepared in a word processor such as Microsoft Word:

- Immediately create a backup set of the original unedited files sent to you by the publisher and safely archive them, preferably on an external device or a remote server.
- Secure the original unedited files on your hard drive in a separate, clearly labeled folder.

- Make a working copy of these original files for your first read-through; rename these working files accordingly and put them in another separate, clearly identified folder.

Next, check to see that the files are compatible with your equipment and inspect them.[14] Open each working file and scroll through its contents with all formatting and any markup displayed. Look for obvious technical problems, such as characters or sections in gibberish, which might denote missing fonts or problems with file conversion or compatibility; correct any obvious formatting errors, such as midparagraph hard returns. (Some editors also use this initial run-through to supply markup for any potentially ambiguous elements, relying on the author's original formatting cues, and to highlight or make note of any conspicuous editorial problems for later attention.) Make sure you have all the files for the document; refer to the table of contents, if there is one. Scan for obvious gaps and for any signs (e.g., embedded comments or redlined revisions) that the digital text is not the final version. Confirm that all nontext items— tables, captions for illustrations, endnotes, and the like—are included. Unless instructed otherwise, remove any embedded tables and graphic elements and sequester them. For book-length manuscripts, these items are usually placed in their own files; for shorter pieces, such as journal articles, they are sometimes placed at the end of the regular text, with section or page breaks inserted between the discrete elements. Some clients prefer to retain embedded tables and graphics.

On-screen copyeditors sometimes receive a reference printout of the document in addition to the files. The electronic manuscript is normally considered the definitive version, but as you scroll through the working files during your initial inspection, loosely collate them against the printout (e.g., comparing first and last sentences in each section of the manuscript) to determine whether any sections or nontext elements in the hard-copy version are obviously missing from the electronic version, or whether these versions significantly differ in other ways—for example, if the author has penciled changes on the paper manuscript that have not been entered in the files. If you find any discrepancies, immediately report them to your editorial coordinator.

Your next step is to perform basic file cleanup routines, unless the publisher has already completed some or all of these preliminary tasks. This cleanup standardizes formatting and keyboarding so that the files are ready for editing and for the subsequent production process. Some editors purchase and use off-the-shelf cleanup tools (examples are listed in the Selected Bibliography), whereas other editors create and use their own *macros,* that is, simple keyboard commands programmed to perform a suite of operations.

Before running any cleanup macros, make sure the *mark-revisions (redlining) feature* of your editing software is turned off; otherwise, the redlining of hundreds of nondis-

14. Copyeditors who work in-house and those who work as independent contractors (freelancers) for publishers will receive compatible files from the publisher. Freelance copyeditors who work directly with authors should discuss file formats and compatibility with prospective clients. These freelancers will also want to examine sample files to evaluate the author's word processing skills. (Yes, there still exist authors who create a paragraph indent by hitting the space bar five times.)

cretionary formatting corrections will distract the publisher or author who later reviews the copyediting. Inspect the default settings in your word processor's autocorrect and autoformatting features and turn off any that will interfere with file cleanup, such as automatic capitalization or formatting of hyperlinks. Confirm the language setting (e.g., for American or British English) in each file to ensure that a spell-check will use the correct dictionary. For large projects, such as chapter books, you may want to consolidate multiple files into a single megafile (excluding graphics and tables) so the cleanup macros need be run only once; this step is unnecessary if you are using cleanup macros that work across all the files in a manuscript directory.

Once this setup is done, run macro-enabled passes through the files to perform any of the following routines that apply to the specific project:

> changing extra spaces between words and sentences to one space
> removing spaces after paragraph breaks
> removing extra line spaces between paragraphs
> changing underlining to italics
> fixing spaces around ellipses
> changing straight quotation marks and apostrophes to *smart* (or *curly*) *quotes*
> correcting the position of commas and periods in relation to closing quotation marks
> removing extra tabs
> replacing hyphens between numerals with *en dashes* (the slightly longer dashes used between numerals in typography)
> deleting spaces around *em dashes* (the typographic equivalent of two typed hyphens signifying an interruption)

These automated cleanup routines and any others created for a given manuscript prepare the files for a subsequent trouble-free import into a page composition program or digital environment.[15] They also allow you to work more efficiently and accurately by eliminating low-level formatting problems before you begin editing in earnest. Note that a few legitimate exceptions to standardized formatting may be miscorrected by such cleanup scripts: for example, the correctly formatted apostrophe in 'cause (for *because*) may default to the opening single quotation mark ('cause). These infrequent exceptions can be restored during your first full pass through the manuscript.

As part of file cleanup, copyeditors often run a preliminary spell-check, noting unusual terms for further review during the first read-through and adding recurrent proper names and legitimate unconventional spellings to their word processor's custom dictionary. In order to get acquainted with the structure of the manuscript and to identify any major organizational issues, copyeditors may also perform some initial tagging

---

15. Formatting files for an e-book may require special attention to certain features, such as ellipses, em dashes, symbols, nonstandard characters, and unmarked section breaks, that may not convert to or display well in an e-book environment.

or styling of various manuscript elements (discussed in chapter 13) during their preliminary run-through.

Once the hard copy has been organized or the files prepared, inspected, and cleaned up, the manuscript is ready for copyediting. Ideally, the publisher's schedule allows enough time for a preliminary skimming of the entire text and two complete editorial read-throughs (*passes*). The preliminary skim is a quick read-through of the manuscript to size up the content, organization, and quality of the writing; to note features that may require special attention (e.g., footnotes, tables, appendixes, glossary); and to identify any weak sections of the manuscript that will require extra time. When time or budget constraints are issues, this preliminary skim may be combined with the previous hard-copy or file inspection, file cleanup, and markup processes. But two thorough passes constitute the universal magic number: no copyeditor is good enough to catch everything in one pass, and few editorial budgets are generous enough to permit three passes (unless the text is only a few pages long).

The next step is to grab a pencil or turn on your word processor's mark-revisions feature and plunge in. Some editors begin by copyediting any technical apparatus—notes, bibliography, tables, figures—as a warm-up exercise before tackling the text. On the first pass through the text proper, copyeditors read very, very slowly. Let me say that again, because it is crucial to your success as a copyeditor: You must train yourself to read v-e-r-y, v-e-r-y slowly—slowly enough to scrutinize each comma ("OK, comma, what are you doing here? Do you really belong here? Why?"), to interrogate each pronoun ("Hey, pronoun, where's your antecedent? Do you two agree in gender and number?"), to cross-examine each homophone ("You there, 'affect'! Shouldn't you be 'effect'?"), and to ponder each compound adjective, adverb, and noun ("Does our dictionary show 'cross section' or 'cross-section'?"). Moreover, you must read slowly enough to catch missing words (a dropped "the" or "a"), missing pieces of punctuation ("We need a hyphen here"), ambiguities in syntax, and gaps in logic.

On your first editorial pass through the manuscript, then, you will want to read as slowly as you can. To slow yourself down, read aloud or subvocalize. An added advantage of reading aloud (or muttering) is that your ear will pick up some discrepancies that your eye will ignore. On this pass, you should look up *anything* that you are unsure of. With your dictionary, style manual, usage guide, thesaurus, and other reference books at your side or bookmarked in your web browser, read up on troublesome mechanical issues, brush up on tricky grammar and usage controversies, and verify your suspicions about factual inaccuracies or inconsistencies in the manuscript as you proceed. If you have any large, global questions—questions that pertain to the manuscript as a whole—make your best effort to get the answers, from your editorial coordinator or from the author, before you begin your second pass.

The second pass through the text is usually a much quicker read for the purpose of incorporating the answers to any global questions that arose on the first pass, catching the mechanical errors you missed, and fixing any errors you inadvertently introduced. On-screen editors will sometimes hide the redlining display on their monitor (but leave the mark-revisions feature on) for this second pass because they can spot their oversights and errors more easily in clean edited text. They may also change the font in the document for this second pass, or even print the document out and reread the text on paper, theorizing that significant changes in the appearance (or the haptic experience) of the document will enhance their perceptual acuity during this second pass. Some editors prefer to avoid a hard-copy pass as wasteful of paper and toner, but others value the fresh perspective it affords. A second-pass review of the hard copy may be warranted, especially for a short document containing critically important information (e.g., recommended doses of prescription drugs) and with a generous editing schedule and budget.

Regardless of method, try to schedule the second pass for a book-length manuscript so that you can read the entire work in a few days, without interruptions. You are more likely to catch inconsistencies if large chunks of the manuscript are residing in your short-term memory. If the text contains tables or charts, you will need to make a separate pass to be sure that all items in the batch are consistent in style and format. This is also the time to verify your markup, to double-check note numbering and placement callouts for tables and figures, to review your queries for tact and efficacy, and, if you are editing on-screen, to run the spell-checker again.

(Some experienced copyeditors reverse this procedure, doing a quick first pass and a slow second pass. During the first pass, they fix all the obvious mechanical errors; the second pass is for less routine matters, issues that they feel can be better addressed after they have read the entire manuscript. On-screen copyeditors may even turn off the redlining or mark-revisions feature in a quick first pass and make only nondiscretionary changes, then turn on the redlining for the second, in-depth pass. I don't recommend this approach to novice copyeditors, however, for two reasons. First, a "quick first pass" is unlikely to be quick. Few mechanical issues are truly routine for beginning copyeditors; confidently identifying "nondiscretionary changes" requires judgment that comes only with experience. Second, copyeditors are deprived of the opportunity to catch any errors they have inadvertently introduced when the in-depth copyediting is done during the second, and final, pass.)

The copyedited manuscript is nearly always sent to the author for review.[16] The author may receive the edited manuscript on paper (some authors are unable to review editing directly on-screen), in the form of a pencil-edited hard copy or as a redlined or clean printout (or both) of the edited files, which the author reviews and marks manually. Alternatively, the author may be sent files for review: password-protected word processing files with redlining activated, or a PDF file enabled for markup and comments. In either digital form the author can review and respond to the editing on-screen without altering the copyeditor's work. Some authors make relatively few changes during

---

16. In some expedited editorial processes, the author review stage is skipped altogether. Clean edited files are sent directly to the typesetter, and any unresolved editorial queries are carried over to typeset pages for the author's response during proofreading. The copyeditor's emendations are presented in the proofs as faits accomplis. This somewhat unconventional abridged process may work for a manuscript receiving only light, nondiscretionary mechanical editing or for text prepared by an employee and legally owned by the company. But it is unlikely to be acceptable for highly technical or professional content or for a manuscript with discretionary changes requiring the author's approval.

their review of copyediting; others may spend considerable time revising, rewriting, and reorganizing. Publishers encourage authors to make any final changes at this stage rather than later in the process, when alterations can be expensive and time consuming.

The author then returns the manuscript to the publisher for *manuscript cleanup*—one final pass made by the copyeditor or the editorial coordinator.[17] If the author has ignored any of the copyeditor's queries or has restored (*stetted*) or added text containing an error, the troublesome passages are resolved in consultation with the author before the manuscript is released for production.

Manuscript cleanup can be fast and straightforward—or fraught. If an author has rejected many suggested changes, ignored queries, or made snide remarks in response to the editor's close attention, cleanup may require a thick skin. Rather than dismissing such reactions as ungrateful and rude, try to be understanding. If you have ever experienced the thousand tiny wounds inflicted on your own prose by a copyeditor (however gentle and skilled), you can probably appreciate the forbearance required to endure another's corrections and queries. Every copyeditor must cultivate empathy for those authors who overreact to the sometimes painful process of editing. Learn to recite the Serenity Prayer during cleanup: "God, grant me the serenity to accept the things I cannot change, courage to change the things I can, and the wisdom to know the difference."

During cleanup, the editor scans every page or file looking for changes by the author and for the author's responses to queries. For that rare paper-and-pencil copyedit, the cleanup editor may have to literally clean messy pages, using an eraser or correction fluid retrieved from the rummage drawer of an old desk, or to retype hard-to-read paragraphs or pages. For an on-screen edit, the editor scrolls through the files, using the software's tools to accept or reject changes or to re-revise text in accordance with the author's instructions. Or, if the author has reviewed and hand-marked a printout of the edited files, the editor transfers the handwritten changes and stets to the files. The editor also reads and lightly edits any material added by the author during review and, as a final step, runs the file cleanup macros and spell-checker once again to pick up any formatting errors or misspellings accidentally introduced during the author-review and cleanup stages.

Occasionally, manuscript cleanup requires the wisdom of Solomon and the diplomacy of Dag Hammarskjöld. These problem cleanups arise when a copyeditor has been overly zealous or has failed to explain persuasively why certain proposed changes are preferable, or when an author is quite attached to unconventional locutions or mannerisms. The cleanup editor cannot override the author, nor ask the author to re-review every rejected change. Instead, the editor needs to rethink each disputed issue and decide whether the point is worth revisiting with the author: Is one of the

---

17. Some publishers reserve cleanup for a senior editor; others expect the copyeditor to do the cleanup because the copyeditor is the person most familiar with the manuscript. Should an author seem extremely dissatisfied with the copyediting, the cleanup may be handed over to another editor, both to spare the copyeditor's feelings and because a fresh pair of eyes may be more objective in resolving the disputes between the copyeditor's suggestions and the author's preferences. Having someone other than the copyeditor do the cleanup may also be preferable when the editorial coordinator wants to get a better sense of the project or evaluate the quality of the copyeditor's work.

4 Cs (clarity, coherency, consistency, and correctness) at stake? Or is the matter one of conflicting preferences about some small point that will not affect readers one way or another?

In other words, cleanup editors have to select their "battles" very carefully. If the cleanup editor is convinced that the author is inviting peril by rejecting a particular piece of copyediting, the proper course is to rephrase (rather than simply repeat) the concern and, if possible, propose one or two additional alternative remedies. In disputes concerning less important issues, however, the cleanup editor should respect the author's preferences and not raise the matter again. After all, it's the author's name, not the editor's, that appears in the byline.

## EDITORIAL TRIAGE

Sometimes a copyeditor is asked to meet what everyone involved in the project knows is an unreasonable deadline for even a light copyedit. In such cases, the copyeditor's first step is to ask the editorial coordinator to help set priorities: which editorial tasks are most important for this particular project, and which niceties must fall by the wayside?

The list of priorities depends on the project, of course; but for most projects, a minimal task list would include attending to those errors that would be most embarrassing to the publisher and those that would be most confusing to readers. Thus the copyeditor would

> correct spelling errors, serious grammatical errors (e.g., faulty subject-verb
>     agreement), and egregious punctuation errors
> query factual inconsistencies
> make sure all initialisms and acronyms are defined
> identify material for which permission to reprint is required
> carefully read the title page, copyright page, and contents page
> check the numbering of footnotes, tables, and figures

In other words, mechanical inconsistencies or discrepancies that do not interfere with communication (e.g., capitalization, hyphenation, use of italics, formatting of lists) would be ignored, as would be almost all matters of diction, syntax, usage, and content. The copyeditor would, however, keep track of the permissions needed (to save the author and publisher from being named in a lawsuit) and would check the contents page and numbering of elements (to save readers the frustration of missing or out-of-sequence items).

If the schedule is a bit more generous, the editor might also

> break up overly long sentences and overly long paragraphs
> revise overuse of passive-voice verbs
> prune repetitions and redundancies

When straining to meet a tight schedule, you may also have to choose between doing two quick passes or doing one slower pass and either forgoing the second pass entirely or doing a selective second pass. During a selective second pass, you could either read only the most important sections of the manuscript or revisit only those paragraphs that you found most troubling on your first pass. (To help you locate these spots, on your first pass you can keep a list, lightly mark an X in the left margin of a hard-copy document, or highlight—or place a hidden comment with—a troublesome passage in an on-screen document.) The choice between one pass or two will depend on the type of material, the priorities list, and your own work style.

This kind of triage is painful: it goes against a copyeditor's nature and training to leave poorly punctuated, convoluted sentences and paragraphs whose logic is inside-out or upside-down. But when time is short, it is more important to have read every page than to have labored over the first half of a project and barely glanced at the rest.

*Triage for technical documents.* In *Technical Editing: The Practical Guide for Editors and Writers,* Judith Tarutz advises technical copyeditors to ask the following kinds of questions when creating a list of priorities for triage: What matters to the readers? What kinds of errors will readers notice and care about? How important is the document to the readers? What kinds of errors are easy to fix within the time constraints? In practice, then, Tarutz says, "Sometimes you'll fix something that's not very important but is so easy to fix that it would be silly not to. And sometimes you need to ignore something that bothers you but it's OK with the customers, it's expensive to change, and it's not important to change. (Just because it bothers you does not make it wrong)" (p. 167).

*Triage for business documents.* An entirely different list of triage priorities is offered by Gary Blake, co-author of *The Elements of Business Writing* and *The Elements of Technical Writing.* Arguing that errors in spelling, grammar, and punctuation will not "send customers out the door"—unless the misspelled word is the customer's name—Blake places all these mechanical issues at the bottom of his ten-point priority list for business writing. At the top of the list, instead, are those substantive issues that defeat the twin purposes of a business document: to inform and persuade readers and to convey the sponsoring organization's authoritativeness and expertise. For Blake the top-priority items are fixing errors in organization, rewording sentences that are inappropriate in tone, and clarifying language that is overly vague—tasks normally considered the focus of heavy, even developmental, editing.[18]

*Triage for legal documents.* In *Legal Writing in Plain English,* Bryan A. Garner outlines a three-step process for editing legal prose. He recommends beginning by simply "clearing out the underbrush," that is, quickly reading through the document to eliminate small, easily repaired problems. Once these distracting weeds have been removed, the

18. In the middle of Blake's list—after revising vague wording and ahead of correcting punctuation errors—are attending to the overuse of the passive voice, fixing overly long sentences and paragraphs, rewriting weasel words and hedging phrases, cutting redundancies, and selecting the correct member of a confusable pair of words; see Blake, "It Is Recommended That You Write Clearly," *Wall Street Journal,* April 3, 1995, p. A14.

editor runs through the document a second time to make "basic edits," sentence-level emendations to tighten the prose. The editor's third pass, if time permits, is a heavy, or developmental, reading: it consists of "edits to refine" and focuses on structure, transitions, and content (pp. 138–39).

These different emphases in triaging business and legal documents underscore the point that outside traditional book publishing, the definitions and expectations for copyediting are often looser.

## ESTIMATES

Because so many people are involved in publishing a piece of text and substantial amounts of money may be at stake, every member of the team must be able to make reliable estimates of time and cost for each task. Copyeditors are typically asked for three estimates: How many hours will the project take? On what date will the copyediting be completed? How much will it cost?

The following rules should help you improve your accuracy in making estimates and help you set reasonable deadlines for yourself.

*Rule 1. Do not make an estimate or confirm anyone else's estimate of how long a copyediting project will take until you have seen the manuscript.* Sometimes a copyeditor is asked to make an estimate after being given a quick description of a manuscript. Unless you have worked with the "describer" before and have great confidence in his or her ability to evaluate a manuscript, your best response is a polite "I'm sorry but I can't give you a useful estimate until I've seen the manuscript." Once you have the manuscript in hand, you can skim it, select representative chunks from different parts (e.g., text, a table, some bibliography), do a sample edit (say, ten pages), and time yourself. In general, the more material you sample, the more accurate your estimate will be. Remember that your estimate has to allow enough time for two passes through the manuscript, although the second pass goes a lot faster than the first. If you will be expected to perform manuscript cleanup after the author's review, estimate this final pass separately. (If you are a freelance editor, best stipulate that you will bill separately for manuscript cleanup, preferably on an hourly basis, since no one can foresee how an author's response to the editing will affect the hours required for this work.)

*Rule 2. Adjust your base estimate to allow extra time for difficult copy.* The heart of an estimate is often based on a pages-per-hour productivity rate. But for hard-copy editing, pages that have 450 words take longer than pages that have the industry-standard 250 words, and if the manuscript for a hard-copy editing job is printed in a difficult-to-read font, you will find your pages-per-hour rate declining over the course of the day as your eyes tire. In a multiauthor work additional time may be required to extrapolate and preserve individual contributors' preferences and idiosyncrasies (if they are to be retained) or to impose one consistent editorial style on multiple contributions prepared in many

TABLE 4. Typical Pace for Copyediting Hard Copy, Two Passes (pages per hour)

|  | Standard Text | Difficult Text |
|---|---|---|
| Light copyedit | 6–9 | 4–6 |
| Medium copyedit | 4–7 | 2–4 |
| Heavy copyedit | 2–3 | 1–2 |

*Standard text:* If hard copy, the text is double-spaced with ca. 250 words to the page. The manuscript is carefully prepared. The content is not technical and includes few or no tables, figures, footnotes, endnotes, or reference citations. The manuscript has no bibliography or a bibliography that is short and well prepared.

*Difficult text:* If hard copy, the count exceeds 250 words a page or the font is difficult to read. The manuscript contains many typographical errors. The content is technical or includes many tables, figures, footnotes, or endnotes. Reference citations are carelessly prepared, inconsistent, or incomplete.

*Cleanup:* The cleanup pass is estimated separately and may take as much as 10 to 25 percent of the time required for the original editing.

different styles. A manuscript with extensive notes and bibliography will require many additional hours of styling and cross-checking, even if the citations are scrupulously prepared. How much of a difference can such factors make? Table 4 suggests a pages-per-hour formula for two passes on a hard-copy manuscript or an electronic manuscript of equivalent length (with 250-word pages as the benchmark); novice copyeditors will—and should—work at a slower pace. Allow extra time for difficult copy (e.g., technical text, tables, footnotes or endnotes, and bibliographies) and poorly prepared files (e.g., idiosyncratic spacing, extraneous formatting codes, improperly formatted extracts).

*Rule 3. As appropriate, allow time for nonediting chores, such as photocopying hard copy, converting or copying files, running file cleanup macros, communicating by phone or email with an editorial coordinator or author, and writing memos.* For some projects, these tasks will take no more than an hour or two. But other projects may require five or more hours of administrative or housekeeping duties. Working directly for an inexperienced indie author, that is, without the mediation of an editorial coordinator, may require substantial additional time if the author expects frequent updates and needs coaching in the basics of editing and production.

*Rule 4. Unless you are extremely experienced in making estimates, always add a fudge factor to your best guess.* Suppose your sampling of a 150-page manuscript suggests that you can complete five pages an hour. Use thirty hours, then, as the base for your estimate. Now add in a fudge factor—from 10 to 20 percent, depending on how confident you feel about your base estimate and how long the project is: the less confident you feel, the larger the fudge factor; the shorter the project, the larger the fudge factor. For a thirty-hour base estimate, a 10 percent fudge factor would be three hours; a 20 percent fudge factor would be six hours. Present your estimate as a range, say, thirty-three to thirty-six hours, or even thirty-six to forty hours.

*Rule 5. Be realistic about how many hours a day you can copyedit and still do a good job.* Most editors find that they cannot copyedit manuscripts for more than five or six hours a day except in times of utmost emergency. Be sure your work schedule includes time for breaks: at least fifteen to twenty minutes every two hours.

*Rule 6. Err on the side of overestimating the amount of time you need.* Because copyediting comes early in the production cycle, a missed deadline can throw off the entire schedule. Don't checkmate yourself by setting too tight a schedule.

*Rule 7. If you are a freelance editor, establish your basic rates in advance.* In preparing cost estimates, freelance editors use different formulas: they may charge by the hour, by the word, by the manuscript page (usually calculated as 250 words), or by the whole job. They may also specify different rates for different types of content, different levels of editing, and different categories of clients. Scientific and technical editing, for example, usually command higher rates than the editing of general interest text. Developmental editing is more handsomely remunerated than copyediting. Government and rich corporate clients may pay more than university presses and nonprofit organizations, and all of these are likely to pay better than the editorial labor contractors that now sometimes mediate between publishing clients and freelance editors.

*Rule 8. Cover your business costs.* Self-employed editors must ensure that their rates cover their overhead—equipment and business services, books and subscriptions, professional education, memberships, conference fees, and the like—and also their income taxes, self-employment payroll taxes, disability insurance, health coverage, sick leave and vacation, and retirement savings. Most freelance editors collect and analyze data on their jobs and make any necessary adjustments in their rates if they are not meeting their income goals; some give themselves regular raises by unapologetically announcing them to clients. Several of the professional editorial associations listed in the Selected Bibliography conduct rates surveys and post the results, and their members generously share information about business practices for self-employed editors. Richard Adin's *The Business of Editing* and Barbara Fuller's *How to Start a Home-Based Editorial Services Business* are among several excellent guides to managing contract work, including how to set rates and prepare estimates.

## ONE PARAGRAPH, THREE WAYS

Let's look at a short example that illustrates both the levels-of-editing concept and the nature of editorial awareness and editorial reasoning. The sample manuscript reads:[19]

> Murphy's Law assures us that no amount of proofreading will uncover all the errors in a work about to be published. The question is, how many re-readings

---

19. This example is based on a passage in Arthur Plotnik's *The Elements of Editing: A Modern Guide for Editors and Journalists* (New York: Macmillan, 1982), p. 7. For the purpose of this example, errors were introduced and other changes were made to the published text.

are reasonable? In my personal experience I have found that two readings of galleys and two of page proofs will catch 99 percent of the errors. Unfortunately the remaining 1 percent are often the mistakes that not only cause embarrassment but trouble. For example, the wrong numbers for ordering merchandise or misspelled names.

Assume that the editorial coordinator has requested a light copyedit. If you want to use the sample to test yourself, copyedit this paragraph. Focus on mechanical issues and make only those changes in wording that are necessary for the sake of correctness and clarity. For this exercise, the house style manual is *Chicago, M-W Collegiate* is the preferred dictionary, and *DEU* is the recommended usage manual.

Let's follow Kate as she copyedits this passage. After skimming the entire manuscript, she carefully reads the first sentence:

> Murphy's Law assures us that no amount of proofreading will uncover all the errors in a work about to be published.

Kate is unfamiliar with the term "Murphy's Law," so she looks it up in the dictionary and ascertains that the usage is appropriate and that the spelling and capitalization are correct. (She incidentally discovers the existence of a corollary that she files away in her memory for possible future use: Muphry's Law, which holds that if you write something criticizing another's editing or proofreading, there will be an error of some kind in what you have written.) Kate wonders whether "assure" (not "ensure" or "insure"?) is the correct word choice and decides that it is after checking these related terms in *DEU*. She detects no mechanical errors in this sentence and makes no changes to it.

Kate moves on to the second sentence:

> The question is, how many re-readings are reasonable?

Uncertain about how to treat a question ("how many re-readings are reasonable?") embedded in a sentence, she picks up the newest edition of *Chicago* (or logs into the online version), goes to the index, and looks under "questions: within sentences." The search leads her to a discussion and examples (at 6.42) that match the syntax of the sentence in the manuscript. She decides to apply the following conventions:

1. The embedded question should be preceded by a comma.
2. The first word of the embedded question should be capitalized, by analogy with a direct quotation; *Chicago* describes this recommendation as a "slight departure from earlier editions of the manual."
3. The question should not be in quotation marks because it is not a piece of dialogue.
4. The question should end with a question mark because it is a direct question.

The author has followed all these conventions except for treatment of "how," the first word of the question, which Kate capitalizes.

She next wonders whether to keep or delete the hyphen in "re-readings." She knows that for words beginning with prefixes, both *Chicago* and *M-W Collegiate* usually prefer the closed forms: *redo, prenatal, postwar,* and so on. But *Chicago* recommends using a hyphen if the absence of one might cause confusion or misreading: *re-cover* (as opposed to *recover*), *co-op,* and *pro-choice.* So the question is, Will "rereadings" be confusing? She thinks not and decides to delete the hyphen.

Kate now scrutinizes the third sentence:

> In my personal experience I have found that two readings of galleys and two of page proofs will catch 99 percent of the errors.

She changes "personal" to "professional"—because "personal experience" is a bit redundant (an individual's experience is, by definition, "personal") and, more important, because the power of the author's observation comes from his professional expertise, not his personal life. She leaves "99 percent" because she remembers *Chicago*'s preference for using a numeral followed by "percent" (rather than the percentage sign, %) in nontechnical copy.

On to the fourth sentence:

> Unfortunately the remaining 1 percent are often the mistakes that not only cause embarrassment but trouble.

Kate adds a comma after "Unfortunately" because a sentence adverb (i.e., an adverb that modifies an entire sentence, not just a single word or phrase) is always followed by a comma. (*Chicago* does not discuss the punctuation of sentence adverbs as such but recommends a comma to set off a transitional adverb that effects a distinct break in continuity.) Next, Kate moves "not only"—to yield "cause not only embarrassment but trouble"—because the items being contrasted are "embarrassment" and "trouble." (Compare: "These errors not only cause embarrassment but jeopardize our credibility." In this example, the items being contrasted are "cause embarrassment" and "jeopardize our credibility," so "not only" precedes "cause embarrassment.") Checking *DEU* again, Kate confirms that "not only . . . but" does not require the addition of "also," which is considered optional and is frequently omitted. So she makes no further changes to the construction.

The fifth sentence brings Kate to a halt.

> For example, the wrong numbers for ordering merchandise or misspelled names.

This is a careless sentence fragment; that is, it is not a fragment serving some rhetorical purpose (which would be fine in the right circumstances; see chapter 4). Kate decides that the least intrusive way to repair the fragment is to change the period before "for example" to a dash. (She turns to *Chicago* to confirm that either a comma or a dash may precede "for example" when introducing a list, with the dash recommended as preferable.) She also changes the order of "wrong numbers for ordering" and "misspelled names" to prevent the misreading of "for ordering merchandise or misspelled names" as one unit of thought. The reordering prevents readers from thinking that one can "order misspelled names." When Kate is done, the last portion of the text reads: "Unfortunately, the remaining 1 percent are often the mistakes that cause not only embarrassment but trouble—for example, misspelled names or the wrong numbers for ordering merchandise."

Kate's light-handed copyedit is shown in figure 1, along with a medium and heavy copyediting of the same passage. The medium-handed and heavy-handed copyeditors, you'll notice, made all the necessary mechanical changes, but they also tried to improve the wording and syntax. In the name of conciseness, they pruned or cut several wordy locutions. But observe that although the heavy-handed copyeditor retained the key points, the edited version is drained of color and personality: gone are Murphy's Law, the posing of the question to be answered, and the author's statement that the recommendation is based on experience. As you might guess, the author of the passage will be quite upset ("You've torn my writing to shreds! You've eliminated every syllable of humanity!") unless the editorial coordinator and the author have previously discussed the desirability of such wholesale cuts.

If your version of this passage looked more like medium or heavy copyediting, you will want to force yourself to lighten up. Do not machete a manuscript or rewrite a document unless you are explicitly asked to do heavy editing or rewriting. If the author's sentences are clear, correct, and serviceable (as this author's sentences are, with the few mistakes caught by our light-handed copyeditor), let them be. Don't rewrite an author's sentence simply because it is not the sentence you would have written. A reminder to this effect is posted on many bulletin boards in publishing offices around the world:

It's ~~hard~~ to **difficult**

resist the ~~urge~~ **temptation**

to ~~change~~ **improve**

someone else's writing.

Resisting this urge will make your life as a copyeditor easier in several ways. First, you will be able to devote more of your attention to your primary responsibilities: when you resist the urge to recast phrases in your own voice, you are more likely to catch mechanical errors, internal inconsistencies, and grammatical mistakes. Second, your relations with authors will be smoother because they will perceive you as an aide, not as a usurper of their authorial powers. Third, both the copyediting and the cleanup will take less time and be less frustrating. Finally, you will neatly sidestep an issue that often troubles novice copyeditors: "How do I maintain the author's style?" That issue will not arise if you focus on copyediting—not rewriting—and if you explain problems to your authors and ask them either to resolve the problems or to select among the alternatives you are posing.

## PROFESSIONALISM AND ETHICS

This overview of what contemporary editors do (and don't do) clearly shows that copyediting has become a highly technical craft. It involves mastery of a body of knowledge and an array of tools and processes, and it requires continuous study and practice.

FIGURE 1. Samples of Light, Medium, and Heavy Copyediting

**[Light]**

Murphy's Law assures us that no amount of proofreading will uncover all the errors in a work about to be published. The question is, ~~how~~How many ~~rereadings~~re ~~readings~~ are reasonable? In my ~~personal~~professional experience I have found that two readings of galleys and two of page proofs will catch 99 percent of the errors. Unfortunately, the remaining 1 percent are often the mistakes that ~~not~~ ~~only~~cause not only embarrassment but trouble——. ~~F~~for example, ~~the wrong numbers for ordering~~ ~~merchandise or~~misspelled names or the wrong ~~merchandise or~~ numbers for ordering merchandise.

**[Medium]**

Murphy's Law assures us that no amount of proofreading will uncover all the errors in a set of ~~proofs.~~ ~~work about to be published.~~ The question is, ~~how~~How many ~~rereadings~~re ~~readings~~ are reasonable? ~~In my personal experience~~I have found that two readings of galleys and two ~~readings~~ of page proofs will catch 99 percent of the errors. Unfortunately, the remaining 1 percent are often the mistakes that ~~not~~cause not only embarrassment but trouble——. ~~For example,~~ ~~misspelled names or incorrect catalog~~ ~~numbers for merchandise.~~the wrong numbers for ordering merchandise or misspelled names.

**[Heavy]**

~~Murphy's Law assures us that no~~No amount of proofreading ~~will~~can uncover all the errors in a set ~~of proofs.~~ ~~work about to be published.~~The question ~~is, how many re readings are reasonable? In my~~ ~~personal experience I have found that two~~Two readings of galleys and two readings of page proofs will catch 99 percent of the errors, ~~but.~~ ~~Unfortunately~~ the remaining ~~1 percent are often the~~mistakes ~~incorrect phone numbers or misspelled names~~ often cause both ~~that not only cause~~embarrassment ~~and~~but trouble. ~~For example, the wrong numbers for~~ ~~ordering merchandise or misspelled names.~~

Long gone is the era when a deft amateur wordsmith, blessed with the spelling gene and equipped with a few sharp pencils and some reference books, could simply hang out a shingle and begin copyediting. Gone, too, is the time when a newly minted English graduate could expect to develop skill in the craft just by apprenticing to a battle-tested in-house editor or by following an experienced copyeditor's hand-marked *foul copy* while proofreading typeset galleys. The apprentice system has all but disappeared as staff editorial positions have dwindled in number, supplanted by the outsourcing or freelancing of many editorial functions. Much proofreading has shifted to authors' shoulders or is now performed *blind* or *cold,* that is, without comparing typeset copy with the previous iteration of marked text that once instructed copyediting novices.

The traditional methods of craft training—as well as their tendency to perpetuate some falsehoods about English grammar and usage, it must be said—have been largely superseded by professional organizations and structured education for editors. (See the listings of editorial organizations and educational programs in the Selected Bibliography.) These have transformed an occupation once populated by talented, largely self-taught amateurs into a profession with a defined body of knowledge and requisite skills. Editorial associations provide advice, support, and collegiality to members, and many help to define terminology for different publishing tasks, to codify standards of proficiency, and to establish fair business practices for freelance editors and the publishers who hire them. Several of these associations also grant formal professional certification to members who qualify on the basis of their experience and their performance on rigorous tests. But nowhere is the transformation of the craft more evident than in the emergence of university-affiliated and independent academic programs offering formal training and certificates recognizing successful completion of a defined curriculum.

This professionalization of editing has also spurred efforts to forge a code of ethics for copyeditors. Practitioners often debate ethical issues in blogs and in exchanges on email lists. Many professional associations in English-speaking countries include guidelines for conduct in their charters and mission statements—for example, the "Code of Fair Practice" of the US-based Editorial Freelancers Association (EFA); the "Professional Editorial Standards" of the Editors' Association of Canada (EAC), now rebranded as Editors Canada; the "Code of Practice" of the UK's Society for Editors and Proofreaders (SfEP); and the "Standards for Editing Practice" of Australia's Institute of Professional Editors Limited (IPEd).[20] (The websites for all these associations are listed in the Selected Bibliography.) Although many editors cite, as their first principle, "Do no harm" (a phrase often misattributed to the Hippocratic oath), no universal oath guides the work of editors. But many proposed codes of ethics for editors share common elements:

20. Readers may wonder why the EAC uses the form *Editors',* whereas the EFA uses *Freelancers* (without an apostrophe), a difference between the genitive (possessive) and attributive forms of the nouns. As *Chicago* (7.27) observes, "Terms denoting group ownership or participation sometimes appear without an apostrophe (i.e., as an attributive rather than a possessive noun)." Chicago style faithfully preserves the names of organizations, regardless of the form used. Thus one finds both possessive and attributive nouns in proper names, such as Laborers' International Union of North America and Department of Veterans Affairs.

Master the core standards—the knowledge, skills, and best practices—of the profession as defined by professional certification boards (where they exist), editorial associations, certificate programs, and publishing curricula.

Represent your training and experience (and acknowledge your limitations) honestly to employers in your résumé, marketing materials, work samples, and tests.

Maintain proficiency through ongoing education. For example, the SfEP stipulates in its "Code of Practice" that "members should make every reasonable effort to maintain, improve and update their skills and knowledge, especially where new technology creates changes in publishing practice. This could include reading trade journals and reference works, requesting feedback from clients, seeking advice from colleagues or attending training courses and conferences."[21]

Be aware of the fundamental legal issues in publishing—copyright and creators' moral rights, permissions, libel, obscenity, and privacy protection—and inform the publisher of any content that requires legal review.

Be aware of the social and ethical issues in publishing—such as discriminatory, culturally insensitive, and offensive language or content—and inform the publisher of any problems. The editor does not act as a censor but as an advisor; the publisher determines an appropriate course of action.

Advise the publisher in writing, clearly but circumspectly, of egregious factual errors, distortions, omissions of essential information, and plagiarism; do not attempt to repair these defects unless explicitly authorized to do so.

Honor confidentiality. Whether or not you sign a formal *nondisclosure agreement* (NDA), protect proprietary and other sensitive information. Avoid revealing the identities of individual clients and displaying their text without permission. Even when seeking needed advice from colleagues, exercise restraint in discussing the defects in authors' manuscripts. Never make a derisive public remark or *any* derisive comment online (even in a private communication) about an author, whether named or unidentified, regardless of provocation. Save it for your diary.

Be scrupulous in all business and financial practices: preparing estimates, setting fees and schedules, forming contracts, communicating with clients, negotiating changes in the scope and terms of a project, subcontracting work, billing, and resolving disputes.

When a manuscript has been prepared in fulfillment of requirements for an academic or professional degree, make sure that the certifying program permits professional editing of the work. Determine the scope of permissible changes before undertaking stylistic or substantive revisions. Many academic departments and graduate offices provide written guidelines for students; some require degree applicants to obtain written authorization before collaborating

21. "Code of Practice," Society for Editors and Proofreaders, https://www.sfep.org.uk, § 3.1.2.

with an editor. Editors Canada posts its own "Guidelines for Ethical Editing of Theses/Dissertations."

Continuous changes in publishing, as in the language itself, will doubtless always demand new knowledge, require new skills, create new tasks and processes, and pose new ethical challenges to editors. To stay in the business, copyeditors must rely on their communities of professionals and on the educational resources available to them.

# CHAPTER 2

# ¶ Basic Procedures

Every copyeditor needs a system for marking changes to the author's text, querying the author and the editorial coordinator, keeping track of editorial decisions, and incorporating the author's review of the copyediting into the final manuscript or electronic files. The traditional procedures for marking, querying, recordkeeping, and cleanup were developed in the pre-computer era. Since then, they have been adapted for editing on-screen. You may sometimes have to rejigger these procedures for use with a new (or unaccommodating) technology or work in an unconventional editing environment, such as nontraditional or indie publishing, but they are essential to any editing process. In this chapter, we'll look at the requisite skill sets and the procedures for paper-and-pencil editing and for on-screen editing using common word processing tools.

## SKILL SETS

### HAND-MARKING SKILLS

Even if you intend to do all your copyediting on-screen, there are several compelling reasons for learning the traditional hand-marking routines. First, a few skills assessments for employment and for freelance work are still administered in paper-and-pencil form. Second, some authors will use traditional copyediting marks when reviewing a printout of your on-screen copyediting. Third, you will need manual skills to handle

> materials for which the author's files prove unusable or for which there are no electronic files—for example, tear sheets from printed sources or even documents prepared on a typewriter (Some nostalgic authors have revived the use of analog writing tools, while others have just never abandoned their old Smith-Coronas.)
> documents that are exchanged by older, paper-based technologies, such as fax and photocopy
> printouts of PDFs
> documents by authors who request hand-marked manuscript and documents created in spreadsheet or presentation software programs with mark-revisions features too cumbersome to use
> copy that has been poured into a sophisticated page-design program (In some advertising firms and other corporate settings, for example, copyeditors may work only on printouts, and although newer page-design applications

support direct entry of editorial corrections, graphic designers may prefer
to maintain control over copyfitting and design by entering editors' hand-
marked corrections themselves.)

text that accompanies maps or other graphics (e.g., callouts, labels, captions) in
the event that these snippets are not supplied in digital form with the main
manuscript

Technology is marching inexorably toward the total digitization of editorial procedures. But even in the twenty-first century, a hoe is sometimes more efficient than
a tractor. In a curious twist, some newer versions of PDF readers enable copyeditors
who are emending PDF documents on-screen to use correction stamps that mimic
hand-marking symbols, or to apply hand-marking symbols directly on-screen using a
mouse, a stylus (electronic pencil), or built-in text editing tools. Especially if you work
in publishing, advises one practitioner, you need to be familiar with the traditional correction marks; the industry is not quite ready to leave them behind.[1]

## COMPUTER SKILLS

Editors working on-screen—that is to say, most editors—must develop scrupulous
routines for file management, backup, and version control. Chapter 1 emphasized the
importance of archiving the author's untouched original files upon receipt and creating
a duplicate set to work on. You should in fact save a complete set of files at each major
stage of the editorial process—say, unedited original files, redlined, author reviewed,
and cleaned up—before you move to the next stage. Also back up in-progress work at
the end of every session and secure each completed stage of work with a backup on an
external hard drive or a remote server accessed over the internet.[2]

Clearly identify each stage, or version, of the project with self-explanatory folder
and file names by devising naming conventions and consistently applying them to all
editing projects. For example, for Patty Pilcrow's three-chapter manuscript "Pleasing
Paragraphs," you might tuck all versions of the manuscript into a master project folder
bearing the author's name and a short form of the title, then store successive versions of
the working copy in subfolders, keying subfolder and file names to both the project and
the specific stage of work. Individual file names can also be formulated to support correct sort order within the directory:

1. Adrienne Montgomerie, "Basic PDF Mark-Up for Copy Editors and Proofreaders," *Right Angels and Polo Bears: Adventures in Editing* (blog), May 31, 2011, http://blog.catchthesun.net/. See the entire six-part series, "PDF Mark-Up for Editors," at this URL. See also the blog post by Colleen Gratzer, "13 Time- and Money-Saving Acrobat Tips," Gratzer Graphics LLC, June 13, 2016, https://gratzergraphics.com/blog/13-time-and-money-saving-acrobat-tips/.

2. A cloud service is also often the most secure way to exchange files with an author, publisher, or composition vendor during the editorial process. Regardless of how files are transmitted, an email alert requesting confirmation of receipt is always advisable.

```
PILCROW_Working Files
    Pilcrow Original_Working_Copy
            a1 Pilcrow_title_orig_working
            a2 Pilcrow_contents_orig_working
            b Pilcrow_ch1_orig_working
            b Pilcrow_ch2_orig_working
            b Pilcrow_ch3_orig_working
            n1 Pilcrow_notes_orig_working
            n2 Pilcrow_bib_orig_working
    Pilcrow Redlined_Working_Copy
            a01 Pilcrow_title_rl_working
            a02 Pilcrow_contents_rl_working
            b Pilcrow_ch1_rl_working
            b Pilcrow_ch2_rl_working
            b Pilcrow_ch3_rl_working
            n1 Pilcrow_notes_rl_working
            n2 Pilcrow_bib_rl_working
etc.
```

Version control is especially critical for a document edited or reviewed by several collaborators. Multiple editors or author-reviewers may work on a single copy of a document in succession—or even simultaneously, as in Google Docs (version control becomes complicated when two people try to change the same thing at once!). With the mark-revisions feature turned on and the document password-protected, the successive changes, identified according to the individual who makes them, are then reconciled in cleanup. Alternatively, several individuals may emend revision-protected copies of the document concurrently; then the several emended versions of the document are combined, using a word processor's merge-documents feature, with any disagreements among the revisers arbitrated by the lead author or editor. Some organizations make use of a sophisticated in-house or commercially available document management system for such collaborative work and create the final draft together in a videoconference. Whether improvised or formal, though, a collaborative system needs three things: a well-defined work process, a way to control versions by tracing the history and differentiating the authorship of changes from multiple sources, and an editorial coordinator or lead editor to reconcile these changes in a definitive final version.

Besides knowing how to organize and back up files and to control versions, editors need to learn how to deploy the many capabilities of their word processing software efficiently. Currently, one of the most prevalent applications for editing is Microsoft Word. Whether working in a PC (Windows) or a Mac environment, editors can acquire or improve their Word skills in the classroom or through a host of online courses, webinars, YouTube videos, printed workbooks, blogs, and the like.[3] (The unrelenting release

3. See, for example, Carol Fisher Saller's helpful "Tech Tips and Editing Resources," *The Subversive Copy Editor Blog,* http://www.subversivecopyeditor.com/blog/. The Selected Bibliography lists many additional resources.

of new versions of Word, as well as the inevitable emergence of other software applications and platforms, will prompt even the most adroit practitioners to go back to school regularly.) A typical curriculum for beginning Word editors might cover the following topics. You can use this rough checklist for evaluating your readiness to grab that mouse:

setting Word *preferences*
adjusting the *autocorrect* and *autoformatting* features
activating the *spell-checker;* deactivating the (much-reviled) *grammar checker*
customizing and creating *dictionaries*
using different document *views*
using *track changes*
using the *compare* documents feature
using the *merge* documents feature
inserting *comments*
using *balloons*
using the *review pane*
creating *styles* and *templates*
writing *macros* and *customizing* the keyboard
using *find and replace;* formulating *wildcard* searches
*protecting* a document from unauthorized changes
*accepting* and *rejecting* tracked changes

In addition to the extensive features available in Word, editors can use customized Word editing tools, for example, macros to perform basic file cleanup (described in chapter 1). Novices should read reviews of off-the-shelf software before purchasing any such add-on tools. Some can save editors considerable time otherwise spent performing routine, mindless chores; others are seriously flawed and roundly criticized. Many are written for the Windows operating system only, so Mac users are sometimes out of luck unless they can duplicate the functionality by creating their own macros. Even without the aid of off-the-shelf editing tools for complex operations, though, editors can access technical support through several email lists and message boards for professional editors. Many advanced Word users in these online communities generously answer questions and help solve problems for colleagues in need of IT assistance.

Although Word is currently the most versatile and widely used editing software, copyeditors may resort to less powerful (and less expensive) word processors, collaborative writing tools, and other applications as the circumstances require. For example, an editor may receive a PDF document for correction and, in a somewhat arduous process using Adobe Acrobat's markup and commenting tools, mark emendations directly on-screen. The graphic designer can subsequently enter the editor's corrections in the document, even copying (rather than rekeying) added or revised text supplied in comments. Regardless of the technology used for on-screen editing—or of any new technologies that may emerge—editors need to establish a process that supports the basic requirements: marking changes, querying, recordkeeping, and manuscript cleanup.

## MARKING CHANGES ON HARD COPY

Every mark a copyeditor makes on the hard copy of a manuscript must be intelligible to the author (who must approve the copyediting), the word processor or typesetter (who must key in the handwritten changes), and the proofreader (who will read the proofs against the marked copy). To accommodate the needs of all these parties, copyeditors must work as neatly as they can. In this job, penmanship counts.

Copyeditors working on hard copy write their corrections in the text proper, reserving the margins for queries to the author (see figure 2). The choice of writing implement depends on how the manuscript will be handled after copyediting. If the entire marked-up copy will be sent to a typesetter for rekeying, the copyeditor may use an ordinary lead pencil. However, if the manuscript will be given to a word processor who will key only the copyeditor's changes into existing production files, the copyeditor may be asked to use a brightly colored pencil or pen. The bright color helps the word processor spot the changes without having to pore over every line of text. In either case, marks on a paper document must always be scannable (light pencil and some colors are thus ill advised): as insurance against damage or loss of the sole copy of a hand-marked manuscript, publishers customarily duplicate it before committing the edited original to the author's hands or to the mail. (Although this precaution is necessary when editing has been done on hard copy, it is obviously inefficient compared with backing up the redlined files of a manuscript that has been edited on-screen.)

No two copyeditors use identical markings, but the conventions shown in figure 3 are universally understood by publishing professionals. It's not safe, however, to assume that all authors will know the system. As a courtesy to your author, you can attach a list of symbols to the copyedited manuscript.

Don't worry about memorizing all the symbols in one or two sittings. Keep a list of the symbols on your desk whenever you are hand-marking a manuscript. It's easier to learn the symbols by using them than by staring at them. In addition to using conventional symbols, you should follow two guidelines:

1. If a word has several errors, cross out the entire word and rewrite it; don't expect others to correctly decode a cryptic string of markings.

*Hard to read:* Government must respect the will of

the people.

*Clearer:* Government must respect the will of

the people

2. When you insert a word or the final letters of a word, write in any punctuation marks that immediately follow.

> *Not:* If you don't write in the punctuation mark~~s~~,
>
> the typesetter might miss **them** ~~it~~.

> *But:* If you don't write in the punctuation mark~~s,~~
>
> the typesetter might miss ~~it~~ **them.**

===

FIGURE 2. Hand-Marked Manuscript

---

One of the basic axioms of financial pla**n**ning is that ~~diversification~~ **from**

reduces volatility and risk. Apparently, many investors agree, for their

movement into asset allocation mutual funds is making this group one of

the fastest growing types of mutual funds.

*[margin note: Add number on rate of growth?]*

Asset allocation, through, can mean different things to different

investors as well as **to** different mutual fund management companies. To

survey the field, **I interviewed** fund managers ~~were interviewed~~ from seven companies.

Among them, a consensus seems to be developing that an asset

allocation fund is an actively managed portfolio with assets in at least

three categories: U.S. stocks, U.S. bonds, and cash. Some funds also invest

in foreign stocks, foreign bonds, or precious metals. Unlike the traditional

"balanced funds," which perennially allocated 50% of their holdings

to stocks, 45% to bonds, and 5% to cash, the asset allocation funds

continuously adjust the proportions of asset classes **in their portfolios** to reflect economic

conditions.

*[margin note:  Ok?]*

FIGURE 2 *(continued)*

¶ This spring, for example, several of the funds ~~are at~~ *have* record ~~high points~~ *amounts* in cash. Citing unusually high short term interest rates and a yield curve that has been flat or ~~in a reverse pattern~~ *inverted* fund managers find cash quite attractive. The yield curve has also prompted large positions in intermediate term bonds.

*Indicate what % is in cash?*

FIGURE 3.  Copyediting Marks

| Mark | Name or Meaning | Example |
|---|---|---|
| ∧ | caret | Use a caret to add letters or *entire* words. |
| ℯ | delete | Use a delete sign to delete letters or a few of words. |
| ◡ or ⌒ | close up | An easy way to remove extra spaces. |
| ℐ or ⌒ | delete and close up | Don't ask the typesetter to guess about whether to close up the space. |
| # or (#) | space | So the words don't run together. Also used to add linespacing. Some copyeditors prefer to use a backslash—or a backslash and a space sign—to indicate a wordspace. So the words don't run together. |
| ∾ | transpose | Transpose a letter or misplaced a word. |
| ••• | stet | Reinstates deleted material. ~~Also~~ used to mean *as is*, to annotate an unusual spelling: Gorge Johnson cain't spell. |
| ∼ | run in | An easy way to correct typing errors or to delete a paragraph break. |

*(continued next page)*

FIGURE 3 *(continued)*

| Mark | Name or Meaning | Example |
|------|-----------------|---------|
| ¶ or ⑾ | para | ¶Adds a new paragraph. |
| | | No marking is needed when the text shows a paragraph indent. |
| ◯ | spell out | When an editor circles ①or ②numerals or an abbrev, the compositor will spell out the circled items. |
| | | When an abbreviation is unusual or could be spelled in several ways, the copyeditor should write out the desired term. *Nineteen ninety* ~~1990~~ was a good year for the ~~NHL~~ *National Hockey League*⊙ |
| ⊙ | period | Dr Kim L Jones delivered the report. |
| | | Copyeditors circle an inserted period to make it more visible; only handwritten inserted periods should be circled. Circling is also used to convert a typed comma into a period. |
| | | Dr Kim L Jones delivered the report. |
| ⌄ | comma | Similarly for visibility editors place a roof over handwritten commas. |
| | | The roof makes the comma more visible. Do not mark a correctly typed comma; mark only handwritten commas and periods that are to be converted into commas. |
| | | She left But he did not. |
| ⌄ | apostrophe | Its just a matter of practice. |
| ⌄ ⌄ | quote marks | You're doing well, she said. |
| ( ) | parens | Parentheses always come in pairs. |
| | | The crosshatches clarify that the character is not a C or an l. |
| = | hyphen | Copyeditors need to handmark hard end-of line hyphens. |
| | | Use the hyphen mark only to insert a hyphen or to indicate that a hyphen appearing at the end of a line is to be retained. Other hyphens need not be marked. |

FIGURE 3 *(continued)*

| Mark | Name or Meaning | Example |
|------|------|------|
| N̲ | en dash | Used in numerical ranges: pp. 45–47. |
| | | Most word processing programs can print an en dash (–) instead of a hyphen, but not all users take advantage of this feature. |
| M̲ | em dash | Your everyday dash--see? |
| | | Most word processing programs can print an em dash (—), but some users type two hyphens instead. |
| / | lowercase | To loWercase a letter or a WORD. |
| ≡ | capitalize | turns a lowercase letter into a capital. |
| ≈ | small cap | So that B.C., a.m., P.M. will be set as |
| | | **B.C., A.M., P.M.** |
| V | superscript | Mark mc2 so that it will be typeset as $mc^2$. |
| ∧ | subscript | Mark O2 so that it will be set as $O_2$. |
| — | italic | Use italics sparingly! |
| | | Typists used to underline words that were to be set in italics, but now word processing programs can print *italic letters*. |
| ⟨ ⟩ | delete italic or bold | Instructs the typesetter to ignore (underlining, printed italics) or (boldface type.) |
| ∿∿∿ | bold | The typesetter will set boldface type. |
| [ | flush left | ⌐ Moves text to align at the left margin. |
| ] | flush right | Moves text to align at the right margin: |
| | | Jane L. Jones |
| ] [ | center | ]This line will be centered.[ |
| \| | align | Combine |
| | | 2 cups fresh basil, chopped |
| | | 1 cup olive oil |
| | | 2 teaspoons chopped garlic |

Copyeditors working on hard copy also mark the location of nonstandard characters, cross-references ("x-refs"), tables and figures, and in-text footnote or endnote numbers. These markings are known as *callouts,* or *placement callouts,* and they are written in the left margin of the manuscript, circled so that the typesetter knows they are instructions, not additional text for insertion.

Nitrate levels at the Shenandoah test sites averaged

(lc "mu") 0.4µg/m³ (see figure 36.7), among the highest in the

(xref)

state.[9] In contrast, sulfate levels at the Shenandoah

test sites were well below the average statewide

(xref) readings (see table 36.4).

## MAKING CHANGES ON-SCREEN

Again, the crucial first step in any on-screen project is to make a working copy of the files from the author's or publisher's set, clearly label the originals as the unedited files, and store these original files in a safe place, with an external backup. Edit only the duplicate files, renamed as your working copy. (The advisory under "Computer Skills" bears repeating: back up your working copy at the end of every session and secure each completed stage of editorial work.) Beyond the usual value of having the original files, with backup, as insurance against meltdowns (hardware, software, computing errors), you may also need the unedited original files while working on the project. Some methods of generating redlined files—files showing both the author's original text and the copyeditor's insertions and deletions (see figure 4)—require both unedited and edited files. The software "compares" the unedited and edited documents and generates the redlined copy as a third, separate document.

Many word processing programs create redlined files as you work by using a *mark-revisions feature.* (In Microsoft Word, the term is *track changes.*) You can view the redlined text on-screen at all times or display the redline markings only when you want to review changes. If you do not want the author to be distracted by the redlining of nondiscretionary changes (e.g., the preliminary file cleanup described in chapter 1 or mandatory corrections), you can turn off the mark-revisions feature before you run the file cleanup macros or the spell-checker and when you make minor mechanical corrections. However, you must turn on the mark-revisions feature for any editorial intervention that could be vetoed or re-revised by the author.

Each word processing program provides options for showing editorial changes on the monitor and in a printout. For example, you can show underlined insertions in red on the screen, display strikeouts in blue, and represent moved copy in green, with a

FIGURE 4. Redlined Text. In this sample the characters that the copyeditor has deleted are marked with horizontal strikeouts, and the characters that the copyeditor has added are double underlined. Even when color is used to differentiate the deletions and additions from the unchanged original text, both on-screen displays of redlined text and hard-copy printouts of redlined text are difficult to read. Thus copyeditors usually work on a clean display, rather than on the redlined display, and some authors forgo the advantage of reviewing a redlined document or printout—that is, the opportunity to see exactly what has been changed—for the ease of reading a clean copy.

~~Murphy's Law assures us that n~~<u>N</u>o amount of proofreading ~~will~~ <u>can</u> uncover all the errors in a <u>set of proofs.</u> ~~work about to be published. The question is, how many re-readings are reasonable?~~ ~~In my personal experience I have found that t~~<u>T</u>wo readings of galleys and two <u>readings</u> of page proofs will catch 99 percent of the errors<u>, but</u>. ~~Unfortunately~~ the remaining ~~1 percent are often~~ ~~the~~ mistakes—<u>incorrect phone numbers or misspelled names</u>—often cause both ~~that not only~~ ~~cause~~ embarrassment <u>and</u> ~~but~~ trouble. ~~For example, the wrong numbers for ordering merchandise or misspelled names.~~

strikethrough for deleted text and double underlining for added or repositioned text.[4] (A one-color printout retains the single and double underlining and strikethrough conventions.) In Microsoft Word, changes can be displayed on-screen entirely in-line or detailed in *balloons* or in a *review pane* alongside the text; in-line changes, balloons, and the review pane can be shown in the printout as well. Some publishers supply their on-screen copyeditors with custom macros that set their preferred conventions.

Your techniques for marking changes on-screen depend on your and your author's viewing preferences. If you prefer to view all edits in-line, change whole words rather than trying to "save" part of a word or phrase so that the redlined screen display and printout will be more legible:

*Hard-to-read redlining:* Th<u>is</u>e~~is~~ ~~reiteration~~<u>ve</u> process~~dure~~<u>dure</u>

*Clearer:* ~~The reiteration process~~<u>This iterative procedure</u>

4. The reviser's name and the date and time of each revision are also embedded in the file. This information appears on the screen in a "sticky note" when a user allows the mouse to linger on a redlined word or passage. The feature enables all parties to determine who made each change to the document, an advantage when one document is sent to several reviewers (e.g., a technical expert, a second writer, and a copyeditor) in sequence—or simultaneously. This personal information, or metadata, can be deleted for security or other reasons.

If you prefer to view the edits in marginal balloons, small changes—case, verb tense, number—can be made to affected letters only. Whole-word changes take up more space: inserting a single letter doesn't create a new balloon, but replacing a whole word does.

You also need to be careful about the wordspacing before and after inserted words. The following markings may look correct on the screen:

It's ~~hard~~difficult to resist the ~~urge~~temptation to ~~improve~~change someone else's writing.

But the printout will read:

It'sdifficult to resist thetemptation tochange someone else's writing.

Certain kinds of changes do not show up on the printout of a redlined document. For example, if you are using a horizontal line strikeout, a deleted hyphen may not appear to have been deleted because the strikeout mark displays or prints over the hyphen; for clarity's sake, you can delete the entire word and type in the hyphenless form. Also, the deletion or addition of a paragraph break is not clearly visible on-screen or in a redlined printout. To alert the author to such changes, you need to add a query.

Finally, watch what happens in redlined files if you move a portion of text that contains a correction:

| *Original* | *Redlined printout* |
| --- | --- |
| Send your comments to | Send your comments to |
| P.O. Box 1 | P.O. Box 1, Anytown CA 94000 |
| Anytown CA 9400 | ~~Anytown CA 9400~~ |

Because the change in the zip code falls within a piece of transposed text, the addition of the fifth digit is not highlighted as a correction in and of itself. To call the author's attention to such a change, you must write a query. Or, if the author will review the copyediting on-screen rather than in a one-color printout, move the copy *before* making the in-line correction: the move and the in-line correction will then be displayed on-screen in different colors. (Another tip: To add one redlined document to another, turn off the track changes feature in both documents before using the Insert File command.) Whether the author reviews the editing on paper or on-screen, though, note that whenever you move a piece of text, the redlined version shows two changes: the deletion of the original words and the insertion of those same words. You may wish to warn your authors about this, lest an author scan the redlined version and think that you have made dozens of extra changes.

## QUERYING

Often a copyeditor needs to address a question, comment, or explanation to the author. Some questions are so important—they pertain to the entire manuscript or to a large chunk of it—that the copyeditor must raise them with the author before completing the copyediting. In those cases, a phone call or an email is warranted. But other questions, comments, or explanations pertain only to a sentence or paragraph, or to a page or small section of the manuscript. These types of communications are collectively called *queries,* and they will accompany the copyedited manuscript when it is returned to the author for review.

For a copyeditor, good querying skills—knowing when to query (and when not to query) and how to query effectively—are as important as a solid grasp of punctuation and grammar. Query too often, and the author may become frustrated with the amount of time needed to read and respond to all your questions, comments, and explanations. Query too infrequently, and the author may not understand the problem you are trying to fix and may stet the error-laden original text, or the author may not catch a slight change in meaning that you have inadvertently introduced, or the author may start to feel that you're taking over the manuscript without so much as a "May I?" Query in a way that confuses or insults the author, and you are unlikely to obtain the cooperation you need to resolve the problem at hand.

*When to query.* Copyeditors write queries to call the author's attention to a problem, to ask for clarification, or to explain a proposed revision whose rationale might not be obvious. For example, copyeditors query when

> the author's meaning is not clear or seems ambiguous
> the copyeditor wants the author to choose among possible rewordings
> the copyeditor wants to explain a complicated revision
> the copyeditor wants to ask the author to provide or recheck a piece of
>     information
> there seems to be an internal contradiction in the text
> the author's argument seems to have a logical error
> the copyeditor knows the topic and has a good reason to question (but with
>     consummate tact) the factual accuracy of a statement

Not every change in a manuscript requires a query. Copyeditors do not query routine mechanical changes that are not subject to the author's veto or re-revision; thus you need not explain the reason for every added or deleted piece of punctuation or for every lowercasing of a word that the author capitalized. Some routine changes, however, may warrant an explanation at first occurrence to reassure the author that the changes are not arbitrary: "AU: Publisher's house style specifies the use of the serial comma here."[5]

---

5. To save time, some copyeditors employ a text-expansion application for boilerplate explanatory queries frequently used in different editing jobs. One such application, TextExpander, for example,

But you should call the author's attention to any mechanical changes that may be controversial, and you must query any mechanical revisions that might affect the meaning of the sentence. For example, your author has written

> This directive is addressed to employees in the following departments:
> order fulfillment, customer service, marketing, media and print advertising.

If house style calls for the final *serial comma* (that is, the comma preceding *and* or *or* in a list) and you automatically place a comma after "media," you might be dividing the "media and print advertising department" into two departments. Here, you must ask the author whether the text should read "marketing, and media and print advertising" or "marketing, media, and print advertising."

A copyeditor also need not write a query to explain minor changes in wording or emendations to repair simple grammatical errors. If the grammatical issue is more esoteric or complex, however, it may be worth an explanation so that the author will know that you are fixing a mistake, not tinkering for the sake of tinkering. For example, if a manuscript is replete with dangling participles, you might write a quick note at the first instance.

Although deciding when to write queries about mechanical and grammatical issues becomes second nature after a while, deciding when to pose substantive queries never becomes wholly routine. Each of the following substantive discrepancies and omissions definitely merits a query:

- Factual inconsistencies within the manuscript. For example, if the population statistics given at the beginning of chapter 2 do not match those in footnote 9 of chapter 3, write a brief, polite query: "Population 17,000 at the beginning of chapter 2, but 12,500 in chapter 3, footnote 9. Please reconcile."
- Points of fact about which you are *verifiably* certain that the manuscript is incorrect. For example, the author gives the date of John F. Kennedy's assassination as November 20, 1963; you clearly remember the event as occurring on your eighth birthday, November 22, 1963, and after verifying your recollection online—memory being a fallible thing—you politely prompt the author to correct the error.
- Inconsistencies between the evidence presented and the author's interpretation of that evidence. For example, suppose your author writes: "Mean test scores for sophomores in the Artview district have risen steadily in the past ten years (see table 1)." You should look at table 1 and query the author if it does not in fact include the mean test scores for sophomores in the Artview district for each of the past ten years or show that the mean score rose each year.
- Inconsistencies between the manuscript and the accompanying diagrams, figures, or photographs. For example, if a caption identifies three people,

---

takes short abbreviations that the editor has defined in the app and expands these into larger snippets of text.

whereas the low-resolution digital image supplied for reference with the manuscript shows only two individuals, you should point out the discrepancy and ask the author to resolve it.

- Incomplete or missing source notes, footnotes or endnotes, or bibliographical items. Sources should be given for all direct quotations other than proverbs, extremely familiar phrases, and well-known literary allusions ("To be or not to be"). Sources should also be provided for facts outside the realm of common knowledge. For example, if the author writes that an obscure mathematical genius named Charles Ellis, not the famous bridge engineer Joseph Strauss, deserves credit for the structural design of the 1.7-mile Golden Gate Bridge, you should ask the author to document this claim.

In deciding whether to pose a substantive query on issues other than these, you need first of all to consider the intended readers: will they be confused, frustrated, or misled by a sentence or passage that bothers you? Next, you need to think about how much additional work you can reasonably expect the author to do at this stage of publication. Every request you make—no matter how polite—places demands on an author's time and patience. For some authors, an accumulation of requests—no matter how small—may be so upsetting that halfway through the manuscript they stop looking at the queries or become so demoralized that they miss their deadline for returning the manuscript. You should also think about the budget and schedule for the publication: is there enough time for the author to respond to all the queries, for those answers to be reviewed, and for the author's additions to be copyedited?

*Length of queries.* Sometimes, a query can be as simple as "OK?" or (if this seems too cryptic) just "OK as edited?" Other times, you will need to write a longer query: an explanation of a proposed revision or a suggestion that the author clarify an ambiguous sentence. The terse request "Please revise" may not give an author sufficient guidance. At least explain the problem, and if you can quickly propose a rewording (or several alternative wordings to choose from), do so.

The best queries are succinct but still polite and specific. When queries are too brief or vague (e.g., "Logic?"), authors may not understand what the problem is or may feel they are being chastised or attacked. Either way—whether you confuse or offend the author—the results will be counterproductive, and you will not get the information you ask for.

When queries are overly long and discursive, in contrast, authors may resent the imposition on their time. You might guess that it will take the author less than a minute to read the query and respond, but consider what happens when author Jack is trying to be conscientious in responding to copyeditor Jill's queries: First, Jack reads (and perhaps rereads) the query. Then he looks at the troublesome spot in the manuscript. Even though Jill's query concerns one sentence, Jack backs up and reads one or two paragraphs before the troublesome sentence and continues to read a paragraph or two past it. Next, he starts to consider the merits of Jill's query: is Jill correct, or has she misunderstood the text or misgauged the audience? This question prompts another rereading of a page or two of the manuscript and another rereading of the query. If Jack concludes that Jill's point is valid, then the time spent reaching that decision and the time to be devoted to revising the manuscript will be chalked up as time well spent. But if Jack concludes that Jill's query is irrelevant or extraneous, he will harrumph (or worse) at having had to go to such lengths so that he could, in good conscience, stet his original sentence.

Think twice about queries that pose a substantive question and invite a yes or no answer. For example, the query "Could you add a sentence to explain what you mean by 'political correctness'?" meets the tests of succinctness, politeness, and specificity. In response to such a query, however, the author could simply scrawl NO. If that would be an acceptable response, then the phrasing of the query is fine. But if you believe that adding the explanation is essential to the readers' understanding of the document, then you will want to phrase your query in a way that helps the author understand the importance of providing the requested explanation. And so you might write: "Because 'political correctness' has become a Rorschach blot onto which everyone projects a personal meaning, readers will want to know what the term means here. Please add a sentence or two to define." Of course, the author is always free to ignore your requests, but this kind of query is harder to shrug off.

*Tone of queries.* Regardless of the temptation to offer occasional humorous or personal asides, avoid a jokey or overly familiar tone in queries, which an author may perceive as unprofessional, even disrespectful. Likewise, queries should never be sarcastic, snide, or argumentative. And they should never adopt the tone of a schoolteacher lecturing a recalcitrant student, or the accusatory "you" of a police officer interrogating a suspect. Above all, queries should not sound as though you might be challenging the author's expertise or intellectual ability. Queries are not the place for complaints or rebukes; use them to describe the problem and to elicit the author's help in resolving it.

Here are some examples of do's and don'ts:

| *Instead of* | *Write* |
|---|---|
| Fix these numbers. | Please reconcile. |
| Where's the referent for "this"? | "this" = the budget or the meeting? |
| "Picasso's portrait" is unclear. | "Picasso's portrait" could mean either "the portrait of Picasso" or "the portrait by Picasso." Clarify? |
| Sometimes you say "pull-down menu," sometimes "drop-down menu." Please be consistent. | If "pull-down menu" and "drop-down menu" are equivalent, let's use the same term throughout this section. Which do you prefer? |
| You never explain how oil prices affected ordinary people. | Will readers follow the sequence here, or would it help them if you explain how soaring oil prices affected the cost of living? |

| | |
|---|---|
| Faulty transition; I don't see how this follows. | Will readers understand how this paragraph relates to the one preceding? |
| This example doesn't really illustrate the point; delete OK? | This example is striking, but it doesn't precisely match the principle. Move it to p. 145 (or delete it?) and supply a stronger example here? Or revise the example for a better fit here? |
| I don't find this convincing. | Will readers trained in structural analysis accept this conclusion as stated? |
| Surely, you can't mean this! | Is this "not" a typographical error (perhaps for "now")? Otherwise, this sentence doesn't seem to follow from what has preceded. |
| Your use of "he" throughout this section implies that all freight expediters are men. Certainly, that is no longer the case. In contemporary usage, the so-called generic he is inadequate. So I rewrote all the sexist sentences. | Scattered revisions to avoid gender bias. OK? Or please re-revise. |

As several of the preceding examples illustrate, it is best to phrase a query in terms of what readers need, want, or expect. Queries worded in this way serve to remind the author that the primary purpose of a publication is to inform, persuade, or entertain and delight readers, and that all editorial decisions should be made with the readers' interests at heart. Also, the "readers first" wording can help you sidestep a potential author-copyeditor battle, in which you are cast as a faultfinding nudge; instead, you and the author become a team working together for the good of the readers. In contrast, your "I don't get this" may provoke an author to mutter a nasty comment about your woeful lack of intelligence rather than to rewrite the confusing passage.

If you find yourself becoming annoyed with the author ("Didn't this guy even reread what he wrote?" "How could she be so careless about her work?"), do not write queries until your mood has improved. It helps to remember that the author did not set out to make your life miserable by purposely mistyping or misspelling dozens of words, that the author may be working under personal or professional constraints unknown to you, and—finally—that if all authors were careful, diligent, and highly skilled, you would be out of work.

Another approach to query writing is to treat the manuscript, no matter how poorly written or prepared, as though it were the author's ugly newborn. That is, regardless of how unprepossessing you may think the baby is, you would never say so to the new mother or father; no—surely, you would find something polite to say. You don't have to coo over a manuscript: insincere praise will quickly be perceived as condescension. But you should be gentle with any criticism, remembering that the manuscript is the product of the author's labor and sweat, hopes and dreams, and that you are being granted the privilege (along with the frustration) of participating in its publication. Point to the author's strengths if possible: "Please clarify this explanation with an entertaining example, as you did in your introductory paragraph."

## PROCEDURES FOR QUERYING ON HARD COPY

A pencil-and-paper copyeditor should ask the editorial coordinator about the publisher's preferred method for queries. Common methods include

- *Bubbles.* If the manuscript has generous margins and the queries are brief, the copyeditor can write *bubble queries* on the manuscript (as shown in figure 2). The advantage of this method is that the copyedited manuscript along with all of the queries can be photocopied easily.
- *Query slips.* Longer comments or questions used to be placed on *flags* (also called *query slips* or *query tags*)—small slips of paper moistened on a gummed edge and then attached to the sides of the manuscript. Today some copyeditors use self-adhesive notes (also known as *sticky notes* or by the trademarked name *Post-its*) for this purpose. Because these notes may fall off in transit, they should always include the manuscript page number (and even the paragraph number) in the corner. Disadvantages of this method are the difficulty of photocopying a hand-marked manuscript with attached sticky notes and the ease with which an author can accidentally dislodge the query notes or simply remove them without responding.
- *Query list.* A more efficient method of posing queries, if they are too detailed or numerous to be handled as bubble queries, is to list them, keyed to the manuscript by page and paragraph number, on separate sheets of paper interleaved with the manuscript or incorporated into a cover letter to the author. Query sheets can be easily photocopied along with the hand-marked manuscript.

## PROCEDURES FOR QUERYING ON-SCREEN

On-screen copyeditors have three choices for writing their queries:

- *Comments.* In Microsoft Word and in most other word processors, you can use the comment feature (see figure 5). Although display options vary with the operating system and software, in Word your comments (queries) can often be displayed in a sidebar by activating Word's balloons, which tethers the comments, together with specified types of changes, to the relevant text. Comments and changes can also be viewed alongside the text in Word's review pane; this split-screen display automatically keys the comments to the relevant text. Both options work best for authors who are comfortable reviewing copyediting on-screen, but if an author prefers hard copy, you can generate a printout with the balloons or the review pane. The review pane prints as a separate document; the balloons print as a sidebar with the text, shrinking the overall

FIGURE 5. Queries in a Microsoft Word File. In Word, copyeditors can write queries using the comments feature. Some versions and settings automatically number the comments and include the commenter's initials. Copyeditors and authors may each choose how they prefer to display the comments: (a) as marginal balloons or (b) as a list in a review pane alongside the document.

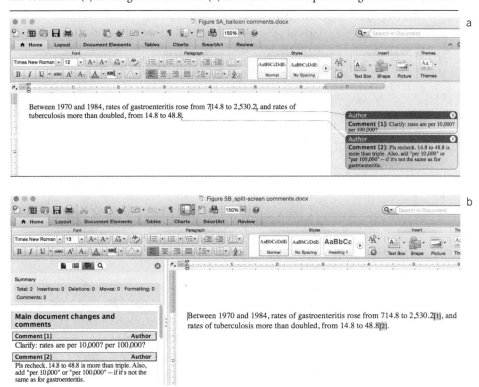

text image to accommodate the sidebar. Some editors temporarily increase the type size of the document or enlarge the right margin to preserve legibility.

- *Footnotes.* You can use a word processor's footnote feature to place your queries in bottom-of-page or end-of-document notes. This method works best for a manuscript without any native notes. But if the manuscript itself contains numbered notes, you can use uppercase letters or nonalphabetical characters (e.g., asterisks) to differentiate the query notes from the author's numbered notes. Although some editors prefer the footnote method, it poses a risk that queries at the foot of the page or end of the document will be overlooked, either by the author when reviewing the editing or by the cleanup editor when preparing the final manuscript for the next stage of production.

- *Embedded queries.* You can place your queries within curly braces in the text proper. Using curly braces, rather than parentheses or square brackets, which the author may have used in the manuscript, will allow you or another editor to search for all the queries during cleanup and remove them from the file. To draw the author's attention to the queries, you can make them boldface or use the color highlighting tool. You can also use separate paragraphs for queries and cast them in a different type font to make them stand out:

Between 1970 and 1984, rates of gastroenteritis rose from 714.8 to 2,530.2,
**{Clarify: 714.8 per 10,000? per 100,000?}**
and rates of tuberculosis more than doubled, from 14.8 to 48.8.
**{Pls recheck. 14.8 to 48.8 is more than triple. Also, add "per 10,000" or "per 100,000"—if it's not the same as for gastroenteritis}**

Although such embedded queries must be easy to spot, don't overdo the typographical emphasis. If you type your queries in all caps, for example, some authors will feel that you are shouting at them. One disadvantage of this method is that interpolated queries, especially if frequent or lengthy, interrupt the flow of the text and may interfere with the author's careful rereading of the edited manuscript. In-text queries also affect the total word count for the document. To overcome these disadvantages, some editors simply embed query numbers in the text (e.g., {**Query1**} or {**Q1**}) and put the queries, keyed to these numbers, in a separate document.

A copyeditor in a conventional publishing environment should ask the editorial coordinator which method is preferred. Although many editors still rely on the second or third method, *Chicago* "no longer recommends using footnotes or bracketed text to insert queries. . . . It is best to avoid adding content that is not intended for publication to the run of text." Instead, *Chicago* advises, "author queries should be inserted using the commenting feature available in most word processors" (2.87). Some publishers use custom macros that include an insert-query feature.

In nontraditional environments, editors sometimes devise or adapt to other on-screen querying systems. An editor working on a short, simple manuscript sometimes just poses questions in an email to the author. An editor working on a complex, multiauthor document may pose queries in a videoconference while the authors view the document together on a shared server (some cloud services facilitate such collaboration). An editor working on a PDF document may use PDF reader tools to query the author.

## STYLE SHEETS

For any project longer than a few pages, you must keep a *style sheet,* a record of your editorial choices. If you are working for a publisher, the editorial coordinator may give you a blank style sheet (either a hard-copy or an on-screen form). If you are editing hard copy on your own, you can create a form based on the sample in figure 6. This template can be adapted for an on-screen project: in the alphabetical section, listings can be recorded willy-nilly in a single column for later computer sorting.

As you copyedit, you must stop every time you make a choice or decision about a mechanical issue (spelling, capitalization, use of numbers, abbreviations, hyphenation) and enter that decision on your style sheet. (If your style sheet must be handwritten, make sure your entries are legible, using traditional copyediting symbols for upper- and lowercase letters and italic and boldface treatment.) Instead of listing every individual change and decision, experienced copyeditors reduce the work of recordkeeping by simply noting the style followed in certain well-defined categories (e.g., "*Chicago* numbers style throughout") and then just recording exceptions (e.g., "Exception: 4 Cs"). But novice copyeditors should err on the side of overdocumentation until they master the intricacies of various editorial styles. As you continue to work through the manuscript, these entries will remind you of your choices and will thus help you enforce mechanical consistency. And when the author's corrections and revisions to the copyedited manuscript arrive on your desk several weeks after you have moved on to another project, you will find yourself repeatedly consulting your style sheet to make sure that the author's additions to the text follow the editorial style of the copyedited manuscript. The designer, typesetter, proofreader, and indexer will also refer to your completed style sheet whenever a question of mechanics arises during production, and it may guide style decisions in later editions or in other books in a series.

To serve all these purposes, your style sheet should have an entry for every decision and choice. Do not stop to record every word that the author misspelled or mistyped; enter only those items that require a decision of some sort. For example, in the following sentence you would correct the errors, but you would not make any entries on your style sheet:

The technical writer is solely respons∧ible for the factual

accuracy of the manuscript, but the editor is expected to

call the write∧rs attention ∧to any internal di∧screpan∧ces.

In contrast, the following sentence doesn't require any corrections:

In 1980 the National Radio Astronomy Observatory (NRAO) completed the Very Large Array, a collection of twenty-seven portable antennas arranged in a Y-shape.

But this one sentence requires four entries on your style sheet:

NRAO (no internal periods)
the Very Large Array (caps, proper name of project)
antennas (plural, *not* antennae)
Y-shape (noun)[6]

---

6. A serif or a sans serif typeface may be used for a letter that indicates a shape:
serif typeface: a V-shaped valley, an A-frame house, an S curve
sans serif typeface: a V-shaped valley, an A-frame house, an S curve
When the publisher's house style calls for sans serif, a copyeditor's style sheet entry would read: Y-shaped (sans serif "Y"). Most publishers, however, view the sans serif font as overly fussy unless the topic is visual acuity ("Three of the children tested could not distinguish a W from a W").

FIGURE 6. A Copyeditor's Style Sheet. In a style sheet for a pencil-edited manuscript, each alphabetic entry may include the manuscript page number of the first occurrence of the term, as exemplified here by the imaginary page number with "ad hoc."

| Author/Title | Smith, Big Book |
|---|---|
| Copyeditor | Amy Einsohn |
| Date | 9/9/99 |
| References | *Merriam-Webster's Collegiate Dictionary*; *Chicago Manual of Style* |

**Special symbols**
European diacritics (é, è, ñ, etc.)

**Permissions/credits needed**
4 lines of poetry by D. Terrell (MS p. 85)
diagram from P. Ricardo (MS p. 172)

**Tables, figures, captions**
Table 1. Title in Headline Style
Figure 1. Artist, *Title of Work* (Museum)

**Dates and numbers**
3 January 1996
1955–1982 (en dash, repeat all digits)
see pp. 123–125 (en dash, repeat all digits)
see chapter 2, table 1, figure 4

**Miscellaneous notes**
downstyle capitalization

page 1 of 4

**Special symbols.** Indicate special characters that appear in the manuscript: diacritic marks, foreign language characters, mathematical signs, and musical or scientific notation.

**Permissions/credits needed.** Indicate pages in the manuscript that contain long quotations of prose (more than 250 words from any source); quotations of song lyrics or poetry; and tables, charts, or photographs that are not the author's work. These notations will remind the author to request written permission from the copyright holder to reproduce the material.

**Tables, figures, captions.** Give examples of the punctuation and capitalization of the titles for tables and figures.

**Dates and numbers.** Record decisions about spelled-out numbers and the use of numerals for dates, ranges, sums of money, and cross-references (see chapter 7).

**Miscellaneous notes.** This copyeditor noted the use of "downstyle" capitalization (see chapter 6).

Some terms require more than one entry on the style sheet. For example, the style sheet in figure 6 has entries for the verb "booby-trap" and the noun "booby trap" because the verb and the noun receive different editorial treatment. There are also two entries for "well received," because this adjective is hyphenated before a noun (a well-received proposal) but not after a noun (the proposal was well received). When the same editorial treatment applies to more than one part of speech, the entry includes a notation for each (see the entries for "inpatient," "online," and "outpatient").

FIGURE 6 *(continued)*

**Footnotes**

P. Small, *Book Title* (City: Publisher, 1995), 36.

Q. Small, "Article Title," *Journal* 3 (1998): 23.


**Bibliography**

Small, Pablo. *Book Title*. City: Publisher, 1995.

Small, Quentin. "Article Title." *Journal* 3 (1998): 21–30.


**Punctuation**

serial comma (a, b, and c)

possessives: Erasmus's concepts

    *but* Moses' leadership


**Abbreviations**

U.S.    U.N.

All acronyms without periods: NATO

Spell out e.g., i.e., etc. (for example, that is, and so forth)

page 2 of 4

**Footnotes.** Provide samples of the format used in the footnotes.

**Bibliography.** Provide samples of the format for bibliographical entries.

**Punctuation.** Indicate whether the serial comma is to be used in this manuscript (see chapter 4). Give examples of the possessive form for proper names ending in *s* (see chapter 5). No need to include standard universal punctuation rules—only ones that admit choices.

**Abbreviations.** Provide a sample of the abbreviations (initialisms and acronyms) that appear in the manuscript, and indicate whether each is to take periods or not. (See chapter 9.)

*(continued next page)*

For each entry, you can also indicate the number of the page (for editing on hard copy) or the name of the file (for editing on-screen) where the term first appears. These notations can be helpful if you have to go back and change something.

## ON-SCREEN STYLE SHEETS

When you are copyediting on-screen, keep the style sheet open as you work. Whenever you come upon an item that belongs on your style sheet, copy and paste the term from the manuscript to the style sheet. On-screen editors sometimes place the alphabetical

FIGURE 6 *(continued)*

| | | |
|---|---|---|
| **A**<br>ad hoc (roman) (MS p. 72)<br>aide-de-camp<br>anti- compounds closed<br>    (antihistamine) *except*<br>        anti-aircraft<br>        anti-intellectual<br>        anti-utopian<br><br>**B**<br>BASIC (computer language)<br>the Bay Area (California)<br>Bible (roman)<br>booby-trap (v)<br>booby trap (n)<br>braille (lc)<br>breakdown (n)<br>break-in (n)<br><br>**C**<br>Capitol Hill<br>catalog<br>childcare (n)<br>co-author<br>coordinate<br>co-opt<br>co-workers<br>Cubism, Cubists<br>curriculums (pl)<br><br>**D**<br>data (pl noun)<br>daycare (n)<br>decision makers | **E**<br>early-twentieth-century (a)<br>engagé (rom)<br>entrepôt<br>ex officio members (rom)<br>ex parte conversation (rom)<br><br>**F**<br>federal government (lc)<br>firsthand (a)<br>focused (*not* focussed)<br>foreign exchange rates<br>foreign language dictionary<br>*Forest* v. *Doe* (court case)<br><br>**G**<br>glasnost (rom)<br>grade 3<br>gray (*not* grey)<br>the Great Depression<br>Great Society programs<br>great-grandparents<br><br>**H**<br>half-life (n)<br>halfway<br>homeowners association<br>houseboat<br>house rules<br><br>**I-J-K**<br>in-house position<br>inpatient (n, a)<br>interagency<br>IQs (pl)<br><br>page 3 of 4 | **Alphabetical ("alpha") list.**<br>Enter choices about spelling,<br>plurals, hyphenation, cap-<br>italization, and italics. For<br>example, choices between<br><br>ad hoc          *ad hoc*<br>catalogue      catalog<br>coauthor        co-author<br>curriculums    curricula<br>day-care        daycare<br><br><br>Copyeditors often use the<br>following abbreviations in the<br>alpha list:<br><br>a = adjective<br>pa = predicate adjective*<br>n = noun<br>v = verb<br><br>s = singular<br>pl = plural<br><br>lc = lowercase<br>UC = uppercase<br><br>rom = roman type<br>ital = italic type<br><br><br>* Predicate adjectives are<br>those that follow the noun<br>(e.g., The play was well<br>received). For more examples,<br>see the Glossary of Gram-<br>mar Terms, s.v. "predicate<br>adjective." |

word list at the top of the document to facilitate copying and pasting as they toggle between the manuscript and the style sheet during editing. Some copyeditors automate this action and populate the style sheet with their chosen style options, such as "Associated Press numbers style" or "Chicago style for possessive forms." When you're done copyediting, you can use the sort feature to alphabetize the items in your word list. There's no need to keep track of page numbers, since you can use the global search feature to locate all mentions of a term, although the file name for a multifile document can help you find the first occurrence of the term more quickly.

FIGURE 6 *(continued)*

| L | Q-R |
|---|---|
| large-scale (a) | Ramadan |
| the Left Bank (Paris) | reelection |
| life cycle (n) | résumé |
| living room furniture | |
| | **S** |
| **M** | self- compounds hyphenated: |
| macroeconomic | self-important |
| mea culpa (rom) | self-sustaining |
| microdot | *Sesame Street* |
| microeconomic | socioeconomic |
| Middle Ages | the South (US region) |
| middle-aged (a) | the Southwest (US region) |
| middle-class (a) | the Sun Belt (US region) |
| millenniums (pl) | systemwide |
| mind-set (n) | |
| multitasking | **T** |
| | *t* test |
| **N-O** | transatlantic |
| New Year's Day | traveler (*not* traveller) |
| Ninth Ward | |
| non- compounds closed: | **U-V** |
| noncompliance | upper-middle-class (a) |
| nonnative fluency | the *Upton* case (court case) |
| *but* non-English-speaking (a) | v. (roman, in court cases) |
| the North Atlantic states | |
| online (a, pa) | **W-X-Y-Z** |
| outpatient (a, n) | well-received (a) |
| | well received (pa) |
| **P** | word processing (n, a) |
| PC-compatible (a) | x-axis |
| pre-computer era | y-axis |
| preenrollment | zlotys (pl) |
| pretest | |
| Purple Heart | |

page 4 of 4

You can also use the search feature to aid decisions about how to handle particular items. For example, early in the manuscript you are puzzled by the author's having capitalized a particular term. You can immediately search the manuscript to locate all the instances of the term and see whether the author has been consistent (indicating a definite preference) or not (indicating the author may not care about the term).

## INFORMAL COMMUNICATIONS
## AND TRANSMITTAL LETTERS

A manuscript prepared for a magazine, journal, corporate publication, or reference work is normally edited to conform to a publisher's rigorous requirements for content and format. The author of such a manuscript is rarely permitted to veto these mandatory changes. But in other kinds of publishing, an author usually has more control. In such cases, you should get the author or editorial coordinator to agree to any substantial rewriting and major changes in editorial style before beginning. A personal meeting, a videoconference, a chat on the phone, or email exchanges, along with a sample of the proposed editing, may be necessary to secure agreement on the overall tack.

A transmittal letter—or, sometimes, a less formal mode of written communication—is customary when the edited manuscript is returned to the author or editorial coordinator for review. As you edit, keep notes of general problems and your observations, questions, and suggestions. You will eventually incorporate these into a memorandum or letter that explains your overall editorial direction and outlines whatever work remains to be done.

This transmittal memo or letter to an author, as well as any other communication, however informal, should be respectful, tactful, and forthright:

- Break the ice: say something nice. A transmittal often begins with a flattering statement about the manuscript. It should be brief and should not sound formulaic or insincere. Perhaps there's not much to admire in the manuscript. If so, try saying something like "I've always been interested in this topic" or "You've tackled a difficult subject" (it's often a good strategy to address the author as "you" when offering praise). Try to convey interest and appreciation without sounding unctuous. Even a wary author is susceptible to flattery.
- Include general instructions for reviewing the editing. Briefly explain how editorial changes and queries are displayed in the on-screen document or redlined printout. If the manuscript has been edited on paper, explain hand-marking conventions and include a key showing the standard hand-marking symbols. Provide directions for responding to queries, approving changes, adding and deleting text, and restoring text that the copyeditor has marked for deletion. Explain the function of the accompanying style sheet. Usually, include a warning about making sure that the edited manuscript is correct and final in every respect to avoid major revisions, delays, and costs in subsequent production. Specify a deadline for the return of the manuscript: the production clock is ticking.
- Explain the basis for editorial decisions. The transmittal usually includes a brief explanation of the basis for decisions regarding editorial style and mechanical corrections. This lets the author know that such changes are authoritative, not whimsical, and refers the author to the expert sources

in the event of a disagreement. For example, you might say, "In settling questions about variant spellings, hyphenation, and conventions for capitalization, number treatment, and abbreviations, I have relied on *Merriam-Webster's Collegiate Dictionary,* 11th ed., and *The Chicago Manual of Style,* 17th ed., the authorities followed by this publisher." (Note that house style may override these or other standard authorities, or a publisher may stipulate that the author's style be followed except where it departs from accepted conventions or good sense.)

- Mention any pervasive style issues. The transmittal usually mentions the major problems of editorial style addressed in the editing, but only in a general way, with an illustrative example or two and reference to the style sheet and queries in the manuscript for elaboration. For example, "The treatment of numbers required special attention because there were so many numbers in the text. In the interest of readability, I adopted the Associated Press style (spelling out only the numbers one through nine) rather than following *The Chicago Manual* (spelling out the numbers one through ninety-nine)."
- Outline larger concerns and further work. The transmittal should spend the most time on larger issues requiring the author's or publisher's close attention or further work. For example, "I have queried inconsistencies in the treatment of Chinese names and terms in the text, with reference to *Merriam-Webster's Biographical Dictionary,* but I cannot claim a specialist's knowledge. I strongly encourage you to reread the manuscript with special attention to romanized Chinese."

*Some Do's:*
- Invoke the needs of the readers. Rather than saying the organization is poor or the writing unclear, suggest that eager-to-learn readers (entry-level students, nonspecialists, whatever) may benefit from the recommended changes in organizational strategy or from simpler, leaner sentences. An author is less likely to respond defensively if the editing is presented not as the correction of faults but rather as a retooling to meet the needs of a readership not quite as smart or knowledgeable as the author.
- Use the strategy of the "average editor." Even if you have subject expertise and can readily grasp the author's meaning, assume the persona of the generalist or another suitable stand-in for the reader. Don't irritate the author by feigning deep incomprehension; just represent the needs of readers who must understand the author's words.
- Be positive and supportive in your comments. For example, don't say, "I've done some rewriting of unclear or awkward passages." Instead, write something like "I've tried to read your manuscript as a stand-in for its future readers and to catch any turns of phrase that might seem unclear or out of tune to them (and, of course, any slips in spelling, syntax, and so forth)."

*Some Don'ts:*

- Don't be overly familiar. The editor-author relationship is a professional one, despite its intimacy. Don't immediately address an author by a first name—or, worse, by a nickname. (While shivering in a thin paper gown during a medical examination of the most private parts of your anatomy, you wouldn't want your physician to first-name you, right?) Instead, wait for the author to first-name you or to sign a communication using only a first name. Some authors will always prefer a formal mode of address, regardless of the length and amiability of your association.
- Don't be condescending. Don't say, for example, "I've tried to bring your writing up to its highest potential." Avoid red-flag words such as "rewritten" and "revised"; instead, employ words such as "suggested" and "proposed," which cede control to the author. Many authors are more receptive to changes if the editing is not presented as a battle of wills: "It's your manuscript; you decide."
- Don't challenge the author's expertise or competence. Avoid setting yourself up as the author's competitor, even if you have substantial knowledge of the subject, and don't step over the line that defines the limits of the copyeditor's authority.

## AUTHOR REVIEW AND MANUSCRIPT CLEANUP

### PROCEDURES FOR HARD-COPY REVIEW AND CLEANUP

For a paper-and-pencil copyedit, the specific instructions in the transmittal letter accompanying the hard-copy manuscript might state:

*Copyeditor's queries.* Please be sure to answer all the queries. Often a "Change OK" or a check mark is all that is needed.

*Additions.* Write any small changes on the manuscript in a color other than that used by the copyeditor; these changes must be readily visible and legible. To add a block of text, clip the newly typed passage to the manuscript page, label the insert, and indicate where the addition belongs: "Insert A (attached) goes here."

*Deletions.* Do not erase or white out anything on the manuscript. If you want to delete text that the copyeditor has added, cross the words out. (Again, please use a color other than that used by the copyeditor.)

*Restorations.* Use "stet" (meaning "let it stand") and a set of dots to indicate deleted or altered copy that you wish to restore to the original wording:

This masterly forgery passed unnoticed until the ~~very~~ end
of the century.

For the author's convenience, these instructions should be accompanied by a handout that explains the meaning of the copyediting symbols and the function of the style sheet if the body of the transmittal letter does not include this information.

During cleanup of hard copy, the copyeditor scans each page of the manuscript to ensure that the author has not introduced mechanical errors while making insertions, deletions, or restorations. Moving page by page, the copyeditor makes sure that

> inserted and restored text follows the spelling, capitalization, and other mechanical preferences shown on the style sheet
> all insertions and restorations are legible, and the location of every insertion is clear
> the sequential numbering of footnotes, tables, figures, and other enumerated elements remains correct even after the author has added, deleted, or restored items
> all cross-references to numbered items are correct
> additions to alphabetized lists are properly placed

Cleanup also entails incorporating the author's responses to the copyeditor's queries. Any queries overlooked by the author should be re-posed and resolved.

Copyeditors should correct any nondiscretionary mechanical errors that they observe while cleaning up the manuscript. But the approval of the author must be sought for any other proposed changes at this stage.

## PROCEDURES FOR ON-SCREEN REVIEW AND CLEANUP

For on-screen copyedits, the author may be sent

> a *redlined printout* of the copyedited manuscript—that is, a printout showing the author's original text and the copyeditor's changes with queries—which the author reviews and annotates on paper; or
> a *clean printout*—that is, a printout showing how the manuscript would read with all copyediting changes accepted—along with a redlined printout, which the author refers to as desired while reading the clean text; or
> a PDF file showing the redlining and queries, which the author can either print out for on-paper review or annotate on-screen using markup tools in a PDF reader; or
> word processing files with track changes activated for the author's on-screen review

The last of these options, on-screen review of the word processing files by the author, is generally the most efficient method: it saves paper, mailing time and costs (and fossil fuel), and the additional labor of keying an author's handwritten revisions into the files during cleanup. But authors vary greatly in their comfort with technology and their ability to work on-screen. Sometimes paper is better.

If word processing files are sent to the author for on-screen review, one of several procedures should be used to prevent the author from silently incorporating changes into the edited files. One method is to password-protect the files for revision so that when the author enters changes in the files, these changes will appear on-screen as red-lined copy in a color scheme other than the one used by the copyeditor; the author's replies to queries will also be differentiated from the editor's comments. Another option is to password-protect the files for revision and instruct the author to cast all revisions as comments or footnotes—but not to make any changes in the body of the text proper. (A word to the wise: Write down that password before you forget it!)

*Incorporating the author's hard-copy corrections.* When the author returns a hand-marked printout, some editors begin by making a backup photocopy or an electronic scan of the pages. Then the copyeditor reviews the author's handwritten insertions, deletions, and restorations and keys them into the files, carefully proofreading the new input. The substantive issues are the same as those for cleaning up a hard-copy man-uscript. It is prudent to run the spell-checker one final time after all the changes have been entered. In addition, you need to be certain that no redlining marks or queries remain in the final files.

*Incorporating the author's on-screen corrections.* The procedures for cleaning up on-screen corrections depend on the system that the copyeditor has used for query-ing and the author has used for responding. Before touching any author-corrected files, the editor should make a working copy and secure the author's original reviewed files untouched, also making the customary backup to an external device or remote server. In the working copy of the author-reviewed files, the editor then accepts or rejects each redlined change in accordance with the author's instructions; incorporates any further changes required by the author's responses to queries, deleting resolved queries along the way; and adds or checks any further revisions introduced by the author. All changes requested by the author must be read for mechanical correctness, and all traces of the editing process—annotations, queries, and redlining marks—must be deleted from the files. Finally, the editor runs the cleanup macros and the spell-checker one last time.

# CHAPTER 3

# ¶ Reference Books and Resources

The contents of your reference collection will depend on the types of material you copyedit, but there are four books (or their digital equivalents) that should always be at your fingertips when you are copyediting: a dictionary, a copy of the publisher's preferred style manual, a thesaurus, and a usage guide. In this chapter we'll look at these basic reference works and then at various types of specialized resources and tools.

## FOUR ESSENTIAL BOOKS

### DICTIONARIES

A copyeditor must have a recent edition of a good dictionary—and must always keep this volume within easy reach. The most popular dictionaries for US editors are *Merriam-Webster's Collegiate, American Heritage College, Random House Webster's College*, and *Webster's New World*. In the publishing industry, these are called college (or collegiate) dictionaries; they are hardbound, roughly seven by ten inches, and about a thousand pages. A paperback dictionary simply won't do for copyediting. Nor can you depend on the dictionary that you received for high school or college graduation unless you are a recent graduate. Hundreds of words enter the language each year, and preferences regarding spelling, hyphenation, plural forms, and other issues change from edition to edition. (Also, don't be misled by the name *Webster* in a dictionary title: the name is not trademarked, and many dictionary makers adopt it simply for its cachet.)

For editors in corporate communications, one of the collegiate dictionaries is usually sufficient. But copyeditors working for book and journal publishers must also have access to an unabridged dictionary. The print editions of *Webster's Third New International Dictionary of the English Language, Random House Webster's Unabridged Dictionary*, and *American Heritage Dictionary of the English Language* have long been the three principal choices from American publishers. You don't have to have one of these twelve-pound monsters on your desk or bookshelf, but you should know where you can find one (public library, office reference room, website) when the need arises. The most comprehensive English dictionary, a word-lover's feast, is the twenty-volume *Oxford English Dictionary (OED)*, which is also available in a two-volume photoreduced compact edition (packaged with the requisite magnifying lens), in several abridged one- and two-volume versions, and online by subscription. The *OED* is a historical dictionary, one containing the core words and meanings in English spanning more than one thousand years and including many quaint and antiquated terms. Definitions are ordered chronologically, according to when they were first recorded in English. The *OED* thus contains far more words and examples of historical usage than any of the American unabridged dictionaries. But watch out for British spellings!

English dictionaries always lag behind actual language change, especially with the global expansion of English through digital technologies and international science and commerce. Lexicographers don't add vocabulary and revise definitions immediately upon discovering a new word or meaning; they wait to determine whether the change has staying power. Even though a few words are quietly added (and eliminated) and some definitions are emended with each reprinting, or *impression,* of a given dictionary edition, the interval between entirely new editions is long. Lexicographers' conservative approach to language change, as well as the time required to research and produce a completely revised edition of a dictionary, means that the moment a new edition is printed, it may already be out of date.

For the trendiest—if sometimes ephemeral—popular culture and technology terms, along with new terms that are still making their way into carefully researched print or online-subscription dictionaries, a free online dictionary may therefore be your best resource. Try the crowd-sourced Urban Dictionary or Wiktionary for the latest slang; zoom to One Look Dictionary Search or Your Dictionary to compare information in several dictionaries at once. But beware! Although the internet offers free access to many general and specialized dictionaries in English and in foreign languages, the entries for standard vocabulary tend to be skimpy, and websites that aggregate the contents of multiple dictionaries may use untrustworthy authorities or older, superseded editions of recognized reference works—sometimes with obfuscating publication details—possibly chosen to avoid steep licensing fees from dictionary publishers.

Conversely, the authoritative free online *Merriam-Webster's Collegiate Dictionary* and online-only *Merriam-Webster Unabridged*—available by subscription along with an ad-free version of the *Collegiate*—are actually more up-to-date than any of their print counterparts. (All three of these online editions are updated regularly, but the subscription *M-W Collegiate* appears to lag a bit behind the free *M-W Collegiate.*) Until recently, the eleventh edition of the print *Collegiate*—which is not merely a slim version of Merriam-Webster's unabridged dictionary but a distinct publication—was the most frequently updated Merriam-Webster dictionary. But in 2011 Merriam-Webster commenced a through-revision of the unabridged print volume, *Webster's Third New International Dictionary* (principal copyright 1961), and it launched the renamed fourth edition, *Merriam-Webster Unabridged,* as an online-only reference. Revisions to this unabridged online dictionary are ongoing; updates are incorporated twice yearly. Until this work is completed, entries in the online *M-W Collegiate* will thus be more up-to-date—*unless* the headword in the *M-W Unabridged* is flagged as "new," signifying a recent entry or update that may supersede information in the online *Collegiate* until the next scheduled round of online *Collegiate* updates.

Similarly, the free online *American Heritage Dictionary of the English Language,* based on the print version of the 2011 fifth edition, is updated annually and is therefore likely to be more current than its older print version. The online *AHD* sometimes includes new words not found either in the online *Merriam-Webster's Collegiate* or in *Merriam-*

*Webster Unabridged;* thus it can serve as a backup dictionary for *Merriam-Webster* users. (The Selected Bibliography lists the official websites for all these online resources.)

These online dictionaries are also more expansive than their print counterparts. *Merriam-Webster Unabridged* lists regularly inflected forms, usually omitted in print editions, which offer only irregular forms to save space. Usage notes and citations (examples of word use found "in the wild") in unabridged online dictionaries are generally more extensive than those in the corresponding print volumes, which are constrained by limits on the number of printed pages.

Take some time to read the front matter of the collegiate dictionary on your desk or the instructions (if provided) for use of the online edition. Besides essays on the history of English and the science of lexicography, provided in most print volumes, you will find some critical explanatory notes in all editions. (Regrettably, they are often abridged online.) You will discover, for example, that not all words are listed, even in an unabridged dictionary. These omissions don't necessarily mean the words are spurious. Although unabridged editions are far larger than their collegiate cousins, they can hardly include the entire English lexicon; furthermore, many print dictionaries exclude regularly inflected forms and self-explanatory combinations of root words with standard prefixes and suffixes. Also, the explanatory notes describe the dictionary's principle for ordering definitions: from the oldest to the most recent in *M-W Collegiate,* for example, and from the most common to the most unusual meaning in *AHD.* And these notes will tell you how to interpret your dictionary's conventions for presenting variant spellings and irregular inflections, for identifying parts of speech, and so forth.

Whichever dictionary you use, don't think of it just as a spelling list with definitions. Dictionaries also contain

> irregular forms (i.e., irregular plurals for nouns, past tenses and past participles for verbs, comparative and superlative forms for adjectives and adverbs)
> guidelines on capitalization, hyphenation, syllabication, and pronunciation
> functional labels (parts of speech)
> usage notes, usage examples, and synonyms
> scientific (Latin) names for plants and animals
> spelled-out forms of common initialisms, acronyms, other abbreviations, signs, and symbols
> biographical information for well-known people
> geographical information (location, population) for major cities and countries
> translations of foreign words and phrases commonly used in English
> lists of common and scientific abbreviations and symbols

## STYLE MANUALS

Next, a copyeditor needs a style manual. Among US book publishers, the most widely used style manual is *The Chicago Manual of Style.* Another well-respected general-purpose style manual, despite its age, is *Words into Type,* which covers much the same material as *Chicago.* The popularity of *WIT* has declined because the publisher has not brought out a new edition since 1974 (there are persistent rumors of a new edition in preparation), so the information about production processes is seriously outdated. But this old classic includes extensive sections on editorial style, grammar, usage, and spelling that are still valued for their rare insights. The greatly expanded *Gregg Reference Manual,* a longtime secretary's companion, has become established as a general reference, particularly for business documents. It provides thorough mainstream advice on style, grammar, and usage, as well as an excellent index. *The New York Public Library Writer's Guide to Style and Usage* offers substantial discussions of usage and grammar as well as editorial style but hasn't been updated since its publication in 1994. Although a handy supplement to other resources, it seems unlikely to supplant *Chicago, WIT,* or *Gregg* in the offices of trade book publishers, scholarly presses, and corporate publication departments.

If you are new to publishing and have never looked at an editorial style manual, *Chicago, WIT,* or *Gregg* is the place to start. These books may initially seem overwhelming: the first two include many topics that don't directly concern copyeditors (e.g., design, typography, composition, paper, and binding), and all three discuss relevant subjects in excruciating detail. Take heart, however, in knowing that you are not expected to memorize every paragraph of the sections in your manual that treat editorial style. You need to read your manual carefully enough to learn the basic rules and conventions—the mechanical points that will arise whenever you copyedit. After all, when you are working on a manuscript, you can't stop at every comma, colon, and semicolon to consult your manual on the common uses of these punctuation marks. Rest assured, though, that even experienced copyeditors pause to check their style manual when they hit a thorny punctuation question.

You also need to read your style manual carefully enough to gain a sense of the kinds of esoteric issues that may arise from time to time in your work. For example, you don't have to remember whether your manual expresses a preference for "Ice Age" or "ice age." But after studying your manual over a period of several weeks, you should remember that, by convention, the names of some geological terms are capitalized. Then, if you come across "Ice Age" or "ice age" in a manuscript, you'll know that you need to pick up your manual, turn to the index, and locate the paragraphs that treat the capitalization of scientific terms.

Some people in corporate communications dismiss *Chicago* and *WIT* as overly pedantic and fussy.[1] But no other reference works cover such a wide array of mechanical issues. Rather than ignore *Chicago* and *WIT,* corporate copyeditors can use these books strategically, as resources that can be followed, adapted, or ignored on a given point. Even for editors working in a tradition-bound scholarly or trade publishing environment, the guidelines set forth in a style manual are not commandments inscribed on clay tablets but recommendations based on best practices. These recommendations will not always suit a particular situation. The goal for editors is to understand the rationale

---

1. Some corporate publication departments rely on *Gregg* or on one of various manuals published by Merriam-Webster. None of these books, however, are sufficiently detailed for copyeditors working in scholarly or trade publishing.

for a style manual's advice, assess how well it fits a project, and then decide whether to conform to, modify, or break with the convention.

Several other major style manuals are more specialized, and the styles they set forth are used only by certain types of publishers and writers:

*AMA Manual of Style.* "AMA style" (the abbreviation stands for American Medical Association) is used by medical journals and medical publishers.

*The Associated Press Stylebook.* "AP style" is used by many newspapers and magazines.

*GPO Style Manual: An Official Guide to the Form and Style of Federal Government Publishing.* "GPO style" (the abbreviation, which previously meant "Government Printing Office," now stands for "Government Publishing Office") is used by many government agencies and also by some private sector businesses.

*Microsoft Manual of Style.* "Microsoft style" is used or adapted by many writers and editors preparing technical instructions for global audiences using digital products.

*MLA Handbook.* "MLA style" (the abbreviation stands for Modern Language Association) is used by literary scholars and some other writers in the humanities.

*Publication Manual of the American Psychological Association.* "APA style" is used by many social scientists.

*Scientific Style and Format: The CSE Manual for Authors, Editors, and Publishers.* "CSE style," named after its publisher, the Council of Science Editors, is used by writers working in biology, chemistry, physics, medicine, mathematics, earth sciences, and the social sciences.

Your public library probably has copies of at least some of these books in its noncirculating reference section.

Style guides also exist for editing even more specialized content—biblical studies, classical music, computing, cooking, sports, and so forth—and are often used to supplement the guidelines of a more general style manual. Colleagues on email lists and social media for copyeditors can usually recommend the most suitable resources for highly specialized subject matter.

## THESAURUSES

The newer thesauruses arrange the main entries in alphabetical order; a few still follow Roget's nineteenth-century schema of categories. Pick any one you like. The best sellers in this category include *Merriam-Webster's Collegiate Thesaurus, Random House Webster's College Thesaurus,* Rodale's *Synonym Finder,* and *Roget's International Thesaurus.* Most of these thesauruses are also published in digital format. The subscription-based online dictionaries *Merriam-Webster's Collegiate* and *Merriam-Webster Unabridged* provide direct access to the online *Merriam-Webster's Collegiate Thesaurus.* Your online search engine can also provide links to several free online thesauruses, which offer different degrees of comprehensiveness and subtlety: as a search engine shortcut, enter the search term *synonym* along with the word to generate a list of websites offering synonyms for the word. If you are working on-screen, your word processing program itself probably includes a thesaurus feature, but the range of synonyms generated by these subprograms tends to be quite limited.

If you're editing content requiring specialized vocabulary—say, a document about vintage carpentry tools or the use of a camcorder—you may need help from a thematically organized *word list* or *visual dictionary*. Rather than using an alphabetical arrangement, these reference works are arranged by broad subject categories (e.g., do-it-yourself and gardening; communications), which are further broken down into major subcategories (e.g., materials, carpentry, plumbing and masonry, . . . snow removal; languages, written communication, photography, . . . telephony). Entries within these subcategories include simple definitions but no alternative spellings, guides to pronunciation, or other standard dictionary information. In a visual dictionary, entries are also accompanied by labeled illustrations of objects. The conceptual organization in word lists and visual dictionaries, especially useful for language learners, can also help editors find the correct words when they know what things are but not what they're called—those clever early twentieth-century carpentry tools in a great-grandfather's toolbox, for example, or the parts of a camcorder that was purchased without an instruction booklet. Well-known word list references include *Random House Webster's Word Menu, Descriptionary,* and *The Describer's Dictionary.* A popular visual dictionary is *Merriam-Webster's Visual Dictionary,* available both in print and (free) online.

## USAGE GUIDES

The authoritative online dictionaries *American Heritage* and *Merriam-Webster Unabridged* provide brief usage commentary with those word entries that especially warrant a cautionary note, but many controversial terms receive no annotation and carry no warning flag. (Usage advice in the print editions may be even more truncated because of space constraints.) For detailed advice and coverage of a wider range of issues, you need to consult a usage guide.

Many editors consider the best guide by far to be *Merriam-Webster's Dictionary of English Usage,* a thousand pages of short articles, from "a, an" to "zoom." Each entry includes a historical overview of the usage issue, comments from the so-called language experts, examples from respected writers, and a good dose of commonsense advice. Editors value this resource for its reliance on the same sound corpus research as that used by the respected Merriam-Webster family of dictionaries[2] and for its scrupulous avoidance of recommendations based solely on the compilers' personal preferences. (Other edi-

2. According to the Merriam-Webster website, the dictionaries' citation files, begun in the 1880s with slips of paper, now include examples of more than 15.7 million words from published material, both print and digital, used in context and covering all aspects of English vocabulary. Citations are also available to Merriam-Webster lexicographers in a searchable database, called a corpus, that includes more than 70 million words drawn from many sources.

tors, to be sure, dislike *DEU*'s "libertarianism.") Unfortunately, this volume hasn't been updated since the mid-1990s and does not cover recent usage issues and developments.

For the latest usage kerfuffles and generally more cautious advice, some editors prefer the hefty *Garner's Modern English Usage*. Bryan Garner builds his work on the "big data" now accessible in vast online linguistic corpora (discussed below), especially those searched with the Google Books Ngram Viewer, and he evaluates the increasing degree of acceptance (or repudiation) of disputed usages on a numbered scale, the Language-Change Index, which he describes in the front matter of his book. While weighing linguistic evidence, though, Garner does not hesitate to make value judgments. He may advise against a usage, despite statistical evidence of its growing popularity, if he deems it "skunked," that is, tainted by the bad odor of long controversy and best avoided by careful stylists so as not to offend discriminating readers' delicate olfactory nerves.

The difference between *DEU* and *Garner's* can be demonstrated by contrasting their entries on the two usage issues mentioned in chapter 1: *data* as a singular mass noun and *hopefully* as a sentence adverb. Both singular and plural uses of *data,* says *DEU,* are "fully standard at any level of formality." *Garner's* demurs: "Perhaps 50 years from now . . . [the singular use of] the term will no longer be skunked: everybody will accept it. . . . But not yet." As for sentence-modifying *hopefully, DEU* advises that "you can use it if you need it, or avoid it if you do not like it. There was never anything really wrong with it." But *Garner's* pronounces the word itself skunked and cautions serious writers against using it under any circumstances at all: "Avoid it in all senses if you're concerned with your credibility."

Some editors working on academic or professional content, where usage tends to be more conservative than in corporate prose, favor *Garner's* precisely for the author's own bottom-line appraisals following a survey of the linguistic data. Others favor *DEU*'s detached, nonjudgmental reports. Editors handling a variety of material may wish to consult both resources to canvass the range of evidence and opinion before making a decision appropriate for a given situation.

You should also be aware of four other usage guides, listed here from oldest to newest, which are so well known that they are often referred to simply by their author's surname:

H. W. Fowler, *A Dictionary of Modern English Usage* (2nd ed., rev. Ernest Gowers)
Theodore Bernstein, *The Careful Writer: A Modern Guide to English Usage*
Wilson Follett, *Modern American Usage: A Guide* (rev. ed., ed. Erik Wensberg)
*Fowler's Dictionary of Modern English Usage* (4th ed., ed. Jeremy Butterfield)

On most issues, Fowler (the 1965 Gowers revision) and Follett tend to take a conservative position. Some of their strictures seem overly formal or dated. In the so-called language wars (see chapter 14), they are known as *prescriptivists* (as in "prescribing what one ought to do"). In contrast, Bernstein and Butterfield (whose 2015 update of Fowler's classic is billed as "a revision for the twenty-first century") lean more toward the *descriptivist* pole. They seem less interested in faultfinding and hairsplitting and more intrigued by examples of the variety of ways in which well-educated writers use, reinvent, and reinvigorate the language.

Another wrinkle: The "English" in Fowler's title refers to British English; the "English" in Bernstein's title refers to American English; and Butterfield's "English" covers British English, American English, and the differences between the two.

Also of interest is Bernstein's *Miss Thistlebottom's Hobgoblins: The Careful Writer's Guide to the Taboos, Bugbears, and Outmoded Rules of English Usage,* an effort "to lay to rest the superstitions that have been passed on from one generation to the next by teachers, by editors and by writers—prohibitions deriving from mere personal prejudice or from misguided pedantry or from a cold conservatism that would freeze the language if it could" (p. xi). Although many of the superstitions persist, the book has been successful enough that both Miss Thistlebottom (the archetypal archconservative English teacher) and hobgoblins routinely enter into conversations on editorial matters.

## LANGUAGE CORPORA

Even the most trusted recent dictionaries and usage guides do not always answer an editor's questions. The information in print editions of such reference works ages as language evolves, and usage manuals that mingle personal opinion with empirical linguistic evidence may not provide clear advice. In resolving a gnarly problem, copyeditors' own intuitions as language-conscious native English speakers are valuable, but the "it sounds funny" (ISF) twitch is not infallible. When neither reference books nor language instincts suffice, another way to survey actual usage is to resort to linguistic corpora, large computer databases of published texts in English. The best of these corpora are based on edited prose and can be searched using refined criteria, such as historical period (nineteenth century, modern, contemporary), type of English (British, American), genre (newspaper, magazine, journal, book), and collocation (recurring pattern of use with other specific words).

Professional linguists and lexicographers are the primary users of language corpora, but copyeditors may consult them as well, especially to decide issues too esoteric for standard reference works, to compare usage in different English dialects or registers (levels of formality), or to study changing or disputed conventions and emerging terms. Surveying the evidence in a corpus of edited writing is hardly an anything-goes approach. When confronted with a vexing question of grammar or usage, editors often poll other editors in the office or online; consulting a corpus of edited prose can show how a multitude of editors have handled the question in preparing text for publication. Although the results may disprove some outdated or unfounded claims in standard references, they also give editors the data needed to exercise judgment, guided by the expectations of different audiences.

Perhaps you need to determine the correct prepositional idiom—which preposition goes with a word—for an expression that cannot be found in the usual printed lists of such idioms. Or perhaps you want to know whether the word *Skype,* referring to a proprietary videoconferencing technology, is disappearing from the English lexicon or, like *Google,* is acquiring a generic meaning. Is it used as a verb? Should it be capitalized? Placed in *scare quotes* to denote an odd, dubious, ironic, or overly colloquial use? Doubtless, lexicographers are busy studying such matters, but language change and regionalisms may move faster than the publication of new dictionaries and usage manuals—for example, when a coinage is introduced into the linguistic gene pool through social media, propagating (and dying out again, or not) overnight. Editors sometimes need answers not found in standard reference works.

Three of the most widely consulted corpora for English are the Corpus of Contemporary American English (COCA), the Corpus of Historical American English (COHA), and the Google Books corpora searched with Google's Ngram Viewer. COCA and COHA are both compiled by the linguist Mark Davies and hosted, along with several corpora for other English dialects, on the Brigham Young University website. The former contains some 520 million words, 1990 to the present (with continual additions), from American English sources—transcribed public radio and television programs and the edited prose of newspapers, magazines, fiction, and academic writing. The latter includes some four hundred million words from printed sources of edited American English, 1800 through the first decade of the twenty-first century. Both offer many options for limiting and refining searches. For example, COCA can show that "data is" occurs far more frequently than "data are" in recorded speech, fiction, and newspaper writing; that the singular and plural treatments of *data* occur about equally in magazine prose; and that the plural use is roughly twice as common as the singular in academic writing.

The Ngram Viewer plumbs a corpus of 155 billion words based on the vast Google Books program, which comprises the digitized contents of participating publishers' contemporary lists and the entire book collections of more than twelve major university libraries, covering British and American English from 1800 to the near-present (some earlier data are flawed by optical scanning errors), with occasional additions. The Google corpus is less scientifically balanced than COCA and COHA but far larger and somewhat easier for first-timers to use. Google Ngram also offers impressive search functionality. Users can narrow their investigation to a particular time frame or dialect (e.g., British or American English), perform wildcard and case-sensitive searches, and specify grammatical inflections, parts of speech, or collocations.

To be sure, research in all these databases and the correct interpretation of results require proficiency and some linguistic savvy.[3] Language corpora are thus best used to supplement the information in dictionaries and usage guides—or just to go spelunking.

3. Users should avoid overinterpreting results that may say more about the contents of a data collection itself than about Standard Written English. At a 2016 conference of ACES (formerly the American Copy Editors Society), a linguistic researcher cautioned his audience about what he called "the poop spike." While investigating the gradual increase in printed references to excrement, he noticed a big spike on his graph for occurrences of the word *poop* during the 1920s and 1930s. Only by examining texts in which these examples appeared was he able to determine that these early instances referred to the "poop deck" on ships. Sarah Zhang describes another "particularly amusing and profane example" in her critique of Google's Ngram Viewer, "The Pitfalls of Using Google Ngram to Study Language," *Wired,* October 12, 2015, https:// www.wired.com/2015/10/pitfalls-of-studying-language-with-google-ngram/.

## ON THE BOOKSHELF

### GRAMMAR HANDBOOKS

The usage guides mentioned above discuss only controversial or difficult points. For a more general review of English grammar and usage, you might want to look at one of these summaries (from the oldest to the most recent):

> *Words into Type,* 3rd ed., pp. 339–404
> Margaret D. Shertzer, *The Elements of Grammar,* pp. 1–47
> Edward D. Johnson, *The Handbook of Good English,* pp. 1–79
> Gordon Loberger and Kate Shoup, *Webster's New World English Grammar Handbook,* 2nd ed., pp. 5–234
> Mark Lester and Larry Beason, *The McGraw-Hill Handbook of English Grammar and Usage,* 2nd ed., pp. 1–108
> Diane Hacker and Nancy Sommers, *A Writer's Reference,* 8th ed., pp. 333–53

Despite its age, *Words into Type* is one of the best of this lot. It offers an excellent sixty-five-page overview of traditional grammar—the eight parts of speech, the classification of basic sentence structures, and a glossary of grammatical terms—with particular emphasis on the subtle and troublesome points that even copyeditors need to study. A strong runner-up, Hacker and Sommers's *Writer's Reference* offers the virtues of brevity and currency. Shertzer's *Elements of Grammar,* a somewhat misleadingly titled work, devotes forty-seven pages to the subject before moving on to other topics of concern to writers. Johnson's *Handbook,* the work of a longtime editor for major book publishers, also offers perspicacious advice in a series of do's and don'ts drawn from a life of copyediting. *Webster's New World* and the *McGraw-Hill Handbook* both provide extensive, if somewhat overwhelming, surveys.

None of these resources is as complete as one might wish, but they will answer most of your fundamental questions. For a more comprehensive conceptual treatment of English grammar, you might explore

> Sidney Greenbaum and Randolph Quirk, *A Student's Grammar of the English Language*
> Rodney Huddleston and Geoffrey K. Pullum, *A Student's Introduction to English Grammar*
> Bryan A. Garner, *The Chicago Guide to Grammar, Usage, and Punctuation*

Written by scholarly linguists, the volumes by Greenbaum and Quirk and by Huddleston and Pullum direct their pedagogical efforts toward advanced college students and teachers. Garner's *Guide,* the most recent of these offerings, specifically addresses professional writers and editors. Like *Garner's Modern English Usage,* this book describes what the author terms standard literary English, the grammatical forms that educated writers and speakers use. It devotes nearly two hundred pages to grammar, with extensive treatment of the traditional parts of speech, syntax (including sections on both sentence diagramming and transformational grammar), and word formation. The book also provides a list of prepositional idioms and an extensive glossary of grammar terms for readers needing clarification of, say, the distinction between a mass noun and a collective noun.

If you are not deterred by the look and feel of the newer college-level English handbooks (some readers find them too heavy on the color graphics, too light on the finer points, and mind-numbingly dull), there are at least a dozen to choose from.

You might also enjoy some of the more lighthearted books on grammar, such as Bill Walsh's *Lapsing into a Comma* or *The Elephants of Style,* and Constance Hale's *Sin and Syntax.*

## GUIDES FOR NEWCOMERS TO PUBLISHING

To learn more about traditional book publishing, from acquisitions to bound books, you might start by reading the chapters of *Chicago* that discuss how manuscripts are prepared, edited, designed, and manufactured. Marshall Lee's *Bookmaking: Editing, Design, Production* covers similar topics in greater detail. William Germano's *Getting It Published: A Guide for Scholars and Anyone Else Serious about Serious Books* describes the publication process for scholars and other authors of "serious books"; it includes a discussion of digital channels and open-access publishing arrangements.

*One Book / Five Ways: The Publishing Procedures of Five University Presses* documents an experiment in the late 1970s: a manuscript on houseplants went through the prepublication process (acquisition, copyediting, production, design, marketing) at five university presses. The manuscript's odyssey is reproduced in the form of copies of all the in-house reports and correspondence. Because the experiment was conducted so long ago, the production processes are obsolete, but here is the rare opportunity to see substantial samples of how five experienced copyeditors handled (on paper) the same manuscript pages.

Seven books written by and for editors provide thoughtful and often entertaining discussions of the craft and practice of editing. Edward D. Johnson worked in New York trade publishing houses for decades, and his *Handbook of Good English,* mentioned earlier as a grammar guide, discusses punctuation (over thirty pages on the comma alone!), other mechanical issues, and diction. Having worked on so many manuscripts, Johnson is exquisitely alert to the slightest nuance of each syllable and mark on the page. One drawback is that the book concludes with a lengthy, hard-to-use "Glossary/Index," rather than a traditional index.

Carol Fisher Saller's *The Subversive Copy Editor* also comes directly from the trenches. Saller, an in-house manuscript editor at the University of Chicago Press, has written with great care, tact, and humor about the day-to-day responsibilities and self-defeating perfectionism of an editor of scholarly books. Dealing with difficult authors, organizing streams of email and computer files, bending rules and mending fences—Saller does it all, and tells you how to be a more productive and (dare it be said?) happier copyeditor.

Mary Norris's *Between You and Me* peers into the quirky editorial culture of the *New Yorker*'s famous copy department, a Lost World where *cooperate* is still spelled with the diaeresis (*coöperate*) and commas are liberally dispensed, as if from a pepper shaker. Norris portrays the *New Yorker*'s inimitable editorial process, eccentric staff, and many celebrated authors—all while sleuthing for the origin of the hyphen in the title *Moby-Dick,* seeking an extinct brand of No. 1 pencil, and making a pilgrimage to the world's only museum for pencil sharpeners. Few contemporary editors will ever wield a No. 1 pencil or enforce the idiosyncratic decrees of Eleanor Gould, the legendary long-time *New Yorker* grammarian and "query proofreader" whose influence still dominates *New Yorker* style. Still, like Saller's essays in *The Subversive Copy Editor,* Norris's sketches evince the deep curiosity and humor that leaven editorial life on any copy desk.

As chapter 1 notes, copyeditors are not expected to reorganize a manuscript. Scott Norton's *Developmental Editing,* however, deftly illustrates how many different ways a nonfiction book, chapter, or article may be structured. Norton's repertoire will help you formulate better queries and suggestions for authors who seem to have lost their way. (Norton will also inspire some of you to move into developmental editing.)

Jack M. Lyon's *Microsoft Word for Publishing Professionals* also benefits from being written by a practitioner specifically for editors. Lyon's mission is to teach you how to customize and turbocharge your version of Microsoft Word by using macros, personal toolbars, and wildcard search-and-replace routines to automate repetitive tasks. He is also the proprietor of Editorium.com, mentioned later in this chapter.

Judith A. Tarutz's *Technical Editing: The Practical Guide for Editors and Writers* is chock-full of copyediting examples, exercises, and advice about teamwork, picking your battles, and setting priorities. Many readers would welcome a revised edition that would speak to the newer technologies in publishing.

For an author's view of the problems caused by overly zealous copyeditors, read Jacques Barzun's "Behind the Blue Pencil: Censorship or Creeping Creativity?" If you can bear his scorn for the "laborious mole" whose "gratuitous tampering . . . knows no bounds," you will receive an excellent lesson in editorial restraint and judgment. To put yourself in a better humor, turn to William Bridgwater's essay "Copyediting."[4] After you pardon his use of the generic *he* and *man* and the antiquated reference to marks on paper (the essay was written in 1962), savor the amusing hyperbole of his concluding paragraph: "The professional copy editor, who sits at his desk with a manuscript planted squarely before him, is not superhuman. He is a humble man in a more or less humble job. Yet upon his shoulders lies the weight of centuries of learning. . . . The little marks he puts on paper are for the betterment of mankind."

Perhaps the best recent overview of contemporary editorial work is offered by the essays in *What Editors Do: The Art, Craft, and Business of Book Editing,* edited by Peter

4. Bridgwater's essay appears in *Editors on Editing: An Inside View of What Editors Really Do,* rev. ed., ed. Gerald Gross (New York: Harper & Row, 1985), pp. 68–88. The 1985 edition, now out of print, is superseded by *Editors on Editing: What Writers Need to Know about What Editors Do,* 3rd rev. ed., ed. Gerald Gross (New York: Grove Press, 1993); essays in this volume discuss the responsibilities and activities of various in-house book editors (e.g., editors in chief, acquisitions editors, and editorial assistants).

Ginna. Contributors describe the many types of editing (acquisitions, developmental editing, copyediting), various market channels (fiction, genre, biography and memoir, academic and reference, and children's publishing), and occupational niches (staff, freelance, agent, self-publisher).

## GUIDES TO EFFECTIVE EXPOSITORY WRITING

Copyeditors are not expected to be skilled rewriters; indeed, heavy-handed copyeditors run into trouble when they take it upon themselves to rewrite a text rather than copyedit it. A copyeditor should, however, have some sense of what constitutes competent expository writing. It goes without saying that such writing is grammatically correct and that clarity, coherency, and consistency are always valued. Beyond that, the characteristics of competent writing vary by field, purpose, and audience. Different standards apply to a journal article on biomedical technology, a monograph on metaphysics, a cookbook, an engineer's manual, and a history textbook for elementary school students.

One way to acquire a sense of the standards for a particular type of writing is to read and analyze excellent examples. If you intend to work primarily in one field, that approach would be reasonable. But if you aspire to be a jack or jill of all trades, you may want to begin by looking at some general guides for nonspecialized writers.

Many people swear by William Strunk Jr. and E. B. White's *Elements of Style,* often referred to simply as "Strunken-White." Copyeditors, however, must realize that *The Elements of Style* presents *a* vision of *a* style of English, one that freely mixes rules, outdated conventions, idiosyncratic preferences, and hokum. Before applying any Strunkian maxim, copyeditors must cross-examine the text: Is recommendation X a hard-and-fast rule that admits no exceptions? Or is it a convention that may or may not be appropriate to the manuscript at hand? Could it be a well-founded nicety, an antique prejudice, or a curmudgeonly crotchet?[5]

Jazzy alternatives to Strunk and White's prescriptions are Constance Hale's *Sin and Syntax* and Arthur Plotnik's flippantly titled *Spunk and Bite.* Both take on the venerable duo, advocating for vivid writing that dares to venture outside Strunkian boundaries. Also more instructive for the beginning copyeditor is Claire Kehrwald Cook's *Line by Line: How to Improve Your Own Writing.* The author, a veteran copyeditor, works through hundreds of shaggy, baggy sentences to illustrate the basic principles of grammar and syntax. On a few points (e.g., the use of *hopefully* and of *everyone . . . their*), time has overtaken Cook, but her examples and explanations are excellent.

---

5. If you are among those who revere *The Elements of Style* as a sacred text, consider the following passage from co-author E. B. White, in his introduction to the volume (p. xv):

> [Strunk] had a number of likes and dislikes that were almost as whimsical as the choice of a necktie, yet he made them seem utterly convincing. . . . He despised the expression *student body,* which he termed gruesome, and made a special trip downtown to the *Alumni News* office one day to protest the expression and suggest that *studentry* be substituted—a coinage of his own.

Studentry?! Even White concedes that studentry is "not much of an improvement," but, he adds, "it made Will Strunk quite happy."

If you're ready for a serious study of the principles of effective prose, look at E. D. Hirsch Jr., *The Philosophy of Composition,* or Joseph M. Williams, *Style: Toward Clarity and Grace.* Neither book is light bedtime reading, but both give detailed analyses of the structural and stylistic elements that enhance or impede the readability of expository prose.

## SPECIALIZED REFERENCE BOOKS

Many copyeditors regularly consult an encyclopedia, a gazetteer, or a dictionary of quotations. Depending on the types of materials you copyedit, you may also turn to a biographical dictionary, foreign language dictionaries, or technical dictionaries.

Every field also has its specialized reference books. Here are a few examples:

Chemistry: *The ACS Style Guide*
Mathematics: Ellen Swanson, *Mathematics into Type;* Nicholas J. Higham, *Handbook of Writing for the Mathematical Sciences*
Medicine: *Dorland's Pocket Medical Dictionary; Stedman's Medical Dictionary; Mosby's Dictionary of Medicine, Nursing, and Health Professions; Merck Manual Consumer Version* (online)
Physics: *AIP Style Manual*
Psychiatry: *Diagnostic and Statistical Manual of Mental Disorders: DSM-5*

## WEBSITES, EMAIL LISTS, DISCUSSION BOARDS, AND BLOGS

Among the many websites that provide information about the practice and business of copyediting are

ACES: The Society for Editing (formerly the American Copy Editors Society): https://aceseditors.org/
Bay Area Editors' Forum (BAEF): http://www.editorsforum.org/
Copyediting.com: http://www.copyediting.com/
Council of Science Editors (CSE): https://councilscienceeditors.org/
Editorial Freelancers Association (EFA): https://www.the-efa.org/
The Editorium: http://www.editorium.com/
Editors Canada (formerly Editors' Association of Canada, EAC): https://www.editors.ca/
Institute of Professional Editors Limited (Australia, IPEd): http://iped-editors.org/
Society for Editors and Proofreaders (UK, SfEP): https://www.sfep.org.uk/

The websites of some of the professional editorial style manuals offer selected editorial tools—including FAQs, examples of citation style, and sample memos and documents—either free or by subscription:

American Medical Association (AMA) style: http://www.amamanualofstyle
    .com/
American Psychological Association (APA) style: http://www.apastyle.org/
Associated Press (AP) style: https://www.apstylebook.com/
Chicago style: http://www.chicagomanualofstyle.org/
Editors Canada style (follows *Editing Canadian English*): https://
    editingcanadianenglish.ca/
Modern Language Association (MLA) style: https://style.mla.org/
US Government Publishing Office (GPO) style: https://www.govinfo.gov
    /content/pkg/GPO-STYLEMANUAL-2016/pdf/GPO-STYLEMANUAL
    -2016.pdf

Whatever your question about copyediting, grammar, or usage (or about a computer-related quandary encountered while working on-screen), one or more of the two thousand subscribers to Copyediting-L are likely to post an answer on this high-volume international electronic mailing list. Subscribers can also access the list's extensive archives. An introduction to the list, with a tab of assorted resources donated by list members, is posted at http://www.copyediting-l.info/. Dues-paying members of EFA can subscribe to its less prolific but ever-helpful email discussion list on the organization's website. Registered members of UK-based SfEP have access to a set of online discussion forums covering all aspects of editing and proofreading. And subscribers to *The Chicago Manual of Style Online* can hang out in its "Users Forum." Several of the professional organizations cited earlier also connect members through social media, including Facebook, LinkedIn, and Twitter. Many editors hobnob on a public Facebook page, Editors' Association of Earth (EAE), which currently boasts more than seven thousand registrants worldwide; some venture into a members-only section, EAE Backroom, where they can let their hair down in privacy. The Selected Bibliography to this book lists these and many additional publishing and technology support sites for editors.

A great many professional editors maintain blogs. A few of the most active, informative, and entertaining are also listed in the Selected Bibliography. Katharine O'Moore-Klopf, the current Copyediting-L list owner, inventories the blogs of the many subscribers to Copyediting-L and regularly updates an extensive bibliography of other professional resources in the "Copyeditors' Knowledge Base" section of her website, KOK Edit. Carol Fisher Saller, the author of *The Subversive Copy Editor,* maintained a blog under that title between 2010 and 2013, then migrated in 2015 to "Editor's Corner," a feature hosted at the *Chicago Manual of Style*'s freely available *CMOS Shop Talk* blog. The latter series is ongoing and is also available, along with an archive of Saller's previous posts, at her resurrected *Subversive Copy Editor* blog (http://www.subversivecopyeditor .com/blog/), a rich resource for editors.

You can keep up with current grammar-related debates, myths, rants, and inquiries on the blog *Language Log,* at http://languagelog.ldc.upenn.edu/nll/, which is co-authored by more than a dozen of the foremost English-language linguists. The archives (going back to 2003) may be searched by keywords or browsed by category.

Besides online English dictionaries and thesauruses, online language corpora, professional websites, email lists, message boards, social media, and blogs, copyeditors rely extensively on other internet resources, including encyclopedias, gazetteers, collections of quotations, biographical references, and technical and foreign language dictionaries. Verifying the English transliteration of a world leader's name, checking bibliographic details, quickly confirming a quotation, converting currency—these and many other tasks are sometimes more efficiently dispatched by firing up a search engine or making a quick trip to a trusted website than by querying an author or searching the reference section of the library.

When consulting an online encyclopedia, many editors stop first at the collaboratively written Wikipedia, although the reliability of individual articles in this crowd-sourced reference must be carefully evaluated. Another widely used storehouse of information is the CIA's World Factbook, an annual online publication with comprehensive information about every country, dependency, and geographic entity in the world. The vast resources of Google Books, Google Scholar, Bartleby.com (a repository of literary classics, including quotations and verse), Project Gutenberg (a source for free e-books), and a host of other repositories are readily available to editors with nimble search skills. Refdesk.com provides links to thousands of information sources, research tools, and other websites. Catalogs for major libraries (e.g., WorldCat and the online catalogs for the Library of Congress and the British Library), abstracting sites, online bookstores, websites of antiquarian booksellers, book search services, and the home pages of peer-reviewed journals and individual authors often provide needed bibliographic details for citations.

Most editors bookmark a handful of useful websites rather than trawl the internet for hours in pursuit of some minor piece of information. In truth, you can easily drown in the vast ocean of online content—or end up in a virtual vortex of debris resembling the Great Pacific Garbage Patch—unless you exercise considerable shrewdness about online navigation and the reliability of web sources. Savvy researchers know to assess information found on the internet by evaluating

> the author, a named individual or institution whose credentials and reputation can be verified
> the publisher or host, often identified through a URL's domain name
> the point of view, especially if there is evidence of advocacy, bias, or commercial motive
> the accuracy of the information, as corroborated by documentation, links to other reliable authorities, and other trusted sources
> timeliness, as evidenced by a recent revision date posted on the site and by active links to other websites

## A CAVEAT

In the pre-internet era, the rule of thumb was that copyeditors were expected to double-check items that appeared in standard desktop reference books: the spelling of the names of well-known people and places, the population of states and countries, the dates of major world events, and the wording of well-known quotations. Copyeditors were not expected to check any other types of facts, information, or quotations: responsibility for content lay with the author. The standard practice was to attach a cover note to the copy-edited manuscript reminding the author to verify all facts, proper nouns, and quotations before returning the manuscript for cleanup.

Now that the internet places terabytes of information at our fingertips, double-checking this or that item seems so easy and so quick that some copyeditors try to track down every detail they can. Indeed, some who are new to the field wrongly assume that verifying facts is among their principal responsibilities. But just as a little knowledge can be a dangerous thing, so can a little Googling.

First, revving up your search engine distracts your attention from mechanical editing and language editing. Second, unless your editorial coordinator has asked you to do some sleuthing, you run the risk of exceeding the project's budget or missing your deadline. Third, copyeditors may lack the subject matter expertise to evaluate the accuracy or value of information on the web. For example, your author may have chosen to cite editions of texts other than those that appear on the web; if you repeatedly point out differences between your author's quotations and the text on the web, you will be wasting your time and your author's. Fourth, even if you are extremely tactful in your queries about content, some authors may feel that you are second-guessing them every step of the way. Rather than applauding your diligence, they may resent your overreaching.

Even though it goes against a copyeditor's heart and soul to leave a stone unturned, copyeditors—especially those new to the field—should be strongly cautioned against wandering into the thickets of content checking unless an editorial supervisor requests this service. Expectations and practices vary widely, of course, and so you will want to discuss this topic before you begin working on a project.

PART 2

¶ Editorial Style

IN THIS PART we first turn our attention to matters of editorial, or mechanical, style: punctuation, spelling, hyphenation, capitalization, numbers, quotations, abbreviations, initialisms, acronyms, and symbols. We then look at the conventions and procedures used in copyediting material that is not running text: tables and graphs, notes and bibliographies, and front and back matter. The final chapter in this part addresses markup (also known as tagging, styling, or typecoding) and design specifications ("specs").

These chapters are intended to raise your editorial awareness and to show you how copyeditors make decisions. They also clarify some of the more difficult points in the major style manuals, identify some of the principal differences among the manuals, and discuss vexing mechanical problems that are not addressed in the manuals.

# CHAPTER 4

# ¶ Punctuation

Many people throw up their hands at the quirks of English punctuation. The linguist David Crystal observes in his *DCBlog* that one reason punctuation presents such challenges to writers and editors is that

> it is trying to do two very different jobs—one phonetic, the other grammatical. On the one hand, people are using it as a guide to how the rhythm of a sentence should sound (if they were to read it aloud); on the other hand, they are using it as a guide to the grammatical structure of a sentence—to what it means. On top of this, there are graphaesthetic considerations of elegance—wanting to avoid too many marks in a sentence, for example. (January 11, 2008)

Modern punctuation—as well as the conventions of spacing between words and the distinction between capital and lowercase letters—originates in early forms of writing and printing. The *diple,* for example, was a right-pointing angle bracket placed in the margins of ancient texts to flag significant passages, possibly the ancestor of modern quotation marks. The *manicule,* or bishop's fist, a small pointing hand, was likewise inscribed (and later printed) in margins to call out points of interest; well into the twentieth century it was featured in the inked "Return to Sender" stamp used by the US Postal Service. The *pilcrow,* or paragraph symbol, marked a change of topic; it now appears on-screen in Microsoft Word documents when formatting is displayed. The *ampersand* (the symbol for *and*) was taught as the twenty-seventh letter of the alphabet during the nineteenth century and remains popular today in logos and ornamental typography. And the *octothorpe* (a.k.a. pound sign, number sign, hash mark, or hash) has lately been repurposed to identify a thread of comments about a given topic on social media sites.

Many quaint symbols have been proposed for addition to our modern repertoire of punctuation marks. Since the invention of the printing press, at least nine different writers and type designers have advocated for the use of a distinctive character to flag irony or sarcasm. The *point d'ironie, percontation point, tilde, sarcasm point, snark, ironieteken, SarcMark*—several differently styled signs have been suggested as aids for readers too obtuse to detect subtle forms of humor without a typographic cue. (The demand for such a mark appears to have declined, at least in casual electronic communications, with the invention of emoticons and emoji.) A twentieth-century Madison Avenue adman vigorously campaigned for the *interrobang,* a fusion of the question mark and exclamation point (‽), to convey a mixture of doubt and surprise, such as that sometimes expressed by a rhetorical question. This mark had its day during the 1960s: American Type Founders actually cast it for a newly designed typeface called Americana, and the

Remington Rand typewriter company offered it as a replaceable key and typehead on the Model 25 electric. Ultimately, the effort to secure a place for this mark in the canon of modern punctuation was defeated by the decline of hot metal composition, the technical limitations of early photocomposition, and cultural resistance to changing the modern writing system. The interrobang still has a cult following—and even a position in Unicode (U+203D), an international standard for character encoding, although few Unicode fonts include the character.[1]

Thus have we inherited fourteen commonly used punctuation marks, along with wordspacing and capitalization, to help make sense of written English: the period, question mark, exclamation point, comma, semicolon, colon, dash, hyphen, apostrophe, (single and double) quotation marks, ellipses, parentheses, (square) brackets, and (curly) braces.

No one would want to read an unpunctuated text. Look at this tiniest of examples:

> tryitonotis

Doesn't that look like some kind of disease, perhaps a rare form of trichinosis? Now, let's add some wordspacing, capitalization, and punctuation:

> "Try it on, Otis."

Suddenly, it's clear that someone is speaking (quotation marks), that the speaker is addressing someone named Otis (proper name, capital *O*; and his name is preceded by a comma indicating direct address), and that Otis is most likely being asked to try on an article of clothing.

Or what about something like:

> what i had had was had began not had begun what was i thinking

Even with wordspacing, this string is hard to decipher until we add all the punctuation:

> What I had had was "had began," not "had begun." What was I thinking?

Punctuation also serves to give structure and coherence to complex expressions. In chapter 114 of *Moby-Dick,* for example, Melville weaves the stages of human life into one long, carefully punctuated sentence:

> There is no steady unretracing progress in this life; we do not advance through fixed gradations, and at the last one pause: through infancy's unconscious spell, boyhood's

---

1. This overview is based on Keith Houston's highly entertaining *Shady Characters: The Secret Life of Punctuation, Symbols, and Other Typographical Marks.* Houston's blog (http://www.shadycharacters .co.uk/) is likewise a rich source of information about the history of punctuation, type design, and the art and craft of bookmaking.

Many writers have facetiously proposed unconventional marks and uses of punctuation. In "A Primer for the Punctuation of Heart Disease" (*New Yorker,* June 10, 2002), for example, Jonathan Safran Foer suggests the following marks to convey his family's style of (non)communication:

- ☐   the silence mark (in conversation)
- ■   the willed silence mark
- ??   the insistent question mark
- ¡   the unxclamation point (indicates a whisper)

thoughtless faith, adolescence' doubt (the common doom), then skepticism, then disbelief, resting at last in manhood's pondering repose of If.

Of course, even the most punctilious punctuation cannot rescue a sentence that is poorly constructed. And, as we will see, in some cases punctuation alone may be too subtle to convey the desired meaning.

This chapter focuses on the most common punctuation problems and will prepare you for a careful reading of the portions of your style manual that discuss punctuation. If you don't recognize one of the grammar terms, consult the Glossary of Grammar Terms at the back of this book.

## CONVENTIONS, FASHIONS, AND STYLE

Eighteenth- and nineteenth-century English authors tended to be profligate with commas and other marks; their style is now called *close punctuation*. "Pick a novel by, say, Charles Dickens," Frances Peck suggests: "Open it to any page and you will see them—dozens of commas, swarming through sentences like ants through spilled syrup."[2] A modern example of close punctuation is the distinctive—some would say idiosyncratic—comma style of the *New Yorker*. In *Between You and Me,* Mary Norris, a longtime member of the magazine's copy department, demonstrates its house style with a sentence from a piece by Marc Fisher:

> When I was in high school, at Horace Mann, in the Bronx, in the nineteen-seventies, everyone took pride in the brilliant eccentricity of our teachers.

This proliferation of commas is by no means capricious, as Norris explains:

> The commas are marking a thoughtful subordination of information. . . . The writer went to only one high school, a very special one-of-a-kind private school that happened to be in the Bronx, and the time that he went there was the nineteen-seventies. None of that is particularly interesting except in the context of a piece that promises to be about the bond between students and teachers. The punctuation is almost like Braille, providing a kind of bas-relief, accentuating the topography of the sentence. (p. 103)

Applying the *New Yorker's* subtle punctuation style might challenge even an experienced editor who had not been tutored in the topography of the sentence by the redoubtable Eleanor Gould, who was the magazine's anointed Grammarian (her official title) for fifty-four years.

The *New Yorker's* close style notwithstanding, the contemporary preference is generally to use as few commas as possible, a style called *open punctuation*. The minimalist approach to punctuation, and especially to comma use, advises, "When in doubt, leave it out." (But this motto does not sanction the omission of optional punctuation when it

2. Frances Peck, "Commas Count: Necessary Commas," *Terminology Update* 35, no. 4 (2002): 9; posted at *Termium Plus,* http://www.btb.termiumplus.gc.ca/.

is needed for clarity.) If Marc Fisher's sentence were copyedited in open style, it might look like this:

> When I was in high school at Horace Mann in the Bronx in the 1970s, everyone took pride in the brilliant eccentricity of our teachers.[3]

Within the realm of open punctuation, some choices, particularly those related to the comma, are more subjective than objective. Some writers, for example, *hear* punctuation. They regard writing primarily as a form of notation for speech, and they punctuate to suggest how the words should be voiced. This vocalizing approach uses question marks, exclamation points, and periods to denote rising and falling tones; commas, semicolons, and colons to speed or slow the pace and rhythm of their prose. One editor who holds this view is Edward D. Johnson. He begins his 138-page discussion of punctuation in *The Handbook of Good English* by suggesting that

> punctuation can be thought of as a means of indicating in writing the pauses and changes of tone that are used in speech to help communicate the meaning of sentences. The marks of punctuation evolved partly as indicators of pause and tone—a comma usually indicates a pause, a question mark usually indicates a rising tone, and so on—and they retain this significance. (p. 81)

Aural punctuators tend to hear a comma as a one-beat pause, a semicolon as a two-beat pause, and a period as a three- or four-beat pause. Some also hear a colon as a pause; for others, a colon signals a sharp accelerando, a signal to speed ahead because something important is coming.

A second group of writers have a highly *visual* sense of punctuation. They are most concerned with how their sentences look on the page, aiming for sentences that are neither overly cluttered by punctuation nor so sparsely punctuated as to look neglected or confusing. Johnson is mindful of this aesthetic consideration as well, grumbling, for example, about the visual litter when an author uses so many quotation marks in a manuscript "that a passage may look as if grass were growing on it" (p. 162). He suggests various workarounds in such circumstances simply to avoid this untidy appearance.

A third approach—and the one taken by all the editorial style manuals—is the *analytical,* or *syntactical, approach,* which instructs editors to punctuate according to grammatical and syntactical units. The advantage of this method is that it does not rely on the ear or eye of the writer or copyeditor, and therefore tends to be less subjective. In a given sentence, the question that syntactical punctuators ask regarding the presence or absence of a comma is not "Do you hear a pause here?" or "Does this look too cluttered?" but "Is this an introductory adverbial phrase?" or "Is this a restrictive or nonrestrictive modifier?"

You will also encounter writers who regard punctuation as an esoteric art and freely combine the aural, visual, and syntactical methods. Most of these idiosyncratic punc-

---

3. In addition to open style commas, most contemporary house styles specify the use of arabic figures rather than words to designate decades if expressed in unabridged form: *the 1970s,* but *the seventies.*

tuators take a wing-and-a-prayer approach and will be pleased by your imposition of order and reasonableness. A few, however, will defend to the death their eccentric ways, proclaiming that the First Amendment guarantees their freedom to punctuate without editorial interference.

When copyediting nonliterary texts, corporate documents, and scientific or technical reports, you can confidently apply the conventions set forth in your style manual. But if your author is an experienced literary or professional writer, you will want to interpret some of the conventions more liberally. Writers who care about punctuation may become quite upset if a copyeditor imposes conventions that are at odds with their own sense of cadence, appearance, or taste. Skillful writers make many discretionary uses of punctuation—and sometimes even choose to violate basic "rules"—to achieve particular effects. Knowing when to give rein to a stylist's creativity with punctuation and when to restrain it requires editorial judgment.

Editorial style manuals and grammar books typically discuss punctuation mark by mark, giving five or ten rules for the period, followed by fifteen or twenty rules for the comma, and so on. They often rely on the concepts and terminology of traditional grammar—the model with eight principal parts of speech and four basic sentence types that many editors learned in school—despite more nuanced descriptions of English advanced by modern linguistics. Although such a model makes for a tidy presentation and is referenced here for simplicity's sake, it tends to obscure some broad functional principles that govern punctuation. In this chapter, we'll look at four major functions and some common conventions, with a few noteworthy exceptions, before examining the more troublesome individual marks.

To master the syntactical approach to punctuation, you must be able to identify various grammatical units. The most important are *independent clauses, dependent clauses* (which, as you'll see later in this chapter, come in two flavors: *restrictive* and *nonrestrictive*), and *phrases*. First, make sure you recall your schoolbook definitions:

> A *subject* is the "doer" (in the *active voice*) or the "receiver" (in the *passive voice*) of the verb's action or state.
>> *Subject with active voice verb: Patty Pilcrow* punctiliously punctuates her paragraphs.
>> *Subject with passive voice verb:* The *paragraphs* are punctiliously punctuated by Patty's grammar checker.
> A *finite verb* is an inflected verb, that is, a verb form marked to show its particular grammatical function; it is not an infinitive (to be, to go, to walk), a *present participle* (being, going, walking), or a *past participle* (been, gone, walked).
> A *clause* is a group of related words that includes both a subject and a finite verb.
>> An *independent clause* is a clause that can stand alone as a complete sentence.
>> A *dependent clause* is a clause that cannot stand alone as a complete sentence.
> A *phrase* is a group of related words that does not contain both a subject and a finite verb.

With these definitions in mind, we can examine the first three principal uses of punctuation: to mark the ends of sentences, to join independent and dependent clauses to form complicated sentences, and to set off phrases within sentences.

## FUNCTION 1: TERMINAL PUNCTUATION

In English every sentence begins with a capital letter and ends with one and only one terminal punctuation mark. The three most common terminal punctuation marks are the period, the question mark, and the exclamation point:

*Statement:* The experiment failed.

*Question:* Did the experiment fail?

*Exclamation:* The experiment failed!

As this trio illustrates, terminal punctuation not only indicates the end of a sentence but also contributes to the meaning of the sentence.[4]

A sentence of dialogue may also end with an em dash (to indicate an interruption) or with a set of ellipsis points (to indicate a thought that trails off). If a speaker's tag (e.g., she said, he murmured) follows the interrupted dialogue, a comma goes after the three-dot ellipsis but not after the stronger em dash:

"We cannot allow—" Then the phone went dead.

His voice was weak. "I have only one regret . . ."

"I have only one regret . . . ," he murmured in a weak voice.

"We cannot allow—" she said. Then the phone went dead.

*Pitfall: Sentence fragments.* A fear of fragments hobbles the practice of many writers and editors. In elementary school most of us learned that sentence fragments—*verbless sentences,* H. W. Fowler calls them—should always be avoided. Not true! In the 1965 edition of his *Modern English Usage* even the conservative Fowler accepts the occasional sentence fragment as "a device for enlivening the written word by approximating it to the spoken"; he lists six rhetorical purposes it can serve to great effect (s.v. "verbless sentences"). Still, fragments should be used sparingly and only for special emphasis:

Must consumers accept this unfair ruling? Not necessarily.

If the project is approved, traffic will increase by 20 percent. Perpetual gridlock.

---

4. Here is a more complex example of how a masterly writer can use punctuation to carry semantic meaning. The author, Adam Gopnik, is comparing the debate on modern art in Paris with that in New York; the former, he explains, is a debate between modernists and antimodernists, the latter a debate between modernists and postmodernists.

> This makes the debate in Paris at once more shallowly conservative—there are people who think it would have been better had Picasso never been born—and more interestingly radical: there are people who think it would have been better had Picasso never been born! ("In the Garden of Bien et Mal," *New Yorker,* April 6, 1998, p. 62)

History has shown that there is only one cure for kleptocracy. More democracy.

Haircuts. Shower curtains. Parking reimbursements. Country club memberships. Use of corporate jets.

Recent criminal and civil court cases involving top executives have brought to the fore an open secret in corporate America: for executives with multimillion-dollar salaries, no company-paid perk is too small—or too big—to accept.[5]

Although verbless sentences may be employed sparingly for rhetorical effect, especially in literary writing and journalism, fragments that result from carelessness should be rewritten:

In the 1980s many farmers were on the verge of bankruptcy. ✗ Because wheat exports had declined.

In the 1980s many farmers were on the verge of bankruptcy because wheat exports had declined.

---

Moderate growth is usually positive for the stock market. ✗ The reason being that stable interest rates and low inflation provide favorable conditions for higher profits.

Moderate growth is usually positive for the stock market because stable interest rates and low inflation provide favorable conditions for higher profits.

---

✗ The gifted copyeditor whose principal virtues include a command of spelling, punctuation, grammar, diction, and usage as well as an ear for idiom.

The principal virtues of a gifted copyeditor include a command of spelling, punctuation, grammar, diction, and usage as well as an ear for idiom.

*Pitfall: Misuse of the terminal question mark.* A question mark indicates that the sentence is a direct question. Note that in a series of short questions the first words may be lowercased, although in a series of longer questions the first words are capitalized in accordance with convention.

Should the project be funded?

The topic for debate was, Should this program be funded?[6]

---

5. Alex Berenson, "From Coffee to Jets, Perks for Executives Come Out in Court," *New York Times,* Feb. 22, 2004.

6. As this example illustrates, the first letter of a formal question is capitalized. In a departure from its previous style guideline, *Chicago* now recommends that other embedded questions also be capitalized, by analogy with dialogue (6.42):

He asked, "Why not?"
He asked himself, Why not?

Note, too, that when a formal question is the subject of a sentence, it retains its question mark:

Should this program be funded? was the topic for debate.

Will this report be completed by Friday? by Monday? later?

Will the package be delivered today? Can it be placed in the lockbox? Should we pick it up at the UPS office instead?

Indirect questions, requests politely phrased as questions, embedded tag questions, and one-word interrogatives take a terminal period. Rhetorical questions—questions to which an answer seems obvious or unnecessary—are normally followed by a question mark. When a rhetorical question does not end with a question mark, the terminal punctuation may indicate that the writer has consciously chosen to use the interrogative form solely to produce an effect or make an assertion, not to elicit a reply.

> *Indirect question:* The question is whether the project should be funded.
>
> *Polite request:* Would you please complete your report by Friday.
>
> *Embedded tag question:* We all believe, don't we, that he will win.
>
> *One-word interrogative:* Employees should not second-guess company policy by asking why.
>
> *Rhetorical question:* It's 97 degrees Fahrenheit. Have you ever felt such heat?
>
> *Two rhetorical questions:* You got a tattoo on your derrière? What would your mother say.

(In this last example the writer is making a statement about the mother's presumed reaction, despite the syntax. Hence the period after the second sentence. And if ever there was an argument in support of the interrobang, it's the first sentence in this example.)

*Pitfall: Placement of terminal punctuation mark for sentences within parentheses.* When a parenthetical sentence stands on its own, the terminal punctuation mark goes inside the closing parenthesis.

> Last year popular fiction accounted for half of all books purchased. (Business and self-help books were the second largest category.)
>
> Even an entire paragraph may be treated as a self-contained parenthetical remark. (See the example in the first chapter of this book.)

When a parenthetical sentence is tucked inside another sentence, the parenthetical sentence does not take a terminal punctuation mark.

> Last year popular fiction accounted for half of all books purchased (business and self-help books were the second largest category).
>
> Three mice died (they refused to eat), and two others lost a third of their body weight.

Occasionally, a tucked-in parenthetical comment consists of two sentences. In that case, the first sentence carries a terminal punctuation mark, but the second does not:

> The terse instructions ("Place tab A into slot B. Secure tab A") were not helpful.

*Pitfall: Placement of terminal punctuation mark for quotations.*  At the end of a quotation, the terminal punctuation mark is placed inside the closing quotation mark. When a quoted question is interrupted by a speaker's tag (as in the fourth example), the question mark still goes at the end of the quotation:

> Jones stated that the manufacturing schedule was "entirely unrealistic."
>
> Jones screamed, "I quit!"
>
> Jones asked, "Where is everyone?"
>
> "What is the penalty," he asked, "if we cannot complete the project on time?"
>
> Who can forget his "Who doesn't like Nascar?" remark?

A question mark or exclamation point that is added as an editorial comment (i.e., an emphasis supplied by the writer) is placed outside the closing quotation mark.

> Jones, of all people, said, "The manufacturing schedule is entirely unrealistic"!
>
> Was it Jones who concluded that "the manufacturing schedule is entirely unrealistic"?

In some circumstances, however, it is preferable to adopt the British convention (also called "the logical convention"): place a punctuation mark within the closing quotation mark only when that punctuation mark is part of the original quotation.[7] For example, in computer manuals, linguistic analyses, and some types of literary criticism, the British convention may be used to enable readers to distinguish between a punctuation mark that is part of the quoted material and a mark that is part of the quoter's sentence. The following pair of sentences illustrates this concern:

> To find all instances of "Judge," but not "judge," check the case-sensitive option and type "Judge."

7. In British practice, single quotation marks (sometimes called *inverted commas*) normally enclose direct quotations; double quotation marks enclose nested quotations, i.e., quotations within quotations. Traditional British style is sometimes reversed in certain academic specialties and in modern British fiction and journalism (*Butcher's Copy-editing*, p. 272; *New Oxford Style Manual*, pp. 162–63).

Owing to the impracticality of determining the original punctuation of quotations without checking the sources, Butcher favors placing *all* punctuation outside closing quotation marks unless an author has scrupulously distinguished between quoted and added punctuation, but she acknowledges that "many publishers follow a rule of thumb that the full point [i.e., period] precedes the closing quote if the quotation contains a grammatically complete sentence starting with a capital letter" (p. 272). *New Oxford* recommends following this rule of thumb. Thus, as *Chicago* (6.9) observes, in practice British style frequently places periods inside closing quotation marks in these circumstances, regardless of the original punctuation.

To find all instances of "Judge", but not "judge", check the case-sensitive option and type "Judge".

The first sentence invites confusion: Are we searching for the word *Judge* or only for *Judge* followed by a comma? Are we to type *Judge* or the word *Judge* followed by a period? Placing the punctuation outside the closing quotation marks prevents these kinds of misunderstandings.

## FUNCTION 2: JOINING CLAUSES

### JOINING INDEPENDENT CLAUSES

Commas, semicolons, colons, and dashes can all be used to join two independent clauses ("IND" in the following examples) to form a *compound sentence*. The choice among these marks is dictated by the nature of the bond. In the language of traditional grammar, there are four types of bonding material—coordinate conjunctions, adverbs, transitional expressions, and punctuation alone—and the rules (with some specific exceptions) are as follows:

IND, coordinate conjunction IND.
   [A comma precedes the conjunction.]

IND; adverb [,] IND.
   [A semicolon precedes the adverb; a comma usually follows the adverb.]

IND; transitional expression, IND.
   [A semicolon precedes the transitional expression; a comma follows the transitional expression.]

IND; IND. *or* IND: IND. *or* IND—IND.
   [Independent clauses may be directly joined by semicolons, colons, or dashes. In IND: IND, the first word of the second independent clause may be capitalized or lowercased (styles vary). For capitalization of the first word of a quotation introduced by a colon, see chapter 8.]

In the following paragraphs, which explain these rules and provide examples, bear in mind that sentence structure, not the use of a particular word, determines punctuation.

When independent clauses are joined by a *coordinate conjunction*—and, but, for, nor, or, so, yet—a comma precedes the conjunction.[8]

8. Since at least the 1950s some writing manuals have used the mnemonic FANBOYS (*for, and, nor, but, or, yet, so*) to teach the traditional list of "coordinating conjunctions." However, contemporary linguists argue that the entire part-of-speech class called *conjunctions* is a muddle and that these seven words do not behave in the same way. As *The Cambridge Grammar of the English Language* explains, only *and, or,* and *but* are true coordinators; *nor* is close; *so* and *yet* are more like conjunctive adverbs such as *however;* and *for* is semantically but not syntactically similar to the subordinating conjunction *because.* Regardless of the oversimplification of the category FANBOYS in traditional grammar, though, all seven words *can* join independent clauses with a comma. But as the subsequent discussion here elaborates, independent clauses can also be joined in a number of other ways *under specific conditions:* the

Dawn was just breaking as they closed their suitcases, and they called for a taxi before the alarm went off.

She made a cup of tea to drink with her oatmeal, but the cat knocked it off the counter.

We were relieved when the trip ended, for it had been a demanding itinerary.

He has never broken a promise, nor has he ever reneged on his debts.

Patty will buy some party decorations, or her sister will bring the old ones stored in the basement.

She phoned to say she'd be late, so we sat down to dinner without her.

They complained about the penalties for exceeding their water ration, yet they continued to soak their lawn daily.

When both clauses are short and there is no chance that readers will misconstrue which elements are joined by the conjunction, the comma may be omitted at a writer's discretion, especially to avoid the impression of "choppiness."

*Comma required:*

Ten people suffered minor injuries, and at least twenty homes near the creek were flooded.

Ten people were injured, but all were released from the hospital by nightfall.

---

*Comma omitted at the writer's discretion:*

Ten people were injured and twenty homes were damaged.

The ball soared and our hopes for victory soared with it.

Come here and I'll show you how to do it.

Let's have lunch and I'll explain my plan.

When independent clauses are joined by an adverb (e.g., however, indeed, moreover, nevertheless, then, therefore, thus), a semicolon precedes the adverb. A comma is usually placed after the adverb, but the comma may be omitted after *then, therefore,* or *thus* when the transition is not abrupt and no emphasis is desired.

The prosecution will appeal the exclusion of the videotape; however, the courts rarely overrule trial judges on evidentiary matters.

The videotaped confession is essential to the prosecution's case; indeed, the government's entire case hinges on the defendant's confession.

The videotape is essential to the prosecution's case; thus the prosecutor is appealing the exclusion of the tape.

---

comma that precedes the "coordinating conjunction" may sometimes be omitted; the comma alone may sometimes suffice, despite the traditional injunction against "comma faults"; and, of course, a semicolon, colon, or dash may be pressed into service.

When independent clauses are joined by a transitional expression (e.g., for example, in addition, in other words, namely, that is), a semicolon precedes the transitional expression, and a comma follows it. Note that a semicolon precedes such transitional expressions *only* when what follows is an independent clause; otherwise, use a comma or (*Chicago*'s preference) a dash, or place the entire phrase with the transitional expression in parentheses.

> The price of airline tickets appears highly irrational; for example, a ticket from New York to Chicago (713 miles) is often less expensive than a ticket from Philadelphia to Detroit (443 miles).

Independent clauses can also be directly joined (with no intervening conjunction or adverb) by a semicolon, a colon, or a dash. The semicolon is the neutral choice and is often used between closely related or antithetical statements. It is somewhat formal—hence unlikely to appear in dialogue representing casual speech—and means something like "and." The colon, also formal, is used when the second clause amplifies or illustrates the first: it means something like "because." The dash signals an abrupt change of thought or tone.

> The past is not dead; it's not even past.

> Minds are like parachutes: they function only when open.[9]

> Half of all advertising is wasted—but no one knows which half.

In *Spunk and Bite* Arthur Plotnik offers an example of the nuances of punctuation between independent clauses:

> During his 1961 inaugural address, President John F. Kennedy uttered these famous two clauses, pausing briefly between them: "And so, my fellow Americans, ask not what your country can do for you [*pause*] ask what you can do for your country."
> But how is that pause to be represented in print? Check enough quotation books, and you'll find five different marks competing for the job: comma, dash, period, colon, and semicolon. . . .
>
> - The comma seems too hurried, too trivializing . . .
> - The dash seems too abrupt . . .
> - A period (full stop) allows time to anticipate the locution and to think, "Yeah, yeah, I get it."
> - And a colon warns of some tedious enumeration.
>
> The semicolon seems just right as a bridge between the two echoing clauses. It calls for a brief rhetorical pause, as before a punch line. (p. 174)

---

9. The first word of an independent clause following a colon is lowercased in Chicago style but capitalized in AP, APA, *WIT,* and New York Times styles:

> Minds are like parachutes: They function only when open.

Chicago calls for capitalization only when a proper name follows the colon or when the colon introduces a question, a direct quotation, or a series of two or more complete sentences:

> You have two choices: You can confess to the crime and negotiate a reduced sentence. You can contest the charge in court and risk receiving the maximum sentence for the crime.

*Pitfall: Run-on sentences.* Contrary to what many writers have been taught in elementary school, the joining of two independent clauses solely with a comma, a *comma splice,* is not *always* an error. Independent clauses may be connected with a comma alone when one has a trio of short independent clauses that all have the same grammatical subject:

> He came, he saw, he conquered.
>
> [Note, however, that if there are only two independent clauses in the series, they cannot be joined solely by a comma: ✘ He came, he saw. Instead, these clauses must be joined by *and* or by a semicolon: He came and he saw. *or* He came; he saw.]
>
> Read the instructions, fill out the form, and submit the completed form to the main office.
>
> [Since the "implied person" of an imperative is always "you," there is no change of subject here. Again, a comma is incorrect when there are only two clauses in the series: ✘ Read the instructions, fill out the form.]

A comma alone is also sometimes used—advisedly—between two short, closely related independent clauses, especially to contrast antithetical statements; to formulate a brief, aphoristic statement; to convey an informal speaking tone, as in dialogue; or to create a special effect in fiction, poetry, and other literary forms. This bonding of independent clauses with a comma rarely appears in formal writing, where a dash, a semicolon, or another revision is often preferable.

> It's not a plane, it's Superman!
>
> The editor proposes, the author disposes.
>
> I think, therefore I am.
>
> She was so changed, she looked like a different person.

Even Strunk and White, in *The Elements of Style,* allow exceptions to the prohibition against comma splices "when the clauses are very short, and are alike in form, . . . or when the tone of the sentence is easy and conversational" (pp. 6–7). In the conservative *Modern American Usage,* Wilson Follett also recognizes that "one kind of sentence profits by joining two or more independent clauses with no more than a comma. Such a sentence should probably have but a single subject, carried forward by a pronoun or else repeated, and the clauses that follow the first should add force to the single idea" (s.v. "sentence, the").

In *The New Fowler's Modern English Usage,* R. W. Burchfield observes that "this habit of writing comma-joined sentences is not uncommon in both older and present-day fiction" (s.v. "comma"). Bryan Garner summarizes the criteria for permissible comma splices in his *Modern English Usage*—but adds a strong cautionary note: "Most usage authorities accept comma splices when (1) the clauses are short and closely related, (2) there is no danger of a miscue, and (3) the context is informal. . . . But even when all three criteria are met, some readers are likely to object" (s.v. "run-on sentences").

In all other cases, a comma alone is insufficient to join independent clauses to form a compound sentence.

✗ He came home, he saw that the refrigerator was empty, he conquered his craving for an anchovy pizza and ate three crackers for dinner.
[These independent clauses are too long to be joined by commas.]

✗ He came home, the refrigerator was empty.
[The change of subject precludes using a comma to join these independent clauses.]

There are many ways to repair a careless run-on sentence:

*Replace each comma with a semicolon:* He came home; he saw that the refrigerator was empty; he conquered his craving for an anchovy pizza and ate three stale crackers for dinner.

*Add a conjunction after each comma:* He came home, and he saw that the refrigerator was empty, and so he conquered his craving for an anchovy pizza and ate three stale crackers for dinner.

*Punctuate each independent clause as a separate sentence:* He came home. He saw that the refrigerator was empty. He conquered his craving for an anchovy pizza and ate three stale crackers for dinner.

*Transform all but one of the independent clauses into dependent clauses:* When he came home, he saw that the refrigerator was empty, which left him little choice but to conquer his craving for an anchovy pizza and eat three stale crackers for dinner.

*Pitfall: Confusion between compound sentences and compound predicates.* Punctuators must distinguish between compound sentences and compound predicates. A *compound sentence* contains two independent clauses; a *compound predicate* is one independent clause in which one subject governs two or more verbs.

*Compound sentence:* The committee will meet tomorrow, and the report will be mailed on Tuesday.

*Compound predicate:* The committee will meet tomorrow and will review the report.

However, a comma is placed before the "and" in a compound predicate if there is a chance that readers will misconstrue which elements are being joined.

The committee will meet tomorrow, and on Tuesday will issue its report.
[Comma prevents misreading of "meet tomorrow and on Tuesday" as a unit of thought.]

In *The Handbook of Good English* (p. 98), Johnson makes the case for inserting a discretionary comma, as an aid to readers, between the elements of a compound predicate when there is a time shift between the actions described by the two verbs:

He resigned[,] and left the room after delivering a fiery speech.

A discretionary comma may also be inserted between the elements of a compound predicate to cue readers properly if the predicates are long and complex, particularly if they contain internal punctuation:

> The *manicule,* or bishop's fist, a small pointing hand, was likewise inscribed (and later printed) in margins to call out points of interest[,] and well into the twentieth century was featured in the inked "Return to Sender" stamp used by the US Postal Service.

*Pitfall: Confusion about* IND; IND *and* IND: IND. The choice between a semicolon and a colon depends on the relationship between the separated clauses. A colon is appropriate when the second clause amplifies the first and the desired traffic signal is "proceed." In most other cases, the semicolon is the better choice.

*Pitfall: Overuse of* IND—IND. The dash between independent clauses is best reserved for special effects: to prepare readers for a punch line or a U-turn.

## APPENDING A LIST TO AN INDEPENDENT CLAUSE

When an independent clause introduces a list, a colon follows the independent clause.

> Three buildings will be demolished: 12 Apple Street, 56 Cherry Drive, and 7 Peach Lane.
>
> Scorers are asked to bring three items: a pencil, a pad, and a stopwatch.

*Pitfall: Misuse of colon before a series.* As just noted, the colon is used to introduce a series that follows an independent clause. A colon is also used to introduce a series when the introductory clause contains a phrase like "the following":

> Scorers are asked to bring the following: a pencil, a pad, and a stopwatch.

In all other cases, however, no colon precedes the list, even if it is set off, or displayed, as a vertical list.

> ✘ Patients should: arrive by 10 A.M., check in at the desk, and go directly to the laboratory.
>
> ✘ The advertising campaign is aimed at: preteens, adolescents, and young adults.
>
> ✘ Scorers are asked to bring:
>    a pencil
>    a pad
>    a stopwatch.

In rare cases the independent clause and the list may be reversed:

> A glass of iced tea, a peach, and an apple: his last meal was spartan and brief.
>    [Following *Chicago,* the first word of the independent clause following the colon is lowercased here.]

More often, a dash rather than a colon follows an introductory list, especially if the appositional list is long and complicated:

> The diple found in medieval manuscripts, the manicule widely used in Victorian printing, the ampersand lovingly crafted by type designers, and the pilcrow, or paragraph symbol, signifying a new topic—all these marks are early forms of modern punctuation.

## JOINING DEPENDENT AND INDEPENDENT CLAUSES

A dependent clause cannot stand alone as a complete sentence. Conventional punctuation relies on the punctuator's ability to distinguish between two types of dependent clauses:

> A *restrictive clause* is one that is essential to the meaning of the sentence as a whole because it limits, or restricts, the meaning or extent of the independent clause.

> A *nonrestrictive clause* is not essential to the meaning of the sentence as a whole; that is, it could be deleted from the sentence without changing the meaning of the sentence.

If you keep these definitions in mind, the punctuation of dependent clauses ("DEP" in the following examples) introduced by subordinate conjunctions (e.g., after, although, because, except, if, unless, when, whether, while) is a matter of applying five rules:

> DEP, IND.
> [A comma follows the dependent clause.]

> DEP, IND and IND.
> [Omit the comma between short independent clauses when the introductory dependent clause applies to both of them.]

> IND R-DEP.
> [There is no comma when the dependent clause is restrictive.]

> IND, NR-DEP. or IND: DEP.
> [A comma sets off the nonrestrictive dependent clause. Or (rarely) a colon introduces a dependent clause that elaborates the statement in the preceding independent clause.]

> IND, NR-DEP, IND.
> [A comma separates the two independent clauses, and a comma follows the interior nonrestrictive dependent clause.]

The following paragraphs explain this stenographic set of guidelines.

When a dependent clause precedes an independent clause, a comma is placed after the dependent clause.

> If the "disk is full" message appears, you must insert a new disk.

> When the mail arrives, the receiving clerk should notify the bookkeeper.

Even though the software creates a backup copy of the active document, weekly backup procedures should be followed.

When a dependent clause precedes two short independent clauses and applies to both, the comma between the independent clauses may be omitted.

When the storm struck yesterday, the winds rose and I secured the shutters.

When a restrictive dependent clause follows an independent clause, no comma is used.

You must insert a new disk if the "disk is full" message appears.
[The *if* clause limits when "you must insert a new disk."]

This warranty covers all moving parts unless the owner is negligent in maintaining the equipment.
[The *unless* clause limits the cases in which "this warranty covers all moving parts."]

When a nonrestrictive dependent clause follows an independent clause, a comma is placed after the independent clause. If the dependent clause elaborates the statement in the preceding independent clause, a colon may be used between the clauses for a formal, dramatic effect.

Weekly backup procedures should be followed, even though the software creates a backup copy of the active document.
[The *even though* clause does not limit when "weekly tape backup procedures should be followed."]

We knew how to recognize the cat's irritation: when her ears flattened.

When a nonrestrictive dependent clause precedes the second independent clause of a compound sentence, commas follow the first independent clause and the interior dependent clause. Do not use a comma immediately *before* the interior dependent clause unless this clause is to be set off as a parenthetical element.

*Choppy:* Dark walls of rock rise steeply from the shores, and, when the weather is calm, snowcapped peaks and blue glaciers are mirrored in the waters of the strait.

*Better:* Dark walls of rock rise steeply from the shores, and when the weather is calm, snowcapped peaks and blue glaciers are mirrored in the waters of the strait.

Sometimes the distinction between a restrictive and a nonrestrictive clause can be quite subtle:

He was annoyed when the phone rang.
[No comma, restrictive, means "The ringing of the phone annoyed him."]
He was annoyed, when the phone rang.
[Comma, nonrestrictive, means "He was annoyed and then the phone rang."]
I don't care if you are happy.
[No comma, restrictive, means "Your happiness does not matter to me."]

I don't care, if you are happy.
   [Comma, nonrestrictive, means "Your happiness is all that matters."]

A similar distinction affects the use or omission of a comma before a *because* clause that follows a negative verb in the independent clause. Given the potential ambiguity of this construction, most editors would revise the following sentences rather than depend on the subtlety of comma use alone to clarify the meaning:

The proposal was not sent to New York, because the meeting had been postponed.
   [Meaning "The proposal was not sent, and the reason it was not sent was that the meeting had been postponed."]
*Better:* Because the meeting had been postponed, the proposal was not sent to New York.

The proposal was not sent to New York because of the impending merger.
   [Meaning "The proposal was sent, but the impending merger was not the reason it was sent."]
*Better:* The proposal was sent to New York, but not because of the impending merger.

He was not killed, because he knew too much.
*Better:* The reason he was not killed is that he knew too much.

He was not killed because he knew too much.
*Better:* He was killed, but not because he knew too much.

When the independent clause preceding the *because* clause is affirmative, in contrast, the presence or absence of a comma causes a slight shift in emphasis. The presence of a comma emphasizes the assertion, while the absence of a comma emphasizes the reason:

All citations to the minutes of committee meetings must include the five-digit record number as well as the date, because the minutes are indexed only by record number.

The results of the third test are invalid because the protocol was not followed.

## PUNCTUATING RELATIVE CLAUSES

Dependent clauses headed by a relative pronoun (that, who, which), a relative adjective (whose), or a relative adverb (when, where) are called *relative clauses,* and the restrictive-nonrestrictive distinction applies to these clauses as well. Here are some examples of restrictive relative clauses:

Dogs that have three legs need special medical care.
   [*That* clause restricts "dogs" to only those dogs that have three legs.]

Adults who are functionally illiterate face many problems.
   [*Who* clause restricts "adults" to those adults who are functionally illiterate.]

She rejected all of his suggestions that were impractical.

[*That* clause restricts "all of his suggestions" to those suggestions that were impractical.]

Here are some examples of nonrestrictive relative clauses:

Dogs, which are members of the canine family, are related to wolves and foxes.
[*Which* clause makes a statement true of all dogs.]

Individuals' federal tax returns, which are due April 15, may be filed electronically.
[*Which* clause makes a statement true of all individuals' federal tax returns.]

Relative clauses that function as *appositives*—that is, they rename the subject or add a new piece of information about a subject that has already been identified[10]—are always nonrestrictive.

Janetta Williams, who is directing the marketing campaign, is arriving tomorrow.

Liberty City, which is in the northeastern corner of the state, will host next year's conference.

The accountants will be busy until April 15, when federal tax returns are due.

As the sample sentences illustrate, nonrestrictive clauses are set off with commas, and restrictive clauses are not. Lest the presence or absence of a comma be too subtle a cue as to the restrictive or nonrestrictive nature of the relative clause, many usage manuals recommend using *that* to signal a restrictive clause and reserving *which* for nonrestrictive clauses. Compare:

Senator Smith opposes new state taxes that will increase the cost of doing business in California.
[Restrictive *that* clause limits "new state taxes" to those taxes that will affect businesses.]

Senator Jones opposes new state taxes, which will increase the cost of doing business in Maine.
[Nonrestrictive *which* clause denotes that "increase the cost of doing business" is true of all the new state taxes.]

The usage manuals, however, admit two exceptions to this convention:

1. When a sentence contains the conjunction *that*, it is preferable to use *which* to introduce a subsequent relative clause, even if it is a restrictive clause.

   Many writers have argued that the distinction which we have been discussing is trivial.

---

10. Commas are also used to set off appositives introduced by *and* or *or:*

I want to thank my sister, and my co-author, for her commitment to this project.
[Means "I want to thank my sister, who is also my co-author."]

The soffit, or underside of the overhang, requires special treatment.
[The *or* phrase introduces a definition of *soffit*.]

2. Euphony may override the *that/which* convention.

It was a sparsely furnished flat which she had rented.

Of course, one could simply delete the relative pronouns to avoid these problems:

Many writers have argued that the distinction we have been discussing is trivial.

It was a sparsely furnished flat she had rented.

## FUNCTION 3: SETTING OFF PHRASES

### INTRODUCTORY PHRASES

The grammatical nature and the length of a sentence-opening phrase determine whether a comma is needed to set off the phrase from the rest of the sentence. A comma is not needed after a two- or three-word introductory phrase that functions as an *adverb*—that is, it indicates time (when?), place (where?), manner (how?), or degree (how much?)— unless there is a chance that readers may misinterpret the comma-less phrase.[11]

*Time:* At noon the staff will meet to discuss new software.

*Place:* Above the panel you will find the safety instructions.

*Manner:* In this way one can solve most quadratic equations.

*Degree:* At length they consented to the request made by the auditors.

---

For July Fourth the company is planning a picnic.

For July Fourth, Jetco is planning a company picnic.
[Comma prevents misreading of "July Fourth Jetco" as a unit of thought.]

---

In all more than 2,000 cases of typhus were reported in the region last year.

In all, cases of typhus decreased by 43 percent between 1991 and 1995.
[Comma prevents misreading of "In all cases" as a unit of thought.]

---

Each spring there is flooding in the valley.

Each spring, rain causes flooding in the valley.
[Comma prevents misreading of "Each spring rain" as a unit of thought.]

These are the general conventions; however, some authors prefer to place a comma after even a short introductory adverbial phrase, usually to supply emphasis or to enforce

---

11. Although no comma is needed after a short introductory adverbial phrase, a comma is used after a sentence adverb or a transitional adverb. For example:

*Sentence adverb:* Unfortunately, the presentation was interrupted by a power outage.
*Transitional adverb:* Next, the recipes are tested in professional kitchens.

A comma may be used after other introductory adverbs to achieve emphasis or to avoid ambiguity: "Typically, we do . . ."; "True, skeptics will wonder . . ."

a pause alerting readers that the sentence's main clause is to come. In contemporary close punctuation (e.g., as practiced by the *New Yorker*), optional commas typically follow short introductory adverbial phrases even when misreading is unlikely and no special emphasis is intended. Many editors abhor these superfluous commas, the remnants of an older style of punctuation, but some authors are devoted to them. Whether a copyeditor deletes or retains the optional commas depends on house style and policy, on the copyeditor's intuitions about the strength of the author's convictions about comma use, and on the sentence and the context—depends, that is, on editorial judgment. For example, the absence or presence of a comma in the following sentences is likely to be of little or no concern to most authors and readers:

Last November, traffic accidents rose unexpectedly.

Over drinks, they made amends.

But when these optional commas cluster in a paragraph, they impose a tiresome stutter-step rhythm that places too much emphasis on the short adverbial phrases:

Last September, we introduced a new quality standard for electric pencil sharpeners. In early December, this standard was reviewed and revised. Since January, the volume of consumer complaints has risen. Each month, between 250 and 350 consumers have requested refunds. At tomorrow's meeting, we must identify the source of the problem.

For longer adverbial phrases and all other types of introductory phrases, the convention is straightforward: place a comma after the introductory phrase.[12] The following examples illustrate this convention:

*Phrase functions as an adverb and is longer than a few words:*

On the first and third Mondays of every month, the reports must be copied and mailed.

In a small town near the Canadian border, hundreds of tourists come every summer to fish.

For the sake of his family and friends, he declined the job offer.

To the best of your ability, try to recall what happened.

---

*Phrase functions as an adjective that modifies the subject of the subsequent independent clause:*

Of the newer photocopiers, the P-12 is the fastest.

With one exception, the programs received excellent evaluations.

---

12. See chapter 14 on avoiding danglers when participles and other modifiers are used as introductory phrases.

*Phrase contains a present or past participle:*

Before using the printer, the operator must check the paper supply and the toner gauge.

Having declined in January, stock prices rose in February.

Redesigned from top to bottom, the car won several awards this year.

This last rule, however, conceals two pitfalls. First: If the sentence uses an inverted word order—that is, if the finite verb precedes the subject in the independent clause—one does not use a comma after the introductory verbal phrase.

Caught in the act of accepting the stolen goods was a clerk who had recently been fired.

Second: When a sentence begins with a *gerund*—a form that looks like a present participle but functions as a noun—the gerund is the subject of the sentence, and one does not want to set off the subject from the finite verb that follows.

*Gerund:* Helping customers solve their problems is a company's most important mission.

*Participle:* While helping customers, service representatives should be polite.

*Gerund:* Driving down Fifth Avenue can be frustrating because the traffic is so heavy.

*Participle:* Driving down Fifth Avenue, motorists should expect delays.

## INTERRUPTERS

The category of interrupters includes all sorts of single words and phrases that flesh out the bare-bones skeleton of a sentence by providing detail, emphasis, transition, or commentary. A restrictive interrupter, which limits the meaning of what it modifies, is not set off from the surrounding sentence by punctuation:

Diseases such as atherosclerosis, arthritis, osteoporosis, hypertension, and Alzheimer's are associated with aging.
[This means not all diseases, but a subset of diseases that includes those listed, are associated with aging.]

However, a nonrestrictive interrupter, which adds information that could be omitted without altering the meaning of the sentence, is set off by a pair of commas. This principle also applies to the punctuation of an interrupter consisting of a complementary or antithetical phrase introduced by an expression such as *in addition to, as well as, but,* or *not* and referring to a following word. But in open style punctuation, the commas may be omitted if the interrupting phrase is short and cannot be misread.

Diseases associated with aging, such as atherosclerosis, arthritis, osteoporosis, hypertension, and Alzheimer's, are seen with increasing frequency in individuals over the age of eighty.

[This means that diseases of aging, of which the ones listed are examples, increase with advanced age.]

Sales of software, according to the store-by-store report, fell sharply last month.

A violent, as well as widely reported, encounter with an inebriated customer led to the clerk's dismissal.

Algernon brought her a lovely, but far too lavishly accessorized and expensive, arrangement of flowers.

*Open style:* The sweet but overpowering smell of incense made her dizzy.

A special exception to the convention of setting off a nonrestrictive interrupter allows the omission of what might be termed *spousal commas*—that is, commas setting off a name used as a short appositive of relationship (e.g., my husband Glenn). This waiver reflects the fact that such phrases are typically spoken without pauses. It also saves copyeditors the task of querying an author ("Have you had other husbands, or is Glenn the only one?") simply to determine whether a name should be punctuated as a no-comma restrictive or a pair-of-commas nonrestrictive interrupter. And the omission of commas helps avoid some potential ambiguities.

*Ambiguous:* My husband, Glenn, and I had dinner at a vegan restaurant downtown.
   [Did three individuals have dinner, or is my spouse's name Glenn?]

*Better:* My husband Glenn and I had dinner at a vegan restaurant downtown.
   [Even if I have only one husband, and his name is Glenn, the omission of the "spousal commas" clarifies that husband Glenn and I had the vegan dinner.]

*Likewise:* McIntyre's son William moved to Chicago in 1919.
   [Did McIntyre have one son or several? Regardless of the answer, the query is unnecessary if the commas with the appositive of relationship are omitted.]

Whereas commas are the neutral choice for setting off interrupters (brief appositives of relationship excepted), dashes and parentheses may be used with interrupters for particular rhetorical effects: dashes emphasize the interrupter; parentheses deemphasize it. Only dashes or parentheses may be used when the interrupter is a self-contained sentence or when it ends with a question mark or exclamation point.

The one—and only—reason to proceed is to recoup the investments we have already made.

Nizhny Novgorod (called Gorky in the Soviet era) is the third largest city in Russia.

Besides conveying emphasis, dashes demarcate the different components of a sentence when the interrupter contains potentially confusing internal punctuation, when the interrupter marks a break in syntax, or when the interrupter is lengthy.

*Interrupter containing internal punctuation:* Regarding the need for more classrooms, the panelists—Bill Jones of Oakland, Carlos Real of San Leandro, and Trey Lee of Hayward—agreed more often than they disagreed.

*Interrupter marking break in syntax:* I must plead the worst of authorial defenses—the perennial limitations imposed by time and space—but will offer several better reasons as well for not treating this issue in detail.

*Lengthy interrupter:* Too often the building's use of interior space—the element that will have the greatest effect on the costs and the most lasting effect on the residents—is left for the last minute.

In addition to de-emphasizing an interrupter that contains a relatively unimportant point, a trivial exception, or a brief list of examples, parentheses are used to supply an acronym, initialism, technical synonym, or translation; to set off a cross-reference; and to provide numerical equivalents. A semicolon may be used to separate different items within parentheses.

In draft mode the output from this printer is 300 dots per inch (dpi); in regular mode, 600 dpi.

The coast live oak (*Quercus agrifolia*) is the dominant native species in this region.

Newspapers in Japan complained about the intensity of American *gaiatsu* (external pressure).

In the first year after the moratorium on condominium conversions was lifted (see section 3), fifty applications for conversion were received by the Hunter County Planning Commission (HCPC; see table 4-1).

The highest point in the park is 1,500 meters (4,920 feet) above sea level.

*Pitfall: Incorrect placement of commas.*  The commas must be placed so that they enclose the interrupter and only the interrupter:

✘ Many of the processes that have contributed to the loss of biotic integrity, including dam construction and the stocking of lakes have been halted in recent years, or are slated for discontinuation.

Many of the processes that have contributed to the loss of biotic integrity, including dam construction and the stocking of lakes, have been halted in recent years or are slated for discontinuation.

You can test for the correct placement of commas preceding and following an interrupter by reading a sentence as though the words enclosed in the commas were not there; the abridged sentence should still make sense. In the preceding example, the incorrectly punctuated sentence fails the test: ✘ Many of the processes that have contributed to the loss of biotic integrity or are slated for discontinuation.

*Pitfall: Interrupters within interrupters.*  When an interrupter itself contains an interrupter, the boundaries of the nested interrupter must be clearly indicated by punctuation marks that are different from those marking the larger interrupter. When the main interrupter is set off by commas, place the nested interrupter in parentheses or dashes:

In the western region, according to Smith's most recent analysis (dated April 1) and the auditor's quarterly report, both shoplifting and returns of damaged merchandise decreased.

DataFlo, which now processes approximately 2,000 terabytes of data—or 10 percent of the market in North Carolina—at its three service centers, is planning to double its operating capacity.

When the main interrupter is set off by dashes, place the nested interrupter in parentheses or commas:

Only one manager—Dana Wilkes (vice-president for marketing) in Topeka—has resigned.

Only one manager—Dana Wilkes, vice-president for marketing, in Topeka—has resigned.

When the main interrupter is in parentheses, place the nested interrupter in brackets, commas, or dashes (or, alternatively, revise to avoid nesting):

Mail the completed application (in-state residents must include Form 568 [Applicants' Statement of Residency] in the packet) by December 1.

Mail the completed application (in-state residents must include Form 568, Applicants' Statement of Residency, in the packet) by December 1.

Mail the completed application (in-state residents must include Form 568—Applicants' Statement of Residency—in the packet) by December 1.

*Better:* Mail the completed application by December 1. In-state residents must include Form 568 (Applicants' Statement of Residency) in the packet.


## FUNCTION 4: INDICATING OMISSION

The fourth principal function of punctuation is to indicate the omission of a letter, portions of a word, an entire word, or a phrase:

| *To indicate* | *Use* |
|---|---|
| dropped letter | apostrophe |
| abbreviation of word | period |
| excision of portion of word | em dash or two-em dash |
| ellipsis within parallel construction | comma or semicolon |
| deletion of word(s) within quotation | ellipsis points |

The use of an apostrophe to indicate a contraction (can't) or a dropped letter (rock 'n' roll) causes few mechanical problems for copyeditors: just make sure that the character *is* an apostrophe and that the apostrophe falls in the correct place. Contractions do, however, raise a stylistic issue. Some publishers and writers insist that contractions have no place in formal writing—with the possible exception of "aren't I," since "am I not" sounds unnatural—but many publishers have dropped or loosened the ban. Even genteel prose, official communications, and professional writing appear to be trending toward greater informality these days, possibly owing to the pervasive influence of blogging and social media. So be sure to ask your editorial coordinator about house policy. If your author's preferences strongly conflict with house policy, discuss the issue with your editorial coordinator before making wholesale changes; publishers will often waive house rules on these kinds of mechanical matters.

Regarding the use of a period to indicate an abbreviation (Dr.), the only issue is whether a particular abbreviation takes a period or not; this topic is discussed in chapter 9.

The use of an em dash (—) or a two-em dash (——) to indicate the excision of a portion of a word is of concern only to scholars (who use the dash to indicate a word that is illegible in a document) and to those publishers who rely on the dash to replace portions of so-called expletives ("This f—ing investigation!" he screamed).

The punctuation of elliptical constructions (that is, constructions in which one or more words are understood and are thus not repeated) requires attention. For simple constructions, a comma suffices in open style punctuation:

> He was born and raised in Iowa City, she in Manitowoc.
>
> Her hair was blond, her eyes blue.

In close style punctuation and in all complex elliptical constructions, semicolons between the clauses and commas at the point of ellipsis are preferable:

> *Close style:* He was born and raised in Iowa City; she, in Manitowoc.
>
> *Close style:* Her hair was blond; her eyes, blue.
>
> *Complex elliptical construction:* Along the south bank of the Grand River, 350 acres of valley oak have been replanted since 1995; along the north bank, 250 acres.

In all such sentences make sure that the meaning is clear, that the parts are parallel in construction, and that no misreading is possible. The following examples fail these tests:

> ✗ He was born in Iowa City but raised in Ames, she in Manitowoc.
>
> ✗ West Lafayette should be Obama country, and Lafayette Clinton country.

A comma may be used in an elliptical construction in dialogue, as in the following example, which omits *that:*

> "The truth is, you're incompetent," he said.

On the use of ellipsis points to indicate the omission of one or more words from a direct quotation, see "Ellipsis Points" in chapter 8.

## MARK-BY-MARK PITFALLS

In addition to the principal functions just enumerated, punctuation serves a variety of what we may call conventional purposes; these are summarized in table 5, and many of them are discussed and illustrated elsewhere in this book. Here, we will look at the most common uses and misuses of the more troublesome punctuation marks: the comma, the semicolon, the colon, and the hyphen, em dash, and en dash.

### COMMAS: THE COPYEDITOR'S NEMESIS

The preceding discussion covers many of the more treacherous perils involving the comma. For a complete inventory of comma rules, see *Chicago* or *WIT*. The most important of these rules and conventions are summarized in table 6, and two of the most troublesome are discussed below.

*Lists and series.* The use of commas to separate items in a series or list causes a surprising number of problems. The first thing to remember is that these commas serve to separate the items; thus there is no comma before the first member of a series:

✗ This photocopier's features include, collating, double-sided copying, and reduction.

This photocopier's features include collating, double-sided copying, and reduction.

And there is no comma after the last member of a series. One exception (noted in *WIT*): When a series in the form *a, b, c* (without a conjunction) directly precedes a verb or clause standing in the same relation to every member of the series, place a comma after each item in the series, including the last one. This special rhetorical device should not be used wantonly; often a conventional conjunction is preferable to the awkward comma.

✗ Yesterday, today, and tomorrow, are the semiannual inventory days.

Yesterday, today, and tomorrow are the semiannual inventory days.

*Exception:* Surprise, disbelief, fear of imminent death, electrified his face.

*Awkward:* The strains of violins, flutes, filled the air.

*Better:* The strains of violins and flutes filled the air.

The other issue concerns the so-called *serial comma* (also called the Oxford comma or the Harvard comma), which is the comma before the *and* or *or* that precedes the last item in a list or series. *Chicago, WIT, APA, CSE,* and *GPO* all either require or strongly recommend the serial comma, but news media and some magazines, following AP style, omit the serial comma—except when it is needed to avoid misreading.

*Serial comma used:* Most book and journal publishers prefer a comma before the coordinate conjunction in a series of three or more items, whether these items are words, phrases, or clauses.

TABLE 5. Punctuation: Principal Conventions

| | |
|---|---|
| To mark the possessive form of a noun | apostrophe or apostrophe followed by *s* |
| To mark the plural form of a(n) | |
| abbreviation that has an internal period | apostrophe followed by *s* |
| nonitalicized lowercase letter | apostrophe followed by *s* |
| word for which adding *s* alone would cause confusion | apostrophe followed by *s* (e.g., do's) |
| To link the members of compound terms | |
| simple compounds | hard hyphen |
| complex compounds (i.e., one or both members are themselves compound terms) | en dash |
| To indicate | |
| a word that continues on the next line | soft hyphen |
| ironic usage or slang | double quotation marks |
| a line break in a run-in quotation of poetry | slash |
| units within a run-in address | comma |
| an unfamiliar foreign term | italics |
| a word used as a word | italics or double quotation marks |
| omission | |
| a dropped letter | apostrophe |
| abbreviation of a word | period |
| excision of a portion of a word | em or two-em dash |
| ellipsis within parallel constructions | comma |
| deletion of words within a quotation | ellipsis points |
| *Dialogue and quotations* | |
| To mark a direct quotation | double quotation marks |
| To mark quoted words within a quotation | single quotation marks |
| To introduce a long, formal quotation | colon |
| To set off the name of the person spoken to | pair of commas |
| To set off the speaker's tag (name and verb) | pair of commas |
| To indicate an interpolation within a quotation | pair of brackets |
| To set off a tag question | comma (e.g., "He's here, isn't he?") |
| Multiple-paragraph quotations | opening quotation mark at the start of each paragraph; closing quotation mark only at the end of the final paragraph |
| *Run-in lists* | |
| To mark the end of an item | comma or semicolon |
| To signal enumerators (numerals or letters) | pair of parentheses |
| To append a summarizing statement to a list | em dash |

TABLE 5 *(continued)*

---

*Titles of works*

| | |
|---|---|
| Title of a short work (e.g., poem, song) | double quotation marks |
| Title of a long work (e.g., book, journal) | italics |
| Title of an unpublished work | double quotation marks |
| To set off a subtitle from a title | colon |

---

*With numerals*

| | | |
|---|---|---|
| To set off thousands in long numerals | comma | 12,345 |
| In hour-minute expressions | colon | 10:30 A.M. |
| In month-day-year expressions | comma | June 23, 1999 |
| To indicate omission of the century | apostrophe | in the '80s |
| In ranges of years | en dash | 1963–1969 *or* 1963–69 |
| For successive years | en dash or slash | 1998–99 *or* 1998/99 |
| In act-scene or chapter-verse citations | period or colon | *Hamlet* 4.2.1 *or* Genesis 4:2 |
| To indicate ratios | colon | a 3:1 mix |
| In fractions | slash | 4/11 |
| In phone numbers | hyphens or periods | 510-555-1212 *or* 510.555.1212 |
| In expressions of units per unit | slash | 3 T/gal |
| To indicate uncertainty or doubt | question mark | 1550?–1593 |
| Word ratios | hyphen or slash | fuel-to-air ratio *or* fuel/air ratio |

---

> *Serial comma omitted:* Most newspaper and magazine publishers omit the comma before the coordinate conjunction in a series of three or more items, whether these items are words, phrases or clauses.

> *But, to avoid ambiguity:* Please state your name, age, sex[,] and housing requirements.

Editors in the book and journalism sectors of the publishing industry expend a great deal of unnecessary energy dueling over the superiority of their respective styles in this matter. Advocates of the serial comma often cite the (apocryphal) dedication "I want to thank my parents, Ayn Rand and God" to illustrate the risk of misreading when this comma is omitted. But even in the streamlined AP style, a discretionary comma would be added here to avoid such a gaffe. True, use of the serial comma reduces the risk of misreading a series; omission of the serial comma requires extra vigilance. Regardless of your personal loyalty to one convention or the other, however, it suffices to ask your editorial coordinator about house style and, if instructed to obey the AP preference, to supply a discretionary comma only when the customary omission of a serial comma would create a miscue.

TABLE 6. Principal Uses of the Comma

**SYNTAX**

*Compound sentence (two independent clauses joined by a conjunction)*
> Separate independent clauses by a comma unless they are very short and unambiguous.
>> The air has become less polluted, and the incidence of respiratory disease has declined.
>> In 1994 sales soared and profits rose.

*Compound predicate (one subject governing two verbs)*
> Use a comma between the subject and the second verb only when it is needed for emphasis or clarity, or when there is a potentially confusing time shift between the actions described by the two verbs.
>> Proofreaders must understand type specs and should learn to detect minute differences in horizontal and vertical spacing.
>> Proofreaders must understand type specs and production and design constraints, and should learn to detect minute differences in horizontal and vertical spacing.
>> Patty parked her Pontiac near the post office, and bought some stamps after lunch.

*Dependent clause preceding an independent clause*
> Place a comma after the dependent clause.
>> If the minimum wage is not increased, the purchasing power of low-wage earners will continue to decline.

*Dependent clause following an independent clause*
> No comma after the independent clause if the dependent clause is restrictive.
>> The purchasing power of low-wage earners will continue to decline if the minimum wage is not increased.
> If the dependent clause is nonrestrictive, place a comma after the independent clause.
>> Senator Poe voted to raise the minimum wage, if that addresses your concern.

*Introductory phrase that contains a participle*
> Set off the phrase with a comma.
>> Before reading the paper, I ate breakfast.
>> Having finished reading the newspaper, I sat down to work.

*Sentence adverb*
> Set off a sentence adverb with a comma.
>> Unfortunately, the results will not be available for another six weeks.

*Transitional adverb*
> Set off a transitional adverb.
>> However, the schedule is very tight.
>> The schedule, however, is very tight.
>> Thus, only one conclusion is logical.
> When the transition is not abrupt and no emphasis is desired, no punctuation is needed.
>> Thus the problem was resolved.

TABLE 6 *(continued)*

Do not set off an adverb that is a qualifier, not an interrupter:

However hard she tried, he criticized her work.

We thus set out to meet our destiny.

*Interrupter*

Set off an interrupter with a pair of commas.

Carla, to her credit, promptly reported the discrepancy.

*Series of parallel items*

Use commas to separate the items in a list or series.

Bring your books, pens, and pencils.

A driver's license, passport, or other official photo ID must be shown to the clerk.

The presence or absence of a comma preceding the *and* or *or* that introduces the final item in the series is a matter of house style. Even when house style does not call for the serial comma, some constructions require a comma to avoid ambiguity.

Please send invitations to Ann and Al, Barb and Bill, Carol, and Dina and Dan.

*Pair or series of adjectives*

Use commas to separate coordinate adjectives.

She gave a thoughtful, constructive speech to a warm, appreciative, well-informed audience.

Do not use commas if the adjectives are not coordinate.

The new blue velvet drapes looked odd behind the overstuffed green leather chair.

Nor did the floor-length blue drapes match the slightly faded handmade wool rug.

*Interdependent clauses*

Separate interdependent clauses with a comma unless the clauses are very short.

The fewer the complications, the faster the project will be completed.

The more the merrier.

*Antithetical elements*

Separate antithetical elements with a comma.

That's my book, not yours, on the table.

## CONVENTIONS
*Direct address*

Set off the addressee.

"Let's eat, Grandma."

"Where, Alice, have you been?"

"Doctor, your next patient is here."

"Hi, John." "Hello, Jane."

"Goodbye, sweetheart, until we meet again."

"Welcome, friends, to this special dinner."

*(continued next page)*

TABLE 6 *(continued)*

The vocative *O* combines with the name of the following addressee.

"O Lord, hear our prayer."

Affirmatives and negatives are followed but not preceded by a comma in both direct and indirect address. The words *yes* and *no* combine with the following terms of direct address in a few set expressions.

"Yes, Virginia, there is a Santa Claus."

He said yes, Santa Claus exists. He said yes.

Yes ma'am, I believe in Santa Claus. No sir, I'm not prevaricating.

*Direct quotation*

Use a comma to separate the quotation from the speaker's tag unless the speaker's tag follows a quotation ending with an exclamation point or question mark.

I said, "Let's go."

"Let's go," I said.

"Right now!" he insisted.

"Where are we going?" she asked.

*Addresses*

In running text, use a comma to separate the street address from the city, and the city from the state.

He lives at 123 Main Street, Oaks, Montana.

*But:* His address is 123 Main St., Oaks MT 59700.

In expressions of the form "City, State," place commas both before and after the name of the state.

Berkeley, California, is a university town.

*Ambiguous:* Shooting in Dallas, Texas kills three police officers.

*Dates*

In the month-day-year date form, place commas before and—unless the date comes at the end of the sentence—after the year.

On June 1, 1998, they signed the document.

The headquarters was moved to Austin on June 1, 1998.

*But:* In June 1998 it didn't rain.

*And:* On 1 June 1998 the document was signed.

*Suffixes with names*

Use a pair of commas to set off a professional, company, or generational suffix from a proper name. A newer convention omits the comma pairs with generational and company suffixes: with these suffixes use a pair of commas or none.

Paul Pilcrow, M.D., will address the convention.

Wilco, Inc., is our supplier.

*Or:* Wilco Inc. is our supplier.

Ralph Merritt, Jr., was born in Wyoming.

*Or:* Ralph Merritt Jr. was born in Wyoming.

*Coordinate and noncoordinate adjectives.* The convention of placing a comma between coordinate adjectives seems to be fading, perhaps because of the trend toward open punctuation, perhaps because the absence of this comma rarely confuses readers, or perhaps because the distinction between coordinate and noncoordinate adjectives is sometimes hard to apply.[13]

In principle, *coordinate adjectives* are those that equally and independently modify a noun, and their coordinate status is marked by the presence of either the word *and* or a comma between them; for example:

a dull and error-filled book *or* a dull, error-filled book

a cool and humid climate *or* a cool, humid climate

Conversely, noncoordinate adjectives do not equally and independently modify a noun; instead, the first adjective modifies the unit comprising the second adjective (or even a third adjective) plus the noun:

a thick green book

a battered old canvas fishing hat[14]

There are three crude "tests" for determining whether a pair of adjectives is coordinate. A pair of adjectives is coordinate if (1) one can place *and* between the adjectives or (2) one can reverse the order of the adjectives and still have a sensible phrase or (3) one can place the adjectives, joined by *and,* in a relative clause following the noun. The phrase "a long, restful vacation" passes all tests (a long and restful vacation; a restful, long vacation; a vacation that is long and restful), and therefore these adjectives are coordinate. But "a long summer vacation" fails these tests (✗ a long and summer vacation; ✗ a summer long vacation; ✗ a vacation that is long and summer), and therefore these adjectives are not coordinate.

---

13. Grammar and usage books often outline an intricate set of rules governing the idiomatic sequence of a series of adjectives in English; these sequencing rules are greatly complicated by semantic nuances and by some specific exceptions—e.g., set phrases (nice old lady, dear little children) that are rarely broken up. Native English speakers usually apply the sequencing rules intuitively. The challenge for writers and editors is to punctuate the sequence of adjectives correctly, which requires differentiating between coordinate adjectives (adjectives perceived as equivalent, i.e., those that separately and equally modify the following noun) and noncoordinate ones. Even experienced editors sometimes puzzle over whether and how to emend a lengthy string of modifiers such as that in ✗ "colorful long silk flowered dresses" ("long, colorful flowered silk dresses"?). A useful discussion of adjective sequence and the punctuation of a series of adjectives can be found in a respected, if somewhat aging (1957), reference: Bergen Evans and Cornelia Evans, *A Dictionary of Contemporary American Usage*, s.v. "adjectives: order in a series."

14. This example comes from Wilson Follett; here is his analysis:

Are the adjectives parallel in *He was wearing his battered old canvas fishing hat*? No, because the hat is not (1) battered, (2) old, (3) canvas, and (4) fishing. Nor could the adjectives be written in a different order (*canvas, old, fishing, battered*). In meaning, the noun is not *hat* but *canvas-fishing-hat.* Does it follow that commas should go after *battered* and *old*? No again, for one of our tests would then produce *battered and old and canvas*—and something stranger still if the sequence of modifiers were changed. Adjectives grouped in this way are not parallel but cumulative, and so are distorted by commas. (*MAU,* s.v. "comma, the")

Sometimes the punctuation of a series of adjectives can change the meaning:

His first scandalous novel was published in 1927.
[He wrote more than one scandalous novel; the first of these was published in 1927.]

His first, scandalous novel was published in 1927.
[The novel published in 1927 was his first, and it was scandalous.]

The coordinate rule also applies to a series of adverbs:

He urgently, repeatedly requested our help.

*Do-nots.* In addition to knowing when a comma is called for, copyeditors need to know when *not* to use a comma.[15] The first three of the following do-nots repeat the syntactical rules discussed earlier in this chapter; the others follow from nonsyntactical conventions.

1. Do not use a comma to join independent clauses.

   ✗ The store is fully stocked, all we need are customers.

   The store is fully stocked; all we need are customers.

   *Exceptions:* When the clauses are very short and they have the same subject, a comma will suffice. Short, closely related independent clauses expressing antithetical ideas or stating an aphorism are also sometimes separated by a comma rather than a stronger mark of punctuation. And in literary writing—for example, to represent dialogue or indirect speech—a comma splice may be used for special effect. (See the discussion of run-on sentences above, under "Function 2: Joining Clauses.")

2. Do not insert a comma between a subject and the second member of a compound predicate.

   ✗ This new method will simplify billing, and save us time.

   This new method will simplify billing and save us time.

   *Exceptions:* A discretionary comma may be inserted between the elements of a compound predicate to prevent misreading, to mark a difference in time between the actions of the two verbs, or to aid readers when these predicates are long and complex, especially if they contain internal punctuation. (See the previous discussion of compound predicates under "Function 2: Joining Clauses.")

15. This list of do-nots is adapted from Harry Shaw, *Punctuate It Right!* (New York: Harper & Row, 1986), and from Joan I. Miller and Bruce J. Taylor, *The Punctuation Handbook* (West Linn, Ore.: Alcove, 1989).

3. Do not use commas to set off a restrictive appositive.

   ✗ The movie, *Casablanca*, is being re-released this year.

   The movie *Casablanca* is being re-released this year.[16]

4. Do not use commas before an indirect quotation.

   ✗ Senior management asked, whether appliance sales were slowing.

   Senior management asked whether appliance sales were slowing.

5. Do not use a comma after a *that* that precedes a quotation:

   ✗ The prospectus states that, "historical returns are not indicative of future performance."

   The prospectus states that "historical returns are not indicative of future performance."

6. Do not use a comma before a quotation that is the direct object of a verb:

   ✗ The sign said, "No Trespassing."

   The sign said "No Trespassing."

   ---

   ✗ The group's motto reads, "All for one, and one for all."

   The group's motto reads "All for one, and one for all."

7. Do not allow a comma to interrupt a *so . . . that* or *such . . . that* construction.

   ✗ The upcoming negotiations are so crucial, that all vacations are canceled.

   The upcoming negotiations are so crucial that all vacations are canceled.

   ---

   ✗ This meeting is such a waste of time, that I think I'll go to the bookstore instead.

   This meeting is such a waste of time that I think I'll go to the bookstore instead.

---

16. For comparison's sake, note that the film's title functions as a nonrestrictive appositive in the following sentences:

Their favorite movie, *Casablanca,* is being re-released this year.

The film that introduced Ingrid Bergman to American audiences, *Intermezzo,* was released in 1939.

8.  Do not place a comma before an opening parenthesis that introduces a comment or a parenthetical source citation.[17]

✗ Many readers dislike double pronouns, ("he or she") and so we do not use them.

Many readers dislike double pronouns ("he or she"), and so we do not use them.

---

✗ Studies of entire communities—such as the Framingham Heart Study in Framingham, Massachusetts, (Kannel 1967) and the Atherosclerosis Risk in Communities (ARIC) Study—investigate the etiology and natural history of diseases.

Studies of entire communities—such as the Framingham Heart Study in Framingham, Massachusetts (Kannel 1967), and the Atherosclerosis Risk in Communities (ARIC) Study—investigate the etiology and natural history of diseases.

9.  Do not place a comma between the members of a pair joined by *not . . . but* or *not only . . . but* [*also*].

✗ He knows not the purpose, but the result.

He knows not the purpose but the result.

---

✗ Patty drives not only a Pontiac, but also a vintage Packard.

Patty drives not only a Pontiac but also a vintage Packard.

✗ Patty is not only driving a Pontiac, but also restoring a vintage Packard.

Patty is not only driving a Pontiac but also restoring a vintage Packard.

*Nuance versus clutter.* Sometimes an author will insert a pair of commas to provide a slight degree of de-emphasis; for example:

The older conventions for using commas, at times, can produce an unpleasant choppiness.

The older conventions for using commas are, for the most part, yielding to a more open style.

Although no commas are required in either of these sentences, no harm is done by their presence, and some writers would argue that the commas improve the cadence of these statements. But watch what happens if the writer combines these sentences and keeps the commas before and after "at times" and "for the most part":

The older conventions for using commas, which, at times, can produce an unpleasant choppiness, are, for the most part, yielding to a more open style.

---

17. A comma may, however, precede a set of parentheses that encloses a numeral or letter in an in-text list.

The minimal installation requires (a) a Pentium processor, (b) 40 MB of available hard disk space, (c) 16K RAM, and (d) a VGA or higher-resolution graphics card.

In this longer sentence, it is preferable in open style punctuation to reduce the number of commas to two, both to eliminate the stutter-step cadence and to visually clarify the boundaries of the nonrestrictive *which* clause:

> The older conventions for using commas, which at times can produce an unpleasant choppiness, are for the most part yielding to a more open style.

*Preventing misreadings.*  Sometimes the syntactical structure of a sentence does not in itself call for a comma, but a comma is needed nonetheless to prevent misreading. For example:

> Whenever possible, actions should be taken to ensure clients' privacy.
>
> To Jane, Harry had nothing to say.
>
> Soon after, the company declared bankruptcy.

*Judgment and taste.*  Even after you have mastered all the comma do's and don'ts, you will continually come across sentences that are not covered by any of the rules. Authors sometimes punctuate aurally, sometimes visually, sometimes syntactically; often they blend these considerations, influenced by such factors as the length of their phrases and clauses, the rhythmical complexity of their words, their nuances of meaning, and their aesthetic preference for lightly or densely punctuated prose. Assuming that house style allows you to exercise some editorial discretion, you must ask yourself whether the presence or absence of a comma will best serve the writer's purposes and the readers' needs: Will the addition or deletion of a comma facilitate or impede the readers' understanding of the sentence? suggest the desired shade of meaning or tone? call undue attention to itself or be perceived as a typographical error? For example, consider the following sentences:

> Her brief, eloquent tribute appears in this month's newsletter.
>
> > [Comma separates the pair of coordinate adjectives.]

---

> Her brief and eloquent tribute appears in this month's newsletter.
>
> Her brief but eloquent tribute appears in this month's newsletter.
>
> > [No comma is required since the adjectives are joined by a coordinate conjunction.]

---

> Her brief yet eloquent tribute appears in this month's newsletter.
>
> Her brief, yet eloquent tribute appears in this month's newsletter.
>
> Her brief, yet eloquent, tribute appears in this month's newsletter.
>
> > [Writer's choice: No comma is required; inserting one comma emphasizes the contrast conveyed by "yet"; inserting a pair of commas de-emphasizes "yet eloquent."]

---

OSS and later CIA personnel were charged with gathering international intelligence.

OSS and, later, CIA personnel were charged with gathering international intelligence.

OSS, and later CIA, personnel were charged with gathering international intelligence.

OSS, and, later, CIA, personnel were charged with gathering international intelligence.

> [Writer's choice: All these punctuation choices are correct; each has a different rhythm and emphasis.]

He floundered in his acting classes. That did not stop him from performing, badly.

The actions of the Federal Reserve governors seem, provisionally, to have worked.

> [Writer's choice: Optional commas are inserted to achieve a desired emphasis or nuance of meaning. For stronger emphasis, "badly" and "provisionally" would be separated by dashes.]

Patty leaped into her Pontiac and, tossing her purse onto the passenger seat along with her parcels, pounded the steering wheel.

> [Punctuation follows strict syntactical rules: no comma separates the parts of a compound predicate; a pair of commas sets off the interrupter.]

Patty leaped into her Pontiac, and, tossing her purse onto the passenger seat along with her parcels, pounded the steering wheel.

> [An optional comma is added between the elements of the compound predicate to reflect a natural speech pause that aids readers in parsing the intricate syntax.]

## SEMICOLONS

Confusion about the use of semicolons arises from the semicolon's dual personality: Sometimes a semicolon serves as a weak period that joins independent clauses more closely together than a period would. But at other times a semicolon functions as a strong comma that separates syntactical elements more definitively than a comma would.

*"Weak period" semicolons.* As we have seen, one use of semicolons is to bind independent clauses together into one sentence. For example, an author writes:

> In most community property states, the income from separate property remains separate property. In a few states, however, the income from separate property is deemed to be community property.

On rereading these sentences, the author feels that they are so closely related—because each sentence makes only part of the point—that they should be joined into one sentence. So the author substitutes a semicolon for the period at the end of the first sentence (and lowercases the first letter of the second sentence):

> In most community property states, the income from separate property remains separate property; in a few states, however, the income from separate property is deemed to be community property.

In theory, any terminal period can be replaced by a semicolon, and any semicolon that joins two independent clauses can be replaced by a period. The artfulness comes in deciding which sentences are so closely linked in meaning that a semicolon is preferable to a period. Rhythm and sentence length also enter into the choice. When the independent clauses are long or complex, a semicolon will technically hold them together, but readers may be confused. When the independent clauses are simple and short, a comma and a conjunction can hold them together, while a semicolon may seem too heavy-handed:

> An anaphylactic reaction is a medical emergency. Prompt care is needed.

> An anaphylactic reaction is a medical emergency, and prompt care is needed.

> An anaphylactic reaction is a medical emergency; prompt care is needed.

*"Strong comma" semicolons.* The semicolon's second personality is that of a strong comma. For example, an author writes:

> The itinerary includes Venice, Florence, and Parma, the jewels of northern Italy, Rome, Naples, and Ravello, in southern Italy, and the islands of Sicily, Sardinia, and Corsica.

In this kind of complex series, the commas are not adequate to help the reader distinguish the different items. If we replace some of the commas with semicolons, readers can see that the trip has three parts:

> The itinerary includes Venice, Florence, and Parma, the jewels of northern Italy; Rome, Naples, and Ravello, in southern Italy; and the islands of Sicily, Sardinia, and Corsica.

Similarly, semicolons are used to mark off the segments of a complex elliptical construction:

> In 1996 we raised $120,000 from 525 donors; in 1995, just under $80,000 from 406 donors.

> The Labor Party won 125 seats; the Freedom Party, 58; and the Dignity Party, 46.

*Some special uses.*  In *Spunk and Bite* Arthur Plotnik suggests several additional uses of the semicolon to achieve particular effects: setting up a sarcastic phrase with a loose *that* or *this,* preceding an introductory word like *namely* or *specifically,* and separating brief, rhetorically balanced (echoing) statements (p. 178):

> Save every penny you earn; that and a winning lottery ticket will buy you a house in San Francisco.

> My doctor recommends a strict regimen of exercise; specifically, get up off the couch.

> The body is weak; the mind is strong.

## COLONS

As we have seen, colons can be used to join two independent clauses to form one sentence or to append a list to an independent clause. It is this second function that causes most of the problems, but the rule is simple enough: use a colon to append a list to an independent clause; do not use a colon if the words that precede the list do not form an independent clause. Thus the colon should be deleted in these sentences:

> ✗ We have to: conduct the inventory, calculate the profits, and submit our proposal.

> ✗ She will write: a production memo, the jacket copy, and a press release.

> ✗ This budget does not include such activities as: proofing, editing, and indexing.

> *But:* This budget does not include the following activities: editing, proofreading, and indexing.

To impart an informal, conversational tone, a writer may sometimes use a deliberate fragment to introduce a full statement following a colon:

> Full disclosure: The subject of this article is a major stockholder in the parent company that owns this magazine.

There are several other conventional uses for the colon. Colons introduce formal quotations (see "Punctuation of Quotations" in chapter 8) and set-off lists, also known as displayed or vertical lists. (For a detailed discussion of how to punctuate set-off lists, including introductory text, see "Lists" in chapter 13.) Colons also follow the salutation in formal business letters and the headings in business memos. They separate hours from minutes in expressions of time, chapter from verse numbers in biblical citations, and titles from subtitles. Colons follow speakers' tags in screenplays and the protocol in internet addresses.

Chicago and GPO styles lowercase the items in a list introduced by a colon as well as the first word of a full sentence following a colon. If a colon introduces a series of full sentences, however, the first word of each is capitalized; Chicago style also capitalizes the first word of a direct question, dialogue, or quotation that is formally introduced by a colon. *WIT* and AP style capitalize the first word of any complete sentence following a colon.

## HYPHENS, EM DASHES, AND EN DASHES

*Soft hyphens.* A hyphen that appears at the end of a line of text to indicate that a word continues on the next line is called a soft hyphen. The epithet *soft* refers to the fact that the hyphen must disappear should the entire word fall on one line. The placement of a soft hyphen is governed by the syllabication of the word and various conventions regarding line breaks in typeset copy; for example, it is incorrect to strand a single letter of a word at the end or the beginning of a line of typeset text.

Copyeditors working on hard copy usually need not concern themselves with whether the soft hyphens are correctly placed, since the line breaks that appear in the manuscript will not appear in the final document. Thus, rather than checking for the correct hyphenation of a word, the copyeditor marks all soft hyphens with a "close-up and delete" sign. Copyeditors working on-screen will not encounter soft hyphens in well-prepared manuscripts, because authors are instructed not to use soft hyphens. If the author has used soft hyphens, the editorial coordinator will usually ask the copyeditor to turn off the hyphenation feature, which will delete the soft hyphens from the files.

You may, however, have occasion to copyedit a manuscript in which the line breaks will carry over to the final document. In that case, you should correct any misplaced soft hyphens. Dictionaries differ somewhat in their syllabication principles, so it's important to consult the house dictionary to confirm the proper location for a soft hyphen. You may also wish to consult *Chicago* or *WIT* on conventions concerning line breaks in long numerals, proper names, and hyphenated words.

The newest wrinkle in end-of-line hyphenation is how to break an email address or a URL. One should never insert an end-of-line hyphen in these clusters. *Chicago* advises that if a URL must break across a line, it should break "*after* a colon or a double slash (//); *before* a single slash (/), a tilde (~), a period, a comma, a hyphen, an underline (_), a question mark, a number sign, or a percent symbol; or *before or after* an equals sign or an ampersand" (14.18). For email addresses, line breaks may appear *before* the at sign (@) or a dot (because a break after the dot may cause the reader to construe the dot as a sentence-ending period).[18]

*Hard hyphens.* Hard hyphens are used to join certain compound words (e.g., self-respect). The epithet *hard* indicates that the hyphen must always appear in print, even when the hyphenated term appears on one line. (Chapter 5 discusses conventions for hyphenating compound words and phrases.) Copyeditors working on hard copy are expected to mark all hyphens that appear at the end of a line of text so that the compositor or word processor will know whether the hyphen is hard or soft.

---

18. For clarity's sake, some publishers italicize email addresses and URLs. A few use boldface for these items, set them in a font that contrasts with the surrounding text, wrap them within angle brackets to define their boundaries, or omit periods when they occur at the end of a sentence. Decisions about such strategies should follow house style and should be made in consultation with the editorial coordinator.

*Clean-Fuel Vehicles*. For details,

see IRS Publication 535, Busi

ness Expenses. If you claim part

of your deduction on Schedule C,

C-EZ, or E, identify as "Clean-

Fuel."

*Em dashes. Em dash* is the technical term for what most people call "a dash." Writers used to key an em dash as two hyphens (--) on the typewriter; many writers still type a dash this way on the computer, but word processing applications usually autocorrect the two hyphens to an em dash (—), the solid character used in typesetting. Copyeditors working on hard copy need not mark em dashes that are consistently typed as either -- or —. On-screen copyeditors may be instructed to substitute the correct em-dash character for any dashes that still appear as two hyphens, or to replace em dashes with a specified code to meet the requirements of the typesetting system. US convention does not use wordspaces before or after an em dash. (British typographic style, however, uses an en dash with wordspaces before and after – like this – to represent an interruption.)

*En dashes.* The quirky creature in this set is the en dash. You have doubtless seen many en dashes in print, although newspapers and some magazines do not use them. An en dash is longer than a hyphen but shorter than an em dash:

hyphen: -        en dash: –        em dash: —

The en dash is used in four situations. First, the en dash replaces the hyphen in certain types of compound adjectives: (1) when one element of the compound is itself a hyphenated term; (2) when one element of the compound is an open (nonhyphenated) two- or three-word term; and (3) when both elements of the compound are open or hyphenated compounds:[19]

(1) One element of the compound adjective is itself a hyphenated term:

The Columbia-Presbyterian–Cornell medical program provides excellent training.

The Woody–Soon-Yi scandal preoccupied the media for many weeks.

(2) One element of the compound adjective is an open two- or three-word term:

Europe's post–World War II economic recovery was primed by the Marshall Plan.

---

19. To avoid "awkward asymmetry," *Chicago* prefers a hyphen, not an en dash, in complex compounds that admit no ambiguity: wheelchair-user-designed environment. For further discussion of the intricacies of hyphenated compounds, see chapter 5.

The San Francisco–based company posted higher-than-expected earnings for the second quarter.

El Niño–related storms caused $200,000 in property damage last week.

These lead soldier–size bronze sculptures will be on display through August.

The conference was held on the University of Wisconsin–Madison campus.[20]

(3) Both elements of the compound adjective contain either open or hyphenated compound terms:

She presented the report at the New York–New Jersey symposium on regional air pollution.

The company is seeking a high-value–low-cost solution to the problem.

But note that in compound adjectives formed by attaching a prefix to a hyphenated element, a hyphen is used:

The airlines are demanding more training for non-English-speaking air traffic controllers.

Wages in these semi-labor-intensive industries are not keeping pace with inflation.

Second, the *peer en dash,* rather than a hyphen, is used in some editorial styles to join equivalently weighted terms in two-word compound adjectives (e.g., risk–benefit ratio, French–American relations, parent–teacher conferences). British convention, as described in *Butcher's Copy-editing* and in the *New Oxford Style Manual,* is to use the peer en dash. Likewise, the American Chemical Society (ACS), CSE, and APA styles specify the peer en dash to link two terms of equal rank (e.g., gas–liquid chromatography, Chicago–London flight). Bryan Garner endorses this style as well in *Garner's Modern English Usage* and in *The Chicago Guide to Grammar, Usage, and Punctuation,* explaining that the en dash connotes movement or tension, an implied "to" or "versus," between the joined terms (e.g., nature–nurture debate, Fischer–Spassky match, Dallas–Toronto route). Along with ACS and CSE, Garner also recommends using a peer en dash in expressions of collaboration and joint authorship (e.g., Young–Laplace equation, Prosser–Keeton text). But *Chicago* uses a hyphen in all these examples.

Third, the en dash is used as a substitute for the word *through* in a range of inclusive numbers or months.

The life of John Smith (1873–1945) is discussed on pages 44–47.

The budget for January–April 1997 appears in the May-June issue of the company newsletter.

---

20. The official names for the campuses of educational institutions with multiple locations take different forms: Wisconsin uses the en dash to connect the institutional name with the campus designation; the University of California uses commas (e.g., University of California, Berkeley); Indiana University omits punctuation altogether (e.g., Indiana University South Bend).

Note that in the second of these examples, "January–April 1997" takes an en dash because it represents an inclusive range of months (i.e., the en dash is a substitute for *through*), but "the May-June issue" takes a regular hyphen because these two months do not represent a range (one would not say "the May through June issue").

Fourth, the en dash may be used to report scores or tallies: "The Mets won, 5–3" or "The court split 5–4."

A howler publicized by Strunk and White in *The Elements of Style* illustrates the value of the en dash, but also its limitations. When the *Chattanooga News* and the *Chattanooga Free Press* merged, "someone introduced a hyphen into the merger, and the paper became *The Chattanooga News-Free Press,* which sounds as though the paper were news-free, or devoid of news" (p. 35). Using an en dash to join the open two-word *Free Press* to its new partner would have helped, though *Chattanooga News–Free Press* still invites snickers.

When marking manuscripts by hand, copyeditors indicate any hyphens in a manuscript that are to be set as en dashes:

The budget for January-April 1997 appears

in the May-June issue of the bulletin.

On-screen copyeditors may be asked only to ensure that the en dash character is correctly typed, or they may be instructed to code en dashes as <–> or <n> or <en>. (Coding is discussed in chapter 13.)

## QUOTATION MARKS: SINGLE AND DOUBLE

The most common use of double quotation marks (to indicate a direct quotation) and of single quotation marks (to set off a quoted word within a direct quotation) cause few problems; these are discussed in "Punctuation of Quotations" in chapter 8.

Double quotation marks can also set off a word that the author is using in a nonstandard or special sense—for example, a piece of slang or technical jargon or a neologism:

> Inevitably, the debate over "squawk radio" turns into a debate about the First Amendment and whether limits may be placed on the freedom of speech.

> The proposed bill would ban "drive-by" deliveries and require insurers to cover the cost of at least a forty-eight-hour hospital stay.

> Emoticons, or "smileys," are those odd combinations of punctuation marks that harried email writers use to indicate their mood at the nanosecond of composition.

> Before a single reporter could ask a single question, the press secretary launched into a well-rehearsed "prebuttal."

Over time, as a word or phrase is naturalized into the language, these quotation marks will disappear.

Double quotation marks may also be used to indicate that the writer is using a word or phrase ironically or sarcastically, or does not mean to legitimize the expression or concept by using the dubious term. These ironic, or distancing, quotation marks are sometimes referred to as *scare quotes, shudder quotes,* or *sneer quotes.*

> Copyeditors should not overlook such "minor details" as punctuation.

> The "evidence" for this claim consists of anecdotes from disgruntled former employees.

A similar effect can be achieved by the use of the expression *so-called* or, replicating so-called air quotes (the gesture accompanying speech) to create an informal tone, by the use of the words *quote-unquote.* In these cases the suspect expression is not placed in quotation marks:

> The so-called evidence for this claim consists of anecdotes from disgruntled former employees.

> The quote-unquote evidence for this claim consists of anecdotes from disgruntled former employees.

Note, however, that quotation marks should not be used to set off clichés:

> ✘ Why do so many Americans persist in struggling to "keep up with the Joneses"?

> Why do so many Americans persist in struggling to keep up with the Joneses?

> ✘ Every young entrepreneur is convinced that he or she can "build a better mousetrap."

> Every young entrepreneur is convinced that he or she can build a better mousetrap.

Quotation marks (or, alternatively, italics) are also used to flag words used as words:

> A similar effect can be achieved by the use of the expression "so-called."

Finally, quotation marks are useful in sorting out a string such as the following:

> During World War I, anti-German sentiment prompted Americans to begin calling sauerkraut "liberty cabbage" and frankfurters "hot dogs."

Copyeditors need to attend to the systematic treatment of styling (italics, quotations, boldface) for words used as words, words used ironically, colloquial terms, foreign words, and special terms requiring definition.

## ENCLOSURES: PARENTHESES, BRACKETS, AND BRACES

Marks used to enclose text include parentheses, brackets, angle brackets, and braces. (In British usage, these marks are referred to, respectively, as round brackets, square brackets, angle brackets, and curly brackets.) Many of the conventional uses of parentheses were demonstrated earlier in this chapter—to set off minor remarks, to supply abbreviations and acronyms (or to explain them), to define or translate terms and expressions, and to supply cross-references. "Parens" may also be used to enclose source citations embedded in text (see chapter 11) and to set off numbers or letters in an itemized list (see "Lists" in chapter 13).

Three somewhat arcane matters concerning the use of parentheses deserve brief mention here. First, successive parentheses may appear back-to-back in text if the content they enclose is unconnected, but often the discrete material can simply be separated by a semicolon within one set of parentheses. Second, when a note number accompanies parenthetical content, the superscript is normally placed outside the closing parenthesis even when the note applies only to the parenthetical content; commonsense exceptions may be made when the note glosses a specific item within the parentheses. And third, in the unlikely event that parentheses enclose several consecutive paragraphs, GPO style stipulates that the opening parenthesis be repeated at the beginning of each new paragraph but the closing parenthesis be supplied only at the conclusion of the entire passage. (*GPO,* which establishes editorial style for many government documents, appears to be the only style guide that even anticipates this possibility.)

The principal use of brackets (a.k.a. square brackets) is to enclose nested parenthetical material, that is, parentheses within parentheses.[21] If the nested material itself contains parenthetical content—a situation best avoided—parentheses enclose this third level of subordination. Brackets are also used for an editorial interpolation, such as a clarifying word or phrase, in a direct quotation or translation (see chapter 8).

Angle brackets, the paired symbols < > on a standard keyboard, have few applications in ordinary nontechnical prose. Some house styles require their use to enclose URLs and email addresses, but this practice has generally declined and is not recommended by *Chicago.* Because angle brackets are rarely deployed in nontechnical writing, some publishers and editors reserve these marks for markup and embedding instructions to typesetters (see chapter 13).

Braces (a.k.a. curly brackets) are primarily used for mathematics, programming, and other specialized purposes.

## MULTIPLE PUNCTUATION

Sometimes more than one punctuation mark is required at a particular spot in a sentence. The following conventions describe American practice in these matters.

### PUNCTUATION WITH CLOSING QUOTATION MARKS

All the principal style manuals except *CSE* recommend what is called American style:

- A period or a comma goes *inside* the closing quotation mark.
- A colon or a semicolon goes *outside.*

---

21. British style allows parentheses within parentheses, according to *Butcher's* and the *New Oxford Style Manual.*

- An exclamation point, question mark, or dash goes *inside* if the mark belongs to the quoted material; *outside* if the mark is not part of the quotation.

*CSE,* however, follows what is called British (or "logical") style: a period, comma, exclamation point, question mark, or dash goes inside a closing quotation mark if it is part of the quoted material, outside if it is not, although actual British practices may vary with house style, for the sake of expediency, and in some academic specialties, fiction, and journalism (see n. 7 in this chapter). Since a section of quoted matter never ends with a semicolon or a colon (if these are in the original, they are suppressed in the quotation), these marks always go outside the closing quotation mark.

## PUNCTUATION WITH A CLOSING PARENTHESIS

Here is a summary of the placement of punctuation marks relative to a closing parenthesis:

- The period goes *inside* when the parenthetical comment is its own complete sentence; otherwise, the period goes *outside.*
- Punctuation marks that are part of the parenthetical comment go *inside;* for example, a parenthetical comment may end with an exclamation point or question mark.
- Since a parenthetical comment cannot end with a comma or a semicolon, these marks always go *outside* the closing parenthesis.

## STRONGER AND WEAKER PUNCTUATION MARKS

When two punctuation marks are called for at the same location, only the stronger is retained. In this sense, a question mark or an exclamation point is "stronger" than a comma or a period.

✘ "Why are you here?," he asked. "Really!," she said.

"Why are you here?" he asked. "Really!" she said.

---

✘ His latest book is *Why Are We Here?.*

His latest book is *Why Are We Here?*

Clarity, however, sometimes demands that this rule be waived. For example, when a title ends with a question mark or an exclamation point, syntactically required commas are not suppressed:

✘ Her best-selling books include *Who Was That Man? Here We Go Again!* and *Don't Be Late.*

Her best-selling books include *Who Was That Man?, Here We Go Again!,* and *Don't Be Late.*

---

✗ "Do You Have a Future in Banking?" the latest pamphlet in the series, is now available.

"Do You Have a Future in Banking?," the latest pamphlet in the series, is now available.

In the first of these pairs, an added comma prevents readers from conceiving of *Who Was That Man? Here We Go Again!* as one title; in the second, the comma clarifies the function of "the latest pamphlet in the series" (a nonrestrictive appositive). In other cases, however, the comma may be safely deleted because the question mark alone is sufficient and unambiguous; for example:

✗ When customers ask "Do you have this in my size?," you should help them.

When customers ask "Do you have this in my size?" you should help them.

## EYEBALLING EVERY MARK

If you are working on a manuscript that will be rekeyed by the compositor, you can trust the compositor to insert the proper characters for apostrophes and opening and closing quotation marks. If you are working on-screen on files that will be processed by a typesetter, you will usually receive files that conform to the typesetter's equipment; for example, the files will contain either typeset-style quotation marks (e.g., " " ' '), sometimes called *smart* or *curly quotes,* or plain marks (e.g., " '), also called *straight quotes.*

However, if you are working on documents that will be printed without any intervention from a compositor (e.g., documents produced on the office laser printer), you will have to carefully scrutinize every piece of punctuation to be sure that the document contains the correct character (see table 7).

TABLE 7. Typed and Typeset Punctuation Marks

|  | Typed Characters* | Typeset Characters |
|---|---|---|
| Apostrophe | I can't go. | I can't go. |
| Single quotes | The 'gestalt' | The 'gestalt' |
| Double quotes | "Go," she said | "Go," she said |
| En dash | Edit pages 2-5. | Edit pages 2–5. |
| Em dash | Here--take it. | Here—take it. |

* Many word processors now default to (or allow the user to set preferences for) smart quotations, directional apostrophes, and em dashes while typing; the en dashes used in typesetting usually require a combination of keystrokes or special coding.

You should also delete any extra wordspacing before or after punctuation marks. The conventions are these:

- One space follows a sentence-ending punctuation mark (period, question mark, or exclamation point).
- One space follows a comma, colon, or semicolon.
- There is no space before or after an em dash or en dash.
- There is no space before or after a hyphen, with the exception of suspended compounds, which are followed by a space: "a two- or three-day delay." When suspended compounds appear in a series, there is no space between the hyphen and the comma: "a two-, three-, or four-day delay."
- There is no space between enclosures (quotation marks, parentheses, brackets) and the enclosed words.
- There is no space between a symbol (dollar sign, cents sign, percentage sign) and a numeral.
- No space precedes or follows a slash in a stenographic construction: and/or, 1997/98.
- One space precedes and follows a slash that indicates the end of a line in a quotation of poetry: "Buffalo Bill's / defunct."

You may also be asked to regularize the punctuation marks that follow italicized or boldface words. Some book publishers still follow what have come to be called traditional conventions:

- Periods, commas, colons, and semicolons are set in the same typeface as the preceding word.
- Question marks and exclamation points are set in the same typeface as the preceding word when they are part of the italicized or boldface term; otherwise they are set in roman:

  > She is rereading that old job-hunting classic *What Color Is Your Parachute?*
  >
  > Has she also seen the book *How to Find Fulfilling Work*?

- Both members of paired punctuation marks (e.g., parentheses, brackets, quotation marks) are set in the same typeface. *Chicago* once recommended (in the 1993 fourteenth edition) that these paired marks be set in italic or bold if the material within them began and ended with italic or bold words, but subsequent editions have endorsed the long-practiced typographic convention of setting these pairs to match the surrounding text.

Newer house styles, including current Chicago style (6.2), call for roman punctuation after italicized or bold words except for a question mark or an exclamation point that belongs to an italicized title: Is *Who Did It?* or *Viva!* better than *Doom*? (Squint hard and you'll see that this terminal question mark is roman.) Paired punctuation marks still must match the style (roman, italic, bold) of the surrounding text, not the style of the enclosed material, except when they enclose all-italic or all-bold display appearing on a separate line.[22]

## CONTROVERSIAL TECHNIQUES

Two techniques intended to save space are widely used in corporate writing but are open to criticism because they sacrifice clarity.

*Slashed constructions.* Some people dislike the appearance of constructions using the slash, or *virgule,* but the deeper issue concerns the meaning of the following types of constructions:

> and/or
> writer/editor
> high altitude/low temperature gear
> are/were
> inner/outer limits

First used in British maritime contracts in the mid-nineteenth century, "and/or" has spread far beyond law offices, sowing confusion and doubt wherever it lands.[23] Today, the sleight-of-hand "*a* and/or *b*" is usually interpreted to mean "*a* or *b* or both," but often the intended meaning is simply "*a* or *b*," or even "*a* and *b*." The "and/or" construction also creates an agreement problem when it joins the elements of a compound subject:

✗ The doctor and/or the hospital is/are responsible for this accident.

Rather than ask readers to piece together the desired relationship between the two items, careful writers and copyeditors avoid the Janus-like "and/or" and supply whatever words are needed to clarify the sentence and remove the convoluted verb agreement.

Similarly, the multiple-choice construction "are/were" can be replaced by a short string of words—"are or were," "once were and still are"—or by a verb that denotes continuity ("remain"). For the bivalent "writer/editor," one can substitute the compound "writer-editor" (to denote a person who is both a writer and an editor) or the disjunctive "writer or editor" (to denote a task that may be performed by either a writer or an editor); these alternatives also avoid the problems created when the slashed term takes a possessive or plural form ("writer/editor's"? "writer's/editor's"? "writer/editors"? "writers/editors"?). And "inner/outer limits" can be transformed into "inner and outer limits,"

22. Keen-eyed readers may notice that this book conforms to the traditional conventions (UC Press's house style) for the font of punctuation following italic and boldface words.

23. The first judicial review of a contract dispute over "and/or" (in England, in the 1850s) concluded with the three-judge panel offering three different interpretations of the meaning of "and/or." In subsequent litigation, three new judges again reached three different opinions—none of which agreed with any of the earlier three. See *DEU,* s.v. "and/or."

"inner or outer limits," "limits, both inner and outer," or "limits, either inner or outer," depending on the intended meaning.

Note also that when a two-word phrase appears on either side of the slash (e.g., high altitude/low temperature gear), a layer of visual confusion ("altitude/low" looks like a syntactical unit) is added to the denotational ambiguity (for high altitudes *and* low temperatures? for high altitudes *or* low temperatures?). For appearance's sake, some publishers add a thin space: high altitude / low temperature gear.

A few multiword slashed constructions have become so well entrenched that there is no risk of misunderstanding; for example, "Here's another good news/bad news quarterly report," "This is one more he said/she said controversy." (Anti-slashers, however, will prefer "another good news, bad news report," "another good-news, bad-news report," or, if the subtle en dash seems clear, even "another good news–bad news report.")

*Parenthetical plurals.* The second stenographic technique open to censure is the use of (*s*) after a noun to indicate that the statement may apply to one or more than one member of the category; for example:

The insured person(s) must take reasonable care in securing the vehicle(s).

When such shorthand migrates from insurance contracts into other contexts, it can not only confuse the reader but also stump the careful writer or copyeditor, especially when an inflected verb or a pronoun follows:

✗ The car(s) is/are insured for its/their full replacement value.

The first riddle is whether "person(s)" or "car(s)" takes a singular verb or a plural verb. In documents that make sparing use of parenthetical plurals, one can finesse this difficulty by avoiding the verb *be* and using only those verbs that have the same form in the third-person singular and the third-person plural (e.g., can, may, must, should, will). The corollary issue is one of pronoun-antecedent agreement for antecedents such as "person(s)" or "car(s)." The better course is to write around the problem and not use pronouns; sometimes rewording with "each," "all," "any," or "every" works.

A final conundrum concerns the form of the parenthetical plural for nouns that take *-ies* or *-es* in the plural. For nouns in the first group, adding (*s*) is sufficient: beneficiary(s). For nouns in the second group, (*es*) is added: loss(es). For nouns whose plurals are wholly irregular, even the most inventive writers yield: no one has yet lobbied for ma(e)n, woma(e)n, or child(ren).

# CHAPTER 5

# ¶ Spelling and Hyphenation

Good spelling skills are essential for a copyeditor. Although copyeditors who work on-screen are rescued from some misspellings by the spell-checking feature, spell-checkers do not distinguish between homophones (principal *and* principle), do not account for spellings determined by usage (resume *and* résumé), may allow variant spellings (catalog *and* catalogue) in the same document, and may flag legitimate spellings as "errors" if they are not included in the word processor's limited dictionary. And, of course, spell-checkers do not highlight a misspelled word if the misspelling is itself a word (from *and* form). Thus spell-checking would not detect any errors in the following sentence: "Too bee oar knot two beet, what is the question."

People who are good spellers not only know how to spell many commonly misspelled words but also

readily look up unfamiliar or unusual words
know which words they *always* have to look up
know that usage affects spelling
are not fooled by homophones
double-check a word in the dictionary before changing it in the manuscript
do not introduce misspellings into a manuscript

The following list should give you a little trouble—but only a little—if you're a strong speller. Don't look at the dictionary yet. Place an **X** next to the words you know are misspelled and put a **?** next to the words you're not sure about. (The answers appear in the next section.)

| | | | |
|---|---|---|---|
| accordian | environment | occasion | sophomore |
| achievement | fallacy | occurred | vaccuum |
| adolescence | leisure | occurrence | weird |
| antiquated | lillies | playwrite | withhold |
| athlete | maintenance | privilege | |
| calendar | mischievious | reference | |
| disastrous | non sequitur | separate | |

One more list—this one intended to bedevil even excellent spellers. Again, place an **X** next to the words you know are misspelled and put a **?** next to the ones you're not sure about. Don't read ahead until you've finished this list.

| | | | |
|---|---|---|---|
| accommodate | fluorescent | liquefy | rarefied |
| acknowledgment | foreword | memento | resistance |
| Albuquerque | fuchsia | millennium | restaurateur |
| anomaly | fulfill | minuscule | rococo |
| asinine | gauge | nickel | sacrilegious |
| cemetery | guerrilla | niece | sergeant |
| coca leaf | harassment | parallel | shepherd |
| consensus | hemorrhage | persistent | siege |
| dachshund | hierarchy | pharaoh | skepticism |
| decaffeinated | idiosyncrasy | Portuguese | stratagem |
| desiccated | indiscernible | preceding | supersede |
| desperate | indispensable | predilection | temperament |
| diphtheria | inoculate | prejudice | tendinitis |
| ecstasy | iridescence | proceed | tenement |
| embarrassment | judgment | proffered | tranquility |
| exhilarate | liaison | publicly | |
| Fahrenheit | lightning | quizzically | |

## IMPROVING YOUR SPELLING SKILLS

Unless you are a letter-perfect speller, you probably didn't get everything right on the first list. There, five words are misspelled. Here are the correct spellings: accordion, lilies, mischievous, playwright, vacuum. And you were probably stymied by at least five or ten words on the second, longer list. All the words on that list are spelled correctly. ("Foreword" = opening section of a book; not to be confused with "forward.")

Don't be dismayed by your mistakes. The purpose of these lists is not to trick you but to remind you that you can't always trust your eyes. It is better to take a moment with your dictionary and look up a word than to assume (or hope) that you know the correct spelling. Here are eight suggestions for improving your spelling skills.

1. *Study lists of hard words.* You can begin with the preceding lists. Tape up photocopies near your desk and skim them once a day (e.g., when you first sit down to work, or when you return from a lunch break). Pronounce the words aloud and practice writing them out in longhand. This triple reinforcement—visual, aural, and muscular—will chisel the correct spellings into your memory.

2. *Keep a list of all the words you look up.* Whenever you look up a word in the dictionary, jot it down. Wait until you have ten or fifteen words and then put *that* list up near your desk. Make a conscious effort to add to your list: whenever you have the dictionary open to look up a word, skim that page to see if there isn't another word worth learning.

3. *Learn spelling rules and exceptions.* A fair number of books have been written for poor spellers, but not for good spellers who want to improve. *WIT* has a section of help-

ful tips, as does Harry Shaw's *Errors in English and Ways to Correct Them,* 4th ed. (New York: Harper & Row, 1993).

4. *Learn something about the etymology of difficult words.* Etymology accounts for many of the oddities of English spelling, as the following examples show.

Why *playwright* but *playwriting* and *copyright*? The word *playwright* (a maker of plays) is based on the word *wright,* an old form of *wrought,* past tense and past participle of *work.* It belongs to a class of similar antique words, such as *wheelwright* (a maker of wheels), *wainwright* (a maker of wagons), and *shipwright* (a shipbuilder). Play*writing,* however, refers to the *writing* of plays; copy*right,* to legal *rights* pertaining to copy.

Why *sacrilegious,* not *sacreligious*? You would think that a word meaning "irreverent toward something sacred" would contain the word *religious.* But the ancestry of the word traces back to the Latin *sacrilegus,* "one who steals that which is sacred," from *sacri* (sacred) + *legere* ("to gather" or "to steal").

Why *supersede* but *precede*? Both words derive from Latin, but

> supersede = *super* (above) + *sedere* (to sit; cf. sedentary)
>
> precede = *pre* (before) + *cedere* (to go; cf. secede)

Unfortunately, etymology cannot account for the fact that three verbs derived from *cedere* are *-ceed* (exceed, proceed, succeed) while all the others are *-cede* (accede, concede, intercede, recede, etc.).

Why one *r* in *iridescence* but two in *irregular*? *Iridescence* derives from the name of the Greek goddess Iris (one *r*), the deity associated with the rainbow. *Irregular* is the prefix *ir-* attached to *regular; ir-* is the form that the prefix *in-* (= not) takes before a stem beginning in *r.*

Why only one *n* in *inoculate* but two in *innocent*? Both derive from Latin, but

> inoculate = *in* (within) + *oculus* (eye; cf. ocular)
>
> innocent = *in* (not) + *nocens* (wicked; cf. noxious)

Why *bisect* but *dissect*? The root of both words is the Latin *sectus* (the past participle of the verb *secare,* "to cut"). But

> bisect = *bi* (two; cf. bicycle) + *sect*
>
> dissect = *dis* (apart; cf. discern) + *sect*

Those two *l*'s and two *n*'s in *millennium*? Another word derived from the Latin, and again the etymology points to the correct spelling:

> millennium = *mille* (thousand; cf. millimeter—two *l*'s) + *annum* (year; cf. annual—two *n*'s)

5. *Pay special attention to suffixes that contain unstressed vowels.* Unless your memory is flawless, take a moment to look in the dictionary when you encounter a word that ends in *-able* or *-ible; -ance* or *-ence;* or *-ar, -er,* or *-or.*

6. *Pay special attention to doubled consonants.* Words that have several consonants, only one of which is doubled, cause a disproportionate number of problems: battalion, Caribbean, desiccated, graffiti, Mediterranean, occasion, Philippines, vaccination.

7. *Watch out for unusual verb forms.* Irregular spellings of the present and past participle forms of verbs are listed in their dictionary entries. Here are some worth noting:

|  | | |
|---|---|---|
| medevac | medevacking | medevacked |
| panic | panicking | panicked |
| picnic | picnicking | picnicked |
| sic (to attack) | siccing | sicced |
| stymie | stymieing | stymied |
| OK | OK'ing | OK'd |
| *But* okay | okaying | okayed |

Beware of extrapolations from these irregular examples to other words. For instance, the spellings of the comparative and superlative forms of the adjective *chic* are standard: chicer, chicest.

8. *Learn some mnemonic devices.* Here are some mnemonic devices once taught in elementary school:

accommodate surely has room for two *c*'s and two *m*'s

affect (noun) = flat demeanor (psychology)
affect (verb) = to alter (produce an effect); rarely: to feign[1]
effect (noun) = result
effect (verb) = to cause to come into being (= to produce)

amend = alter
emend = edit out errors (= improve)

complement = to complete
complementary = interdependent ("complementary colors")
compliment = I like hearing them
complimentary = positive ("complimentary review"); gratis
    ("complimentary tickets")

principle = rule
principal = is your pal; is the main agent or actor; is the adjective

stationary = stay still
stationery = for letters

---

1. The two verbs *affect* are homonyms. The first, meaning "to produce an effect" (e.g., to affect the outcome), derives from the Latin verb *afficere* ("to influence"); the second, meaning "to feign" (to affect a French accent), derives from the Latin verb *affectare* ("to strive after").

## VARIANT SPELLINGS

Some words can be spelled more than one way: likable *and* likeable, *or* tying *and* tieing. Such pairs are called *equal variants,* and either spelling is acceptable in a manuscript. For equal variants, the copyeditor's job is to note on the style sheet which variant the author has used and to enforce consistency throughout the manuscript.

For other words, your dictionary will show one spelling as the *primary variant,* or preferred spelling, another as a *secondary variant* or as a British variant. American publishers expect copyeditors to change British variants to US spellings (e.g., metre *to* meter), but some publishers will accept American secondary variants (e.g., epilogue *and* epilog).

Read the explanatory notes accompanying your dictionary to understand how the lexicographers treat variant spellings. In *M-W Collegiate,* for example, equal variants are separated by *or,* and secondary variants are separated from primary variants by *also:*

> *Equal variants:* Shakespearean *or* Shakespearian
>
> *Primary and secondary variants:* cancellation *also* cancelation

Because dictionaries list words in alphabetical order, the first spelling shown for a pair of equal variants is usually determined by alphabetization, not by the prevalence of usage. A separate entry for a variant spelling, if provided, will refer you to the preferred spelling:

> jibe *var of* GIBE
>
> metre *chiefly Brit var of* METER

Note, however, that outdated and highly abridged dictionaries don't always show variants. To peruse alternative spellings, you must consult a current, authoritative dictionary, such as the online edition of *M-W Collegiate* or *M-W Unabridged,* the most comprehensive (and convenient) of all the Merriam-Webster dictionaries. The following pairs of words are shown as equal variants in *M-W Unabridged* and in the online edition of *M-W Collegiate.* Nonetheless, many book publishers have unshakable preferences among these pairs; these industry-wide preferences are indicated by an asterisk.

| | |
|---|---|
| afterward | afterwards |
| catalog | catalogue |
| diagrammed* | diagramed |
| excludable | excludible |
| fulfill* | fulfil |
| judgment* | judgement (chiefly British) |
| programming* | programing |
| résumé* | resume |
| salable | saleable |
| theater* | theatre |
| toward* | towards |

The following list is also based on the online *M-W Unabridged;* other dictionaries may show different preferences for some of these words.

| *Preferred spelling* | *Secondary variant* |
|---|---|
| acknowledgment | acknowledgement |
| adviser | advisor |
| anesthetic | anaesthetic (chiefly British) |
| descendant | descendent |
| epilogue | epilog |
| forgo ("do without") | forego (but *forego* is correct when the meaning is "come before" or "precede": "a foregone conclusion") |
| mustache | moustache |
| naïveté | naiveté |

Of course, a self-reinforcing effect is in play here. The lexicographers' decision to label a spelling as a secondary variant is based on the prevalence of that spelling in publications from which evidence of usage is culled. But once a spelling is labeled a secondary variant, it is less likely to appear in print.

Clipped forms, or *clippings,* sometimes also have variant spellings. Clippings are shortened forms usually created by pruning syllables from the front, middle, or back of a longer word. Both the short and the full forms of the word may be recorded as separate entries in a dictionary. Some clippings are legitimate alternatives to their full versions in all but the most formal prose: we are so accustomed to *bus, exam, lunch, memo, movie, phone, taxi,* and *tie* that we nearly forget (or never realized) they are truncations of *omnibus, examination, luncheon, memorandum, moving* (or *motion*) *picture, telephone, taxicab,* and *necktie.* Other clippings are suitable only for casual writing: consider, for example, *bra, burger, deli, flu, fridge, gym, pro, sitcom,* and *typo.*

Most clippings pose simple questions for editors: whether they are appropriate for the level of formality, or *register,* of a given manuscript, and whether they will be intelligible to readers, especially if these are nonnative speakers of English. Some clippings, moreover, have several spellings. For the verb *synchronize,* for example, should an editor use the clipped forms *sync, synced,* and *syncing,* or *synch, synched,* and *synching* (both sets are listed as variants in the online *M-W Collegiate*)? An ongoing debate among editors concerns the alternative spellings for the shortened form of *microphone: mic* or *mike?* The online editions of *M-W Collegiate* and *AHD* list both spellings (flagged as informal in *AHD*) without designating either as the primary variant. *Garner's* recommends the older form *mike* for suitably informal writing, arguing that *mic* may be misread as "mick"; the *AP Stylebook,* which many journalists follow, now accepts *mic.* In such contested cases, you should ask the editorial coordinator whether house style specifies a preferred variant—or spell out the word in full.

## BRITISH SPELLING

If you have read many books and publications printed in Britain or Canada, British spellings may look correct to you. (To be sure, some perfectly good British spellings—such as *bussed* and *vice-like* for the US forms *bused* and *viselike*—may mislead a US readership in the absence of a self-explanatory context.) But, as noted above, the house style of most American publishers calls for US spelling. Table 8 indicates some of the major differences. In addition to the differences itemized there, a distinctively British convention is to double the final consonant when adding inflections to words such as *focus, marvel, signal,* and *travel* (hence *focussed, marvellous, signalled,* and *traveller*).

TABLE 8.  Differences between American and British Spelling

| Lexical Features | | Examples | |
|---|---|---|---|
| American | British | American | British |
| -am | -amme | program | programme |
| -ber | -bre | caliber | calibre |
| -ction | -xion | connection | connexion |
| -e- | -ae- | anemia | anaemia |
| -e- | -oe- | fetus | foetus |
| -ed | -t | misspelled | misspelt |
| -ense | -ence | offense | offence |
| -eu- | -oeu- | maneuver | manoeuvre |
| -f- | -ph- | sulfur | sulphur |
| -ice | -ise | practice | practise |
| -ize | -ise | recognize | recognise |
| -ol- | -oul- | smolder | smoulder |
| -or | -our | color* | colour |
| -ow | -ough | plow | plough |
| -ter | -tre | center | centre |
| -yze | -yse | analyze | analyse |

*American spelling calls for *color, honor, labor, neighbor,* and the like, but note the trio *glamour, glamorous,* and *glamorize.* Practice was long divided on retaining the British spelling for proper nouns: *Chicago* has consistently favored "the Labour Party," but *The Associated Press Stylebook* (s.v. "spelling") didn't drop its recommended "Labor Party" in favor of the British form until about 2005. The *Wall Street Journal* adopted the British spelling in 2007; the *New York Times*, in 2009. The political designation "Labour" is also used in reference to New Zealand; however, Australia's party uses the spelling "Labor."

In US spelling the consonant is doubled only when the stress falls on the syllable containing the consonant; thus *focused, marvelous, signaled,* and *traveler,* but *rebelled, propeller.* (To be sure, exceptions abound: *programmed, diagrammed.*) Canadian English generally follows British conventions of orthography but incorporates some US traits. For guidance you should turn to authoritative print or online references, such as *M-W Collegiate* or *AHD* for US spellings; to the applicable current Oxford English dictionary for British or Australian orthography; and to the frequently cited second edition of the *Canadian Oxford Dictionary,* supplemented by the tables on orthography in *Editing Canadian English,* for the mixed spelling style of Canadian English.

## HOMOPHONES

A copyeditor must also be aware of *homophones,* that is, words pronounced identically or quite similarly but spelled differently. You are probably a whiz at the simpler homophone pairs and triplets, able to spot misuses of *there* and *their,* or of *to, two,* and *too.* (A special plea: Watch out for the often overlooked confusables *it's/its, who's/whose, you're/your, they're/their,* and especially *than/then!*) Most editors can easily distinguish between such forms, yet oversights are so frequent that nearly every copyediting test includes a few to snare the unwary.

You should also be able to distinguish between more troublesome pairs and triplets:

| | | |
|---|---|---|
| accept | except | |
| adverse | averse | |
| affect | effect | |
| aid | aide | |
| allusive | elusive | illusive |
| ascent | assent | |
| baited | bated | |
| bazaar | bizarre | |
| canvas | canvass | |
| capital | capitol | |
| censure | censor | sensor |
| complement | compliment | |
| disc | disk[2] | |
| discreet | discrete | |
| emigrant | immigrant | |
| eminent | immanent | imminent |
| ensure | insure | |
| gorilla | guerrilla | |
| grisly | grizzly | |
| hoard | horde | |

2. In the computer industry, *disk* is reserved for *hard disk, floppy disk,* and *diskette,* while *disc* is the preferred spelling for media such as compact discs (CDs), digital video discs (DVDs), and laser discs (*Microsoft Manual of Style,* pp. 279, 280; *The Yahoo! Style Guide,* p. 448).

| | | |
|---|---|---|
| incidence | incidents | |
| leach | leech | |
| mantle | mantel | |
| palate | palette | pallet |
| pedal | peddle | |
| rack | wrack | |
| review | revue | |
| silicon | silicone | |
| troop | troupe | |
| undo | undue | |
| yoke | yolk[3] | |

If you are unsure about any of these words, grab your dictionary and bone up. (A favorite homophonic mix-up: One author wrote about a doctor cutting the "naval chord.")

Homophone confusion is especially common in set phrases whose original meaning may now be obscure. The substitution of a plausible word or phrase that sounds like the original expression is so pervasive in writing that the linguist Geoffrey Pullum has given this type of error a name: *eggcorn,* from the mangled saying "Mighty oaks from little eggcorns [acorns] grow."[4] Here are some common eggcorns:

| *Eggcorn* | *Correct phrase* | *Original meaning* |
|---|---|---|
| baited breath | bated breath | bated = held in abeyance; restrained |
| beyond the pail | beyond the pale | pale = an area enclosed by pales, or stakes |
| chaise lounge | chaise longue | longue = long (French) |
| change tact | change tack | tack = course or direction (sailing) |
| free reign | free rein | rein = strap used to control an animal |
| here! here! | hear! hear! | "Hear him!" to express agreement |
| hold one's piece | hold one's peace | peace = silence (from the Book of Common Prayer, "Solemnization of Matrimony") |
| hone in on | home in on | home = to move, to aim toward |
| hew and cry | hue and cry | hue = outcry |
| just desserts | just deserts | deserts = deserved reward or punishment |
| pass mustard | pass muster | muster = gathering of troops for inspection |
| phased by | fazed by | fazed = disconcerted |
| shoe-in | shoo-in | shoo = to drive in a given direction |
| slight of hand | sleight of hand | sleight = use of dexterity or cunning |

3. A White House tweet (December 8, 2017) to recognize Human Rights Day hailed "those suffering under the yolk of authoritarianism"; it was promptly retweeted worldwide and prompted a frenzy of comments containing puns about eggs.

4. *Mondegreens,* the misheard lyrics of songs and poems, are a subset of eggcorns. They derive their name from the rendering of the line "laid him on the green" as "Lady Mondegreen" in the ballad "The Bonnie Earl O'Murray."

| soft-peddle | soft-pedal | pedal = foot-operated lever, as on a piano |
|---|---|---|
| straightlaced | straitlaced | strait = narrow, cramped |
| tow the line | toe the line | toe = to place one's toe at or on |
| to the manor born | to the manner born | manner = position or custom by birthright |
| veil of tears | vale of tears | vale = valley |
| vocal chords | vocal cords | cords = long, flexible strands |

Some eggcorns occur so often in print that the misconstrued versions begin to acquire legitimacy through a sort of folk etymology and are then recorded in dictionaries alongside the original versions. For example, *M-W Collegiate* online lists, without a demur, both the original expression *to the manner born* (from Shakespeare's *Hamlet*) and the eggcorn *to the manor born*. *AHD* online, however, does not sanction the second variant. Both dictionaries recognize *chaise lounge,* as either an equal (*M-W Collegiate*) or a secondary (*AHD*) variant of *chaise longue*. But *Garner's* sternly rejects the upstart *to the manor born* and dismisses *chaise lounge* as "distinctly low-rent." Although dictionaries may reflect the increasingly frequent occurrence of a given eggcorn in their language corpora, you should follow the guidance of your usage manual in choosing the preferred form unless or until a spurious variant becomes accepted usage. (Language change happens.)

## FOREIGN WORDS AND PHRASES

Foreign words and phrases now naturalized in English writing retain their original spelling (when imported from a language that uses the Latin alphabet), often retain their diacritical marks (accents), and are set in roman type.

From French: carte blanche, de rigueur, déjà vu, fait accompli, faux pas, hors
    d'oeuvre, laissez-faire, raison d'être (*secondary variant:* raison d'etre),
    vis-à-vis
From German: ersatz, gestalt, realpolitik, weltanschauung, zeitgeist
From Italian: a cappella, alfresco, cappuccino, espresso, punctilio, virtuoso
From Japanese: hara-kiri, hibachi, samurai, tempura
From Latin: ad nauseam, de facto, in loco parentis, in medias res, in memoriam,
    modus operandi, persona non grata, sine qua non, sui generis, vice versa
    (et cetera, et cetera, et cetera)
From Spanish: aficionado, gringo, guerrilla, junta

Over time, foreign language borrowings lose some of the characteristics of their source languages, such as diacritical marks, but some features may persist to aid pronunciation (see, e.g., *garçon, jalapeño, naïveté*) or to differentiate the imported words from English ones with similar spellings (cf. *resume* and *résumé, expose* and *exposé, pâté* and *pate*). Unless an assimilated word has been completely bleached of diacritics through long use in English, omitting them is a spelling error.[5] *M-W Collegiate* or another authoritative dictionary can provide guidance concerning correct spelling.

Languages written in the Latin alphabet employ a great many diacritics. The marks most commonly encountered in English text are these: acute accent, breve, caron (a.k.a. háček), cedilla, circumflex, double acute accent, diaeresis, dot above, grave accent, macron, ogonek, ring above, tilde, and umlaut. Even the less common diacritical marks on this list—as well as ligatures and other characters occasionally found in English—can be keyed using Unicode-compliant software, such as Microsoft Word. Editors handling copy that includes unusual diacritics must develop proficiency in using Unicode, as described more fully in "Markup On-Screen" in chapter 13. (*Chicago*, tables 11.1–5, supplies lists of Unicode numbers; the complete set may be consulted at the Unicode Consortium website, https://www.unicode.org/.) Unicode characters are stable, regardless of the form of output, provided the typesetting and output systems and the fonts chosen by the production designer support these characters.

In contrast to naturalized foreign terms, nonnaturalized terms are set in italics. When a nonnaturalized import appears repeatedly in the text, it is set in italics on first mention and usually in roman thereafter unless it could be confused with an identically spelled English word that has an entirely different meaning (e.g., Spanish *actual,* "current," and English *actual*). If a familiar foreign term and an unfamiliar one appear in the same passage, *Chicago* recommends italicizing both, or neither, for the sake of consistency within the passage of text.

One test of naturalization is whether the term appears in the main section of the dictionary. Yet some entries in the Foreign Words and Phrases appendix to the print edition of *M-W Collegiate* (words with a foreign language label, such as "French phrase," in the online *Collegiate*) would pass muster in roman type for certain audiences: de profundis, dies irae, sans souci, sayonara. Here again, a copyeditor must gauge the readership: If the term is set in roman, will readers be confused? If the term is set in italics, will readers be surprised?

A special cautionary note applies to foreign language terms used as part of English place names, misuse of which can create a redundancy discernible to a speaker of the originating language. Some recurrent errors cited by both *Chicago* and standard dictionary authorities are these:

| *Redundant* | *Correct* | *Explanation* |
|---|---|---|
| Mount Fujiyama | Mount Fuji; Fujiyama | *fujiyama* = mountain formed by volcanic material |
| Mount Mauna Loa | Mauna Loa | *mauna loa* = long mountain |
| Rio Grande River | Rio Grande | *rio* = river |
| Sierra Nevada Mountains | Sierra Nevada | *sierra* = mountain range |

5. But note that AP style omits all diacritics: "Do not use any diacritical or accent marks because they cause garble for some users" (*AP Stylebook,* s.v. "accent marks"). This interdiction owes to the technical limitations of a vast, sometimes antiquated, and poorly integrated media infrastructure: transmission of copy by wire services, display of text on various newsroom computer systems, and the additional burden of handling any "nontransmitting symbols" by overworked copydesks. New York Times style, however, permits six diacritics: the acute, grave, circumflex, cedilla, tilde, and umlaut.

Other geographical names, however, may become established in English through long usage despite a redundancy. The Mississippi River takes its name from an Ojibwe word meaning "great river." The locale in Los Angeles called La Brea Tar Pits receives dictionary approval—and has a website so named—despite the redundancy (*la brea* means "pitch" or "tar" in Spanish).

Common nouns imported from foreign languages may also present challenges for proper usage if they have not yet been completely Englished. But words of long standing in the English lexicon, even it they seem exotic, are usually treated just like other English words. For example, despite a common belief that the expression *hoi polloi* (from Greek, meaning "the many") is redundant when used with the definite article in English, both *M-W Collegiate* and *AHD* accept this usage. *Garner's* and *DEU* point out that "the hoi polloi" has been around since about 1850.

Longer foreign phrases may be set in roman and enclosed in quotation marks; the translation may be appended in parentheses.

> The poem is a meditation on the proverb "Una mano no se lava sola" (A single hand cannot wash itself), although the phrase never appears in the poem itself.

If you are unable to verify the spelling and grammar of foreign phrases, remind your author to double-check them.

## PROPER NOUNS AND ADJECTIVES

Copyeditors are expected to verify or to query the spelling of every proper noun (person, place, organization, etc.) and proper adjective that appears in a manuscript. The spelling of well-known names can be verified in the dictionary—either in the main section or in separate biographical and geographical listings. On some projects, it is more efficient to consult basic or specialized reference books and reliable online sources than to query the author or to hope that the author will identify all errors during the review of the copyediting.

For a manuscript containing relatively few proper nouns whose spelling you cannot verify, you should query each unverified spelling with a simple "Spelling OK?" For a manuscript with dozens of unfamiliar, unverifiable proper nouns, you need not bother querying each. Instead, explain to the author in a cover note that he or she should take extra care to double-check the spelling of all proper nouns.

Proper nouns that are translated into English from foreign languages may have more than one form or spelling. In articles and books addressed to nonspecialists, Spanish kings and princes may be called Peter, Charles, Philip, or James; readers of scholarly texts, however, will expect to see Pedro, Carlos, Felipe, and Jaime. Transliterated names—names converted to the Latin alphabet from a language using a different writing system—pose many additional choices: the variants on "Tchaikovsky" (the form shown in *M-W Collegiate*) are legendary; reputable publishers have used at least four different transliterations of the group variously known as Hezbollah, Hizbollah, Hizbu'llah, and Hizballah.

Sometimes the choice of variants is political rather than orthographic. For example, after the breakup of the Soviet Union, some of the newly independent states changed the spelling of their names to reflect the local preferences; thus, Belarus (formerly Byelorussia), Kyrgyzstan (formerly Kirgizia), Moldova (formerly Moldavia), and Tajikistan (formerly Tadzhikistan). Politics and ideology are also at issue in some controversies over names ("the Falkland Islands" versus "the Malvinas"). In such cases, when the author's spelling or choice of names differs from that in your reference books, it is better to query the author than to change the manuscript.

Authors of historical works usually retain the place names that prevailed during the period under discussion. The city today known as Saint Petersburg would be called Petrograd in a study of the Russian Revolution but Leningrad in a study of World War II.

Unlike other foreign words, foreign proper nouns are not italicized.

The Biblioteca Nacional is in Madrid.

The Rue des Ursins is on the Île de la Cité.

## PLURALS

All the major style manuals discuss the conventions regarding the formation of plurals. Here are some explanations and pointers to complement those discussions. (Chapter 9 provides additional guidelines for pluralizing abbreviations.)

*Common nouns.*  Your dictionary is your best source for the spelling of common nouns and their plurals. Many common nouns form the plural by adding *s* or *es* to the singular. A few nouns undergo vowel changes in the plural (men, women, feet, geese, teeth, mice, lice), and several take the Anglo-Saxon *en* (children, oxen). The nouns most likely to cause trouble are those with singular forms ending in *f* (halves, leaves, wolves, *but* dwarfs,[6] roofs), in *fe* (knives, lives, wives, *but* safes), or in *o* (echoes, heroes, potatoes, *but* egos, embryos, portfolios).

When your dictionary lists two plurals for a common noun, read the entire entry to discover if the two forms have different uses. For example, *staff* has two plurals: *staffs* for groups of people and *staves* for musical notation. *Indexes* are alphabetical lists, but *indices* is the plural form used in mathematical contexts. *Brothers* are siblings, but *brethren* are members of a fellowship. *Buses* are large motor-driven passenger vehicles, but *busses*— at least in American English—are usually kisses. And *mediums* are persons claiming to have paranormal powers, but *media* are artistic materials, digital storage devices, or forms of mass communication. Also, although some dictionaries show *appendixes* and *appendices* as equal variants, many book publishers prefer *appendixes* for denoting the back sections of a book.

6. Despite J. R. R. Tolkien's use of the form *dwarves* (possibly as a parallel to *elves*), *dwarfs* is the definitive plural form according to the second edition of *OED* (1989). Since that *OED* entry the alternative plural *dwarves* has become established in several authoritative dictionaries as a secondary form or an equal variant.

Other difficulties arise for nouns borrowed from the classical languages but naturalized into English. As such borrowings become Englished, regularly formed plurals often develop alongside the irregular (original plural) forms, coexisting in the dictionary as variants. For some of these nouns, the regular and irregular plurals are labeled as equal variants, joined by *or* in the Merriam-Webster and American Heritage suites of dictionaries. The following variants are listed here following the online *M-W Collegiate* order, in which equal variants are presented alphabetically unless the first is slightly more common than the second.

| | |
|---|---|
| antenna | antennae *or* antennas |
| apex | apexes *or* apices |
| aquarium | aquariums *or* aquaria |
| automaton | automata *or* automatons |
| cactus | cacti *or* cactuses |
| formula | formulae *or* formulas |
| memorandum | memoranda *or* memorandums |
| millennium | millennia *or* millenniums |
| narcissus | narcissi *or* narcissuses |
| podium | podiums *or* podia |
| stadium | stadia *or* stadiums |
| terminus | termini *or* terminuses |
| vertebra | vertebrae *or* vertebras |

Provided the equal variants do not have different meanings, as in the examples cited previously, editors following *Chicago* normally choose the first form listed. But equal variants are equally acceptable if the chosen forms are used consistently. Editorial discretion may be exercised in consideration of a given readership. Most readers—possibly excepting those with a formal classical education—are likely to stumble over the exotic plurals *termini, aquaria, podia,* and *apices.* Ham radio operators use *antennas,* business executives write *memorandums,* and fans watch sports or attend rock concerts in *stadiums.*

Other nouns derived from classical languages still take the Latin- or Greek-style plural, listed either as the only plural form or as the primary variant in the online *M-W Collegiate.* (An emerging regular English plural form, if any, is identified by *also.* Granted, some of these secondary variants may sound barbaric to the classically trained ear.)

| | | |
|---|---|---|
| -a → -ae | alga | algae; *also* algas |
| | alumna | alumnae |
| | fauna | faunae; *also* faunas |
| | larva | larvae; *also* larvas |
| | minutia | minutiae |
| | nebula | nebulae; *also* nebulas |
| -is → -es | analysis | analyses |
| | axis | axes |

|              | basis        | bases                          |
|--------------|--------------|--------------------------------|
|              | crisis       | crises                         |
|              | ellipsis     | ellipses                       |
|              | diagnosis    | diagnoses                      |
|              | hypothesis   | hypotheses                     |
|              | oasis        | oases                          |
|              | parenthesis  | parentheses                    |
|              | synopsis     | synopses                       |
|              | synthesis    | syntheses                      |
|              | thesis       | theses                         |
| -on → -a     | criterion    | criteria; *also* criterions    |
|              | ganglion     | ganglia; *also* ganglions      |
|              | phenomenon   | phenomena                      |
| -um → -a     | addendum     | addenda; *also* addendums      |
|              | erratum      | errata                         |
|              | ovum         | ova                            |
|              | phylum       | phyla                          |
| -us → -i     | alumnus      | alumni                         |
|              | bacillus     | bacilli                        |
|              | fungus       | fungi; *also* funguses         |
|              | locus        | loci                           |
|              | nucleus      | nuclei; *also* nucleuses       |
|              | radius       | radii; *also* radiuses         |
|              | stimulus     | stimuli                        |
| *but*        | ignoramus    | ignoramuses (after the hero of the play *Ignoramus*) |
|              | octopus      | octopuses[7]                   |
| -us → -era   | genus        | genera; *also* genuses         |
|              | opus         | opera; *also* opuses           |

Some words—for example, *bacteria, desiderata, errata, memorabilia*—are used most often in the plural; the trick is to remember that they take a plural verb. Allegiances remain divided about the singular or plural nature of several other borrowings from Latin and Greek. The debate over *data* (see chapter 1) is the best known of these. Other squabbles concern *insignia* (the Latin plural of *insigne,* but often treated as a singular

---

7. *Garner's* declares that this regularly formed English plural outranks the spurious *octopi* by a ratio of three to one in the Google Books Ngram Viewer. Although the bogus plural is listed as a variant in most dictionaries—in fact, as an equal variant in *M-W Collegiate* online—according to Garner this plural is based on the erroneous assumption that to form the plural of *octopus* (from the Greek), one should follow the pattern of Latin nouns such as *alumnus → alumni*.

in English and given the English plural *insignias*) and *media* (a plural in Latin, often treated as singular in such phrases as "the print media"). The noun *fauna,* often treated as a plural, is traditionally singular and takes a singular verb. The case of *kudos,* a singular noun in classical Greek, is more curious. Sometime in the 1940s, English speakers, believing that the final *s* indicated a plural, invented a singular form (*kudo*) and began to treat *kudos* as a plural. Both forms appear in *M-W Collegiate* online, which upholds the singular as an example of a back-formation.

For nouns and phrases derived from languages other than Latin and Greek and now naturalized into English, check your dictionary for irregular plurals. In French phrases, for example, the noun, along with the adjective that modifies it, is pluralized, but not a noun that is part of an accompanying prepositional phrase. Here are some samples of plural nouns and phrases from modern languages:

| | |
|---|---|
| adieu | adieus *or* adieux |
| beau | beaus *or* beaux |
| bon mot | bons mots *or* bon mots |
| cherub | cherubim (though *cherubs* is preferred when the meaning is figurative—that is, to denote chubby, rosy-faced people or images of winged children) |
| concerto | concertos *or* concerti |
| coup de grâce, | coups de grâce, |
|    coup d'état, |    coups d'état, |
|    coup d'oeil |    coups d'oeil |
| cul-de-sac | culs-de-sac; *also* cul-de-sacs |
| faux pas | faux pas |
| libretto | librettos *or* libretti |
| nouveau riche | nouveaux riches |
| seraph | seraphim *or* seraphs |
| weltanschauung | weltanschauungs *or* weltanschauungen |

For foreign nouns that have not been naturalized into English, the plural is formed by adding a roman *s* after the italicized noun:

the *keiretsu*s [Japanese for "distribution conglomerates"]

the *sottopassaggio*s [Italian for "underpasses"]

Or one may revise the wording to avoid pluralizing the foreign word: the *keiretsu* associations.

*Compound nouns.* The plural of a hyphenated compound noun is usually formed by adding *s* to the noun member of the compound: courts-martial, runners-up, sisters-in-law. The plurals of solid compounds, however, are regular: handfuls, spoonfuls, tablespoonfuls, teaspoonfuls. For open compounds, the preference is to pluralize the head noun: attorneys general, notaries public. When in doubt, consult your dictionary.

*Proper nouns.* The plural of most proper nouns is regularly formed:

The property is owned by the Arroyos, the Bachs, the Beaches, and the Roths.

But the plural of a proper noun ending in *y* takes an *s:*

There are three Marys and two Larrys in this department.

*Exceptions:* the Rocky Mountains, the Rockies; the Allegheny Mountains, the Alleghenies; Teletubby, Teletubbies.

The plural of a proper noun ending in *s* (even one already ending in *es*) takes *es:*

We invited the Wellses and the Joneses to dinner.

Nonetheless, to add *es* to form the plural of *McDonald's* seems to invite an odd pronunciation. Sometimes, one can write around the problem by adding a noun after the proper name: "Two new McDonald's restaurants opened last week—in Belarus and Tahiti." In other situations, it seems best to treat *McDonald's* as an invariant:

Large corporations—the Intels, the IBMs, and the McDonald's—can achieve significant economies of scale.

The plural of a proper name ending in a silent *s* or *x* is also usually treated as an invariant or, alternatively, avoided by rewording:

Two original Degas graced her foyer.

*Better:* Two original works by Degas graced her foyer.

Editors sometimes puzzle over the correct plural forms for product names. You may put blackberries on your breakfast cereal, but a company gives (well, used to give) new executive employees free BlackBerrys. Just as you would write that you know two Larrys (not two Larries), the plural of a product name, even one based on a common noun, is formed, like the plural of other proper nouns, by adding *s* or *es*. You may also ogle iPads in the computer store, despite the fact that Apple, like virtually all trademark owners, prefers (but cannot require) that its product names be used only as adjectives. But who would ogle "iPad devices" in the computer store? (See chapter 6 for more about the unconventional capitalization and the handling of trademarks and product names.)

*Abbreviations.* Most abbreviations are made plural by adding an *s:* vols., B&Bs, CDs, HMOs, IDs.[8] However, when a publisher's style or convention calls for abbreviations to carry internal periods, *'s* is added to form the plural: H.M.O.'s, M.D.'s. Such plurals are rarely used in formal writing; in most cases, a copyeditor would substitute the spelled-out form:

---

8. *Garner's* (s.v. "plurals: acronyms and abbreviations") cautions against the overthinking that causes writers to avoid plural forms of abbreviations they wrongly assume already stand in for plural terms: FAQ = a frequently asked question or a document containing such questions, hence *FAQs;* POW = a prisoner of war, hence *POWs;* RBI = a run batted in, hence *RBIs;* WMD = a weapon of mass destruction, hence *WMDs.*

*Overly colloquial:* She has two M.A.'s.

*Better:* She has two master's degrees.

*But:* A panel of M.B.A.'s gave their opinions of the new auditing procedures.

In the last example, one has to retain the abbreviation because there are no graceful substitutes: "a panel of people holding master's degrees in business administration" is far too clunky.

Unlike other abbreviations, acronyms usually omit the internal periods and are pronounced as words (NAFTA, NATO, UNESCO, WYSIWYG).[9] Plurals of acronyms are thus formed in the same way that the plurals of other proper nouns are formed, by adding *s* or *es* to the unchanged base: NIMBYs, PINs, POTUSes, WASPs. Commonly used acronyms may eventually become distinct words and lose their capitalization (and sometimes even the memory of their origins):

gif: graphics interchange format
laser: light amplification by stimulated emission of radiation
radar: radio detecting and ranging
scuba: self-contained underwater breathing apparatus
snafu: situation normal, all fouled up (*M-W Unabridged*'s euphemism;
     the online *Collegiate* and *AHD* specify the original f-word used to form the
     expression)
sonar: sound navigation and ranging
taser: Thomas A. Swift's electric rifle (a trademarked name, sometimes
     capitalized)

These mutated acronyms form their plurals as common nouns (gifs, lasers, snafus, tasers). Thus, as *NIMBY* is increasingly lowercased in writing (nimby), the base word may be changed with the addition of a plural inflection (nimbies). Watch for it.

*Letters of the alphabet.* Some letters can be made plural by adding an *s* (the three Rs), but often an apostrophe is needed to assist reading, especially when the letters are lowercased:

How many students received A's?

Are all the i's dotted and the t's crossed?

Mind your p's and q's.

*Some oddities.* The convention of using 's to form the plurals of numerals, abbreviations, symbols, and words representing sounds or used in set phrases has largely yielded to the practice of simply affixing an *s* (1980s, URLs, &s, oohs and aahs, whys and where-

---

9. As *Butcher's Copy-editing* and the *New Oxford Style Manual* explain, British convention sometimes lowercases all but the initial letter of an acronym (Nato, Unesco), although UK house styles vary. *Chicago* recommends the all-caps treatment—even when the words on which the acronym is based are common nouns—unless the acronym becomes established as a discrete word in the dictionary.

fores, ifs and buts). The plural form of a word used as a word usually appends *s* or *es* in roman type to the italicized base word (*however*s and *thus*es). For the sake of readability, a handful of expressions may retain apostrophes, but authorities are divided on these forms: for example, *Chicago* recommends *dos and don'ts,* whereas the *AP Stylebook* specifies *do's and don'ts* (the form used in this book), preserving visual symmetry at the expense of logic by using an apostrophe to create the first plural but not the second. Other contested forms include *how-tos* versus *how-to's* and *no-nos* versus *no-no's.* (But for *yes* and *no, M-W Unabridged* simply gives, as variants, "*yeses also* yesses" and "noes *or* nos.") For such curious forms, follow house style or your style manual as instructed; otherwise, use your editorial judgment in choosing the plural form more likely to be immediately intelligible to readers.

## POSSESSIVES

*Possessive form of common nouns.* All the style manuals agree on the following principles for creating the possessive forms for common nouns:

> Singular common noun that does not end in *ess:* add an apostrophe and an *s.*[10]
> cat → cat's

> Plural common noun that does not end in *s:* add an apostrophe and an *s.*
> children → children's

> Plural common noun that ends in *s:* add an apostrophe only.
> cats → cats'

But there is some dissension about forming the possessive of a singular common noun that ends in *ess. WIT* notes that "some prefer *witness', countess',* and the like" but recommends *witness's* and *countess's* as more accurately reflecting spoken English. The *AP Stylebook* previously advised looking at the word that follows and recommended "the witness's answer" but "the witness' story," to avoid a sibilant hiss in the latter combination; this quirky exception to AP style's general rules for the formation of possessives was retracted in the 2017 edition of the *AP Stylebook.* Still, writers and copyeditors in corporate publications departments usually avoid *business's* as the singular possessive by substituting another noun (firm, company) to produce a more euphonious and less controversial sentence. Recasting is likewise desirable to avoid such ambiguities as the possessive form of *maître d'* (maître d's), which is identical to the plural form. In this instance, one can simply use the full phrase (the maître d'hôtel's duties); otherwise, an "of" construction (the duties of the maître d') often provides an alternative to a cumbersome or misleading formulation.

---

10. However, both *Chicago* and *WIT* advise dropping the possessive *s* in some set expressions ("for goodness' sake"). *Chicago* (7.20) also recommends dropping this *s* in the possessive of a singular noun ending in *s* which has the same form as the plural (e.g., corps, measles, series, species) or else rewording to avoid the possessive: this species' survival *or* the survival of this species.

*Possessive form of proper nouns.* The formation of the possessive for proper nouns (both personal and place names) that end in *x, s,* or *z* is fraught with peril. According to *Chicago* 14 (1993), "how to form the possessive of polysyllabic personal names ending with the sound of *s* or *z* probably occasions more dissension among writers and editors than any other orthographic matter open to disagreement" (6.30). *Chicago* 15 offered two pages of rules, exceptions, and options, but *Chicago* 16 settled on one simple principle, which *Chicago* 17 reiterates: form the possessive of all singular proper nouns, including names ending in *s, x,* and *z,* by adding an apostrophe and an *s;* form the plural possessive by adding an apostrophe to the plural proper noun. Examples of singular possessive forms include the following: Illinois's policy, Marx's essay, Jesus's parables, Moses's anger, Euripides's plays, Camus's novels. Examples of plural possessive forms include these: the Obamas' daughters, the Lopezes' home, the Coxes' ranch.

A more traditional convention—described in the fourteenth edition of *Chicago* (at 6.27) and later abandoned—is to add an apostrophe and an *s* to form the possessive of all proper nouns except *Jesus, Moses,* and classical names with "an unaccented ending pronounced *eez.*" Thus: Dylan Thomas's poems, Jasper Johns's paintings, *but* Jesus' parables, Moses' anger, Achilles' heel, Euripides' themes.

Some in-house style guidelines, however, call for adding only an apostrophe to form the possessive of any proper name ending in *s:* Dylan Thomas' poems, Jasper Johns' paintings.

How should one construct the possessive of a proper noun that is already a possessive—say, the department store Macy's? Seriously, Macy's's? There are three options for avoiding this risible form: (1) simply use the unchanged name, that is, treat it as an invariant form (Macy's clearance sale); (2) add "a" or "the" to use the name as an attributive noun (a Macy's clearance sale, the Macy's clearance sale); or (3) reword to avoid the problem altogether (a clearance sale at Macy's). The same principle applies to other institutional and place names containing the possessive inflection: for St. John's University one can refer to St. John's faculty, the St. John's faculty, a St. John's faculty member, or the faculty of St. John's.

Another brain teaser: What is the possessive form of Red Sox? Some argue that since the team name is a playful spelling of the plural word *socks,* the apostrophe alone should be used, just as it is for the possessive of plural common nouns ending in *s* (socks', *hence* the Red Sox' chances of a victory). Others maintain that the possessive form of the team's name should obey the simple rule established for other proper names, including those ending in a sibilant (e.g., Marx's, *hence* the Red Sox's chances of a victory). Or, one could choose Door Number Three: the chances of a victory by the Red Sox. Sometimes the best way to solve a problem is to avoid it.

*Possessive form for inanimate objects.* In some quarters, a peculiar hobgoblin is afoot: since inanimate objects cannot own anything, one should not attach *'s* to an inanimate noun. The origin of this hobgoblin is uncertain (see *DEU,* s.v. "genitive"), but Wilson Follett and his disciples have insisted on it with such fervor that some copyeditors become queasy when they spot such common forms as "Florida's governor" or "the nation's capital." Follett (*MAU,* s.v. "possessives") vilifies both expressions as "false [possessives]," but he is wrong. They are venerable instances of the *genitive case* (the traditional name for the possessive), and they cannot be *false* possessives because they are not possessives at all. *DEU* (s.v. "genitive") blesses and even supplies a set of fancy names for them (objective genitive, descriptive genitive, genitive of purpose, group genitive). Trust your ear and your common sense: the car's engine *and* the tree's roots, *but not* the computer's user *or* the eggs' carton.

*Possessive for duration.* The possessive form is used for units of time that indicate duration.[11]

> We took three weeks' vacation.
>
> *But:* She handed in her paper two weeks early. *And:* She is five months pregnant.

You can test for the correct form by imagining a sentence in which the unit of time is singular:

> I took a week's vacation. [*Not* a week vacation] *So:* I took three weeks' vacation.
>
> I finished my paper a week early. [*Not* a week's early] *So:* I finished my paper two weeks early.

*WIT,* however, concludes that in some expressions "the idea of possession is so remote" that the unit of time functions as an adjective: "a two weeks waiting period." But surely that is better put as "a two-week waiting period."

*Joint possession.* For shared possession add 's to the second name only: John and Jane's daughters. (Compare this expression with one designating separate possession: John's and Jane's competing theories.) But if one of the joint possessors is represented by a pronoun and one by a noun, both forms are possessive: his and Jane's daughters; John's and her daughters.

*Double genitives.* Expressions such as "a friend of David's" or "a colleague of mine" are called *double genitives* (sometimes *double possessives*) because they use both a possessive (David's, mine) and an "of" phrase. Despite a common belief that the double possessive is redundant, this construction is a long-standing English idiom used to refer to animate objects when the meaning is "one of several" or "some of the whole category." Compare these:

> He is a friend of the college.
>> ["College" is inanimate.]
>
> Joe's friends gathered for the memorial service.
>> [An unrestricted category, "Joe's friends," gathered for the memorial service.]

---

11. One also hears this use of the possessive in "ten dollars' worth of gas" or "a dollar's worth." In print this expression is rarely used: rather than "millions of dollars' worth of devastation," one usually sees "millions of dollars in devastation." No apostrophe is required if numerals are used: "$125,000 worth of costume jewelry."

Friends of Joe's gathered for the memorial service.
  [Some of Joe's friends gathered for the memorial service.]

David's friend knocked on the door.
  [A specific unnamed (or previously named) friend knocked on the door.]

A friend of David's knocked on the door.
  [One of David's friends knocked on the door.]

As the last four examples show, there is a subtle difference of meaning between the single and double genitive forms. The double genitive also facilitates another important distinction: the ambiguous "Jasmine's photograph" can be resolved to either "a photograph of Jasmine" or "a photograph of Jasmine's," that is, one of several photographs belonging to Jasmine.

*Possessive form of words in italics or in quotation marks.* To form the possessive of an italicized word, *Chicago* recommends adding a roman apostrophe followed by a roman *s*: *Newsweek*'s circulation. If one cannot rewrite a sentence to avoid using the possessive form for a word that appears within quotation marks, the apostrophe and the *s* are placed outside the closing quotation mark: "Lord Randal"'s rhymes and rhythms. In a *New Yorker* review of the film *W.,* whose title it styles as "W.," the magazine uses "W."'s for the possessive.

*Attributive nouns.* According to the *AP Stylebook,* the apostrophe may be omitted when a plural head noun ending in *s* functions as an adjective rather than as a possessive—in other words, when the relation between the plural head noun and the second noun could be expressed by the preposition *for* or *by* rather than the possessive *of* (e.g., editors guild, employees lunchroom, ironworkers union, users guide). If the plural form of the head noun does not end in *s,* however, AP style requires the apostrophe: the people's republic, a children's hospital.

    *Chicago* is much more restrictive regarding this elision of the apostrophe in plural nouns used attributively: *Chicago* 7.27 mandates the apostrophe (editors' guild, employees' lunchroom, ironworkers' union, users' guide) unless the term is an official proper name that does not use the apostrophe (Northwest Editors Guild). The special treatment of plural nouns used attributively, along with the divided opinion of style guides on the legitimacy of this form, explains the absence of the apostrophe in some formal institutional names (even under *Chicago*'s strict style) and the inclusion of the apostrophe in others:

| | |
|---|---|
| Consumers Union | *but:* |
| Department of Veterans Affairs | Actors' Equity Association |
| Diners Club | Bay Area Editors' Forum |
| Editorial Freelancers Association | National Rural Letter Carriers' Association |
| *Publishers Weekly* | |

Note that several set expressions using plural attributive nouns are recorded in dictionaries: *M-W Collegiate* online recognizes *citizens band* and *teachers college.*

## ONE WORD OR TWO?

*Open, hyphenated,* and *solid* (or *closed*) are basic terms in copyediting jargon:

> An *open compound* is written as two words: high school, near miss, common sense.
> A *hyphenated compound* links the words with a hard hyphen: half-life, self-confidence.
> A *solid compound* is written as one word: schoolteacher, headache, textbook, commonsensical.

Some compound forms are fixed: *Chicago* uses the established form *copyediting,* for example. Other compounds change over time, becoming fixed through frequent use: *Chicago* 17 (7.89) now recognizes the nouns *decision-making* and *head-hunting* as permanent compounds, although previous editions listed the former as open. But many compound forms are determined by their grammatical function and their position in a sentence: *problem solving* is open as a noun (engage in problem solving) but hyphenated as an adjective preceding a noun (problem-solving approach); the adjective *time consuming* is hyphenated before a noun (time-consuming tasks) but not after the noun (these tasks are time consuming). Hyphens also help sort out complex modifiers: her all too brief letter *but* her all-too-brief public service career.

A copyeditor's first resource for the treatment of a compound is the dictionary, where established forms, *permanent compounds,* are listed. But, as the editors of *M-W Collegiate* explain, "Variation in the styling of compound words in English is frequent and widespread. It is often completely acceptable to choose freely among open, hyphenated, and closed alternatives (as *life style, life-style,* or *lifestyle*). However, to show all the stylings that are found for English compounds would require space that can be better used for other information. So this dictionary limits itself to a single styling for a compound" (p. 10A)—specifically, the most widely used styling found in that dictionary's language corpus. But other authoritative dictionaries, which rely on different data sets, may offer different (or more) stylings of a given compound. Consider the many forms of the term *x-ray* in just two standard sources:

> *M-W Unabridged*
>> *Noun:* X-ray; *also* X ray
>> *Verb:* x-ray; *often* X-ray
>
> *AHD* (online)
>> *Noun:* x-ray *or* X-ray; *or* x ray *or* X ray
>> *Verb:* x-ray *or* X-ray

Choosing a suitable compound form challenges the confidence of editors who want to believe that there is only One Right Way! Perhaps no copyediting decision places a greater importance on both a rigorous process and the exercise of editorial judgment. In view of often differing advice from language authorities, best practice in styling compounds is to approach decision-making systematically but with a degree of flexibility.

First, editors should select one trustworthy, up-to-date dictionary (or use only the one specified by house style) and rely on it throughout an editing project. Bear in mind that even the collegiate, unabridged, print, and online editions of a given dictionary may differ because they are distinct publications with different reprint and update cycles. Compound forms are always in flux, so they may have several legitimate spellings, but sticking with one reliable source will ensure consistency. Switching dictionaries—or even switching the edition of a given dictionary—midproject may result in a muddle. Also, in every dictionary search for a compound term, editors must take care to identify the correct part of speech, since styling may vary accordingly: *cutoff, layout,* and *markup* are noun forms, whereas *cut off, lay out,* and *mark up* are verbs.

If the prescribed dictionary does not include the compound term in question, copyeditors should next turn to a designated backup source, for example, *M-W Unabridged* when *M-W Collegiate* fails to list a word. If neither dictionary provides help, editors should then consult their style manual for guidance governing the formation of *temporary compounds* (e.g., note taking). *APA* condenses its hyphenation advice—most pertaining to adjectival forms—into a few pages. *WIT* devotes twelve pages to general guidelines and sixteen models of noun and adjectival compounds based on word types (e.g., colors), grammatical structures (e.g., compounds formed with the present participle), and specific prefixes and suffixes (e.g., the suffix *-like*). *Chicago*'s invaluable hyphenation guide distills the patterns for temporary compounds into twelve pages with four lengthy tables—well thumbed in every editor's print edition of the manual and usually bookmarked in their online edition—that organize model compound forms into several useful categories. Although the specific advice and the level of detail in these style guides differ, all agree on several general principles:

1. Do not use unnecessary hyphens (post office regulations, *not* post-office regulations), which create visual clutter.

2. Do use hyphens if necessary to assist reading or to prevent a miscue (fast sailing ship *or* fast-sailing ship?).

3. In styling a compound form, consider the syntax of the sentence; for example, a compound unit modifier is usually hyphenated if it precedes the modified word but unhyphenated if it follows the word (a thought-provoking discussion *but* a discussion that is thought provoking).

Besides consulting a dictionary and a style manual and weighing the possibility of misreading, editors must consider authors' preferences and the conventions familiar to a given readership. A business writer might favor the golem-like *decisionmaking* (listed as a newish secondary variant in *M-W Unabridged*) over an open or hyphenated form; a technical writer might choose *logon* instead of *log-on* or *log on,* and *filetype* rather than *file type.*

As noted, the hyphenation of compounds changes over time. New compounds typically enter the language in open or hyphenated form; if the term gains currency, the wordspace or hyphen disappears and the term becomes solid. Thus *copy editor* and *copy-editor* yield to *copyeditor*. Citing this principle, some tech editors advise, "When in doubt, close it up": *email, homepage, menubar.*

Above all, copyeditors must remember that hyphenation alone cannot rescue a writer's careless or compulsive agglomerative clusters. A writer's shoot-from-the-hip, over-the-top, pull-out-all-the-stops hyphenated style is likely to evoke one of those heaven-help-me-why-am-I-reading-this-book reactions in most readers. A bushel of hyphens won't ease the course though a steeplechase of adjectives and nouns. Rewriting is the only solution.

## COMPOUND ADJECTIVES: ATTRIBUTIVE AND PREDICATE

Adjectives that precede the noun they modify are called *attributive adjectives;* adjectives that follow the noun are called *predicate adjectives.* When an attributive adjective is two words or longer, the possibility of misreading often arises. For example, a sign outside a restaurant reads "No Smoking Section." Some patrons will assume that the restaurant does not have a section in which diners can smoke ("there is no smoking section"); others will assume that the restaurant has a section in which smoking is prohibited ("there is a no-smoking section").

Here is another example of the difference a hyphen can make:

He is taking care of four year-old boys.

She is taking care of four-year-old boys.

In styling compound attributive adjectives, copyeditors must thus analyze the terms to make sure they modify the following noun as a unit. "The time to peak effect" (meaning the time it takes to reach peak effect) is correct; "the time-to-peak effect" is wrong. A moisturizing lotion is recommended "for normal to dry skin" (meaning a range of skin types), not "for normal-to-dry skin." Likewise, compare "lowest possible rating" ("lowest" modifies "possible") with "lowest-ranking employee"; "worst imaginable result" ("worst" modifies "imaginable") with "worst-case scenario."

Every style manual has a long section on compound adjectives, and each has its peculiarities and preferences. The following guidelines summarize the most important concepts.

*Two-word attributive adjectives.* Two-word attributive adjectives are usually hyphenated:

low-rent district     full-service bank     freeze-dried coffee
tax-free trade     all-out effort     acid-forming
sad-eyed gaze     working-class     compounds
hot-water faucet     families

There are, however, three principal exceptions to this rule.

*Exception 1.* When the attributive adjective is a common open compound noun,[12] a hyphen is used only if needed to avoid ambiguity:

|  |  |
|---|---|
| income tax refund | word processing files |
| real estate transaction | city planning department |
| mass transit routes | baby boom generation |
| high school student | social service providers |
| post office regulations | |

*But:*

|  |  |
|---|---|
| end-user manuals | free-trade agreement |
| hard-sell tactics | real-number theory |
| short-story writer | top-dog status |
| free-market system | secret-police organization |
| loose-cannon mentality | emergency-room visits |
| poison-pill provisions | rare-book dealer |

*Exception 2.* When the first member of the compound adjective is an adverb ending in *ly,* the compound is open: a highly cultivated sense of irony, an openly hostile attitude. (But a compound adjective formed with *early* is an exception to this exception: early-onset Alzheimer's disease.) Compound adjectives with adverbs that do not end in *ly* (e.g., often, ever, much) can also be left open if there is no ambiguity: a much cultivated sense of irony, an often hostile attitude.

*Exception 3.* Adjectives derived from foreign phrases are not hyphenated (in any position) unless the term is hyphenated in the original language:

|  |  |
|---|---|
| à la carte menu | per capita consumption |
| ex parte motion | |

*But:*

|  |  |
|---|---|
| beaux-arts style | papier-mâché construction |
| tête-à-tête negotiations | |

Do hyphenate a multilingual attributive adjective: *béisbol*-crazed teenagers, *flâneur*-inspired style.

*Phrases used as adjectives.* Adjectives that consist of short common phrases are hyphenated when used attributively:

|  |  |
|---|---|
| off-the-record remark | spur-of-the-moment decision |
| over-the-counter drugs | black-and-white photographs |

12. What constitutes a "common open compound noun" or risks ambiguity when used attributively is often a matter of house style and editorial judgment. For example, even though *soft tissue* is an established medical term and is listed as an open noun compound in the online *AHD,* the official journal of the American Medical Association, *JAMA,* stipulates that to avoid confusion the adjectival form should be hyphenated when it precedes a noun: soft-tissue injury. Yet *head injury,* unlisted in either *M-W Unabridged* or *AHD,* is usually treated as an open form when used attributively: head injury patient.

In these formulations the hyphens join only the words that constitute the modifying string: higher-than-expected earnings *but* higher-than-expected quarterly earnings.

Unusual short phrases may be hyphenated or placed in quotation marks:

big-box stores *or* "big box" stores

strong-comma semicolon *or* "strong comma" semicolon

When a longer commonplace phrase is pressed into service as an attributive adjective, practice varies. The goal is to provide clarity with a minimum of clutter. To this end, writers and copyeditors have enlisted commas, hyphens, en dashes, quotation marks, and even the ever-controversial slash.

Tickets will be distributed on a first come, first served basis.

It was a typical he-said, she-said dispute.

We need a high-touch–low-tech solution.

She introduced me to a succession of here-today-gone-tomorrow boyfriends.

His lips curled into a "been there, done that" sneer.

This is another good news/bad news story.

*Adjectives of quantity.* Compound adjectives that consist of a number and a unit of measurement are hyphenated. A compound consisting of an ordinal number and a superlative-degree adjective is hyphenated before the noun but open following it.

|   |   |
|---|---|
|   | a one-word reply |
|   | a 105-pound dog |
|   | thirteenth-century art |
|   | a twelve-ounce can |
|   | a 350-page book |
|   | a five-hundred-page monograph |
|   | an eight-hundred-million-dollar pill |
|   | the second-to-last runner |
| *But:* | The runner finished the race second to last. |
|   | a late-tenth-century relic |
|   | a twenty-six-mile race |
|   | a 5-percentage-point decline |
|   | a twenty-first-century notion |
|   | a twenty-one-gun salute |
|   | a two-hundred-foot-high cliff |
|   | the fourth-highest murder rate |

There is no hyphen, however, between a numeral and an abbreviation for a unit of measurement, between a numeral and *percent,* or between a numeral with a currency symbol and the following term:

a 10 km race
a 7.75 oz bottle
a 7 percent lead in the polls
an $800 million pill
*Exception:* Scientific style often calls for hyphens in numerals and abbreviated units of measurement. *APA* (4.31) gives the example "a 5-mg dose."

*Suspended compound adjectives.*  A space follows the hyphen in a suspended compound adjective:

right- or left-handed users
fifteen- and thirty-year mortgages
micro- and macroeconomics
125- and 185-pound cartons

In a series of suspended compounds, no space intervenes between the hyphens and the commas:

first-, second-, and third-graders
35-, 45-, 55-, and 65-year-olds

(*Note:* In a phrase like "ten-to-fifteen-minute traffic delays," the "ten to fifteen" constitutes a unit—an approximation of length of the backup—and it is therefore not a suspended compound; nor is "a four-by-six-inch envelope" or "a six-by-six-foot cell.")
     Suspended compounds of the form "water-based and -soluble paint" or "servicemen and -women" are licit but likely to confuse and irk readers; substitute "water-based and water-soluble paint" or "servicemen and servicewomen" (or, to avoid the gendered terms altogether, "service members"). Ungainly suspensions warrant revision, even though some make it into print: "Mr. Stone and Ms. Berloff . . . keep their distance from post-—or, for that matter, pre-—9/11 politics" (*New York Times,* August 9, 2006).

## COMPOUND ADVERBS

Compound adverbs rarely cause problems, but be on the lookout for ambiguous combinations:

He too readily agreed.
*Better:* He, too, readily agreed.
     [*Means* He also agreed.]

He too-readily agreed.
     [*Means* He agreed too readily.]

She is requesting yet more arcane information.
     [*Means* additional information that is arcane]

She is requesting yet more-arcane information.
[*Means* information that is more arcane]

---

Scientists predict more extreme weather events.
[*Means* more weather events that are extreme]

Scientists predict more-extreme weather events.
[*Means* weather events that are more extreme]

## COMPOUND NOUNS

There isn't much rhyme or reason to many of the conventions for compound nouns; for example, *M-W Collegiate* online shows *crossbones, cross-purpose,* and *cross section; break-in, breakout, breakup; walk-in, walk-on, walkout, walk-up.* And since few writers pause to check the preferred hyphenation of a word that is easy to spell (e.g., girl friend *or* girlfriend? half hitch *or* half-hitch?), even good writers tend to mix various forms within a document. To ensure consistency within a document, the copyeditor should always take a moment to look up compound nouns in the dictionary and to enter the desired form on the style sheet.

Sometimes, though, copyeditors must break with convention and depart from the dictionary in order to avoid compounds that will appear inconsistent or call attention to themselves. For example, *M-W Collegiate* online shows *windowsill.* But it might seem odd to read "I dusted off the windowsill and the window seat." Here, "window sill" would call less attention to itself. And although residents of Baltimore and Philadelphia have lived for many generations in rowhouses, rows of attached dwellings, *M-W Unabridged, M-W Collegiate* online, and *AHD* all still spell the term "row houses." The *Baltimore Sun* style guide, in keeping with local custom, specifies the solid compound.

Sometimes, too, it is worthwhile to think about how a compound noun is pronounced and how it functions. Nicholson Baker's thoughts about function coalesced in a discussion with a copyeditor over *pantyhose, panty hose,* and *panty-hose.* Baker had used the closed compound, and the copyeditor proposed the open form, which was the only form shown in *M-W Collegiate* online. Baker responded, "My feeling was that . . . *pantyhose* . . . constitutes a single, interfused unit of sense, greater than the sum of its parts, which ought to be the criterion for jointure."[13]

13. The author-editor exchange appears in Baker's "The History of Punctuation," in *The Size of Thoughts: Essays and Other Lumber* (New York: Random House, 1996), which describes the hyphenation minefield from the point of view of a careful, fastidious writer:

> And yet, though the suggested space [in *panty hose*] seemed to me mistaken, I could just as easily have gone for *panty-hose* as *pantyhose*—in fact, normally I would have campaigned for a hyphen in this sort of setting, since the power-crazed policy-makers at Merriam-Webster and *Words into Type* have been reading too much Joyce in recent years and making condominiums out of terms . . . that deserve semi-detachment. . . . Evolution proceeds hyphen by hyphen, and manuscript by manuscript—impelled by the tension between working writers and their copy-editors, and between working copy-editors and their works of reference. (pp. 81–82)

Here again, if writers and copyeditors are completely deferential to the choices shown in the dictionary, the lexicographers' observations about which forms are most frequently used will not reflect the

## PREFIXES AND SUFFIXES

Most words formed with common prefixes (e.g., anti-, bi-, hyper-, mega-, mid-, multi-, non-, over-, post-, pre-, proto-, re-, sub-, un-, under-) are closed up. But combinations with capitalized terms (anti-American), numerals (mid-1990s), and compound terms (non-English-speaking) retain the hyphen, as do forms that would be ambiguous or hard to read if spelled solid. Suffixes (e.g., -fold, -less, -like, -wide) are closed if the terms are listed as solid compounds in the dictionary; otherwise, they retain the hyphen.

> anti-intellectual, semi-independent (to avoid a double *i*)
> co-edition, co-op, co-opt
> de-emphasize, de-escalate, de-ice
> mid-ocean, mid-thirteenth century (noun), mid-thirteenth-century (adjective),
>     mid-thirties
> pro-democracy, pro-choice, pro-government, pro-life
> re-aerate, re-interview
> re-cover, re-form, re-sign (as distinct from *recover, reform,* and *resign*)
> un-ionized (as distinct from *unionized*)

> guru-like, hobo-like, lava-like
> industry-wide
> yacht-less

The "hard to read" standard, of course, introduces a subjective element. Here many writers and copyeditors find *Chicago* and *M-W Collegiate* far too stingy in the allocation of hyphens. *Chicago* does mention the difficult-to-read test but recommends such spellings as *midcareer, midthirties, neoorthodox,* and *nonevent.* The list of *co-* compounds in *M-W Collegiate* (which Chicago style follows) seems almost bizarre to some editors: cocaptain, cochair, cocurator, coheir, costar, coworker. Fortunately, the *AP Stylebook* (s.v. "co-") offers a sane alternative: "Retain the hyphen when forming nouns, adjectives and verbs that indicate occupation or status." Thus: co-author, co-captain, co-chair, co-conspirator, co-curator, co-heir, co-star, co-worker.[14]

Compounds consisting of a prefix and a hyphenated term are hyphenated:

> non-English-speaking students
> un-air-conditioned auditorium

---

actual preferences of writers (in this case, for "pantyhose") but rather the compromises writers make with dictionary entries ("panty-hose") or with their copyeditors' suggestions to abide by the dictionary ("panty hose").

14. Instead of a hyphen, the *New Yorker*'s house style specifies a diaeresis to prevent the misreading of some—but not all—prefixed compounds in which identical vowels fall together: coöperate, reëlect, *but* zoological. (Although the diaeresis looks like an umlaut, it serves a different purpose, denoting that the marked vowel begins a new syllable.) These antiquated spellings were established early in the history of the magazine and continue as a cherished tradition to this day. Mary Norris's sketch of the *New Yorker*'s idiosyncratic treatment of other compound terms ("The dictionary is a wonderful thing, but you can't let it push you around, especially where compound words are concerned") is well worth reading (*Between You and Me,* pp. 114–24).

post-cease-fire negotiations
preflight-de-icing equipment

Compounds consisting of a prefix and a proper noun or a proper adjective are hyphenated:

anti-American sentiments
in mid-July
pre-Newtonian physics

If the proper noun is itself a two-word item, an en dash is used:

anti–New York sentiments
pre–World War II borders

A departure from editorial orthodoxy concerns the use of the prefix *mid-,* which forms a solid or hyphenated compound with the following word or (more rarely) is used as a freestanding noun or adjective. *Chicago* counsels that the prefix be closed with a common noun that follows (midcentury, midfield) but hyphenated if the following term is a proper noun, a numeral, or a multipart compound (mid-Atlantic, mid-1990s, mid-twentieth century, mid-twentieth-century politics). But what is the recommended treatment of constructions in which *mid* is separated from the word it modifies: mid- to late 1990? mid-to-late 1990? mid to late 1990? In response to a query, in *Chicago's* online "Style Q&A" the Chicago editors sanction all of these as legitimate choices, provided the meaning is clear, but specify *Chicago's* preferences (see "Time" in chapter 7).

## CYBERJARGON

Dozens of computer-related compounds have entered everyday life, and current practice is sharply divided, with preferences changing as technologies mature. For example, *E-mail* was common in the mid-1990s but by the early 2000s had all but disappeared, leaving editors and writers to haggle over *e-mail* versus *email.* (*Chicago* and other major style guides have now embraced the solid form.) The term *Web site* has yielded to the solid compound *website,* along with *webcam, webcast,* and *webmaster; webpage* is recognized as solid in *AHD* online but is still listed as an open form in the online *M-W Collegiate.*

If cyberjargon is covered in the publisher's in-house guidelines, you will of course follow the conventions shown there. But if you have to make an independent decision, look to the author's preference and the strength of the author's feelings as well as to the intended readership and the purpose of the document. Most often your overriding concern should be, Which forms are likely to be clearest to the readers? In corporate publishing, however, conveying an up-to-date image is sometimes deemed more important than clarity; in these cases, the publications department may prefer the sleeker all-lowercase closed compounds (homepage, voicemail, website).

## SPELL-CHECKERS

All word processing programs include a spell-checking feature. For short documents that contain few unusual words and few proper nouns, spell-checking is fast and convenient—though not reliable. As noted at the beginning of this chapter, spell-checkers do not identify a misspelled word if the misspelling is itself a word, do not distinguish between homophones, do not account for spellings determined by usage, and may include variant spellings and hyphenations that are inconsistent with the house dictionary—or may exclude the house's preferred forms. Spell-checkers also fail to identify a writer's cut-and-paste errors on the computer, in which parts of several versions are inadvertently conflated. An autocorrect tool, if not disabled in the word processor, may even introduce errors, sometimes called *Cupertinos* after the habit of some older autocorrect features to suggest—or even default to—*Cupertino* as a "correction" for *cooperation*. (Cupertino, California, is the current home of Apple.) Cupertinos come in two flavors: real words miscorrected into other words owing to a gap in the spell-checker's dictionary, and misspelled words changed to the wrong word when the correct one is not listed as the spell-checker's first suggestion.

To save yourself some embarrassment, you can create an exclusion dictionary: a list of words that you want your spell-checker to flag even though they are legitimate words. For example, if you add *pubic, thee,* and *widows* to your exclusion dictionary, your spell-checker will stop three times in the following sentence: "The pubic library ordered thee licenses for Widows XP."

For long documents that contain many unusual words, spell-checking can be tedious. You can save some time by clicking the "ignore all" option, which instructs the computer to ignore all instances of the currently flagged word in the document. Or you can click "add," which permanently adds the word to the main dictionary or to a supplementary dictionary that you have created. Add-on spelling modules are available for some technical fields and many foreign languages.

Because bibliographies and reference lists are filled with proper names, spell-checking these sections is a slow process, and some copyeditors do not run the spell-checker on these sections.

*On-screen edits.* When you copyedit on-screen, running the spell-checker is one of your routine tasks. Most copyeditors run the spell-checker before editing the file—so that they will not have to correct each misspelling as it arises—and again after editing the file. The spell-checker is run one final time during cleanup, after the author's changes have been incorporated into the file.

*Hard-copy edits.* If you can obtain the author's files, running the spell-checker before or after you copyedit may help you catch a few hard-to-spot typos.

# CHAPTER 6

# ❡ Capitalization and the Treatment of Names

Proper nouns and proper adjectives are always capitalized, but there are two conventions for treating words that are not indisputably proper. *Down style* favors the sparse use of capital letters; in *up style* many more nouns and adjectives are uppercased:

| *Down style* | *Up style* |
|---|---|
| The president announced | The President announced |
| The Truman administration | The Truman Administration |
| After the secretary of state left | After the Secretary of State left |

Up style is used by some newspapers and magazines, but down style predominates in book publishing.[1]

You can save yourself a lot of time if you raise questions about capitalization with your editorial coordinator or the author after you've skimmed the manuscript and before you begin working on it. The fourteenth edition of *Chicago* (1993) asserts that "most authors . . . do not feel strongly about capitalization" (7.4), an opinion wisely omitted in subsequent editions. Indeed, *Butcher's Copy-editing* (1996), the Cambridge University Press style manual, explicitly counters that "many authors have strong feelings about capitalization" and advises editors to "follow their system if they have a sensible one" (p. 126).

The truth may well lie somewhere in the middle: some authors do not have strong opinions about capitalization; others regard capitalization not merely as a matter of typography but as an issue of giving or denying status to a term. The conventions in some academic, professional, and technical fields also differ from the down-style preferences shown in *Chicago* and *WIT*. Thus you should use your style manual as a starting point but always be willing to accommodate both an author's invincible preferences and the current conventions in the author's field. Making reasonable, consistent choices is more important than adhering to every guideline set forth in a general-purpose style manual. So that you and others can keep track of your decisions about capitalization, you should always record those decisions on your style sheet.

---

1. In "Let's Kill All the Copy Editors" (*New York Times*, October 6, 1991), William Safire takes a gleeful poke at book publishers' preference for down style, which he labels "a case of the lowers": "We are not going to turn into slaves of e. e. cummings." In November 1999, however, the *New York Times* abandoned up style for down. Also, although Cummings used unconventional capitalization in his poems, he normally capitalized his name; see Norman Friedman, "NOT 'e. e. cummings,'" *Spring* 1 (1992): 114–21.

Here are some pointers about the most common headaches that arise in the area of capitalization and the treatment of names.

## PERSONAL NAMES AND TITLES

By convention, all personal names (first, middle, and last names as well as nicknames and the suffixes *Jr.* and *Sr.*) are capitalized. Also, the suffixes *Jr.* and *Sr.* were traditionally preceded and followed by a comma, but the newer convention eliminates these commas:

> *Older convention:* Pemberton Smythe, Jr., was appointed the chairman of the board.

> *Newer convention:* Pemberton Smythe Jr. was appointed the chairman of the board.

Policies vary, however, in the treatment of individuals who prefer that their names be lowercased. Here's Bill Walsh's spirited defense of using standard capitalization despite the individual's preference (but on Cummings's preference, see note 1 to this chapter):

> Sure, before "k.d. lang" there was "e.e. cummings." But, as most good dictionaries . . . and *New York Times* style recognize, these are logos. The names are K.D. Lang and E.E. Cummings. To bow to the artists' lowercase demand . . . deprives readers of a crucial visual cue. . . . [Although] when you print "K.D. Lang" or "E.E. Cummings" without a footnote explaining your departure from the norm . . . many readers will simply assume you made a mistake.
>
> But Bill, you may ask, don't people have the right to be called whatever they choose? Well, ideally, yes. . . . [But] how about another ordinary citizen . . . who insists that his name is I'M!!!A!!!NEAT!!GUY!!? . . . It's impossible to be a consistent liberal on this issue—you have to draw the line somewhere, and I choose to draw it quicker than most.[2]

But some publishers defer to the lowercasers' preference. *Chicago* (8.4), for example, advises that "unconventional spellings strongly preferred by the bearer of the name or pen name (e.g., bell hooks) should usually be respected in appropriate contexts." When a lowercased name appears occasionally in a text, one tries to avoid having the name at the start of a sentence. Thus:

> *Awkward:* bell hooks is the pen name of Gloria Watkins.

> *Preferable:* Gloria Watkins uses the pen name bell hooks.

To be sure, this strategy is cumbersome for lowercased names that appear frequently throughout a document. In such situations, the copyeditor should consult with the

2. Until his death in 2017, Bill Walsh was the copy chief of the national and business desks at the *Washington Post;* this passage comes from the "Curmudgeon's Stylebook" section of his popular website The Slot (http://www.theslot.com/), a vast, eclectic collection of rules, pointers, and rants on matters editorial. The eagle-eyed reader will notice that Walsh closed up personal initials ("k.d." and "K.D."), which is the treatment mandated by the *AP Stylebook.* The next subsection discusses conventions for the spacing of personal initials.

author and the editorial coordinator before deciding whether to uppercase the first letter of the name at the beginning of a sentence. In source citations a lowercased name should be preserved out of respect for the author's choice: if a bibliographic entry reads "hooks, bell," do not capitalize it or add "[*sic*]."

*Treatment of initials, given names, and surnames.* Most style manuals call for spacing between initials in a personal name: A. B. Cherry (*not* A.B. Cherry).[3] But there are no spaces between personal initials that are not followed by periods (FDR, LBJ). Some manuals also recommend closing up initials that follow a first name (Thomas A.J. Castle), and initials that come in a set of three (J.R.R. Tolkien). In *CSE* style—which eliminates periods whenever possible—personal initials in running text carry internal spacing (Dr S E Ralph), and in bibliographical citations are closed up (SE Ralph).

Initials for a hyphenated first name use the initials for both parts of the name and retain the hyphen, for example, "J.-P. Sartre" for "Jean-Paul Sartre." Practices vary for initials of surnames with prefixes, such as McGovern, MacAuley, and O'Brien. Some writers use just the first initial (M., O.); others, McG., MacA., and O'B. If there are no specific house guidelines, chose a style that is clear and consistently applied.

Some publishers expect their copyeditors to ask the author to supply the full name (not just the initials and surname) of an individual the first time that person is mentioned in a document. After the first full-name mention, the surname alone usually suffices. Compound surnames, whether hyphenated or not, use both parts of the surname on subsequent references:

| | |
|---|---|
| Ralph Vaughn Williams | Vaughn Williams |
| Katharine O'Moore-Klopf | O'Moore-Klopf |
| José Ortega y Gasset | Ortega y Gasset |

For famous individuals, the complete form of the surname can usually be determined by consulting an authoritative biographical dictionary or encyclopedia; for minor celebrities, by asking the author or investigating the prevailing usage in print documents or online.

Excepted from the convention of providing the full name at first reference are extremely well known people whose surnames are distinctive (Shakespeare, Darwin, Poe), persons who are best known by their initials rather than their full names (T. S. Eliot, A. A. Milne, J. D. Salinger, H. G. Wells, E. B. White), and persons best known by only one name (Michelangelo). In addition, the sensitive copyeditor will consider the intended audience, the function of the name within the document, and the cadence of the sentence. In a scholarly book about a twentieth-century Spanish poet, for example, there is no need to insert the first names of artists who appear in a whirlwind cluster like the following:

---

3. Some publishers prefer a thin space, rather than a regular wordspace, between personal initials. If you are working on hard copy, you may be asked to add the instruction "thin #" for the typesetter. If you are working on-screen, you may be asked to insert a special code or to use your word processing program's *hard space* character (also called a *nonbreaking space*). The hard space will prevent the typeset line or reflowing text from breaking between the initials.

> When he returned to Madrid, he resumed his acquaintances with Picasso, Dalí, Buñuel, Salinas, Jiménez, Guillén, and Aleixandre. That winter, at a conference in Moscow, he met Eisenstein, Gorky, Prokofiev, and Malraux.

Since the author's purpose here is simply to suggest the number and variety of artists known by the Spanish poet, and since readers of this kind of specialized work are likely to recognize all these surnames, there is no reason to clutter the text with a rash of given names.

Conversely, a given name alone may be more appropriate in some contexts, such as a passage in a biography that refers to several family members with the same surname. A paragraph describing Henry James's family relations, for example, might differentiate the James siblings as "Henry," "William," and "Alice," whereas a passage focused on Henry James alone might use his surname.

Judgment is also required when determining whether to provide a surname that can easily be inferred from the context:

> George Rumple's youngest son, Arthur, was killed in the line of duty while serving as a police officer in Martinez.

If Arthur's surname differs from that of his father, it should be provided. If he shares his father's surname, repeating it here would ordinarily seem superfluous. But if the document is to be distributed and indexed electronically, a search engine might still require specifying Arthur's full name to facilitate searches on "Arthur Rumple."

*Personal nicknames.*   An epithet used as part of or in place of a proper name is capitalized and sometimes placed in quotation marks when embedded within the proper name:

> Stan "the Man" Musial; Stan the Man
>
> August "Ham and Eggs" Jemenez; Ham and Eggs Jemenez
>
> Joyce "Big J" Harris; Big J

*Particles.*   There are no surefire rules for the capitalization of particles (de, de la, van, von) in personal names, nor for retention or omission of the particle when referring to the person by surname alone. The capitalization and surname-only treatment of the names of well-known individuals can be found in a dictionary or a one-volume or online encyclopedia; preferred forms may be specified in the designated style manual, which should be consulted for house style. The conventions for more obscure personal names must be determined by asking the author to verify the treatment.

| | |
|---|---|
| Thomas De Quincey | De Quincey |
| Charles de Gaulle | de Gaulle (*Chicago; M-W Collegiate* also lists "Gaulle") |
| Alexis de Tocqueville | Tocqueville |
| Vincent van Gogh | Van Gogh (*Chicago; M-W Collegiate* has "van Gogh") |
| Ludwig van Beethoven | Beethoven |

When a lowercased particle appears as the first word in a sentence, it is capitalized. When a lowercased particle appears at the beginning of an entry in an alphabetical listing (e.g., a directory, index, or bibliography that uses an inverted order for names), the particle remains lowercased.

Determining the correct initials to represent names containing particles often requires a query to the author or a bit of research: Nicholas deBelleville Katzenbach (a US attorney general under President Lyndon B. Johnson) was referred to as Nicholas deB. Katzenbach in his *New York Times* and *Washington Post* obituaries; Ira De Augustine Reid (a prominent sociologist) published some early books under the name Ira De A. Reid but in later books spelled out his full middle name. (Individuals may change the form of their name over a lifetime: Ralph Le Roy Merritt to Ralph LeRoy Merritt, then Ralph Leroy Merritt, and finally Ralph L. Merritt.)

*Titles and offices.* In down style, a person's title or office is capitalized only when it directly precedes a personal name and is part of the name. Applying this style requires you to distinguish between a formal title and a title that functions merely as a descriptive tag (often with an explicit or implied "the" or with another modifier), even when it appears immediately before the name, as in the last three examples below:

> In 1862 President Lincoln announced . . .

> In 1862 the president announced . . .

> In 1862 the American president announced . . .

> Lincoln, before he was elected president, announced . . .

> In 1862 [the] American president Lincoln announced . . .

> In her speech [the] former secretary of state Hillary Clinton proclaimed . . .

> [The] California senator Kamala Harris declared . . .

In the last three examples, the names function as restrictive appositives rather than as formal titles: *which* American president? *which* former secretary of state? *which* California senator? In some up styles, you would capitalize the descriptions in the last two instances, which can be construed as titles.

*Adjectives based on personal names.* The most common suffixes for transforming a personal surname into an adjective are *-esque, -ean, -ian,* and *-ic.* The proper adjectives are always capitalized:

> Audenesque, Disneyesque, Lincolnesque, Reaganesque

> Aeschylean, Lockean, Sartrean

> Aristotelian, Chekhovian, Emersonian, Freudian, Hegelian

> Aristophanic, Byronic, Napoleonic, Pindaric, Platonic, Ptolemaic

Surnames ending in *w, eau,* or an unpronounced consonant call for some adjustment: Shaw, Shavian; Thoreau, Thoreauvian; Foucault, Foucauldian. Some names take other suffixes: Calvinist, Thatcherite. And some adjectival forms have equal (*or*) or secondary (*also*) variants listed in the dictionary: Caesarian *or* Caesarean; Aristotelian *also* Aristotelean; Coleridgean *also* Coleridgian; Lockean *also* Lockian.

For the adjectival forms of well-known names, consult your dictionary; for other names, consult with your author and trust your ear. When names can take different suffixes, the variants may convey a slight difference in tone: to most Americans, *Clintonesque* sounds a bit grander than *Clintonian*. The device of transforming a proper name into an adjective should be used with care. If an individual is not of sufficient stature to merit adjectivalization, some readers will take the usage to be satiric or parodic.

*Terms derived from personal names.*  Many terms derived from personal names are lowercased: braille, caesarean birth, fallopian tube, *but* Molotov cocktail. Units of measurement named after individuals are also lowercased: joule, newton, pascal, watt. In medical terminology for diseases, the possessive form of the name (but not the adjectival and other forms) is usually capitalized: Achilles' tendon, Huntington's disease, Down's syndrome, Tourette's syndrome, Crohn's disease, Parkinson's disease, *but* parkinsonian, parkinsonism. Note, however, that CSE style omits the possessive altogether in capitalized eponymous disease names: Huntington disease, Down syndrome, Tourette syndrome, Crohn disease, Parkinson disease.

## ASTRONOMICAL TERMS AND GEOGRAPHICAL NAMES

All style manuals offer detailed discussions of astronomical terms and place names. The following pointers address the most common issues.

*Astronomical terms.*  Capitalize *earth, moon,* and *sun* when they refer to celestial bodies, but usually lowercase them in nonastronomy contexts:

> Lars von Trier's film *Melancholia* depicts the final days of Earth as it approaches collision with a newly discovered planet long concealed from detection by the Sun.

> He moved out of the sun and into the shade.

> The moon was obscured by the clouds.

> Jim is the salt of the earth.

*Areas of the globe.* Geographical coordinates and imaginary boundaries are usually lowercased (prime meridian, equator). Other distinct areas of the globe are capitalized (Arctic Circle, Antarctic Circle, Tropic of Cancer, Tropic of Capricorn, *but* the tropics).

*Proper place names, nicknames, popular and historical place names.*  Proper names, nicknames, and conventional or historical names of places are all capitalized: San Francisco, the Bay Area, New York, the Big Apple, New Orleans, the Big Easy, Minneapolis, Saint Paul, the Twin Cities, the European Union, Euroland, the Pacific Coast (*but* the

Pacific coastline), the Northwest Passage, the Northwest Territories. The full formal name of a political entity is capitalized (the State of California, the Commonwealth of Virginia);[4] generic use to specify a geographical entity is lowercased (the state of California).

*Directions.* Directional nouns and adjectives are capitalized when used with a place name to identify a distinct region, for example in an economic, cultural, or political context: West Africa, sub-Saharan Africa, Central Europe, Southeast Asia, South Asia, the Midwest, the South, the East Coast, the West Coast. When directional terms merely indicate orientation, they are not capitalized: west Africa, central Europe, south Texas, eastern Pennsylvania, northern Oregon. Political jurisdictions whose official place names include directional terms are capitalized following an authoritative gazetteer: South Africa, North Carolina.

*Terms derived from geographical names.* Many terms derived from geographical names are lowercased: arabic numerals, french fries, manila envelope, venetian blinds. (The capitalization of *Scotch tape* has nothing to do with Scotland; by convention, brand names are capitalized.) Despite the capitalization of some of these terms in *M-W Collegiate* (e.g., Arabic numerals, French horn, French toast, Scotch whisky), Chicago style lowercases many such names when they are used in a nonliteral sense, that is, in the sense of *having qualities or features of,* rather than literally *originating from,* the place named. Hence: "We had swedish meatballs and brussels sprouts with a pleasing California burgundy for dinner."

*Name changes.* In Europe, in particular, the political map has been remade in recent years. Thus you may need recourse to such terms as "the former West German capital," "the former East Germany," and "the former Soviet Union." Likewise, the Cold War–era term "Third World" has given way to (politically) "nonaligned nations" or, more often, "the Global South," comprising the "developing nations" or "emerging nations" in Africa, Asia, and Latin America.

*Names for residents of states in the United States.* GPO recommends the following forms for state residents:

| | | |
|---|---|---|
| Alabamian | Floridian | Kentuckian |
| Alaskan | Georgian | Louisianian |
| Arizonan | Hawaiian | Mainer* |
| Arkansan | Idahoan | Marylander |
| Californian | Illinoisan | Massachusettsan* |
| Coloradan | Indianian* | Michiganite* |
| Connecticuter* | Iowan | Minnesotan |
| Delawarean | Kansan | Mississippian |

4. Kentucky, Massachusetts, Pennsylvania, and Virginia are officially designated commonwealths rather than states.

| | | |
|---|---|---|
| Missourian | North Dakotan | Texan |
| Montanan | Ohioan | Utahn (*adj.*, Utahan) |
| Nebraskan | Oklahoman | Vermonter |
| Nevadan | Oregonian | Virginian |
| New Hampshirite | Pennsylvanian | Washingtonian |
| New Jerseyite* | Rhode Islander | West Virginian |
| New Mexican | South Carolinian | Wisconsinite |
| New Yorker | South Dakotan | Wyomingite |
| North Carolinian | Tennessean | |

*For these somewhat awkward forms, other books suggest "Nutmegger" (Connecticut), "Hoosier" (Indiana), "Down Easter" (Maine), "Bay Stater" (Massachusetts), and "Michiganian" or "Michigander" (Michigan). Natives of New Jersey often prefer "New Jerseyans" (Andy Hollandbeck, "Angelenos and Demonyms," *Copyediting*, March 21, 2018, https://www.copyediting.com/). Paul Dickson discusses these controversies, among others, in *Labels for Locals: What to Call People from Abilene to Zimbabwe*, a dictionary of demonyms, nouns and adjectives that denote residents of cities, states, and countries around the world. (For good measure, the book also has entries for hypothetical residents of the planets in our solar system.)

*Names for residents of countries.* Many print and online resources offer lists of noun and adjective forms designating nationalities. Here's a selection from the recommendations in *GPO* for nouns denoting nationality:

| | |
|---|---|
| Afghan(s) | Mozambican(s) |
| Argentine(s) | Nepalese (*sing. and pl.*) |
| Bahamian(s) | Nigerois (*sing. and pl.*)† |
| Bangladeshi(s) | Pakistani(s) |
| Belizean(s) | Portuguese (*sing. and pl.*) |
| Briton(s) (*collective pl.*, British)* | Salvadoran(s) |
| Filipino(s) | Senegalese (*sing. and pl.*) |
| Greenlander(s) | Swiss (*sing. and pl.*) |
| Icelander(s) | Thai (*sing. and pl.*) |
| Iraqi(s) | Togolese (*sing. and pl.*) |
| Lao *or* Laotian (*pl.*, Laotians) | Vietnamese (*sing. and pl.*) |
| Liechtensteiner(s) | Yemeni(s) |
| Luxembourger(s) | Zimbabwean(s) |

*Briton* and *British* are used to denote the residents of England as well as those of the United Kingdom. (The United Kingdom comprises the island of Great Britain—England, Scotland, and Wales—and Northern Ireland.)
†Refers to residents of Niger, not Nigeria. "Nigerois" (nee-zher-WAH) is the somewhat archaic term used by old-schoolers; more common and up-to-date is "Nigerien" (nee-ZHER-yen). Both terms are acceptable; just don't call your friend in Niamey a Nigerian (nai-JEER-ee-un).

*Names for residents of cities.* Some city dwellers claim unusual identities:

| | | | |
|---|---|---|---|
| Glasgow | Glaswegians | Los Angeles | Angelenos |
| Halifax | Haligonians | Manchester | Mancunians |
| Liverpool | Liverpudlians | Sydney | Sydneysiders |

## RACIAL AND ETHNIC GROUPS

The capitalization of racial and ethnic groups remains a contentious topic. (On controversies over the names themselves, see "Bias-Free Language" in chapter 15.) *Chicago* and *WIT* both recommend lowercasing designations based on skin color (black, white), though *Chicago* notes that at times these terms are capitalized, following an author's or publisher's preference. All the manuals recommend capitalizing the names of ethnic and national groups, and most advise omitting hyphens in compound designations: African Americans, Chicanos, Chinese Americans, First Nations or First Peoples (Canada), Hispanics, Indigenous Australians, Italian Americans, Native Americans.

Sometimes such capitalization decisions are purely political, but at other times the issue is one of achieving an editorial consistency that looks logical to readers who are unfamiliar with the strictures enunciated in the style manuals. Thus, when the name of one group is capitalized, a copyeditor may decide to ignore the style manual and capitalize the names of all analogous groups:

> *Original:* The number of black, Latino, and Native American applicants rose last year.

> *Revision:* The number of Black, Latino, and Native American applicants rose last year.

> *Or:* The number of African American, Latino, and Native American applicants rose last year.

Note: Some writers and editors now prefer the gender-neutral *Latinx,* duly recorded in the online *M-W Collegiate.*

## NAMES OF INSTITUTIONS AND COMPANIES, TRADEMARKS, AND BRAND NAMES

The full proper names of institutions are capitalized. So, too, are their shortened forms when used to stand in for the previously identified full forms:

> The City of Sacramento Department of Parks and Recreation is developing this historical site. Any complaints about construction noise should be addressed to Parks and Recreation.

Thus it is acceptable (and common practice in institutional and business documents) to substitute, for example,

> the University *for* the University of California

> the Foundation *for* the Woodrow Wilson Foundation

> the Park Service *for* the National Park Service

provided the short version has been clearly established as proxy for the full formal name.

But the shortened names of institutions are lowercased when they are simply used descriptively:

The Alameda County Sheriff's Office announced that . . .

*But:* He filed a report with the sheriff's office.

When referring to a university or other institution as a legal entity in self-contained copy, such as an imprint on a title or copyright page, capitalize the full formal name exactly as specified by the institution's guidelines (The Johns Hopkins University, The Regents of the University of California); in running text, lowercase any official "the" (the Johns Hopkins University, the Regents). For institutions that deliberately exclude "the" from their brand name (University of California Press), follow house style in official proclamations but supply a lowercased "the" in running copy if required for readability.

The treatment of such institutional names is usually straightforward, but business and product names and terms sometimes have unusual typographic features. Always ask your author to verify the spelling and capitalization.

*All capitals:* UMAX Technologies
[*Chicago* releases editors from any obligation to replicate such all-caps treatments.][5]

*All lowercase:* nook, adidas
[*Chicago* "draws the line . . . at names in all lowercase; in order to signal that such a term is in fact a proper noun, an initial capital should be applied even midsentence" (8.154).]

*Midcap or intercap (a.k.a. camel cap):* WordPerfect, LaserJet, PowerPoint
[*Chicago* counsels preserving such internal capitalization.]

*Numerical character:* 7-Eleven

*Lowercase letter:* eBay, iPhone
[*Chicago* now permits retention of an initial lowercase letter in a headline or at the start of a sentence and recommends revision when it is desirable to avoid the situation.][6]

*No internal periods:* IBM, AT&T, Dr Pepper

Although novelists often use (and overuse) brand names as an aid to characterization, careful expository writers use generic names unless they are discussing a particular product.

---

5. As Bill Walsh once pointed out: "Your credit card may say VISA, your athletic shoes may say NIKE, but this is just because the companies chose an all-caps presentation for the brand names. That doesn't mean you write the words that way, any more than you would write WEBSTER'S NEW UNIVERSAL UNABRIDGED DICTIONARY just because that's what it says on the spine" (http://www .theslot.com/).

6. An aside: When the first letter of a technical term such as *fMRI* or *tPA* begins a sentence, recasting the sentence or spelling out the term is preferable to capitalizing the initial letter, according to the consensus of an exchange on *Chicago*'s online "Forum." But contractions with an initial elision (*'tis* for "it is," *'ere* for "here") are capitalized at the start of a sentence: "'Tis the season to be jolly."

*Careless usage:* Please keep all kleenexes and cokes away from the xeroxing machine.

*Better:* Please keep all tissues and cans of soda away from the photocopier.

*But:* We are ordering three new Xerox copiers and two LaserJet printers.

All editorial style manuals recommend that trademarks be capitalized. But strict adherence to this convention is likely to startle readers, many of whom are unaware that Dacron, Dumpster, Formica, Frisbee, Jell-O, LISTSERV, Mace, Muzak, Orlon, Ping-Pong, Post-it, Realtor, Styrofoam, Teflon, Touch-Tone, Wi-Fi, and Wite-Out (a name recognizable to those old enough to remember typewriters) are trademarks. Trademark owners urge writers not only to capitalize trademark names but also to restrict these terms to adjectival uses (Kleenex facial tissues, *not* Kleenex). There is no legal obligation to do either. Few editors heed the grammatical prescription, and once a trademark is so common as to be listed in the dictionary as a generic term, some editors will lowercase the name (that's no more than a band-aid approach; the teflon president; he shook like jello).[7] But others choose to follow all trademark protocols or to substitute a descriptive term for the trademark (electronic mailing list, *not* LISTSERV).

The more common trademarks appear in the dictionary, with "trademark" in the slot used to indicate the part of speech. *M-W Collegiate* online shows *xerox* as a transitive verb ("to copy on a xerographic copier") and *Xerox* as a trademark for a xerographic copier.[8] A newly updated entry in the online *M-W Unabridged* lists the verb form *Google* (with the secondary variant *google*), derived from the trademarked name of the popular internet search engine and well on its way to generic use. (Google's executives may in fact welcome this evidence of its market dominance: terms derived from Bing, Microsoft's rival search engine, are nowhere to be found in the dictionary.) For additional information on trademarks, you may wish to consult the website of the International Trademark Association (INTA), https://www.inta.org/Pages/Home.aspx. Unfortunately, this site no longer provides free access to its handy trademark checklist, but it posts several "Public Resources," including "Trademark Basics" and "A Guide to Proper Trademark Use for Media, Internet and Publishing Professionals."

Despite INTA's advice, there is no requirement to include such designations as ™ (trademark), ℠ (service mark), ® (registered trademark), or © (copyright) in running text unless a document is published by the trademark owner. The holder of a mark must use the appropriate symbol at least once in each publication, but others need not. Indeed, it is preferable to avoid these symbols because they may interfere with the linespacing of a finished document.

---

7. The capitalized *Dumpster,* for example, is rapidly losing ground to the lowercase generic term, and the figurative expression *dumpster fire* (less commonly, *Dumpster fire*) was recently added to the online *M-W Collegiate.* Because all the style manuals are so insistent on capitalizing trademarks and brand names, some editors may feel a bit guilty (or defiant, depending on mood) when they lowercase them. But it seems that they are in excellent company: Edward D. Johnson, who proudly upholds many proprieties that others dismiss as overly finicky, confesses, "When I find a figuratively used trademark lowercased in a book I am editing, I am apt to pretend I don't know it should be capitalized, though I can't conscientiously recommend this course" (*The Handbook of Good English,* p. 233).

8. *M-W Collegiate* does not have an entry for the noun *xerox* (a photocopy). All the manuals advise using the generic terms *copy* and *photocopy.*

## CYBERJARGON

Google was incorporated in 1998; in twenty years the name has shed its capitalization, gone generic, and become a verb form. Cyber terms emerge and change (or vanish) with remarkable speed. Even in nontechnical content, rapid mutations—especially toward lowercasing, treatment as solid compounds, and soldering onto other words—are common. For example, *internet* and *web* are now often lowercased; *email* and several compound forms with *web* now tend to be spelled solid. Can *ebook, webmail,* and *logon* be far behind? Follow house style or your chosen style manual, or, in the absence of specific guidelines, consult an up-to-date, authoritative dictionary to determine the current treatment of cyberjargon. These selected forms are conventional at the moment:

> CD-ROM, CD-ROMs[9]

> e-book, e-commerce, *but* email (an update in *Chicago* 17)
>> *At the beginning of a sentence:* E-books
>> *In headline-style titles:* E-Books *or* E-books

> *file extensions:* .eps, .gif, .jpg, .pdf, .rtf, .tif *or* .tiff, .zip
> *file formats:* EPS, GIF, JPEG, PDF, RTF, TIFF, ZIP
> hypertext markup language, HTML
> the internet (an update in *Chicago* 17), the net
> local-area network, LAN
> multipurpose internet mail extensions, MIME
> username, user ID
> Wi-Fi (a trademark; but, increasingly, wi-fi)
> the World Wide Web, the web, web browser, webpage (*AHD*'s preference), webcast, webmaster, website

Publishers of computer manuals have devised various conventions for capitalizing the names of items on the screen display and on the keyboard, for example:

> *Names of keys:* ALT, CTRL, ESC, TAB, ENTER, *or* Alt (*or* Option), Ctrl (or Command), Esc, Tab, Enter (*or* Return), Caps Lock, Shift
> *Names of cursor keys:* Down Arrow, Up Arrow, Home, PgUp, PgDn
> *Labels on the menu bar:* File, Edit, View, Table, Help

## TITLES OF WORKS

The conventions regarding the capitalization of titles apply to the capitalization of complete works (books, corporate reports, magazine articles, recorded albums, cartoon

9. Well, OK, *so* 1990s!

strips, poems, songs, works of art) and titled sections of complete works (chapter titles, headings within books and documents). There are two basic styles for capitalizing titles. The first is called either *headline style* or *UC/lc* (shorthand for "uppercase and lowercase"), and the second is called *sentence style* or *initial cap only*. Note that the title case feature in Microsoft Word does not conform to either of these conventions.

Both styles are acceptable for the treatment of headings in a document as long as they are used consistently. Here, *consistently* does not mean "exclusively." The two styles may be combined in one document—major headings in headline style, subheadings in sentence style—as long as all items in a given class are treated consistently. *Exception:* When a chapter title or heading contains a quotation, the quotation may be set in sentence style, even if the other chapter titles and headings are set in headline style:

> Redefining Patriotism: "Ask not what your country can do for you"

> "Shall I compare thee to a summer's day?": Metaphors and Clichés of Our Time

## HEADLINE STYLE

In headline style, one capitalizes the first and last words of a title or subtitle. Subtitles are most often introduced by a colon (*Sticks and Stones: The Magic of Names*). Sometimes a dash is used, in which case what follows is not usually considered a subtitle and may begin with an uncapitalized word ("Willa Jan—the Greatest Player"; *Chicago* 8.164). In addition, one capitalizes all interior words except articles (a, an, the), coordinate conjunctions (and, or, nor, but, for, yet, so),[10] prepositions, the *to* in infinitive forms, scientific terms that begin with a lowercase letter (pH, mRNA), and scientific (Latin) names that are lowercased in running text (*E. coli*).

There are contending conventions regarding prepositions. *Chicago* recommends lowercasing prepositions regardless of length, some publishers use a "four-letter rule," and others use a "five-letter rule":

| *Chicago style* *(lowercase all prepositions)* | *Four-letter rule* *(uppercase prepositions of four letters or longer)* | *Five-letter rule* *(uppercase prepositions of five letters or longer)* |
|---|---|---|
| Running for Cover | Running for Cover | Running for Cover |
| Life with Father | Life With Father | Life with Father |
| Driving through Maine | Driving Through Maine | Driving Through Maine |

Whichever preposition rule you adopt, you need to remember that many common prepositions may function as nouns, adjectives, or adverbs, and when they do, they should be capitalized in a title.

---

10. For correlative conjunctions, the leading element is capitalized, and the trailing element is lowercased: Mayor Urges Either Fare Hikes or Service Cuts; Riders Demand Both Fare Cuts and Better Service; Riders Demand Not Only Fare Cuts but Better Service.

*Lowercase the prepositions:* Poverty in America in the 1960s

*Uppercase the nouns:* The Ins and Outs of Office Etiquette

*Uppercase the adjectives:* The In and Out Trends This Year

*Uppercase the adverbs:* Taking In the Sights, Taking Over the City

Take in, take over—as this last example shows, an erstwhile preposition that is an inseparable part of the verb, forming an idiomatic expression called a *phrasal verb,* is capitalized in a title. Other examples:

Cat Beats Up Dog in Domestic Altercation

Nonagenarian Looks Up Girlfriend from High School

*WIT* also recommends capitalizing compound prepositions (apart from, just before, out of, owing to) in titles.

A common error in applying headline-style capitalization is the failure to capitalize the verb *is*—the word is so tiny that editors sometimes overlook it! Another pesky little word is *as,* which may function as a preposition, adverb, subordinate conjunction, or pronoun. *Chicago* advises always lowercasing *as* in a title. Or you can parse the title:

*Lowercase the preposition:* Working as an Editor

*Uppercase the adverb:* Twice As Good

*Uppercase the conjunction:* Do As the Pros Do

*Uppercase the pronoun:* Tears Such As Angels Weep

The style manuals differ in their approach to hyphenated words in a title. *Chicago* calls for capping all elements of a hyphenated term except for the articles, coordinating conjunctions, prepositions, and elements attached to a prefix (unless the element is a proper noun or adjective):

Over-the-Counter Remedies

An Up-and-Down Ride for Investors

Anti-intellectualism in Post-Restoration Drama

Twenty-First-Century Architecture

E-commerce and Texting among Non-English-Speaking Students

*WIT* takes a different approach. When a spelled-out number is hyphenated, all terms after the first are lowercased. In a permanent compound—that is, a compound term that would be hyphenated even if not serving as a unit modifier—only the first term is capitalized.

Twenty-five Years of History

Miracle on Forty-second Street

My Son-in-law Is from Mars

Success: The So-called Bitch Goddess

As noted in chapter 4 (see "Controversial Techniques"), slashed constructions pose various semantic problems. When they appear in titles, however, the slash does not interfere with the regular rules for capitalization:

> Capitalization Quandaries for the Modern Writer/Editor
>
> Peace and/or Justice
>
> Slash/Slant/Virgule: Boon or Bane

When slashed constructions are printed in display type, a thin space may be inserted before and after the slash for appearance's sake.

## SENTENCE STYLE

In sentence style, one capitalizes the first word of the title, the first word of a subtitle, and those words that would be capitalized in regular text (i.e., proper nouns, proper adjectives, and the pronoun *I*). The following examples illustrate the treatment of hyphenated and slashed words:

> Self-esteem in the American workplace
>
> The post–World War II economic miracle
>
> Slash/slant/virgule: Boon or bane?

*Typographical treatment.* Within running text, the titles of books, newspapers, magazines, journals, movies, operas, recorded albums, works of art, and cartoon strips are set in italics. For newspapers and periodicals, lowercase "the," using roman type, even when it appears in the actual masthead, unless the word is integral to the title (the *New York Times; The Nation*). Do not capitalize or italicize "magazine" unless this word is part of the official title of a periodical publication (*Time* magazine; the *New York Times Magazine*). The titles of short literary works (poems, essays, short stories, and magazine and journal articles) and short musical works (songs) are set in roman type and placed in quotation marks.

Capitalize but do not italicize the title of a website, even if it is analogous to a print publication, unless it is the online version of a printed work (hence: Wikipedia, *Encyclopaedia Britannica Online*). But sometimes an editor following these guidelines cannot determine whether a website has—or once had—a print existence. "When in doubt," *Chicago* advises, "treat the source as if there is no printed counterpart" by omitting italics (8.191). Also, do not capitalize the URL; lowercase any initial "the" in running text (http://www.editorium.com/, the Editorium). Capitalize named sections and pages of websites and use quotation marks ("Editorium Update Newsletter"). Italicize titles of blogs (*CMOS Shop Talk*), by analogy with print periodicals, and use quotation marks for titles of individual blog posts ("Chicago Style Workout 21: Word Usage, Part 4"), by analogy with articles therein.

Applying these guidelines to the treatment of website names and other web content in a given document, *Chicago* adds, requires the exercise of editorial judgment. For example, if readers cannot distinguish between a website title and the identical title of its print analogue (even though the online and print editions can differ), the editor may need to specify the version in the running text (the online *Merriam-Webster's Collegiate Dictionary*). Or the editor and readers may be distracted by seeming inconsistencies in a passage containing a mix of differently styled web and print titles, in which case standardizing their treatment might be desirable.[11]

Some newspapers and magazines follow AP style by setting all print titles in roman type and enclosing them within quotation marks; names of websites and computer applications are capitalized without quotations (Facebook, Foursquare).

## NAMES OF PLANTS AND ANIMALS

The capitalization of the common names of plants and animals is somewhat anarchic, and copyeditors should always consult a dictionary. Copyeditors who routinely work on scientific papers, field guides, and similar projects will want to acquire specialized reference books.

By convention, the scientific (Latin) names of plants and animals are always italicized, and the genus is capitalized, while the species and subspecies are lowercased, even in title-style headings and titles: *Escherichia coli; Ursus americanus; Heteromeles arbutifolia macrocarpa*. On second reference, the genus name is usually abbreviated, with only its first letter given: *E. coli; U. americanus; H. arbutifolia*. Specific common (English) names are sometimes capitalized (Whooping Crane, Bald Eagle), whereas types are lowercased (cranes, eagles).

The abbreviations *sp.* (species; plural, *spp.*), *ssp.* (subspecies), *var.* (variety), and *cv.* (cultivar) are set in roman type: *Ceanothus* sp.; *Acer negundo* ssp. *californicum; Delphinium decorum* var. *patens; Pelargonium peltatum* cv. Claret Crousse. Note that variety names are lowercased and italicized, while cultivar names are capitalized and set in roman type. In some editorial styles, cultivar names are placed in single quotation marks and the abbreviation *cv.* is not used: *Pelargonium peltatum* 'Claret Crousse.' Hybrids are indicated by a multiplication sign: *Salvia* × *superba*.[12]

Domain, phylum, class, order, and family names are capitalized and set in roman type: Hominidae, Mammalia.

---

11. In this book, references to the online editions of *Merriam-Webster's Collegiate Dictionary* and *American Heritage Dictionary of the English Language* are italicized; when it is necessary to differentiate them from the identically titled print editions, they are further identified in the text as the online versions. *Merriam-Webster Unabridged,* the retitled online successor to *Webster's Third New International Dictionary of the English Language, Unabridged,* is likewise italicized.

12. A space always precedes the ×, but whether or not a space belongs after the × depends on how the hybrid name was derived (see *CSE*).

# CHAPTER 7

# ¶ Numbers and Numerals

A publication's editorial style for the treatment of numbers includes guidelines for

> when to spell out a quantity and when to use a numeral
> how to treat common numerical expressions (e.g., cardinals and ordinals,
> fractions, percentages, money, time, addresses, and phone numbers)
> how to express units of measurement
> how to use roman numerals
> how to treat inclusive numerical ranges
> how to style mathematical expressions

The two broad sets of conventions for the treatment of numbers are called *technical* (or *scientific*) style and *nontechnical* (or *humanistic*) style. Technical style is used in technical and scientific writing, of course, but also in other types of documents that typically have many numbers and quantities in them, including statistical and financial material, cookbooks, and do-it-yourself carpentry books. Nontechnical style, in contrast, is often used for pieces that have relatively few numbers in them.

## WORDS OR NUMERALS?

In both technical and nontechnical documents, one rule is absolute: a sentence must never begin with a numeral. Thus a copyeditor must either spell out the numeral or reword the sentence.

> *Original:* 10,500 pages of depositions were submitted by the plaintiff.
>
> *Revision:* Ten thousand five hundred pages of depositions were submitted by the plaintiff.
>
> *Or:* Some 10,500 pages of depositions were submitted by the plaintiff.
>
> *Or:* The plaintiff submitted 10,500 pages of depositions.

---

> *Original:* 1998 was a disappointing year for wheat exporters.
>
> *Revision:* The year 1998 was a disappointing one for wheat exporters.
>
> *Or:* Nineteen ninety-eight was a disappointing year for wheat exporters.
>
> > [The *AP Stylebook* does permit "1976 was a very good year," but no other manuals endorse this practice.]

Beyond this restriction, technical and scientific publishers—and most newspapers and magazines—prefer numerals to spelled-out numbers because numerals are easier to read and locate (they stand out from the sea of surrounding words) and because they take up less space than spelled-out numbers.[1] Most style manuals and in-house guides for technical texts prescribe spelling out only whole numbers less than ten that do not represent precisely measured quantities. Thus, in "We performed the five experiments within a 6-week period," a numeral appears before the unit of measurement "weeks," but a spelled-out word is used for the number of experiments, which is deemed to be a matter of counting rather than the specification of a precisely measured quantity. *CSE* calls for numerals for anything that can be counted or measured; thus "We performed the 5 experiments within a 6-week period."[2] *APA* specifies that numerals be used for quantities that "denote a specific place in a numbered series" (e.g., grade 8, trial 3) and for "each number in a list of four or more numbers" (e.g., "Participants were allowed to make 1, 2, 3, or 4 choices"). And AP style spells out one through nine but stipulates numerals for ten and above and for all units of measure, ages, and other conventional numerical expressions listed in the *AP Stylebook*.

In contrast, the convention for nontechnical texts outside the sphere of journalism is to spell out whole numbers less than 101—except for percentages, years and dates, page numbers, and chapter numbers—and to spell out large numbers that can be expressed in two words (e.g., thirty-three thousand, five million). To aid readers, numerals are normally used for large numbers requiring more than two words, but such numbers may also be spelled out, at an editor's discretion, for the sake of consistency with similar numbers in the surrounding text. In that case, commas are avoided in the spelled-out number (six hundred seventy-two, one hundred three thousand), and *Chicago* recommends omitting "and" (✗ six hundred *and* seventy-two, ✗ one hundred *and* three thousand).

| *Scientific or technical text* | *Humanistic or nontechnical text* |
| --- | --- |
| Students were tested at ages 5, 7, and 9. | Students were tested at ages five, seven, and nine. |
| The satellite traveled 23 million miles. | The satellite traveled twenty-three million miles. |
| The average speed of the test vehicles was 25 mph. | The average speed of the test vehicles was twenty-five miles per hour. |
| Participants' guesses ranged from 60 to 672 jellybeans. | Participants' guesses ranged from sixty to six hundred seventy-two jellybeans. |

1. In some banking and legal documents, sums of money are expressed by a numeral followed by the spelled-out form: The underwriting fee will be $2,500,000 (two and a half million dollars). According to Bryan Garner, this convention arose as a safeguard against fraudulent alterations in such documents (*Legal Writing in Plain English,* p. 115).

2. For ordinal numbers, *CSE* recommends spelling out "first" through "ninth."

In spelled-out numbers, hyphens are used only to join the parts of a two-digit number: forty-five, forty-five thousand, forty-five million, nineteen forty-five, twenty forty-five.

In both technical and nontechnical documents, all numerical values of the same class or type are treated similarly in the text.

> *Technical document:* We ran 5 trials in January, 9 in February, and 12 in March. [Since numerals are used for all two-digit numbers in a technical document, the twelve trials in March must be expressed as a numeral. Because the five trials in January and the nine in February are numerical values of the same class—number of trials run—these must also be expressed as numerals, even though they are less than ten.]

> *Nontechnical document:* Next year 325 local officials will attend the national meeting. California is expected to send the largest contingent, 28 delegates; Rhode Island, the smallest, 2 delegates. The meeting will last two days and will include six hours of workshops.
> [The 325 in "325 local officials" has to be a numeral, so numerals must be used for all numbers that refer to the officials (28 delegates, 2 delegates). But the number of days and the number of hours of workshops are not in the same category as officials and delegates, and these small numbers are spelled out.]

In nontechnical documents one tries to avoid having two unrelated numerals in a row. (Many technical documents also observe this convention in order to prevent misreading.) A copyeditor can add a word between the two numerals, spell out one of the numerals, or reword the sentence. Sometimes, syntax permitting (as in the first example below), a simple comma can separate the numbers.

> *Original:* In 1968 125,000 marchers protested the decision.

> *Revision:* In 1968, 125,000 marchers protested the decision.

> *Or:* In 1968 about 125,000 marchers protested the decision.

> [*About, approximately,* and *some* are the usual choices here. The context may also permit *an estimated, more than,* or *less than.*]

---

> *Original:* We ordered 120 12 V batteries.

> *Revision:* We ordered 120 twelve-volt batteries.

> [The decision to spell out "12" precludes the use of the abbreviation for *volt. Chicago*'s convention is this: always use a numeral before an abbreviated unit of measurement and preserve the space between these elements even when they are used adjectivally.]

---

> *Original:* The 2002 162-game schedule will be announced next week.

> *Revision:* The 162-game schedule for 2002 will be announced next week.

*But:* Her scores on the four tests were 85, 88, 84, and 93.

[Here the back-to-back numerals are fine because they are of the same class—test scores.]

*But:* While we . . . are lost in the quagmires of ostentatious parlor game parallelism (Is Iraq Vietnam or the intifada? Is 2004 1920 all over again?), many Americans have decided that it's time to persevere and win.

[In this exception—from David Brooks, "Looking through Keyholes," *New York Times,* April 27, 2004—the conjunction of years underscores the "parlor game parallelism."]

You may also encounter some nontechnical authors who follow *WIT* in spelling out all numerals other than years when they appear in dialogue or any other transcription of speech. *WIT* is the only style manual that makes this recommendation, but some authors feel strongly about it, arguing that speakers speak in words, not numerals. Although the logic of this argument is shaky—speakers' utterances may be transcribed in various ways—copyeditors are usually expected to honor the author's preference in the matter.

## PUNCTUATION OF NUMERALS

All style manuals recommend placing a comma to set off the last three digits of a five-digit numeral; some manuals also recommend placing a comma in four-digit numerals, except those that represent addresses, page numbers, test scores, and years (1600 Pennsylvania Avenue, page 1021, 1550 on the SATs, the year 2000, *but* 20,000 B.C.E.). The five-digit convention tends to prevail in technical documents, the four-digit convention in nontechnical documents.

If you work with international authors, you should be aware of two other conventions for punctuating long numerals. In an older British style, a period was used in lieu of a comma in long numerals, and a raised dot in lieu of a decimal point. In what is called Continental style, a space is used in long numerals, and a comma is used to indicate decimals (thus, for example, Europeans use a comma, not a decimal point, in €15,25). Compare:

| *Style* | *Long numerals* | *Decimal numerals* |
|---------|-----------------|--------------------|
| American | 12,345,678 | 3.1416 |
| British (old style) | 12.345.678 | 3·1416[3] |
| Continental | 12 345 678 | 3,1416 |

All the style manuals recommend placing a zero before a decimal expression that is less than one (e.g., 0.2) unless the numeral is of a category whose value cannot exceed

---

3. Editors still sometimes encounter these conventions, but the *New Oxford Style Manual* and *Butcher's* now endorse the American conventions in nontechnical text and recommend a nonbreaking thin space between groups of numerals in technical text.

one (e.g., probabilities, correlations, levels of statistical significance). The leading zero offers a friendly alert that the subsequent numeral is less than one (because readers may easily overlook a decimal point, especially in smaller type sizes). When such a decimal appears before a spelled-out unit of measurement, the unit is stated in the plural, as it would be pronounced:

0.25 inches
0.75 square feet
0.2 kilometers
0.5 liters

The number of digits expressed after the decimal point depends on the context. In nontechnical work, rounding off to one or two decimal places is usually sufficient. In technical work, however, some values are conventionally expressed to three, four, or more decimal places, and copyeditors working on technical documents should not delete any digits from these lengthy decimals. When an author has been inconsistent in expressing values of the same class or type, the copyeditor should query the internal discrepancy ("Two decimal places or three for test values? Revise for consistency").

## CARDINALS AND ORDINALS

*Cardinal numbers* are used for counting and specifying quantities (one, two, three); they answer the question "How many?" *Ordinal numbers* are used for designating position in an ordered sequence (first, second, third). A simple mnemonic for remembering this distinction: cardinal = playing card; ordinal = order. The general rules for using either words or numerals for cardinal numbers apply to ordinals as well: the forty-fifth parallel, the two hundredth anniversary, the 103rd Regiment. When ordinals are expressed in numerals, the endings *st, nd, rd,* and *th* are affixed as adscripts, not as superscripts, despite the common default setting of some word processors: 1st, 2nd, 3rd, 4th, *n*th (italic *n*), *not* 1$^{st}$, 2$^{nd}$, 3$^{rd}$, 4$^{th}$, *n*$^{th}$. The convention of omitting the *n* and the *r* in *nd* and *rd* (2d, 3d), common in legal writing, is no longer recommended in Chicago style.

## FRACTIONS

*Nontechnical text.* In nontechnical text, fractions are treated like other numbers: those that can be spelled out with one-word or two-word numerators and denominators are spelled out. But *Chicago, WIT,* and *APA* each have slightly different recommendations for the hyphenation of spelled-out fractions; these require careful study. If house style does not mandate strict adherence to one of these manuals, you might want to adopt the following rules:

- Place a hyphen between the numerator and denominator of a spelled-out fraction when neither of these numbers is itself hyphenated: one-third, two-fifths, fifteen-sixteenths, eleven-hundredths, three and three-quarters, twenty-five and one-half.
- Omit the hyphen between the numerator and denominator when either of these itself contains a hyphen: twenty-five hundredths, five sixty-fourths.
- Apply these two rules to all fractions, whether they function as nouns, adjectives, or adverbs:

  *Noun:* Two-thirds of the children answered the question.
  *Adjective:* A two-thirds majority is required.
  *Adverb:* The work was two-thirds completed.

Mixed numbers (i.e., a whole number followed by a fraction) may be spelled out (if short) or set as numerals:

The final report was five and one-half inches thick.

*Or:* The final report was $5\frac{1}{2}$ inches thick.

Converting a mixed fraction into a decimal expression (5.5 inches thick) produces neater copy but may imply a finer degree of precision than desired.

Common fractions are usually typeset as a single character (e.g., $\frac{1}{2}, \frac{1}{3}, \frac{1}{4}, \frac{3}{4}$); these are called *case fractions,* or *piece fractions.* Unusual fractions may be set as *built-up fractions* (e.g., 11/16, 27/64); a space (not a hyphen) is used to separate a built-up fraction from a whole number: 5 9/32 inches.

*Technical text.*  Fractions rarely appear in technical text; usually the decimal form is preferred. When fractions are used, the fraction is spelled out if it is not a precisely measured quantity.

In one-third of the trials, the results were not statistically significant.

Two-thirds of the subjects received a placebo.

*But:* The test cards were $2\frac{1}{2}$-by-$4\frac{1}{4}$ inches.

*Or:* The test cards were $2\frac{1}{2}$-by-$4\frac{1}{4}$ in.


## PERCENTAGES, PERCENTAGE POINTS, BASIS POINTS, PERCENTILES, AND PORTIONS

To express percentages, a numeral and the percentage sign are used in technical documents; in nontechnical text, the convention is to use a numeral and the word *percent.*

*Technical:* Over the 6-month period, the cost of employee benefits declined by $50 per employee, which reduced overhead by 2.5%.

*Nontechnical:* Over the six-month period, the cost of employee benefits declined by fifty dollars per employee, which reduced overhead by 2.5 percent.

Some economic indicators expressed in percentages are, by convention, rounded to whole numbers; others are given to one or two decimal places. Follow the rounding rules and use the number of decimal places appropriate for the context and audience; aim for consistency in percentages of the same class.

Percentage ranges should likewise be treated consistently within a document:

*Technical:* 20% to 30%  *or*  20%–30%  *or*  20–30%

*Nontechnical:* 20 percent to 30 percent  *or*  20 to 30 percent  *or*  20–30 percent

Copyeditors who work with documents that contain percentages should remember the following:

- When a quantity doubles, that is an increase of 100 percent (*not* 200 percent); when a quantity triples, that is an increase of 200 percent.
- When a quantity decreases by half, that is a drop of 50 percent.
- A quantity can increase by more than 100 percent, but it cannot decrease by more than 100 percent (because once the quantity has decreased by 100 percent, it is reduced to zero).

Percentage points are also expressed in numerals.

*Technical:* In one 18-month period (mid-1979 to late 1980), the prime rate rose by 9 percentage points, from 11.5% to 20.5%.

*Nontechnical:* In the past month, the governor's popularity rating dropped by 12 percentage points, from 57 to 45 percent.

As these examples illustrate, percentage points are used to quantify the change between two percentages by subtracting the smaller percentage from the larger (e.g., 20.5 − 11.5 = 9). But to say that the prime rate increased by 9 percentage points is *not* the same as saying it increased by 9 percent: had the prime rate increased by 9 percent, the higher rate would have been only 12.5% (11.5 + [9% × 11.5] = 12.535).

Basis points, which are used in the banking and financial industries, are also expressed in numerals. A basis point is one-hundredth of a percentage point. When interest rates rise by half a percentage point (e.g., from 5.50 percent to 6.00 percent), that is an increase of 50 basis points, and when rates rise by a quarter of a percentage point (e.g., from 6.00 percent to 6.25 percent), that is an increase of 25 basis points.

Percentiles are expressed in numerals as well:

Students in the Eden district scored in the 75th percentile on the statewide reading test.

Note that percentiles are measured "from the top": to score in the 99th percentile is to score better than 99 percent of all the people who were tested. Thus no one is ever in the 100th percentile (it is impossible to score better than 100 percent of test takers), and those in the 10th percentile down through the 1st percentile are those who performed the worst.

Finally, remember that *portion* simply means "part." Hence, "Henry contributes a greater portion of his salary than of his investment income to charity" does not necessarily mean that Henry contributes more salary dollars than investment income dollars to charity, because his salary may be far lower than his investment income.

## MONEY

*Monetary units.*  Monetary units are lowercased: dollar, franc, mark, peso, euro. Proper adjectives that modify these units are, of course, uppercased: the Canadian dollar, the Turkish lira, the Malaysian ringgit.

Some financial publications use the three-letter codes of the International Standards Organization (ISO) to refer to those units of currency that are heavily traded on international markets. These codes are uppercased:

> The CAD is expected to decline against the USD as the JPY strengthens this winter.
> [CAD = Canadian dollar; USD = US dollar; JPY = Japanese yen.][4]

*Amounts of money.*  In technical or scientific text, sums of money are expressed in numerals, accompanied by the symbol for the unit of currency.

> 85¢ (*or* $0.85)
> $25,000
> $33 million
> $1.5 billion to $1.8 billion

ISO style uses the form *amount [space] three-letter code:*

> 500 CAD

Commonly used symbols and abbreviations for overseas currencies include these:

| | |
|---|---|
| British pound | £100 |
| Canadian dollar | Can$100 *or* C$100 |
| euro | €100 |
| Japanese yen | ¥100 |

Most style manuals show no space between a foreign currency symbol and the numeral that follows (£100, €100, ¥100) but a wordspace or thin space after an abbreviation for a foreign currency (Fr 100, R 100).

---

4. Other codes in this system include AUD (Australian dollar), CHF (Swiss franc), DKK (Danish krone), EUR (euro), GBP (British pound), HKD (Hong Kong dollar), MXN (Mexican new peso), NZD (New Zealand dollar), RUB (Russian ruble), and SGD (Singapore dollar). There is no ISO currency code for Bitcoin, although XBT is commonly used; the alternative abbreviation, BTC, violates ISO standards because "BT" is the country code for Bhutan. See, e.g., the list at Countries-ofthe-World.com (https://www.countries-ofthe-world.com/world-currencies.html).

For contemporary overseas amounts, provide a rough US dollar equivalent, especially if readers are unlikely to be familiar with the currency or the conversion formula. (More precision, along with the applicable exchange rate, is needed in financial copy.) For some older amounts, a contemporary cost equivalent may assist general readers.

The ticket cost ¥1000 (roughly $9).

When Fred Divita began as a laborer on the Golden Gate Bridge in 1934, he earned ninety cents an hour (about sixteen dollars an hour in 2017).

Try to avoid awkwardly worded equivalents by rewording:

*Awkward:* a ¥1000 (roughly $9) ticket

*Better:* a ¥1000 ticket (roughly $9) *or* a ticket costing ¥1000 (roughly $9)

In nontechnical text, the occasional mention of a sum of money that can be expressed in one or two words is spelled out:

A subscription to the local newspaper costs less than thirty-five cents a day.

The manufacturer is requesting a five-dollar increase in the wholesale price per unit.

The rental fee is thirteen hundred dollars a month.

However, when round sums of money cluster in a sentence or paragraph, numerals are used:

The initiation fee has tripled, from $200 to $600, and monthly dues have doubled, from $40 to $80.

Similarly, large sums of money are expressed in numerals:

Last year the median price of a home in San Francisco exceeded $900,000.

For arranging the $8 billion buyout, the brokerage firms earned $80 million in fees.

The surplus for this fiscal year is estimated at $53 billion to $71 billion.

As the last example shows, clarity requires that ranges not be condensed unless space is at an absolute premium. In running text, "$53 billion to $71 billion" is preferable to "$53 to $71 billion" or "$53–71 billion."

## TIME

*Noon and midnight.* A persistent point of confusion—not only among copyeditors but also in the world at large—concerns the relationship between noon, midnight, 12 A.M., and 12 P.M. Many of us were taught

12:00 P.M. [noon]        12:00 A.M. [midnight]

But one also sees

　　　　12:00 M. [noon]　　　　12:00 P.M. [midnight]

or even

　　　　12:00 N [noon]　　　　12:00 M [midnight]

The confusion can, in part, be attributed to etymology. Since A.M. and P.M. stand for *ante meridiem* (literally, "before midday") and *post meridiem* ("after midday"), neither abbreviation serves to express the exact moment of noon or midnight.

To avoid misunderstanding, the airlines, railroads, and other time-sensitive organizations never use the precise hour of 12:00 in their schedules: planes and trains arrive at 11:59 A.M. or 12:01 P.M. The solution for copyeditors is to spell out "noon" and "midnight":

The meeting was scheduled to begin at noon, but it did not start until 12:25 p.m.[5]

Between 10 p.m. and midnight, four emergency calls were received.

Revise redundant expressions—"2 A.M. in the morning" or "11 P.M. at night." House style dictates the form of the abbreviation (e.g., A.M., AM, a.m., AM, or a.m.).

When times of day are spelled out, hyphenate only those cardinals that are ordinarily hyphenated: one fifteen, two thirty, three forty-five, four fifty-five.

*Time zones.* Time zones are styled as follows:

The speech will air at 9:15 p.m. EST (6:15 p.m. PST).

The plane landed in Paris at 6 p.m. (noon EST).

The abbreviations for time zones within the continental United States are

| EST, EDT | eastern standard time, eastern daylight time |
| CST, CDT | central standard time, central daylight time |
| MST, MDT | mountain standard time, mountain daylight time |
| PST, PDT | Pacific standard time, Pacific daylight time |

There are no abbreviations for Alaska standard or daylight time (one hour earlier than Pacific time) nor for Hawaii standard time (two hours earlier than PST; three hours earlier than PDT).[6]

The other common time-zone abbreviation is GMT (Greenwich mean time), the time at the Royal Observatory in Greenwich, England, located at 0° longitude. Local

---

5. *Or* twelve twenty-five. Other spelled-out forms: ten *or* ten o'clock *or* ten in the morning; two in the afternoon, six in the evening, nine at night; five after ten, ten fifteen, ten thirty, ten forty-five.

6. If you are copyediting materials that mention times in different parts of the country or the world, be sure to account for the vagaries of daylight savings time (DST), which is not uniformly observed. Hawaii, for example, does not switch to daylight time in the spring.

times may be expressed in relation to GMT; for example, GMT+8 or GMT–2. Astronomers and other physical scientists often use the notation UTC (coordinated universal time) in lieu of GMT.

*Dates.* In running text, a full date is usually written in the following form: June 1, 1997. But some publishers prefer or will accept what is called the European convention: 1 June 1997. In both styles the day of the month is expressed as a cardinal number, not an ordinal: on June 1, on 1 June. The historic date September 11, 2001, is usually styled, in both noun and adjectival uses, as September 11 or 9/11 ("Nine-eleven" to begin a sentence), never as September 11th.

In tables, footnotes, and other places in which space is at a premium, dates may be expressed wholly in numerals: 6/1/97 *or* 06/01/97. If you are working with international authors, you may encounter dates styled according to the European convention, in which 1 June 1997 is shortened to 1/6/97, 01/06/97, or 1.vi.97. When in doubt, you should ask the author which convention applies, although scanning the manuscript will usually supply the answer: if you spot numerals between 1 and 31 in the first position and only the numerals 1 through 12 appear in the second position, then the author has used the European system.

Depending on the type of materials you copyedit, you may also come across the following notations:

| | |
|---|---|
| FY 98–99 *or* FY 98/99 | *FY* stands for "fiscal year" and is used when an organization's fiscal year spans two calendar years (i.e., July 1, 1998, through June 30, 1999). Typically, only the final two digits of the year are used in this construction: FY 00–01, FY 01/02. |
| AY 1998–99 | *AY* stands for "academic year" and is used by educational institutions. Typically, four digits are used for the first year in the range, and two digits or four digits for the last: AY 1999–2000; AY 2001–2002 *or* AY 2001–02. |
| 1997-06-01 | A ten-character format (eight numerals, two hyphens) is used in computer documents that follow ISO conventions. The sequence is year-month-day. |
| dd-mm-yy | An eight-character format (six numerals, two hyphens) is used in some software programs. The example here signals that dates are expressed as day-month-year, with two characters allotted to each factor (01-06-97). Alternatively, dates can be formatted mm-dd-yy or yy-mm-dd. |

*Decades, centuries, and spans.* In styling references to decades, editors must decide whether to spell out the full year date (or its clipped form) or to use numerals, how to append the plural *s* in numerical representations, and whether to supply an initial apostrophe to indicate omitted numerals:

| | | |
|---|---|---|
| the nineteen nineties | the 1990s | the 90s |
| the nineties | the 1990's | the '90s |

All of these (and some other) forms are recognized in various style manuals, but the trend is to favor numerals, especially in the condensed style of modern journalism, and to omit apostrophes except when numerals are elided. *WIT* (1974) illustrates an older style still favored by some authors and publishers, whereas *Chicago* (2017) recommends the most streamlined forms:

| | |
|---|---|
| *Chicago* | the nineteen nineties *or* the nineties (if clear in context)<br>the 1990s *or* the '90s* |
| *AP* | the 1990s *or* the '90s* |
| *Gregg* | the nineteen-nineties *or* the nineties<br>the 1990s *or* the '90s* |
| *WIT* | the nineties<br>the 1990's |

*Note that an apostrophe, not a left single quotation mark, precedes the numeral.

The first decade of the twenty-first century presents a special challenge. Should this decade be written as "the 00s"? "the '00s"? "the aughts"? "the ohs"? "the zeros"? "the zips"? "the naughties"? An undated reply to a query on *Chicago*'s online "Style Q&A" doesn't completely resolve this question but suggests that "in writing, 'the '00s' perhaps looks OK" even if the form defies euphonious pronunciation; alternatively, an editor may use the numerical date range 2000–2009 if "the first decade of the twenty-first century" seems overlong. The *New York Times* favors "the '00s."

Another brainteaser involves the expression of ranges with the adjective *mid,* which is both a combining form and a freestanding word. *Chicago*'s "Style Q&A" sanctions the following, listed in order of preference:

mid- to late 1950s
> [*Mid* is used as a prefix; the suspended expression means "mid-1950s to late 1950s."]

mid to late 1950s
> [*Mid* is used as a synonym for "middle"; the expression means "middle to late 1950s."]

mid-to-late 1950s
> [*Mid-to-late* is used as a unit modifier; this treatment prevents a possible misreading of the stray hyphen in the first example.]

Spans across centuries are styled thus:

> from the mid-nineteenth to the early twentieth century
>
> in the late nineteenth and early twentieth centuries
> [Note the plural "centuries."]

*Dates as attributive adjectives.* Some writers and copyeditors have been taught never to use a date or year as an attributive adjective; for example, they would write not "the November 4 election" or "the 2002 election" but instead "the election on November 4" or "the election of 2002." The taboo may stem from an overly broad interpretation of a subtle point made by Jacques Barzun: the phrase "her 1972 fall from a horse" implies that she had a series of falls, just as "the 1920 marriage of Countess Haha" suggests repeated marriages at suitable intervals.[7] Barzun traces the "vulgar practice" to a "legitimate one" used by scientific journals (e.g., In his 1905 paper on relativity, Einstein . . .) but still pleads for the "more elegant" use of "of" (In his paper of 1905, Einstein . . .). It would seem, then, that one is free to use a date or year as an attributive adjective as long as the event *is* one of a repeated series (the 2002 election), the adjective is not overly long or awkward, and the document does not require Barzunesque elegance.


## STREET NUMBERS AND PHONE NUMBERS

*Numbered street names.* In running text, numbered street names are spelled out or expressed as numerals according to the publication's general rule for numbers.

> *Technical style:* We interviewed 15 men aged 18 to 35 who were waiting for the bus at 12th Street.

> *Nontechnical style:* The center of the neighborhood's business district is Twelfth Street. The repair shop is on Telegraph Avenue between Fifty-First and Fifty-Second Streets.
> [The capitalization of the second part of the spelled-out ordinal numbers and the plural "Streets" here are both features of Chicago style.]

In lists or directories of addresses, numerals are usually used, although numbered street names may be spelled out:

| | | |
|---|---|---|
| 123 First Street | *or* | 123 1st Street |
| 45 Fortieth Street | *or* | 45 40th Street |
| 1 Sixty-Eighth Street | *or* | 1 68th Street |

*Phone numbers.* There are several conventions for expressing US phone numbers. The trunk prefix 1, which is not always required to "dial" a number, is usually omitted; the area code, which may be optional for local calls, is sometimes placed in parentheses:

---

7. "Vulgar, Vulgarity, Vulgarisms," in *A Word or Two Before You Go . . .* (Middletown, Conn.: Wesleyan University Press, 1986), p. 66.

212-555-0123      (212) 555-0123      212 555 0123

Another convention uses periods between the groupings of numerals (e.g., 212.555.0123), but *Chicago* (9.57) now discourages this form.

Phone numbers may be preceded or followed by an indication of the type of transmission available:

Fax 212-555-0134      212-555-0123 (phone)

As demonstrated above, when a made-up phone number is needed as an example, the convention is to use the three digits once reserved for information (555) followed by four digits between 0100 and 0199.

For phone numbers that are expressed in words, the text should include the numerical equivalent as a courtesy to readers who have telephones on which the letters are less legible than the numerals:

Call 555-NEWS (555-6397)

For dialogue, use numerals or write out the number, depending on house style: "Please call 911" or "Please call nine-one-one."

For toll-free phone numbers, the long-distance access code 1 is usually included (because all callers must dial the 1):

1-800-123-4567      1 888 123 4567      1.877.123.4567

If the publication is to be distributed outside the United States, a non-toll-free number should be added, because 1-800, 1-888, and 1-877 numbers are not accessible outside the country.

For international phone numbers in publications addressed to US readers, the listing may include the international access code (e.g., 011 for international calls from the US or Canada), the one- through three-digit country code, the one- through four-digit city code, and the local phone number. Spaces rather than hyphens are typically used between numerical groupings:

(011) 39 42 123 4567      011 39 42 123 4567

Overseas local phone numbers may contain six, seven, or eight digits, and different countries and localities have developed different conventions for printing local phone numbers:

123 456      1234 567      1234 5678      12 34 56 78      12345678

For documents that will be circulated outside the United States, the phone number should begin with a +, which is the placeholder for the applicable international-access prefix, and the country code (with no space between them), then the city code and local phone number: +39 42 123 4567.

Calling instructions may also make mention of the two nonalphanumeric keys on the phone pad: the pound sign (#) and the star (*).

In all cases, the copyeditor should scrutinize all instances of 1 (one) and I (capital *i*) and 0 (zero) and O (capital *o*).

## UNITS OF MEASUREMENT

*Technical text.* In technical text, a quantity is expressed as a numeral, and the unit of measurement may be spelled out or abbreviated. Depending on conventions in the author's field and the units in which the measurements were taken, quantities may be expressed in US units, in metric or SI units,[8] or in both when judged necessary for the intended audience. If a field team took measurements in feet, for example, the text would read:

> The sample was taken 190 feet north of Starkweather Pond.
>
> *Or:* The sample was taken 190 ft (58 m) north of Starkweather Pond.

But if the surveyors took the measurements in meters, the text would read:

> The sample was taken 58 meters north of Starkweather Pond.
>
> *Or:* The sample was taken 58 m (190 ft) north of Starkweather Pond.

When metric equivalents are given, the copyeditor may be asked to spot-check the equivalents; table 9 provides rough conversion factors for this purpose.

*Scientific notation.* Scientific notation allows writers to express very small and very large numbers in a succinct format. The system is based on the powers of ten:

$$10^1 = 10 \qquad 10^{-1} = 0.1$$
$$10^2 = 100 \qquad 10^{-2} = 0.01$$
$$10^3 = 1,000 \qquad 10^{-3} = 0.001$$
$$10^4 = 10,000 \qquad 10^{-4} = 0.0001$$

(*Note:* When 10 is raised to a positive power, the number of zeros after the 1 is the same as the power: the long form of $10^8$ has eight zeros after the 1. When 10 is raised to a negative power, the number of digits after the decimal point is the same as the power: the long form of $10^{-8}$ has seven zeros followed by a 1.)

In scientific notation, a large or small quantity is expressed as a numeral between 1 and 10 multiplied by the desired factor of 10.

$$6.25 \times 10^{11} = 6.25 \times 100,000,000,000 = 625,000,000,000$$
$$4.53 \times 10^{-8} = 4.53 \times 0.00000001 = 0.0000000453$$

---

8. SI (Système international d'unités, or International System of Units) is an expanded version of the metric system that is used by scientists. *Chicago, APA,* and *CSE* all discuss SI conventions, and detailed guidelines are elaborated in National Institute of Standards and Technology, *Guide for the Use of the International System of Units (SI),* NIST Special Publication 811, 2008 Edition, http://physics.nist .gov/cuu/pdf/sp811.pdf.

TABLE 9.  Rough Metric Conversion Factors

|  | From US to Metric | From Metric to US |
|---|---|---|
| Length | 1 mile = 1.6 kilometers | 1 kilometer = 0.6 miles |
|  | 1 yard = 0.9 meters | 1 meter = 1.1 yards |
|  | 1 foot = 0.3 meters | 1 meter = 3.2 feet = 39 inches |
|  | 1 inch = 2.5 centimeters | 1 centimeter = 0.4 inches |
| Area | 1 square mile = 2.9 square kilometers | 1 square kilometer = 0.4 square miles |
|  | 1 acre = 0.4 hectares | 1 hectare = 2.5 acres |
| Weight | 1 pound = 0.5 kilograms | 1 kilogram = 2.2 pounds |
| Capacity | 1 liquid quart = 0.9 liters | 1 liter = 1.1 liquid quarts |
|  | 1 gallon = 3.8 liters | 1 liter = 0.3 gallons |
| Temperature | To convert Fahrenheit to Celsius, subtract 32 and multiply by 5/9. | To convert Celsius to Fahrenheit, multiply by 9/5 and add 32. |

*Note:* These rough conversion factors should be used only to spot-check equivalences that appear in a manuscript. They are not accurate enough for calculating conversions.

*Nontechnical text.* In nontechnical text, round quantities under 101 are usually spelled out, as are the units of measurement, although the use of numerals with units of measurement is a common exception:

> He is six feet four inches. *Or:* He is six feet four. *Or:* He is six four. *Or:* He is 6 feet 4 inches.

> We need fifty-five pounds of flour and twenty-two pounds of butter.

*Names of large numbers.* Large numbers are usually expressed in numerals and words; here are the terms for large numbers:

| million | 1,000,000 | [6 zeros] |
|---|---|---|
| billion[9] | 1,000,000,000 | [9 zeros] |
| trillion | 1,000,000,000,000 | [12 zeros] |
| quadrillion | 1,000,000,000,000,000 | [15 zeros] |
| quintillion | 1,000,000,000,000,000,000 | [18 zeros] |

9. In British English 1,000,000,000 was traditionally called a milliard or a thousand million, and a billion was equivalent to a million million (1 followed by twelve zeros). According to the *Oxford English Dictionary,* however, the US value for a billion has been increasingly used in Britain since 1951, though the older sense is still common. In the 2015 edition of *Fowler's,* Jeremy Butterfield reiterates the advice of his predecessor, R. W. Burchfield, that "it is now best to work on the assumption that [a billion] means 'a thousand millions' in all English-speaking areas, unless there is direct contextual evidence to the contrary" (s.v. "billion"). Similarly: "[Trillion] normally means now a million million . . . both in AmE and BrE" (s.v. "trillion").

The numeral that precedes the word should be larger than 1, unless the use of a decimal facilitates comparisons, or consistency within a sentence or paragraph requires the numeral 1:

> The cost overruns to date are $800,000. [*Not* $0.8 million]

> The project was budgeted at $3.5 million, but cost overruns to date are estimated at $0.8 million.

*Prefixes for very small and large numbers.* In expressions of very small or large quantities, prefixes may be used to modify the unit of measurement:

> A millisecond is 0.001 seconds (one-thousandth of a second).
> A microsecond is 0.000001 seconds (one-millionth of a second).
> A nanosecond is 0.000000001 seconds (one-billionth of a second).

> A kilobyte is 1,000 bytes (one thousand bytes).
> A megabyte is 1,000,000 bytes (one million bytes).
> A gigabyte is 1,000,000,000 bytes (one billion bytes).
> A terabyte is 1,000,000,000,000 bytes (one trillion bytes).

## ROMAN NUMERALS

Roman numerals are rarely used in regular text, unless the topic is kings (Louis XIV), popes (Leo V), historic inscriptions (the cornerstone reads MDCCLVI), Super Bowls (Super Bowl XII), or the front matter of a book (page ix). Some journals use roman numerals on their covers for the volume number, but the arabic form is always used in citations and bibliographies.

The system has seven basic units, which may be written in uppercase or lowercase:

| | |
|---|---|
| I (*or* i) = 1 | C (*or* c) = 100 |
| V (*or* v) = 5 | D (*or* d) = 500 |
| X (*or* x) = 10 | M (*or* m) = 1,000 |
| L (*or* l) = 50 | |

These basic units are combined in the following ways:

> When a unit is followed by an identical or a smaller unit, the two values are added.
> When a unit is followed by a larger unit, the smaller unit is subtracted from the larger unit. This rule prevents the appearance of four identical units in succession; thus IV (*not* IIII) = 4.
> The units I, X, C, and M may be repeated in succession; the units V, L, and D are not.
> When a bar appears over a unit, the unit's value is multiplied by one thousand.

Table 10 shows a representative sample of roman numerals.

TABLE 10. Roman Numerals

| | | | | | |
|---|---|---|---|---|---|
| I | 1 | L | 50 | DCCC | 800 |
| II | 2 | LX | 60 | CM | 900 |
| III | 3 | LXX | 70 | M | 1,000 |
| IV | 4 | LXXX | 80 | MCD | 1,400 |
| V | 5 | XC | 90 | MD | 1,500 |
| VI | 6 | C | 100 | MDCCC | 1,800 |
| VII | 7 | CL | 150 | MCM | 1,900 |
| VIII | 8 | CC | 200 | MCMXCIX | 1,999 |
| IX | 9 | CCC | 300 | MM | 2,000 |
| X | 10 | CD | 400 | MMI | 2,001 |
| XX | 20 | D | 500 | $\overline{\text{V}}$ | 5,000 |
| XXX | 30 | DC | 600 | $\overline{\text{X}}$ | 10,000 |
| XL | 40 | DCC | 700 | $\overline{\text{C}}$ | 100,000 |

## INCLUSIVE NUMERALS

There are three conventions for treating inclusive numerals. In most contexts, any of these systems is acceptable as long as it is used consistently in a document. The first style is to simply show all the digits in the second number of the range:

See pages 22–25, 100–102, 105–109, 441–449, 481–503, and 1000–1004.

The second style, which conserves some space, calls for showing only those digits that change in the second number:

See pages 22–5, 100–2, 105–9, 441–9, 481–503, and 1000–4.

The third style, the one recommended by *Chicago,* is a bit more complex, with the repetition and elision of digits in the second number depending on the nature of the first number in the range:

*For a number with two digits, show all digits:* See pages 22–25.
*For a multiple of 100, show all digits:* See pages 100–102, 300–315, and
  1000–1004.
*For a number that exceeds 100 and ends in 01 through 09, show the changed digit
  only:* See pages 105–9 and 1001–9.
*For a number that exceeds 100 and ends in 10 through 99, show at least the
  last two digits and show all digits that change:* See pages 441–49, 481–503,
  1333–35, and 1388–402.

In ranges that consist of roman numerals or of dates labeled B.C. or B.C.E., all digits should be repeated:

pp. xiv–xvii      195–120 B.C.      20,000–15,000 B.C.E.

In technical copy that includes signs, the sign is usually repeated:

10%–12%        $35–$55 million        44°–48°F

If house style calls for no repetition of signs in ranges, the sole sign should be logically placed:

10–12%        $35–55 million        44–48°F

*Chicago,* however, advises repeating the symbol or abbreviation if it is closed up to the numeral but not if it is open: 35%–40% *but* 2 × 5 cm.

Inclusive ranges should not be used when one of the quantities is a negative number.

## MATHEMATICAL SIGNS AND SYMBOLS

If you work extensively with mathematical texts, you will want to consult a specialized style guide (several are mentioned in chapter 3). All copyeditors, however, may come across simple mathematical expressions and should be aware of a few conventions governing them.

Operational signs should be preceded and followed by a wordspace or a thin space, as should signs functioning as quasi verbs:

$2 + 2 = 4$        $8 \times 8 < 100$        $6 \cdot 5 = 30$        $99 \div a = 33$

$h = 5$        $p < .001$        $a \approx b$

But when signs do not represent an operation, there should be no space between the sign and the numeral:

The low temperature for the day was −13°F, and the high was +2°F.

The central bank kept the peso within its ±2.5% trading band.

All the samples exceeded the standard of <10,000 ppm.

This supplement provides ~20% of the user's daily protein requirement.

When a lowercase letter represents an unknown quantity, it is italicized:

$x − 5 = 23$        $y + z^2 = 125$

When a lowercase letter is used as an abbreviation, it is set in roman:

Gift boxed. 16w × 5d × 11h. 4 pounds.

sin = o/h        cos = a/h        tan = o/a

In mathematical expressions, parentheses appear within brackets—the reverse of the convention for prose:

*Math:* $[(25 − a) \times (b/2)]$

*Prose:* The study was attacked for "chaotic design" and "slapdash follow-up" (Briggs, *Guide to Evaluation* [Major City: Big Press, 1972], 382).

Copyeditors working on hard copy should clarify for the word processor or typesetter which symbols are intended.

*Chicago* further advises that if type is to be reproduced from an author's hard copy, handwritten clarifications should identify mathematical symbols not only by name but also by Unicode number (e.g., "minus sign [U+2212]," "multiplication sign [U+00D7]," "prime [U+2032]") to avoid—or when necessary correct—conversion problems in different digital environments. Unicode tables are available in *Chicago* and online.

Copyeditors working on-screen must ensure that mathematical symbols are correctly keyed, using their word processor's list of special characters or typing the correct Unicode number to replace any makeshift substitutions, such as an en dash for a minus sign or an apostrophe for a prime symbol.

## AMBIGUOUS NUMERICAL STATEMENTS

A statement such as "The value of the property has increased tenfold since 1991" simply means that the original 1991 value is multiplied by ten. The suffix *-fold* forms a solid compound with a spelled-out number and a hyphenated compound with a numeral (10-fold).

But when describing an increase or decrease between two numerical values, watch out for momentary miscues and possible misreadings:

> The cost of a subscription is expected to go up from two dollars to three dollars per week.
> [Does this mean that the old cost was two dollars and the new cost will be three dollars? or that the *increase* over the current cost, which is unspecified, will be somewhere between two and three dollars?]

> The stock value fell from $45 to $30 per share.
> [Does this mean that the old stock value was $45 and the new value $30? or that the per-share *decline* in the unspecified stock value ranged between $45 and $30?]

To avoid such ambiguities, give the *to* figure first:

> The cost of a subscription is expected to go up to three dollars from two dollars per week.

> The stock value fell to $30 from $45 per share.

Likewise, when expressing comparisons numerically, beware of equivocal and overly complicated formulations. A statement such as "The new chip runs five times faster than the old one" uses a common English idiom that is often understood to mean, simply, "multiplied by five," although some usage guides strongly recommend the more mathematically precise "five times as fast as" because it cannot be misunderstood.[10] But consider the statement

The old chip runs five times slower than the new one.

Huh? Expressions such as "five times slower than" are time-honored English idioms, according to *DEU* (s.v. "times"), which quotes Jonathan Swift for good measure ("I am resolved to drink ten times less than before"). Some readers will mentally translate this statement, perhaps after some head scratching, into

The old chip runs at one-fifth the speed of the new one.

Likewise,

The proposed geothermal power plant would emit 35 times less carbon dioxide per kilowatt than a traditional coal-fueled plant

might be interpreted, with a bit of difficulty, as

The proposed geothermal power plant would emit 1/35 the amount of carbon dioxide per kilowatt as a traditional coal-fueled plant.

But such statements border on nonsense. They are best avoided in writing, and many usage guides advise revision to spare readers the mathematical acrobatics required by these formulations. Consider the difficulty posed by this passage for a reader:

Among Mormon high-school seniors only ten per cent of boys and eighteen per cent of girls say that they have had sexual relations—respectively seven times and three times lower than comparable national figures. (Lawrence Wright, "Lives of the Saints," *New Yorker,* January 21, 2002, 51; "high-school" and "ten . . . eighteen per cent" are features of *New Yorker* house style)

Similarly, a statement such as

The port commission underestimated the cost of the memorial by 93 percent

might momentarily stump a reader unfamiliar with the conventions of financial analyses: does this mean that the real cost was a 93 percent increase over the estimate (i.e., 193 percent of the estimate)? that the estimate was 93 percent under the real cost (i.e., 7 percent of the real cost)? A simple revision clarifies the statement:

The cost of the memorial exceeded the port commission's estimate by 93 percent.

10. The argument sometimes invoked in newsrooms over "times more than" and similar formulations goes thus: if $x$ = processor speed, then "five times faster than $x$" means "$x + 5x$."

## STYLE SHEET ENTRIES

To ensure consistency throughout the manuscript, copyeditors should make entries on their style sheets that state the principles applied and that provide examples of the different categories of numbers, numerals, and quantities that appear in the manuscript.

First, you should note a general principle for which numbers are to be spelled out:

Spell out all numbers under 10 (or under 11).

*Or:* Spell out all numbers under 101 and all large numbers that can be expressed in two words, except for percentages, years and dates, and chapter and page numbers. Also, use numerals when quantities cluster in a paragraph.

*Or:* Treatment of numbers (words vs. numerals) follows the in-house style manual, pages 11–18.

Then, for each type of numerical expression that appears in the manuscript, you should provide an example and, as needed, a guiding principle:

*Dates:*   June 1, 1997   June 1   June 1997

*Decades:*   the 1990s   the mid-1960s   the late 1940s

*Academic years:*   1997–98   2000–01 *but* 1999–2000

*Abbreviations:*   A.D. 100   300 B.C.   a.m.   p.m.

*Inclusive page ranges:*   pp. 123–125 (include all digits)

*Cross-references:*   see chapter 12   see part 5   see figure 17

*Money:*   Spell out round amounts under $100,000; use numerals for amounts $100,000 and over:
>    twenty-five dollars, thirty thousand dollars
>    $900,000, $1 million, $2.5 million

*Percentages:*   72 percent   72.5 percent

*Decimals:*   Include leading 0 for decimals less than one: 0.5 percent

*Latitude and longitude:*   23°52′ W

# CHAPTER 8

# ¶ Quotations

The author of a manuscript is responsible for the accuracy of direct quotations from printed matter, interviews, and speeches. Rarely are copyeditors provided with the original documents and asked to verify or spot-check the word-by-word accuracy of quotations in a manuscript, although well-known quotations can be quickly verified in *Bartlett's Familiar Quotations* (the 1919 tenth edition, available for free on Bartleby.com, can be used to check older sources) or a similar authoritative print or online compendium. But beware of unreliable sources: the internet is awash with erroneous and misattributed quotations! And even though editors are not expected to authenticate quotations in a manuscript, they must exercise judgment in evaluating and tactfully querying excerpts that appear to be used in a misleading or tendentious way.

Whenever a direct quotation appears in a manuscript, copyeditors are expected to

query or correct any obvious spelling errors in the quotation

call to the author's attention any odd wording within the quotation that suggests that words were mistyped, deleted, or otherwise miscopied

enforce consistency in deciding which quotations are run into the text and which quotations are set off as extracts (block quotations)

make sure that opening quotation marks have closing mates and that quotation marks within quotation marks are handled correctly

make sure that the syntax of the quoted matter fits the surrounding text

mark ellipsis points correctly and delete unnecessary ellipsis points

ensure that the quotation is attributed to its source

Editors should never alter quotations from printed sources to conform to house style; they are permitted to style (but *not* to reword) speeches or quotations from oral interviews.

All the major style manuals offer extensive guidelines on these issues; here, we will survey the principal points.

## MISSPELLINGS IN THE SOURCE DOCUMENT

A direct quotation need not reproduce innocent misspellings or typographical errors that appear in the original document; instead, these errors may be silently corrected.

*Source document containing a typo:* Copyeditors are expected to delete unnecessary elipsis points.

*Manuscript quoting source document:* The guidelines call for deleting "unnecessary ellipsis points," but they do not define "unnecessary."

In a work of literary criticism or historical analysis, however, the original spelling is usually reproduced. Alternatively, the author should explain—in the preface, in a footnote, or in a parenthetical comment—that the spelling has been modernized or standardized.

A misspelling in the original document should also be reproduced when the fact that there was a misspelled word is at issue—for example, in a document that discusses the carelessness with which the original document was prepared. To alert readers that the misspelling occurred in the original, an author may insert an italicized *sic* (Latin, meaning "thus") within brackets:

The memo from the principal included a request that teachers "devote less time to science and arithmatic [*sic*] and more time to reading, penmanship, and spelling."

If there are many misspellings in the original document, it is usually preferable to insert a footnote or a parenthetical comment to that effect rather than to sprinkle snarky *sic*s throughout the quotations from that document. Such a comment might read

I have here reproduced all the misspellings contained in the original document.

*Or:* The original document is replete with misspellings, and these are reproduced here.

## ODD WORDING IN THE SOURCE DOCUMENT

Direct quotations from printed material must be reproduced verbatim; a copyeditor may never revise the wording of a direct quotation from a printed source. If a quotation sounds awkward or incorrect, ask the author to recheck the quoted material against the source. Should the transcription prove to be accurate, the author's choices are to (1) let the quotation stand without emendation or explanation, however odd it may sound; (2) add a bracketed *sic* after the troublesome phrase; (3) add clarifying words and place these within brackets; (4) add a comment, either in the text proper or in a footnote, stating that the transcription, however awkward, is correct; or (5) replace all or part of the direct quotation with a paraphrase.

When the material being quoted is spoken—not written—language, acronyms and abbreviations should be rendered in their conventional written form.

*Spoken version:* "Mister Ralph Snider the third will now discuss the newest scuzzy technology."

*Print version:* "Mr. Ralph Snider III will now discuss the newest SCSI technology."

Some publishers also encourage, or even require, copyeditors to make minor changes to correct a speaker's grammar, to eliminate false starts, and to delete voiced hesitations ("uh," "well," "you see").

> *Original comment:* "The number of consumer complaints about our products are decreasing."
>
> *Print version:* "The number of consumer complaints about our products is decreasing."

---

> *Original comment:* "The introduction of the 405 line, I mean, uh, the 4055 line, of course, is expected to increase revenues by 10 percent."
>
> *Print version:* "The introduction of the 4055 line is expected to increase revenues by 10 percent."

It is never acceptable, however, to tamper with the truth under the guise of editorial cleanliness. Under no circumstances should copyeditors make changes in direct quotations that alter the speaker's meaning or that serve only to make the speaker "look better."

If the original quotation is horribly mangled by false starts, labyrinthine syntax, jargon, or grammatical errors, the text should paraphrase the speaker's point.

> *Original:* Addressing the council, General Smith said, "High tech—spy satellites and computer-enhanced infrared photography and electronic intercepts and all those Star Wars gadgets—well, we live in an age where that kind of envelope-pushing technology affects decision-making at the national security–type level, and then we begin to downgrade human judgment, but technology is no substitute for well-informed, well-trained officers."
>
> *Revision, using paraphrase:* General Smith warned the council of the dangers of allowing advanced technological gadgetry to supersede human judgment in national security decisions. "Technology," he said, "is no substitute for well-informed, well-trained officers."

## RUN-IN AND SET-OFF QUOTATIONS

Short quotations (quotations of a sentence or less) are usually run into the text, and longer quotations (two or more sentences) are usually set off as extracts. The distinction between "short" and "longer" in this case is rather arbitrary: *Chicago* suggests setting off quotations of one hundred words or more, *WIT* puts the cutoff at five lines, and *APA* calls for setting off quotations longer than forty words. Many publishers have in-house rules that define "longer" as more than, say, six or eight lines. Sometimes even shorter quotations are treated as extracts so that readers can easily compare them; multiparagraph quotations, however brief, are also usually set off as block quotations.

## CREATING AN EXTRACT

To change a run-in quotation into an *extract,* or *block quotation,* a copyeditor who is working on hard copy must

> indicate where the set-off block is to begin and end
> typecode the block to indicate that it is an extract (a typical code is EX)[1]
> delete the opening and closing quotation marks that surround the block
> change any single quotation marks within the block to double quotation marks

For example, the manuscript reads:

> "Whatever infrastructure is provided will be used to
>
> capacity," Gilliam argues. "Traffic, for example, always
>
> expands to fill the capacity of a freeway, creating a
>
> 'demand' for more freeways. And the population inevitably
>
> expands to the limit set by the infrastructure--no matter
>
> how high that limit is."

Here the author correctly uses double quotation marks for the beginning and end of Gilliam's words and single quotation marks for quotation marks appearing in Gilliam's original statement. If this quotation is to be set as a run-in quotation, you would not need to mark anything. But for the sake of example, let's turn this run-in quotation into an extract. The marked hard copy would look like this:

> "Whatever infrastructure is provided will be used to
>
> capacity," Gilliam argues. Traffic, for example, always
>
>  expands to fill the capacity of a freeway, creating a
>
> demand for more freeways. And the population inevitably
>
> expands to the limit set by the infrastructure--no matter
>
> how high that limit is.

1. Markup alerts the designer and compositor to the presence of text that requires special formatting: e.g., extracts, lists, chapter titles, and headings. (Markup is discussed in chapter 13.) Extracts may

The compositor will then follow the designer's specifications (specs) for the EX code; the resulting printed text might look like this:

> "Whatever infrastructure is provided will be used to capacity," Gilliam argues.
>
> > Traffic, for example, always expands to fill the capacity of a freeway, creating a "demand" for more freeways. And the population inevitably expands to the limit set by the infrastructure—no matter how high that limit is.

The copyeditor working on-screen will achieve the same results by inserting hard returns before and after the extract, inserting the start and end codes for the extract or styling the extract using the word processer's style template (see "Markup On-Screen" in chapter 13), and fixing the quotation marks.

Notice that when a quotation is set as an extract, opening and closing quotation marks are not added; instead the typography indicates that the material is a direct quotation. Thus an extract will begin with an opening quotation mark only if the material being quoted happens to begin with an opening quotation mark:

*Source:*

> "That dog don't hunt" has become an all-too-familiar refrain in Washington this year, nuzzling out all other animals in the Capitol Hill menagerie. What accounts for the migration of the dependable duck, which for decades has been relied on to "look like a duck and quack like a duck"? Where are our 800-pound gorillas? (And why do they never weigh in at 700 or 900 pounds?)

*Quotation from source:*

> After expressing relief at the disappearance of the "soccer moms," Whitson turns to another set of clichés:
>
> > "That dog don't hunt" has become an all-too-familiar refrain in Washington this year, nuzzling out all other animals in the Capitol Hill menagerie. What accounts for the migration of the dependable duck, which for decades has been relied on to "look like a duck and quack like a duck"? Where are our 800-pound gorillas? (And why do they never weigh in at 700 or 900 pounds?)

## CREATING A RUN-IN QUOTATION

To change an extract into a *run-in quotation,* a copyeditor working on hard copy must

add a run-in curlicue and write a circled "run-in" instruction
add opening and closing double quotation marks around the entire quote
change any internal double quotation marks to single quotation marks

---

be differentiated from running text by one or more typographical devices: extra indention (from the left, the right, or both), extra leading (space) above and below the extract, reduced leading within the body of the extract, or a smaller type size. The publication's designer makes decisions about the typographical treatment.

For example, the manuscript reads:

> "Whatever infrastructure is provided will be used to
>
> capacity," Gilliam argues.

> Traffic, for example, always expands to fill the capacity
>
> of a freeway, creating a "demand" for more freeways.
>
> And the population inevitably expands to the limit set
>
> by the infrastructure--no matter how high that limit is.

Here the author has correctly formatted the extract and has correctly used double quotation marks to set off the word that was in quotation marks in the original. If you want to turn this extract into a run-in quotation, you would need to mark your hard copy as shown here:

> "Whatever infrastructure is provided will be used to
>
> capacity," Gilliam argues.
>
> Traffic, for example, always expands to fill the capacity
>
> of a freeway, creating a "demand" for more freeways.
>
> And the population inevitably expands to the limit set
>
> by the infrastructure--no matter how high that limit is.

*run in*

And the resulting printed text would look like this:

> "Whatever infrastructure is provided will be used to capacity," Gilliam argues. "Traffic, for example, always expands to fill the capacity of a freeway, creating a 'demand' for more freeways. And the population inevitably expands to the limit set by the infrastructure—no matter how high that limit is."

The copyeditor working on-screen can run in a set-off quotation by deleting the author's hard return, deleting the extract styling or any coding and extra indention before the extract, and fixing the quotation marks.

## EDITING A PULL QUOTE

A *pull quote* is a brief, striking excerpt copied, or "pulled," from the main text of a document and treated as a graphic element. Its purpose is to attract uncommitted readers who are scanning the piece, to spotlight a key point, and, like an illustration, to relieve the visual fatigue caused by perusing yards of prose. Type designers often differentiate pull quotes from the surrounding text by using a larger or otherwise distinctive typeface, a special color scheme, and other graphic devices. This eye-catching ploy is familiar to all readers of magazines and newspapers; it is also used in annual reports, brochures, and websites and, less often, in books.[2]

House styles differ in their requirements for reproducing the original text verbatim and for attributing the source of a pull quote. Many publishers permit pull quotes to be prudently shortened or paraphrased for the sake of copyfitting and impact—after all, the full quotation can be found in the body of the document—but some discourage this practice or caution against condensing a sensitive statement that may be misconstrued out of context. (In February 2011 the *Guardian* was obliged to apologize for a misleading and offensive pull quote about Palestine attributed to the former Israeli foreign minister Tzipi Livni.) Words pulled from an author's own narrative text normally do not need to be placed in quotation marks and may usually be modified somewhat as long as the meaning is unchanged; attribution is not necessary. Direct quotations from another individual cited by the author in the body of the document should retain quotation marks and should remain faithful to the original wording, although some publishers allow minor omissions and adjustments, without the customary ellipses and brackets, as long as the meaning is not altered. Attribution for direct third-party quotations should always be supplied with pull quotes. The editor should check all pull quotes against the text versions to ensure that they accurately reproduce both the words (exactly or judiciously abridged) and the sense of the original.

Pull quotes, a type of "floating" text, are positioned in the final document shortly before or near the original version. The editor should provide a placement callout, for example, "<Pullquote 1 about here>," to guide the typesetter.

## PUNCTUATION OF QUOTATIONS

### PUNCTUATION PRECEDING A QUOTATION

No punctuation is required before a quoted word or short phrase that is integral to the sentence structure.

---

2. Although the most widely used term is *pull quote,* some journalists use *lift-out pull quote, pullout,* or *callout.* (In book publishing the term *callout* usually refers to an instruction designating the placement of a table or an illustration or, occasionally, to a label identifying a feature in an illustration.) A pull quote, which repeats content from the main text, is different from other types of "floating" text—e.g., tables, chronologies, lists of key terms, study questions, and other pedagogical features given special treatment in a textbook.

Mme Ratignolle dismisses Edna, saying that "she is not one of us; she is not like us."

Otherwise, run-in quotations may be introduced by a comma or a colon. The choice reflects the syntax of the introductory phrase, the length of the quotation, and the degree of formality that is desired. A comma is the usual choice to introduce a short quotation, maxim, or expression following a verb such as *to say, to exclaim, to note,* or *to write.*

As Heraclitus wrote, "Nothing endures but change."

A colon is the usual choice to introduce a long quotation following a complete independent clause.

Today we remember Thomas Paine's stirring words: "These are the times that try men's souls. The summer soldier and the sunshine patriot will, in this crisis, shrink from the service of their country; but he that stands it *now,* deserves the love and thanks of man and woman."

A colon is also used when the introductory tag contains "the following" or "thus."

Heraclitus wrote the following: "Nothing endures but change."

Set-off quotations may be preceded by a comma, a colon, or a period, depending on the syntax of the introductory tag.

As Carolyn Heilbrun notes,

To denounce women for shrillness and stridency is another way of denying them any right to power. . . . Ironically, women who acquire power are more likely to be criticized for it than are the men who have always had it. (*Writing a Woman's Life* [New York: W. W. Norton, 1988], p. 16)

Despite all that these women accomplished, their autobiographies downplay or ignore the very qualities that enabled them to be successful:

Well into the twentieth century, it continued to be impossible for women to admit into their autobiographical narratives the claim of achievement, the admission of ambition, the recognition that accomplishment was neither luck nor the result of the efforts or generosity of others. . . . Their letters and diaries [reflect] ambitions and struggles in the public sphere; in their published autobiographies, however, they portray themselves as intuitive, nurturing, passive, but never—in spite of the contrary evidence of their accomplishments—managerial. (Carolyn Heilbrun, *Writing a Woman's Life* [New York: W. W. Norton, 1988], p. 24)

"Above all," Carolyn Heilbrun explains, in women's autobiographies "the public and private lives cannot be linked."

We hardly expect the career of an accomplished man to be presented as being in fundamental conflict with the demands of his marriage and children; he can allow his public life to expand occasionally into the private sphere without guilt or disorder. These women are therefore unable to write exemplary lives: they do not dare to offer themselves as models, but only as exceptions chosen by destiny or chance. (*Writing a Woman's Life* [New York: W. W. Norton, 1988], p. 25)

Sometimes a colon is used directly after a verb of saying when the introductory phrase formally introduces a literary quotation set off from the text.

As Thomas Paine wrote in *The Crisis* (1776):

These are the times that try men's souls. The summer soldier and the sunshine patriot will, in this crisis, shrink from the service of their country; but he that stands it *now,* deserves the love and thanks of man and woman.

If necessary, the editor should help the author to vary—or to avoid excessive variation in—these introductory phrases.[3] The editor should also suggest rewording passive-voice tags ("As noted by Heilbrun") as active constructions ("As Heilbrun notes").

## SINGLE AND DOUBLE QUOTATION MARKS

When a quotation occurs within running text, an opening double quotation mark appears at the beginning of the quotation and a closing double quotation mark appears at the end. If a quotation extends over a paragraph break, an opening double quotation mark appears at the beginning of each paragraph, and a closing double quotation mark appears only at the end of the last paragraph in the quotation.[4] (In expository works, however, a multiparagraph quotation is usually printed as an extract.)

In addition to making sure that each opening quotation mark has its closing mate, the copyeditor must ensure that the author has used the correct mark. In US practice, the outermost marks are double quotation marks, and single quotation marks are used to indicate a quotation within a quotation.

According to Gilliam, traffic "always expands to fill the capacity of a freeway, creating a 'demand' for more freeways."

In the rare event that a third level of quotation is embedded within the other two, double quotation marks are used:

At his deposition, Mr. Vine stated: "John asked, 'Shall I change "unaccustomed" to "not accustomed" in the Miller contract?' I replied, 'Suit yourself. You always do.'"

If you are editing files on-screen, also make sure that the correct style of single and double quotation marks is used. Most professionally typeset copy features smart, or curly, quotes (see "Eyeballing Every Mark" in chapter 4). You may need to search and replace the document's straight quotes if file cleanup routines haven't already corrected them.

---

3. Inexperienced writers, especially in fictional dialogue, sometimes resort to an entire thesaurus of speech tags (say, utter, declare, state, remark, announce, observe, mention, note, comment, claim, maintain, assert, confess, grin, grimace, etc., etc.) in a misguided pursuit of "elegant variation." In fact, such tags are nearly invisible to readers, and the relentless cycle of synonyms is merely distracting.

4. The *AP Stylebook* offers a refinement of this principle that requires a closing quotation mark at the end of the first paragraph of a multiparagraph quotation if the words within quotation marks at the end of that first paragraph do not constitute a complete sentence.

## SYNTACTICAL FIT

When a quotation is embedded within an author's sentence, the copyeditor should ascertain that the syntax and grammar of the quotation mesh with the surrounding sentence and that the placement of the quotation marks does not fracture the phrasing of the sentence or the quotation. In the following example, the shift in tenses is unsettling:

> *Awkward:* In devising their classification scheme, Potrero and Sanchez wanted to ensure that it "accounts for patterns of intraspecific genetic variation measured by DNA analysis, allozyme analysis, and virulence studies."

In revising the sentence to fix the tense shift, the copyeditor must not introduce a new problem by interrupting the inseparable "account for":

> *Awkward:* In devising their classification scheme, Potrero and Sanchez wanted to ensure that it would account "for patterns of intraspecific genetic variation measured by DNA analysis, allozyme analysis, and virulence studies."

The better solution here is to move the quotation marks to a less intrusive location:

> *Revision:* In devising their classification scheme, Potrero and Sanchez wanted to ensure that it would account for "patterns of intraspecific genetic variation measured by DNA analysis, allozyme analysis, and virulence studies."

Partial quotations from interviews can create problems with pronouns:

> *Awkward:* Danno confessed that "during the recession, I turned to shoplifting and purse snatching."
>
> *Revision:* Danno confessed, "During the recession, I turned to shoplifting and purse snatching."

In some cases, revising the wording around the quotation will produce the best fit with the context:

> *Awkward:* Occasionally, Hugo promulgates silly, idiosyncratic preferences as though they were divinely inspired rules. He insists that writers use "no semicolons. Semicolons indicate relationships that only idiots need defined by punctuation. Besides, they are ugly."
>
> *Revision:* Occasionally, Hugo promulgates silly, idiosyncratic preferences as though they were divinely inspired rules. "No semicolons," he insists. "Semicolons indicate relationships that only idiots need defined by punctuation. Besides, they are ugly."

Another approach is to interpolate a bracketed syllable or word so that the quotation fits the context.

> *Awkward:* As early as the 1950s, "middle-class Americans' twin obsessions with automobiles and single-family homes conspire to make housing less affordable."

*Revision:* As early as the 1950s, "middle-class Americans' twin obsessions with automobiles and single-family homes conspire[d] to make housing less affordable."

Notice that the syntax of the sentence as a whole determines the punctuation immediately preceding and following the quotation:

In Emerson's words, "A foolish consistency is the hobgoblin of little minds, adored by little statesmen and philosophers and divines."

In Emerson's words, "A foolish consistency is the hobgoblin of little minds."

"A foolish consistency," Emerson says, "is the hobgoblin of little minds."
[Here, "Emerson says" is an interrupter set off from the full quotation by a pair of commas, after which the quotation continues with the lowercase "is."]

Emerson argues that "a foolish consistency is the hobgoblin of little minds."

Emerson disparages "a foolish consistency" as "the hobgoblin of little minds"; this sort of consistency, he explains, is motivated by "a reverence for our past act or word."

As these examples show, in most instances authors may silently change the capitalization of the first word in a quotation to suit their own syntax. Thus, if a brief quotation is embedded within a sentence, the author will lowercase the first word of the quotation, regardless of how it appeared in the source document. Similarly, if the quotation appears at the head of the author's own sentence, the author will uppercase the first word of the quotation.

*Source:* Proper words in proper places, make the true definition of a style.

*Quotation from source:* Swift defines style as "proper words in proper places."

*Or:* "The true definition of a style," according to Swift, is "proper words in proper places."

In literary criticism, legal documents, and other texts in which precise reproduction is important, the changed letter is placed in brackets.

*Source:* Rule 5.8.1. Proof of service may be made by declaration of the person accomplishing the service.

*Quotation from source:* According to Rule 5.8.1, "[p]roof of service may be made by declaration of the person accomplishing the service."

*Or:* "[D]eclaration of the person accomplishing the service" constitutes proof of service under Rule 5.8.1.

## ELLIPSIS POINTS

Sometimes an author wishes to quote only a portion of a sentence. By convention, *ellipsis points* (three spaced periods) replace the omitted words.

*Source:* The half-year convention does not apply to residential real property, nonresidential real property, and railroad gradings and tunnel bores. It treats all property placed in service (or disposed of) during any tax year as placed in service (or disposed of) on the midpoint of that tax year.

*Quotation from source:* Under the half-year convention, the company must treat "property placed in service . . . during any tax year as placed in service . . . on the midpoint of that tax year."

But no ellipsis points are needed when the abridged quotation consists of words that are contiguous in the source document—that is, when no intervening words have been omitted.[5]

*Source:* But all copy editors show a common bias: vigilance breeds suspicion, and the suspect is the writer. What he has set down is ipso facto questionable and incomplete; anything not utterly usual is eccentric and reprehensible; what the editor would prefer is preferable.

*Quotation from source:* In "Behind the Blue Pencil: Censorship or Creeping Creativity?" Jacques Barzun warns copyeditors against what he calls "a common bias," the source of which is the very vigilance that copyeditors covet: "Vigilance breeds suspicion, and the suspect is the writer." Mistrustful of "anything not utterly usual," the copyeditor wrongly turns into an intrusive semi-ghostwriter.

[No ellipsis points are needed before or after any of the quoted phrases here because each phrase is intact.]

On hard copy, the periods in an ellipsis are spaced:

*Correct manuscript:* "property placed in service . . . during any tax year"

*Incorrect manuscript:* "property placed in service...during any tax year"

*Marked hard copy:* "property placed in service⎰⁝⎱during any tax year"

*Will be typeset as:* "property placed in service . . . during any tax year"

5. Leading ellipsis points (e.g., ". . . and for no other purpose") and trailing ellipsis points (e.g., "the limitation shall be disallowed . . .") are used only in textual criticism and legal work, where precise reproduction is crucial, and in fictional dialogue to denote faltering or interrupted speech ("I . . . I can't . . ."). With trailing ellipsis points, there is no space between the final ellipsis point and the closing quotation mark.

Copyeditors working on-screen may be asked to insert three spaced periods, an ellipsis code, or a special nonbreaking ellipsis character that consists of three tightly spaced dots (...).[6]

Some publishers, including most scholarly and academic presses, follow a more rigorous convention regarding what are sometimes called three-dot and four-dot ellipses. Under this convention, when the cut material is located within one sentence in the original document, the quoter inserts a three-dot ellipsis. But when the cut material spans a sentence boundary in the source document, a four-dot ellipsis—that is, a period followed by a three-dot ellipsis—is used. The period (first ellipsis point) in a four-dot ellipsis is closed up with the preceding text regardless of where the period falls in the source document, as the following example illustrates.

> *Source:* The limitations on lines 5 and 11 apply to the taxpayer, and not to each separate business or activity. Therefore, if you have more than one business or activity, you may allocate your allowable section 179 expense deduction among them.

> *Quotation from source:* According to the instructions for Form 4562, "the limitations on lines 5 and 11 apply to the taxpayer. . . . If you have more than one business or activity, you may allocate your allowable section 179 expense deduction among them."

Authors who are unaccustomed to working with quoted material may use three dots or four dots willy-nilly. Sometimes you will be able to tell from the context whether a three-dot or a four-dot ellipsis is called for. Otherwise, write a query that explains the convention and ask your author to revise the manuscript as necessary.

In the relatively unusual situation in which ellipsis points appear in the original document, this fact should be indicated in a footnote or in a bracketed or parenthetical comment.

> His last letter to his son began, "Dear Sonny, Lead . . . and they will follow [ellipsis in the original]. But don't never ever look back—not because someone might be gaining on you, but because there might not be anyone there. Hah! Ain't that rich!"
> > [Here the comment is placed in brackets because it falls within a set of quotation marks.]

> Just as Jetsen is on the verge of revealing who committed the heinous crime, he turns to his cousin and says, "But I digress . . ." (ellipsis in the original), and the chapter ends.
> > [Here the comment follows the direct quotation and is placed in parentheses.]

Bracketed ellipsis points may be used in a translation to indicate that the ellipsis is the translator's, not the author's.

---

6. In traditional typesetting, the space before and after each dot in an ellipsis is one-third of an em wide—in other words, narrower than a wordspace. (See Glossary of Copyediting Terms, s.v. "em.")

It was then (even as we yet see it used) a custom that the kinswomen and women neighbors of the dead should assemble in his house [. . .] and he with funeral pomp of chants and candles was borne away on the shoulders of his peers to the church chosen by himself before his death.

## BRACKETS

Brackets—not parentheses—are used to enclose any material that the quoter wishes to interpolate into the quotation or to add for the purposes of clarification or explanation.

The principal's memo called for greater attention to "spelling and reading comperhension [*sic*]."

*Merriam-Webster's Dictionary* states that the noun is "often attrib[utive]."

A local aid worker said, "The UNHCR [United Nations High Commissioner for Refugees] could have done more to avert this disaster."

"Errare humanum est [To err is human]" was his sole defense.

According to the press release, "The assistant vice-mayor in charge of community relations [Dinai Smithers] will be reassigned for the duration of the investigation."

The start-up company's motto is "A terabyte [one trillion bytes] on every desktop."

Heine's last words were "Of course he [God] will forgive me; that's his business."

"We must never forget it is a *constitution* we are expounding [emphasis in the original]."

"The power to tax involves the power *to destroy* [emphasis added]."

"Vision requires distance; one cannot see a thing if one is too close to it [translation mine]."

If more than one person has made insertions—explanatory comments, for example, from both a translator and an academic editor—tags identifying each interpolator should be added, with a note explaining the convention on first appearance.

[mǎ, "horse," not mā, "mother" —Trans.]

[pun intended —Ed.]

Empty brackets are used in legal writing and in some literary criticism to indicate the deletion of part of a word (for example, a change in a verb form). Or, provided it's acceptable for the reader to think the word has been interpolated, the whole word may be placed in brackets.

*Original reads:* insists

*Quoted version reads:* insist[ ]

*Or:* [insist]

Alternatively, the lead-in to the quotation may simply be rewritten to fit the grammar of the original quotation.

In contrast, parentheses appear within quotation marks only when parentheses were used in the source document.

> The tax code is quite clear on this point: "The contribution must be made by the due date (including extensions) for filing the tax return."

Sometimes you will be able to tell that your author has used parentheses where brackets are called for; otherwise, write a query that explains the convention and ask the author to revise the manuscript as necessary.

## CITING SOURCES

Quotations of extremely well known phrases need not be formally attributed to their sources, but all other quotations—with the exception of casual snatches of conversation—must be. In documents that contain many quotations, a formal system of attribution (either footnotes or endnotes, or in-text references keyed to a reference list) is used; see chapter 11.

In documents that contain few quotations, however, sources may be cited in the text proper. For some classic works of Western culture and literature—for example, the Bible, Shakespeare's plays—abbreviations may be used unless, in the editor's judgment, these citations should be spelled out for lay readers or for global readers who may be unfamiliar with the conventions described (with small variations) in *Chicago,* the *MLA Handbook, The SBL Handbook of Style,* or other manuals.

> The passage in 1 Cor. 5 is . . .

> "Your glorying is not good. Know ye not that a little leaven leaveneth the whole lump?" (1 Cor. 5:6 AV)

> *Ham.* 1.5.35–37

Other in-text citations must include at least the author and title of the work. The publisher, city of publication, date of publication, and page number may also be provided if the publisher requires, or readers expect, a greater degree of rigor in source attributions.

> In *The Devil's Dictionary,* Bierce defines "accordion" as "an instrument in harmony with the sentiments of an assassin."

> "Why do you sit there looking like an envelope without any address on it?" (Mark Twain, quoted by Nancy McPhee, *The Book of Insults, Ancient and Modern*).

The Russian word *razbliuto* denotes "the feeling a person has for someone he or she once loved but now does not" (Howard Rheingold, *They Have a Word for It* [Los Angeles: Tarcher, 1988], 62).[7]

As these examples show, the parenthetical citation is punctuated as part of the sentence; thus the terminal period follows the closing parenthesis. In contrast, when a parenthetical citation accompanies an extract, the citation is placed after the final period in the quotation.

From his reading of many of the explorers' accounts, Barry Lopez concludes:

> The literature of arctic exploration is frequently offered as a record of resolute will before the menacing fortifications of the landscape. It is more profitable I think to disregard this notion—that the land is an adversary bent on human defeat, that the people who came and went were heroes or failures in this. It is better to contemplate the record of human longing to achieve something significant, to be free of some of the grim weight of life. That weight was ignorance, poverty of spirit, indolence, and the threat of anonymity and destitution. This harsh landscape became the focus of a desire to separate oneself from those things and to overcome them. In these arctic narratives, then, are the threads of dreams that serve us all. (*Arctic Dreams,* p. 310)

7. A footnote (literally) to this example: There is no such word in Russian. In an April 2005 "On Language" column for the *New York Times Magazine,* William Safire praised Christopher Moore's promotion of this worthwhile term in *In Other Words: A Language Lover's Guide to the Most Intriguing Words around the World* (New York: Walker, 2004). But according to subsequent blog posts by investigating linguists on *Language Hat* and *Language Log,* Moore had probably picked it up from Rheingold, who in turn had based his definition on J. Bryan III's 1986 book *Hodgepodge: A Commonplace Book* (New York: Atheneum); these investigators eventually traced the spurious word to an episode of the 1960s TV show *The Man from U.N.C.L.E.* Thus, like internet memes, are linguistic rumors spread. See Steve Dodson, "Razbliuto? Nyet!," *Language Hat,* April 17, 2005, http://languagehat.com/razbliuto -nyet/; Benjamin Zimmer, "*Tingo* and Other Lingo," *Language Log,* September 28, 2005, http://itre.cis .upenn.edu/~myl/languagelog/archives/002500.html.

# CHAPTER 9

# ¶ Abbreviations and Symbols

Abbreviations and symbols are shortcuts that help authors save space. By uncluttering the text, these shortcuts can also facilitate comprehension. Consider, for example, the following sentence, which is to appear in a document for the general public:

> Researchers are examining samples of deoxyribonucleic acid in an effort to determine why some people who test positive for human immunodeficiency virus do not develop acquired immune deficiency syndrome.

Here, replacing the three scientific terms with abbreviations will help readers because most nonscientists are more familiar with the abbreviations than with the spelled-out forms.

> *Revision:* Researchers are examining DNA samples in an effort to determine why some people who test positive for HIV do not develop AIDS.

Indeed, despite the schoolbook injunction "Never use abbreviations in formal writing," some abbreviations are routinely used:

- Courtesy titles (Mr., Mrs., Ms.) are never spelled out when they precede a proper name. (In any case, there is no spelled-out equivalent for "Ms.")
- Military, political, and other titles are commonly abbreviated when they precede a full name (Gen., Lt. Col., Sen., Rep., Dr.) though the full title is usually spelled out when only a surname is given.
- Following a proper name, suffixes (Jr., Sr.) are always abbreviated, as are academic degrees (BA, MS, PhD) and "Esq."
- The following designations related to time are always abbreviated: A.M. (*or* a.m.), P.M. (*or* p.m.), B.C.E. (*or* BCE), B.C. (*or* BC), C.E. (*or* CE), A.D. (*or* AD). Different publishers specify using or omitting periods and styling with capital, lowercase, or small capital letters (see below, under "Time").
- As adjectives, "US," "UN," and "UK" (now written without periods in *Chicago*) are frequently preferred to the unabbreviated forms; *Chicago* now also accepts "US" as a noun, provided the meaning is clear in context.
- Business suffixes are almost always abbreviated: Inc., Co., Ltd., LLC, PLC, S.A. (Société anonyme), AG (Aktiengesellschaft).
- Most style manuals recommend or accept the abbreviation "St." in the names of cities (St. Louis, St. Paul).

- Abbreviations appear in the names of many corporations (ABC, A&P, CBS, IBM); indeed, for some companies (AT&T, 3M, USX) the abbreviation is the official corporate name.
- Some technology products (CD-ROM, VCR) and scientific terms (DNA, LSD) are referred to by their initials, and dictionaries label these terms as ordinary nouns. Similarly: AM and FM radio, UHF and VHF television channels, UFOs.
- In some contexts the initials for well-known phrases are used: OK, RIP (*or* R.I.P.), RSVP, SOS, QED (*or* Q.E.D.).

Many symbols are likewise standard in formal writing, particularly in professional and specialized text. For example:

- The dollar sign ($) is used when sums of money are expressed in numerals.
- The percentage sign (%) is used in technical and financial documents, and in tables in nontechnical documents (see "Words or Numerals?" in chapter 7).
- The ampersand (&) is used in the names of companies.
- The section sign (§) and the paragraph sign (¶) are used in references to legal documents.

The various style manuals each recommend slightly different editorial conventions for the treatment of abbreviations and symbols. As in all matters of editorial style, the three overarching concerns for the copyeditor are that (1) the document is internally consistent, (2) the document conforms to recognized conventions in the author's field, and (3) the editorial style facilitates readers' comprehension of the document.

In this chapter we'll look at some of the everyday problems that abbreviations and symbols pose for copyeditors. Copyeditors who work on scientific and technical documents should consult *CSE* and the specialized style manuals listed in chapter 3.

## ABBREVIATIONS

Abbreviations come in several types:

*initialisms,* formed by the first letters of the words in a phrase and pronounced as separate letters (NSA, FBI)
*acronyms,* formed by the first letters of the words in a phrase and pronounced as words (NASA, FEMA)
*contractions,* formed by eliding the middle letters of a word (Dr., Sr.)
other shortened forms, created by clipping off the ends of words (Rev., Prof.)

In fact, some abbreviations are created by combining these methods or by substituting letter sounds or numbers for some part of the word or phrase: JPEG ("jay-peg") for "Joint Photographic Experts Group"; XML ("ex-em-ell") for "extensible markup language"; P2P ("pea-to-pea") for "peer-to-peer." Other abbreviations fuse parts of several words from the full term to form a portmanteau: *hazmat* for "hazardous material." And some abbreviations are treated either as initialisms or as acronyms, depending on pronunciation: URL ("you-are-ell" or "earl") for "uniform resource locator"; FAQ ("eff-ay-cue" or "fack") for "frequently asked question(s)"; *CMOS* ("see-em-oh-ess" or "see-moss") for *The Chicago Manual of Style*.

Regardless of how shortened forms are constructed or pronounced, all fall under the general rubric *abbreviations*.[1]

In the editorial styling of all abbreviations, the three major considerations are capitalization, punctuation, and plural formation. The conventions for styling acronyms and initialisms generally differ from those for other types of abbreviations in these matters and are discussed later. Before looking at acronyms and initialisms, we can make some observations about the other types of abbreviations and some specific issues concerning them.

*Capitalization:* With the exception of initialisms and acronyms, the capitalization of abbreviations typically follows the capitalization of the spelled-out terms. For example, the abbreviations of personal titles and proper nouns are capitalized, but the abbreviations of most common nouns are not:

The report was submitted by Dr. John Osgood Jr.

Gusts along the coast exceeded 72 knots (83 mph).

The police arrested Hapgood Smythe (a.k.a. Sticky Fingers).[2]

Contemporary scholarly style discourages the use of "op. cit." in notes.

If a sentence begins with a lowercase abbreviation, capitalize the first letter or rewrite:

Dpi, or dots per inch, is a measure of the resolution of a printed image.

*Or:* Dots per inch, or dpi, is a measure of the resolution of a printed image.

*Punctuation:* Excepting acronyms and initialisms, most abbreviations take terminal periods;[3] the following do not:

---

1. Although some style manuals use *acronym* more broadly to describe any abbreviation constructed from the first letters of the words in a phrase, whether a proper name or a common term, this discussion maintains a distinction between initialisms and acronyms. Some house styles treat these types of abbreviations differently.

2. Who would have thought this little term could take so many forms! The online editions of *M-W Collegiate, M-W Unabridged,* and *Webster's New World College Dictionary* list "aka"; the online *AHD,* "AKA." *Chicago* and *The New York Times Manual of Style and Usage* recommend "a.k.a."; the *AP Stylebook,* "aka."

3. In British style, no period follows a contraction, that is, an abbreviation whose last letter is the same as the last letter in the full word: Dr Smith *but* Capt. Smith; vol. 1 *but* vols 2–4. US publishers typically instruct their copyeditors to "Americanize" a document that follows the British convention.

*French courtesy terms:* Mme Dupris, Mlle Dupris (*but* M. Dupris)
*Units of measurement:* ft, sq ft, mi (*but* in.)—to avoid confusion with the word
   *in*),[4] cm, kg, mL, kHz
*Rates of measurement:* mph, dpi, cps (cycles per second)

Abbreviations that have internal periods do not take internal spaces:[5]

   a.k.a.      at 8 A.M.      e.g.      i.e.

A comma is not required in a company name with "Inc." or "Ltd.," regardless of the
form employed in the company's own official documents, and minimalist punctuators
often prefer to omit it. But if the comma is retained, following the company's own style,
use a pair of commas to set off the abbreviation from surrounding text.

> The rising value of shares in Widget International Inc. makes the company an
> attractive investment.

> *Or:* The rising value of shares in Widget International, Inc., makes the company
> an attractive investment.

*Plural formations:* Some abbreviations have regular plural forms (vol., vols.; chap.,
chaps.; Dr., Drs.); others have irregular plurals (p., pp.; f., ff.; Mr., Messrs.). All units of
measure are invariant: in., ft, cm, g.

## COMMON LATIN ABBREVIATIONS

Many publishers allow the common Latin abbreviations "etc.," "e.g.," and "i.e." only in
parenthetical references and in footnotes. Copyeditors working under this policy are
expected to substitute an equivalent English term for the abbreviation or to delete it,
depending on the context. The standard substitutes for these Latin abbreviations are
these phrases:

| *For* | *Substitute* |
|---|---|
| e.g. | for example |
| etc. | and so on *or* and so forth *or* and the like; |
|  | *less often:* et cetera [no italics] |
| i.e. | that is |

Note the distinction between *e.g.* and *i.e.,* often confounded by authors (and copyeditors).

---

4. In nonscientific texts, *Chicago* recommends periods after all US units of measure (in., sq. ft.,
mi.), but it notes that when these abbreviations are used in scientific copy, they usually appear without
periods.

5. *Chicago* 17 recommends not using periods for abbreviations with capital letters, even if lowercase
letters appear within the abbreviation: US, UN, DC, PhD. Although *Chicago* endorses two-letter postal
codes for abbreviated names of states in notes and bibliographical entries (see the subsequent discussion in "Abbreviations for States"), it recommends retaining internal periods in the adjective *U.S.* in
documents that use traditional state abbreviations: N.Y, N.J., N.M.

The following examples illustrate several ways to handle these abbreviations:

*Original:* Consider planting evergreens, e.g., pines, firs, and cedars.

*Revision:* Consider planting evergreens—for example, pines, firs, or cedars.

*Or:* Consider planting evergreens: pines, firs, and cedars, for example.

*Or:* Consider planting pines, firs, cedars, or other evergreens.

---

*Original:* Arrange the reports in chronological order: January, February, etc.

*Revision:* Arrange the reports in chronological order: January, February, and so on.

*Or:* Arrange the reports in chronological order, from January through December.

---

*Original:* Connect the 15-pin output to the DIS port, i.e., the display adapter.

*Revision:* Connect the 15-pin output to the DIS port (i.e., the display adapter).

*Or:* Connect the 15-pin output to the DIS port (that is, the display adapter).

When house style allows these abbreviations to appear in running text, you must make sure that the abbreviations are correctly used and punctuated; for example:

Consider planting evergreens, e.g., pines, firs, and cedars.

Consider planting evergreens (e.g., pines, firs, and cedars).

---

Connect the 15-pin output to the DIS port, i.e., the display adapter.

Connect the 15-pin output to the DIS port (i.e., the display adapter).

---

Wilco ships nuts, bolts, hand tools, etc. by overnight mail.[6]

Wilco ships small orders (nuts, bolts, hand tools, etc.) by overnight mail.

The abbreviation "etc." requires special care. Since "etc." is short for the Latin *et cetera,* which means "and the others" or "and the rest," the expression "and etc." is always incorrect:

✘ Reread the front matter (title pages, copyright page, contents page, preface, and etc.).

Reread the front matter (title pages, copyright page, contents page, preface, etc.).

Moreover, *etc.* should not come at the end of a list introduced by a form of *including* or by *such as,* both of which denote that the list is not exhaustive:

---

6. Traditional editorial style recommends that *et cetera, etc., and so on,* and similar expressions be set off by a pair of commas, but some minimalist punctuators style these expressions like any other final element in a series. *Chicago* 17 now permits the omission of the second comma when the abbreviation "etc." and its English equivalents are used in running text.

✗ The analyses account for factors that include age, sex, marital status, etc.

The analyses account for factors that include age, sex, and marital status.

The other Latin abbreviation in common use is "v." (versus), which may be set in roman or italic:

*Wilkins* v. *California* is a landmark case in patent law.

*Or: Wilkins v. California* is a landmark case in patent law.

In contexts other than law, "versus" is usually spelled out, but the abbreviation ("vs." in nonlegal contexts) may be used in parenthetical expressions.

A few other Latin abbreviations sometimes appear in manuscripts (for bibliographical abbreviations, see table 11 later in this chapter).

| | | |
|---|---|---|
| c. *or* ca. | circa | approximately (used before a date: c. 1530) |
| cf.[7] | confer | compare |
| fl. | floruit | flourished (used before a date: fl. 900 B.C.) |
| N.B. | nota bene | mark well, note (used before a caveat or explanation) |
| viz. | videlicet | namely, to wit |

## ABBREVIATIONS FOR STATES

There are two systems for abbreviating the names of states and territories of the United States. In what has come to be called the traditional system, most of the shorter names are not abbreviated (Alaska, Guam, Hawaii, Idaho, Iowa, Ohio, Utah), and the longer names have two- to five-letter abbreviations (Calif., Conn., N.Y., Wash.). The second system uses the postal codes, a set of two-letter, all-upper-case, no-internal-period abbreviations: AK, CA, CT, GU, HI, ID, IA, NY, OH, UT, WA.

Despite the efficiency of postal abbreviations, it seems prudent to avoid them in the titles and running text of publications intended for global audiences, including online publications with an international following. Would someone in France know the difference between AK and AL in a headline, newspaper dateline, or business location? Indeed, many US residents confuse

AK (Alaska), AL (Alabama), AR (Arkansas), AZ (Arizona)
MA (Massachusetts), MD (Maryland), MI (Michigan), MN (Minnesota),
    MO (Missouri), MS (Mississippi)
NE (Nebraska), NV (Nevada)

These abbreviations make sense for mail delivered by the US Postal Service—and perhaps for domestic newspapers because of limited space—but they are not universally reader friendly.

---

7. This abbreviation is often used erroneously to mean "see."

Still, some publishers use these postal abbreviations whenever abbreviations are permitted. In that case, they are either written without any commas or set off from the surrounding text with a pair of commas.

We will open a branch office in Ann Arbor MI in June.

*Or:* We will open a branch office in Ann Arbor, MI, in June.

Publishers that have not adopted the postal code system often use the following conventions:

1. Running text. No abbreviations of states in running text except for addresses and parenthetical expressions of political affiliation (see items 2 and 3 below):

    The new factory will be built in Worcester, Massachusetts.

2. Addresses. Use the postal abbreviations in addresses:

    Send questions and comments to PO Box 101, Anytown MA 01222.

3. Political affiliation. In parenthetical expressions, use the traditional abbreviations for states:

    Senators Jeanneanne Mei (D-N.J.) and Carla Hoving (R-Nev.) are sponsoring the bill.
    [Note: This journalistic convention uses D (*or* D.) for Democrats, R (*or* R.) for Republicans, and I (*or* I.) for independents, followed by a hyphen and an abbreviated state name.]

4. Notes and bibliography. *Chicago* favors the use of postal code abbreviations for states in notes (footnotes or endnotes) and bibliographical entries, although some house styles stipulate conventional state abbreviations:

    *Footnote:* Keith Wilson, *Life Goes On* (Marshall, MA: Little Press, 2000), 11–12.

    *Bibliography:* Wilson, Keith. *Life Goes On.* Marshall, MA: Little Press, 2000.

TIME

The following abbreviations are never spelled out: A.M., P.M., B.C.E. (*or* B.C.), C.E. (*or* A.D.).[8] But the use of capitalization and periods varies with house style. Some publishers prefer small capital letters (*small caps*) for these forms (A.M., P.M., B.C.E., B.C., C.E., A.D.) and may omit periods from the era designations. *Chicago* sets the times of day lowercase

---

8. Writers designate eras based on their tradition, academic specialty, or personal preference (*Chicago* 9.34). Many Western scholars favor the more inclusive terms *BCE* and *CE*, which do not explicitly refer to the birth of Christ, but some usage guides still recommend the older *BC* (before Christ) and *AD* (*anno Domini*, "in the year of the Lord") as "the better choice because they are clear to more readers" (*Garner's*, s.v. "B.C.").

with periods (a.m., p.m.) and capitalizes chronological eras without them (BCE, BC, CE, AD).

A traditional publishing convention calls for "BC" (*or* B.C. *or* B.C.) to follow the year, but "AD" (*or* A.D. *or* A.D.) to precede the year, since it stands for *anno Domini* (in the year of the Lord):

> The shrine was built in 50 BC and destroyed in AD 40.

Outside scholarly publishing, this convention seems to be losing ground to a preference for placing the abbreviation after the year: 50 BC, 40 AD. Note that the designation *AD* is used only when *BC* appears nearby in the text.

In works addressed to general readers, some of the less well known abbreviations for eras may need to be spelled out on first mention:

BCE    before the Common Era (a nonsectarian synonym for BC)

CE    of the Common Era (a nonsectarian synonym for AD)

BP    before the present (used in astronomy and cosmology; by convention, "present" = AD 1950)

AH    *anno Hegirae*, "in the year of the Hegira" (used in the Islamic calendar; Muhammad's Hegira occurred in AD 622); this abbreviation precedes the date

JD    Julian date (used in astronomy; represents the number of days between January 1, 4713 BC, and the date in question)

There is no need to spell out these abbreviations in texts addressed to specialists.

## UNITS OF MEASUREMENT

In nontechnical text, units of measurement are abbreviated only when space is at a premium (e.g., in tables) or when the abbreviations facilitate comprehension (e.g., when numerical data cluster thickly in a paragraph). In technical text, abbreviations are used more freely.

Abbreviations of units of measure named after people are capitalized. The abbreviations of other units of measure are lowercased—except the abbreviation for *liter,* which is an uppercase "L" (a lowercase "l" is too similar to the numeral 1).

| A | ampere | ft | foot |
|---|---|---|---|
| Hz | hertz | kg | kilogram |
| J | joule | m | meter |
| K | kelvin[9] | mi | mile |
| L | liter | mol | mole |
| Pa | pascal | s (SI abbrev.) | second |
| W | watt | sec (US abbrev.) | second |

9. The unit *kelvin* is lowercased, but both the abbreviation (K) and the name of the scale (the Kelvin scale) are capitalized. Temperatures expressed in kelvins do not carry a degree sign: Water freezes at 273 K (32°F) and boils at 373 K (212°F). (Note that *Chicago*'s convention has no space before or after a degree symbol with an abbreviated unit of measurement but includes a space when the abbreviation directly follows the numeral.)

Care must be taken in the capitalization of abbreviations for prefixes used in the metric and SI systems.[10] The prefixes larger than *kilo-* are uppercased; the others are lowercased. For example:

| T | tera- | (1 trillion × the base unit) | k | kilo- | (1,000 × the base unit) |
| G | giga- | (1 billion × the base unit) | c | centi- | (0.01 × the base unit) |
| M | mega- | (1 million × the base unit) | m | milli- | (0.001 × the base unit) |

In scientific and technical measurements, the official SI abbreviation for *kilo-*, one thousand times something, is always lowercase "k," never capitalized "K." But in nontechnical writing a capitalized "K" is sometimes used as an informal abbreviation for one thousand (*not* for kelvin) in contexts where the unit of measurement is understood: a 10K run (10 kilometers), a 700K disk (700 kilobytes). When referring to disk capacity in computers, however, the prefix *kilo-* (usually abbreviated as a capitalized "K") signifies a binary thousand (1,024); a kilobit is abbreviated Kb, a kilobyte KB.

Uncommon units of measurement should be spelled out on first mention in documents intended for general readers, but such units need not be spelled out in documents intended for specialists.

*For general readers:* The best of the dot-matrix printers produced noticeably stippled text at 72 dots per inch (dpi); today, the standard laser printer provides a crisp 600 dpi.

*For general readers:* The lead levels in 102 of the 150 samples exceeded 8 parts per million.
[The abbreviation "ppm" should be supplied only if the document contains further references to this unit.]

*For specialists:* The lead levels in 102 of the 150 samples exceeded 8 ppm.

When measurements are given in both US and SI units, the equivalences are enclosed in parentheses.

The shards were found 328 ft (100 m) from the fence.

The shards were found 100 m (328 ft) from the fence.

The boiling point of this compound is 800°F (445°C).

The boiling point of this compound is 445°C (800°F).

On his homebuilt 1920 Indian Scout motorcycle, the New Zealander Burt Munro set a world land-speed record of 183.59 mph (295.453 km/h).
[Note the different conventions for abbreviating *miles per hour* and *kilometers per hour*.]

---

10. SI (Système international d'unités; International System of Units), which is based on the metric system, is the international standard in science and technology. *Chicago*, *APA*, and *CSE* all discuss SI conventions.

When an abbreviated unit of measurement appears in a compound adjective preceding a noun, the compound is not hyphenated:

a 20 ft wall      a 13 m tube      a 10 km race      a 5 kg carton

## SOURCE CITATIONS

If you are copyediting text that contains footnotes, in-text references to source materials, or a bibliography, you may encounter or want to use the abbreviations shown in table 11. Although *ibid.* ("in the same place") is still widely used in scholarly documentation, *Chicago* now recommends a short-form citation instead of this abbreviation in publications intended for a digital environment, because the previous note specifying source details may not be displayed with the linked note containing only the abbreviation.

## ACRONYMS AND INITIALISMS

*Capitalization, punctuation, and typography.* All the major style manuals recommend that abbreviations described as acronyms and initialisms be set in uppercase letters with no internal periods: WHO, MRI, CPR. However, a newer convention for styling acronyms, long observed in some British publications, has been adopted by many US newspapers, and it seems likely to spread to corporate and book publishing:

*Full caps for initialisms:* NFL, HMO, NAACP
*Full caps for three- or four-letter acronyms:* RAM, GATT
*Initial cap only for acronyms of five or more letters:* Nafta, Erisa

Some publications differentiate the treatment of acronyms and initialisms in other ways. The *New York Times* uses periods with initialisms (U.A.W.), except for some well-known terms commonly rendered without periods (CBS, DSL, OMG); it omits periods with acronyms, which are fully capitalized if they have four letters or less (NATO) and upper-and-lowercased if they are longer (Unesco). The *New Yorker* uses full capital letters and periods for initialisms standing for proper names (I.R.A.); full capitals without periods for initialisms standing for common nouns (MRI); and small caps for acronyms (PET scan), even at the beginning of a sentence, with some exceptions involving hyphenated acronyms (C-SPAN). The resulting typographic incongruities, like the quaint use of the diaeresis (coöperation), are hallmarks of the magazine's house style:

PET scans, functional MRIs, and other types of brain imaging can investigate the neural bases of visual imagery.

Groups like ETA and the I.R.A. have committed reprehensible acts of violence.

The floor debate was typical C-SPANnery.

*Plural formations.* If an acronym or initialism stands for a singular item, the plural is formed regularly, by simply adding an *s*.

TABLE 11. Bibliographical Abbreviations

| Singular | Plural | Meaning |
| --- | --- | --- |
| cf. | — | compare. Used to direct readers to compare (not simply to "see" or "see also") a source that presents an alternative interpretation or point of view: Cf. Ludi, *Rights and Privileges,* p. 35. |
| chap. | chaps. | chapter |
| ed. | — | edition; editor; edited by |
| | eds. | editors |
| et al. | — | and others. Used in some styles of documentation to refer to a work that has multiple authors: Barton et al. repeated this experiment. There is no period after "et" because the Latin *et* (and) is a complete word. |
| f. | ff. | and following. Used to refer to pages: See pp. 67f. and pp. 234ff. (The plural "pp." is because the reader is being referred to more than one page.) Or, if the publisher's style calls for the omission of "p." and "pp.": See 67f. and 234ff. There is no space between the numeral and "f." or "ff." |
| fig. | figs. | figure |
| ibid. | — | in the same place. Used in some styles of documentation to indicate that the source of a quotation or piece of evidence is the same as the source previously cited. Usually appears only in notes and is capitalized when it is the first word in a note: 8. Ibid., p. 15. Or, if "p." is not used: 8. Ibid., 15. *Chicago* advises against using this abbreviation for documents intended for digital publication. |
| l. | ll. | line. Many publishers discourage authors from using "l." and "ll." because these abbreviations too closely resemble the numerals 1 and 11. Some authors use "v." (pl. "vv."), "verse," instead. |
| n. | nn. | note (i.e., footnote or endnote) |
| no. | nos. | number (i.e., issue of a magazine or journal) |
| p. | pp. | page |
| pt. | pts. | part |
| s.v. | s.vv. | *sub verbo* (pl. *verbis*; "under the word[s]"); see under. Used to refer the reader to an entry in a dictionary or an encyclopedia: *Webster's New World*, s.v. "comprise." |
| vol. | vols. | volume |

He studied leveraged buyouts (LBOs) and initial public offerings (IPOs).

My girlfriend pointedly ignored my frequent SOSs at the singles bar.

But if the initials themselves stand for a plural item, do not add an *s*:

NIH = National Institutes of Health

CDC = Centers for Disease Control

Usage remains unsettled for "WMD" and "FAQ." *M-W Collegiate* online defines "WMD" as "weapons [plural] of mass destruction," and, for what it's worth, so does the *Department of Defense Dictionary of Military and Associated Terms* (s.v. "WMD"): The United States and the UK asserted that Saddam Hussein possessed large stockpiles of WMD. *AHD* online defines the term as "weapon [singular] of mass destruction," thus capable of taking a plural inflection: The soldiers searched for WMDs. Likewise, the abbreviation "FAQ" can mean either a list of frequently asked questions (Did you peruse the FAQ for a solution?) or a single frequently asked question on a list with many such questions (Yes, I scanned the FAQs but didn't find an answer).

Do initialisms that stand for a plural item take a singular or plural verb? The answer may depend on the meaning. Consider the uses of "EPS" (earnings per share) and "MIS" (management information systems):

EPS is used to evaluate . . .
    [*Meaning* earnings per share as a discrete measurement]

Our MIS is under review . . .
    [*Meaning* management information systems as a whole]

Our competitors' MIS are better . . .
    [*Meaning* competitors' discrete management information systems]

*Formation of nonce words (a.k.a. verbing and nouning).* The formation of verbs and nouns from initialisms is acceptable only for informal contexts: OK's, OK'd, OK'ing, cc'ing, CBer, and similar improvisations have no place in formal or professional writing—unless deliberately used for a particular (often humorous) effect.

*Familiar versus unfamiliar.* Acronyms and initialisms that appear in the alphabetical section of a standard dictionary (e.g., AIDS, DNA, LSD, REM, VCR) need not be introduced or spelled out, even on first mention. This principle also applies to the distilled terms for well-known organizations (e.g., AFL-CIO, CIA, FBI, IRS, NATO, YMCA). Nonetheless, if the intended audience includes readers in other countries or readers unlikely to be familiar with the abbreviated terminology, spell out all such shortened forms on first use. The watchword is "When in doubt, spell it out."[11]

---

11. Some acronyms and initialisms are, in fact, orphans; that is, the original full name has been entirely discarded in favor of the abbreviation, sometimes for reasons of branding: the American Association of Retired Persons is now AARP, the Future Farmers of America is FFA, and Kentucky Fried Chicken has become KFC. For unfamiliar or potentially ambiguous orphan abbreviations, the editor may still need to identify the former full name parenthetically: AAA (formerly the American Automobile Association).

In documents addressed to scientists, technical specialists, and other professional experts, acronyms and initialisms that are standard in the field may usually be used without any introduction. For example, an accountant writing a report addressed to other accountants can confidently use FASB, IRR, and ROI.[12] But when the intended audience for the document is broader (say, readers in other specialties or in other countries), all such terms should be formally introduced.

*Parenthetical introduction.*  The traditional way to introduce an acronym or initialism is to place it in parentheses after the first mention of its spelled-out equivalent in the running text and also in any stand-alone sections, such as abstracts, figure captions, tables, or appendixes, where readers need to understand the shorthand without scouring the main text to rediscover the definition.

> The courthouse was picketed by Mothers Against Drunk Driving (MADD) following the jury's failure to convict the driver. Several members of MADD were arrested.

> The International Monetary Fund (IMF) will announce its decision next month. Analysts predict that the IMF will reinstate the funding package only if the government presents a credible budget that includes substantial cuts in social welfare programs.

> The technology for optical character recognition (OCR) has improved in the last five years. But even when OCR is 99.99 percent accurate, scanned documents will contain 1 error per 10,000 characters, or about 1 error on every third page.[13]

When introducing an acronym or initialism on first mention would interrupt a compound or force an otherwise awkward parenthetical expression, either the sentence should be rewritten or the introduction of the short term should be delayed until its second mention.

> *Awkward:* If you have a fever and you either have traveled to a severe acute respiratory syndrome (SARS)–affected area or have in the past ten days been around a person who has SARS, your doctor may suspect the disease.

---

12. FASB = Financial Accounting Standards Board; IRR = internal rate of return; ROI = return on investment.

13. Under the influence of the *AP Stylebook,* some nonjournalists have adopted a convention that does away with the parenthetical introduction of acronyms and initialisms. The AP rule is to spell out the term on its first mention in the text and to use the short form thereafter; if the term standing alone will be puzzling to readers, then the spelled-out term is always used. Under this system, the examples would read:

> The courthouse was picketed by Mothers Against Drunk Driving following the jury's failure to convict the driver. Several members of MADD were arrested.

> The International Monetary Fund will announce its decision next month. Analysts predict that the IMF will reinstate the funding package . . .

> The technology for optical character recognition has improved in the last five years. But even when OCR is 99.99 percent accurate, scanned documents will contain . . .

*Revision:* Your doctor may suspect severe acute respiratory syndrome (SARS) if you have a fever and you either have traveled to a SARS-affected area or have in the past ten days been around a person who has SARS.

---

*Awkward:* Any retirement plan opened by an account executive (AE; except those who hold Series 11 licenses) must be reviewed by the AE's branch manager.

*Revision:* Any retirement plan opened by an account executive (AE)—except those who hold Series 11 licenses—must be reviewed by the AE's branch manager.

*Or:* Any retirement plan opened by an account executive (AE) who does not hold a Series 11 license must be reviewed by the AE's branch manager.

If the first mention of the spelled-out term is possessive or plural in form, the parenthetical acronym that follows must be possessive or plural as well. If the result is awkward, the sentence should be rewritten.

*Awkward:* The Food and Drug Administration's (FDA's) position is . . .

*Better:* The position of the Food and Drug Administration (FDA) is . . .

---

Users of the linguistic corpus can search for specific parts of speech (POSs).

*Or:* Users of the linguistic corpus can search for a specific part of speech (POS).

For terms better known by their short form than by their full name, some publishers prefer that the abbreviated term precede the spelled-out one on first mention:

The CPU (central processing unit) is often called the brain of the computer.

Newcomers are advised to read the list of FAQs (frequently asked questions).

As all the preceding examples illustrate, only proper nouns and proper adjectives are capitalized in the spelled-out version of an acronym or initialism.

Ideally, an acronym or initialism is introduced shortly before it is repeatedly used in the document. For example, an organization may be mentioned in a long list on page 5 of the text, but if that organization is not discussed in detail until page 25, it is preferable to introduce the shortened term on page 25 rather than on the first mention of the organization. Alternatively, the term can be introduced on page 5 and reintroduced on page 25. In very long documents, especially those using many unfamiliar abbreviations, readers will appreciate seeing the spelled-out term on the first mention in each chapter or long section.

There is usually no need to use an acronym or initialism at all if the full term appears only a handful of times in a document, because the space to be saved is not worth the strain placed on the reader's memory. Occasionally, however, an author may introduce an abbreviated term solely so that readers who come across it in another context will recognize it.

*Alphabet soup.* Writers and copyeditors must guard against "alphabet soup," strings of confusing nonce forms that will confuse readers.

*Alphabet soup:* MDFs scored higher than MDMs on the DI.

*Revision:* Moderately dysthymic females scored higher on the depression inventory than moderately dysthymic males.

---

*Alphabet soup:* The CDF-SPP map shows both the CCDs and the smaller CBGs within the LAWD.

*Revision:* The map produced by the Strategic Planning Program of the California Department of Forestry shows both the county census divisions and the smaller census block groups within the Los Angeles Water District.

This last example could be rewritten to introduce one or two abridged terms, but readers will be overwhelmed by five new terms in one sentence:

*Confusing:* The map produced by the Strategic Planning Program (SPP) of the California Department of Forestry (CDF) shows both the county census divisions (CCDs) and the smaller census block groups (CBGs) within the Los Angeles Water District (LAWD).

*Revision:* The map produced by the Strategic Planning Program of the California Department of Forestry shows both the county census divisions (CCDs) and the smaller census block groups (CBGs) within the Los Angeles Water District.

*Or:* The map produced by the Strategic Planning Program of the California Department of Forestry (CDF) shows both the county census divisions and the smaller census block groups within the Los Angeles Water District (LAWD).

*International organizations.* Some international organizations are best known by acronyms and initialisms that derive from their non-English names. In such cases, it is preferable to include both the organization's proper name and the English translation of the name. Although a bit cumbersome, this system prevents readers from puzzling over the relationship between the abbreviation and the translated name.

The PRI (Partido Revolucionario Institucional; Institutional Revolutionary Party) ruled Mexico for decades.

The initial study was conducted by researchers at CERN (formerly the Conseil Européen pour la Recherche Nucléaire, or European Council for Nuclear Research, now the European Organization for Nuclear Research).

Some publications use less formal constructions to provide the additional information:

The conference is being sponsored by the GSI (which stands for the German Gesellschaft für Schwerionenforschung, or Society for Heavy Ion Research).

In Sunday's election the Institutional Revolutionary Party, best known by its Spanish acronym PRI, lost its majority in the House of Deputies.

*A or an?* When an indefinite article precedes an acronym or initialism, the choice between *a* and *an* follows from the pronunciation:

> a FAQ file ("fack"; but "an FAQ file" with the alternate pronunciation
>     "eff-ay-cue")
> an FTC commissioner ("eff-tee-cee")
> an IRA plan (pronounced either "eye-are-ay" or "eye-ruh"; either way, the article
>     is "an")
> an LED display ("ell-ee-dee")
> an MPEG application ("em-peg")
> an NAACP spokesperson ("en-double-ay-cee-pee")
> an ROTC program (officially, "are-oh-tee-cee"; but "a ROTC program" with the
>     occasional alternate pronunciation "rot-cee")
> an SEC ruling ("ess-ee-cee")
> a SEP-IRA plan ("sep-eye-ruh")
> a UNESCO project ("you-neh-sco")
> a URL ("you-are-ell"; but "an URL" with the less common pronunciation "earl")

If you do not know how an acronym or initialism is pronounced, ask your author or editorial coordinator for help.

*Redundonyms.* In speech, people often use an acronym or initialism followed by a word that is actually a part of the abbreviation:

> ATM machine (ATM = automated teller machine)
> GRE exam (GRE = Graduate Record Examination)
> HIV virus (HIV = human immunodeficiency virus)
> PIN number (PIN = personal identification number)
> UPS service (UPS = United Parcel Service)

In writing, such redundancies are best avoided.

A former redundonym, "SAT test," is no longer a redundonym. In 1997 the College Board, the company that administers the exam, announced that SAT was not an initialism. "The SAT has become the trademark; it doesn't stand for anything."[14]

*Pronunciation cues.* There are several conventions for representing the pronunciation of an acronym:

> ASCII (pronounced "ass´-key")        ASCII (pronounced ASS-key)
> ASCII (rhymes with "passkey")        ASCII (rhymes with *passkey*)

14. Scott Jeffe, in Peter Applebome, "Insisting It's Nothing, Creator Says SAT, Not S.A.T.," *New York Times,* April 2, 1997, p. A16, national edition. Originally, *SAT* stood for "Scholastic Aptitude Test"; after years of dispute about whether the test measures aptitude, as opposed to skills, the exam was rechristened "Scholastic Assessment Test."

As in all other matters, consistency within a document is crucial, whichever convention is used.

*List of abbreviations.*  As a kindness to readers, long documents that incorporate many acronyms and initialisms often include an alphabetized list of abbreviations. In a book this list may appear in the front matter or in the back matter; in a shorter document, the list may appear in a footnote or an endnote or in a separate section that precedes or follows the main text.

## SYMBOLS AND SIGNS

A handful of symbols and signs are in common currency:

> nonalphanumeric characters found on the standard keyboard:
> @   #   $   %   &   *
> degree sign, for temperature and longitude and latitude: °
> single and double prime signs, for feet and inches as well as longitude and latitude:
> ′   ″
>
> section and paragraph signs, for citations from legal and technical documents:
> §   ¶

Generally, no spacing intervenes between the sign and the numeral in the following types of expressions.

| | | | | | |
|---|---|---|---|---|---|
| *Currencies:* | $525 | 65¢ | £123 | ¥10,568 | €110 million |
| *Percentages:* | 15% | 8.4% | 0.5% | $2\frac{1}{2}$% | |
| *Citations:* | § 1457(a) | ¶ 5(c–e) | §§ 123–36 | ¶¶ 1–10 | |
| *Linear measurements:* | 6′ | 5′2″ | 3′6″ × 2′8″ | | |
| *Latitudes and longitudes:* | N 50°45′35″ (*or* 50°45′35″ N) | | | | |
| | E 85°20′10″ (*or* 85°20′10″ E) | | | | |
| *Temperatures:* | 61°F (*or* 61 °F) | 16°C (*or* 16 °C) | | | |

*Notes:* The *AMA Manual of Style,* the standard reference for many biomedical journals, stipulates that no spaces should appear between the unit of measure, the degree symbol, and the Celsius or Fahrenheit designation; *Chicago* (at 10.58) concurs. Following SI usage, however, *CSE* specifies a space before (but not after) the degree sign. In legal citations following *Bluebook* and the revised *Chicago* forms, the section symbol has spaces before and after.

Spacing between values and electrical unit symbols depends on the field and the publisher's style:

> kilovolt:   1 kV *or* 1kV        megawatts:   2.2 MW *or* 2.2MW

The US National Institute of Standards and Technology (NIST) and Canada's National Research Council (NRC), which follow SI rules, insert a space between the number and the unit. This is the most common approach in the sciences but not in every field of engineering. When in doubt, query the editorial coordinator or, in the absence of a style guide, insert a space.

No spacing is used in abbreviated terms with the ampersand: A&P (supermarkets), S&P (Standard and Poor's), R&D (research and development).

Copyeditors working on hard copy may need to call out for the compositor the names of the following signs and symbols.

| | |
|---|---|
| # | number sign, pound sign, hash mark, hash, octothorpe |
| £ | pound sign (British currency) |
| € | euro glyph (single European currency) |
| ¥ | yen sign |
| & | ampersand |
| @ | at sign |
| * | asterisk |
| ( ) | parentheses |
| [ ] | brackets, square brackets |
| { } | braces, curly brackets |
| < > | angle brackets |
| « » | guillemets (a style of quotation marks used in some European languages) |
| / | slant, slash, virgule, solidus |
| \ | backslash |
| \| | pipe, vertical bar |
| † | dagger |
| ‡ | double dagger |
| ¶ | paragraph sign (formerly called *pilcrow*) |
| § | section sign |
| ° | degree sign |
| ‖ | parallels |
| ☜ ☞ | index symbols, manicules, pointing hands, bishop's fists, etc. |

Greek letters appearing in Latin text must also be identified for the typesetter—e.g., A or α (alpha), Ω or ω (omega). A list of the capital and lowercase Greek letters can be found in an authoritative dictionary; *Chicago* provides the complete alphabet (with Unicode numbers for on-screen editors) at table 11.4.

Copyeditors working on-screen must correctly insert any nonstandard symbols—those that cannot be typed directly on their keyboard—as Unicode characters by using keyboard combinations or the software's symbol browser, or by consulting internet resources to find the correct hexadecimal codes to key in or symbols to copy and paste. Editors should never improvise symbols by substituting, for example, an apostrophe for a prime symbol, angle brackets for guillemets, or an en dash for a minus sign. *Unicode,* a platform-independent international standard for the character encoding of world languages and symbols, is supported by most contemporary computer operating systems and internet browsers and by many software applications. Still, most fonts support only a subset of the vast Unicode character set. Thus, when a manuscript contains non-QWERTY accents, alphabets, and symbols, the editor should list these items for the production designer's evaluation during font selection and should avoid changing fonts during editing, which could cause these characters to display incorrectly.

*Chicago* discusses additional symbols in chapters on foreign languages and mathematics, and *APA* has several lists of symbols used in the social sciences. Copyeditors who work with scientific or technical material should consult *CSE* or a specialized handbook.

*APA* offers the following guidelines about beginning a sentence with a symbol: "Never begin a sentence with . . . a symbol that stands alone (e.g., α). Begin a sentence with . . . a symbol connected to a word (e.g., β-Endorphins) only when necessary to avoid indirect and awkward writing. In the case of chemical compounds, capitalize the first letter of the word to which the symbol is connected" (p. 111). For example:

> *In regular running text:* The effects of λ-hydroxy-β-aminobutyric acid were measured.

> *At the start of a sentence:* λ-Hydroxy-β-aminobutyric acid has several unusual properties.

# CHAPTER 10

# ❡ Tables, Graphs, and Art

The problems that copyeditors encounter in handling tables, graphs, and art depend on how well the author understands the construction of these elements and on how much care the author has taken in their preparation. Ideally, tables and graphs offer an efficient way to present a large amount of information, most often numerical data. And various types of art—line drawings, maps, charts, photographs—can be used to present information or to provide ornamentation.

However, because tables, graphs, and art are more expensive to produce than running text, most publishers ask authors to exercise some restraint, with the number and complexity of these items depending on the nature of the project. Although a field guide to Pacific Coast birds, for example, will contain many illustrations (line drawings, black-and-white photographs, color photographs, and maps), the biography of an ornithologist may have no illustrations or just a handful of photographs.

The two questions a copyeditor should always ask about any table, graph, chart, map, or photograph are these: What specific purpose is this item intended to serve? Is this particular item the best way to serve that purpose? You must be able to answer these questions in order to correctly handle the item. But unless you are providing a full menu of production services to an indie author, you need not concern yourself with the technical quality of an illustration; the publisher's production staff will evaluate that. The production staff will also arrange to have charts or maps redrawn by graphic artists.

## TABLES

All the major style manuals discuss the construction and formatting of tables and provide some tips on simplifying complex tables. Copyeditors who deal with relatively simple tables may need no guidance beyond that offered in *Chicago* or *WIT*. *CSE* and *APA* offer more sophisticated treatments of various types of scientific and statistical tables.

When working on a manuscript that contains more than a few short tables, you will usually have to make three passes through the tables—either on-screen or on hard copy:

*Pass 1.* Look at a table when it is first mentioned in the text.

- Make sure that the table "tells" a worthwhile and intelligible story. Although tables are meant to be read in conjunction with the text, a table should be understandable on its own.

- Check the relationship between the text and the table: Does the table present the information that the text says it presents? Is all the information in the table relevant to the discussion in the text? Does any information in the table seem to contradict the text?

*Pass 2.* At a convenient point, stop reading the manuscript and copyedit the table.

- Check the numbering and location of the table.
- Impose mechanical consistency (spelling, capitalization, punctuation, use of abbreviations).
- Scan the data in the table for internal inconsistencies.
- Verify that all information taken from other sources is attributed.
- Query an unusually small or large table that may need to be reconceptualized.

*Pass 3.* Read all the tables in the manuscript as a batch.

- Make sure all elements (e.g., table numbers, titles, column heads, footnotes) are consistent in format. (The elements of a table are illustrated in figure 7.)

Let's look at each of these tasks in turn.

## EVALUATING THE STORY

The function of a table is to provide information in a format that is more efficient or effective than a prose description of the information would be. For example, the information presented in the table in figure 7 would be harder to comprehend if it were presented in a sentence-by-sentence, animal-by-animal report of the experiment: "Of the 9 camels tested, 7 (or 78%) tested positive. Of the 36 cows tested, 6 (or 17%) tested positive . . ."

When a table does not appear to be efficient or effective, however, the copyeditor should suggest that the information be given in the text proper and that the table be dropped. For example, consider table 12.

TABLE 12.  Turnout in Anytown Mayoral Elections, 1994–1998, by District

|            | 1994  | 1996  | 1998  |
|------------|-------|-------|-------|
| District 1 | 58.4% | 54.0% | 58.3% |
| District 2 | 69.8  | 67.9  | 70.0  |
| District 3 | 67.7  | 68.8  | 70.1  |

FIGURE 7.  Parts of a Table

| | Table 1. Virus-Neutralization Tests on Sera from Mammals and Birds | | | Table title |

| | | Number | Positive | | Column heads / Spanner head / Decked heads |
|---|---|---|---|---|---|
| Table number | Table 1. Virus-Neutralization Tests on Sera from Mammals and Birds | | | | Table title |
| | Species | Tested | $N$ | % | |
| Stub head | Species | Tested | $N$ | % | |
| Cut-in head | Mammals | | | | |
| Stub entries | Camel | 9 | 7 | 78 | |
| | Cow | 36 | 6 | 17 | |
| | Donkey | 15 | 7 | 47 | Cells |
| | . . . | . . . | . . . | . . . | |
| | Sheep | 64 | 15 | 23 | |
| Subtotal | Total mammals | 466 | 187 | 40 | |
| | Birds | | | | |
| | Chicken* | 24 | 4 | 16 | Indicator for footnote that applies to an entire row |
| | Crow | 163 | 102 | 65 | |
| | Duck | 14 | 2[†] | 14 | Indicator for footnote that applies only to one cell |
| | . . . | . . . | . . . | . . . | |
| Subtotal | Total birds | 420 | 170 | 40 | |
| Grand total | Grand total | 886 | 357 | 40 | |

Stub head · Cut-in head · Stub entries · Subtotal · Grand total (left-margin labels)

Source note

*Source:* Chris T. Author, *Book Title* (New York: Big Books, 1990), 536–37.

Footnotes

*Note:* All tests and retests were performed under IASA standards.

*Chickens were retested by PSA-3 analysis.
[†]Retest results were inconclusive for 2 additional ducks.

Because the array in table 12 is both short (four lines of text) and narrow (four columns), all the information could easily be displayed in a multicolumn list:

|  | 1994 | 1996 | 1998 |
|---|---|---|---|
| District 1 | 58.4% | 54.0% | 58.3% |
| District 2 | 69.8 | 67.9 | 70.0 |
| District 3 | 67.7 | 68.8 | 70.1 |

Table 13 presents a different type of difficulty. Although it sorts the numbers of voters and nonvoters by gender—as its title promises—the raw numbers do not tell the entire story. Readers cannot easily ascertain whether voting is more common among men or among women, nor how great the gender gap might be.

In other words, the real story in table 13 lies in the percentages (not the raw numbers) of voters and nonvoters. One could improve the table by adding columns that supply the percentages or by replacing the raw numbers with the percentages, as shown in table 14.

But consider how easily the information in table 14 could be conveyed in one sentence:

In the April primary election, 60.0 percent of the registered men but only 56.9 percent of the registered women voted.

Or, if greater visual emphasis is desired, the information can be presented as a simple two-column list, omitting the redundant "Did Not Vote" category altogether. (If you

TABLE 13. April Primary Election: Turnout among Registered Voters, by Gender

|  | Voted | Did Not Vote | Total |
|---|---|---|---|
| Men | 2,111 | 1,404 | 3,515 |
| Women | 1,904 | 1,440 | 3,344 |
| Total | 4,015 | 2,844 | 6,859 |

TABLE 14. April Primary Election: Turnout among Registered Voters, by Gender

|  | Number of Registered Voters | Voted | Did Not Vote |
|---|---|---|---|
| Men | 3,515 | 60.0% | 40.0% |
| Women | 3,344 | 56.9% | 43.1% |
| Total | 6,859 | 58.5% | 41.5% |

know the percentage of registered voters who voted, you can easily determine the percentage who didn't vote.)

Among registered voters, men were more likely than women to turn out for the April primary.

|  | *Voted* |
|---|---|
| Men | 60.0% |
| Women | 56.9% |

If you come upon a table that contains many different types of data and is referred to repeatedly in the manuscript over a series of pages, you can suggest to the author that it be broken into several less complicated tables. (Problems related to a table's physical size, rather than its complexity, are discussed later in this chapter.)

## RELATIONSHIP BETWEEN TEXT AND TABLE

The discussion of a table should not simply describe the table nor repeat vast portions of the data given in the table. Rather, the discussion should, as needed, prepare the reader to understand the table; summarize the importance, meaning, or value of the data presented in the table; or explain the implications of the data. Suppose your author writes:

> For each member of the OECD, table 2.2 shows the population (column 1), population density per square mile (column 2), per capita gross national product (column 3), per capita annual income (column 4), and life expectancy (column 5).

Since the table does show all these items, and each column in the table carries a heading that identifies it, this entire sentence could be deleted.

Another example. Your author writes:

> For at least a decade after the depression, the rate of population growth declined substantially. The birthrate dropped (see table 15), from 31.5 per thousand in 1920, to 28.7 per thousand in 1930, to 24.7 per thousand in 1935, and began to recover modestly only in 1945 (25.2 per thousand). In addition, emigration increased and immigration came to a halt.

TABLE 15.  Birthrates and Death Rates, 1915–1950
(per 1,000 inhabitants)

|  | Birthrate | Death Rate |  | Birthrate | Death Rate |
|---|---|---|---|---|---|
| 1915 | 35.1 | 15.5 | 1935 | 24.7 | 12.5 |
| 1920 | 31.5 | 14.7 | 1940 | 24.0 | 10.7 |
| 1925 | 30.9 | 13.6 | 1945 | 25.2 | 10.3 |
| 1930 | 28.7 | 12.2 | 1950 | 28.9 | 10.1 |

(Note the doubled-up stub entries in table 15.) You could delete the redundant data in the text and write a query to the author to explain the change:

> For at least a decade after the depression, the rate of population growth declined substantially. The birthrate dropped ~~(see table 13), from 31.5 per thousand in~~ between 1920~~, to 28.7 per thousand in~~ and 1930, ~~to 24.7 per thousand in 1935,~~ continued to decline through 1940, and began to recover modestly only in 1945 ~~(25.2 per thousand).~~ (see table 15). In addition, emigration increased and immigration came to a halt.

*In-text cross-references.* *Chicago* recommends lowercasing in-text references to tables and portions of them: see tables 3 and 4; see tables 1.6 through 1.9; see table 12, column 2. *WIT, APA,* and *CSE* uppercase in-text references to tables (e.g., see Tables 3 and 4) and are silent on the issue of how to treat portions of tables.

*Percent versus percentage.* When referring to percentages that are shown in tables, conservative usage favors the noun *percentage* (not *percent*): The percentage of absentee voters has continued to increase.

## NUMBERING AND PLACING TABLES

All tables in a manuscript must be numbered consecutively, by either single numeration (Table 1, Table 2, Table 3) or double numeration, where the first digit represents the chapter number and the second digit represents the table's relative location within that chapter (Table 1.1, Table 1.2, Table 1.3).[1] The numbering should match the order in which the tables are first referred to in the text. In other words, it is not acceptable to have the first in-text reference to table 3 precede the first in-text reference to table 2. Once a table has been introduced, it may be referred to again at any time. If there is only one table in the document, it is usually labeled Table 1 in a scholarly or professional context but may be unnumbered in a less formal context, with an in-text reference simply reading "see table." Avoid (or revise) references to "the table above" and "the table below," since the placement of the table will depend on the final layout in a printed work and may be meaningless in a digital publication without a fixed-page format.

In hard-copy manuscripts, all the tables must be removed from the running text and gathered in a separate batch, one table to a page, at the end of the manuscript. If the tables are interspersed throughout the manuscript, you may need to photocopy the originals (one table to a page), mark for deletion the tables interspersed in the manuscript, and call out the approximate location of each table in the left margin. These placement callouts are usually done in red pencil (so they can be easily spotted) and are placed in boxes (like other editorial instructions):

---

1. Under both systems, tables that appear in an appendix take the lettered designation of the appendix as their first element. Thus the tables in appendix A are numbered Table A.1, Table A.2, and so on; the tables in appendix B are labeled Table B.1, Table B.2, and so on.

For many working-class families, real wages fell by as much as 50 percent between the depression of 1913 and the Armistice in November 1918 (see table 8.4). The falling standard of living and a tightening labor market proved a politically explosive combination.

In on-screen manuscripts, the procedure is similar—all the tables are gathered in a separate file (or several files when there are many long tables), and an in-text code is inserted at the end of a paragraph to alert the compositor to the location of each table:

> For many working-class families, real wages fell by as much as 50 percent between the depression of 1913 and the Armistice in November 1918 (see table 8.4). The falling standard of living and a tightening labor market proved a politically explosive combination. <Table 8.4>

For the compositor's convenience, the location of each table is called out on the hard copy if it accompanies the files. When the tables are complex or poorly prepared, you may be asked to copyedit them on the hard copy rather than on-screen.

## MECHANICAL EDITING

*Table numbers.*  Some publishers have a preferred house style for the format and terminal punctuation of the table numbers that precede the table title. For example:

> *All caps, followed by a period:* TABLE 1. World Population, 1996
>
> *Upper- and lowercase, followed by a colon:* Table 1: World Population, 1996
>
> *Uppercase and small caps, followed by one or more wordspaces:*
> Table 1    World Population, 1996

Other publishers allow authors to use any reasonable style for table numbers, as long as it is applied consistently.

*Table titles.*  Titles should be accurate and brief. If the table is part of a scholarly or serious nonfiction work, the table title should be an objective statement of the table's contents and should not express value judgments or conclusions about the data (*not* "SAT Scores Drop between 1960 and 1995" *but* "SAT Scores, 1960–1995"). In business reports and newsletters, in contrast, a table title may function as an eye-catching interpretive headline ("Sales Soar in 2018").

The capitalization and terminal punctuation of the table titles should follow house style. If there is no house style, be sure the author has been consistent in these matters. Typically, the title is set in one of the styles shown here, with no terminal punctuation following.

*Headline style:* Per Capita Personal Income in Canada, Mexico, and the United States, 1995

*Sentence style:* Per capita personal income in Canada, Mexico, and the United States, 1995

*All caps:* PER CAPITA PERSONAL INCOME IN CANADA, MEXICO, AND THE UNITED STATES, 1995

As these examples illustrate, long titles are cumbersome and hard to read when set in all caps, so an all-caps style is best reserved for a piece in which all the table titles are short. (The rules for headline style and sentence style capitalization are discussed under "Titles of Works" in chapter 6.)

*Squibs.* A *squib* is a short parenthetical indicator placed after the table title to identify an element that pertains to the table as a whole. For example, in a table itemizing a state's annual budget, it is preferable not to clutter the table with six-, seven-, eight-, and nine-digit numbers. Instead, a squib—"($ Millions)"—is placed after the table title. Tables 16 and 17 illustrate how much space this device can save.

Some publishers prefer to set squibs in headline style, and others prefer sentence style:

| *Headline style* | *Sentence style* |
|---|---|
| (in Constant 1985 Dollars) | (In constant 1985 dollars) |
| (in Thousands of Persons) | (In thousands of persons) |
| (in Japanese Yen) | (In Japanese yen) |

Whichever style is used, all squibs in the manuscript must be treated consistently. (Another use for squibs, to express the baseline for a statistical index, is discussed later in this chapter.)

TABLE 16.  State Budget, 1995–1997

| Department | 1995 | 1996 | 1997 |
|---|---|---|---|
| Education | $14,500,000 | $16,700,000 | $17,300,000 |
| Health | 800,000 | 900,000 | 1,100,000 |
| Transportation | 125,600,000 | 141,100,000 | 136,400,000 |

TABLE 17.  State Budget, 1995–1997 ($ Millions)

| Department | 1995 | 1996 | 1997 |
|---|---|---|---|
| Education | 14.5 | 16.7 | 17.3 |
| Health | 0.8 | 0.9 | 1.1 |
| Transportation | 125.6 | 141.1 | 136.4 |

*Stub.* The *stub* is the far left-hand column of a table, which defines the horizontal variables. Stub items should be arranged logically. For example:

in chronological or reverse chronological order (earliest to latest; most recent to oldest)
in alphabetical order
in size order (largest to smallest; smallest to largest)
in geographical order (northeast to southwest; north to south; distance from the sun)
according to a conventional series (colors of the spectrum; zoological families)

When the stub consists of a set of numerical ranges (e.g., age cohorts), these ranges should not overlap. For example, because the ranges shown here in stub A overlap, readers cannot tell whether the 20-year-olds were counted in the 15–20 group or in the 20–25 group. A copyeditor would have to ask the author to review the data presented in the table and to select the correct ranges (either stub B or stub C).

| A (illogical) | B (logical) | C (logical) |
|---|---|---|
| 15–20 | 15–20 | 15–19 |
| 20–25 | 21–25 | 20–24 |
| 25–30 | 26–30 | 25–29 |

The capitalization of stub entries should also follow house style; if there is no house style, either headline style or sentence style may be used. *Exception:* Scientific terms that begin with a lowercase letter (pH, mRNA) should not be capitalized in the stub.

*Column heads.* Column heads should be brief, logically arranged, and consistently styled for headline or sentence caps. If all cells in a column contain percentages, the percentage sign (%) may be placed in parentheses after the column heading; similarly, if the numbers in a column represent dollars, a dollar sign ($) may be used. (Alternatively, the % or $ may be placed in the first cell in the column or in each cell.)

If different units are used in different columns, the units are placed in parentheses after the column headings, as in table 18. Everyday units of measurement may be abbreviated and placed in parentheses after the column head; unusual abbreviations should be spelled out in a footnote to the table.

| TABLE 18. Oceans of the World | | | |
|---|---|---|---|
| | Area (sq mi) | Average Depth (ft) | Greatest Depth (ft) |
| Pacific | 164,000,000 | 13,215 | 35,820 |
| Atlantic | 81,815,000 | 12,880 | 30,246 |
| Indian | 75,300,000 | 13,002 | 24,460 |
| . . . | . . . | . . . | . . . |

If you copyedit science or social science manuscripts, you are likely to come across tables in which N, *N,* or ɴ appears in a column head. By convention, N is used to indicate the number of subjects or participants in an experiment or survey. Some publishers call for an italic *N;* others prefer a small cap ɴ. Always ask your editorial coordinator which convention to follow.

*Body of a table.* Although the author is responsible for the accuracy of the data in the tables, copyeditors are expected to scan the entries, looking for any obvious typographical errors and querying any apparent inconsistencies or illogicalities. For example:

- All cells in a column should be of the same type and unit.
- If decimal numbers are used, all items in a column should be given to the same number of decimal places, and the column should be marked to align on the decimal point. *Note:* A copyeditor cannot simply add zeros to fill out a column; the editor must ask the author to decide how many decimal places are appropriate to the table and ask the author to supply the correct numbers.
- If four-digit and larger numbers appear in a table, the commas in each column must align.
- Any words in the body of a table must match the editorial style of the document (capitalization, hyphenation, spelling, and the like). Short text entries in table cells usually do not have terminal punctuation, but if cell entries contain full sentences, they should be followed by periods (see table 1 in this book for an example). Any unusual abbreviations or symbols should be defined; these explanations are usually placed in a footnote to the table.
- The notation "n.a." (or "na," "*na,*" or "NA") may be used to mean "not applicable" or "not available," but this abbreviation should not be used for both meanings in the same table or series of tables. When "n.a." stands for "not applicable," "n.av." can be used for "not available." In tables intended for readers familiar with statistical data, there is no need to spell out these abbreviations. In tables intended for nonspecialist readers, *Chicago* recommends leaving the cell blank or inserting an em dash. Some publishers add an unnumbered footnote to the table: n.a. = not applicable.

*Source notes.* If the information presented in a table is not the result of the author's research (lab experiments, fieldwork, surveys), the source(s) of the data must be stated in a note directly below the table (see figure 7). Source notes are not needed, however, for standard mathematical and financial tables (e.g., tables of square roots, logarithms, geometric functions, or mortgage amortizations). Multiple sources are usually listed in the order matching the appearance of the data in the table (either column by column, from left to right, or row by row, from top to bottom).

Source notes are labeled "Source" (or "Sources" when more than one source is named). Depending on the designer's preference, the label may be set in italics or in boldface, in uppercase and small caps, or in some other distinctive style. Some designers prefer a colon after the label "Source"; others use a period.

*Footnotes.*  When copyediting the footnotes to a table, you must first determine which columns, rows, or cells the note refers to. If you are not sure, you must query the author.

Notes that apply to an entire table are placed directly below any source note and are introduced by the label "Note" (or "Notes" when there is more than one). This convention avoids the placing of a footnote superscript or an asterisk after the title of the table. (Most publishers discourage or ban the placement of footnote indicators in display type; *CSE,* however, permits footnote indicators in table titles.) The location of other footnote indicators depends on the content of the note:

| *When a footnote applies to* | *Place the footnote indicator* |
|---|---|
| all entries in a column | in the heading for that column |
| all entries in a row | in the stub entry for that row |
| only one cell | in that cell |

When the same footnote text applies to more than one column, row, or cell, the same footnote indicator should be repeated in all the relevant locations in the body of the table, as shown in table 19. Once you have sorted out where each footnote indicator belongs (column head, stub, or cell), make sure that the order of the footnotes matches their appearance in the table, reading from left to right across the column heads, the column subheads, and then the cells. (*CSE,* however, calls for an entirely different hierarchy for assigning footnotes to tables.)

The content of the table determines the system most appropriate for numbering or lettering the footnotes. Three systems are in common use:

*Numbering:* 1, 2, 3, 4, 5, 6
*Lowercase lettering:* a, b, c, d, e, f
*Asterisk-dagger system:* *, †, ‡, §, ‖, #

The number, letter, or character within the table is conventionally set as a superscript (e.g., $^1$, $^a$, $^*$). At the beginning of the footnote itself, the marker may be set as a superscript, with no punctuation following it (see figure 7); numerals and lowercase letters may also be set as regular characters followed by a period (see table 19).

When a table contains numerals, it is preferable to use lowercase lettering or the asterisk-dagger system because numbered footnotes invite confusion: $123.56^7$. But the asterisk-dagger system cannot be used if any of the tables in the manuscript contain probability footnotes of the form $^*p < .05$ (discussed in the next subsection). In such tables, the asterisk is reserved for the probability footnotes, and it is best to use lowercase letters for the other footnotes.

Whichever system is used, the footnotes in each table begin at the start of the sequence (i.e., the first footnote in each table is labeled 1, a, or *). In other words, the sequence of footnote indicators is never carried over from one table to the next, and

TABLE 19. Unemployment and Mean Annual
Wages, 1954–1957

| | Unemployed as % of Labor Force[a] | Mean Annual Wages | |
|---|---|---|---|
| | | Urban[b] | Rural[c] |
| 1954 | 10.4 | n.a. | n.a. |
| 1955 | 11.5 | $6,221[d] | $5,258 |
| 1956 | 17.7 | 6,717[d] | 5,527 |
| 1957 | 13.4 | 7,049 | 6,342[e] |

*Source:* Jan Smith, *The Economy of Dystopia* (New York: Economics Institute Press, 1965), 122–23.

a. Males over age 16.

b. Urban index based on 10 largest cities and their suburbs.

c. Rural index based on provinces of Jefferson, Adams, and Fillmore.

d. Estimated from incomplete data.

e. Extrapolated from data collected in March 1958.

the sequence of footnote numbers in the running text is never interrupted by any numbered footnotes in a table.[2]

*Footnotes stating probabilities.* When scientists conduct experiments to determine the correlation between two or more variables (i.e., the frequency with which those variables are observed to accompany one another), they subject the correlation to statistical tests in order to ascertain whether the correlation is meaningful (significant) or is merely the result of coincidence. The statistical strength of a correlation is expressed in terms of its probability level, which is conventionally represented as $p$ (a lowercase italic "p"). If the statistical test of significance (a complex set of mathematical operations) shows that a correlation has a 5 percent or smaller chance of being a random coincidence, that correlation is said to have a $p$ that is less than 5 percent; in scientific shorthand, this level of confidence in the result is expressed as $p < .05$. If the correlation has a 1 percent or smaller chance of being random, then $p < .01$, and so on. (No zero precedes the decimal point in these expressions because $p$ by definition is always less than one.) In the body of a table, the correlations that are not statistically significant carry no marker; the correlations that are statistically significant at the weakest level of confidence are marked by a single asterisk; two asterisks mark correlations that have a stronger level of confidence. The $p$ levels are stated in footnotes that follow the table. Notice that in the following example, a portion of a table showing correlations, probability footnotes set on the

2. If the author integrated the tables into the manuscript (rather than treating them as separate items) and if the text and the tables both contain numbered notes, then—most unfortunately—the word processing program will have conflated all the numbers, and you will have to segregate the tables and renumber all the notes in the running text and in each table.

same line are separated by space; if they are run together on the same line, *Chicago* recommends that they be separated by semicolons.

| | | | |
|---|---|---|---|
| .670* | .879** | .612 | .345 |
| .322 | .823* | .989** | .278 |
| .415 | −.124 | .455 | .977* |

*p < .05     **p < .01

*Statistical indexes.* You may also come across tables that have squibs or footnotes containing a year or date, an equals sign, and the numeral 100, for example: (1990 = 100). This kind of shorthand—used by economists, historians, and financial writers—indicates the base year (here, 1990) for a statistical index.

In constructing a statistical index, one assigns the value 100 to a specific point in time (either a year or a month and a year), and values for other periods of time are expressed relative to that baseline. This system enables readers to make immediate comparisons: an index number of 200 means that whatever quantity is being measured has doubled since the period when the baseline was set at 100. For example, if 1980 is the base year for wheat exports, and the index number for 1995 is 200, then wheat exports doubled between 1980 and 1995.

Among the most widely cited indexes is the US Consumer Price Index (CPI), the monthly indicator of the level of retail prices based on the cost of everyday goods and services. Each month the US Bureau of Labor Statistics adds up the cost of a fixed list of consumer items, which is then represented in relation to the cost in the baseline year. Consider these hypothetical figures:

| | Dollar Cost | Index |
|---|---|---|
| March 1984 (baseline) | $250 | 100.0 |
| March 1985 | $265 | 106.0 |
| March 1986 | $277 | 110.8 |

By dividing each month's price by the baseline and multiplying the quotient by 100, one arrives at the index equivalent ($265/$250 = 1.06; 1.06 × 100 = 106), which expresses the percentage increase or decrease relative to the baseline:

106 = 6% increase since the baseline date

110.8 = 10.8% increase since the baseline date

90 = 10% decrease since the baseline date

A table that presents index numbers must indicate the baseline period. By convention, this statement of the baseline is always placed in parentheses, and it appears in one of three places: as a squib following the title of the table; after the appropriate column heading; or as an unnumbered, unasterisked footnote to the table.

| *Baseline as squib:* | Table 8.1. Retail Gasoline Prices, 1965–1995 (1965 = 100) | |
| *Baseline in column head:* | Consumer Price Index (1984 = 100) | Real Wages (1984 = 100) |
| *Baseline in footnote:* | (January 1988 = 100) | |

*Horizontal and vertical rules.* Typically, horizontal rules are placed above and below the body of a table, below spanner heads, and below the column heads (see figure 7). Most publishers ask their copyeditors to delete vertical rules, but sometimes the rules are retained (or added) for tables that have many columns. Check with your editorial coordinator regarding the convention to be observed.

## ODD-SIZE TABLES

Exactly how a table will look on the printed page is the responsibility of the designer, who will select the typeface, type size, margins, column widths, and so on. But if you copyedit books, you will need some general sense of how large a table can fit on a typeset book page. That way, you can make suggestions to the author for revising overly large tables, avoid making suggestions that will result in cumbersome tables, and alert the designer to potential difficulties. Here are some rules of thumb based on a typical book page of six by nine inches. Of course, smaller pages will accommodate less text, and larger pages will accommodate more. (If you are puzzled by the mention of fonts and point sizes in these guidelines, return to this list after you have read chapter 13.)

*Width*
- A table typed in an 11-point font that fits on an 8½-by-11 manuscript page (with 1-inch margins left and right) will comfortably fit on a 6-by-9 book page.
- If the body of the typeset table will be in 8-point type, a 6-by-9 book page can accommodate 80–85 characters per line. A character count of the widest lines in a table should allow at least 2 characters for the spacing in between adjacent column heads.
- If necessary, the table can be set in 8-point type and photoreduced by a small percentage.
- An overly wide table may be run broadside (also called landscape), although some publishers discourage or ban broadside tables. A 6-by-9 book page can accommodate a broadside table that is 125–35 characters wide and 20–25 lines long.
- A very wide table cannot be run across two printed pages; such an arrangement poses almost insurmountable difficulties in binding.
- A very narrow table can be run doubled up (see table 15 earlier in this chapter).

*Length*

- If a double-spaced table typed in an 11-point font fits on two 8½-by-11 manuscript pages (with 1-inch margins top and bottom), it will fit comfortably on one book page.
- If the body of the table will be set in 8-point type, a 6-by-9 book page can accommodate 50–55 lines of text.
- Very long tables can be continued over to the next page. The column heads are repeated at the top of the continuation page, along with the table number and a "continued" line: Table 20 (*continued*). (Repeated column heads and a "continued" line are not required, however, for a long table to be set as a broadside—that is, presented in landscape format—and positioned across a facing-page spread in the printed book.) If column heads must be repeated and a "continued" line added for the runover portion of a table, the editor should flag the table for the production designer's attention.

## ODD-SIZE COLUMNS

Tables that have many words may pose special problems in composition. For example, although the text of table 20 fits across the page, the last column is so narrow that the table looks ungainly. To produce a better-looking table, one could

decrease the number of columns by combining compatible items
decrease the number of characters in any column head that is substantially wider than the data in the column; "stack" the column head, that is, run it as several lines; or, as a last resort, ask the production designer to set the column head on an angle
use common abbreviations
use common symbols

Table 21 shows the result of applying these techniques to table 20. (A fine point: The titles of tables 20 and 21 are capitalized according to sentence style, reflecting the preference of most scientific journals and books.)

## READING TABLES AS A GROUP

During your final pass, you want to look at all the tables as a group in order to double-check the consistency in the treatment of titles, squibs, use of measurement units in column heads, use of horizontal and vertical rules, styling of source notes, placement of dollar and percentage signs, and the like. Note that some publishers want abbreviations spelled out in *each* table, not just the first one in the sequence of tables, so that every table is comprehensible as a stand-alone document.

TABLE 20. Genetic variation within populations of mammal species in the western United States

| Taxonomic Name | Common Name | Heterozygosity* | Sampling Range | Number of Sites | Researchers |
|---|---|---|---|---|---|
| *Dipodomys agilis* | Pacific kangaroo rat | 0.040 | Western United States | 12 | Wilson, Kline, and Stonefield (1995); Wilson and Kline (1996) |
| *Dipodomys deserti* | Desert kangaroo rat | 0.010 | Western United States | 14 | Alvarez and Messinger (1993) |
| *Canis latrans* | Coyote | 0.052 | Southern California | 17 | Singh, Yarnell, and Whapper (1992); Singh and Rosen (1993) |
| *Microtus californicus* | California vole | 0.220 | California Coast Range | 21 | Eden and Paradise (1991); Johnson (1992) |

*Heterozygosity is the proportion of heterozygous genotypes per site per individual.

TABLE 21. Genetic variation (heterozygosity) within populations of mammal species in the western United States

| Taxonomic Name (Common Name) | H* | Sampling Range/ Number of Sites | Researchers |
|---|---|---|---|
| *Dipodomys agilis* (Pacific kangaroo rat) | 0.040 | Western US/12 | Wilson, Kline & Stonefield (1995); Wilson & Kline (1996) |
| *Dipodomys deserti* (Desert kangaroo rat) | 0.010 | Western US/14 | Alvarez & Messinger (1993) |
| *Canis latrans* (Coyote) | 0.052 | S. Calif./17 | Singh, Yarnell & Whapper (1992); Singh & Rosen (1993) |
| *Microtus californicus* (California vole) | 0.220 | Calif. Coast Range/21 | Eden & Paradise (1991); Johnson (1992) |

*H = heterozygosity, the proportion of heterozygous genotypes per site per individual.

## GRAPHS

All graphs must be read for sense, consistency, and editorial style.[3] The procedures are similar to those for tables:

- Make sure that the information or conclusions stated in the text match the data shown in the graph.
- Check the sequence and numbering. Graphs are usually labeled with other visual elements as Figure 1, Figure 2, Figure 3, and so on. When a manuscript contains many graphs, charts, photographs, drawings, or maps, however, each type may be labeled in a separate sequence: graphs labeled Graph 1, Graph 2, and so on; charts labeled Chart 1, Chart 2, and so on; photographs and line drawings labeled Figure 1, Figure 2, and so on; maps labeled Map 1, Map 2, and so on.
- If you are working on hard copy, call out the location of each graph in the margin of the manuscript:

  GRAPH 5 ABOUT HERE

  If you are working on-screen, insert a callout code at the end of a paragraph:

  \<Graph 5\>

- Edit the titles and captions for consistency and mechanical style (spelling, hyphenation, capitalization).
- Make sure every graph has a source line. If the graph is reproduced from a published work that is under copyright, the author may also need to request written permission to reprint the graph from the copyright holder and include a permission credit.[4]
- Check to see that each part of each graph is clearly and correctly labeled and that graphic representations of information are intelligible.

---

3. Copyeditors are usually not expected to comment on the construction of an author's graphs; construction issues include the selection of graph type (e.g., pie, line, bar), selection of scale values, and use of linear or logarithmic scales. However, if you are interested in these topics, you might look at Edward R. Tufte's *The Visual Display of Quantitative Information.* In addition to describing the principles that govern graphical excellence, Tufte demonstrates numerous ways to maximize what he calls "data-ink" (the ink in a graph or chart that represents nonredundant information) and to eliminate what he calls "chartjunk" (overly busy or excessive graphical decoration).

4. *Chicago* 4.91 differentiates between "a single graph, table, or chart that simply presents data in a straightforward relationship," which ordinarily does not require permission, and "reproduction of a graph or chart embellished with pictorial elements," which does. Regardless of whether the degree of "expressive input" in the original necessitates permission, however, a source citation is obligatory. When devising attribution and permission lines for graphics, authors must identify the degree of distance between their image and the original. "Source" means the graph is the work of the originator and requires a full citation and "by permission" line. "Adapted from" likewise means the graph is primarily that of the originator and also requires a source citation and possibly a permission credit. "Data source," "Based on," and "After" mean the data, concepts, or core ideas are the originator's, but the development and graphic interpretation are the author's; a citation is required but permission is unnecessary.

*Pie charts:* Each slice of a pie chart (see figure 8) should have a label identifying the sector and the percentage it comprises, and the percentages should total 100 (slightly more or less if the percentages have been rounded).

*Bar graphs:* For bar graphs (see figures 9–11), the tabs should be in a logical order, the scale line must be labeled and the units (dollars, tons) stated, and the scale line must begin at zero and have tick marks at reasonable intervals.

*Line graphs:* For line graphs (see figures 11–13), the different types of lines must be sufficiently distinctive and legible at the size the graph will be printed or displayed; the lines may be of different weights or of different character (solid, dashed, dotted). When the units on an axis represent numerical quantities, the scale line for that axis usually begins at zero (for example, see the price data represented on the Y-axes in figure 11). However, the range of the numerical values sometimes makes it impractical to start the scale line at zero (for example, see the two Y-axes in figure 12). When the units on an axis do not represent numerical quantities, the scale line does not begin at zero (for example, see the time-interval data on the X-axes in figure 11).

*Scatter charts:* For scatter charts (see figure 13), the symbols for each variable, in both the chart and the legend, must be distinctive and legible at the size the chart will be printed or displayed.

*Glyphs:* All the glyphs in a pictogram should be equal in width and height; unequal glyphs produce a misleading impression. For example, each of the following lines contains five glyphs, but the glyphs in the third line are noticeably larger.

- As a last pass, read through the graphs as a batch to be sure that they are consistent.

FIGURE 8.  Copyediting a Pie Chart. The copyeditor must make sure that

- the pie chart is correctly numbered and appropriately titled
- each slice is labeled, and the labels are consistent with the manuscript's editorial style (e.g., spelling, capitalization, hyphenation, use of italics)
- the percentage share is shown for each slice, and all percentages are shown to the same number of decimal points
- the percentages total 100 or very close to 100 (Sometimes the percentages do not equal 100 because the numbers are rounded.)
- the size of each slice appears to match its percentage of the pie
- contiguous slices are visually distinctive
- a source line is included (For a chart reproduced from a published or unpublished work, the author may also need to obtain written permission from the copyright holder; see "Publishing Law" in chapter 15.)

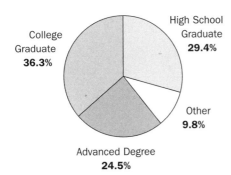

Figure A. Educational Background of AXY Employees

College Graduate **36.3%**

High School Graduate **29.4%**

Other **9.8%**

Advanced Degree **24.5%**

*Source:* AXY Company survey, June 1995.

Chart number and title

The capitalization of the labels for slices may be either initial cap only (sentence style) or upper- and lowercase (title style).

Percentages may be placed next to the labels or within the slices.

Source line

FIGURE 9. Parts of a Bar Graph

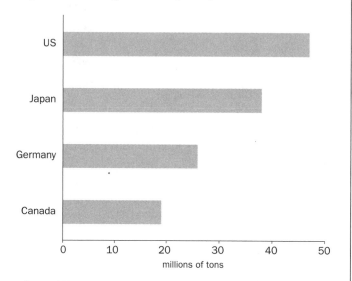

Figure B. World's Largest Gizmo Importers, 1993

Figure number
and title

Items in the tab, here
arranged from largest
to smallest

Axis begins at zero;
tick marks guide the
reader; label indicates
unit of measurement.

Source line

FIGURE 10. Sliding-Bar Graph. Sliding-bar graphs can depict complex relationships. Figure C, for example, shows the variation in the company's total sales from quarter to quarter, the variation in each region's sales from quarter to quarter, and the share of sales achieved by each region during each quarter. Note how much more difficult it is to discern the various relationships when the same information is presented in tabular form.

| | Sales ($ million) | | | |
|---|---|---|---|---|
| | 1Q96 | 2Q96 | 3Q96 | 4Q96 |
| North | 85 | 65 | 50 | 90 |
| South | 70 | 45 | 40 | 50 |
| East | 20 | 40 | 30 | 25 |
| West | 45 | 30 | 20 | 10 |
| Total | 220 | 180 | 140 | 175 |

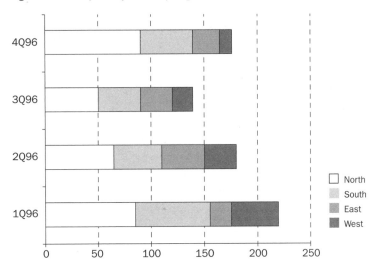

Figure C. OurCo Quarterly Sales, by Region ($ million), 1996

FIGURE 11.  Line Graph. Line graphs are useful for depicting trends or changes over time. Figure D-1, for example, shows the stock prices for four companies during a trading day. A bar graph, in contrast, can present only selected, discontinuous data points for each stock; figure D-2 presents the prices at four moments during the day. Note also that trends in each stock are easy to track in the line graph but hard to discern in the bar graph.

Figure D-1. Intradaily Stock Prices for Companies A, B, C, and D on July 1, 1998

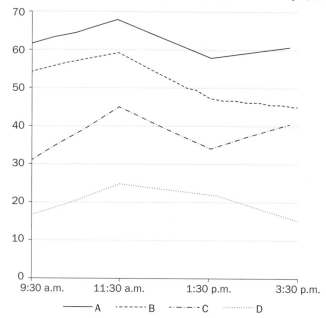

Figure D-2. Intradaily Stock Prices for Companies A, B, C, and D on July 1, 1998

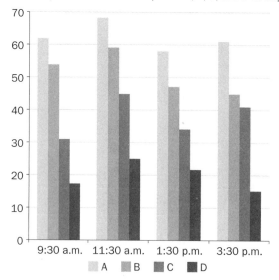

FIGURE 12.  Line Graph with Two Y-Axes. Figure E shows the trading range of the Italian lira against the US dollar (USD) and the German mark (DEM) over a five-month period. The number of lire per dollar is shown on the vertical axis to the left (called Y-1), and the number of lire per mark is shown on the vertical axis to the right (called Y-2).

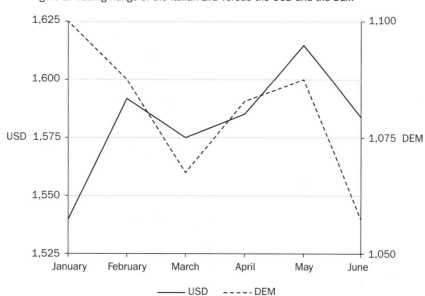

Figure E. Trading Range of the Italian Lira versus the USD and the DEM

FIGURE 13.  Simple Scatter Chart. Figure F-1 is a scatter chart that shows the competitive rankings of three mutual funds in the four quarters of 1998. Because the X-axis data points are discontinuous (the funds were ranked once a quarter) and the Y-axis data points are discontinuous (no fractional rankings are possible), the scatter chart presents the data accurately, while a line graph (figure F-2) distorts the data.

Figure F-1. Quarterly Performance Rankings of Mutual Funds USABX, USACX, and USADX in 1998 (3 = best-performing fund)

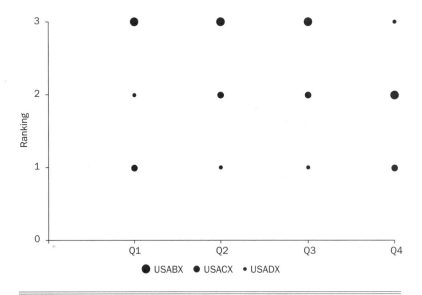

Figure F-2. Quarterly Performance Rankings of Mutual Funds USABX, USACX, and USADX in 1998 (3 = best-performing fund)

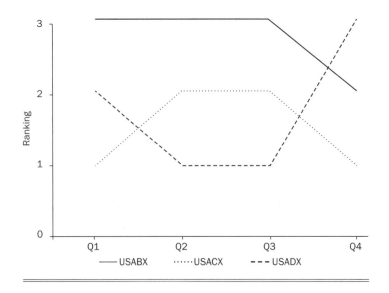

## ART

When a manuscript contains drawings, maps, or photographs, the manuscript given to the copyeditor should be accompanied by photocopies, thumbnails, or low-resolution digital images for reference. The procedures are similar to those for tables:

- Make sure that the author's comments on the illustration reflect what the illustration shows. If the text turns our attention to "the building in the upper right of figure 6," check to see that there is a building in the upper right of figure 6. If the author mentions the blue circle in figure 12, verify that the illustration is to be printed in color; if not, the text should be reworded.
- Check the sequence and numbering of the illustrations. Art can be through-numbered in a manuscript (figure 1, figure 2, figure 3, etc.) or numbered by chapter (figure 1.1, figure 1.2, figure 2.1, figure 2.2, etc.). Illustrations in appendixes are usually identified by the appendix letter (figure A.1, figure A.2, . . . figure E.6). As noted in the discussion of graphs, when a manuscript contains many different types of art (graphs, charts, photographs, drawings, maps), each type may be labeled in a separate sequence (figure 1, figure 2, map 1, map 2, etc.).
- If you are working on hard copy, call out the location of each illustration in the margin of the manuscript:

  FIG 2 ABOUT HERE

  If you are working on-screen, insert a callout code at the end of a paragraph:

  &lt;Figure 2&gt;

- Make sure every substantive illustration has a caption and edit the captions for consistency and mechanical style (spelling, hyphenation, capitalization). Decorative illustrations, in contrast, usually do not carry captions.
- Make sure every substantive illustration has a source line, including a permission credit (if required); edit this copy for consistency and mechanical style. Source and permission credits for decorative illustrations, in contrast, are usually placed on the copyright page, in the acknowledgments, or elsewhere in the text.
- Copyedit any text that appears within an illustration (e.g., labels of parts, cities on maps, legends and keys) that will be redrafted for the publication. If "Seville" appears throughout the text, then the label for that city on the map of Spain should read "Seville," not "Sevilla." However, if a historical map is being photographically reproduced (and not redrawn), the labels on the old map must suffice.
- Make sure the illustration and caption supply all the information readers need in order to interpret the illustration (e.g., magnification for a

microscopic view, legend for a map, identification of principal persons in a photograph).

- If a list of illustrations is to appear in the front matter, correlate the numbering and captions for the art against that list. Shortened captions may be used in the list of illustrations.

## USE OF "ALT TEXT"

Publishers concerned about preparing content accessible to people with disabilities need to add text alternatives ("*alt text*") for tables and illustrations in electronic formats. *Chicago* recommends several resources to editors seeking further information and explains that "properly marked-up text and captions will enhance accessibility; . . . alternative text will help readers who use text-to-speech and related tools understand the nature and content of the illustration" or table (3.28, 3.88).

# CHAPTER 11

# ❡ References

An author must provide a source for every direct quotation (other than an extremely well known quote) and for every table, graph, and illustration that is reproduced from someone else's work.[1] Sources must also be cited for all facts, statistics, conclusions, and opinions that the author obtained from someone else's published or unpublished work. But sources are not needed—and should not be given—for facts that are in general circulation.

The means by which an author cites the source of a quotation, paraphrase, or piece of evidence taken from another work depends on

the conventions within the author's profession or field
the intended audience for the work (e.g., scholars, professionals, general readers)
the number and complexity of citations in the author's manuscript
the preferences, if any, of the publisher

All journals and magazines impose their house style on contributors for uniformity within their issues. Some book and corporate publishers do so as well, especially for multiauthor collections and works in a series. Other publishers allow authors to use whatever citation system they prefer—provided it is not too idiosyncratic—if it is suitable for the intended readership and is consistently applied.

When a document has only a few citations, these may be incorporated into the running text (see "Citing Sources" in chapter 8). For example, popular magazines do not usually include formal references; instead, brief but sufficient attributions are supplied parenthetically or are mentioned within the text, with minimal source information that often omits full publication details and page numbers:

The brilliant scholar Maisie Meow once claimed (in *Me and Meow*) that cats don't have owners—they have staff.

"Cats don't have owners—they have staff," claimed the brilliant scholar Maisie Meow in her 2017 study, *Me and Meow.*

Popular trade nonfiction often includes chapter-based readings or references—mini bibliographical essays—either placed at the ends of chapters or gathered at the back of

---

1. Lengthy quotations and the reproduction of tables or illustrations may require permission from the originator in addition to a reference citation or credit line, but *Chicago* (4.91) suggests that the noncommercial reproduction "of a single graph, table, or chart that simply presents data in a straightforward relationship, in contrast to reproduction of a graph or chart embellished with pictorial elements, should ordinarily be considered fair use." See "Publishing Law" in chapter 15.

the book. When a book surveys a large field (e.g., US history, 1776–present), it may include a general discussion of key works to avoid enormous chapter bibliographies.

For documents that contain many citations, one of three systems of attribution is used: *author-date* (also called *name-year*), *reference notes,* or *citation-sequence.* As you will see, each of these systems has complicated conventions governing the order, punctuation, and capitalization of items, as well as the use of italics, quotation marks, and parentheses, and each system admits many variations in editorial styling.

For copyeditors, then, reference citations require an almost excruciating attentiveness to detail. Be prepared: in a manuscript with extensive documentation, you may spend more hours on styling and cross-checking citations than on all other editorial tasks combined. Nor has citation management software (applications such as EndNote and Zotero) appreciably improved authors' preparation of such scholarly apparatus. Authors may use this software to extract online citation data and to generate notes and bibliographies, but these tools work best with recent books and articles and with other common publication formats. They are not designed to format citations for the many oddball sources mentioned in some manuscripts—the proceedings of an annual conference or meeting, the title of a book series, a single volume in a multivolume work, an archival collection, an unpublished manuscript, a government document, an oral history, informal digital content, or other nontraditional sources (e.g., a text message or a video game).[2] Authors—with or without the assistance of citation management software—are often unable to master the many esoteric forms described in major style manuals such as *Chicago.* So if you specialize in editing scholarly content, you need to know the documentation chapters of the relevant style manuals inside out in order to work efficiently.

Always consult with your editorial coordinator about the publisher's preferred style and the publisher's policy for manuscripts that do not conform to that preference. Also, ask whether you are expected to verify or spot-check the accuracy of the citations. Usually the answer to this last question is no, although some editorial coordinators instruct on-screen editors to confirm URLs. You should not spend your time verifying entries unless you are explicitly instructed to do so (and accordingly remunerated) or you encounter a specific tangle that you simply must unknot before you return the manuscript to the author.

## AUTHOR-DATE SYSTEM

In the author-date system, the source is cited in the running text, usually in parentheses. The in-text citation includes the surname of the author, the year of publication, and,

---

2. *Chicago* 14.5 warns authors that notes and reference lists generated by such software "are only as good as the data that generate them and the software used to format them." The results may be inaccurate, omit essential data (or include redundant or superfluous details), format citations incorrectly, and include unwanted codes, such as fields and hyperlinks. *Chicago* strongly advises authors to review the output for consistency, accuracy, and completeness before manuscript submission; regrettably, some authors rely entirely on the self-driving citation software.

as needed, a page, chapter, or table number. (Any suffixes, professional titles, or editorial roles accompanying the surname in the original source—"Jr.," "II," "M.D." or "MD," "Esq.," "ed.," "trans.," etc.—are omitted in this parenthetical in-text citation.) If multiple sources are cited parenthetically, a semicolon separates the discrete sources within the parentheses, as shown in the second example that follows.

> British usage differs from American usage: "the educated American's strong feeling [is] that *different from* is idiomatic and hence inviolable" (Follett 1966, 129).

> Similar findings have been reported in the rain forests of Brazil (Johnson 1991, chap. 5; Peters and Lynn 1996).

> Jones (1988, table 6.6) observed no relation between megadoses of vitamin C and resistance to influenza.

At the end of a document containing author-date citations, there must be an alphabetized reference list (or a list of works cited) that supplies the complete publication data for each citation.

The author-date system is quite common in the social sciences and the natural sciences but is rarely used in the humanities. *Chicago, APA,* and *CSE* all present detailed advice on the formatting of in-text citations and the reference list. Each book, however, takes a slightly different approach to the editorial styling of these items. In editorial jargon, the three variants are called *Chicago* author-date, *APA* author-date, and *CSE* name-year.

## FORMATS FOR IN-TEXT CITATIONS

The syntax and content of the author's sentence govern the location of the in-text citation. Some finesse is required in placing the parenthetical source details as unobtrusively as possible. Here are some of the most common formats, shown in Chicago style with notes that highlight the most important differences between *Chicago, APA,* and *CSE.*

> Sometimes the complete citation is provided in parentheses. *Chicago* and *CSE* recommend the following formats; *APA*, however, always requires a comma after the surname in a parenthetical citation: (Gallegos, 1993).

> *Reference to an entire work:* A report on the *m* allele (Gallegos 1993) . . .

> *Reference to a chapter in a work:* A report on the *m* allele (Gallegos 1993, chap. 1) . . .
> *Note:* In APA style: (Gallegos, 1993, Chapter 1).

> *Reference to specific pages in a work:* A report on the *m* allele (Gallegos 1993, 11–13) . . .
> *Note:* APA uses "p." before a page number and "pp." before a page range. *CSE* uses "p" (without a period) before all page numbers and page ranges.

> *Reference to specific pages in a volume:* A report on the *m* allele (Gallegos 1995, 2:211–15) . . .

*Reference to a work that is in press:* A report on the *m* allele (Gallegos forthcoming) . . . *or* A report on the *m* allele (Gallegos in press) . . .[3]

*Reference to an undated work:* A report on the *m* allele (Gallegos n.d.) . . .
[The abbreviation "n.d." is used in many forms of citation to signify "no date."]

Sometimes the author's name is mentioned in the text proper, with the remaining source details in parentheses. (Note the handling of the citation when the author's name appears in the text in possessive form.) Occasionally, full source details are embedded in the running text.

Gallegos (1993) describes the *m* allele.

Gallegos (1993, chap. 1) describes the *m* allele.
*Note:* In APA style: Gallegos (1993, Chapter 1).

Gallegos (1993, 11–13) describes the *m* allele.
*Note:* In APA style: Gallegos (1993, pp. 11–13). In CSE style: Gallegos (1993, p 11–13).

Gallegos (1995, 2:211–15) describes the *m* allele.

Gallegos (forthcoming) describes the *m* allele.
*Note:* In APA style: Gallegos (in press).

Gallegos (n.d.) describes the *m* allele.

Gallegos's (1993) description . . .

Early descriptions of the *m* allele (e.g., Gallegos 1993) . . .

The description in Gallegos 1993 . . .

Multiple citations

Two later studies (Wong 1996, 1997) report . . .
*Note:* In APA style, a comma would follow each surname in a parenthetical citation: (Wong, 1996, 1997).

Two later studies (Wong 1996, 15; 1997, 27) report . . .
*Note:* In APA style: (Wong, 1996, p. 15; 1997, p. 27). In CSE style: (Wong 1996, p 15; 1997, p 27).

The reanalyses of these data (Ellington 1994a, 1994b) show . . .

Other studies (Mays 1989, 1996; Byrd 1995) have shown . . .

As both Mays (1989, 1996) and Byrd (1995) have shown . . .

---

3. By convention, "in press" means that the work is in production; "forthcoming," that it has been accepted for publication; "in preparation," that the work has been sent to the publisher but has not yet been accepted. "Preprint" refers to a peer-reviewed preliminary version of a work; it may differ from the final, published version.

Multiple authors

The findings of Willy and Wally (1994) were not confirmed by later testing (Apple and Berry 1996; Apple, Berry, and Cherry 1997).

*Note:* Within parenthetical references *APA* substitutes an ampersand for "and": The findings of Willy and Wally (1994) were not confirmed by later testing (Apple & Berry, 1996; Apple, Berry, & Cherry, 1997).

Institutional author

A nationwide survey by the National Food Institute (1997) . . .

A nationwide survey (National Food Institute 1997) . . .

Personal communications (including letters, interviews, telephone conversations, and email)

As I. R. Felix (pers. comm., July 31, 1996) suggests, . . .

Unattributed book or article

One other intriguing hypothesis has been suggested (*Book Title* 1996, 215–35), but . . .

According to a recent report ("Article Title" 1999), . . .

*Note:* In CSE style, "Anonymous" is placed in the author slot for an unattributed work: According to a recent report (Anonymous 1999), . . .

## REFERENCE LIST

An alphabetized reference list must appear at the end of a document that contains author-date citations. Each item in the list contains four blocks of information: (1) the name of the author(s) or editor(s), inverted for ease of alphabetization, (2) the year of publication, (3) the title of the work, and (4) the place of publication and the publisher's name. The formats shown here are typical, but they admit numerous variations.

*Author(s) and year.* Each entry begins with the name of the author(s) or editor(s) and the year of publication; these blocks are separated by a period. Chicago style inverts only the first name in a multiple-author entry. Authors' names are listed in the exact form in which they appear on the title page or in the byline of the source, including any suffixes with surnames and any editorial roles; professional degrees and institutional affiliations are omitted.[4] However, the full name may be supplied in the entry (unless this violates house style), even though only initials are given with the surname in the source, if the information is necessary to identify the author. Works by authors who have changed their name should be listed under the name used in the cited publication; following that entry, a listing may be added to supply a "see also" cross-reference to entries under the alternative name.

---

4. An exception is sometimes made for "MD" in listings of medical works.

*One author:* Babble, Alan B. 1992.

*Two authors:* Banana, Quincy, and Susan L. Cream. 1993.

*Three authors:* Berle, Merle M., Lyndon D. Mindon, and Paul Olds. 1995.

*Institution:* Canadian Broadcasting System. 1994.

*Unattributed work: Concise Columbia Encyclopedia.* 1994.

*Editor:* Dylan, Dee, ed. 1997.

In APA style for reference lists, (1) the author's first and middle names are replaced by initials, (2) all authors' names in a multiauthor citation are inverted, (3) an ampersand replaces "and," (4) the notation "ed." (or "eds." for multieditor works) is treated as a separate block (i.e., it begins with a capital letter and ends with a period) and is placed in parentheses, and (5) the year is placed in parentheses:

Babble, A. B. (1992).

Banana, Q., & Cream, S. L. (1993).

Berle, M. M., Mindon, L. D., & Olds, P. (1995).

Canadian Broadcasting System. (1994).

*Concise Columbia encyclopedia.* (1994).

Dylan, D. (Ed.). (1997).

(The lowercase *e* at the beginning of "encyclopedia" is not an error; APA style uses sentence capitalization for book and article titles. As the examples show, APA reference list style also uses periods after parenthetical dates and the parenthetical "Ed[s].")

In CSE style, (1) no periods appear after personal initials, (2) all names are inverted, (3) the surname and initials are not separated by a comma, (4) "and" is not used in multiauthor cites, and (5) the notation "editor" (or "editors" for multieditor works) is treated as part of the name block (i.e., it is preceded by a comma and followed by a period):

[Anonymous]. 1994.

Babble AB. 1992.

Banana Q, Cream SL. 1993.

Berle MM, Mindon LD, Olds P. 1995.

Canadian Broadcasting System. 1994.

Dylan D, editor. 1997.

(In CSE style, "[Anonymous]" appears in the author slot for an unattributed work, such as the *Concise Columbia Encyclopedia*.)

When two or more works by an author were published in the same year, a lowercase letter is appended to the date in the reference list:

Rightsalot, Abby. 1989a.

Rightsalot, Abby. 1989b.

Rightsalot, Abby. 1989c.

(In Chicago style, the second and subsequent instances of the author's name in a reference list were once replaced by a three-em dash: ———. 1989b. But *Chicago* now recommends repeating the name because three-em dashes do not correctly sort in computerized lists, may obscure notations such as "ed." or "trans.," and may not function properly in digital publications.)

The corresponding in-text citations would be

Only one study (Rightsalot 1989a) examined . . .
*Note:* In APA style: (Rightsalot, 1989a).

Rightsalot (1989b, 1989c) concludes that . . .

*Title.*   The third block consists of the title of the work. The two principal styles for formatting titles are called humanities style (which uses the headline style of capitalization) and scientific style (which uses sentence-style capitalization).[5] When the cited work is an article, the name of the journal, volume number, and page numbers follow the article title.

Humanities style

> Book: *Petrographic Analysis of Cherts.*
> Article: "Anorexia Nervosa in Teenage Boys." *Journal of Anatomy* 33 (July): 514–24.

Scientific style, *APA* version

> Book: *Petrographic analysis of cherts.*
> Article: Anorexia nervosa in teenage boys. *Journal of Anatomy, 33,* 514–524.

Scientific style, *CSE* version

> Book: Petrographic analysis of cherts.
> Article: Anorexia nervosa in teenage boys. J Anat. 33:514–24.

As these examples illustrate, the various author-date styles also differ in the typographic treatment of book, article, and journal titles.

*Publication data.*   The fourth block of the entry consists of the publication data, which is intended to provide interested readers with sufficient information to locate the source.

For a book, one supplies the city of publication and the name of the publisher. (Variant: All entries provide only the publisher's name.) When the place of publication is not a major city, the abbreviated name of the state or the full name of the country is given:[6]

---

5. Newspapers take headline style a step further in capitalizing the first word of every line in a multiline headline. This design choice should not be imitated in references to the article. For example:

**New Wines**    *Citation:* "New Wines from France and Spain," *Daily Planet,*
**From France**   March 8, 1998, p. 14.
**And Spain**

6. Some publishers create an in-house list to guide editors in identifying cities that require further information. The *AP Stylebook*'s list of well-known (stand-alone) US and international cities under

Major city

New York: Bigtop Books.

Washington, DC: Topnotch & Wheedle.

Paris: Livres populaires.

Other places

Williams, N.D.: Great Plains Press.

Lublin, Poland: Katowice.

For self-published books and books published or distributed through commercial self-publishing platforms, the place of publication may be omitted if it is not specified in the front matter and is not known. The designation "Self-published" and sometimes the commercial vendor or platform take the place of a publisher's name and are followed by the year of publication.

Self-published, 2018.

*Or:* Self-published, CreateSpace, 2018.

For an article in a journal, magazine, or newspaper, the place of publication is given only when needed to help readers locate obscure publications.

## COPYEDITING PROCEDURES

If you are working on the hard copy of a manuscript that uses the author-date system, you must copyedit the reference list *before* you work on the text. (The reason will become apparent when you read steps 2 and 3 below.) If you are working on-screen, however, you may choose to ignore this precaution, since you can always use the global search to locate entries that require further attention.

*Step 1.* Scan the entire reference list to verify that the entries are in alphabetical order. Special conventions govern the alphabetization of multiple surnames, foreign names, and names beginning with particles (de, Della, von) and with *Mac, Mc, St.,* and *Saint.* For example, hyphenated American and British surnames are alphabetized under the first element of the surname, but nonhyphenated American and British surnames are alphabetized under the last element. Thus *Jean Dorr-Winston* is alphabetized under *Dorr,* while *Ann Smith Jones* is alphabetized under *Jones.* You can use the online Library of Congress catalog as a resource for alphabetizing unusual names: Dr. Seuss, for example, is listed there under "Seuss, Dr.," with a cross-reference to Theodor Seuss Geisel. *Chicago* and *CSE* describe other special conventions; for an extended discussion, see Nancy Mulvany, *Indexing Books.*

---

"Datelines" can guide copyeditors in the absence of a house style. Otherwise, an editor must decide case by case which cities are "major." The context sometimes enables readers to infer the correct city of publication without further identifying details:

Spear, Sheik S. *Oregon's Shakespeare Festival at Eighty.* Eugene: University of Oregon Press, 2015.
Wallace, Percy. *My Life as a Don.* Oxford: Oxford University Press, 2016.

*Step 2.* Scan the entire list again and notice whether there are two works by the same author(s) in the same year, for example:

Blythe, A. L. 1988. *In Praise of Proofreaders.* New York: Ashcan Press.

Blythe, A. L. 1988. *In Praise of Copyeditors.* Chicago: Veritas Press.

In this case, you need to rearrange the two entries so that the titles are in alphabetical order and then label the first entry 1988a and the second entry 1988b. When you are copyediting the manuscript, you must remember to call your author's attention to all in-text citations that refer to Blythe 1988 so that your author can change them to either "Blythe 1988a" or "Blythe 1988b."

*Step 3.* Scan the entire list again and notice whether there are two authors with the same surname, for example:

Roberts, Ellen M. 1995. *Paranormal Psychology.* Boston: ESP Press.

Roberts, Jack L. 1989. *Psychometrics.* Los Angeles: Southland Books.

When you are copyediting the manuscript, you will have to make sure that all in-text references to these authors include an initial:

E. Roberts (1995) and J. Roberts (1989) provide differing views of this phenomenon.

*Step 4.* Copyedit the entries. Read each entry slowly so that you can spot any typographical errors. (Because reference lists contain so many proper names, on-screen copyeditors usually do not run the spell-checker on the reference list.)

Then read the entry a second time to make sure that it is properly formatted and styled. Follow your editorial coordinator's recommendation for either imposing the house style or using the style the author has chosen. If the author's style is not one you are familiar with, write out sample entries based on the first few in-text citations and reference list entries and annotate each style choice and piece of punctuation:

*In-text citation:* (Doe 1999, 125–129)
　　[No comma after surname; comma after date; no "p." or "pp."; repeat all numerals in page ranges.]

*Reference list entry, book:* Doe, A. A. 1999. *Title of book: Subtitle of book.* City, Sta.: Publisher.
　　[Author's initials only, with periods; title and subtitle in sentence capitalization, italic; nonpostal state abbreviations.]

*Reference list entry, article:* Doe, A. A. 1999. Title of article: Subtitle included too. *Journal title* 5(2): 125–129.
　　[Title and subtitle in sentence capitalization, roman, without quotation marks; journal title in sentence capitalization, italic; roman for volume(issue); space after colon; repeat all numerals in page ranges.]

These samples will help you learn the style and make it easier for you to spot inconsistencies.

As you are reading, pay special attention to the logic of page ranges (an article cannot have appeared on pages 45–32 or pages 45–45 of a journal) and to the consistent styling of the page ranges. (The ranges should follow one of the three systems described in "Inclusive Numerals" in chapter 7.) Be alert, as well, for internal inconsistencies. For example, the following discrepancy in volume numbers (3 or 13?) merits a query:

Babs, R. R. 1997. "Study Skills for High School Students." *Teachers Journal* 3: 12–18.

Morgenstern, L. 1997. "Journal Writing." *Teachers Journal* 13: 115–26.

*Step 5.* Make notations on your style sheet about the styling of in-text citations and reference list entries. If the author has followed one of the formats in *Chicago, APA,* or *CSE,* make a note to that effect on your style sheet, under "Footnotes" and "Bibliography"—or "Citations" and "Reference List" (see figure 6, in chapter 2). But if you had to select a format and impose it on the manuscript, transfer your previous scratch notes on sample entries to the style sheet. These samples will be helpful to the author during the review of the copyediting, when entries may need to be added; the samples will also refresh your memory during cleanup.

When you have finished copyediting the reference list, begin working on the manuscript. Each time you come across an in-text author-date citation, check it against the reference list. If there is no corresponding entry in the reference list, ask the author to supply one.[7] Also, query any discrepancy between an in-text citation and the reference list (e.g., author's name, date, page ranges).

## REFERENCE NOTE SYSTEM

In the reference note system, the sources are placed in notes keyed to the running text by asterisks or superscript numerals. The notes themselves may appear at the bottom of the page (*footnotes*) or gathered together at the end of the article, document, book chapter, or book (*endnotes*).[8] For example:

*Running text:* British usage differs from American usage: "the educated American's strong feeling [is] that *different from* is idiomatic and hence inviolable."[1]

*Note:* 1. Wilson Follett, *Modern American Usage: A Guide* (New York: Hill & Wang, 1966), p. 129.

---

*Running text:* Similar findings have been reported in the rain forests of Brazil.[2]

*Note:* 2. See, for example, A. R. Johnson, "Microclimatology in the Southern Rain Forests," *Journal of Meteorological Studies* 3 (1987): 35–42; S. S. Peters and

---

7. Personal communications (letters, interviews, phone conversations, email exchanges), however, are usually not included in the reference list, since readers will not be able to locate these items.

8. Authors often call their reference notes "footnotes" regardless of the intended placement in the publication. To avoid confusion, however, publishers differentiate between *footnotes* and *endnotes* (a.k.a. *backnotes*).

W. Lynn, "Mating Habitats of the South American Zao-zao," *Journal of Avian Studies* 2 (1988): 58–63.

---

*Running text:* Jones observed no relation between megadoses of vitamin C and resistance to influenza.*

*Note:* *K. C. Jones, "Vitamin C Revisited," *Journal of the Institutes of Health* 32 (1988): 45.

Notice that reference notes are written and punctuated so that all the information about the source is contained in one sentence. As these examples show, the in-text note indicator is set as a superscript, but the number in the text of the note is not. Unfortunately, the default setting in some word processing programs produces superscripts in both locations.[9] The use of "p." and "pp." to indicate page numbers, as shown in the first example, is optional; many authors and publishers prefer to eliminate these indicators. *Chicago* omits them provided no ambiguity results.

When a document contains a bibliography that lists all the works cited in the document, complete publication data need not be given in the notes. Instead, each note may contain the author's surname, a short form of the title, and the relevant page number(s):

1. Follett, *Modern American Usage,* 129.

2. Johnson, "Microclimatology," 38; Peters and Lynn, "Mating Habitats," 61.

*Jones, "Vitamin C Revisited," 45.

Some publishers, however, prefer that a full citation appear in the first note that mentions a source. In subsequent notes, only the surname and short title are given, with any applicable page numbers. When consecutive notes cite the same source, it was once customary to use the abbreviation *ibid.* (for *ibidem,* "in the same place"), along with any changed page numbers, in the second note. But *Chicago* now discourages this practice and recommends continued use of a short-form citation because electronic formats that link one note at a time do not allow readers to identify the previously cited source with ease.

To reduce the number of notes that refer to one or more often-cited works, an author may (1) provide a complete citation for the work in a note on the first reference to the work, (2) mention in that note that future references to the work appear in the text and are indicated by a short title or acronym, and (3) thereafter reference the work in parenthetical in-text citations. For example:

*Running text:* British usage differs from American usage: "the educated American's strong feeling [is] that *different from* is idiomatic and hence

---

9. To fix these errant superscripts, copyeditors working on hard copy can write a global instruction for the typesetter ("Within the notes, set all note numbers on the line followed by a period") and also hand-mark the first example or two in each chapter or section of the manuscript. Copyeditors working on-screen for a publishing house will usually find that the production editor has already updated the author's files to correct the improperly placed superscripts. Copyeditors working on-screen for corporate publishers or for self-publishing authors should consult their word processing program's help files for advice on redefining the numbering style for footnotes or endnotes.

inviolable."[1] . . . Cross-Atlantic differences in the choice of prepositions lead Americans to "tinker with," while the British "tinker at" (*MAU,* p. 259).

*Note:* 1. Wilson Follett, *Modern American Usage: A Guide* (New York: Hill & Wang, 1966), p. 129. Future references to this work are denoted by *MAU* and appear in the text.

Here's an alternative wording for the note and an alternative treatment of the title:

1. Wilson Follett, *Modern American Usage: A Guide* (New York: Hill & Wang, 1966), p. 129; hereafter cited as *Usage.*

As this example illustrates, a short title need not include the first word(s) of the full title; also, although a short title may contain an adjective, it must contain a noun. In addition, all the words in a short title must appear in the same order as in the full title:

Full title: *A Manual for Writers of Term Papers, Theses, and Dissertations*

Short title: *Manual for Writers* or *Manual* but not *Manual for Term Paper Writers*

A short title is usually preferable to an unwieldy acronym. For example, *Metaphors We Live By* should be shortened to *Metaphors* rather than *MWLB.*

Notes are the preferred citation system for writers in the humanities, and they are favored by some historians and social scientists. *Chicago* offers the most detailed discussion of the various formats. In the humanities, another widely used style guide for notes is the *MLA Handbook.* (Since *APA* requires the author-date system and *CSE* calls for either author-date or citation-sequence, neither of these manuals discusses reference notes.)

## LOCATION OF IN-TEXT NOTE INDICATOR

The in-text superscript or asterisk is preferably placed at the end of a sentence or, if necessary, at the end of a clause. It follows all punctuation marks except the dash. Another exception: *WIT* places the note signal inside a closing parenthesis if the reference applies only to the parenthetical content. Even in such cases *Chicago* places the note signal outside the closing parenthesis, barring the rare situation in which the note pertains to a discrete term within the parentheses.

*Awkward:* Many educators,[5] working in diverse settings, report considerable success with this method.

*Revision:* Many educators, working in diverse settings, report considerable success with this method.[5]

Only in the rarest of cases should a sentence contain more than one note indicator.

*Awkward:* Scores improved in math classes,[6] science classes,[7] and history classes.[8]

*Revision:* Scores improved in math classes, science classes, and history classes.[6]
[Within this new note 6, the references would be divided by subjects: On scores in math, see . . . ; on science, see . . . ; on history, see . . .]

Each chapter of a book (or section of a long document) begins with note 1. Footnotes in tables, sidebars, and figures use separate, self-contained sequences: they are not integrated into the sequence of numbered notes to the text and often use a different system of note signals, such as the asterisk-dagger or letter sequence (see the discussion of table footnotes in chapter 10).

Many publishers prohibit the placement of an in-text note indicator in a line of display type (e.g., a chapter title, author byline, first- or second-level subhead, table title), although *Chicago* accepts note indicators in the titles of journal articles and in subheads within articles or book chapters. The remedy for a misplaced indicator depends on the context and the content of the note.

*Problem:* Manuscript has a note indicator after the chapter title, article title, or author byline.

*Solution:* Delete the note indicator but retain the text of the note and treat it as an unnumbered note. If the notes are to be printed as footnotes, this unnumbered note should be placed at the bottom of the first page of the chapter or article. If the notes are to be printed as endnotes, this unnumbered note precedes the numbered notes in the endnote section.

*Problem:* Manuscript has a note indicator within or at the end of a display heading.

*Solution:* Move the note indicator to the end of the first sentence of text under that heading and edit the note accordingly (e.g., "The title of this section is taken from . . .").

*Problem:* Manuscript has a note indicator within or at the end of a table title.

*Solution:* Delete the indicator from the table title. If the note applies to the entire table, label it "Note" and place it before the numbered, lettered, or asterisked footnotes to the table. If the note applies to only a portion of the table, place the note indicator in the appropriate stub line, column heading, or cell. (See figure 7 and table 20, in chapter 10, for examples.)

Note signals should never be used in a displayed equation, where any kind of indicator would be confusing. An explanation can be moved into the text proper, either before or after the equation.

## KEY PHRASE ENDNOTES

Some trade publishers use reference notes for documentation without any note indicators in the text. Instead, the references appear at the end of the book, keyed to the text by page number and a relevant phrase from the text.

5     In national polls . . . : *New York Times,* "Taxes and the Middle Class," Sept. 5, 1997, p. 12.

8     Judges proposed . . . : Allegra Thom, "Legal Rights of Pregnant Women," *Reproductive Rights,* 2 (10), July 1995, p. 17.

9     "Improving prenatal care . . .": Dr. Corinna Somes, letter to author, Aug. 15, 1997.

Publishers sometimes favor these *key phrase endnotes,* or *incipit notes,* in the belief that general readers are intimidated by superscript note signals in the text.[10] The trade-off is that serious readers must check the endnotes constantly just to determine whether something in the text is sourced or annotated. In addition, the production labor required to create key phrase endnotes is painstaking. Each key phrase must be cross-checked against the wording in the text during copyediting and updated every time the affected text is altered. A hard-copy copyeditor may also be asked to indicate which lines in the manuscript are linked to the reference notes; the final page listings cannot be completed until the final page proofs are available. An on-screen copyeditor may be asked to code the text so that the correct page references can be generated automatically.

## PLACEMENT OF REFERENCE NOTES: FOOTNOTES VERSUS ENDNOTES

Some journal and book publishers routinely favor either footnotes or endnotes. Other publishers make the decision case by case, weighing various editorial and design issues. These decisions are usually made before the manuscript is released for copyediting, but sometimes copyeditors are asked to participate in them. There are two primary editorial considerations:

> *Intended readership:* Readers of academic and scholarly books usually prefer footnotes to endnotes because the former allow them to skim the notes without losing their place in the text. But popular wisdom says that general readers are either reluctant or unwilling to purchase a nonfiction trade book whose feet are hemmed with ribbons of tiny type; thus most trade books place (the shop term is *bury*) the notes containing sources and references at the back of the book.[11]
>
> *Content of the notes:* Footnotes are preferable for *discursive notes*—that is, notes including material other than references and sources—because readers will be able to glance at, if not scrutinize, this material without jumping to

---

10. The term *incipit notes* is a misnomer based on the assumption that the key phrase invariably consists of the *incipit,* or beginning words, of the annotated sentence. In fact, a key phrase may consist of a substantive phrase taken from the heart of the sentence.

11. If the text contains substantive notes—commentary, asides, or brief excurses—the author may be asked to integrate them into the text proper. Or the publisher may recommend two sets of notes: substantive notes as footnotes under the asterisk-dagger system, and reference notes as endnotes (either numbered or keyed to the text by page and line number).

the back of the book. However, tables, charts, complex math and musical examples, and similar elements cannot be run as footnotes. There are four ways to handle such elements: (1) the author can move the element into the text proper; (2) the author can decide to delete the problematic element; (3) all the notes can be run as endnotes, which can easily accommodate complex elements; (4) a table or chart can be treated as an appendix, and a cross-reference to the appendix can be placed in a footnote or in the text proper.

In terms of design, the choice between footnotes and endnotes depends on the quantity and length of the notes as well as the desired visual style for the publication. If the notes are few, short, and widely dispersed, treating them as footnotes will not substantially affect the overall look of the final document or book. But if the notes are many, long, or densely clumped at various intervals, designers favor endnotes. In oversize books that have wide margins, the notes may be run in the outer margin as *sidenotes*.

## BIBLIOGRAPHIES

A bibliography is a list, alphabetized by the authors' surnames, of the works cited in a document, article, or book. When the notes include all the information a reader needs to locate the work being cited, the author need not provide a bibliography. But some publications, particularly those intended for classroom use or academic research, include a bibliography as an additional tool for students and scholars.

Bibliographical entries provide the same information as notes, but in a different form. The author's name is inverted for ease in alphabetizing the list and finding entries, and each of the three blocks—author's name, title of the work, publication data—is followed by a period.

*Note:* 1. Wilson Follett, *Modern American Usage: A Guide* (New York: Hill & Wang, 1966), p. 129.

*Bibliography:* Follett, Wilson. *Modern American Usage: A Guide.* New York: Hill & Wang, 1966.

---

*Note:* 2. See, for example, A. R. Johnson, "Microclimatology in the Southern Rain Forests," *Journal of Meteorological Studies* 3 (1987): 35–42; S. S. Peters and W. Lynn, "Mating Habitats of the South American Zao-zao," *Journal of Avian Studies* 2 (1988): 58–63.

*Bibliography:* Johnson, A. R. "Microclimatology in the Southern Rain Forests." *Journal of Meteorological Studies* 3 (1987): 35–42.

Peters, S. S., and W. Lynn. "Mating Habitats of the South American Zao-zao." *Journal of Avian Studies* 2 (1988): 58–63.

## COPYEDITING PROCEDURES

At some point during the copyediting, you need to make a separate pass through all the notes in order to ensure that the numbering is correct and the styling is consistent. The best time to do this pass is usually after you have finished your first pass through the entire manuscript, including the bibliography (if there is one). Here's one way to proceed:

*Step 1.* Copyedit the manuscript. When you come upon an in-text note indicator, turn to the text of the note. Read the note for sense and relevancy, and correct any obvious errors. Also, some publishers ask copyeditors who work on hard copy to call out all in-text note markers (superscript numbers or asterisks):

> British usage differs from American usage: "the
>
> educated American's strong feeling [is] that *different*
>
>  *from* is idiomatic and hence inviolable."[1]
>
> Similar findings have been reported in the rain forests
>
>  of Brazil.[2]

Many copyeditors call out the notes (whether asked to or not) when working on hard copy because the callouts make it easier to page through the manuscript and verify that all numbered notes are in sequence.

*Step 2.* Copyedit the bibliography. First, scan the bibliography to make sure the entries are in alphabetical order.[12] Then read entry by entry and correct or query all typographical errors, illogical items (e.g., a page range of 45–43), and incomplete entries.

*Step 3.* Copyedit all the notes. During this pass, read each reference citation in the notes against the bibliography. Query any inconsistencies, discrepancies, and incomplete entries.

*Step 4.* If the in-text note indicators are numbers, page through the manuscript and the notes to make sure the numbering is correct.

*Step 5.* Make your second pass through the manuscript. If you add or delete any notes during your second pass, recheck the numbering sequence when you are done.

If the manuscript has an unwieldy number of notes and if time permits, you may want to try to reduce the number of notes by combining those that fall in the same para-

---

12. Some authors divide their bibliographies into sublists by topic or by chapter, and such divisions are sometimes helpful for readers. When an author has arranged the items by type (e.g., primary sources, secondary sources) or has separate lists for books, articles, and archival materials, you should ask your editorial coordinator whether to retain these sublists or ask the author to consolidate them. A helpful definition of primary and secondary sources may be found at Ithaca College Library, https://libguides.ithaca.edu/research101/primary.

graph or by introducing short titles and in-text citations, as described earlier in this section.

## CITATION-SEQUENCE SYSTEM

The citation-sequence system uses in-text superscripts for references, but—unlike the reference note system—only one work appears in each numbered note and that number serves to identify that source throughout the entire document. In other words, 1 is assigned to the first source mentioned in the text, 2 is assigned to the second source, and so on. In the reference list at the end of the document, the items are numbered and are listed in order of their first mention in the text (i.e., the reference list is not alphabetical).

If you've never seen a document that uses the citation-sequence system, you will likely be puzzled at first: multiple superscripts may cluster together, and superscripts may appear out of numerical sequence.

> Occupational injuries are underreported for agricultural workers in all regions of the country.[1-3] Underreporting is most serious for itinerant workers,[2,4] and for younger workers.[3]

The [1-3] after the first sentence refers the reader to items 1, 2, and 3 in the reference list. The sources for the comment about itinerant workers are items 2 and 4 on the reference list, and the source for the comment about younger workers is item 3.

The principal advantage of the citation-sequence system is that the running text is not interrupted by long strings of parenthetical references. Look what happens, for example, when the two earlier sentences about occupational injuries are rewritten in author-date style:

> Occupational injuries are underreported for agricultural workers in all regions of the country (US Department of Labor 1996a; Angeles 1997; Myrmia and Wilkerson 1998). Underreporting is most serious for itinerant workers (US Department of Labor 1996a; Hollingshead 1998) and for younger workers (Myrmia and Wilkerson 1998).

The principal editorial disadvantage of the citation-sequence system is that the entire reference list and all in-text superscripts must be renumbered if the author adds or deletes a reference at the last minute.

The citation-sequence system is used in some natural science, social science, and medical literature, especially in articles for professional journals. *CSE* presents a comprehensive description of the system and the formatting of the reference list; neither *Chicago* nor *APA* mentions the citation-sequence system.

## COPYEDITING PROCEDURES

Barring the last-minute addition or deletion of a reference that necessitates renumbering throughout, the citation-sequence system poses the fewest problems for the copyeditor:

there are no in-text citations to be checked against the reference list, and there is no alphabetization task (since the items in the reference list appear in the order they have been cited in the document). All of the following tasks may be done before or after copyediting the manuscript.

*Step 1.* Check the numerical order in the reference list. Make sure that no numerals are skipped or repeated.

*Step 2.* Scan the document to check the sequence of the in-text superscript numerals. Look for the first appearance of each numeral; these first appearances must be in sequence, although any numeral may reappear at any time. Also, make sure that multiple citations are correctly punctuated: inclusive numerals are linked by an en dash (e.g., [2-5]); two consecutive numerals and noninclusive numerals are separated by commas without any wordspacing after the commas (e.g., [1,2] or [2,3,8]).

*Step 3.* Copyedit the reference list. Read each entry carefully so that you can spot any typographical errors. Then reread the entry to check the format. These entries should be styled according to the models presented in *CSE,* another specialized scientific style manual, or an in-house style guide. For example, in CSE style:

> 1. Winters AA. Air pollution, water contamination, and public health. New York: Eco Books; 1998. 525 p.

> 2. Spring BY, Fall CZ, editors. Genetic diversity within species. Boston: T Riley; 1996. 1234 p.

> 3. Summers DE, Mamori I, Jackson J. A controlled trial of quality assurance. Am J Clin Lab 1995 Jan;85(2):125–37.

> 4. Hunter Applied Physics Laboratory. Standards for mapping subatomic particle behavior. Int J Phys 1997;12:785–804.

## CITATION OF DIGITAL SOURCES

Editorial conventions for citing electronic sources are evolving as more content is published in digital form—instead of, in advance of, or in addition to print. If parallel analog and digital versions exist, they may differ, and an online version can be modified without notice. When authors consult a digital document, they should cite this version even though it appears to be identical to (e.g., a PDF of) the print version. Many of the conventions described above for styling blocks of information in reference lists, reference notes, and bibliographies have been adapted for online and other digital publications, but some specific new issues arise in citing digital sources.

### AUTHORS' NAMES

For posts on social media, email lists, and online forums, the author's real name, if known, should be provided, followed by the author's screen name in parentheses:

*Twitter author:*
Eliot Marshall (@FireMarshall205)

## TITLES

As mentioned in chapter 6, *Chicago* specifies headline-style capitalization for the titles of most online sources—websites and databases, webpages, blogs and titled blog posts—by analogy with print sources. But for text messages and for untitled posts on social media, mailing lists, and online forums, *Chicago* recommends using the text or partial text of the post as a title and applying sentence capitalization. As in running text, titles of online works in references are set in roman or italic or are enclosed in quotation marks according to the type of source:

Title of website without a printed counterpart: in roman

Wikipedia
Google Scholar

Title of online edition of a printed work: in italics

*Merriam-Webster Unabridged*
*The Chicago Manual of Style Online*
the online *Encyclopaedia Britannica*

[If the existence of a printed counterpart to an online publication is in doubt, "opt for roman," *Chicago* 14.206 advises. When the titles of the print and online editions are identical, specify the version cited.]

Page or section of a website: in quotation marks

"About the Unabridged," *Merriam-Webster Unabridged*
"Forum," *The Chicago Manual of Style Online*
"Hypatia: Mathematician and Astronomer," *Encyclopaedia Britannica* (online)

Title of blog: in italics

*Language Log*
*CMOS Shop Talk*

Title of blog post: in quotation marks

"Three Social Media Habits for a Better World," *CMOS Shop Talk*

Untitled text or post on a social media platform, list, or forum: in quotation marks

"The White House put out a statement on Friday hailing 'those suffering under the yolk of authoritarianism,'" Twitter

## PUBLICATION DETAILS

For e-books, self-published or otherwise, the application, device, or file format is also specified:

Self-published, Amazon Digital Services, 2018. Kindle.

New York: W. W. Norton, 2017. iBook.

## PAGE NUMBERS AND OTHER LOCATORS

Except for photographic or PDF replicas of printed publications, e-books and other electronic works lack fixed pages: on-screen text scrolls; e-book text reflows with the user's choice of reading device and text size. Accordingly, a chapter number or section heading must suffice as a locator unless the content contains numbered paragraphs, line numbers, or other precise coordinates, or the publisher's digital format includes page numbers that correspond to the printed edition.

## URLS FOR ONLINE SOURCES

For online works, the URL follows the customary blocks of information, and either precedes or follows a "posted on" or "modified on" date, a time stamp, or, when required, a retrieval date. Among the style questions for citing URLs are whether

> to set the URL off from surrounding text in some way, such as enclosing it in angle brackets or using italics
>
> to include the protocol (e.g., http://, https://, ftp://)
>
> to include the prefix "www" when it is part of the domain name
>
> to use a period or other terminal punctuation following the URL
>
> to supply the retrieval, or access, date (the date on which the author retrieved the information from the online source)
>
> to specify restricted access for any source that limits access to members or paying subscribers

*Typographic treatment of URLs.* Most styles have now dropped the use of enclosing angle brackets and other special typographic treatment of URLs. Otherwise, style manuals offer slightly different formatting advice. *Chicago* includes both the protocol and the "www" prefix, includes any trailing slash as "part of the URL" (14.17), and follows the URL with a period. *APA* likewise includes the protocol and the "www" prefix but omits a terminal period, "to prevent the impression that the period is part of the URL" (p. 192). *MLA* omits the protocol but includes a terminal period. *CSE* includes the protocol, "www," and terminal period.

> *Chicago:* http://www.chicagomanualofstyle.org/.
>
> *APA:* http://www.chicagomanualofstyle.org
>
> *MLA:* www.chicagomanualofstyle.org.
>
> *CSE:* http://www.chicagomanualofstyle.org.

*Durable URLs. Chicago* and *MLA* explicitly advise against using the short URLs provided by commercial web-based services, such as TinyURL and Bitly, that generate aliases for long URLs and redirect, or link, them to the original URL. Although these aliases are widely used in social media communications, they are not appropriate for serious citation: they do not contain the domain information necessary for readers to assess the authoritativeness of the sources cited, and the commercial companies that create them can vanish, along with the utility of their short-form links. Even content identified by full URLs can disappear entirely or move to a new web location without a forwarding address, a change commonly called reference rot or link rot. Editors should ask the author to supply a DOI (Digital Object Identifier) when available or, lacking that, a *permalink,* sometimes called a persistent or stable URL and so identified within the online source document. DOIs, which are often used for online scholarship, help readers locate a document even if it migrates to a new URL; permalinks are also more stable than the often-lengthy URLs copied or "shared" from a web browser's address bar. To be sure, durable links are not always available—it's the Wild West out there on the internet. But the provision of as many conventional publication details as possible for online sources still enables readers to search the web or to plumb the depths of the Internet Archive for superseded (or suppressed) webpages.

*Access restrictions. Chicago's* online "Style Q&A" counsels against noting access restrictions in reference list entries because such restrictions are not mentioned for other types of sources; also, these restrictions may change. For sources at locations that limit access to members or subscribers, it may be preferable for the author simply to identify the database unless the URL links nonsubscribers to useful metadata for the source.[13] Even for unrestricted sites, a domain name (e.g., http://www.bartleby.com/) or the name of a database (e.g., Great Books Online) may sometimes be preferable to a mile-long URL, provided the site offers a robust search function and the citation includes the full publication details for the source.

*Retrieval (access) dates.* Some publishers prefer that reference citations include retrieval dates, whereas others see little use for these dates and request them only for certain types of online documents. *Chicago* considers retrieval dates "of limited value" (14.12) but recommends them for citations of online content that may be quickly superseded, such as frequently updated survey results or a crowd-sourced dictionary of contemporary slang. And it *requires* retrieval dates for citations of online sources for which no publication or posting date, revision date, or time stamp can be identified. *APA* tells authors not to include retrieval dates unless the source material is likely to change over time. *MLA,* on the other hand, considers retrieval dates an important indicator of the version consulted, given the volatility of online content; like *Chicago,* it regards the date of access as "especially crucial if the source provides no date specifying when it was produced or published" (p. 53). *CSE* includes retrieval dates in all reference citations. Specifications for the placement and styling of retrieval dates vary in these manuals.

13. Metadata, the digital information about a document, includes the sorts of details normally accompanying a journal article or printed on a book's cover or jacket: e.g., title, subtitle, author, author biography, other contributors, edition, publisher, publication date, ISBN, price, description of content, and subject categories. See Glossary of Copyediting Terms.

*Examples.* Here are sample citations for electronic sources from *Chicago* and *APA:*

*Chicago* author-date reference list

> Kossinets, Gueorgi, and Duncan J. Watts. 2009. "Origins of Homophily in an Evolving Social Network." *American Journal of Sociology* 115:405–50. https://doi:10.1086/599247.

> Stolberg, Sheryl Gay, and Robert Pear. 2010. "Wary Centrists Posing Challenge in Health Care Vote." *New York Times,* February 27, 2010. http://www.nytimes.com/2010/02/28/us/politics/28health.html.
> [In reference list entries for newspaper and magazine articles, *Chicago* repeats the year of publication with the month and day.]

*APA* author-date reference list

> Herbst-Damm, K. L., & Kulik, J. A. (2005). Volunteer support, marital status, and the survival times of terminally ill patients. *Health Psychology, 24,* 225–229. doi:10.1037/0278–6133.24.2.225

> Sillick, T. J., & Schutte, N. S. (2006). Emotional intelligence and self-esteem mediate between perceived early parental love and adult happiness. *E-Journal of Applied Psychology, 2*(2), 38–48. Retrieved from http://ojs.lib.swin.edu.au/index.php/ejap

*Chicago* reference note system

> *Note:* 1. Gueorgi Kossinets and Duncan J. Watts, "Origins of Homophily in an Evolving Social Network," *American Journal of Sociology* 115 (2009): 405–50, https://doi:10.1086/599247.

> *Bibliographic entry:* Kossinets, Gueorgi, and Duncan J. Watts. "Origins of Homophily in an Evolving Social Network." *American Journal of Sociology* 115 (2009): 405–50. https://doi:10.1086/599247.

*Chicago, APA, MLA,* and *CSE* give detailed advice about the formatting of bibliographical entries for online documents. You can also adopt the following simpler formats, omitting the access date when it is not required:

Individual work

> Author. *Title of Work.* Publisher, year. [Access date.] URL.

> Ortega, Marilena. *Four Corners.* Sylvan Online, 2015. Accessed April 1, 2016. http://www.sylvan.org/corners/.

Part of a work

> Author. "Title of Selection." *Title of Complete Work.* Publisher, year. [Access date.] URL.

> Weber, Israel. "GUIs." *Encyclopedia of Design.* ComputerForm Publications, 1996. Accessed January 30, 1997. ftp://cfp.com/encycd/218/html.

Journal, magazine, or newspaper article

> Author. "Title." *Periodical Title* volume:issue (year), paging or indicator of length. [Access date.] URL.

> Dennison, Michael. "Selecting a Web Browser." *Online Consumer Review* 2:3 (2015), 5 paragraphs. Accessed March 8, 2016. http://www.ocr.com /brow~denn/html.

Editorial style for citing digital sources will doubtless continue to change. Ask your editorial coordinator about house policy, and consult your style manual or in-house style guide for current practices.

# CHAPTER 12

# ¶ Front Matter, Back Matter, and Running Heads

Copyeditors who work on books and book-length documents may be called upon to handle *front matter* (the materials that appear before the first page of the text proper) and *back matter* (the materials that appear at the end of the volume). For the sake of brevity, in this chapter *book* is used to refer to any publication in the form of a traditional book.

## FRONT MATTER

Most printed books have at least four pieces of front matter (also called *preliminaries* or *prelims*), and some e-book formats retain these elements and their traditional order. (Web publications may relegate prelims to the margins of the core content.) These prelims are often supplied by the publisher, but the copyeditor may be charged with preparing them using the publisher's template.

The *half-title page* (sometimes called the *bastard title*) displays the main title of the book only. The half-title is a holdover from the early days of printing, when the page was used to protect and identify the unbound book block. The half-title continues to be used in traditional bookmaking, serving as a sort of foyer to the book proper, but it is sometimes eliminated by cost-cutting publishers to reduce the total page count.

The *title page* gives the essential publishing information: title and subtitle (differentiated by typography rather than by a colon between them); edition, if other than the first; all authors' names; all editors' and translators' names, if applicable; the publisher's name and the publisher's logo, if any; and the cities in which the publisher's main offices are located. A self-publishing author can adopt these conventions, omitting the publisher's name unless a company name or imprint for the author's publishing venture has been devised or a commercial self-publishing service supplies its own imprint.

The *copyright page* includes the copyright notice with the publisher's imprint, which may include the publisher's location and home page URL; Library of Congress Cataloging-in-Publication (CIP) data; the International Standard Book Number (ISBN); a Digital Object Identifier (DOI) if the book has one; and details of the book's publishing history (e.g., earlier editions with year dates). This busy page may also include an impression line, consisting of two rows of numerals identifying the number and year of the given printing;

a "Printed in [country]" line; and a statement about paper durability. Sometimes brief acknowledgments of permissions and grants and, if the book is
a translation, bibliographical information about the original work are also
added. (For design-intensive publications, such as fine arts books, a publisher may move some of this intricate "plumbing" to the back matter.) The
copyright page for a self-published book should include at least a copyright
statement and a list of any ISBNs (e.g., for hardcover, paperback, and digital
editions). The author may also add personal contact information in lieu of
a publisher's imprint and, for an e-book that has been updated, any applicable "last modified" date or (by analogy with iterations of software) a version
number.

The *table of contents,* which carries the heading "Contents" (rather than "Table
of Contents"), consists of one or more pages listing the chapters or sections
and the opening page number for each. Serving as both a map and a marketing tool, the table of contents may be more or less detailed, depending on
users' needs. The "TOC" for a textbook or instruction manual, for example,
might include one or more subhead levels along with chapter listings. Some
books and reports have two tables of contents: a simple contents page with
chapter or section titles only and an expanded list including all the subheads.

The prelims for technical reports and book-length business documents often use condensed formats: no half-title page, title and copyright data placed on the cover or on
a title page, and a table of contents. In many business reports, an *executive summary*
immediately follows the title page and precedes the contents. This self-contained section
summarizes the issue addressed in the report and outlines the findings and recommendations without reciting all the supporting data contained in the full report; the concise form of this summary allows a busy manager to make a decision without reading
further.

In traditional book design, the half title and title are printed on right-hand (*recto*)
pages, and the table of contents begins on a right-hand page; the copyright page appears
on a left-hand (*verso*) page, the back side of the title page. By convention, all front matter is numbered with lowercase roman numerals, and page numbers (also called *folios*)
are suppressed (that is, not printed) on the half-title, title, and copyright pages. Thus for
a book having only these four elements, the order and paging would be

| | | | |
|---|---|---|---|
| right page | half-title page | i | (folio suppressed) |
| left page | [blank] | ii | (folio suppressed) |
| right page | title page | iii | (folio suppressed) |
| left page | copyright page | iv | (folio suppressed) |
| right page | table of contents | v | (folio suppressed or expressed on opening page, depending on house style) |
| left page | continuation of contents or blank | vi | (folio expressed if text appears on the page; folio suppressed if page is blank) |

If the book is part of a series, a list of other books in the series may be placed on page ii. Page ii may also be used for a list of other works by ("Also by") the same author, a list of contributors (for a multiauthor work), or a *frontispiece* (an unnumbered illustration).

When the manuscript contains a dedication page or an *epigraph* (a brief quotation conveying the theme of the work) it is usually placed on page v, and the table of contents begins on the next right page, which would be page vii.

After the table of contents, any or all of the following items may appear, in the following order:

list of illustrations
list of tables
foreword
preface
acknowledgments
introduction
list of abbreviations
errata[1]

Here are the copyeditor's tasks:

- Check the order and page numbering of the front matter.
- Proofread the half-title, title, and copyright pages. Although these pages contain few words, they are important words, and careful proofreading is essential. (The annals of publishing are full of tales about misspellings of authors' names and embarrassing typos in book titles.)
- Style the dedication and epigraph, if any. The dedication can be a simple "For Amy"; although longer dedications are acceptable, the heading "Dedication" and the phrase "Dedicated to" are superfluous. An epigraph should end with a terminal punctuation mark: silently change a colon, comma, or semicolon to a period, or use ellipsis points if they work better. Brief source information (the author's name and the title of the work suffice) is provided below the epigraph. An epigraph page does not bear the heading "Epigraph."
- Read the table of contents against the manuscript, making sure that every section of the manuscript (front matter, chapters, back matter) is listed in the contents and that the chapter titles and subtitles in the contents exactly match those that appear at the opening of each chapter.
- Make sure that the pieces of front matter are correctly titled.

  The table of contents should be titled "Contents" (*not* "Table of Contents"). Similarly, a list of illustrations should be titled "Illustrations"; a list of

---

1. Or "erratum" if there is only one serious error to correct. Only errors causing severe confusion and discovered too late in the production process to emend in a last correction cycle warrant an errata list. Corrections may be posted online or placed in the front matter or back matter of the book.

tables, "Tables"; and an acknowledgments page, "Acknowledgments."
(Note the preferred spelling: no *e* between the *g* and the *m*.)

An introductory piece written by someone other than the author is labeled
"Foreword." (Note the spelling and remember the mnemonic "a *word*
that comes be*fore*.") A book-length work may have several forewords.
If so, each should have a different name: Publisher's Foreword, Translator's Foreword, Note from the ———.

An introductory piece written by the author is titled either "Preface" or
"Introduction." Typically, a preface is a short piece (one to three book
pages) containing remarks of a personal nature (reasons for writing the
book, acknowledgments). A longer piece is usually treated as an introduction. An introduction that includes substantive material essential
to the book, however, is not placed in the front matter; instead, it is
treated as the first (unnumbered) chapter of the body of the book, and
it carries arabic page numbers.

- Correlate any list of illustrations, tables, or maps against the caption copy
for those items. Is everything numbered correctly? Are the entries on the list
consistent in content, format, and editorial style?
- Advise the author of ways to consolidate the amount of front matter: If the book
has only a few tables, charts, or maps, the front matter need not include lists of
these elements. If the acknowledgments are brief, they can be moved to the end
of the preface or the introduction; if they are exceptionally lengthy, they can
sometimes be moved to the back matter.[2]

Besides preparing correct front matter, self-publishing authors need to take responsibility for supplying and maintaining basic *metadata* for their sales channels (see Glossary of Copyediting Terms). If they use a commercial self-publishing service, they can
often provide a description and keywords, sometimes with the editor's help, along with
other metadata by using the service's account management tools.

## BACK MATTER

Back matter is traditionally presented in the following order, with each item beginning
on a right-hand page unless space is at a premium:

2. The convention of expressing gratitude for advice and assistance during writing can be a tour de
force of style, gracious humor, or sly irony. But sometimes acknowledgments degenerate into condescension, sentimentality, false modesty, or name-dropping disguised as extravagant praise of colleagues.
Copyeditors understandably hesitate to challenge an author's deeply personal declarations of indebt-
edness, but they should alert the editorial coordinator if the length and tone of the acknowledgments
seem embarrassing—especially because acknowledgments are often added late in the production process, evading the publisher's customary scrutiny. An author who will not throttle the prose, even on the
advice of the publisher, may at least be persuaded to move the acknowledgments to a less conspicuous
place in the book.

| | |
|---|---|
| Appendix(es) | Instead of being given a chapter number, appendixes are labeled Appendix A, Appendix B, and so on. The title of the appendix follows: |

Appendix A. Field Data from Malaysia

Appendix B. Field Data from Thailand

| | |
|---|---|
| Notes | If the book has endnotes, they are printed here, chapter by chapter. When the endnotes include many acronyms or short titles for often-cited texts, a list of abbreviations precedes the notes. |
| Glossary | |
| Bibliography | May also be called Selected Bibliography, References, or Works Cited |
| Index | |

All back matter pages carry arabic folios.

## APPENDIXES

An appendix gives the reader additional content that would be distracting in the body of the book, and it affords greater flexibility with rules of style and page layout. For example, an appendix might consist of facsimiles of letters and other primary documents, a chronology or genealogy, a long and unwieldy table, a word list, or a questionnaire or other survey document. An appendix offers deeper understanding of a topic covered in the text; it does not simply contain table scraps left over from the author's research after the manuscript is written.

An appendix is sometimes published online instead of, or in addition to, appearing at the back of the book. Sometimes a chapter appendix immediately follows the specific chapter to which it pertains.

For the copyeditor, working on an appendix is just like working on regular text. But other types of back matter require special attention. In chapter 11, we discussed copyediting notes and bibliographies; here are some tips for working with glossaries and indexes.

## GLOSSARIES

A glossary provides clear, succinct definitions of key terms used in the text. Even if these terms are always explained when first mentioned in the text, and are indexed, they should be included in the glossary, with concise definitions allowing users to continue reading the text without further distraction. (Some glossaries include cross-references to the fuller discussions in the text to aid those readers seeking more information.) An author must exercise good judgment in selecting terms for the glossary: specialized terms already familiar to readers need not be glossed, whereas new and arcane ones should be included.

The copyediting of a glossary usually requires four passes. The first pass is a quick skimming of the manuscript to get a general sense of the author's definition-writing style. Typically, a definition opens with a concise sentence fragment that captures the essence of the term being defined. Subsequent sentences in a definition may be fragments or grammatically complete; when a term has more than one definition, each definition begins with a concise sentence fragment. During this first pass, note any definitions that are significantly more or less detailed than the others. These entries may require some substantive editing or a query to the author asking for a rewrite.

The second pass consists of reading down the main entries to be sure they are in alphabetical order. (For a discussion of some quirks of alphabetical order, see the penultimate section in this chapter, "Alphabetization.")

The third pass of the glossary is the occasion for careful copyediting, entry by entry. Each entry consists of the term being defined and one or both of the following: a definition (or definitions) and a cross-reference to other entries in the glossary. If no definition appears, the cross-reference begins with *See,* which redirects the user to a more common synonym, a more generic (or more specific) term, or a variant spelling; if the term is defined, the cross-reference begins with *See also, Contrast,* or *Compare* (normally italicized unless what follows, e.g., a foreign language term, is in italics).

At the designer's discretion, each part of the entry—term, definition, cross-reference indicator, cross-referenced term—may receive a different typographical treatment; for example:

| Term | Lowercase, boldface, followed by a period. |
|---|---|
| Definition(s) | Initial capital letter and terminal period. |
| | Technical terms within the definition are italicized. |
| | Multiple definitions are numbered (1), (2), and so on; each ends with a period. |
| Cross-reference indicator | Italics for indicator: *See* or *See also.* |
| Cross-referenced term | Lowercase and set in roman type. |
| | Multiple references are separated by a semicolon. |
| | Cross-reference is followed by a period. |

The resulting glossary will look like this:

**negative.** (1) A photographic image in which light values are reversed (i.e., black appears as white); *see also* positive. (2) Film used in photo-offset.
**numerals.** *See* arabic numerals; roman numerals.
**nut.** Printer's term for an *en. See also* em; molly.

If instructions for styling the entries do not accompany the manuscript, ask the editorial coordinator for advice.

So, on the third pass, as you read each entry,

make sure that the terms, definitions, and cross-references are styled
  consistently
copyedit the spelling, capitalization, hyphenation, and punctuation of the
  definitions
query or correct definitions that are wordy, tautological, or unclear
check every cross-reference to be sure the cross-referenced term appears in the
  glossary

Copyeditors are usually not expected to verify that every term listed in the glossary appears in the manuscript or that every technical term in the manuscript is included in the glossary.[3] Based on your understanding of the intended audience, however, you may want to suggest terms that could be added to or deleted from the glossary.

The fourth pass is a quick read-through to catch any overlooked errors.

## INDEXES

An index is not merely a concordance, an alphabetical list of all the words used in a work. Nor can it be replaced by the full-text search capability of a digital work. Rather, an index is an intellectual construction, a systematic arrangement of terms enabling users to locate information in a document, with cross-references, the grouping of related concepts, and other analysis. It serves as a critical tool for users' research, reference, and recovery of half-remembered content. It also serves as a marketing and sales tool: bookstore customers may peruse an index while deciding whether to purchase a book, and some bookselling websites give shoppers access to digital indexes for the same reason. Most nonfiction works need an index.

Indexing requires a different mind-set and different skills from copyediting, although some ambidextrous freelancers provide both services. Authors, too, sometimes prepare their own indexes, especially if the task requires subject expertise. Some authors are naturals at indexing their own work, but their knowledge of the content does not automatically endow them with the highly specialized skills necessary to prepare a useful index. And there are no shortcuts in this labor-intensive work. The best indexes are written by professional indexers.

Since an index cannot be prepared until the final pagination of the publication has been determined, the index never accompanies the manuscript. Copyeditors who work solely as manuscript editors are thus spared the task of handling indexes. But someone has to read and copyedit them, and that someone needs to have a very careful eye and a good sense of the conventions for indexes.

3. *Exception:* In some manuscripts—for example, training manuals, reference books, and technical reports—technical terms are given special typographical treatment (e.g., bold or italic type), and readers are told that all such terms are defined in the glossary. In such cases, the copyeditor is expected to make sure that all specially marked terms do appear in the glossary.

Copyediting an index usually requires four passes. The first pass is delightfully simple: race through the index and make sure there is a blank line before the first entry that begins with a *b,* the first entry that begins with a *c,* and so on. To save space, short indexes (a page or two) are often set without this additional linespacing.

The second pass sounds simple: read down the main entries to check the alphabetical order and the capitalization style (either all entries begin with a capital letter or only those entries that are proper nouns and proper adjectives begin with a capital letter). In practice, there are several tricky issues in alphabetization, described in the next section of this chapter.

The third pass is for the slow, careful reading and copyediting of the entries, entry by entry. There are eight key tasks—and one optional, time-consuming chore—at this stage:

1. Correct all typographical errors. Check any unusual spellings, capitalization, and hyphenation choices against the page proofs.

2. Make sure the wording of the main entries matches readers' expectations. For example, in a consumer guide that covers automobiles, large appliances, and small appliances, readers interested in tips on buying a new car are likely to look under "cars, new," not under "new cars."

3. If the entry has subentries, the subentries should be concise, with the key term first, and should be parallel in form.

   *Not parallel:* quotations 12–18; accuracy, 14; capitalizing, 15; using ellipsis
       points in, 16
   *Parallel:* quotations, 12–18; accuracy of, 14; capitalization of, 15; ellipsis
       points within, 16
   *Or:* quotations, 12–18; accuracy, 14; capitalization, 15; ellipsis points, 16

   A subentry may include prepositions or conjunctions that link it to the main entry and form a grammatical phrase (e.g., "accuracy of [quotations]," "ellipsis points within [quotations]"), but the imprecise "concerning . . ." and "relating to . . ." should be avoided. Subentries may also represent logical subdivisions of the main entry (e.g., "accuracy," "ellipsis points").

4. If the entry has subentries, check the order of the subentries. Most often, subentries are arranged in alphabetical order, but sometimes numerical order or chronological order (e.g., for indexing biographical or historical content) is preferable.

   *Numerical order:* amended returns, filing procedures: form 1057, 285–90;
       form 1124, 293–300; form 1335A, 310–15; form 5252, 415–17
   *Chronological order:* tombs, design of: in First Dynasty, 17–35; in Second
       Dynasty, 267–92; in Third Dynasty, 389–402

5. Check the punctuation within each entry. The conventions for a standard run-in index[4] are these:

> Use a comma to separate portions of an inverted main entry: diseases, tropical.
> Place a comma after the main entry when the entry is immediately followed by a page number; place a colon after the main entry when the entry is immediately followed by a subentry heading.
> Place a comma after a subentry heading (to separate it from the page numbers that follow).
> Use a semicolon to separate successive subentries.

Place internal cross-references (i.e., cross-references that apply to only one subentry) in parentheses at the end of the subentry; lowercase and italicize the cross-reference indicator (*see* to redirect readers to the applicable entry; or *see also* to refer them to additional entries):

> magazines: binding of, 25–26; citation of (*see* articles, magazine); titles of, 121–23

Terminal cross-references (i.e., cross-references that apply to the entire entry) carry an initial capital letter and are set in italics. The text immediately preceding the cross-reference takes a terminal period. When the cross-reference is to a specific term, that term is set in roman type (unless it is normally set in italics); when the cross-reference is to a class of terms, the entire cross-reference is set in italics.[5]

> legal citations: in bibliographies, 238–42, 251; in footnotes, 230–37. *See also* laws
> legends. *See* captions and legends
> planets. *See names of individual planets*

There is no punctuation at the end of an index entry.

6. Scrutinize the page numbers in the entry and subentries:

> A series of page numbers should be in ascending order: 16, 23, 145.
> Page ranges must be logical: 34–35 (*not* 34–34 *or* 35–34 *or* 34035).
> The treatment of page ranges should be consistent, following one of the three systems shown in "Inclusive Numerals" in chapter 7.

---

4. In a run-in index, the subentries are set in the same paragraph as the main entry (as illustrated by all the examples in this chapter); the first line of each entry is set flush left, and the remaining lines are indented (this style is called "flush and hang"). Alternatively, an index may be set in indented style, in which each subentry begins on a new indented line.

5. In both internal and terminal cross-references, *see* redirects readers to synonyms, pseudonyms, and variant spellings and is used when the entry contains no page locators; *see also* points to related topics and is used when the entry includes locators.

Overly large page spans, for example, "50–68," are unhelpful because they are too broad for readers to find what they're looking for. If possible, ask the author or indexer to provide subentries.

7. Verify that terms listed in cross-references do appear in the index. If you encounter a pair of entries such as

> fire safety. *See* smoke detectors
> smoke detectors, 198, 211–12

you can replace the cross-reference with the page numbers, because the page numbers take up less space than the cross-reference:

> fire safety, 198, 211–12
> smoke detectors, 198, 211–12

Make sure such double postings have the same page numbers.

8. If an entry has many subentries but few page numbers, consolidate the entry. For example,

> termites, 205–6; damp-wood, 205; dry-wood, 205; identifying, 205–6; subterranean, 206

could be shortened to

> termites, 205–6

The optional task at this stage, time permitting, is to rewrite any entries that have long strings of pages numbers without subentries to guide the reader. Some publishers use "the rule of five," others "the rule of seven," to determine what constitutes an overly long string of unanalyzed page locators. *Chicago* offers a few paragraphs of helpful advice; for a comprehensive discussion, see Nancy Mulvany, *Indexing Books*. Be warned, however, that this task can be extremely time consuming. So, too, can trimming an index bloated with trivia and useless page locators for nonsubstantive references to (passing mentions of) indexed terms. Repairing a conceptually deficient or thin index—for example, one with poorly formulated, nonintuitive, redundant, or scanty categories—is an exercise in self-flagellation. Salvaging a computer-generated concordance—an unfiltered list of words in the document, with page locators—is an impossibility. Leave these jobs to the author or to a replacement indexer, who may start from scratch rather than attempting to rescue the inadequate work.

If you clear (or evade) the hurdle of a defective index, the fourth copyediting pass should be a relatively quick scanning to make sure that you have not inadvertently inserted an error and have not overlooked anything.

## ALPHABETIZATION

Checking the order of entries in bibliographies and reference lists (see chapter 11) and in glossaries and indexes is not quite as simple as reciting the alphabet. First, determine which system of alphabetization has been followed:

*Letter by letter versus word by word.* Listings must be consistent in using either the letter-by-letter system or the word-by-word system of alphabetization. Under the word-by-word principle, terms are alphabetized by the first full word in the entry; thus "San Francisco" would precede "sanctuary." Under the letter-by-letter principle, wordspaces are ignored; thus "sanctuary" would precede "San Francisco." Among the style manuals, *Chicago* and *CSE* offer the best guidance on alphabetization. For the most thorough treatment of the topic for indexers, see Mulvany, *Indexing Books.*

*Personal names.* Surnames beginning with particles (e.g., de, Della, La, van) or with *Mac, Mc, St.,* or *Saint,* and foreign names present special problems in capitalization and alphabetization. For example, Ludwig van Beethoven is alphabetized under *b* (Beethoven, Ludwig van), but Willem de Kooning is alphabetized under *d* (de Kooning, Willem). The best references to consult are *Chicago, CSE,* and Mulvany's *Indexing Books.*

*Numerals.* Main entries that begin with numerals are alphabetized as though they were spelled out: an entry for the television program *60 Minutes* would appear after "sixpenny nails" and before "sizing." In a bibliography, an unsigned article titled "1939: The Beginning of the End" would be alphabetized under the spelled-out number "nineteen." But when there are many numerical terms to be listed, as in an index, they may be placed together in numerical order at the beginning of the index, preceding the *a*'s.

*Nonalphabetical characters.* Main entries that consist of nonalphabetical characters are collected at the beginning of the listings, in a group preceding the *a* words, and are also double-posted (i.e., duplicated) in their spelled-out form (for the names of common nonalphabetical characters, see chapter 9). For example, in an index:

> #, use of, 19, 25 [Would also appear under "hashtag," "pound sign," or "number sign."]
> < >, in commands, 12 [Would also appear under "angle brackets."]
> &, syntax for, 38 [Would also appear under "ampersand."]
>
> AAs, 128
> abacus, 2
> abbreviations, 76–78
> acronyms, 82, 87, 125

There is no consensus on how to order a list of nonalphabetical characters that precedes the *a* words. Sometimes these characters are arranged by name (although nonalphabetical characters often have several names, depending on context: e.g., @ = "at" or "per"). Sometimes they are placed in numerical order using their ASCII code equivalents.[6] Sometimes the proprietary algorithms embedded in indexing software automatically sort terms.

## RUNNING HEADS (AND RUNNING FEET)

*Running heads,* also called *headers,* are the short titles appearing at the tops of pages (when they are positioned at the bottoms of pages, they are called *running feet* or *footers*); along with page numbers, or folios, they help readers navigate a book-length document. The copyeditor may be expected to prepare running head copy for a manuscript or simply to check and, if necessary, correct or update running head copy supplied by the editorial coordinator.

The content of running head copy is dictated by the nature of the publication, by the needs of readers, and by house style. The print edition of *M-W Collegiate,* for example, uses the first and last words defined on each page of the dictionary. Many publishers still follow the tradition of using book titles as verso running heads, but Chicago style avoids this, because titles may change during production, necessitating extensive corrections in proofs. Instead, the print *Chicago* lists the chapter title and first paragraph number on verso pages and first-level subhead and last paragraph number on recto pages.

Although the content of running head copy has many variations, certain conventions prevail in bookmaking. Running heads are never used on blank pages, with full-page illustrations or tables, or on display pages, such as half-title, title, copyright, dedication, epigraph, part-title, and section- or chapter-opening pages. Some typical configurations for pages that bear running heads are these:

|  | *Verso* | *Recto* |
|---|---|---|
| Front matter *(as applicable)* | Contents *(if multipage)* | Contents |
|  | Illustrations *(if multipage)* | Illustrations |
|  | Tables *(if multipage)* | Tables |
|  | Maps *(if multipage)* | Maps |
|  | Preface | Preface |
|  | Acknowledgments | Acknowledgments |
|  | Introduction | Introduction |
|  | Abbreviations *(if multipage)* | Abbreviations |
| Body text *(as applicable)* | Part Title | Chapter Title |
| *or:* | Book Title | Chapter Title |
| *or:* | Chapter Title | Chapter Title |
| *or:* | Chapter Title | Chapter Subtitle |

6. Each nonalphabetical character in the basic ASCII set has a two- or three-digit number; for example, the pound sign (#) is 35 and the open angle bracket (<) is 60. But readers are unlikely to know this system and will still have to skim the entire list to find the item wanted.

| | | |
|---|---|---|
| *or:* | Chapter Title | First-Level Subhead |
| *or, for a multiauthor volume:* | Chapter Author's Name | Chapter Title |
| Back matter *(as applicable)* | Notes to Pages 000–000 | Notes to Pages 000–000 |
| *or:* | Notes to Chapter 00 | Notes to Chapter 00 |
| | Appendix X | Appendix Title |
| | Glossary | Glossary |
| | Bibliography | Bibliography |
| | Index | Index |

Running head copy with the accompanying folio must not exceed the width of the page of type. If running head copy is excessively long, the editor may need to shorten it to fit, taking care to preserve key terms and to secure the author's approval of the truncated version. For possible running heads in electronic formats, short forms for chapter and section titles can be specified as part of the markup of the files.

# CHAPTER 13

# ¶ Markup

Many manuscripts contain material other than sentences and paragraphs of running text. The most common of these elements are book, article, and chapter titles; heads and subheads; extracts; tables; and captions for illustrations.

Decisions about the physical appearance of these elements—e.g., typeface, type size, indention, vertical and horizontal position and spacing—are the province of the publication's designer. But the copyeditor must often identify for the designer which elements appear in the manuscript and where each is located; this process of pinpointing the elements that require special formatting is variously referred to as *markup, tagging, styling,* or (a term carried over from editing on paper) *typecoding.* The designer then supplies specifications (called *specs*) that detail the desired treatment of those elements.

In the pencil-editing era, markup was done by hand-marking these special elements on the hard copy, using the publisher's set of descriptive, easily remembered (mnemonic) labels, usually called *typecodes:* for example, CN (for chapter number) and CT (for chapter title). At the end of the job, the copyeditor would prepare a complete list of the typecodes applied in the manuscript, with page numbers for representative (and aberrant) examples of each, to guide the designer's preparation of specs. In the great shift to on-screen editing, these typecodes were repurposed as *generic codes:* for example, <cn> and </cn> (beginning and end of chapter number, respectively), <ct> and </ct> (beginning and end of chapter title). Although manuscripts were still occasionally hand-marked, most copyeditors began to key these codes directly into the author's files (or to verify and correct codes previously inserted into the files by a production editor), conforming to increasingly rigorous tagging protocols demanded by computer technology.

In recent years, however, many book publishers have abandoned the manual entry of generic codes on-screen as well, instead *styling* the elements, that is, applying predefined formats, called *styles,* in Microsoft Word or other proprietary software. These styles are mapped to a design template during production.[1] Other publishers use a formal markup language, such as *XML* (extensible markup language), which can be mapped to multiple

---

1. *Styling* a manuscript by using a word processor's styling feature (e.g., Microsoft Word's Style menu) means applying predefined or customized formatting to different elements in the files, e.g., a "Title" style for a title, a "Body Text" style for body text, and a "Caption" style for a picture caption. The visual appearance of a manuscript so styled should not be mistaken for the final design of the publication; rather, this software-assisted styling, like generic coding, simply identifies and differentiates the manuscript elements and maps them to the designer's template, which determines the appearance of the finished product. Such software-assisted styling should also not be confused with *editorial styling*—the treatment of punctuation, spelling, capitalization, numbers, quotations, abbreviations, tables and graphs, and references—as described in chapters 4 through 12.

design templates suitable for different publishing environments (e.g., print, e-book, PDF, web). XML markup is likely to be preferred in the production of complex reference works published in many print and digital formats, especially if they have rigorous indexing requirements and frequent revisions—for example, dictionaries, encyclopedias, and, of course, the redoubtable *Chicago*.

Regardless of whether markup is done on paper or on-screen, the preparation of a manuscript for editing usually includes some preliminary markup (see "The Editorial Process" in chapter 1). Turning the pages or scrolling through the cleaned-up files of an unedited manuscript, the copyeditor typically surveys its overall structure and features while beginning to tag or style headings and other major elements. This initial markup sometimes reveals issues of logic and organization evident in an aerial sweep over the manuscript though not always detectable on the ground during the subsequent sentence-level copyediting—for example, chapters or sections of conspicuously different lengths, overly long headings, an irrational hierarchy of subheads, an excessive use of extracts, or an inconsistent treatment of formatted lists. Thus a discussion of markup necessarily includes advice about some structural deficiencies that may be disclosed in the process.

## MARKUP OF HARD COPY

When copyeditors worked on hard copy, they were usually asked to mark up, or type-code, the elements with a colored pencil. As figure 14 shows, the copyeditor also marked the beginning and end of any element whose boundaries were unclear in the manuscript. Typecodes were written in the left margin—or to the left of an indented item—and circled.

Every publisher had its own set of hard-copy typecodes, and a list of these codes was given to the copyeditor. In book publishing the following mnemonic labels were typical, and some publishers continue to use them in on-screen editing.

| *Part openings* | | | *Chapter openings* | |
|---|---|---|---|---|
| PN | part number | | CN | chapter number |
| PT | part title | | CT | chapter title |
| PST | part subtitle | | CST | chapter subtitle |
| PEP | part epigraph | | CEP | chapter epigraph |
| PES | part epigraph source line | | CES | chapter epigraph source line |

| *Heads (headings) within the document* | | | *Display text within the body of the document* | |
|---|---|---|---|---|
| A | first-level head[2] | | EX | prose extract (block quote) |
| B | second-level head | | PX | poetry extract |
| C | third-level head | | EQ | equation |

2. Alternatively, heads are coded as 1, 2, and 3; see the discussion later in this chapter.

FIGURE 14.  Markup of Hard Copy

 1    Lump Sum Distributions from Qualified Plans

 All's well that ends well.

William Shakespeare

A qualified plan is an employer-sponsored retirement plan that meets certain standards set in the Internal Revenue Code. The three principal types of qualified plans are

 *Pension plans*, which include money purchase pension plans, defined benefit pension plans, Keogh plans, and 401(k) plans

*Profit-sharing plans*

*Stock bonus plans*

Payout of retirement benefits from a qualified plan

Most qualified plans give a retiring employee several choices for receiving his or her accrued benefits:

- In a series of equal periodic (annual, semiannual, quarterly, monthly) payments.
- Through a variable or fixed annuity contract purchased from an insurance company.
- Through a life annuity contract purchased from an insurance company.
- In a lump sum distribution (defined in the next subsection).

The qualified plan agreement also specifies how an employee's accrued benefits are to be handled if the employee, before reaching retirement, becomes disabled, leaves the company, or dies, or if the plan is discontinued by the employer.

Lump sum distributions

Many qualified plans allow participants the option, under certain conditions, of receiving in one lump sum the entire amount credited to their retirement account.

FIGURE 15. Markup of a Table

 Table 1. Virus-Neutralization Tests on Sera from Mammals and Birds (Performed under IASA standards)

| Species | Number Tested | Positive | |
|---|---|---|---|
| | | $N$ | % |
| **Mammals** | | | |
| Camel | 9 | 7 | 78 |
| Cow | 36 | 6 | 17 |
| Donkey | 15 | 7 | 47 |
| **Birds** | | | |
| Chicken* | 24 | 4 | 16 |
| Crow | 163 | 102 | 65 |
| Duck | 14 | 2[†] | 14 |

*Source:* Chris T. Author, *Book Title* (New York: Big Books, 1990), 536–37.

*Chickens were retested by PSA-3 analysis.

[†]Retest results were inconclusive for 2 additional ducks.

**Lists**

UNL   unnumbered list[3]
NL    numbered list
BL    bulleted list
MCL   multicolumn list

*Documentation*

FN    footnote
EN    endnote

**Back matter**

BMT   back matter section title
BIB   bibliography text
AN    appendix number
AT    appendix title

*Figures*

FGN   figure number
FGC   figure caption

Copyeditors were also expected to code the elements in each table. The coding in figure 15 is based on the following set of typical codes:

3. The formatting of lists is discussed later in this chapter.

| TN | table number | T1 | table first-level head |
|---|---|---|---|
| TT | table title | T2 | table second-level head |
| TST | table subtitle | TB | table body |
| TSQ | table squib | TS | table source line |
| TSH | table stubhead | TFN | table footnote |
| TCH | table column head | | |

## MARKUP ON-SCREEN

Copyeditors working on-screen today may be asked to key generic codes into the files or to verify the codes that have been inserted by an in-house production editor. Alternatively, copyeditors may be instructed to apply or to confirm formatting in the manuscript based on a template of styles created in the word processing application. The markup procedures depend on the publisher's production process, and the instructions given to the copyeditor normally include a list of the codes or a template with the styles, along with an explanation of the procedures. The following examples illustrate the general principles and some commonly used conventions. Figure 16 shows one system for inserting generic codes into the files of the manuscript page hand-coded in figure 14. Figure 17 shows the application of a word processor's style feature to the same excerpt.

### MARKING UP TEXT ELEMENTS

Codes keyed directly into the files are short mnemonic combinations. There are various systems for formatting these codes. Some place the codes in angle brackets, others use curly brackets or other delimiters, and still others use special characters before and after the code:

| Element | Angle brackets | Curly brackets | Special characters |
|---|---|---|---|
| chapter number | <CN> | {CN} | @cn: |
| chapter title | <CT> | {CT} | @ct: |

The end of the element is indicated either by a </> or <\> code (which may be accompanied by a repeat of the opening code) or by a hard return, depending on the system:

<CN>1</><CT>Rules of the Road</>

<CN>1</CN><CT>Rules of the Road</CT>

{CN}1{\}{CT}Rules of the Road{\}


@cn:1
@ct:Rules of the Road

FIGURE 16. On-Screen Markup Using Generic Codes. In this sample the running text is the default setting and so it carries no codes. Uppercase paired codes are used for text elements, lowercase paired codes for character attributes (features such as italics and boldface). The line breaks are generated by the hard return codes in the word processing program.

<CN>1<CN><CT>Lump Sum Distributions from Qualified Plans<CT>

<CEP>All's well that ends well.<CEP>

<CES>William Shakespeare<CES>

A qualified plan is an employer-sponsored retirement plan that meets certain standards set in the Internal Revenue Code. The three principal types of qualified plans are

<UL><i>Pension plans,<i> which include money purchase pension plans, defined benefit pension plans, Keogh plans, and 401(k) plans

<i>Profit-sharing plans<i>

<i>Stock bonus plans<i><UL>

<A>Payout of retirement benefits from a qualified plan<A>

Most qualified plans give a retiring employee several choices for receiving his or her accrued benefits:

<BL>In a series of equal periodic (annual, semiannual, quarterly, monthly) payments. Through a variable or fixed annuity contract purchased from an insurance company. Through a life annuity contract purchased from an insurance company. In a lump sum distribution (defined in the next subsection).<BL>

The qualified plan agreement also specifies how an employee's accrued benefits are to be handled if the employee, before reaching retirement, becomes disabled, leaves the company, or dies, or if the plan is discontinued by the employer.

<B>Lump sum distributions<B>

Many qualified plans allow participants the option, under certain conditions, of receiving in one lump sum the entire amount credited to their retirement account.

FIGURE 17. On-Screen Markup Using Styles. In this sample, prepared in Microsoft Word, the system supplies mnemonic codes along with visual formatting as the copyeditor marks the elements using the word processor's styling tools. This particular customized interface allows the copyeditor to verify correct markup easily. (The visual formatting, however, is only a tool to aid the copyediting process; the production designer determines the final appearance of the published document.) Here, regular paragraphed general text ("<GT>") is differentiated from general text with no indent ("<GT-ni>") that immediately follows headings; items in unnumbered lists are identified as first, middle, or last ("<UL-f>," "<UL-m>," "<UL-l>"). Publishers do not always expect this degree of specificity in markup, but specialized digital content, such as an online reference work, may require it. (See the examples in the online supplement to *Chicago,* "How Books and Journals Are Produced," linked at 1.117.)

<CN>1

<CT>**Lump Sum Distributions from Qualified Plans**

<CEP>All's well that ends well.

<CEPSN>William Shakespeare

<GT-ni>A qualified plan is an employer-sponsored retirement plan that meets certain standards set in the Internal Revenue Code. The three principal types of qualified plans are

<UL-f>*Pension plans,* which include money purchase pension plans, defined benefit pension plans, Keogh plans, and 401(k) plans

<UL-m>*Profit-sharing plans*

<UL-l>*Stock bonus plans*

<H1>**Payout of retirement benefits from a qualified plan**

<GT-ni>Most qualified plans give a retiring employee several choices for receiving his or her accrued benefits:

<BL-f>• In a series of equal periodic (annual, semiannual, quarterly, monthly) payments.

<BL-m>• Through a variable or fixed annuity contract purchased from an insurance company.

<BL-m>• Through a life annuity contract purchased from an insurance company.

<BL-l>• In a lump sum distribution (defined in the next subsection).

<GT>The qualified plan agreement also specifies how an employee's accrued benefits are to be handled if the employee, before reaching retirement, becomes disabled, leaves the company, or dies, or if the plan is discontinued by the employer.

<H2>*Lump sum distributions*

<GT-ni>Many qualified plans allow participants the option, under certain conditions, of receiving in one lump sum the entire amount credited to their retirement account.

When elements are instead coded by using a word processor's styling feature, each element is defined as a distinct style in the word processor's style template and then applied consistently throughout the manuscript. The on-screen system may be designed to display generic codes along with distinctive formatting of various elements, but these features of the user interface merely allow the copyeditor to verify that elements have been correctly styled. What matters in subsequent production is what's under the hood. (Subscribers to *The Chicago Manual of Style Online* can compare figures 1 and 2 in the online supplement "How Books and Journals Are Produced," showing two views of a manuscript page from *Chicago:* the user-friendly interface the copyeditor sees and the XML-coded plain text version exported from the styled and edited files.)

## CODING CHARACTER ATTRIBUTES

*Attributes* are features that apply to typed characters: boldface, italics, small capitals, subscripts, superscripts. In many production systems, the copyeditor need only verify that the author's word-processed formatting is correct. For example, assume that house style calls for an italic comma after a word in italics. In the following sentence, you would make sure that the second comma (the one at the end of the novel's title) is an italic comma:

> *Author's coding:* His best novel, *For Whom the Bell Tolls,* is also his most personal.

But some production systems require the copyeditor to delete the author's word-processed formatting and substitute special attribute codes:

> *Attribute coding:* His best novel, <I>For Whom the Bell Tolls,<I> is also his most personal.
>
> *Or:* His best novel, <I>For Whom the Bell Tolls,<i> is also his most personal.
>
> *Or:* His best novel, <I>For Whom the Bell Tolls,</> is also his most personal.

As these examples show, attribute codes come in pairs, one to start the feature, the other to turn off the feature. In some systems, the "turn-off" code is always </> or <\>. In other systems, the closing code is a repeat of or a variant on the opening code:

> <BF>Amendment 1.<bf> The term of city council members shall be four years.
>
> H<SUB>2<sub>O<SUB>2<sub> is highly unstable.
>
> Who can fail to appreciate the poetry of E = mc<SUP>2<sup>?

## CODING OR ENTERING SPECIAL CHARACTERS

Some manuscripts contain characters that do not appear on a standard QWERTY key-board, such as European diacritics and punctuation marks, non-Latin alphabets, some mathematical expressions, and scientific symbols. Authors and copyeditors can insert many of these characters by using special keyboard combinations (for example, the Alt or Option key plus a character key in Microsoft Word), selecting them from the symbols lists and tables in their word processing program, or keying the correct hexa-decimal codes for these characters in Unicode, an international cross-platform stan-dard for character encoding.[4] Improvised characters—for example, angle brackets for guillemets—are not acceptable; these characters may not survive the transition from one format (e.g., print, website, e-book) to another. If the author's files contain such jerry-rigging and the publisher has not cleaned them up before editing, a copyeditor may be asked to replace the counterfeits using the correct Unicode numbers to ensure that the special characters are retained in the production process.

Most contemporary computer operating systems and internet browsers and many software applications now support Unicode. Even so, Unicode-compliant type fonts typ-ically offer only a subset of the vast Unicode character set. Thus, when a manuscript con-tains non-QWERTY characters, the editor must list them so the production designer can select a suitable font; the editor should also avoid changing fonts during editing, which could cause the characters to display incorrectly in the files. *Chicago* includes sev-eral charts listing Unicode numbers, and the complete set is available at the Unicode Consortium website (http://www.unicode.org/). Many internet resources describe how to enter hexadecimal codes with different operating systems and applications.

## PROCEDURES

If codes are keyed into the files, the copyeditor is expected to make sure the coding is correct. This step includes checking to see that

> there are no typographical errors within the codes
> there is no extra wordspacing before or after the codes
> there is no extra linespacing before or after displayed elements
> punctuation that is to be set in italic or bold is correctly coded[5]

---

4. By convention, Unicode numbers described in running text are prefixed by "U+"; for example, U+00B1 represents the plus-or-minus sign (±).

5. In traditional typesetting, periods, commas, colons, and semicolons are set in the same style as the word that immediately precedes them. Question marks and exclamation points are set in italic or bold only if they are part of the expression preceding:

> The best children's book this season is Anderson's *Why Is the Sky Blue?*
> How can one explain the enduring popularity of *Gone with the Wind*?

Both members of paired marks (i.e., parentheses, brackets, quotation marks) are set in the same type-face, and they are set in italics or bold only when all the text within them is italic or bold.

*Chicago* now recommends a newer convention: all punctuation, including paired marks, is set in the style of the surrounding text. Exceptions: a question mark or exclamation point that is part of an italicized (or bold) term; parentheses or brackets appearing alone on a separate line and enclosing all-italic or all-bold text.

all paired codes have closing mates

all codes used in the manuscript appear on the master list that will be sent
    to the compositor

If elements are coded using the word processor's style feature, the copyeditor must scrutinize the edited manuscript to ensure that each element has a discrete style and that the
formatting is consistently applied.

## HEADS AND SUBHEADS

In addition to marking up the heads and subheads, a copyeditor must regularize the
capitalization of these heads, using either headline style or sentence style (see "Titles of
Works" in chapter 6). Both headline style and sentence style may be used in the same
document as long as all heads of the same level are treated consistently.

Some coding systems use letters (A, B, C) to indicate levels of heads, and other
coding systems use numerals (1, 2, 3). Under both systems, the code assigns a level of
importance to each head; the codes are *not* used to count up the number of heads in a
section. Thus a chapter may have nine first-level heads, all of which are coded A (or,
alternatively, coded 1).

As for the frequency of heads and subheads, the number that is "just right" depends
on the nature of the document and the intended readership. For most nonfiction trade
books, one head every four or five pages is probably sufficient; more-frequent heads
may give the text a choppy feel. Reference books, textbooks, and computer manuals, in contrast, may require several heads and subheads per page. For journal articles
printed in two-column formats, one head per column may be appropriate. Content
intended for the web requires frequent headings to break the text into easily skimmed,
bite-size chunks, since web users typically scan rather than read a piece from start to
finish.

The length and balance of headings must also be considered. When headings are
long (two or three lines of type), they disrupt the appearance of the page. When they are
short (two to four words), they are both more effective and more aesthetically pleasing.
Headings that are balanced in length and parallel in grammatical structure help readers
map the progress of a discussion through its visible scaffolding. Consider how the following scheme might baffle a reader:

Why Are Dogs Such Great Pets?
    Dogs Coevolved with Humans
    Small Dogs
    Large Dogs
    Diets for Dogs
    Medical Insurance for Dogs
    Werewolves

Cats
> Long-Haired Cats
> Short-Haired Cats
> Hairless Cats Are Best If You Have Allergies or Don't Like Vacuuming

This bizarre outline points to another issue sometimes disclosed when a copyeditor marks up head levels in a manuscript. After standardizing capitalization and checking the frequency and length of heads and subheads, you should make sure the heads in each chapter or section are logical. All first-level heads should be of roughly equivalent "weight." For example, a chapter on house pets could have first-level heads like those shown on the left; the set on the right is illogical.

| *Logical* | *Illogical* |
|-----------|-------------|
| Dogs | Dogs |
| Cats | Small dogs |
| Hamsters | Cats |
| Rabbits | Long-haired cats |
| | Hamsters |
| | Harvey, the Invisible Rabbit |

Because "small dogs" is a subset of "dogs," "small dogs" would have to be a second-level head, and logic suggests that if there is a second-level head for small dogs, the chapter should also have a second-level head for large dogs—and quite possibly one for medium-size dogs. Similarly, "cats" and "long-haired cats" are not logically equivalent, because the second is a subset of the first. And if there is to be a section on long-haired cats, logic requires a section on short-haired cats as well. Thus, one would expect to see

| First-level head: | Dogs |
|-------------------|------|
| Second-level head: | Small dogs |
| Second-level head: | Medium-size dogs |
| Second-level head: | Large dogs |
| First-level head: | Cats |
| Second-level head: | Short-haired cats |
| Second-level head: | Long-haired cats |
| Second-level head: | Hairless cats |
| First-level head: | Hamsters |
| First-level head: | Rabbits |

The small dogs and long-haired cats exemplify a second issue concerning the logic of heads. As a rule—though this rule admits some exceptions—for each level of head used, there must be at least two instances of that level. Thus when a document or chapter contains first-level heads, there must be at least two such heads in the document. And if second-level heads are used in a section that begins with a first-level head, there should be at least two second-level heads within that section, and so on. Like the schoolbook rule for making outlines, this principle is based on the premise that it is illogical to have only one subordinate item or subtopic within a category:

| *Logical* | *Illogical* |
|---|---|
| Dogs | Dogs |
|    Small dogs |    Small dogs |
|    Large dogs | Cats |
| Cats |    Long-haired cats |
|    Short-haired cats | Hamsters |
|    Long-haired cats | |
| Hamsters | |

The use of only one subdivision under a higher-level heading may indicate that the hierarchy of information is unclear. Most style manuals counsel against such asymmetry. *APA* stipulates, "Use at least two subsection headings within any given section, or use none (e.g., in an outline, you could divide a section numbered 1 into a minimum of A and B sections; just an A section could not stand alone)" (p. 62). *CSE* concurs: "In general, a heading should be followed by at least 2 subheadings at the next level down, not by a single subheading" (pp. 512–13). *Chicago,* too, states that "when a section of text is subdivided, there should ideally be at least two subsections," but adds that "occasionally . . . a single subdivision may be called for—for example, to emphasize a unique case or a special consideration" (1.56). A single subdivision may also be required for a special section, such as chapter endnotes.

Some publishers follow two other conventions for heads:

*A head cannot immediately follow a chapter opening.* This prohibition largely reflects an aesthetic preference—that a page with a display head directly below the chapter opening display is unattractive—although some editors also argue that it is illogical to immediately divide the content of a chapter into subtopics before introducing the chapter's overarching main topic.

*Heads cannot be stacked. Stacked heads* occur when a head is immediately followed by a subordinate head, with no intervening text; for example:

DOGS

*Small dogs*

Small dogs have become very popular in recent years, especially among apartment dwellers. But even the smallest dogs require daily care and regular exercise.

The ban on stacked heads is likewise based partly on aesthetics and partly on logic, the objection raised by the latter being that one should not discuss a subtopic before saying something about the topic as a whole. Chicago style, however, permits stacked heads.

## LISTS

There are four basic formats for displayed lists: numbered, unnumbered, bulleted, and multicolumn. Numbered lists are best used when the items are instructions to be done in sequence, when the numbers denote some type of hierarchy (e.g., The ten largest markets are . . .), or when the subsequent discussion refers back to items on the list (e.g., In the third situation . . .). Otherwise, the numbers serve little purpose other than to clutter the text, and unnumbered or bulleted lists are preferable. Bulleted lists are extremely popular in corporate communications, less so in scholarly writing, where unnumbered lists predominate. A multicolumn list may contain unnumbered, numbered, or bulleted items.

The capitalization and punctuation of items in a displayed list depend on the nature of the items in the list:

- When at least one item is a complete sentence, all the items are punctuated as though they were complete sentences. Thus each item begins with a capital letter and ends with a period.
- When all the items are single words, phrases, or sentence fragments, each item is treated as a sentence fragment. Thus each item begins with a lowercase letter (unless the first word is a proper noun or adjective) and carries either no terminal punctuation or a comma or semicolon. When the items carry terminal punctuation, the last item ends with a period.

In documents that contain many displayed lists, some publishers prefer that all lists be formatted by the first principle except when each item in a list consists of a single word, in which case the second system is used.

Regarding the punctuation of the regular text that introduces a displayed list, *Chicago* and *WIT* recommend the following:

- When the introductory text includes the phrase "as follows" or "the following," the lead-in should end with a colon.
- When the introductory text is the beginning of a sentence that is concluded by the items in the list, the lead-in should carry no terminal punctuation (as in item 8 below), unless a comma or a colon is desired after "for example" or "that is."
- In all other cases, the lead-in text may end with a colon or a period.

Here's a checklist for copyediting displayed lists:

1. Mark up the list, following the publisher's coding scheme for numbered, unnumbered, bulleted, and multicolumn lists. Make sure that the compositor can discern the beginning and end of the list and the boundaries of each item on the list.

2. Verify that all items are in their correct order (e.g., alphabetical, numerical, chrono-logical, geographical), or determine that there is no logical ordering principle that can be imposed upon the items.

3. Make sure that the items are parallel in structure (logic, syntax, length, importance).

4. Check the logic, syntax, and length of any subitems.

5. Enforce consistency in the capitalization of items.

6. Regularize the punctuation preceding the list, at the end of each item, and at the end of the list.

7. Enforce consistency in the choice of item markers:

Bullets

| | | | |
|---|---|---|---|
| circular, closed (filled) | ● | • | · |
| circular, open | ○ | ○ | ○ |
| square, filled | ■ | ■ | ▪ |
| square, open | □ | □ | ▫ |

Special characters ☞ ✓ ☆ ❑

Uppercase or lowercase letters (followed by a period).

Numerals (followed by a period).[6] In long lists, the numerals should align on the last digit, not the first:

| *Correct alignment* | | *Incorrect alignment* | |
|---:|---|---|---|
| 1. | wheat | 1. | wheat |
| 2. | rice | 2. | rice |
| 10. | textiles | 10. | textiles |
| 110. | paper | 110. | paper |

In publishing jargon, the vertical alignment of numerals on the last digit is called *clearing for 10s*. When copyeditors working on hard copy come upon an incorrectly aligned list, they write a circled instruction to the compositor: "Clear for 10s." Copyeditors working on-screen are expected to insert the publisher's stipulated generic codes or templated styles for the items in a vertical list. Parenthetical enumerations are best reserved for run-in lists; in display lists, long columns of parenthetical numbers or letters are unattractive.

8. Check for consistency in the

leading (linespacing) above and below the list
indents
spacing between the item marker and the start of the item text

---

6. An alternative style calls for extra wordspacing, rather than a period, after the numerals in a numbered list:

1 wheat
2 rice
10 textiles

Of course, not every enumeration or series need be treated as a displayed list. When a list has only three or four items, each of which is short, it is often preferable to set it as a run-in list; for example:

*Awkward:* Our analysis is based on

> the USGS survey,
> the USFS survey, and
> field research we conducted in 1997.

*Revision:* Our analysis is based on the USGS survey, the USFS survey, and field research we conducted in 1997.

*Or:* Our analysis is based on (1) the USGS survey, (2) the USFS survey, and (3) field research we conducted in 1997.

But sometimes even a short list containing short items may be displayed, for the reader's convenience:

In order to complete this form, you will need

> your 1999 federal income tax return
> your 1999 state income tax return
> a stub from a recent paycheck

Multiple-choice tests are styled like unnumbered vertical lists: unless all the items are complete sentences, lowercase the first word of each item (except for a proper noun or adjective) and omit periods.

Markup of the elements of a manuscript may be done by

(a) hand-marking the hard copy using the publisher's descriptive labels

(b) keying generic codes into the files

(c) styling the elements using a word processor's style feature

(d) using a formal markup language, such as XML

(e) any of the above methods

## DESIGN SPECS

While the copyeditor is busy working on the content of a manuscript, the designer is making decisions about how the final product will look—decisions about the typefaces, the treatment of illustrations, (for printed publications) the jacket design and paper, and so on. At several points, the paths of the copyeditor and the designer cross. As we have seen, it is the copyeditor who informs the designer—either in a formal memo or through notes on the style sheet—that the manuscript contains unusual alphabetical or nonalphabetical characters (e.g., mathematical symbols, foreign language characters or diacritical marks, music notation) or elements other than straight running text (e.g., heads, tables, extracts).

In large publishing outfits, the designer usually works with the editorial coordinator or a production editor rather than with the copyeditor. In a small, paper-based business, however, a copyeditor may still be asked to interpret and transfer a designer's specs to a paper manuscript. And in the world of indie publishing, an editor may collaborate directly with a designer or may provide not just editing but also production support by ensuring that the designer's technical instructions have been correctly followed. Even if you are never asked to work directly with a designer, you should have at least a basic understanding of design specs, developed in the era of print but still used by some designers working on-screen.

## SYSTEMS OF MEASUREMENT

Designers and compositors use three traditional systems of linear measurement: inches, points and picas, and em and en spaces.

*Inches.* Inches are used to specify the *trim size* (the size of the document's pages) and occasionally to specify the dimensions of the *type page* (the trim size minus the top, bottom, and side margins) and the margins.

*Points and picas.* *Points* and *picas* are units unique to publishing. Just as there are twelve inches to a foot, there are twelve points to a pica. But when one expresses picas and points in terms of inches, the equivalences are awkward, because the pica is based on the eighteenth-century French precursor of the modern centimeter:

> 1 pica = 0.1656 inches
> 6.039 picas = 1 inch
> 1 point = 0.0138 inches
> 72.464 points = 1 inch

For a copyeditor's purposes, the following rules of thumb suffice:

> 6 picas ≈ 1 inch
> 72 points ≈ 1 inch

The metric equivalences are equally awkward; the following approximations are used:

> 1 pica ≈ 4.2 millimeters
> 1 point ≈ 0.35 millimeters

The varied uses of points and picas are described on the following pages.

*Em and en spaces.* The size of an *em* space depends on the size of the type being used. If the text is set in 8-point type, an em space is 8 points wide; if the text is set in 24-point type, an em space is 24 points wide. An *en* space is half the width of an em space.

Em and en spaces are most often used to indicate the width of paragraph inden-
tions (e.g., "Indent 1 em") and to measure other small amounts of lateral spacing. For
example, a *thin space,* one-fifth (sometimes one-sixth) of an em, is a small, nonbreaking
space sometimes used between the personal initials preceding a surname (T. S. Eliot) or
between nested quotation marks to provide a smidgen of separation ("Call me 'Spike'").
A *hair space,* which is thinner still, is a nonbreaking space sometimes inserted between
typeset characters that are touching, as when italic and roman characters crash. All these
typographic refinements, which originated in print culture, have Unicode numbers, but
some word processing applications don't support them, so they are sometimes manually
coded ("T.<th#>S. Eliot") in the files or added in composition.

## SPECS FOR BOOK PAGES

The dimensions of the pages of a book are expressed in inches: 6 × 9 inches. These
dimensions constitute the trim size, the size of the entire book page.

The dimensions of the type page (the trim size minus the margins on all four sides)
may be expressed in inches or in picas: 25 × 43 picas.

The size of the margins is also expressed in inches or in picas. Each book page has
four margins: the top (*head*), the bottom (*foot*), the inside (*back* or *gutter*), and the outside (*fore-edge*) margin. The back margin is the right margin of a left-hand page of a
book, but the left margin of a right-hand page of a book—a necessary distinction so the
pages can be properly bound.

The *text page* or *text area* (the area covered by the body text, excluding running head,
running foot, and page number) is usually given in picas, as are the margins between
columns on a multicolumn page.

## SPECS FOR RUNNING HEADS,
## RUNNING FEET, AND PAGE NUMBERS

In the specs, the designer indicates the location of the running heads (also called headers) or running feet (footers) and page numbers (folios): how far across the page, in relation to the margins, these elements start or end, and how far up or down the page they
are to be placed.

The horizontal location of the running elements is stated with reference to the left
and right margins of the text area. Three common horizontal locations are flush left
(beginning at the left margin), centered (centered across the text area), and flush right
(ending at the right margin). The instruction "fl. out." calls for the element to be placed
flush outside: on a left-hand page the element begins at the left margin, and on a right-
hand page the element ends at the right margin. Similarly, the instruction "fl. in." calls
for the element to be placed flush inside: on a left-hand page the element ends at the
right margin, and on a right-hand page it begins at the left margin.

Some designers indicate the vertical location of the running heads or running feet
by reference to the type page: "Running heads at top outside of type page." Other designers indicate how much vertical space is to fall between the header or footer and the

text area with reference to the *baseline,* an imaginary line on which the typeset characters sit. This vertical space is specified by the number of points from the baseline of the type in the running head to the baseline of the type in the first line of text, or from the baseline of the last line of text to the baseline of the running foot. For example, the instruction "16 pts b/b" calls for sixteen points of vertical space between the two baselines.

The location of folios is specified with reference to the inner or outer margin and to the top or bottom margin. Page numbers that appear at the bottom of the page are called *drop folios.* The spec may also call for *modern,* or *lining, figures* (or numbers) or *old-style figures* (sometimes abbreviated *o.s.* or *OS*). Lining figures sit on the baseline. Old-style figures have ascenders and descenders, parts of the character that extend, respectively, above the mean line or below the baseline of the type:

| | | |
|---|---|---|
| *Lining figures:* | 123456789 | 123456789 |
| *Old-style figures:* | 123456789 | 123456789 |

## TYPE SPECS

In the type specs, the designer indicates the face, weight, style, and size of the type for each element in the document. Here are some examples of each of these attributes:

*Face:* Franklin Gothic, Times Roman, **Gill Sans**, Minion

*Weight:* light, regular, **medium,** condensed

*Style:* roman, *italic,* **bold**

*Size:* 8 point, 10 point, 12 point

The designer also specifies the amount of *leading*—that is, the amount of vertical space between lines of type. (*Leading* is pronounced "ledding," because linespaces were once created by inserting strips of lead.) The size of the type and the amount of leading are expressed in points.[7]

| Notation | Meaning | Amount of leading |
|---|---|---|
| 8/9 | 8-point type on a 9-point form | 1 point |
| 9/11 | 9-point type on an 11-point form | 2 points |
| 10/13 | 10-point type on a 13-point form | 3 points |
| 24/28 | 24-point type on a 28-point form | 4 points |

7. In traditional typography, type size is measured from the bottom of the descenders (e.g., the lowest point of the letters *g j p y*) to the top of the ascenders (e.g., the highest point of the letters *b d f h*). The height of lowercase letters that have neither ascenders nor descenders (e.g., *a c e i m*) is called the *x-height.*

The specs for running text also indicate the size of the paragraph indent (para indent), expressed in picas ("para indent 1 pica") or em spaces ("para indent 1 em #").

## INTERPRETING TYPE SPECS

Here are some sample type specs and their "translations."

*Running text (also called* general text *or* main text*).* The designer writes

> Main text: Garamond roman, 10/13 × 25 picas × 42 lines, para indent 1 pica.
> No para indent following display type.

This spec means: Set the text in 10-point Garamond type, roman, with 3 points of leading. Each line of type will be 25 picas wide, and each page will run 42 lines deep. Each paragraph will be indented 1 pica, except that the first paragraph after a line of display type (e.g., chapter title, heading, subheading) will be set flush left. Since no instruction is given regarding *justification* (the even alignment of text at the left and right margins), the compositor will assume that the left and right margins are to be justified. To obtain text that is justified at the left margin but not at the right margin, the designer would write "ragged right," "rag right," or "rag r."

*Running heads.* The designer writes

> Running heads: 6 pt. Bodoni, small caps, centered, 36 pts b/b to text line.

This spec means: Set the running heads in 6-point Bodoni type, all small capitals, and centered on the text page. The baseline of the running head should sit 36 points above the baseline of the first line of running text.

*Prose extracts.* Extracts (block quotes) are differentiated from regular text in one or more of the following ways: (1) set on a narrower line (i.e., with wider margins) than regular text, (2) set with additional leading above and below the block, (3) set in a smaller point size than regular text, (4) set in the same point size but with less internal leading. In the following spec, the designer ensures that the extracts will be centered on the page but 2 picas narrower than the regular text:

> Prose extract: Bembo ital, 9/11 × 25 picas, indent 1 pica each side, leading 16
> pts b/b above & below.

This spec means: Set the prose extracts in 9-point Bembo italic with 2 points of leading. Each extract will run 23 picas wide (25 picas minus the 1 pica indent on each side), and there will be 16 points of linespacing base to base between the regular text and the first line of the extract, and again between the last line of the extract and the following first line of regular text.

*Chapter titles.* The specs for chapter titles must indicate which of the three capitalization styles is to be used:

| Style | Abbreviations | Example |
|---|---|---|
| All uppercase (all capitals) | UC<br>All caps | TYPE SPECS FOR FRENCH EDITORS |
| Capitals and lowercase (headline style) | UC/lc<br>Clc<br>C & lc | Type Specs for French Editors |
| Initial capital only (sentence style) | Init cap only<br>Init cap | Type specs for French editors |

So, the designer writes

Chapter title: 24/27 × 25 picas, Goudy bold, Clc, flush left, sink 6 picas.

This spec means: Set the chapter titles in 24-point Goudy bold type. The capitalization style is capitals and lowercase. Set the chapter titles flush with the left margin and 6 picas below where a regular text page would start.

*Displayed math equations.* The designer writes

Displayed equations: 10/12 Baskerville, centered, runovers indented 2 ems, 18 pts b/b between successive equations; 24 pts b/b above and below.

This spec means: Displayed equations are to be set in 10-point Baskerville, with 2 points of leading, centered across the text page. *Runover lines* (the second and following lines of a long item, also called *turnovers* or *turned lines*) are to be indented 2 ems. When several equations follow one another, the spec asks for 18 points base to base between them. There will be 24 points base to base above and below each set of equations.

*Index.* Most indexes to books and manuals are set two columns to a page, so the specs must give the width of the columns and the amount of space between them. A typical index spec might read:

Index text (2 cols): 8/9 Times Roman × 12 picas × 40 lines; rag r; 1 pica between cols; runover 1.5 em indent.

This spec means: Set the index in 8-point Times Roman with 1 point of leading. Each of the two columns will be 12 picas wide and 40 lines long, and each column will have a ragged right margin. There is to be 1 pica between the columns. Runover lines are to be indented 1.5 ems.

PART 3

# ¶ Language Editing

IN PART 3 WE MOVE beyond mechanics to look at grammar and usage (chapter 14) and selected stylistic and substantive issues (chapter 15). Here, as in mechanical matters, copyeditors are expected to correct or query whatever is incorrect in the manuscript, but the differences between correct and incorrect are sometimes harder to discern. On many points of grammar and usage, for example, even the experts offer conflicting advice. Thus copyeditors need to be able to distinguish between inviolable rules and personal stylistic preferences, with the goal of enforcing the former and respecting the author's choices in the latter. Chapter 14 surveys the major battles in the grammar and usage wars as well as the gaffes most often committed even by good writers.

The final challenge for copyeditors is to ensure that the text is clear and unambiguous at all levels—from individual words to sentences, paragraphs, sections, and chapters. Chapter 15 examines matters pertaining to organization, expository style, plain language and accessibility mandates, global English, English as a foreign or second language (EFL or ESL), and bias-free language. The last section of the chapter summarizes four legal topics (libel, privacy, obscenity, and copyright) of concern to copyeditors, as well as the issue of plagiarism.

# CHAPTER 14

# ¶ Grammar and Usage: Principles and Pitfalls

Even if you haven't formally studied English grammar, you know countless aspects of grammar as an English speaker. You would never say or write "I are hungrily very," no matter how many hours had passed since your last meal. Not all questions of grammar are that simple, of course, but many tangles are easily resolved once you know the rules and conventions. In some cases, however, the rules are unclear or disputed, and the experts offer conflicting analyses. The number of these disputes—and the passion, indeed the moral fervor, they sometimes inspire—is far greater than you might imagine, until you begin to pore over the shelves of grammar and usage books in the library or in a well-stocked bookstore (if you can find one). For example, the editors of *DEU* describe their work as an examination of "common problems of confused or disputed English usage" (p. 4a)—and note that their volume treats some five hundred such problems.

"Many of the rules that have been codified into 'grammar' uphold an ideal, not a reality," writes the lexicographer Kory Stamper in *Word by Word*. Thus what is referred to as Standard English "*is based on a mostly fictional, static, and Platonic ideal of usage*" (p. 50). Lexicographers and linguists recognize numerous variations in English as functions of regional dialect and social group (as defined by, e.g., education, socioeconomic status, or age), the type of discourse (formal, informal, intimate), the medium of communication (spoken, written, digital) and its purpose, and the speaker's or writer's attitude toward the audience and the topic. These language professionals also faithfully record and study contemporary English speakers' continual inventiveness, including their appropriations from foreign languages, subcultures, and jargon. But the manuals consulted by copyeditors rarely differentiate dialectical or class-marked choices, analyze nuances of register and medium, or tolerate innovation. Instead, as the linguist Arnold Zwicky points out, most advice literature

> tends to focus . . . on informal vs. formal variants (to disparage the former), spoken vs. written variants (to disparage the former), variants that are (or are perceived to be) innovative, and arcana like split infinitives, stranded prepositions, *which* vs. *that*, sentence-adverbial *hopefully*, and singular *they*. . . . Some people judge the disfavored variants to be signs of ignorance or lack of education. The list of these disfavored variants is huge.[1]

Like the etiquette books of old, some advice manuals censure departures from Standard English by resorting to disparaging, if occasionally droll, explanations connoting moral turpitude, stupidity, weakness of character, or low caste. So-called greengrocer's

---

1. Arnold Zwicky, "Crazies Win," *Language Log*, May 13, 2008, http://languagelog.ldc.upenn.edu/.

apostrophes—apostrophes such as the ones incorrectly used to form plural nouns on hand-lettered signs outside mom-and-pop stores (potato's, apple's)—are denounced as a "satanic sprinkling" of errors. (No copyeditor would allow these nonstandard plurals to remain in a written document, but such errors hardly justify demonizing innocent shop owners or vandalizing their signs in the dark of night.) Split infinitives are said to reveal "ignorance and sloppiness," despite the fact that the injunction against them is wholly specious. The spelling *chaise lounge,* now recorded in *M-W Unabridged* as an equal variant with the original (c. 1906) French form, *chaise longue,* is facetiously branded "low-rent."[2] Even while acknowledging the falsehood or obsolescence of some long-cherished rules and finicky distinctions, commentators may caution writers to heed these rules and to avoid the stigmatized terms altogether, lest readers judge them to be careless or illiterate.

Following the advice of such language authorities, generations of copyeditors have corrected *convince* to *persuade* (or vice versa), revised statements with *blame* and *graduate,* unsplit infinitives, rewritten prepositional endings to sentences, changed *while* to *whereas* in expressions of contrast, swapped *that* for *which* in restrictive clauses, and so on. These hundreds of tiny differentiations, thought to be the special knowledge of copyeditors, are also the ones that give them their not entirely undeserved reputation for pedantry among authors, who sometimes describe copyediting as the *which*-hunt.

To be sure, many guidelines that editors follow are legitimate. Conventions for formal writing serve the goals of precision and elegance, and they build the trust of readers. But some guidelines are entirely spurious, despite their perpetuation in the advice literature and in editing folklore. Still others are theoretical, the sorts of prescriptions that are based not on the actual practice of educated writers but on what some commentators think is more logical or more desirable. Some rules once held sway but are now obsolete or in a state of transition. And some rules are not rules at all, but preferences, appropriate for, say, a scholarly or professional paper but incongruous in a catalog for camping gear. In threading the narrow path between the collective habits of native speakers, as accurately described in dictionaries, and the socially constructed conventions of Standard English codified in these manuals of grammar and usage, copyeditors must ever be guided by flexibility, pragmatism, and good judgment.

The perplexities associated with emending errors in a manuscript are compounded when an author and a copyeditor have different positions about what constitutes correct English. In *Style: Toward Clarity and Grace,* Joseph M. Williams describes the contours of this plight.

> A few especially fastidious writers and editors try to honor and enforce every rule of usage; most careful writers observe fewer; and there are a few writers and editors who know all the rules, but who also know that not all of them are worth observing and enforcing, and that they should observe other rules only on certain occasions.

2. Lynne Truss, *Eats, Shoots and Leaves: The Zero Tolerance Approach to Punctuation* (2003; repr., New York: Avery, 2006), p. 1; Edward D. Johnson, *The Handbook of Good English,* p. 71; Bryan Garner, *Garner's Modern English Usage,* s.v. "chaise longue." *Chaise longue* remains the favored spelling in British English.

What do those of us do who want to be careful writers?

We could adopt the worst-case policy: follow all the rules all the time because somewhere, sometime, someone might criticize us for something. . . . And so, with a stack of grammar books and usage manuals close by, we scrutinize every sentence for all possible "errors." . . . But once we decide to follow all the rules, we deprive ourselves of stylistic flexibility. And sooner or later, we will begin to impose those rules—real or not—on others. . . .

But selective observance has its problems too, because that requires us to learn which rules to ignore, which always to observe, and which to observe in some circumstances and to ignore in others. This freedom to choose is further complicated by the fact that those who invoke every rule of grammar always seem to have the moral upper hand: they claim to be dedicated to precision, and they seem to know something about goodness that we don't. Conversely, if we know enough to dismiss some "rule" of grammar as folklore, we risk being judged permissive by those who are ignorant of the history of our language. (p. 178)

Here we hit upon several inevitable occupational hazards. Almost daily, copyeditors confront minor episodes of "damned if you revise, damned if you don't." Although some authors will respect your expertise, accept all your revisions, and thank you profusely for fixing their mistakes, others will view grammatical revisions on the copyedited manuscript as a challenge to their intellectual ability or professional identity. Or, conversely, they will fault you for "overlooking" things that only Miss Thistlebottom would find unacceptable. Some authors will defend their personal tics and preferences as constitutionally guaranteed forms of self-expression or will accuse you of needlessly nitpicking and tampering with wording they find unobjectionable ("It's clear enough. Readers will know what I mean"). Others will dismiss your judicious restraint as ignorant and careless ("You didn't fix all my split infinitives!"). You must not only know the rules and conventions but also unlearn fake ones—and sometimes reeducate authors about them as well. You may have to negotiate between effective communication and formally correct but unclear or awkward grammar. You must constantly judge whether a lively invention or a colloquial construction will seem sloppy or imprecise in print, and when punctilious grammar should yield to an author's vivid, eccentric style.

Moreover, on some points of grammar both authors and copyeditors can invoke the equally impressive authority of equally impressive experts who happen to disagree. For the working copyeditor, deference is the better part of valor: if the author's preference is at all acceptable, it should be respected. But when your desk is free of manuscripts and you have time to mull, you might want to think a bit about how you go about choosing your experts and the reference books you rely on. Is the newest grammar and usage book always to be trusted, or is there a value in sometimes sticking with the dog-eared classics? Is Expert A's attack on a certain expression based on a functional rationale (the expression is unclear or ambiguous) or on some airy pretension to elegance? Is Authority B honestly trying to help readers write with greater clarity and precision, or is he (for few of them are shes) promulgating pedantry for pedantry's sake or playing an erudite game of "Gotcha!" in which the reader is always the loser? Does Maven C have any real expertise or just the chutzpah to remake the language in his image and the arrogant self-confidence of a lone prophet on a moral crusade? Is Guru D someone who values idiomatic English or someone who would replace "put one's best foot forward" with "put one's better foot forward" on the grounds that one cannot use the superlative when only two items are being compared? (See *DEU,* s.vv. "best foot forward" and "superlative of two.")

In this chapter we'll take a peek at the main contenders in the ongoing battle over English grammar and usage and then look at a basket of problems that vex even experienced copyeditors. If you want to brush up on some of the less (and more) contentious topics, turn to one of the grammar or usage books mentioned in chapter 3. Better still, turn to several: on contested points, always get a second opinion.

(If you're hoping that your word processing program's grammar checker will save you any time or spare you any errors—forget it. Even for the shortest of texts, these checkers are time consuming and frustrating. They routinely ignore simple errors, repeatedly question unmistakably correct constructions, and suggest substitutions that are flat-out wrong. Most copyeditors simply disable the grammar checker. Separately sold grammar-checking applications are equally flawed, despite advertising hype, and such software has been roundly panned in copyeditors' reviews.)

## WHOSE GRAMMAR?

As noted, one source of difficulty for people who care about written language is that even the experts sometimes disagree. In broadest terms, the battle is between the descriptivists, who seek to document how language *is* used, and the prescriptivists, who champion an edenic vision of how the language *should be* used. A principal charge against the descriptivist position, summarized by John Updike, is that it "proposes no ideal of clarity in language or, beyond that, of grace, which might serve as an instrument of discrimination."[3] Across the battlefield, Steven Pinker dismisses the prescriptivists' finicky discriminations and differentiations as bosh: "Most of the prescriptive rules of the language mavens make no sense on any level. They are bits of folklore that originated for screwball reasons several hundred years ago and have perpetuated themselves ever since. For as long as they have existed, speakers have flouted them, spawning identical plaints about the imminent decline of the language. . . . The rules conform neither to logic nor to tradition, and if they were ever followed they would force writers into fuzzy, clumsy, wordy, ambiguous, incomprehensible prose."[4]

3. John Updike, "Fine Points," *New Yorker* (December 23 and 30, 1996), p. 145. In this review of R. W. Burchfield's edition of H. W. Fowler's classic, retitled *The New Fowler's Modern English Usage,* Updike offers a spirited defense of Fowler's brand of prescriptivism ("a dynamic guidance that promises a brighter future, rather than a helpless wallow in the endless morass of English as it was and is").

4. Steven Pinker, *The Language Instinct,* p. 373. The passage appears in the chapter "The Language Mavens," a deft skewering of the contemporary state of a tradition by which "the manuals tried to outdo one another by including greater numbers of increasingly fastidious rules that no refined person could afford to ignore." Similar terrain is covered, more sedately and with an emphasis on written English, by Williams in *Style,* chapter 10.

This characterization of opposing camps is, of course, a bit overstated. The best language advisers, while disagreeing on specific points of usage, might now represent themselves as "descriptive prescribers" or "prescriptive descriptivists"—both informed and literate, but never rigid. As the language maven Bryan Garner said of his prescriptivist mantle: "We could go a long way toward reconciling the language wars if linguists and writers . . . would stop demonizing all prescriptivists and start acknowledging that the reputable ones have always tried to base their guidance on sound descriptions." Indeed, both camps peruse linguistic evidence, and both repudiate the peevish, unfounded superstitions touted by those moralistic popularizers who publish new advice books every year and write the *New York Times* to complain about split infinitives.

Perhaps the real difference between the so-called prescriptivists and descriptivists is this: The former collect their evidence from what Garner labels "the actual usage of educated speakers and writers," that is, a select subset of English speakers.[5] They extrapolate their advice from this prestige dialect and also tend to resist linguistic changes that, in their judgment, blur useful distinctions or defy logic. The latter plumb language corpora reflecting broad linguistic diversity and active language change. They acknowledge the legitimacy of different dialects, the vernacular of different social groups, the use of different registers for different audiences, and the messy inventiveness of English itself. Like their prescriptivist brethren, they accept the desirability of adopting a classic style (the construct called Standard English) for formal and professional prose, but they are more inclined to talk about "appropriate register" and "judgment" than about "rules" and "errors."

More-detached commentators describe the prescriptivist ethos as originating in the desire of British elites, beginning in the late sixteenth century, to confer grandeur on the English language and the burgeoning English Empire through the imitation of classical Latin and the august Roman Empire: "The best historical model of an influential empire with a language to match was Rome; and in this period, the perfection of the Latin language was still seen as closely connected to the success of Roman political expansion. So (the reasoning went), for England to achieve equivalent political success, its language had to be rendered as 'perfect' as Latin—preferably by coaxing it into the model of Latin, making it as much like Latin in form as possible."[6]

The legacy of this post-Elizabethan imperial ambition is still with us, in the form of, among other niceties, the taboo on ending sentences with prepositions. For it was John Dryden who, in 1672, proclaimed that English sentences were no longer to end with prepositions, because those of Cicero and his brethren did not—and, after all, to have a

5. The Garner quotations in this and the preceding paragraph are from his interesting exchange with Robert Lane Greene (a correspondent for *The Economist*) concerning the language wars, "Room for Debate: Which Language and Grammar Rules to Flout," *New York Times*, September 27, 2012, https://www.nytimes.com/roomfordebate/2012/09/27/which-language-and-grammar-rules -to-flout.

6. Robin Tolmach Lakoff, *Talking Power: The Politics of Language* (New York: Basic Books, 1990), p. 289.

sentence-ending preposition was to violate the term's etymological soul, the Latin *prae-* ("in front of" or "before") and *ponere* ("to put" or "to place"). Henceforth, only a scoundrel would place a preposition anywhere that was not *pre-*.

Then, with the rise of literacy and formal education in the eighteenth century, "correct grammar" became a mark of education and manners—and of their presumed corollary, moral rectitude. To enter polite society, the emerging merchant class sought to emulate the cultivated speech and writing of the aristocracy, sometimes with the aid of letter-writing guides and grammars published to further their social aspirations. Antecedents to the modern-day usage manuals, these eighteenth-century English grammars, Stamper points out, "were thus the linguistic complements to the etiquette books, . . . [in which] good manners, good morality, and good grammar all go hand in hand" (*Word by Word*, p. 43).

The American Revolution may have freed the colonies from British rule (and British spelling), but not from the anxieties of imperial and social striving. Instead, linguistic prescriptions and proscriptions multiplied over the centuries, as each new generation promulgated its view of decorous usage. Since the time when Dryden is alleged to have confessed that "he sometimes had to translate an idea into Latin to find the correct way to express it in English,"[7] scores of commentators have added their own inventions, discoveries, and pet peeves to the list of acts that an educated writer dare not commit. Sometime in the mid-nineteenth century, for example, the taste masters decided that infinitives were no longer to be split in the King's and Queen's English, because Latin infinitives, consisting of a single word, could not be split.

Thus as you gingerly tiptoe around the land mines that dot the prescriptive-descriptive battlefield, you will encounter dozens of "rules" that were never really rules, just the personal preferences or prejudices of someone bold enough to proclaim them to be rules. Despite what may have been drilled into you (or one of your authors) in high school, well-respected writers, editors, and experts in contemporary American usage routinely break (and even scoff at) the following taboos:

- Never begin a sentence with *and, but, or, also,* or *however.*
- Never end a sentence with a preposition.
- Never split an infinitive.
- Never use *which* to refer to an entire preceding clause.

*But* maybe we don't know what we're talking about. Or perhaps our sole intention is to *further* addle your brain by breaking the rules, *which* would be a despicable betrayal of your trust. *However,* even if you should happen to feel betrayed, it is now time for us to confront the vexatious creatures one by one.

7. Robert McCrum, William Cran, and Robert MacNeil, *The Story of English* (New York: Viking, 1986), p. 129; see also *DEU,* s.v. "preposition at end."

## SUBJECT-VERB AGREEMENT

The textbook statement of *subject-verb agreement* seems simple enough: a singular subject takes a singular verb, and a plural subject takes a plural verb. According to the professional grammarians, however, there are three, sometimes competing, principles of subject-verb agreement in modern English: formal agreement, notional concord, and attraction (or proximity).

Formal (or grammatical) agreement is the fancy name for the textbook rule just stated. But not all subjects neatly proclaim themselves to be singular or plural, and in some situations the overt grammatical form of the subject conflicts with our sense of the intended meaning. In these cases, we tend to discard formal agreement and rely on notional concord, selecting the verb that matches the meaning, not the overt grammatical form:

> Fifty pages of manuscript are sitting on his desk.
> [Answers the question *How many?*]

> Fifty pages of manuscript is a day's worth of work.
> [Answers the question *How much?*]

Grammarians have also observed that certain constructions "sound right" to educated native speakers of English, even though the constructions defy both formal and notional agreement. Such constructions exemplify the principle of attraction (or proximity), under which the verb tends to take the form of the closest subject. But as *DEU* cautions, "Proximity agreement may pass in speech and other forms of unplanned discourse; in print it will be considered an error" (s.v. "agreement, subject verb: the principle of proximity"). Sometimes revision to avoid the awkward construction altogether is the best course.

> ✗ For those who attended the second day of the annual meeting, there was an early morning panel and afternoon workshops.

> *Better:* An early morning panel and afternoon workshops were held for those who attended the second day of the annual meeting.

An elementary principle of subject-verb agreement is that the grammatical subject determines the number of the verb. Even with the linking verb *to be,* nouns that appear in the predicate have no bearing on the number of the main verb—with the disputed exceptions discussed at paragraph 31 below. Thus the following sentences are correct:

> The only sign of Christmas was the stockings on the mantel.

> My favorite vegetable is potatoes.

> The best weight-loss diet is raw carrots and water.

The singular verbs (*was* and *is*) are needed here because the subjects of the verbs ("the only sign of Christmas," "my favorite vegetable," "the best weight-loss diet") are singular; "stockings," "potatoes," and "raw carrots and water" are irrelevant because they are in the predicate. Note that these sentences are *not* inversions of

The stockings on the mantel were the only sign of Christmas.

Potatoes are my favorite vegetable.

Raw carrots and water are the best weight-loss diet.

In these versions, the plural subjects "stockings," "potatoes," and "raw carrots and water" require plural verbs; the singular predicates "the only sign," "my favorite vegetable," and "the best weight-loss diet" do not affect subject-verb agreement.

The following paragraphs summarize thirty-one common perplexities and controversies in subject-verb agreement; for a detailed discussion and more examples, see the several entries under "agreement, subject-verb" in *DEU*. But one day, despite all your diligence, you will meet a sentence that sounds wrong no matter which verb form you use. A bit of rewriting can rescue you: select a verb that has the same form in the singular and the plural—for example, an auxiliary verb (can, may, might, should, will) or a past-tense verb other than *was* or *were*.

1. *All; any.* As subjects, *all* and *any* may take either a singular or a plural verb. When *all* refers to a plural count noun, it takes a plural verb; when it refers to a noncount noun, it takes a singular verb.[8]

   All have resigned from the advisory council.

   The jewelry was hidden in the refrigerator: all is accounted for despite the burglary.

   When a noun phrase with *all* is the subject of the verb *to be* and is followed by a plural complement, the linking verb is singular.

   All I want for my fiftieth anniversary is diamonds.

   All they saw was trees.

   The verb form with *any* is determined by the meaning: "any single one" (singular verb) or "some" (plural verb).

   Does any of us have the right to judge?

   Are any of your students in the play?

2. *All [of], half [of].* (The *of* is optional and may be omitted.) As predeterminers, *all* and *half* may take either a singular or a plural verb. When the subject is a plural count noun, the verb is plural; when the subject is a noncount noun, the verb is singular.

   All the students have arrived.

   All the jewelry has been stolen.

---

8. A *count noun* has a plural form and in the singular can be used with an indefinite article (members, a member). A *noncount noun* does not ordinarily have a plural form and cannot be used with an indefinite article or a number (e.g., jewelry: you cannot say "a jewelry" or "two jewelries").

Half the voters are undecided.

Half the food is spoiled.

3. *And.* A pair of singular nouns joined by *and* requires a plural verb, with two exceptions:

(a)   Appositive nouns (equivalent terms with the same referent) joined by *and* are treated as singular.

Such an injustice and inequity is intolerable.

The sole object and aim of my campaign is to reunite the party.

(b)   Nouns joined by *and* to form a collective idea or unitary whole are singular.

Bacon and eggs is her favorite breakfast.

The bread and butter of our business is summer tourism.

The Stars and Stripes flies over the parade ground.

Notice, too, how *and* may be used in an elliptical construction:

Consumer and business confidence remain high.

Here, *remain* is plural, even though *confidence* is singular, because the subject is "consumer [confidence] and business confidence." To use a singular verb would imply that there is an entity known as "consumer and business confidence." Likewise, in the following sentences, the plural subjects require plural verbs despite the omission of the words shown in square brackets:

What I say and [what I] do are none of your business.

Classical [music] and folk music are his favorites.

Both French [cuisine] and Spanish cuisine emphasize fresh ingredients.

For verb agreement when the second term of a compound subject with *and* is set off by parentheses, dashes, or commas, see paragraph 26 ("Punctuation with a compound subject").

4. *As well as* and other *quasi-coordinators* (*accompanied by, added to, along with, combined with, coupled with, in addition to, no less than, together with, with,* and similar expressions). Prescriptive grammar handbooks treat a pair of singular subjects joined by *as well as* or another quasi-coordinator as invariably singular, but descriptive analyses show that actual usage is mixed. The most liberal advice on the first of these terms comes from *DEU* (s.v. "as well as"): when a singular verb sounds better, use commas to set off the phrase joined to the subject by *as well as;* when the plural verb sounds better, do not set off the phrase with commas.

For copyeditors, a style manual, as well as a dictionary, is useful.

A style manual as well as a dictionary are always on his desk.

But *DEU* stands alone in endorsing a plural verb with *as well as* under any circumstances, and it offers no recommendations regarding other quasi-coordinators. A cautionary note concluding *DEU*'s "as well as" entry recommends discretion if an author or editor wishes to avoid the risk of irritating readers: "If your instinct does not lead you to prefer one approach over the other . . . , choose commas and a singular verb. That will offend no one."

Singular subjects joined by other quasi-coordinators take singular verbs; as a parenthetical phrase, the term following the quasi-coordinator is usually set off from the formal subject by a pair of commas.

> The recent divestiture, combined with rising costs, is expected to affect profits.

> *Or rewrite:* The recent divestiture and rising costs are expected to affect profits.

5. Collecting noun phrase. In recent years, notional agreement has gained the upper hand: *collecting noun phrases* usually take a plural verb, although they may take a singular verb when the collecting noun (rather than the items being collected) imposes itself as the main idea.

> A host of competitive offers have been received.

> A fraction of the students cause these disruptions.

> A group of sports fans gather in the bar nightly.

> A galaxy of movie stars attend the yearly event.

> A wide range of violations were observed.

> A rash of flight cancellations, weather events, and security alerts have forced many American businesses to reassess whether to send employees abroad.

> *But:* A set of keys is on the desk.

> *But:* A panel of physicians has convened to plan the next conference.

Some staunch formalists hold out for the irreproachable singular verb in all these cases. But even if you are a formalist, it is better to revise than to follow the rules of concord ad absurdum, especially when pronoun agreement is added to the mix.

> *Awkward:* A new generation of philanthropists is rushing to spend its money before it dies.

> *Better:* New philanthropists are rushing to spend their money before they die.

6. Collective idea. Notional agreement is the norm: no matter the grammatical form a collective idea takes, it requires a singular verb.

> Do you think that three cars is enough for one family?

> Eight hundred words is at least a hundred words too long for this summary.

7. Collective noun. *Collective nouns* (e.g., administration, class, committee, couple, jury, majority, management, minority, population, staff, team) are singular when the members of the collectivity are deemed to be acting as a group, plural when the members are acting as individuals. (Take care to ensure that any pronouns agree in number.)

> The couple is in therapy.
>
> The couple argue about their money.
>
> The committee has made its decision.
>
> The committee have signed their names to the resolution.

When the plural sounds unnatural, the sentence should be revised.

> *Awkward:* The orchestra are tuning their instruments.
>
> *Better:* The members of the orchestra are tuning their instruments.

The names of organizations and companies, even if they are plural in form, also take a singular verb (and singular pronouns) when the reference is to the organization rather than to its members.

> The Boy Scouts of America trains its participants in the responsibilities of citizenship.
>
> General Motors is dedicated to serving its customers.

An exception is made for the names of sports teams. Because many teams have plural names (Chicago Bears, Oakland Athletics, San Francisco Giants), plural verbs seem natural. Names of sports teams that are singular in form (Miami Heat, Oklahoma City Thunder, Orlando Magic, Utah Jazz) also take a plural verb (and pronouns to match), according to the *AP Stylebook* (s.v. "collective nouns"). But a city name used alone to refer to a team takes a singular verb, along with singular pronouns and other terms that must follow suit.

> The Miami Heat are competing for third place and expect to become the new NBA champions.
>
> Miami is competing for third place, and it [*or* the team] expects to become the new NBA champion.

Whereas American English generally treats collective nouns as singular (sports teams excepted) unless a plural sense predominates, British English sometimes tips the other way. Names of institutions, firms, and (as in AmE) sports teams—including cities serving as shorthand for them—may take plural verbs (and pronouns to match) in BrE.

> MI5 are investigating the incident.
>
> Barclays are expanding the services offered by their international branches.
>
> Manchester were the winners of the third match.

8. *Each.* The pronoun *each* takes a singular verb, even when its antecedent is plural.

> Each reflects a different view of what constitutes the good life.
>
> The two sides are deadlocked in negotiations, and each has offered few concessions.

When the adjective *each* follows a plural noun or pronoun, the verb is plural.

> We each are entitled to our own opinions.

9. *Each of.* In formal agreement *each of* takes a singular verb. Actual usage is mixed: when notional agreement prevails, a plural verb is sometimes used, though rarely in formal prose.

> Each of these arguments is well reasoned.
>
> Each of these principles have stood the test of time.

10. *Either . . . or.* When two subjects, one singular and one plural, are joined by these correlative (paired) conjunctions, the verb agrees with the nearer subject.

> Either the supervisor or the workers watch the site during the lunch break.
>
> Either the workers or the supervisor watches the site during the lunch break.

But when these correlatives join personal pronouns, the results can be awkward. Revision is often preferable.

> *Awkward:* Either he or I am responsible.
>
> *Better:* Either he is responsible, or I am.

11. Fractions. In such constructions as "two-thirds of *x*," the verb agrees with *x*.

> Two-thirds of the work is done.
>
> Two-thirds of the guests are here.

12. Inverted, or transposed, word order. In regular word order the subject precedes the verb. Inverted order occurs after an introductory adverbial phrase or in an interrogative. Although the verb precedes the subject in these examples, the subject determines the number of the verb.

> In the employee handbook is a sample expense voucher.
>
> Also in the handbook are procedures for submitting expense vouchers.
>
> Across the street are two broken parking meters.
>
> Who are John and Mary Smith?

13. *Many a.* Expressions with *many a* are notionally plural but grammatically singular.

Many a cat video has entertained office drudges who are supposedly hard at work.

14. Money. Amounts of money are singular when a specific sum is named, plural when the sum is vague.

> Eighty-five dollars is too high. Seventy-five dollars is a fair price.
>
> Billions of dollars were wasted, and millions are unaccounted for.

15. *More than one* x. Although notionally plural, the subject "more than one *x*" takes a singular verb.

> More than one candidate was disappointed.

16. *Neither . . . nor.* Formalists insist that a pair of singular nouns joined by *neither . . . nor* is singular.

> Neither the president nor the secretary was at the meeting.

Notionalists allow the pair of singular subjects to be treated as singular or plural, depending on the emphasis desired.

> Neither the president nor the secretary were at the meeting.

But *DEU* considers formal agreement "the safe choice" (s.v. "neither").
> When a pair of subjects, one singular and one plural, is joined by *neither . . . nor,* the verb agrees with the nearer subject.

> Neither money nor men were lacking.
>
> Neither men nor money was lacking.

17. *None of.* When the noun following *none of* is singular, the verb is singular. When the noun following *none of* is plural, either a singular or a plural verb is acceptable.

> None of the work was finished.
>
> None of the workers are here.
>
> None of these books seems [*or* seem] appropriate for this course.
> [None (*meaning* not one) seems; but none (*meaning* not any) seem.]

18. *Not only . . . but [also].* (The optional *also* may be omitted.) When subjects are joined by the *correlative conjunctions* "not only . . . but [also]," the subject that follows "but [also]" determines the number of the verb.

> Not only the high winds but also the flooding is wreaking havoc.
>
> Not only the flooding but also the high winds are wreaking havoc.

19. Nouns ending in *ics*. *Acoustics, economics, mathematics, physics, politics,* and *statistics* are singular when referring to a subject or field of study; otherwise, they are plural.

> Economics is a dismal science, politics a dismal craft.

> These statistics look incorrect. His politics are distasteful. The acoustics are excellent.

20. *Number of* x. "The number of *x*" takes a singular verb; "a number of *x*," a plural verb.

> The number of magazines devoted to technology is increasing.

> A number of magazines devoted to technology are available.

21. *One in* x. Formalists recommend a singular verb, arguing that "one" is the subject.

> One in two marriages ends in divorce.

Notionalists allow for a singular or a plural verb.

> One in nine Americans lives in California.

> One child in five is not covered by health insurance.

> One in five children are not covered by health insurance.

22. *One of those* x *who*. Formalists insist on a plural verb, arguing that "those *x*"— not "one"—is the true antecedent of "who" and thus determines verb agreement.

> Mlynar, one of the few non-Russians who know Grachev well, denies the report.

Notionalists hold out for a singular verb.

> Mlynar, one of the few non-Russians who knows Grachev well, denies the report.

This controversy rages on, leaving authors and copyeditors free to use either verb— and sure to be condemned by someone no matter which verb they use.[9]

9. William Safire ("On Language," *New York Times Magazine,* July 6, 1997, p. 12) reported having received a one-word note ("Ouch!") from William F. Buckley in response to a column he wrote that began "'Conduct unbecoming an officer and a gentleman' is one of those phrases that sounds as if it comes out of Kipling." Safire spotted the problem: "The ouchifying word was the verb *sounds.*" Soon, a second message arrived, this one from Alistair Cooke, who homed in on "as if it comes out of Kipling." In Cooke's view, Safire's sentence should have read "'Conduct unbecoming an officer and a gentleman' is one of those phrases that sound as [it would sound] if it came out of Kipling." In "Culpa for mea: 13 gaffes in 2002" (*New York Times,* January 5, 2003), Safire apologized for making the same mistake again: quoting his own error, "Henry [Kissinger] is one of the few who has the trust of the keepers of secrets," he said it should read "few who have." But Safire did not question the nature of this game of "Gotcha!" To wit, if Safire, who for decades wrote a weekly column on language, did not catch himself in the act

23. *One or more* x. The expression *one or more* always takes a plural verb.

> One or more files are missing.
>
> One or more of these reports are out of sequence.

24. *Or.* A pair of singular nouns joined by *or* almost always takes a singular verb.

> Heavy editing or rewriting is not needed.

On rare occasions, however, the intended meaning ("this or that or both") may take a plural verb.

> After I draft a questionnaire, I send it to Doris or Elizabeth, who review and correct it.
>> [The singular *reviews* and *edits* would mean that only Elizabeth reviews and edits.]

When *or* joins one singular and one plural subject, the verb agrees with the nearer subject. This rule applies even when the subjects differ in person, although rewording may be preferable if the result sounds awkward.

> The au pair or the parents take the children to the park.
>
> The parents or the au pair takes the children to the park.
>
> *Awkward:* He or I am going to the grocery store.
> *Better:* He is going to the grocery store, or I am.
> *Or:* One of us is going to the grocery store.

25. Percentages. After the construction "*x* percent of *y*," the verb is singular if *y* is a singular noun or a collective noun, and the verb is plural if *y* is a plural noun.

> Thirty percent of her practice is devoted to tenant law.
>
> Forty percent of the town's population is illiterate.
>
> Eighty percent of older voters are undecided.

"The percentage of" takes a singular verb. "A percentage of" takes a singular or plural verb, depending on the number of the noun in the following prepositional phrase: for example, after the phrase "a large percentage of *z*," the verb is singular when *z* is a singular or a noncount noun, plural when *z* is plural.

> The percentage of underemployed copyeditors is large.
>
> A large percentage of copyeditors are underemployed.
>
> Because of faulty handling, a large percentage of food is wasted.

---

of breaching subject-verb agreement, and if his copyeditor at the *New York Times* didn't spot the "error" either, then perhaps the Rule is not inviolable, but just a matter of preference.

A large percentage of the electorate has registered absentee.

A large percentage of voters have registered absentee.

26. Punctuation with a compound subject. When the second term in a pair of subjects joined by *and* is set off with parentheses or dashes (used to demarcate an interrupter, or parenthetical expression), the verb agrees in number with the first term only.

The reason for his dismissal (and the details of the case) remains confidential.

The thrill of defying the rules—and the risk of discovery—motivates this behavior.

But when the second term is set off by a pair of commas (used at an author's discretion to force a slight pause for purposes of emphasis or style), the punctuation does not affect the plurality of the subject.

The accumulation of tiny clues, and especially the eccentric character of the detective, hold the reader's attention until the final page.

27. *There is, there are; here is, here are.* In constructions with these *expletives,* the verb usually agrees with the anticipated subject.

There is nothing we can do.

There are many ways to approach the problem.

Here is my favorite song.

Here are Tom, Dick, and Harry.

However, when an expletive construction anticipates a (formally plural) compound subject whose first element is singular, usage is mixed. The verb often takes the singular form under the principle of attraction, or proximity. This grammar may raise Miss Thistlebottom's eyebrows, but it is highly idiomatic. If the idiomatic construction seems unsuitable for the context, for example, in professional writing, a plural verb can be substituted; if the plural verb sounds unnatural and stilted, recasting may be the better course.

In our school, there is a computer lab and a language lab.
*Awkward:* In our school, there are a computer lab and a language lab.
*Better:* Our school has a computer lab and a language lab.

The sky was dark. There was no moon and few stars.
*Awkward:* The sky was dark. There were no moon and few stars.
*Better:* The sky was dark. No moon and few stars were visible.

28. Time. The singular verb is used when referring to a period of time.

Thirty minutes is too long a commute.

Five years is now the average "time to degree" for undergraduate students.

The 1950s is often regarded as a golden age for television.

29. Titles of works. Titles of works always take a singular verb.

Dickinson's *Selected Poems* is a fine introduction to her work.

30. *Variety of. Variety of* takes a singular verb when preceded by the definite article (the variety of), a plural verb when preceded by the indefinite article (a variety of).

The variety of magazines is astonishing.

A variety of magazines are available.

31. *What* clause. The misconception is that a *what* clause always requires a singular verb, but this is not the case. When a *what* clause is the subject of the main verb, the verb in the *what* clause is usually singular, but, following the principle of attraction, the main verb in the sentence can agree in number with the predicate noun.

What is needed is a simpler way to estimate production costs.

What troubles us are the frequent cost overruns.

When the predicate noun consists of two or more terms, the main verb again follows the principle of attraction: it is generally singular if the terms in the predicate noun are singular and plural if these terms are plural.

In Scandinavian crime fiction, what commands the close attention of readers is the investigators' teamwork, their dogged dedication, and the society that produced the criminal act.

What galls us are his frequent outbursts of temper, his accusations, and his denials.

Sometimes, however, the choice between a singular or plural verb in the *what* clause itself conveys a difference of meaning that carries through to the form of the main verb.

What is usually the wettest ninety days of the year has brought only six inches of rain.
    [The focus is on a single period of time, the wettest ninety days.]

What are usually the wettest ninety days of the year have brought only six inches of rain.
    [The focus is on the individual ninety days.]

What thrills him most is attention and controversy.
    [That which thrills him most is attention and controversy.]

What thrill him most are attention and controversy.
    [The things that thrill him most are attention and controversy.]

TABLE 22. Principal Parts of Common Irregular Verbs

| Base Form | Past Tense | Past Participle |
|---|---|---|
| bear | bore | borne |
| begin | began | begun |
| bid (to command) | bade, bid | bidden, bid |
| dive | dived, dove* | dived |
| drink | drank | drunk |
| fit | fitted, fit | fitted, fit |
| forbid | forbade, forbad | forbidden |
| forgo | forwent | forgone |
| get | got | got, gotten[†] |
| hang (a person) | hanged | hanged |
| hang (a picture) | hung | hung |
| lay (to place) | laid | laid |
| lead | led | led |
| lie (to falsify) | lied | lied |
| lie (to recline) | lay | lain |
| light | lit, lighted | lit, lighted |
| plead | pleaded, pled | pleaded, pled |
| prove | proved | proved, proven[‡] |
| put | put | put |
| rise | rose | risen |
| shine (to emit light) | shone | shone |
| shine (to polish) | shined | shined |
| shoot | shot | shot |
| sink | sank | sunk |
| sneak | sneaked, snuck** | sneaked, snuck |
| spring | sprang, sprung | sprung |
| stride | strode | stridden |
| strive | strove, strived | striven, strived |
| swim | swam | swum |
| thrive | thrived, throve | thrived |
| weave | wove, weaved | woven, weaved |

*DEU: "Dive is a weak verb with the past tense dived. In the 19th century it developed a past tense dove—probably by analogy with drive, drove. . . . Although dived is somewhat more common in writing in the U.S. and is unusual in British English, dove is an acceptable variant." The past tense of nose-dive, however, is always nose-dived.

[†]In British English, got predominates (he has got); in American English, both gotten and got are used as past participles—gotten to mean obtain (he has gotten the response he wanted), and got to denote possession (he has got a gun).

[‡]Prescriptivists stipulate that proved is the only correct past participle form (it has proved true), proven only an adjective (a proven remedy). Descriptivists, however, unequivocally state that both forms are fully standard as past participles.

**In a usage note (s.v. "sneak"), M-W Collegiate observes that "snuck has risen to the status of standard and to approximate equality with sneaked." AHD describes the form as "an Americanism first introduced in the 1800s as a nonstandard regional variant," adding that "it is now used by educated speakers in all regions," although the more traditional form sneaked "predominates in British English."

When *what* is the object in a *what* clause that serves as the subject of the sentence, problems arise only when the predicate is plural.

What the company has done is laudable.

What the directors are asking for is [*or* are] new policies on overtime.

In sentences like this last example, usage is divided, and some writers and copyeditors prefer to finesse the issue by revising.

## TROUBLESOME VERBS

Table 22 lists common irregular verbs that sometimes cause trouble, even for native speakers of English. Many excellent books of English grammar offer extensive catalogs of irregular inflections (see, for example, Garner's *Chicago Guide to Grammar, Usage, and Punctuation,* pp. 74–81), and a good dictionary provides the past tense and past participle forms with entries for all irregular verbs. These forms may vary, depending on the meaning (hung a portrait, hanged a cattle rustler) or on the use of the verb in a literal or a figurative sense (wove a basket, weaved through traffic). American and British English forms may also differ (spelled, spelt).

Compounds whose base is an irregular verb do not always hew to the irregular base inflections in forming their past tense and past participle. The inflected forms of these compound verbs should be verified in the dictionary—or avoided altogether if they seem awkward:

backlight: backlighted or backlit

highlight: highlighted (*not* highlit)

input: inputted *or* input

troubleshoot: troubleshot

Some verbs have unusual and variant forms that also should be checked in the dictionary: medevac (medevacked *also* medevaced); sic (sicced *or* sicked); picnic (picnicked); OK (OK'd *or* OK'ed *or* okayed); sync (synced *or* synched).

Of the irregular verbs, perhaps *lay* (the transitive verb meaning "to place something down") and *lie* (the intransitive verb meaning "to recline") cause the most difficulties. A useful mnemonic is to hear the long "a" sound in *lay* and *place* and the long "i" sound in *lie* and *recline:*

Lay (place) the book on the table.

If you're tired, lie (recline) down for a while.

Notice that even though "Now I lay me down to sleep" is referring to the act of reclining, the verb in this sentence is transitive—the direct object of *lay* is *me.*

Once you've sorted out the transitive and intransitive verbs, be sure to use the correct past tense:

He laid the book on the table before he lay down.

I had lain in bed for an hour before falling asleep.

The verbs *may* and *might* also cause some confusion because they crisscross in several situations.

- *Might* is the past tense of *may.*

  We feared that we might have to postpone the project.

- *Might* is a polite alternative to *may* in the present tense.

  Might I be of some assistance?

- Both *might* and *may* are used to describe unlikely future events, with *might* denoting less certainty.

  Due to bad weather, the flight to Toronto may be delayed, and it might be canceled.

- *Might have* is used to denote a counterfactual past event (that is, an event that did not take place).

  He might have won the election, had he been a better debater.

  The company might have shown a profit last quarter, had the price of oil remained low.

- *May have* is used to denote a speculation about a past event.

  He may have won the election; the absentee votes are still being counted.

  The company may have shown a profit last quarter; we are awaiting the earnings report.

A handful of other verbs sometimes cause trouble, not because they are irregular but because they have cousins. About some look-alike pairs, there are no usage disputes: no one has proposed that *precede* may be used to mean *proceed,* or that *absorb* and *adsorb* are synonymous. But the correct use of the following verbs is sometimes challenging or hotly contended.

*Affect; effect.* As a verb, *affect* means (1) "to influence" or (2) "to pretend"; *effect,* "to cause," "to bring about."

  Biased media coverage affects public opinion. When newscasters affect impartiality in one-sided reports, how can activists effect honest discussion of issues?

*Appraise; apprise.* *Appraise* means "to set a value on something"; *apprise,* "to inform."

  The estate dealer will appraise the collection and apprise the heirs of any offers to purchase it.

*Assure; ensure; insure.* Copyeditors, especially in the business and financial services sectors, are usually expected to enforce the traditional distinctions among these words. To *assure* is to alleviate doubt; to *ensure* is to make certain; and to *insure* is to cover by insurance. Thus:

> Your broker will review your portfolio quarterly to ensure that it continues to meet your investment goals. However, we can offer no assurances about the short-term performance of your portfolio. If you are concerned about market volatility, you may wish to consider investing in an FDIC-insured savings account.

Nonetheless, it is worth noting the following comment in *M-W Collegiate* (s.v. "ensure"):

> ENSURE, INSURE, ASSURE, SECURE mean to make a thing or person sure. ENSURE, INSURE, and ASSURE are interchangeable in many contexts where they indicate the making certain or inevitable of an outcome, but ENSURE may imply a virtual guarantee <the government has *ensured* the safety of the refugees>, while INSURE sometimes stresses the taking of necessary measures beforehand <careful planning should *insure* the success of the party>, and ASSURE distinctively implies the removal of doubt and suspense from a person's mind <I *assure* you that no harm will be done>.

*Born; borne.* Both are past participles of the verb *to bear. Born* is used, in a literal or figurative sense, only as the past participle of the passive *to be born* (She was born in 1950) or as a related adjective (born-digital publications, American-born children). *Borne* is the active past participle for *give birth to* (She has borne three children) and for all other senses of the verb *to bear* (They have borne the sorrow for many years). More examples:

> Her wisdom is born of experience
>
> Baby, we were born to run.
>
> Our efforts have borne fruit.
>
> Cholera is a water-borne disease.

*Bring; take.* From a speaker's or writer's point of view, *bring* implies movement toward, *take* implies movement away from; these verbs roughly track with *come* and *go*. The common error is to use *bring* when *take* is clearly preferable:

> ✗ When you go to Hawaii, be sure to bring your water wings.

When the point of view is unclear or irrelevant, either *bring* or *take* may be used. The choice implies the speaker's point of view, and native English speakers rarely err.

> Should I bring a sweater [when I come to your house]?
>
> Should I take a sweater [when I go to your house]?

*Complement; compliment.* The verb *complement* means "to complete"; *compliment* means "to praise or flatter."

A pistachio scarf is the final touch; it complements the tangerine outfit.

The photographer complimented the woman's pistachio scarf.

*Compose; comprise.* Wilson Follett's summary (*MAU,* s.v. "compose, comprise") neatly illustrates the distinction at issue:

> The whole comprises the parts;
> The parts are comprised in the whole;
> The whole is composed of its parts;
> The parts compose the whole.

In this schema, *compose* is a synonym for "constitute," and *comprise* a synonym for "include," "embrace," or "take in." According to *DEU,* however, *comprise* has been used since the late eighteenth century to mean "constitute," and this denotation did not come under attack until the early twentieth century. Yet *M-W Collegiate* rightly cautions those who would use *comprise* to mean "constitute" and suggests that they "choose a safer synonym such as *compose* or *make up*" (s.v. "comprise").

*Convince; persuade.* In conservative usage, *convince,* meaning "to satisfy by argument or evidence," is followed by a prepositional phrase with *of* or by a dependent clause with *that; persuade,* meaning "to induce to action," is followed by an infinitive with *to.*

> My son convinced me of the superiority of cats as pets.
>
> My son convinced me that cats make superior pets.
>
> He persuaded me to adopt a rescue cat from the local shelter.

The kerfuffle concerns the increasing use of *convince* with the infinitive in place of *persuade:*

> My son convinced me to adopt a rescue cat from the local shelter.

This specific usage began to attract the ire of commentators in the 1950s despite the long history of the polymorphous *convince.* In *Fowler's,* Jeremy Butterfield writes that the proscription "is a classic example of a change in construction that is acceptable to the many and repugnant to the few" (s.v. "convince"). Copyeditors need only be aware that some authors and readers may expect this distinction to be observed, whereas others may be utterly oblivious to it.

*Flaunt; flout.* To *flaunt* is to display ostentatiously; to *flout* is to show contempt and disregard for. Thus one flaunts one's wealth and flouts another's rules. However, according to a usage note in *M-W Collegiate* (s.v. "flaunt"), *flaunt* has acquired a second meaning—"to treat contemptuously"—which "undoubtedly arose from confusion with *flout* [and yet] the contexts in which it appears cannot be called substandard." Muddying the waters a bit is the following observation in *DEU* (s.v. "flaunt, flout"):

All [usage commentators] regard the use of *flaunt* to mean "flout" as nothing less than an ignorant mistake. Many of them also note with dismay or astonishment that . . . it occurs even among the well-educated. . . . Nowhere is there the least suggestion, however, that its common occurrence among the highly educated makes it at all defensible. Even those commentators who are relatively liberal in other matters take a hard line when it comes to *flaunt* and *flout*. . . .

It is an oversimplification, however, to say that the use of *flaunt* to mean "to treat with contemptuous disregard" is merely the result of confusion. Certainly this sense originated from confusion of *flaunt* with *flout,* but those who now use it do so not because they are confused—they do so because they have heard and seen it so often that its use seems natural and idiomatic. . . .

Nevertheless, the notoriety of *flaunt* used for *flout* is so great, and the belief that it is simply an error is so deep-seated and persistent, that we think you well-advised to avoid it, at least when writing for publication.

And avoid it copyeditors do.

*Gibe; jibe.* To *gibe* is to deride; *to jibe* means to agree. Both words have the same pronunciation, and, to confuse matters further, *M-W Collegiate* lists the spelling *jibe* as an equal variant with *gibe* (*AHD* labels it a secondary variant). Usage guides recommend differentiating the spellings and thus the meanings.

The winner gibed me about my pathetically low score.

My tally jibes with yours.

*Home; hone.* To *home in on* is to aim for, to target; *to hone* is to sharpen. Both terms may be used figuratively, but the conflation of these terms (in *to hone in on*) is a common error. Compare the uses:

Homing in on discrepancies in the defendant's alibi, the prosecutor honed the case for conviction.

*Imply; infer.* To *imply* is to suggest or hint; *to infer* is to deduce. The common error is using *infer* for *imply.* Following an essay of nearly two and a half pages on the historical and dialectical complexities of this pair of verbs, *DEU* (s.v. "infer, imply") concludes that in writing "the distinction is easy enough to observe" and counsels doing so.

The news report strongly implied that the councilmember had embezzled funds.

Listeners inferred this allegation from the details in the story.

*Lend; loan.* In figurative expressions, only *lend* will do: "Lend me your ears" or "Lend me a hand." In literal expressions, both verbs are acceptable, although *lend* tends to be the choice in more formal writing, probably because *lend* is the inevitable choice in contemporary British English. (See *DEU,* s.v. "loan, lend," on how *loan* fell out of use in England after the seventeenth century and is now regarded by the British as an Americanism, and by some misinformed Americans as nonstandard.)

*Rack; wrack; wreak.* The verbs *rack* and *wrack* are often confused. The mostly archaic *wrack,* meaning "to wreck," sometimes appears as a variant spelling of *rack* in stock expressions, such as "to wrack the body with pain" and "to wrack one's nerves [*or* memory]," but the only fully sanctioned contemporary use of *wrack* is in the set phrase "wrack and ruin," in which the sense of wreckage is clear. Most commentators prefer *rack,* meaning (literally or figuratively) "to cause great suffering," in such expressions: "to rack one's brains," "to rack the body with pain," "nerve-racking." The verb *wreak,* "to cause," rarely wreaks confusion, but this trio of verbs can wreak havoc with grammar checkers.

## SPLIT INFINITIVES

Most language experts label the prohibition against splitting an infinitive (that is, allowing a word to come between the *to* and the verb) a bugaboo, but they advise writers and editors to continue to enforce the ban because readers expect them to do so. As noted earlier in this chapter, the fetish seems to have sprung from the desire that English emulate Latin, and Latin's one-word infinitives are, so the counterargument goes, unsplittable. (But that's not entirely true either, according to one Latinist: *amare,* "to love"; *amari,* "to be loved"; *amavisse,* "to have loved"; *amatus esse,* "to have been loved"; *amaturus esse,* "to be about to be loved.")

Copyeditors may choose one of two paths. The safer is to ascertain whether the author is a pro-splitter or an anti-splitter and to respect the author's preference. The riskier path is to try to educate the anti-splitter in those cases when the refusal to split an infinitive produces an unclear or ungainly sentence. For this purpose, citing the following authorities may prove useful. First, you could show your author a page or two from Theodore Bernstein's *The Careful Writer.* Bernstein offers several instances in which splitting is preferable, even if one is an anti-splitter by nature:

1. When avoiding the split infinitive produces ambiguity. "The Thanksgiving Day setback was sure to defer further American hopes of keeping pace with the Soviet Union in lunar exploration." Does "further" modify "defer" or "hopes"? All would be clear if it read "to further defer." . . .

2. When avoiding the split infinitive is almost impossible. "Rumania's Communist rulers expect the nation's industrial output to more than double in the next five years"; "The Governor has decided to all but give up on his minimum wage bill"; "He refused to so much as listen to the prisoner's appeal."

3. When avoiding the split infinitive produces clumsiness or artificiality. . . . "The Premier proceeded to admonish sharply the ten die-hard Opposition speakers." A reader can only wonder why "sharply" is in that position. Another unnatural placement: "The objective is apparently almost to double coffee consumption in the Soviet Union in the next three years." Only fear of the taboo prevented these writers from saying the natural things: "to sharply admonish" and "to almost double."

. . . When an infinitive contains an auxiliary—a part of the verb *to be* or *to have*—even the most hair-splitting anti-infinitive-splitter does not contend that an adverb cannot stand before the main verb. Complete sanction is given to such a construction as "His aim in life was to be constantly improving." (pp. 426–27)

The second authority you could bring to bear is Wilson Follett, long regarded as among the most conservative of modern authorities. Invoking George Bernard Shaw, Follett handily dispatches the prohibition: "Of the split construction, Bernard Shaw wrote: 'Every good literary craftsman splits his infinitives when the sense demands it'" (*MAU*, s.v. "split infinitive").

The misguided fear of split infinitives has even led some usage authorities to insist that adverbs can never "interrupt" any verb consisting of an auxiliary and a principal verb form (as in, e.g., is now walking, has frequently walked, would often walk). But they can and do: we can easily demonstrate that this injunction is wrong.

## SUBJUNCTIVE MOOD

Obituaries for the *subjunctive* date from the late eighteenth century, according to *DEU* (s.v. "subjunctive"), and at least one linguist has concluded that "English has no subjunctive," only special uses of the base forms of verbs (Heaven help us *and* I demand this be discussed) and special uses of *was* and *were* (If I were king).[10] Be that as it may, most usage and grammar handbooks recommend that careful writers be attentive to the subjunctive mood, and these manuals use "subjunctive mood" to describe the *be* in "be that as it may" and in "recommend that careful writers be attentive."

### FORMS OF THE SUBJUNCTIVE

The feeling that the subjunctive has all but disappeared in modern English (or that it does not exist at all) in part reflects the fact that the subjunctive forms are hard to spot. For all verbs except *be,* the subjunctive forms differ from the indicative forms only in the third-person singular:

| *Present indicative* | *Present subjunctive* |
| --- | --- |
| I go | I go |
| you go | you go |
| he goes, she goes | he go, she go |
| we go | we go |
| they go | they go |

Thus the subjunctive is noticeable in "We recommend that he go alone" but invisible in "We recommend that they go with him."

For the verb *be,* the situation is more complicated. First, the present subjunctive differs from the present indicative in all persons. Second, *be* is the only verb to retain what

10. Frank Palmer, *Grammar* (Middlesex, England: Penguin, 1971), pp. 195–96.

most grammarians call a subjunctive past tense (though, as we will see, the uses of this tense have everything to do with uncertainty and counterfactuality and nothing to do with the past). The forms are

| *Present tense* | | *Past tense* | |
|---|---|---|---|
| INDICATIVE | SUBJUNCTIVE | INDICATIVE | SUBJUNCTIVE |
| I am | I be | I was · | I were |
| you are | you be | you were | you were |
| he is, she is | he be, she be | he was, she was | he were, she were |
| we are | we be | we were | we were |
| they are | they be | they were | they were |

Some grammar books also use the term *subjunctive* to describe the appearance of *should* (the past tense of *shall*) and *would* (the past tense of *will*) in dependent clauses that state future or hypothetical events:

They doubt he would ever go alone.

They wondered if he should go alone.

But other grammarians categorize such *should*s and *would*s as past-tense indicative forms that are enlisted as auxiliary verbs in expressions of future conditional events.

## USES OF THE SUBJUNCTIVE

The subjunctive appears in various set phrases, phrases so formulaic that their subjunctiveness usually passes unnoticed:

| | | |
|---|---|---|
| The public be damned | Far be it from me | Lest it be thought |
| Heaven (*or* God) forbid | Come what may | Be that as it may |
| The devil take him | Heaven (*or* God) help him | If need be |
| Perish the thought | Suffice it to say | As it were |
| If I were you | Would that it were so | So be it |
| God bless you | Long live the king | God save the queen |
| Thy kingdom come | The Force be with you | Woe betide |

Such phrases are so fixed (some say "fossilized") that they do not cause native speakers any problem.

A second use of the subjunctive also causes few problems. The subjunctive is required in *that* clauses following verbs of command, demand, suggestion, recommendation, wish, request, or necessity.

The director insisted that he audition for the role.

The senator urged that the vote on the amendment be postponed.

The defense asked that the witness be excused.

I wish [that] I were on vacation right now. I wish I were in Hawaii. I wish it were not true that I had already used all my vacation days.

This committee recommends that the board adopt the plan before the end of the year.

It is imperative that the meeting begin at once.

If her conclusions about reading comprehension are correct, then it is important that the instructions be printed in bold type.
[A necessity: The instructions must be printed in bold type.]

*But:* If her conclusions about reading comprehension are correct, then it is important that the instructions are printed in bold type.
[A fact: The instructions are printed in bold type.]

Note that British English sometimes uses the auxiliary verb *should* with the infinitive form of the verb in such sentences.

The director insisted that he should audition for the role.

Third, the subjunctive form *were* (the so-called past tense of the subjunctive) may be used in dependent clauses expressing a condition of uncertainty in the future. Here, matters of nuance and tone come into play:

*Subjunctive:* If he were to take this case, how many hours would it require?

*Indicative:* If he takes this case, how many hours will it require?

The subjunctive emphasizes the uncertainty of the condition, because readers will silently add the implicit qualification: we read "If he were to take this case" and supply the tacit "which is not to say that he will, but *if* he were to do so." The indicative form of a statement expressing future uncertainty is now common in speech and informal writing; the subjunctive conveys a more decorous tone than does the unadorned indicative in such constructions, and it remains the norm in formal prose.

The final use of the subjunctive is the one that causes careful writers and copyeditors the most grief. The principle is, Use the subjunctive form *were* to emphasize that a condition is contrary to fact or hypothetical.

She speaks as though he were out of the room.

If Mexico were not just across the border from the United States, its domestic economy would be even more troubled.

Many small businesses would face bankruptcy if Congress were to revise the tax laws.

When no special emphasis on the counterfactual or hypothetical quality of the statement is desired, the indicative is often used.

The debate over the land permit could be resolved if there was a consensus about the value of mixed-use zoning.

Many small businesses will face bankruptcy if Congress revises the tax laws.

Much of the confusion concerning this last use of the subjunctive results from the mistaken assumption that most clauses introduced by *if* are contrary to fact and therefore might benefit from a subjunctive. This is not at all the case. For example, when an *if* clause introduces a condition that has not yet come to pass, an indicative verb is mandatory:

> If each employee is informed of company policy on email, there are likely to be few complaints.

> If her calculations are correct, the project will come in under budget.

An *if* clause may also express a condition whose truth or falsity is unknown, and in this case too the indicative is called for:

> She did not answer when asked if she was in favor of the restrictions.

> But if he is not responsible for the error, who is?

> We wondered if she was aware of the deadline.

And when an *if* clause refers to a condition in the past whose truth or falsity is unknown (in the grammarians' jargon, "a real past possibility"), the indicative is used:

> If he was aware of her plans, he knew nothing of the details.

Nor do *as if* and *as though* always transport us to the realm of the counterfactual:

> Doug looks as though he is ill. *Or:* Doug looks as if he is ill.

> Wendy looks as though she were ill. *Or:* Wendy looks as if she were ill.

The indicative form *is* in the sentences about Doug conveys the writer's belief that Doug is ill, but the subjunctive form *were* in the sentences about Wendy expresses the writer's observation that Wendy looks sickly even though she is not ill.

## DANGLING PARTICIPLES

There is no dispute about the impropriety of dangling one's participles, yet some days you will find dangling participles everywhere you turn, even in manuscripts by able writers. Because this class of errors is so prevalent, every copyeditor needs to develop a special alertness. The problem arises when a sentence begins with a modifying phrase containing a participle but the subsequent independent clause does not begin with the subject that is performing the action denoted by the participle. (Two exceptions to this rule against dangling participles—absolute participles and nominative absolute participle constructions—are discussed later.) For example:

> ✗ While writing the memo, the phone rang and interrupted me.

Here, the phone is doing the writing as well as the ringing. One remedy is to provide the correct subject for "writing" in the opening clause:

> While I was writing the memo, the phone rang and interrupted me.

A second remedy is to begin the independent clause with a subject capable of performing the writing:

> While writing the memo, I was interrupted by the phone ringing.
> [On "the phone ringing" versus "the phone's ringing," see the final paragraphs of "Case of Nouns and Pronouns" later in this chapter.]

Similarly,

> ✘ Although watched by 25.8 million viewers, the program's ratings disappointed the advertisers.

Because it was the program, not the program's ratings, that was watched by millions of viewers, the sentence should read:

> Although the program was watched by 25.8 million viewers, the ratings disappointed the advertisers.

Dangling is inevitable when the independent clause begins with "there is [or are]" or "it is":

> ✘ Relieved of responsibility for the Woodrow project, there is no reason for us to delay the end-of-quarter review.

Again, one solution is to introduce the correct subject in the first clause:

> Now that we have been relieved of responsibility for the Woodrow project, there is no reason for us to delay the end-of-quarter review.

Another solution is to rewrite the independent clause:

> Relieved of responsibility for the Woodrow project, we have no reason to delay the end-of-quarter review.

Dangling is also inevitable when the independent clause is headed by a gerund:

> ✘ Having been reprimanded for tardiness, buying a clock was her first priority.

One solution is to add a subject that will serve as the subject for both verbs in the sentence:

> Having been reprimanded for tardiness, she made buying a clock her first priority.

Another solution is to expand the participial phrase into a clause and to place the subject in this clause:

> Because she had been reprimanded for tardiness, buying a clock was her first priority.

And dangling often results when the independent clause is in the passive voice:

> ✘ Driving down the street, the Empire State Building was seen.

The solution is to change the passive construction into an active one and supply an appropriate subject:

Driving down the street, we saw the Empire State Building.

## ABSOLUTE PARTICIPLES

The *absolute participles* pose an exception to the anti-dangling rule. Because absolute participles function as prepositions or adverbs, they do not have a grammatical subject.

*Regular participle:* Given a block of wood and a knife, he carved a small deer.

*Absolute participle:* Given the limits of this plan, the alternative proposal seems more practical.

---

*Regular participle:* Judging on the basis of speed and style, the panel awarded the trophy to the second skater.

*Absolute participle:* Judging from these early returns, the margin of victory will be 10 percent.

Among the most common absolute participles:

| | | | |
|---|---|---|---|
| according | concerning | granted | providing |
| acknowledging | considering | granting | reading* |
| admitting | depending | including | recognizing |
| allowing | excepting | judging | regarding |
| assuming | excluding | leaving | respecting |
| barring | failing | looking | speaking† |
| beginning | following | owing to | taking‡ |
| conceding | given | provided | viewing |

\* In expressions such as "reading from left to right."
† In expressions such as "broadly speaking."
‡ In expressions such as "taking into account."

The use of "based on" as an absolute participle, although "virtually universal," is still "opposed on cogent grounds by a few linguistic stalwarts," according to *Garner's Language-Change Index* (s.v. "based on"; on this index, see "Usage Guides" in chapter 3).

✗ Based on her report, the panel approved the director's request.

*Better:* On the basis of her report, the panel approved the director's request.

Even the tolerant *DEU* (s.v. "based on") discourages this usage, although "the sin . . . is a venial one." (Like other usage manuals, *DEU* sometimes resorts to metaphors of morality when discussing errors of grammar and usage.)

## NOMINATIVE ABSOLUTE PARTICIPLE CONSTRUCTIONS

Nominative absolute participles are another exception to the anti-dangling rule. A *nominative absolute participle* is a grammatically independent (absolute) part of a sentence that functions as an adverbial modifier of the main clause and contains its own subject and a present or past participle. It may occur at the beginning, in the middle, or at the end of a sentence.

His heart fluttering with anticipation, he entered the classroom.

He walked to his desk, his satchel clutched to his chest, and took his seat.

He picked up the pencil, his hand trembling with anxiety.

If overused, such absolute constructions can sound stilted and Latinate (Caesar having sent a messenger to Rome, the army rested until morning), but some nominative absolutes are set phrases in English.

All things considered, our team did well in the Olympic trials.

We're planning a hike and picnic on Labor Day, weather permitting.

Note that absolute constructions can also be formed without participles:

The test over, he raced to the playground.

He ran across the soccer field, his red hair ablaze in the sun.

## DANGLING AND MISPLACED MODIFIERS

A similar stricture against dangling applies to sentences that begin with other types of modifying phrases. The word that heads the second clause must be the element that is being modified by the phrase in the first clause. For example:

✗ Unlike meat or poultry, the federal government does not inspect fish.

True, the federal government is unlike meat or poultry, but this should read "Unlike meat or poultry, fish is not inspected by the federal government" or "Fish, unlike meat or poultry, is not inspected by the federal government." Similarly:

✗ With one hundred years of experience, you can count on Sears.

On hearing this advertisement, "you" (or I) can only say, "Sorry, Sears, I don't have one hundred years of experience."

Rewriting such sentences can be a challenge, especially when, as with advertising copy, you must preserve the shrewdly calculated emphasis and tone of the original. Here are some revision strategies.

- Rewrite the main clause using the term modified by the introductory phrase as the subject.

✗ As a scientist, his laboratory is his home away from home.

As a scientist, he considers his laboratory a home away from home.

✗ Fresh out of law school, finding a job was difficult for Kim.

Fresh out of law school, Kim was having difficulty finding a job.

✗ As a valued customer, we are writing to inform you of your eligibility for additional services with your account.

As a valued customer, you are eligible for additional services with your account.

- Expand the modifying phrase into a clause:

✗ Once over the Gulf, forecasters expect Hurricane Harvey to gain strength.

Once Hurricane Harvey is over the Gulf, forecasters expect it to gain strength.

- Reposition the modifying phrase:

✗ A former general who revels in the image of blunt-spoken maverick, the latest criticism was especially stringent, even for Mr. Clippard.

The latest criticism was especially stringent, even for Mr. Clippard, a former general who revels in the image of blunt-spoken maverick.

✗ At almost $5 billion a year, critics charge that the program is too expensive.

Critics charge that the program, at almost $5 billion a year, is too expensive.

- Change the adjectival modifier to an adverbial one:

✗ Even with an excellent credit history, the bank denied John's request for a loan.

Despite John's excellent credit history, the bank denied his request for a loan.

- Break up the sentence if the emphasis can be preserved. (In this example, the solution resorts to the use of a fragment, a common technique in marketing copy.)

✗ With the broadest range of cellular calling plans, no one serves you better than PhoneCo.

PhoneCo—offering the broadest range of cellular calling plans. No one serves you better.

*Misplaced modifiers* are not always located at the head of a sentence, and they do not always result simply from a failure to put modifiers adjacent to—or at least close to—the phrases they modify, as advice manuals sometimes suggest. Rather, miscues result from the complex ways that native English speakers parse sentences: linguists refer to such miscues as modifier attachment problems. The linguist Arnold Zwicky demonstrates with three examples and proposes a different solution for each:[11]

11. The following discussion is indebted to Zwicky, "Not Your Usual Modifier Attachment Problem," *Language Log,* February 22, 2006, http://languagelog.ldc.upenn.edu/.

✗ A resident reported a large animal in a tree with tall and pointed ears.

Because "in a tree" and "with tall and pointed ears" both describe "a large animal," reversing the order of these prepositional phrases hardly solves the problem:

✗ A resident reported a large animal with tall and pointed ears in a tree.

The solution requires a more substantial revision, such as

A resident reported that a large animal with tall and pointed ears had been sighted in a tree.

The second example from Zwicky:

✗ Last night, Domanico presented a history of the hospital district and how the hospital is governed to dispel misconceptions that the public might have had.

In this example, "to dispel misconceptions that the public might have had" is meant to modify the entire preceding clause, but a reader may interpret it as attaching to "how the hospital is governed." Moving the modifier to the head of the sentence, where it clearly modifies the entire main clause, solves the problem.

Last night, to dispel misconceptions that the public might have had, Domanico presented a history of the hospital district and how the hospital is governed.

Zwicky's third example:

✗ Ruisdael's canvases of Bentheim Castle, for instance, which he [Ruisdael] saw on a trip to the Dutch-German border, are invariably acclaimed.

Can the painter have seen his own canvases of Bentheim Castle on a trip to the Dutch-German border? Or did he see the castle and later paint it? Here, the clause "which [Ruisdael] saw on a trip to the Dutch-German border" incorrectly attaches to "Ruisdael's canvases" merely because of the intervening "for instance." Once this interpolation is omitted, the modification becomes clear.

Ruisdael's canvases of Bentheim Castle, which he saw on a trip to the Dutch-German border, are invariably acclaimed.

Zwicky's examples show that misplaced modifiers cannot always be corrected simply by moving them as close as possible to the things they modify. Repairing attachment problems requires different strategies and a finely tuned ear for English syntax.

Here are a few more out-of-joint sentences and corrections, for good measure:

✗ This novel is a haunting tale of deception, sexual domination, and betrayal by one of South America's most important writers.

This novel by one of South America's most important writers is a haunting tale of deception, sexual domination, and betrayal.

✗ Neonatologists seldom see healthy babies once they begin their subspecialty training.

Once neonatologists begin their subspecialty training, they seldom see healthy babies.

✘ The Century Building has been reincarnated after years of disuse as a beautiful bookstore.

After years of disuse, the Century Building has been reincarnated as a beautiful bookstore.

✘ Both prosecutors and defense attorneys will present jurors with evidence.

Both prosecutors and defense attorneys will present evidence to jurors.

✘ They are editing a national newsletter for parents of teenagers based in Seattle.

They are editing a Seattle-based national newsletter for parents of teenagers.

✘ We spoke with Michael Hart, the founder of Project Gutenberg, which began putting books whose copyrights had expired online 32 years ago and has made nearly 9,000 books freely available.

We spoke with Michael Hart, the founder of Project Gutenberg, which began putting public domain books online 32 years ago and has made nearly 9,000 books freely available.

### ROVING *ONLY*

The common modifier that causes the most trouble is *only*. The general rule is to place the *only* directly before the noun, adjective, or verb it is to modify. Each of the following sentences, for example, has quite a different meaning:

Only CanDo Company works to serve the interests of its client.

CanDo Company works only to serve the interests of its client.

CanDo Company works to serve the interests of its only client.

Writers and editors striving for exactitude hew to the strict guideline regarding the placement of *only*. But language experts agree that the rule may yield to idiomatic expression:

I can only try to explain the problem.

She only thought she was being helpful.

Their newest offer can only be called an insult.

Still, beware of possible ambiguity when the placement of *only* produces different interpretations:

Only he said he loved her.

He only said he loved her.

He said only he loved her.

He said he loved her only.

Also, note that the meaning of a sentence changes when *only* comes in the final position. Compare:

> The experiment was conducted only yesterday.
>
> The experiment was conducted yesterday only.

## SQUINTING MODIFIERS

A related, final example of a pitfall in the placement of modifiers:

> The copyeditor who can do this well deserves praise.

Did you read "who can do this well" or "well deserves praise" in this sentence? An ambiguous modifier such as this, usually an adverb or adverbial phrase, is sometimes called a *squinting modifier* because it can modify either what precedes or what follows.

> Jogging uphill quickly improves your stamina.
>   [Quickly jogging uphill? Improves your stamina quickly?]
> Changing jobs often affects your financial situation.
>   [Changing jobs often? Often affects?]

A copyeditor's job is to make sure that readers don't have to choose between interpretations.

## LINGUISTS' RESERVATIONS

Would that the rules about *dangling modifiers* were as simple as many usage commentators suggest! The sometimes contrived and manifestly flawed specimens cited in manuals of grammar and usage (and, yes, some of the examples in this chapter) often provoke an instant bark of laughter. Yet many danglers encountered in the wild are glossed over by copyeditors, even in thoughtfully curated and edited prose, and almost as many go unnoticed by readers. Consider this paragraph from the *New York Times:*

> In another time, it wouldn't have been too hard to guess where Frances Harris would have ended up going to college. She has managed to do very well in very difficult circumstances, and she is African-American. Her high school, in the Oak Park neighborhood of Sacramento, was shut down as an irremediable failure the spring before her freshman year, then reopened months later as a charter school. Midway through high school, her father developed heart problems and became an irritable fixture around the home. . . . In Harris's senior year, her mother lost her job at a nursing home and the family filed for bankruptcy. (David Leonhardt, "The New Affirmative Action," *New York Times Sunday Magazine,* September 30, 2007, p. 76)

You may reasonably ask whether Homer—or the copyeditor—nodded in this case. But should a copyeditor quibble over "midway through high school" when it clearly refers to the subject of the paragraph, Frances Harris, rather than to her father?

In *The Sense of Style,* Steven Pinker explains that "the missing subject of a modifier is identified with the protagonist whose point of view we are assuming as we read the sentence, which is often, but need not always be, the grammatical subject of the main clause. The problem is not one of ungrammaticality but of ambiguity." He continues by proposing a middle ground for copyeditors:

> The decision of whether to recast a sentence to align its subject with the subject of a modifier is a matter of judgment, not grammar. A thoughtlessly placed dangler can confuse the reader or slow her down, and occasionally it can lure her into a ludicrous interpretation. Also, even if a dangler is in no danger of being misinterpreted, enough readers have trained themselves to spot danglers that a writer who leaves it incurs the risk of being judged as slovenly. So in formal styles it's not a bad idea to keep an eye open for them and to correct the obtrusive ones. (p. 211)[12]

Thus the best usage advice about danglers is pragmatic: "correct the obtrusive ones" in order to avoid misleading or alienating the reader.

## GARDEN-PATH SENTENCES

The same practical advice applies to misunderstandings created by *garden-path sentences,* so called because they lead readers astray, or "down the garden path," even though the sentences are grammatically correct. Often-cited examples:

The man who hunts ducks out on weekends.

The old man the boat.

The cotton clothing is usually made of grows in Mississippi.

Because English speakers parse sentences serially—so the theory goes—readers are initially lured into an interpretation leading to a dead end or resulting in a clearly unintended meaning. Then they must return to the beginning of the sentence and reanalyze its components. Linguists study the garden-path phenomenon, and some wordsmiths in need of a hobby enjoy collecting garden-path headlines as entertainment—Squad Helps Dog Bite Victim, Eye Drops Off Shelf, Juvenile Court to Try Shooting Defendant, French Left Torn in Two in Row over EU Constitution.

## PRONOUN-ANTECEDENT AGREEMENT

Like subject-verb agreement, pronoun-antecedent agreement relies on what appears to be a straightforward principle: every pronoun must have a clear, unambiguous antecedent and must agree with that antecedent in gender and in number.

---

12. Readers will doubtless note that Pinker uses the "generic *she*" in this passage. This strategy for avoiding *he* when referring to a singular antecedent of unspecified gender is gradually being replaced by "singular *they*," as a subsequent section discusses.

## SINGULAR *THEY*

During the 1990s, however, a revolution occurred in the treatment of pronouns whose antecedents are indefinite pronouns, such as *anyone, anybody, everyone, everybody, no one, nobody, someone,* and *somebody.* Through the 1980s most grammar and usage books insisted on "Everyone took his seat." The rationale was that *everyone* and these other indefinite pronouns were incontrovertibly singular and that the subsequent pronoun must therefore also be singular; in the absence of a common-gender third-person singular pronoun in English, the correct choice, so went the argument, was the third-person singular masculine form—the "generic *he*." A few well-respected voices pointed to the illogic of viewing these indefinite pronouns as invariably singular and masculine and to the impossibility of using the generic *he* in tag questions ("Everyone brought a pencil, didn't he?").[13] Gradually, more voices objected on the grounds of gender bias. ("Anyone registered in the medical school may bring his partner to the reception"?)

The tide has turned, and many newer dictionaries and usage guides now recognize the legitimacy of using the plural pronoun *they* (*their, them*) after an indefinite subject: Everyone took their seat; Anyone may bring their partner to the first class; Everybody ran when they heard the siren; No one brought any money with them. Usage notes in *M-W Unabridged* and the online *M-W Collegiate* and in the online *AHD* (s.v. "they") register the trend toward acceptance of the so-called singular *they,* as do the somewhat cautious remarks in *Garner's:* "In all varieties of World English, resistance to the singular *they* is receding" (s.v. "concord"). Much of this resistance, Garner adds, has come from speakers of American English; singular *they* "is already more or less standard" in British English (s.v. "sexism"). The *New Oxford Style Manual* (p. 29) and *Fowler's* (s.v. "they, their, them") also attest to this greater tolerance of singular *they* in BrE. To assuage those who continue to denounce the construction as a new barbarism, *DEU* (s.v. "everybody, everyone") notes that the use of plural pronouns in reference to indefinite subjects has a four-hundred-year history in English literature and that this form appears in the majority in Merriam-Webster's files of twentieth-century citations.

Style manuals have slowly come around to acceptance of the usage as well. In 1993 the fourteenth edition of *The Chicago Manual of Style* urged "the 'revival' of the singular use of *they* and *their,*" citing "its venerable use by such writers as Addison, Austen, Chesterfield, Fielding, Ruskin, Scott, and Shakespeare" (pp. 76–77, note 9). The fifteenth and sixteenth editions half-reversed course, however, repudiating the singular *they* but allowing an indefinite pronoun that "carries a plural sense" to serve as a plural antecedent: "Nobody could describe the music; they hadn't been listening to it" (5.64 in both editions). Despite *Chicago's* temporizing, several influential publications have since adopted the singular *they* as house style. In 2015, Bill Walsh, the longtime keeper of

---

13. Jacques Barzun, never accused of being permissive, argued the point as early as 1946: "It seems clear that good sense requires us to say 'Everybody took their hats and filed out.' . . . If *everybody* aren't plural now, it's high time they were"; in "Mencken's America Speaking," reprinted in *A Word or Two Before You Go . . .* (Middletown, Conn.: Wesleyan University Press, 1986), p. 162. (We'll look at "their hats" versus "their hat" in a moment.) Professional linguists have long taken issue with the position that indefinite pronouns are invariably singular: see, for example, Geoffrey K. Pullum, "Everyone Knows Each Other," *Language Log,* April 26, 2008, http://languagelog.ldc.upenn.edu/.

editorial guidelines for the *Washington Post,* added it to his newspaper's stylebook. The 2017 edition of the *AP Stylebook* endorses the usage "when alternative wording is overly awkward or clumsy," while maintaining that "rewording usually is possible and always is preferable" whenever a revision can be devised (s.v. "they, their, them"). The eleventh edition of the *AMA Manual of Style* reportedly will also permit the use of singular *they.* And *Chicago* 17 again concedes that singular *they* is acceptable in speech and informal writing and is "showing signs of gaining acceptance in formal writing" as well, although this manual still recommends avoiding the usage in formal prose by writing around the problem whenever possible (5.48, 5.256, 5.255).[14]

Steven Pinker provides a final twist on the topic, in effect making the whole problem vanish by explaining that

> *everyone* and *they* are not an "antecedent" and a "pronoun" referring to the same person in the world, which would force them to agree in number. They are a "quantifier" and a "bound variable," a different logical relationship. *Everyone returned to their seats* means "For all X, X returned to X's seat." The "X" does not refer to any particular person or group of people; it is simply a placeholder that keeps track of the roles that players play across different relationships. . . . The *their* there does not, in fact, have plural number, because it refers neither to one thing nor to many things; it does not refer at all. (*The Language Instinct,* pp. 378–79)

The singular *they* is also sometimes used after an antecedent noun of unspecified gender or a pair of nouns of different genders joined by *or.* It may also be used for a person whose identity, including gender, must be concealed or whose gender is unknown or nonbinary. Except in the last of these situations, these constructions are not sanctioned in formal prose, although they are common and acceptable in speech and informal writing. Revision is often preferable.

Every student does their best.

John or Mary thinks they can do it by Friday.

My informant wishes to conceal the nature of their association with the corporation.

The gender-nonconforming character Taylor disrupts the hypermasculine hedge fund world with their addition to the cast in the second season of the television show *Billions.*

Although the singular *they* may be used after a preceding indefinite pronoun when the gender of the referent is unknown, *he* or *she* should be used when the context makes the gender of the antecedent clear.

---

14. Increased tolerance of the singular *they* may have been driven in part by the need for a common-gender singular pronoun in writing about people who identify as neither male nor female and who ask not to be referred to as *he/him* or *she/her.* Despite continued resistance to the singular *they* by *The Economist,* the *New Yorker,* and the *New York Times,* these publications all allow exceptions to respect gender-nonconforming individuals' stated preference for epicene pronouns, as does *Chicago* 17. (See "Bias-Free Language" in chapter 15.) *APA* and *MLA* remain silent on the entire issue.

✗ If someone is pregnant, I recommend that they take a folic acid supplement.

If someone is pregnant, I recommend that she take a folic acid supplement.

Like the singular *you,* the singular *they* takes a plural verb.

When someone loves you, they always know your favorite song.

Usage guides equivocate somewhat on the question of whether the reflexive pronoun corresponding to the singular *they* should be *themselves* or (gasp!) *themself. DEU* notes that *themself* was standard well into the sixteenth century, gradually yielding to *themselves,* but now appears "to have been deliberately chosen as a gender-neutral singular reflexive pronoun, taking the place of *himself or herself,*" although this usage is not well established (s.v. "themself"). *Fowler's* traces the same reemergence of *themself,* "a remarkable by-product of the search for gender-neutral pronouns. . . . It is a minority form, but one that turns up from time to time in Britain, North America, and doubtless elsewhere. . . . The final battle for a set of gender-free pronouns will probably be fought over *themself,* but it is hard to see what could comfortably replace it" (s.v. "themselves"). In a discussion of singular *they, Chicago* parenthetically mentions *themself* as a "non-standard" alternative to *themselves* (5.48).

For copyeditors, the singular *they* is sure to remain a sticky wicket. Some authors will denounce the usage as barbaric, and a copyeditor has little to gain (and much to lose) by attempting to impose the newest old fashion on a reluctant author. Conversely, those copyeditors who are disconcerted by the construction—the authorities' blessing notwithstanding—are advised to keep their preferences to themselves when they encounter an author who embraces the construction. Copyeditors who find this use of *they* distasteful need not use it in their own writing but should avoid imposing their preference on authors.

## MISSING ANTECEDENTS

Among the other pronoun-antecedent pitfalls that await the unwary, the most obvious is a pronoun whose intended antecedent is absent:

> *AWOL antecedent:* The governor described his health-care proposal to an enthusiastic crowd of banner-waving supporters. It was one of the best-attended campaign rallies of the year.

Readers will intuit that the "it" at the start of the second sentence is supposed to refer to the rally. But looking backward from "it," the closest singular noun is "crowd," and the desired antecedent, "rally," is nowhere to be found.

> *Revision:* The governor described his health-care proposal to an enthusiastic crowd of banner-waving supporters at one of the best-attended campaign rallies of the year.

> *Or:* The governor described his health-care proposal to an enthusiastic crowd of banner-waving supporters. This campaign rally was one of the best attended of the year.

An unanchored *this* at the start of a sentence often invites confusion:

> *Unanchored pronoun:* During June, consumer prices rose sharply, unemployment declined, but wages remained flat. This has perplexed some economists.

The reader is left to wonder how broadly to interpret this sentence-opening "this." Are the economists perplexed only by the last item in the list (flat wages) or by the simultaneous occurrence of flat wages, lower unemployment, and rising consumer prices? To avoid such ambiguities, careful writers and copyeditors add a noun after a leading *this* to name the desired referent:

> *Revision:* This trio of indicators has perplexed some economists.

> *Or:* This unexpected combination has perplexed some economists.

## POSSESSIVE ANTECEDENTS OF PRONOUNS

Can a noun in possessive form serve as the antecedent of a pronoun? Some readers may recall a foofaraw over whether the following sentence on the 2003 PSAT (Preliminary SAT, a trial run for the standard assessment of college readiness) contains a grammatical error:

> Toni Morrison's genius enables her to create novels that arise from and express the injustices African Americans have endured.

According to the Educational Testing Service, this sentence is error-free; according to those who challenged the ETS's answer key, it contains a solecism. The challengers cited several usage authorities, including Follett, who have argued that a pronoun cannot take as an antecedent a noun in the possessive case. Since possessives are adjectives, the reasoning goes, they can't be referred to by pronouns. But if you accept this logic, a perfectly idiomatic sentence such as "John's wife kissed him" is grammatically incorrect. Balderdash! say the linguists.[15] Poppycock! says Theodore Bernstein, who demolished this bogus rule in *Miss Thistlebottom's Hobgoblins* (p. 115). *Chicago* likewise dismisses it as spurious (5.29). Writers and editors need only exercise care in avoiding potential ambiguities: "John's friend said he was in a car crash" (was John or John's friend in a car crash?).

## SINGULAR OR PLURAL?

When the subject is a corporation or other group, writers sometimes shift between singular and plural pronouns in referring to the organization:

---

15. See, for example, Arnold Zwicky, "More Theory Trumping Practice," *Language Log*, May 22, 2008, http://languagelog.ldc.upenn.edu/. By a similar false logic, any delayed antecedent might be subject to criticism, even if the meaning is clear and the construction idiomatic: "At his first recital, John performed perfectly."

*Shifting pronouns:* Today IBM announced that it would be ready to ship its new line of computers by February 1. Citing pent-up demand, weak competition, and a falling dollar, they are predicting strong sales in the European market.

It is usually best to treat a corporation as a singular subject and to reword clauses in which "it" cannot serve as the subject:

*Revision:* Today IBM announced that it would be ready to ship its new line of computers by February 1. Citing pent-up demand, weak competition, and a falling dollar, company executives are predicting strong sales in the European market.

A pronoun referring to a collective noun (e.g., crowd, battalion) is singular unless the emphasis is on the individual members.

The crowd wildly applauded its approval of the comedian's stand-up routine.

After the performance the crowd scattered to their cars.

Sports teams require not only a plural verb (see the previous discussion under "Subject-Verb Agreement") but also plural pronouns, even when the team's name is singular in form.

If the Utah Jazz are to succeed at the offensive end of the floor, they'll need Rodney Hood to take his game to another level.

## IMPERSONAL *ONE*

Many writers avoid *one,* feeling it is overly formal. When *one* does appear, British grammarians insist that the subject *one* always be followed by the pronoun *one*:

*British style:* One is entitled to do as one likes as long as one does not betray one's promises.

But American grammarians advise us to avoid an endless train of *one*s and either turn to *he* (or *he or she* or another workaround) or recast the sentence:

*American style:* One is entitled to do as he likes as long as he does not betray his promises.

*Better:* We are entitled to do as we like as long as we do not betray our promises.

*Or:* People are entitled to do as they like as long as they do not betray their promises.

## DISTRIBUTIVE POSSESSION

A final logical conundrum related to pronoun-antecedent agreement remains insolvable:

It was a horrible dream. I saw a roomful of people, each of whom was picking their nose and shouting at their spouse.

Some grammarians follow Follett (*MAU*, s.v. "number, trouble with") and reject "their nose" and "their spouse" because, they explain, not everyone in the room shares the same nose and spouse. But, the counterargument runs, the plural "their noses" and "their spouses" would suggest that some or all of these people have more than one nose and one spouse apiece: "To avoid ambiguity a singular noun is often used with a plural possessive when only one of the things possessed could belong to each individual" (*WIT*, p. 357). In *The Handbook of Good English*, Edward D. Johnson offers this example:

> We each brought our own lunch.

"The singular *lunch*," he explains, "is permissible by a principle sometimes called *distributive possession*; each member of the possessing group possesses one . . . of the possessed items" (pp. 45–46; italics added). *Fowler's* offers contrasting examples to demonstrate that either a plural or a singular noun may sometimes be acceptable:

> We watched the proceedings that led to her resignation with sadness uppermost in our minds.
>
> *Or:* We watched the proceedings that led to her resignation with sadness uppermost in our mind.

"In some contexts," *Fowler's* observes, "a singular noun is often idiomatic" (s.v. "distributive"). The singular generally works best with abstractions that each possessor has in the singular:

> The police examined the surveillance video of the robbers to determine their identity.
>
> Two freestyle climbers fell to their death.
>
> They could see the ancient city in their mind's eye.

## CASE OF NOUNS AND PRONOUNS

*Case* refers to the form of a noun or pronoun that indicates its function in a sentence:

- The *nominative case* is used for the subject of a verb and for a predicate noun.
- The *objective case* is used for the object of a verb and for the object of a preposition.
- The *possessive* (or *genitive*) *case* indicates ownership (my hat), origin (my offer), or purpose (girls' shoes).

## FORMATION OF CASES

The case forms of nouns present few problems (see "Possessives" in chapter 5).

*Singular*

| NOMINATIVE | OBJECTIVE | POSSESSIVE |
|---|---|---|
| boy | boy | boy's |
| girl | girl | girl's |
| child | child | child's |

*Plural*

| NOMINATIVE | OBJECTIVE | POSSESSIVE |
|---|---|---|
| boys | boys | boys' |
| girls | girls | girls' |
| children | children | children's |

The pronouns, however, sometimes cause difficulties.

| | NOMINATIVE | OBJECTIVE | POSSESSIVE |
|---|---|---|---|
| Personal | I | me | my, mine |
| | you | you | your, yours |
| | he | him | his |
| | she | her | her, hers |
| | it | it | its |
| | one | one | one's |
| | we | us | our, ours |
| | they | them | their, theirs |
| Indefinite | everyone | everyone | everyone's |
| | somebody | somebody | somebody's |
| | each other | each other | each other's* |
| | one another | one another | one another's* |
| Relative | who | whom | whose |
| | whoever | whomever | whosever |
| | which | which | whose, of which[16] |
| | that | that | — |

*Always singular.

16. Bernstein, *Careful Writer*, p. 479: "Since *which* has no genitive of its own, it is only fair to let it borrow *whose* when the loan is useful to avoid clumsiness. It is nonsense to compel one to write, 'The car, the carburetor, brakes, and steering wheel of which need overhauling, is to be sold at auction.' . . . And never forget that banner 'whose broad stripes and bright stars' have inspired us all these many generations." Thus, *whose* need not refer to a person.

AWKWARD CASE USE

Some sentences use correct case forms but sound awkward:

> This experiment will put your and my hypotheses to the test.
> [Correct, although "your hypotheses and mine"—or "your hypothesis and mine" if each person has only one hypothesis—would sound more natural to most readers.]

> A group of us taxpayers protested.
> [The objective case is needed because the pronoun is the object of the preposition "of."]

Since being correct is only half the goal, it is perhaps best to revise.

> *Revision:* Our taxpayers' group protested.

> *Or:* Our taxpayers group protested.
> [This second revision treats "taxpayers" as an attributive noun rather than as a possessive; see "Possessives" in chapter 5.]

## *WHO* AND *WHOM*

*Who* is both an interrogative pronoun and a relative pronoun. The nominative form *who* serves as the subject of a clause or the complement of a linking verb: Who loves you? I will ask who she is. Is she the woman who saw you? The objective form *whom* serves as the object of a verb or preposition, or as the subject of an infinitive: Whom do you love? I will ask whom she represents. Is she the woman whom you saw? To whom should we submit our application? I don't know whom to ask.

Like the subjunctive mood, the objective case pronoun *whom* is widely claimed to be moribund. Speakers and writers grapple with it, hypercorrect for it when a simple *who* is the right choice, and joke about how pompous it sounds when used correctly. (The writer and humorist Calvin Trillin is often quoted as saying that "*whom* is a word invented to make everyone sound like a butler.") To many ears, some informal constructions can sound absurdly priggish with the grammatically correct *whom:*

> It's not what you know; it's whom you know.

> Whom are you going to trust—me or a stranger?

Thus many contemporary English speakers find it more natural to say

> Who do you love?

> I will ask who she represents.

> Is she the woman who [*or* that] you saw?
> *Or:* Is she the woman you saw?

> Who should we submit our application to?

> I don't know who to ask.

Even the sternest of contemporary usage commentators concede that, in all but the most formal prose, an invariant *who* may sometimes be acceptable for interrogatives and indirect questions, as the subject of an infinitive, and as the object of a preposition when the preposition is placed at the end of the sentence:

*Informal:* Who do I write if I have a question?
*Formal:* Whom do I write if I have a question?

*Informal:* She asked me who I knew at the celebration.
*Formal:* She asked me whom I knew at the celebration.

*Informal:* I know exactly who to blame for this catastrophe.
*Formal:* I know exactly whom to blame for this catastrophe.

*Informal:* Who do you wish to speak to?
*Formal:* To whom do you wish to speak?

Despite the decline of *whom* in speech and informal writing, its use remains strong in some set expressions and in informal constructions where it occurs directly after a preposition or serves as the object in a relative clause:

To whom it may concern . . .

The principal questioned the students, one of whom admitted to triggering the sprinkler system.

Police arrested the driver whom witnesses reported as having struck the pedestrian.

But in formal discourse (lectures, speeches, presentations) and in professional writing, case distinctions are rigorously maintained—or *whom* is avoided altogether if it seems unacceptably stilted.

Correct case use in relative clauses creates the greatest challenge. The appearance of *who* (or *whoever*) and *whom* (or *whomever*) at the head of a subordinate clause often sends writers into a tizzy. The rule is straightforward: when *who* introduces a subordinate clause, the correct case of *who* depends on its function in that subordinate clause. When in doubt, try substituting *he* or *him* in the relative clause as a test.

Smith is the candidate who we think will win.
   [We think he will win (nominative case); "we think" is a parenthetical interpolation that does not affect the case of *who,* the subject of the subordinate clause → the candidate who (we think) will win.]

Jones is the candidate whom we hope to elect.
   [We hope to elect him (objective case) → the candidate whom we hope to elect.]

This book offers sound advice to whoever will accept it.
   [He will accept it (nominative case); in the subordinate clause, "whoever" functions as the subject of "will accept." The object of the preposition *to* is the entire clause "whoever will accept."]

In such sentences, wary writers sometimes skirt the whole *who/whom* dilemma by substituting *that* or omitting the relative pronoun altogether:

Jones is the candidate that we hope to elect.

*Or:* Jones is the candidate we hope to elect.

An aside: The relative pronoun *that* is perfectly acceptable in such references to people. Conversely, the relative pronoun *who* (or *whom*) may be used to refer to animals, especially when they are individualized, for example, by being named.

In determining the appropriate choices for a manuscript, copyeditors must assess both the level of formality and the author's preferences. The advice offered for singular *they* and other matters of unsettled usage applies here as well: in their own writing, copyeditors may choose to observe (or ignore) the fading grammatical conventions governing *who* and *whom,* but they should avoid imposing their preference on authors who, duly advised of the risk of being judged either careless (by eschewing *whom*) or pretentious (by insisting on its traditional use), have followed another course.

While assessing case use, take a moment to make sure the antecedent of the *who* or *whom* is secure:

A leading American scholar on the Pilgrims, who lived in the Dutch town of Leiden before setting out for America in 1620, has been ordered to leave the Netherlands.
  [The "American scholar" competes with "the Pilgrims" as the antecedent of "who."]

## ME, MYSELF, AND I

It's me? It's I? Pronouns linked to a subject by the verb *to be* ordinarily take the same case as the subject. In speech and informal writing, however, English has long tolerated objective-case pronouns in short constructions with "it is" and "this/that is": it is me; that's him. These constructions, according to *Garner's,* are "fully acceptable" (s.v. "it is I; it is me"). But in formal prose and in longer sentences, some punctilious writers still prefer to use the nominative case: it is I who am responsible; if I were he, I would resign.

The pronoun *myself* is normally used as a reflexive or an emphatic form:

I call myself the Rodeo Queen.

I went to Portland by myself.

My companion enjoyed the film, but I myself couldn't even follow the plot.

*Myself* is also commonly used as part of a group of names or nouns serving as the subject or object of a verb or the object of a preposition. *Fowler's* considers these uses equally "beyond reproach" (s.v. "myself"), as does *DEU,* although stricter commentators discourage it in formal writing:

The robbery was planned by Amanda, Henry, and myself.

*Or:* The robbery was planned by Amanda, Henry, and me.

All usage commentators counsel against using the word simply as an "elegant" or "modest" substitute for *I* or *me:*

✗ My husband and myself will be delighted to accept your invitation.

✗ Your book is an inspiration to myself.

The common expression *between you and I* (for *between you and me*), roundly censured in grammar and usage manuals, has long served as a shibboleth separating the literati from the illiterati. No copyeditor would allow this solecism to remain in a manuscript (unless it was used deliberately in dialogue or as a joke). But similar constructions—linguists call them nominative conjoined objects—can deceive even conscientious and highly educated speakers, such as the Supreme Court justice who in an interview said, "He spent all that time listening to José and I dissect the Puerto Rican colonial spirit."[17] In this sentence the speaker treats the conjoined objects ("José and I") as the notional subject of the following verb phrase, "dissect the Puerto Rican colonial spirit." Even a graduate of Yale Law School can choose the wrong case because of treacherous syntax, especially in unscripted conversation.

Copyeditors, beware of conjoined terms with *I* and *me*!

## POSSESSIVES

"Possessives" in chapter 5 describes the distinction between separate possession (Melissa's and Peggy's tools) and joint possession (Melissa and Peggy's tools). When joint possession combines a noun and a pronoun, however, both terms must be marked as possessive:

✗ We sold Harvey and my pickup truck.

We sold Harvey's and my pickup truck.

The *double possessive* (a.k.a. *double genitive*), also described in chapter 5, uses both "of" and a following possessive noun or pronoun. It is a venerable idiom in English and is unlikely to trip up an author or copyeditor who avoids overthinking the construction: a friend of Amy's, a friend of mine.

How do you form the possessive of a noun immediately followed by an appositive, that is, a noun or noun phrase that explains or amplifies what precedes it?

✗ Leonard Bernstein, the conductor of the New York Philharmonic's, performance . . .

Barbara Wallraff, a longtime columnist and editor at *The Atlantic,* once tackled this conundrum and concluded that a nonrestrictive appositive construction (one set off

17. David D. Kirkpatrick, "Judge's Mentor: Part Guide, Part Foil," *New York Times,* June 22, 2009, p. 1.

by a pair of commas) would have to be revised, whereas a restrictive appositive (one restricting, or limiting, the meaning of the following term and therefore not set off by a pair of commas) could take the long-deferred possessive apostrophe:

> The New York Philharmonic conductor Leonard Bernstein's performance . . .

---

✗ The leader of the transcendentalists, Ralph Waldo Emerson's, ideas . . .

The transcendentalist leader Ralph Waldo Emerson's ideas . . .

"I wouldn't call that a beautiful sentence," Wallraff remarked about the latter construction, "but it is a grammatical one."[18]

## DISPUTED USAGES

Now for four disputed usages. First up: Grammarians disagree about which case should follow the expression "everyone but." As Theodore Bernstein points out, the *but* in "everyone but" may be regarded as a conjunction (and therefore followed by a pronoun in the nominative case) or as a preposition (and therefore followed by a pronoun in the objective case). His advice neatly splits the difference:

> 1. If the pronoun is at the end of the sentence, regard *but* as a preposition and put the pronoun in the objective case ("Everyone laughed at the quip but him"). Not only is this grammatically acceptable, but in addition it sounds inoffensive since normally a [pro]noun at the end of a sentence is in the objective case. 2. If the pronoun appears elsewhere in the sentence, put the pronoun in the same case as the noun to which it is linked by the *but* ("Everyone but he laughed at the quip"; "The quip, directed at no one but him, fell flat"). (*Miss Thistlebottom's Hobgoblins*, p. 93)

A similar dispute concerns the correct case following *than*. Usage advisers argue over whether *than* functions as a conjunction and should therefore be followed by a pronoun in the nominative case, or as a preposition, which should be followed by an objective-case pronoun. Some commentators maintain that the word can function as either part of speech: the conjunction prevails in writing, especially in formal prose; the preposition, although censured by many prescriptivists, characterizes speech and colloquial communication.

*Formal:* No one loves you more than I.

*Informal:* No one loves you more than me.

Because of the bivalent nature of this little word, all usage guides caution against possible misunderstandings.

---

18. Wallraff, *Word Court* (San Diego: Harcourt/Harvest, 2000), pp. 143–44. In the same passage, Wallraff writes entertainingly about the "picnic's grandmother" construction, so called after an example picked up from *WIT*: "the girl who gave the picnic's grandmother." Wallraff's advice: Recast!

He admires Roosevelt more than I.
[He admires Roosevelt more than I do.]

He admires Roosevelt more than me.
[He admires Roosevelt more than he admires me.]

Another tiny word that trips the unwary is *not*. Not I *or* not me? not we *or* not us? not she *or* not her? not they *or* not them?—when the negation attaches to the subject of the sentence, what case should the pronoun use? Once again, language advisers distinguish between formal writing, which preserves the traditional nominative form, and informal communication, which favors the objective case and often places the negation at the end of the sentence:

*Formal:* She, not he, wrote the report.
*Informal:* She wrote the report, not him.

*Formal:* They caused the accident, not he.
*Informal:* They caused the accident, not him.

*Formal:* We were the clinicians, not he.
*Informal:* We were the clinicians, not him.

The last disputed usage arises from the fact that a gerund is usually preceded by a possessive noun or pronoun.

May's singing is atrocious.

The staff objected to his having made a change in the agenda.

But this rule is not invariable. Witness the following examples: "without a shot being fired," "long odds against that happening," and "Imagine children as young as twelve years old being haled into court!"[19] Or consider the head-scratching apostrophes in these sentences, from letters to the editor in the *New York Times:*

There is a technological solution to the problem of digital photographs' being easy to alter. (September 6, 2001)

Students' not eating a healthy lunch is certainly not new to our nation's high achievers. (June 2, 2008)

And there's a further wrinkle: although the *-ing* forms that function as gerunds are (usually) preceded by possessive pronouns, the *-ing* forms that function as verbal participles are preceded by objective pronouns. Fortunately, in *The Elements of Style* Strunk and White come to the rescue with a pair of sentences that elucidate this mystery:

---

19. Bernstein, *Miss Thistlebottom's Hobgoblins*, p. 104. Rebutting Fowler's insistence that the genitive always precedes the gerund, Bernstein writes: "In the clause 'Which will result in many having to go into lodgings,' [Fowler] suggested making it *many's*, and in the sentence 'It is no longer thought to be the proper scientific attitude to deny the possibility of anything happening,' he favored altering it to *anything's*. The suggested changes can hardly be called English."

Do you mind me asking a question?

Do you mind my asking a question?

In the first sentence, the queried objection is to *me,* as opposed to other members of the group, putting one of the questions. In the second example, the issue is whether a question may be asked at all. (p. 13)

In his classic (1965) edition of *A Dictionary of Modern English Usage,* H. W. Fowler labeled the "me asking" construction a *fused participle,* and abhorred it. Follett devoted two double-column pages to the topic and issued what remains the definitive opinion (reworded but not substantively altered in the Erik Wensberg update of *MAU*):

> One sort of statement . . . calls for a pronoun and excludes a possessive adjective: *The idea of me standing in the pulpit in my uncle's robes and delivering his sermon was too much, and I began to laugh.* Here *me* insists upon being the central idea; *my standing* would give a misleading emphasis to *standing,* the action expressed by the participle. By the same logic, when the statement requires more stress on the action than on the agent, the possessive should be used: In *What I cannot stand is some journalist calling a politician "Bob,"* it is clear that the speaker's objection is not to journalists but to what one sort of journalist says, the *calling.* Hence *some* journalist's *calling a politician "Bob."* (s.v. "fused participle")

## PARALLEL FORM

*WIT* defines *parallelism* as "the principle that parts of a sentence that are parallel in meaning should be parallel in structure. Two or more sentence elements in the same relation to another element should be in the same form" (p. 384). In the following example, two sentence elements, a subject and a predicate nominative, are connected by a linking verb:

✗ Thinking is to blog.

To think is to blog.

Although constructions with copulative verbs sometimes have defects in parallel structure, especially when gerunds and infinitives are involved, faulty parallelism occurs more frequently in series, in constructions with correlative (paired) conjunctions, and sometimes in antithetical expressions.

The terms in a series—a list of items joined by a coordinate conjunction—are said to be parallel when they all belong to the same part of speech; that is, each member in the series is a noun, a verb, an adjective, or an adverb:

✗ She likes swimming, playing tennis, and to run marathons.

She likes to swim, play tennis, and run marathons.

*Or:* She likes swimming, playing tennis, and running marathons.

Parallelism, however, does not require that all the items in the series be identical in length. In the following examples, the items are parallel (they are all nouns), even though some are one-word nouns and others are noun phrases:

> She spent her vacation reading, writing letters in French, and lying on the beach.

> The documents must be checked for spelling, punctuation, and the correct use of abbreviations.

Normally, parallelism with articles and prepositions in series should also be observed, although a stylist may consciously relax this guideline for purposes of rhythm, tempo, or emphasis:

> *Not:* the French, the Italians, Spanish, and Portuguese

> *But:* the French, the Italians, the Spanish, and the Portuguese

> *Or:* the French, Italians, Spanish, and Portuguese

---

> *Not:* in spring, summer, or in winter

> *But:* in spring, summer, or winter

> *Or:* in spring, in summer, or in winter

Parallelism with correlative conjunctions—pairs of conjunctions, such as *either . . . or, neither . . . nor, both . . . and, not only . . . but [also]*—poses the greatest difficulty for writers.

> ✗ The passive voice may be used either for variety or to emphasize the activity accomplished rather than the agent who accomplished it.

> The passive voice may be used either to achieve variety or to emphasize the activity rather than the agent who accomplished it.

---

> ✗ My neighbor not only recycles bottles and cans but she also drives an electric car.

> My neighbor not only recycles bottles and cans but also drives an electric car.

> *Or:* Not only does my neighbor recycle bottles and cans but she also drives an electric car.

Antithetical statements with *but not* and *not . . . but* also require parallel syntax.

> ✗ Eleanor likes singing folk songs but not to perform karaoke.

> Eleanor likes singing folk songs but not performing karaoke.

---

> ✗ He has not gone missing but resigned.

> He has not gone missing but has resigned.

As a conjunction, the antithetical expression *rather than* (meaning "and not") requires that parallel syntax be maintained; as a preposition, *rather than* (meaning "instead of") does not need parallelism.

*Conjunction:* I am speaking to you as your friend rather than as your lawyer.

*Preposition:* Rather than skimming a summary in a blog post, I prefer to peruse the long-form magazine article.

But parallel structure alone may not ensure clarity:

> Critics of internet filtering devices question whether they are appropriate shields against offensive material or high-tech censorship.
>> [The writer wants to oppose "appropriate shields" and "high-tech censorship," but the syntax suggests "shields against offensive material" as opposed to "shields against high-tech censorship."]
>
> He should eat nothing but tasteless TV dinners and clean latrines.
>> [The writer wants to link the verbs "eat" and "clean," but the sentence can be misread as saying that "he" should "eat" two things only: "tasteless TV dinners" and "clean latrines."]

In complex sentences, the preference for parallelism is sometimes relaxed. *DEU* (s.v. "faulty parallelism") offers the following example, from an essay by E. B. White, a well-respected English prose writer and co-author of *The Elements of Style:* "I have written this account in penitence and in grief, as a man who failed to raise his pig, and to explain my deviation from the classic course of so many raised pigs. The grave in the woods is unmarked, but Fred can direct the mourner to it unerringly and with immense good will." To insist on schoolbook parallelism here—to have Fred directing mourners "without error and with immense good will" or "unerringly and cheerfully" or some such—would be to distort the meaning and mar the dignity of the moment. Nor is there any way to force "and to explain" into line with what precedes it.

## MORE MUDDLED SYNTAX

Disjointed syntax, especially in comparisons, is often overlooked. The author may shrug, "Readers will know what I mean!" Indeed, readers may unconsciously compensate for faulty syntax, but the effort is taxing, and they may misinterpret the sentence.

When *like* and *unlike* introduce comparisons, both balanced syntax and logic frequently go awry.

✘ Like Canadians, Americans' attitude toward genetically modified foods is one of suspicion.

Like Canadians, Americans are suspicious of genetically modified foods.

---

✘ Unlike traditional unionized jobs, gig workers have no job security.

Unlike traditional unionized jobs, gig work offers no job security.

Other faulty comparisons are caused by faulty ellipsis, the omission of essential words from the construction:

✘ This year awards were more lavish than previous years.

This year awards were more lavish than they were in previous years.

*Or:* This year awards were more lavish than in previous years.

---

✘ The gymnast performed as well or better than expected.

The gymnast performed as well as or better than expected.

---

✘ My short story is as short or shorter than yours.

My short story is as short as or shorter than yours.

---

✘ Obesity kills far more Americans than terrorists.

Obesity kills far more Americans than terrorists do.

Some mangled comparisons defy interpretation. The following sentence sounds intelligible until you begin to think about it:

✘ In Michigan and Minnesota, more people found Mr. Bush's ads negative than they did Mr. Kerry's.

[More people found Mr. Bush's ads negative than found Mr. Kerry's ads negative? People found Mr. Bush's ads more negative than Mr. Kerry's?][20]

Other syntactical errors are caused by *syllepsis,* the use of a word that agrees grammatically with only one of two terms by which it is governed.

✘ I have not and will not yield to these demands.

I have not yielded and will not yield to these demands.

*Or:* I have not yielded to these demands, nor will I.

---

✘ He either will or has already voted yea.

He either will vote or has already voted yea.

*Or:* He either will vote yea or already has.

The opposite of omitting essential words is unnecessary repetition, as in the common error of prepositional doubling:

✘ A habit of which I am guilty of is procrastination.

A habit of which I am guilty is procrastination.

*Or:* A habit I am guilty of is procrastination.

---

20. This example is discussed by Geoffrey K. Pullum, "More People Than You Think Will Understand," *Language Log,* December 27, 2009, http://languagelog.ldc.upenn.edu/.

## ADJECTIVES AND ADVERBS

We are usually taught that *adjectives* are words that modify a noun or pronoun, and *adverbs* are words that modify an adjective, verb, or another adverb. The circularity of the latter point aside (an adverb is a word that modifies an adverb?), these schoolroom definitions ignore the so-called copulative, or linking, verbs—verbs that express a state of being rather than an action; for example: be, become, feel, seem, smell, sound, taste. Although an adverb is used to modify a verb expressing an action, a copulative verb is followed by an adjective:

> I am fine; he became sad; she feels bad; they felt ill; you seem happy.

> This fish smells bad; the band's new song sounds good; the soufflé tastes delicious.

> Identical twins may look different, sound different, and walk differently.
> [*Walk* is not a copulative verb, so an adverb is required. For euphony, the final item could be changed to "have different ways of walking."]

Some verbs may be used in both a copulative and a noncopulative sense:

> *Copulative:* She looked happy.

> *Noncopulative:* She looked happily at the page proofs of her first novel.

---

> *Copulative:* He felt hesitant.

> *Noncopulative:* He felt hesitantly for his keys.

*Garner's* (s.v. "adjectives") cautions that identifying copulative verbs requires the analysis of specific sentences, not the memorization of a list of verbs: "Often unexpected candidates serve as linking verbs." Examples of "unexpected candidates" abound:[21]

> The children acted innocent.
> Colors come alive.
> Get ready.
> She grew impatient with him.
> The children held still.
> The woman lay motionless.
> You can rest secure.
> He stood firm.
> The milk turned sour.
> The takeover appears imminent.
> The room fell silent.

21. The following list, possibly created by Mary Beth Protomastro, is from an unsigned newsletter article, "The Missing Linking Verbs," *Copy Editor,* February and March 1993, n.p.

John is going bald.
The fog hangs heavy over the city.
Please keep quiet.
Reports proved false.
The crabgrass is running wild.
Stay alert.
The chairman waxed sentimental.

The copulative-noncopulative distinction is one of the issues in the multiple controversies concerning the pairs "feel good" and "feel well," "look good" and "look well," and "feel bad" and "feel badly." These disputations are too tortuous to even summarize here; excellent guidance is provided by the lengthy entries in *DEU* (s.vv. "feel bad, feel badly" and "good").

## COMPARATIVE AND SUPERLATIVE FORMS

The adjectives and adverbs whose comparative and superlative forms are irregular (e.g., bad, worse, worst; little, less, least) cause few problems. Rather, difficulties tend to arise with some of the regularly formed comparatives and superlatives. When in doubt, consult your dictionary. The typical forms are these:

*Base form has one syllable*

large, larger, largest
soon, sooner, soonest

*Exception:* Base form is a participle
lost, more lost, most lost
told, better told, best told

*Base form has two syllables, with the stress on the first syllable*

able, abler, ablest
bitter, bitterer, bitterest
clever, cleverer, cleverest
cruel, crueler, cruelest
early, earlier, earliest
gentle, gentler, gentlest
happy, happier, happiest
narrow, narrower, narrowest
simple, simpler, simplest

*Also: Un-* forms of some of these bases
unhappy, unhappier, unhappiest

*Other base forms*

difficult, more difficult, most difficult
efficiently, more efficiently, most efficiently

But there is no definitive rule for the construction of comparative and superlative forms: the idiomatic forms for specific words are learned by reading well-wrought prose and checking an authoritative dictionary. Some adjectives have both inflectional forms (e.g., commoner, commonest) and periphrastic ones (e.g., more common, most common). Consider, for example, *handsome, pleasant, polite:* when these words function as adjectives, according to *M-W Unabridged,* they "usually" or "often" add *-er* and *-est;* the periphrastic forms are also used. In cases such as these, a writer or editor must choose between the alternative forms by considering euphony and style.

## ABSOLUTES

There are also disputes about whether certain adjectives and adverbs are absolute (that is, they cannot be used in the comparative or the superlative and cannot be modified by the intensifier *very*). As *DEU* points out (s.v. "absolute adjectives"), most adjectives and adverbs do not lend themselves to comparison or intensification, and each generation of usage experts proposes its list based on its notions of semantics and logic. Today, the most controversial of the adjectives are *perfect* (at which point someone always cites the "more perfect union" promised by the US Constitution) and *unique*. As to the former, *DEU* (s.v. "perfect") cites many examples of "more perfect" and "most perfect" and notes that it has been "in respectable use from the 14th century to the present." As to the latter, *DEU* (s.v. "unique") notes that the definition "one of a kind," which invites the label of absolute adjective, is not the sole meaning of the term. *Unique* also denotes "distinctive" or "unusual," and these meanings certainly admit comparison and intensification.

## FUNCTION AND FORM

Another problem related to adjectives and adverbs arises from the fact that neither "adjectiveness" nor "adverbiality" is a quality inherent to a word. *Home,* for example, may function as a noun (This is our home), as an adjective (Taste our home cooking), or as an adverb (We went home). Because nouns may function as adjectives (the technical term for a noun that modifies a subsequent noun is *attributive noun*), "government offices" is just as correct as—and many would say preferable to—"governmental offices." Attributive nouns are usually singular (eye strain), but they are plural if the noun is invariably plural (arms control) or is part of a set phrase (admissions policy).

A number of adjectives are formed by adding either *-ic* or *-ical:* analytic/analytical, fanatic/fanatical, ironic/ironical, philosophic/philosophical. Some of these pairs have different meanings:

| | |
|---|---|
| classic symptoms | classical literature |
| comic drama | comical behavior |
| economic forecast | economical shopping |
| electric personality | electrical wiring |
| historic event | historical fiction |
| lyric soprano | lyrical description |

With the exception of the adverb *publicly,* however, the corresponding adverbs for both spellings are formed by the addition of *-ically:* classically, comically, economically.

But not all adverbs end in *ly:* for example, *clean, deep, fast, free, loud, much, near, quick, slow, tight,* and *well* can function as adverbs or as adjectives. The dual function of these so-called flat adverbs is recorded in reliable dictionaries. Some flat adverbs have *ly* forms as well (cleanly, deeply, freely, loudly, nearly, quickly, slowly, tightly), and these are sometimes preferred in formal writing:

*Informal:* Drive slow! Take it slow, my friend.

*Formal:* We drove around the block slowly.

But some of these paired adverbial forms have different meanings or specific idiomatic uses:

Children ride free.
   [Children ride without charge.]

Citizens may speak freely.
   [Citizens may speak without restraint.]

---

We must dig deep to discover the murderer's motive.
   [We must dig to a great (figurative) depth to discover the motive.]

We care deeply for our family pets.
   [We care profoundly or intensely for our family pets.]

Native speakers usually get these idioms right without even thinking. Editors need only avoid the sort of overthinking that leads to hypercorrection, that is, the addition of an unnecessary *ly* in the belief that adverbs must invariably take this form. In *The Careful Writer* (s.v. "overrefinement"), Bernstein cautions against "the Adverb Syndrome," the affectation of adding an unnecessary inflection ("muchly") or tampering with established idioms:

✗ I'm taking it easily this summer.
I'm taking it easy this summer.

✗ She's sitting prettily after inheriting her father's estate.
She's sitting pretty after inheriting her father's estate.

✗ The watch runs slowly.
The watch runs slow.

## MORE IMPORTANT AND MORE IMPORTANTLY

A final problem relating to adjectives and adverbs concerns the choice between *more important* and *more importantly* as a sentence modifier. In *The Elements of Style,* Strunk and White discourage the use of the adverbial *more importantly* in favor of the adjectival form, and many usage advisers have followed suit. But today's commentators accept these expressions as interchangeable. *Garner's* dismisses the prejudice against *more importantly* as "picayunish pedantry" (s.v. "more important[ly]").

> When working at your computer, make sure you are sitting in a comfortable position and maintaining a good posture. Your eyes should be level with the screen. More important, you should take five- to ten-minute breaks at least once an hour.

> *Or:* More importantly, you should take five- to ten-minute breaks at least once an hour.

## FEWER AND LESS

The schoolbook rule is this: use *fewer* for numbers and countable nouns; use *less* for quantity, measure, degree, and noncountable nouns. Thus, fewer apples, fewer books, and fewer cats, but less advice, less beef, and less comity. The conventional distinction is often codified in the mnemonic "Fewer cows, less milk."

*DEU*, however (s.v. "less, fewer"), notes that this "rule" was invented by Robert Baker, the author of *Reflections on the English Language* (1770): "Almost every usage writer since Baker has followed Baker's lead, and generations of English teachers have swelled the chorus. The result seems to be a fairly large number of people who now believe *less* used of countables to be wrong, though its standardness is easily demonstrated." The examples in *DEU* include "less than" preceding amounts with plural nouns and numbers (e.g., distances, sums of money, units of time, and statistical enumerations) and the idiomatic constructions "no less than," "*x* objects or less," and "one less *x*." The criterion for differentiating these words is not the presence or absence of numbers and count nouns, but rather the meaning: does the sentence refer to a countable number or to a unitary quantity?

> *Distance:* The closest store is less than 250 yards from here.

> *Money:* She made less than three hundred dollars at the flea market.

> *Time:* Teachers who have taught for less than five years are eligible for the stipend.

> *Statistics:* Less than 10 percent of applicants passed the test.

> *Idiom:* They were instructed to write a personal essay of five hundred words or less.

In the following examples either *less* or *fewer* may be appropriate, depending on the intended meaning.

> Seasonal workers are usually employed less [*or* fewer] than 150 days a year. [According to Follett (*MAU*, s.v. "fewer, less"), in this sentence "the ideas of quantity and number are hardly distinguishable. . . . Here 150 days can be felt as either a specified number of days or a unitary measure of time (as *less than half a year* would be)."]

Fewer [*or* Less] than one in four voters requested absentee ballots.

[Here, "one in four voters" may be construed as either a countable number or a unitary amount.]

Your troubles are less [*or* fewer] than mine.

[Both locutions are acceptable, though not identical in meaning. "Your troubles are less than mine" means "Your troubles are not as great as mine," and "Your troubles are fewer than mine" means "Your troubles are not as numerous as mine."]

As these examples show, native speakers and writers of English use *less* with count nouns in many constructions: the simple "rule" is misleading if it is too rigidly applied.[22] In some sentences, *fewer* might be preferable in formal prose; in others, no native speaker would choose anything but *less*. Although authors and editors are often quite passionate about this point of usage, it's inadvisable to be overzealous in emending idiomatic expressions.

## PREPOSITIONS

The most memorable dismissal of the hobgoblin about never ending a sentence with a preposition is attributed to Winston Churchill. When rebuked for this putative solecism, he is said to have retorted, "That is the type of arrant pedantry up with which I shall not put." The rebuttal is valid, even though the Churchill quotation, which has many variants and no verifiable source, is probably made up. Note this perfectly natural sentence: *made up* is an example of a *phrasal verb*, a two-part verb that includes a preposition or adverb. Some so-called prepositional endings to sentences are attached to phrasal verbs; others represent writers' efforts to produce natural, idiomatic English rather than stilted Latinate prose.

*Awkward:* About what are you writing?

*Better:* What are you writing about?

Although the superstition about prepositional endings is still afoot in some quarters (see *DEU,* s.v. "preposition at end"), the more pressing issue for copyeditors is to ensure that the author has selected the correct preposition. Few features of English are more challenging to nonnative speakers than prepositional idioms; even native speakers of English sometimes muddle them. In addition to consulting your dictionary, you might want to review the fourteen-page list "The Right Preposition" in *WIT,* which runs from "abashed: at, before, in" to "zeal: for, in"; or check out the section "Prepositional Idioms" ("aberration: from, of" to "zealous: about, in, for") in Garner's *Chicago Guide to Grammar, Usage, and Punctuation.*

22. One of William Safire's "On Language" columns in the *New York Times* reportedly convinced the Safeway supermarket chain to change the signs over its express checkout lanes from "10 items or less" to "10 items or fewer." Surely this hypercorrection violates an English idiom! *Garner's* proposes an alternative revision: "10 or fewer items." That works too.

Many people think that prepositions, like other "function words," constitute a relatively small list: *about, at, before, by, for, from, in, into, of, off, on, to, under, with,* and so forth. In fact, more than two hundred prepositions exist in English, and the list is ever expanding, with foreign imports (à la, après, apropos, chez, ex, in re, sans, via, vis-à-vis), reanimated antiquities (afore, athwart, ere, twixt), and novelties (post, as in: Post the 2008 financial meltdown . . .). The following paragraphs list a few troublesome prepositions and commonly confused pairs.

*All, all of.* In formal writing the predeterminer *all* is often used without the trailing preposition (all the children), except when the following term is a personal pronoun (all of us) or a possessive noun (all of John's luggage). Informal writing and speech, however, sometimes use the *of* before nouns (all of the children, all of that aggravation); it's not an error, but a matter of style.

*Awhile, for a while.* "For a while" is a set prepositional phrase; "awhile" is an adverb and is never preceded by "for."

> Let the paint dry for a while; then apply a second coat.
>
> Stay awhile!
>
> She said she would be gone for a while.
>
> *Or:* She said she would be gone awhile.

*Beside, besides.* The preposition *beside* means "alongside"; *besides* means "except" or "in addition to."

> The faithful dog lay beside the slain knight.
>
> No one besides Phyllis had the combination to the safe.
>
> Who did John invite besides us?

*Between, among.* The oversimplified guideline for distinguishing these prepositions holds that *between* is properly used for relationships involving two things, *among* for relationships involving more than two. Nonsense! *Between* describes one-to-one relationships, regardless of the number of entities involved, whereas *among* describes collective, vague, and diffuse relationships.

> Talks between the world's nuclear powers have been scheduled.
>
> The inheritance was divided equally between the three siblings.
>
> The wrecked car came to rest among the trees.
>
> The gossip among the employees focused on the latest office romance.

*Compare with, compare to.* "Compare with" describes the usually literal similarities and differences between things, point by point; it is the expression that predominates in APA style and in most scientific writing. "Compare to" describes similarities of a figurative nature.

Compared with the job benefits once secured by union teamsters, the perks offered to contract drivers are negligible.

Shall I compare thee to a summer's day?

*Couple, couple of.* As a noun meaning "a pair" or, more indefinitely, "a few," *couple* must be followed by the preposition *of* (a couple of beers). The adjectival use of *couple,* that is, without the trailing preposition (a couple beers), emerged in the late twentieth century. Although condemned by some advisers, this usage is now commonplace in informal writing and speech: most English speakers probably hear it a couple of times a day.

*Due to.* Some traditionalists still parse *due to* as the adjective *due* followed by the preposition *to,* rather than treating *due to* as a compound preposition like *because of* or *owing to.* In the traditionalists' view, the adjective *due* must have a noun to modify, and thus *due to* is correct only as a substitute for *attributable to:*

The delays at the Denver airport were due to bad weather in Chicago.

But this preference is largely ignored, and all but the most fastidious purists allow *due to* as a substitute for *because of* or *owing to:*

Planes were delayed at the Denver airport due to bad weather in Chicago.

*Into, in to.* The preposition *into* is used with a verb of motion to indicate entry, insertion, or inclusion (movement toward the inside of a place). One prays "Lead us not into temptation"; one goes into a building, jumps into a lake, drives into a garage, or enters into a pact. *Into* is also used to indicate

*involvement:* check into the facts; take into account
*occupation:* go into teaching
*condition:* get into trouble, get into a fight
*extent:* far into the night
*direction:* look into the sky
*contact:* run into a wall
*transformation:* turn into a frog

In contrast, *in to* is the adverb *in* (an adverb because it "completes" the meaning of a verb, e.g., hand something in) followed by the preposition *to,* which links the verb to an indirect object:

They turned themselves in to the police.

He handed the memo in to his supervisor.

We refused to give in to his demands.

*On line, in line, online.* All across the country, people stand *in* line; but in the greater metropolitan New York area, people stand *on* line. Both expressions are acceptable.

Manufactured items are produced *on* an assembly line—never *in* one. *Online,* an adverb, means "connected to a computer network."

*Onto, on to. Onto* is used to indicate movement to a position on or atop something: they ran onto the field; he wandered onto the grounds; the cat jumped onto the desk. *Onto* is also used to indicate attachment: hook this wire onto the nail. And *onto* is used colloquially to mean "aware of": she's onto his methods; they're onto us. In contrast, *on to* is the adverb *on* followed by the preposition *to:* please hold on to this; pass the news on to her; they flew on to London.

*Toward, towards. Toward* predominates in American English, *towards* in British English. Both spellings are legitimate and may be used interchangeably, but most US copyeditors—sometimes to the annoyance of authors—consistently enforce the former spelling in manuscripts prepared for US readers.

*Unlike in, unlike with.* Fowler (1965) and other commentators have criticized these informal adverbial constructions, but they are widespread in both British and American English: "Unlike in US libel cases, the truth of a defamatory statement may not be recognized as sufficient legal exoneration in British courts." In formal prose they are often replaced by "in contrast to," "as distinct from"—or simply "unlike" without the trailing preposition, provided the revision does not result in a faulty comparison such as the one exemplified under "Dangling and Misplaced Modifiers" above. As a preposition, *unlike* takes an objective-case noun or pronoun, just as constructions with the preposition *like* do: unlike me, my brother completed college.

*Until, till, 'til.* Both *until* and *till* are legitimate prepositions and may be used interchangeably, although *till* is a tad less formal. *'Til* is a fake contraction with literary pretensions. Don't use it except facetiously.

*Versus.* From the Latin, meaning "toward," this preposition is now used to mean "in opposition to," "in contrast to," or "as an alternative to" and is fully standard. (A search for "versus" in *The Chicago Manual of Style Online* returns more than 130 hits; searches for "vs." and "v." produce additional results, the former for abbreviations in *Chicago's* index, the latter for examples of legal citations.) Stylists recommend maintaining parallel structure for the terms contrasted or opposed using *versus.*

> *Poor:* According to the 2000 US Census, median household income in Aspen was $53,750 versus $47,203 in Colorado and $41,994 nationally.

> *Better:* According to the 2000 US Census, median household income was $53,750 in Aspen versus $47,203 in Colorado and $41,994 nationally.

*Via.* From the Latin, *via* originally meant "by way of a location, a route" (flew to Milan via Paris); in its extended use the word denotes "by means of" or "through the agency of" (via courier, via the internet). The latter usage was at one time disparaged but is now standard.

## MISCELLANEOUS BUGABOOS

"Step on a crack, break your mother's back!" Many child editors learned to dodge cracks on the sidewalk after hearing this rhyme—or after being inducted into the Cult of Copyediting, with its secret knowledge and quaint customs. Gradually editors uncover the half-truths and superstitions, the spurious rules that Theodore Bernstein called hobgoblins, and begin to discard them along the way. The following is an excerpt from a seasoned editor's long list of untruths that were discarded on her journey.

*And.* The belief that a sentence should never begin with *and* or another coordinate conjunction (the traditional "FANBOYS" list is *for, and, nor, but, or, yet, so*) was once widely taught to young writers in elementary school. But there is no foundation for this belief. And conscientious writers everywhere use these brief words to connect ideas.

*As.* English has a causal *as* and a temporal *as.* Some would banish the causal conjunction for the sake of the temporal one. Instead, writers should confine the weak-kneed causal *as* to sentences in which there is no possibility that readers will mistake it for the temporal *as:*

> *Temporal:* As the overnight temperatures dropped, the road became icy and slick.

> *Causal:* As Lila had no need for another hammer, she walked past the display without stopping.

> *Ambiguous:* As the rain continued into the evening, Pat felt morose.

And because *as* is so weak an indicator of causality, it seems too lightweight when the cause-and-effect relation concerns a matter of any import:

> *Inappropriate:* As the parts are no longer available, the entire unit has to be replaced.

> *Inappropriate:* As the earthquake caused the double-deck freeway to collapse, new seismic-safety regulations are under discussion.

*As, like.* In the 1950s a bit of a brouhaha erupted when a cigarette maker claimed that its product tasted "good, like a cigarette should" rather than "as a cigarette should." In the parsers' analysis, a conjunction must be used to link the clauses "Winston tastes good" and "a cigarette should," and the most punctilious parsers insisted that *like* was a preposition, not a conjunction. *DEU* (s.v. "like, as, as if"), however, notes that *like* has been used as a conjunction "for more than 600 years. . . . A noticeable increase in use during the 19th century provoked the censure we are so familiar with. . . . [Since then] the belief that *like* is a preposition but not a conjunction has entered the folklore of usage. . . . Be prepared."

If you don't want to make waves, you can apply the following conventions:

- Use *as, as if,* or *as though* to express similarities or comparisons that involve a verb.

  Mark the proofs as shown in the example.

  We are pledged to upholding democracy, as were our forebears.

  They sing as if they were angels.

  He played the concerto as though possessed by the spirit of Stravinsky.

- Use *like* to express similarities or comparisons that involve a noun.

  This example is like the previous one.

  They sing like angels.

  His music is like Stravinsky's later work.

*Cannot help but.*   Follett approves of three idioms for expressing inevitability—"I cannot help doing it," "I cannot but do it," and "I can but do it"—but excoriates a fourth, "I cannot help but do it," as a "grammarless mixture" (*MAU,* s.v. "help"). Both grammar and logic, however, yield to idiom, as illustrated by the citations in *DEU,* which labels all four constructions standard (s.v. "cannot but, cannot help, cannot help but").

*However.*   Beginning a sentence with *however* was once branded a grammatical error, but it's not. A sentence-opening *however* is merely cumbersome if one of the more streamlined coordinators (*but, yet*) will do the job. But when *however* is used to contradict or qualify the entire preceding sentence, the initial spot is natural. The placement is a matter of style and emphasis, but burial deep within the sentence is usually not recommended.

*Since.*   Just as English has a bivalent *as,* so English is also blessed with the temporal *since* and the causal *since:*

   *Temporal:* Since 1990 the state has constructed twelve new prisons.

   *Causal:* Since new prisons provide jobs, town officials courted the state prison commissioners.

Because *since* has these two meanings, some prescriptivists urge writers to shun the causal *since,* lest readers mistake a causal *since* for a temporal one. But banning the causal *since* deprives writers of a much-needed tool: a causal conjunction that is weaker than *because* and stronger than *as.* The sensible course is to avoid using *since* in sentences in which the temporal and causal meanings contend:

   *Ambiguous:* Since the state has spent so much money on prisons, the education budget has suffered.

   *Ambiguous:* Since the female prison population has doubled, the number of children in foster care has increased by 35 percent.

*Which.* Commentators once held that the relative pronoun *which* must refer to a specific antecedent and could never represent an entire preceding clause. Untrue. A writer need only be concerned to avoid ambiguity, for example, when the relative pronoun might be interpreted as referring either to the entire preceding clause or to a specific noun at the end of the clause, as in

> OSHA did not play an active role during the recovery operation, which is typical in emergency responses.
> [*Which* = recovery operation? *Which* = OSHA did not play an active role during the recovery operation?]

In fact, *Garner's* (s.v. "which") acknowledges some special stylistic uses of *which* at the head of an incomplete sentence: to add emphasis to a conclusion following an especially long sentence or a series of sentences, or to create a dramatic effect following a short sentence.

*While.* All dictionaries acknowledge that *while* has a temporal meaning ("during the time that" or "at the same time that"), a concessive meaning ("although"), and a contrastive meaning ("whereas"). *DEU* (s.v. "while") notes that although the earliest meanings of *while* are temporal, "senses unrelated to time have been established in English since Shakespeare's time." Nonetheless, some prescriptivists reject the use of *while* as a synonym for *although* or *whereas.* Follett's judgment is among the more vitriolic: "To write that something happened today *while* something else happened ten years ago is to work hard at achieving contradiction" (*MAU,* s.v. "while").

But all the other experts agree with *Fowler's* (s.v. "while") that "contrived, if amusing, examples apart, the temporal, concessive, and contrastive uses of *while* . . . do not create ambiguity" in most circumstances. For copyeditors, then, the task is not to eradicate the concessive or contrastive *while* but to make sure that no ambiguity follows in its wake. Also, as Bernstein points out (*Miss Thistlebottom's Hobgoblins,* p. 85), careful writers and editors reject the use of *while* to mean "and":

> ✗ The older computers have been moved to the basement, while the new ones are in the main office.

# CHAPTER 15

# ❡ Beyond Grammar

There is no easy way to catalog all the types of structural, conceptual, and stylistic problems a copyeditor encounters. In this chapter, we'll look at how copyeditors handle common problems in several broad areas: organization; point of view; expository style; plain language compliance; accessibility considerations; global English; bias-free language; and publishing law.

## ORGANIZATION

The overall structure of a piece (whether a report, an article, or a book) is dictated by its central purpose. As you read a manuscript, be sure you can discern the structure of the entire piece and each major section of the text. Look at the table of contents and the opening and closing paragraphs of each chapter (for a book), the headings and subheadings (for an article), or the opening sentences of each paragraph (for a short essay). Copyeditors are usually instructed not to fix large-scale structural deviations—doubling back, omissions—but are expected to bring them to the author's attention. Easily repaired minor structural errors should be corrected and flagged for the author's attention.

### FORMS OF ORGANIZATION

*Alphabetical order* is useful for directories, inventories, glossaries, and catalogs. Note, however, that if the work is to be translated into another language, the alphabetized elements—with the exception of personal names—will have to be reordered. For example, the alphabetical sequence "England, France, Germany, Spain" would have to be reordered as "Alemania, España, Francia, Inglaterra" if the document were to be translated into Spanish.

*Chronological order* is useful for historical studies, biographies, memoirs, and step-by-step how-to manuals. Within a broadly chronological framework, some biographers, historians, and memoirists incorporate flashbacks or flash-forwards. When used effectively, these out-of-sequence episodes can emphasize key points or create tension, drama, or suspense. The pitfalls, however, are that poorly handled flashbacks and flash-forwards may confuse the reader, loosen the narrative tension, or require the author to spend too much time backtracking or repeating information.

*Numerical order* can be used to organize analyses of alternative proposals or choices: from smallest to largest, from least expensive to most expensive (or vice versa).

*Spatial order* can be used to organize geographical surveys (from northeast to south-west), fashion books (from head to toe), and auto repair manuals (from front fender to back bumper).

*Degree of difficulty* is a principle used in many instructional books: the easiest topics are presented first, and succeeding sections build on those basic topics.

A *system-by-system* approach is often used for studies of complex physical organisms, social systems, or manufacturing processes and procedures. For example, a medical book might describe the circulatory system, the nervous system, the digestive system, and so on. A book on the federal government's role in ensuring free speech might have three principal parts: the executive branch, the legislative branch, and the judicial branch.

Short documents may follow the contours of the author's method of inquiry:

> *Compare and contrast.* After an overview of the subject or theme, the author points out the similarities and differences between A and B. The author then analyzes how or why A and B differ and explains the significance of those differentiating factors.
>
> *Observations and predictions.* The author describes the investigative methods (e.g., lab experiments, fieldwork, library research), presents the pattern of observations, offers an explanation for that pattern of findings, and explains the significance of that pattern or makes predictions based on that pattern.
>
> *Problem and solution.* The author defines a problem, explains how the quantitative or qualitative dimensions of the problem were measured, describes a solution to the problem, and discusses how the solution resolved (or can be expected to resolve) all or part of the problem.
>
> *Argument.* The author proposes a thesis and presents the data or reasons (usually from most important to least important) that support his or her point of view. Counterarguments may also be presented and disposed of.

Other arrangements are possible. For example, recipes in a cookbook can be arranged

> in alphabetical order (from abalone to zucchini)
> in diurnal order (from breakfast to after-dinner snacks)
> in seasonal order (from springtime meals to wintertime meals)
> course by course (appetizers, main dishes, salads, desserts)
> by difficulty of preparation (from hard-boiled eggs to Beef Wellington)
> by geographical provenance (from northern Europe to southern Europe and northern Africa)
> by cooking technique (boiling, broiling, sautéing, pan frying)
> by food groups (breads, meats, fruits, vegetables)

Sometimes an author's ordering principle is not transparent. For example, a discussion of the traditional list of planets in our solar system (i.e., including the "dwarf planet" Pluto) may treat the planets in any of the following sequences:

| A | B | C |
|---|---|---|
| Earth | Mercury | Jupiter |
| Jupiter | Venus | Saturn |
| Mars | Earth | Neptune |
| Mercury | Mars | Uranus |
| Neptune | Jupiter | Earth |
| Pluto | Saturn | Mars |
| Saturn | Uranus | Pluto |
| Uranus | Neptune | Mercury |
| Venus | Pluto | Venus |

Obviously, sequence A relies on alphabetization. But only copyeditors who remember their elementary school science will immediately detect that sequence B presents the planets in order of their mean distance from the sun, from the closest to the farthest, and even most of that select editorial group is likely to be stumped by sequence C, which presents the planets in order of their period of rotation, from the shortest to the longest. The best editorial response to a set of items whose order appears random is to query the author ("What is the ordering principle here? Are these items in order?") rather than to assume that reordering is needed.

Items presented in lists, tables, and other arrays should also be in order, whether alphabetical, chronological, numerical, spatial, or according to some other scheme. For example, each of the following lists needs to be reordered.

| Electoral votes (1996) | | Atlantic coastline (miles) | |
|---|---|---|---|
| Alabama | 9 | Maine | 228 |
| Alaska | 3 | New Hampshire | 13 |
| Arkansas | 6 | Massachusetts | 192 |
| Arizona | 8 | Rhode Island | 40 |
| Colorado | 8 | New Jersey | 130 |
| California | 54 | New York | 127 |

Since the list of states by electoral strength appears to be alphabetical, Arizona must precede Arkansas, and California must precede Colorado. (However, if a query to the author establishes that the ordering principle is the number of electoral votes, only Alabama is out of place.) The list of North Atlantic coast states, however, does not appear to be intended as an alphabetical list. Rather, it seems that the author is following the coastline from north to south. Thus the copyeditor would request an entry for Connecticut (after Rhode Island) and move the entry for New Jersey down, after the entry for New York. Or the copyeditor might suggest an alternative ordering scheme if it better serves the readers.

An inept strategy for organizing written content into bulleted lists has become commonplace, owing to the popularity of contemporary presentation software—applications such as PowerPoint and Keynote. Excessive use of bullet-point lists, especially without a narrative context, has become so widespread in writing for business, government, and education that the affliction has sometimes been described as *PowerPoint-itis* (or *Keynote-itis*). To be sure, lists of items can serve many legitimate purposes, including pedagogical ones: this book makes frequent use of lists. But slides supporting an oral presentation in which a speaker elaborates on displayed bullet points do not directly translate into an appropriate format for readers of discursive text. Such lists may be suitable for writing on the web because readers often quickly scan webpages for pertinent information, but text intended for print and other narrative-form publications to be read closely must supply context and transitions. Editors should prompt authors to elaborate list items or, better still, to convert them into running text.

## EMPHASIS

The major points in a piece should be emphasized by their prominent location and the length of their treatment. Relatively minor points should receive minor attention. Detours from the main points, dead ends, straw-man arguments (that is, weak points raised solely to be refuted), and irrelevant details should be severely restricted or eliminated.

Copyeditors should query minor infractions of these principles: "Paragraphs on semiconductors seem off the point here—consider moving (perhaps to p. 12), trimming, or deleting." If you encounter serious problems, consult your editorial coordinator before you spend time suggesting major structural changes.

In some types of texts, the issue of placement is more than a matter of logic or aesthetics. For example, in training or instructional materials that describe hazardous procedures, any warnings or precautions should precede—not follow—the description of the step to be taken.

*Original:* Insert the probe into slot A (see diagram 2). Make sure the unit is unplugged before you insert the probe.

*Revision:* Unplug the unit. Insert the probe into slot A (see diagram 2).

*Or:* WARNING: Unplug the unit before you begin the following procedure.
   Insert the probe into slot A (see diagram 2).

## CROSS-REFERENCES

Some kinds of documents require or benefit from cross-references that lead readers to look at (or recall) another part of the text. As chapter 10 notes, each table and figure in a document is given a number, and a cross-reference is placed in the text to direct the reader's attention to the item. Similarly, appendixes to a document are labeled (Appendix A, Appendix B, etc.) and introduced in the main body of the text by means of cross-references.

Cross-references may also be used to refer readers to chapters and other parts in a book or to sections in a document. When copyeditors encounter such cross-references, they are expected to verify that each is correct and to revise the cross-references if sections of text are relocated or cut during the editing.

Some publishers strongly discourage, or even prohibit, authors from using cross-references to specific page numbers because they entail extra work in the page proofs for print publications and are worthless in digital publications that don't preserve a fixed-page layout. The issue for a printed book is that the correct page numbers cannot be inserted until the document is in final page form. At that time, the proofreader must locate all the placeholders for page-number cross-references (e.g., "see pages 00–00" or "see pages ▮▮–▮▮"), replace the placeholders with the correct page numbers, and hope that no further repagination of the document will be made. So that the replacement of the placeholders will not require adding or subtracting characters from a line of text (and possibly producing bad line breaks, widows, or orphans), the thoughtful copyeditor tries to estimate the correct number of digits for each page-number placeholder. Thus if the cross-referenced page falls toward the end of a book-length manuscript, the placeholder should have three digits ("see page 000"), not one or two. Because page-specific cross-references are meaningless in e-books without fixed page numbers, they should be avoided in manuscripts intended for digital publication.

In some documents, cross-references by chapter may not be very helpful to the reader. If the chapters are long, for example, or if the cross-reference is only to a small portion of a chapter, a cross-reference by chapter number alone will not help readers locate the relevant section of text (especially if the document does not have an index). One way to provide for closer cross-references without using page numbers is to direct readers to a major heading within a chapter:

> The technical specifications are given in chapter 5, under "CPU Specs."

> For more information, see "Crossing the Frontier" in chapter 12.

Another way to provide for close cross-referencing without resorting to page-number references is to insert section numbers, or even paragraph numbers, in the document. For example, most cross-references in *Chicago* are of the form "see 6.24–27," where *6* is the chapter number and *24–27* the section numbers. This system obviates the need for page-number placeholders but does require the rechecking of all cross-references if sections are cut or moved during copyediting or cleanup.

Casual cross-references sometimes just rely on "above" and "below" to identify local content appearing earlier and later in the text, respectively. In print documents, more precise cross-references—for example, to tables, figures, or equations by number—are preferable because the placement of such floating elements "above" or "below" their cross-references cannot be confirmed until pages are composed. In digital formats, the terms "above" and "below" may be irrelevant for tables and graphics accessed by means of an embedded link. But this casual convention is handy when greater specificity is not possible and there is no confusion about what is meant. Writers may use (but should avoid overusing) such generic signals to avoid creating the impression of inadvertent repetition ("As I mentioned above . . .") or to point to an important building block in an argument ("A second approach is suggested below . . .").

## SIGNPOSTING

Despite the convenience of such tools for cross-referencing, good writers avoid too much *signposting,* the use of phrases that refer backward or forward to other parts of the text. Although an occasional cross-reference can help the reader follow the thread of a complex argument or a long document, the use of unduly frequent or long signposts is dizzying, and copyeditors should help writers eliminate these cross-references.

> *Disorienting:* As we have seen in chapter 1 and will examine in more detail in chapters 4 and 6 . . .

> *Disorienting:* But this point is getting ahead of the argument, and we will return to it after we have laid the proper groundwork.

> *Disorienting:* Now that we have seen the three major causes of the citizens' discontent—high property taxes, poor municipal services, and unresponsive local officials—and the role of the two major grassroots groups, the Community Action Caucus and the Citizens Taskforce, we need to consider the relationship between local politics and regional issues.

Frequent thickets of signposts may also indicate faulty overall organization. In such cases, the solution is to recommend that the author consider reordering the pieces of the document to better serve the reader.

## POINT OF VIEW

The misguided advice of some grade school English teachers has taught many a writer to avoid first-person singular pronouns altogether. Although an objective point of view is often desirable in formal and professional prose, the unqualified proscription against *I* (*me, my, mine*) can result in evasive language, sometimes with ludicrous effect:

> The present writer argues that . . .

> It is the opinion of this book that . . .

Or the scrupulous avoidance of first-person pronouns may require excessive recourse to passive voice constructions:

> It is argued in this book that . . .

> It is concluded in this paper that . . .

Some solo writers adopt "the editorial *we*" as a depersonalizing strategy, but this convention is appropriate only when a writer is actually representing or reporting on behalf of a group. *APA,* among other style guides, recommends that *we* be used only for the multiple authors (and *I* for the single author) of a publication. *We* is otherwise potentially confusing and possibly presumptuous: does it refer to all individuals in a field of study or endeavor? to all of humanity? Either replacing the first-person plural pronoun with a specific noun or clarifying the pronoun referent offers a simple solution:

*Not:* We conducted a survey . . .

*But:* The principal investigators conducted a survey for this report . . .

*Not:* We often agree that . . .

*But:* Counselors often agree that . . .

*Not:* We seek . . .

*But:* As analysts, we seek . . .

The second-person pronoun, *you,* is frequently recommended for cookbooks, instructions, and other how-to books. The *Microsoft Manual of Style,* for example, coaches writers and editors to adopt *you* when preparing Microsoft's technical documentation: "Second person supports a friendly tone because it connects you with the user. It also helps avoid passive voice because it focuses the discussion on the user" (p. 9).

Writing guides, like couples counselors, invariably caution authors to avoid not only excessive *I*s but also accusatory *you*s:

*Not:* If you forget to back up your computer daily, you risk losing all your work.

*But:* Protect your work by remembering to back up your computer daily.

Regardless of the point of view adopted, it should be maintained consistently. Sudden appearances of *I, me, my,* and *mine,* for example, can be distracting in a document framed in the third person.

## EXPOSITORY STYLE

As chapter 3 notes, there are several useful books on expository style, but most of them are, quite naturally, addressed to writers. For copyeditors, however, the task is not to develop one's own style nor to revise a manuscript to meet one's own taste. Rather, the task is to decide which kinks or knots in someone else's writing seem likely to disrupt communication with the intended readers and then to revise those patches as unobtrusively as possible.

These judgments are among the most difficult a copyeditor makes, and they require a careful assessment of both the author's purpose and the intended audience. As long as a sentence is grammatically correct, for example, minor stylistic infelicities will not trouble or perplex most readers of a technical report or a business document, although a series of off-kilter sentences may confuse or distract all but the very determined. But readers of scholarly books and serious trade books are likely to have higher expectations and may dismiss the work of an author who disappoints them.

Judgments about issues of style also require copyeditors to undertake a bit of self-examination. Before making discretionary changes to a manuscript, you might pause a moment to ensure that your proposed revisions are motivated by an effort to help the author improve the manuscript for the sake of the readers—not by a desire to prove that you are a better writer than the author is, not by the need to make every document conform to your tastes, and not by the fear that any sentence left unmarked will leave you open to criticism for not having sufficiently high standards.

For copyeditors, the perils of doing too much rewording often outweigh the hazards of doing too little: every time you make a change, you run the risk of misinterpreting the author's meaning, inadvertently introducing an error, frustrating the author's goodwill, and overshooting your editorial schedule or budget.

The amount of time a copyeditor spends unkinking and unknotting sentences and paragraphs thus depends on the nature of the project and the level-of-edit instructions that accompany it. Here, we focus on common problems that can be corrected with minimal intervention.

## DICTION

The standard advice on *diction,* or word choice, is the Fowler brothers' five-part dictum: "Prefer the familiar word to the far-fetched, prefer the concrete to the abstract, prefer the single word to the circumlocution, prefer the short word to the long, and prefer the Saxon word to the Romance."[1] Many high school and college students encounter these preferences, converted into commandments, in Strunk and White's *The Elements of Style* ("Avoid fancy words"; "Use definite, specific, concrete language"; "Omit needless words"; "Use figures of speech sparingly"; "Prefer the standard to the offbeat") or in George Orwell's essay "Politics and the English Language."[2]

Unfortunately, some copyeditors take these proposals too seriously and enforce them with a self-defeating rigor. Self-defeating because the author who uses the occasional far-fetched word, abstraction, circumlocution, or polysyllabic Latinate term will question the judgment of a copyeditor who appears to be "dumbing down" the text. The goal for the copyeditor is not to eradicate every unusual or unnecessary word and thereby turn every sentence into a predictable procession of neat monosyllables. Rather, the goal is to identify those patches of text in which so many far-fetched, abstract, or polysyllabic words cluster that the reader either loses the thread of the discussion or questions the expertise, skill, or judgment of the writer.

*Level of diction.* A writer's word choices set the tone for a piece (formal, informal, colloquial). In general, slang and colloquialisms are suitable only in highly informal pieces,

---

1. H. W. Fowler and F. G. Fowler, *The King's English,* 3rd ed. (1931; repr., London: Oxford University Press, 1973), p. 11.

2. Working from the premise that ridding ourselves of bad linguistic habits is the first step toward clear thinking and "political regeneration," Orwell proposes six rules:

  (i)   Never use a metaphor, simile or other figure of speech which you are used to seeing in print.
  (ii)  Never use a long word where a short one will do.
  (iii) If it is possible to cut a word out, always cut it out.
  (iv)  Never use the passive where you can use the active.
  (v)   Never use a foreign phrase, a scientific word or a jargon word if you can think of an everyday English equivalent.
  (vi)  Break any of these rules sooner than say anything outright barbarous.

"Politics and the English Language" (1946), in *A Collection of Essays by George Orwell* (New York: Doubleday Anchor, 1954), p. 176.

while sesquipedalian Latinisms are rarely appropriate outside academic journals. Still, a well-chosen word from a level that is noticeably higher or lower than the rest of the piece can add a touch of emphasis, realism, or humor. But when an unimportant word calls too much attention to itself, a copyeditor may replace it or ask the author to select a substitute from a short list of synonyms.

Under the guise of making life easier for readers, some copyeditors change a word merely because they are unfamiliar with it and had to look it up in the dictionary. This impulse seems misguided. Obviously, unusual words have no place in instructions for handling a toxic spill; emergency crews do not carry dictionaries to disaster sites. But for articles and books addressed to educated adults, there is no reason to restrict the author to some hypothetical list of five or ten thousand common words. As long as the word appears in the dictionary (abridged or unabridged) and the author has used it correctly, there's no reason for you to replace it.

But when you are copyediting books designed for young readers or for readers whose native language is not English, you may be asked to restrict the vocabulary to a "grade-appropriate" list or to those words that appear in a particular abridged or bilingual dictionary. Likewise, editors of content intended for a global readership that includes nonnative English speakers should replace culture-specific idioms with simple, direct language. Nonliteral idioms—that is, colloquial phrases used by a specific language community to mean something other than what the words literally say—can confuse nonnative speakers, not to mention machine-translation software. There's no easy way to explain (or to robo-translate) such phrases as "keep tabs on," "go bananas," "chip on the shoulder," or "bought the farm."

*Neologisms.* "Robo-translate"? Either consciously or inadvertently, writers often deploy the rich inventiveness of English to coin new terms. Some nonce words, such as *robo-translate* (combining *robo-*, "automatic," with a base word), serve a momentary purpose and quickly fade into obscurity—if they are not immediately stamped out by a zealous copyeditor. Others, like *mansplaining,* inspired by the writer Rebecca Solnit ("Men Explain Things to Me"), spread rapidly in the general culture, especially through social media. If coinages endure, they are eventually recorded in dictionaries. (In September 2017 Merriam-Webster announced the addition of some 250 new words and definitions to its dictionary, including *ransomware,* malware that disables a computer until a ransom is paid, and *froyo,* frozen yogurt.) New words often take root in the language owing to their brevity, novelty, or specificity. They may be more compact than earlier expressions, they may seem exceptionally hip or clever, or they may connect to a specific context (e.g., technology) or group (e.g., women) and offer a nuance of meaning not provided by existing vocabulary.

Among the most common neologisms are conversions and back-formations, the creation of new words either by using old words in new ways (an ask, a disconnect) or by removing an affix (to enthuse, to liaise, to burgle, to incent). Copyeditors are rightly wary of authors' lexical inventiveness, especially of the penchant for "*verbing* nouns" (an example of that very thing), but they need not trounce every novelty just because it's not in the dictionary (yet). Even unabridged dictionaries do not include every word in the language, and new words may swim in the linguistic soup for several decades before being classified and recorded by a lexical authority. Although prescriptivist usage mavens and language peevers are often resistant to linguistic innovation, a copyeditor's job is not to censor all novel vocabulary but rather to judge whether a new word is clear and effective or distracting and inappropriate in tone.

*Jargon.* Word choice also gives cues to the readers about the author's conception of them. Shop talk, jargon, and lingo should be reserved for publications aimed at a specialized audience that is familiar with the argot. Academic writers may use *reference* and *problematize* as verbs; psychologists and counselors may recommend or practice *active listening.* When such terms are used in documents intended for a general readership—perhaps to give readers the flavor of conversation in the field—translations should be appended, either in parentheses or introduced by a "that is" or a "which means." At times, you will need to ask the author to supply a sentence or two that explains to lay readers the significance of the jargon. For example, the manuscript reads

> Some economists have revised their estimate of the NAIRU from 6 percent to as low as 5.3 percent.

If the piece is for a specialized audience, you might assume that readers will recognize NAIRU or you might ask the author to supply the spelled-out form of *NAIRU.* But if the piece is for a general readership, you would ask the author both to spell out *NAIRU* and to add an explanation of what NAIRU is. In response, the author might offer the following:

> According to basic economic theory, low rates of unemployment put upward
> pressures on wages, and higher wages translate into higher rates of inflation.
> The healthiest economy, therefore, is one which has the lowest rate of unem-
> ployment that does not cause inflation to accelerate. Some economists have
> revised their estimate of this magic number, known as NAIRU (nonaccelerating
> inflation rate of unemployment), from 6 percent to as low as 5.3 percent.

Beware of jargon that has different meanings to specialists and lay readers. To lawyers, *actionable* signifies "affording ground for legal action or a lawsuit," whereas to ordinary mortals trying to sound officious it simply means "providing a basis for action" or "capable of being put into practice." To psychologists, the phrase *steep learning curve,* derived from a graph plotting knowledge acquisition against time, means "easy to learn," because the rapid acquisition of substantial knowledge forms a steep curve on the graph; to general readers, however, the phrase has come to mean the very opposite, "difficult to learn," because steep hills are hard to climb. In medicine and pharmacology, the distinction between a *dose* and a *dosage,* terms often used interchangeably by nonspecialists, is critical. In computer manuals, *choose, select,* and *click* signify different actions.

*Noun stacks.* Writers who value concision, especially in business, technical, and government documents, often attempt to compress their prose by stacking successions of attributive nouns in front of the words they modify: customer satisfaction evaluation procedure, control panel software installation guide, employee benefits package exclusions consultant. (This mannerism is so prevalent in some fields that humorists have constructed four- and five-column tables of assorted terminology and invited users to generate new jargon, just for laughs, by randomly selecting one word from each column.) Clusters of four or more nouns are difficult to parse, even for native English speakers and industry or government insiders. Sometimes the meaning can be deciphered only with an author's help. Most writing guides advise breaking apart these stacks, when possible, by hyphenating unit modifiers, using possessives, and expanding clusters of nouns into prepositional phrases and relative clauses: procedure for evaluating customer satisfaction? guide for installing the control-panel software? consultant who interprets exclusions from the package of employee benefits?

*Deadwood.* Some words and phrases add bulk, but nothing of substance, to the text. The occasional redundancy or circumlocution is fine and may even be commendable if it emphasizes a key point or provides a bit of relief in a patch of extremely dense text. But copyeditors should help authors prune brambles that obscure the meaning or force the reader to work too hard for too little gain.

*Redundancies*

| | | |
|---|---|---|
| adequate enough | habitual custom | prejudge in advance |
| big in size | important essentials | serious danger |
| bisect in two | joint cooperation | sufficient enough |
| close proximity | major breakthrough | total annihilation |
| descend down | paramount | trained professional |
| eliminate altogether | importance | violent explosion |
| few in number | past history | warn in advance |
| final outcome | persist still | |
| follow after | plan in advance | |

*Circumlocutions*

| | |
|---|---|
| a large proportion of (= many) | in spite of the fact that (= although) |
| are in possession of (= have) | in the not too distant future (= soon) |
| as being (e.g., regarded as being the best = regarded as the best) | in the vicinity of (= near) |
| | made a statement saying |
| as of now (= now) | (= stated, said) |
| as of yet (= yet) | provide a description of (= describe) |
| as to (e.g., debate as to = debate [on]) | put in an appearance (= appear) |
| at present (= now) | take into consideration (= consider) |
| at this point in time (= now) | was of the opinion that |
| for the time being (= now) | (= believed, thought, said) |
| in this day and age (= now) | was witness to (= saw) |

Notice, for example, what pruning can do for this briar:

> In spite of the fact that a large proportion of parents are at this point in time of the opinion that schools need trained professional nurses, there is a serious danger that funding for these jobs will be eliminated altogether in the not too distant future. [Forty-six words.]

> Although many parents now believe that schools need nurses, funding for these jobs may soon be eliminated. [Sixteen words.]

Leaner writing is often produced by weeding out excess nominalizations (especially nouns formed from verbs by adding *-tion*) and the accompanying prepositional phrases with *of*. But the effort to prune deadwood should never dissolve into knee-jerk deletions. Surely "methods that are new at this point in time" sounds better than "methods that are new now" or (gasp!) "the now new methods." Nor should a copyeditor insist that authors always avoid the copyeditor's pet-peeve phrases. Some copyeditors, for example, routinely eliminate the "of" in "all of," "any of," "both of," and "half of" even though these variants are acceptable and are sometimes crucial to syntactic structure. Other editors may strike the first two words of almost every "in order to" and delete any "that" that they believe is not absolutely required. While such practices are useful when space is at a premium, in most cases these deletions do not substantially improve the author's sentence. Worse still, although such elisions may save a few millimeters of space, the resulting text can be confusing or ambiguous, especially for nonnative English speakers and for international readers deciphering a machine-translated version. For example, the following sentence is clear and correct:

> Congress modified the administration's proposal in order to exempt small businesses.

If a parsimonious copyeditor deletes the "in order," the meaning is ambiguous:

> Congress modified the administration's proposal to exempt small businesses.

Likewise, the omission of "that" in the following sentence makes parsing difficult, even for proficient English speakers:

> Some security analysts fail to recognize sufficiently the human beings who use computers constitute the greatest security risk.

In sum, you must continuously weigh the value of brevity against the value of clarity:

> The thoughtful writer strives not for mere conciseness, but also for ease of communication. Many of the little phrases that brevity buffs think unnecessary are the lubrication that helps to smooth the way for your message to get across. (*DEU,* s.v. "in order to")

*Clichés.* In the universe of clichés, the only place lines are drawn is in the sand; all opinions are considered or humble, and all plans are best laid; each swoop is fell, every end is bitter, and every peeve is pet. Writers and copyeditors are always told to shun clichés, but this maxim is overly broad and unenforceable. The occasional cliché is almost unavoidable and does little harm; after all, set phrases become set because they are use-ful. (Why reinvent the wheel?) Moreover, a phrase that is a cliché to one clique of read-ers may seem fresh and vivid to another, if the expression has not yet migrated beyond the in-group into general circulation. Then, too, given the pace at which phrases become shopworn, even the diligent cliché stomper can barely keep up. The honest answer to the question "What is a cliché?" is either the tried-and-true "I know it when I see it" or the equally hackneyed "If it looks like a duck and quacks like a duck . . ."

Thus copyeditors should aspire not to eradicate every cliché but to curb the follow-ing common abuses of clichés. First, you should propose new wording to authors who too often turn to canned phrases or who try to put an awkward twist on a cliché: "one cannot see the proverbial forest for the trees" or "an exercise in pedagogical futility" or "a cog in an unforgiving machine." (But good twists do exist: "Hedda Hopper knew not just where all the bodies were buried in Hollywood but under how much dirt.")

Second, you should ensure that the author has chosen the correct cliché and has not inadvertently mangled the commonplace expression or conflated several clichés. "To go back to square one" (to start at the beginning) is not the same as "to stand at ground zero" (the target of a nuclear attack). One does not "lift an eye" but rather "bats an eye[lash]" or "lifts [or raises] an eyebrow." A promise to "stay on top of" an issue in order to "get to the bottom of it" is hardly reassuring. And let us not "ignore the white elephant in the room" or "change dark horses in midstream."

Third, you should test to see if the sentence would be improved by the deletion of the deadwood part of the set phrase. For example, would the sentence seem more vivid if "vanish into thin air" were reduced to "vanish," "bewildering variety" to "variety," "built-in safeguards" to "safeguards," or "at first blush" to "at first"?

Fourth, because clichés are, by definition, ready-made, they are inappropriate in describing events of magnitude or gravity. The use of a commonplace at such a moment suggests that the author is an insensitive wretch, incapable of sincere emotion:

> Adding insult to injury, the first jolt of electricity to reach the condemned man was not strong enough to be fatal.

> Words fail to express the sights that greeted the soldiers as they entered the death camps.

Even in circumstances that are not matters of life and death, the predictability of a cliché undermines the authenticity of the idea being expressed.

> It goes without saying that our company will spare no effort to iron out the difficulties in our distribution procedures.

You should also be on the alert for incongruous clichés, which will elicit groans or chuckles from careful readers:

> The highway bill is water over the dam now, unless we can light a fire under Senator Snowe.

> In the rapid-fire debate, Jones's arguments in favor of gun control were right on target.

In order for them to mend fences, they will have to escape the quicksand of inertia.

If Jefferson were alive, he would be rolling over in his grave at this revisionist interpretation.

> [This formula has become popular, but if Jefferson were alive, why would he be in his grave?]

This legislation is intended to level the playing field without leading us down the slippery slope of reverse discrimination.

Overfamiliarity with such stale phrases often desensitizes authors to their inappropriate or incongruous use. Authors may also misjudge the extent to which these formulaic expressions are likely to baffle nonnative English speakers and translators in content that is intended for an international readership. Editors should evaluate the obstacles that richly figurative, culturally specific clichés may pose for such readers and should revise accordingly.

*Euphemisms.* Another class of words that writers and copyeditors have long been advised to avoid is euphemisms. Like the ban on clichés, the ban on euphemisms has merit, but applying it requires judgment and care, not ruthless slashing. Euphemism is an essential rhetorical tool that writers use to exert some form of "spin control." The Reagan White House floated "revenue enhancements" (for "taxes"), and the best-known euphemism of the 1970s, also from Washington, was the comment by Ron Ziegler, then President Nixon's press secretary, that certain earlier statements from his office were "inoperative" (that is, "lies"). One of the longest chains of euphemisms comes from corporate America, where employees have been terminated, laid off, riffed (from "reduction in force"), and downsized—but never fired—as a result of restructuring, reengineering, or rightsizing.

It is easy to poke fun at political and bureaucratic euphemisms, but harder to answer the questions, Why all the fuss about euphemisms? What harm is done by a bit of sugarcoating? What difference does it make whether the trash is picked up by garbage collectors, refuse haulers, sanitation crews, or waste management engineers? What's wrong with an expression intended to spare us from offensive or unpleasant utterances? The issue for copyeditors thus becomes retaining those of the author's euphemisms that contribute to the author's purpose and deleting those that detract from it. The former category includes euphemisms sincerely intended to spare readers' feelings; the latter category includes euphemisms that readers will perceive as silly or deceptive and that will undermine their faith in the author's credibility. Perhaps political journalists and their editors confront the greatest challenges in finding that middle ground: collateral damage *or* noncombatant deaths? targeted killings *or* assassinations?

Because framing the terms of an argument is crucial to making an argument, the line between euphemism and persuasive rhetoric is a fuzzy one. Compare the following two paragraphs, both of which discuss how the trade treaties NAFTA and GATT have affected employment, wages, and prices in the United States:

The free-trade opportunities offered by NAFTA and GATT have enabled manufacturers to maximize productivity by relocating employment. This redeployment has, in turn, created redundancies in the more industrialized nations, which will provide substantial insurance against wage-driven inflationary spirals. Thus inflation should remain below 3% a year.

In the wake of NAFTA and GATT, US manufacturers have closed factories in the United States and moved their operations to low-wage enclaves in Mexico and Southeast Asia. The resulting high level of unemployment in the United States leaves American workers with no leverage in requesting cost-of-living increases. Thus the purchasing power of the average worker's wages will remain stagnant or will continue to decline.

Clearly, the first author wants readers to view NAFTA and GATT as wholly positive: the treaties provide opportunities, enable companies to maximize productivity, and offer substantial insurance against inflation. For the second author, NAFTA and GATT have been a disaster: jobs have vanished; higher unemployment means that companies do not have to raise wages to attract workers, and those workers who have jobs feel insecure and are reluctant to demand higher wages; in the end, working people's wages barely keep up—or fail to keep up—with price increases.

As you might imagine, the first author will ignore a copyeditor who suggests replacing any of the pleasant terms with unpleasant ones ("layoffs," "unemployment," "wage stagnation"), just as the second author will ignore any suggestions to add a cheering sentence about the upside of flat wages, such as the prospects for low rates of inflation. To earn and maintain the goodwill of authors, you must respect the author's right to frame opinions and arguments in charged terms.

How euphemistic or how charged a statement should be, of course, depends on the purpose of the document and the intended readership.[3] Here a copyeditor may do the author a great service in pointing out wording that seems too euphemistic or too emotional or language that seems evasive rather than persuasive. Spin control and damage control may belong in the advertising, marketing, and public relations toolbox, but outside those domains most readers will resent feeling manipulated rather than informed.

3. An example from politics. In 1997, residents of Houston who wanted the city to discontinue its affirmative action policy proposed the following ballot measure:

The City of Houston shall not discriminate against or grant preferential treatment to any individual or group on the basis of race, sex, ethnicity or national origin in the operation of public employment and public contracting.

The mayor of Houston, who favored continuing the city's affirmative action policy, proposed a rewriting of the measure:

Shall the Charter of the City of Houston be amended to end the use of preferential treatment (affirmative action) in the operation of the City of Houston employment and contracting?

In preelection polling, 68.1 percent of the respondents said they were for the first measure, but only 47.5 percent said they favored the second measure; Sam Howe Verhovek, "Houston to Vote on Affirmative Action," *New York Times*, November 2, 1997, p. 16, national edition. The proposition that appeared on the ballot was quite similar to the second version and was defeated (the yes vote was 45 percent).

*Connotation.* Many words and phrases have shadings that are not precisely conveyed by their dictionary definitions. For example, although "thanks to" is a close cousin of "owing to," "due to," and "because of," any note of thankfulness is inappropriate in a sentence about disaster: "Thanks to winter storms, the wheat harvest was ruined." Similarly, "eligible for" is a poor choice in "Though only sixteen, he is eligible for the death penalty"; rather, "he is subject to the death penalty."

*Denotation.* Obviously, communication between a writer and a reader collapses when a writer uses a word that does not mean what the writer seems to think it means.[4] Common misuses that arise from homophones (words that sound alike but have different spellings and meanings) are discussed in chapter 5. Heteronyms and homographs (words that are spelled alike but have different meanings and pronunciations) can also cause confusion, especially in the compressed language of headings: Consumer Content = consumers' data or their contentment? Lead in Acme Hamburger Recipes = metal or preeminence?

Other problems arise from incorrect assumptions about parts of words. In traditional usage

> *bemused* does not mean "amused"
> *disinterested* does not mean "uninterested"
> *enervate* does not mean "stimulate the nerves"
> *enormity* does not mean "immensity"
> *fitful* does not mean "fit"
> *fortuitous* does not mean "fortunate"
> *fulsome* does not mean "full"
> *impracticable* does not mean "impractical"
> *inflammable* does not mean "not flammable"
> *noisome* does not mean "noisy"
> *nonplussed* does not mean "indifferent" or "bored"
> *sensuous* does not mean "sensory"
> *sinuous* does not mean "sinewy"
> *tortuous* does not mean "torturous"

---

4. Remember Humpty Dumpty in chapter 6 of *Through the Looking Glass:*

[Humpty Dumpty:] "There's glory for you!"

"I don't know what you mean by 'glory,'" Alice said.

Humpty Dumpty smiled contemptuously. "Of course you don't—till I tell you. I meant 'there's a nice knock-down argument for you!'"

"But 'glory' doesn't mean 'a nice knock-down argument,'" Alice objected.

"When *I* use a word," Humpty Dumpty said, in rather a scornful tone, "it means just what I choose it to mean—neither more nor less."

"The question is," said Alice, "whether you *can* make words mean so many different things."

"The question is," said Humpty Dumpty, "which is to be master—that's all."

Lewis Carroll, *Through the Looking Glass and What Alice Found There* (Philadelphia: Henry Altemus, 1897), p. 123

Some problems arise from carelessness:

> *aggravate* does not mean "annoy"
> *exponential* does not mean "a lot" or "dramatic"
> *heartrending tales* break (*rend*) the heart; they do not *render* (extract fats and oils from) the heart
> *parameters* does not mean "perimeters"
> *regretfully* does not mean "regrettably"
> *respectively* does not mean "respectfully"
> *temblors* (not the nonword *tremblors*) cause the earth to tremble
> *uncharted waters* are those that have not been mapped; they are not *unchartered*

And some arise from an oversimplified sense of a complex denotation:

> *anxious* does not mean "eager" (any more than *anxiety* means "eagerness")
> *continuous* does not mean "continual"
> *ironic* does not mean "coincidental"

To be sure, in some cases the differences between such "confusables" are disappearing through repeated conflation of their meanings. Although some authors and readers still scrupulously observe these distinctions, *M-W Collegiate* now recognizes the disputed meanings of *bemused, continuous, enormity, fortuitous, fulsome,* and *parameters* as legitimate; several standard dictionaries duly record the first or second definition of *disinterested* as "uninterested," despite ongoing disapproval of this sense in all but the most liberal usage guides. The sole recourse for a copyeditor is to learn about the most commonly contested "pairs and snares," as the 1965 edition of H. W. Fowler's *Dictionary of Modern English Usage* calls them, and to judge whether the author's style and meaning, the readers' expectations, or the level of formality justifies intervention. The online *AHD* often supplies usage notes and warning labels with troublesome entries.

*Rollercoastering.* Some writers have little sense of the physicality of words. Because they do not hear or feel the *under* in *underlie* or the *over* in *overcome,* they do not perceive the rollercoaster movement in a phrase like "the underlying problem in overcoming poverty" or "this overemphasis on internal structure underlines fundamental problems," and they see nothing amiss in "over the long run, these short-term problems can be solved." Copyeditors should suggest revisions that are less disorienting.

*Pet peeves.* Every copyeditor has at least a short list of words he or she simply detests. Among the words that raise the most hackles are the noun or verb *impact* when used to describe anything other than a car crash; the verbs *enthuse, liaise,* and *interface;* nonce modifiers ending in *wise,* such as *businesswise* and *spacewise;* and *-ize* verbs such as *prioritize* and *operationalize.* The charges against these words range from "ugly and unnecessary—we already have a name for it" to "dreadful back-formation" and "corruption of the language by illiterate bureaucrats."

But when examined, these rationales wobble and collapse. Why is a particular combination of letters or sounds any uglier than some other combination of letters or sounds? Since some of the beauty and utility of English derive from its wealth of synonyms and near synonyms, what's wrong with having a few more? And aren't back-formations also part of the richness of the language?

For authors, the matter is a simple one: authors may freely exert their prerogative to banish whatever words they dislike. For copyeditors, however, the decision to banish an unlikable word should be based on something other than the copyeditor's own prejudices. Before you outlaw a word because *you* don't like it, do a bit of research in *DEU* or a trusted usage guide. You may find a sound argument for replacing a controversial word, or you might be persuaded to reconsider your bias against a word.

## VERBS

Verbs are the muscle of a sentence. Strong writers let finite verbs—rather than participles and verbal phrases or adjectives and adverbs—do the work of the sentence. As the following examples show, when verbs convey the action, sentences become a bit crisper. By pointing an author to the correct verb, copyeditors can also rescue text that suffers from an overabundance of "is" and "are" or "was" and "were."

*Weak:* The primary focus of this workshop is recent developments in computer scanning.

*Better:* This workshop focuses on recent developments in computer scanning.

---

*Weak:* This is a difficult problem that is going to require months of research.

*Better:* This difficult problem will require months of research.

---

*Weak:* This house is old and is in danger of collapsing during an earthquake.

*Better:* This old house could collapse during an earthquake.

---

*Weak:* Smith's report is a most valuable contribution to our understanding of hypoxemia.

*Better:* Smith's report contributes greatly to our understanding of hypoxemia.

---

*Weak:* The results of our field testing are that the new manufacturing process is more cost-effective than current procedures.

*Better:* Our field testing shows the new manufacturing process to be more cost-effective than current procedures.

---

*Weak:* There was a strong disagreement between the two sides over the estimate of damages.

*Better:* The two sides strongly disagreed on the estimate of damages.

---

*Weak:* Before the commencement of the program, there was a brunch served for the guests.

*Better:* Before the program began, the guests were served brunch.

---

*Weak:* After completing an inspection of the factory, the engineers still could not provide an explanation for the malfunction.

*Better:* After inspecting the factory, the engineers still could not explain the malfunction.

## PASSIVE VOICE

Some well-meaning people have truncated Orwell's rule "Never use the passive where you can use the active" to "Never use the passive." But the passive voice has its place. The passive is the correct choice when the doer of the action is indefinite, unimportant, or unknown:

> Video conferencing capability is no longer considered a luxury in home offices.
>
> Each panelist was identified by institutional affiliation and field of expertise.
>
> No other problems were reported.

The passive is also preferable when the result of the activity is more important than the performer:

> These statistics are drawn from thirty field tests.
>
> Temperature and humidity readings were made at 9 A.M., noon, and 3 P.M.
>
> Hundreds of dead seabirds were sighted near the oil spill.

Unpleasant messages are often framed in the passive:

> Three hundred workers were let go, and dividend payments were cut.

The passive voice may also be advisable when a long subject with modifiers delays the predicate, thus straining a reader's ability to parse the sentence; when a reader's attention must remain focused on the topic placed in the subject position, which happens to be the very thing "being done to"; or when the passive voice serves a transition or emphasizes a word by placing it at the head of the sentence.[5]

But the passive voice is wordy, and its use can create intentional or unintentional mysteries:

> It has been determined that . . . [Who determined it?]
>
> It has been alleged that . . . [Who made the allegation?]
>
> Mistakes were made . . . [Who made the mistakes?]

---

5. In *The Sense of Style,* Steven Pinker demonstrates these tactical uses of the passive by analyzing a Wikipedia entry on *Oedipus Rex* (pp. 132–35).

For clarity and brevity, then, strong writers tend to prefer the active voice and reserve the passive voice for one of the purposes mentioned above or for the sake of cadence or variety. In turn, copyeditors are expected to help authors avoid the overuse or awkward use of the passive, but this effort should be tempered. For readers, the judiciously placed passive construction can provide welcome relief from an onslaught of sentences in the active voice.

## SUBORDINATION

Copyeditors should query or revise strings of short sentences that sound like a grade-school primer:

> *Choppy:* To initiate an action from a dialog box, click on a command button. The three command buttons are OK, Cancel, and Help. These command buttons are most often located at the bottom of the dialog box. Sometimes, though, they are located at the right border of the dialog box.

Decide which points are most important and subordinate the incidental details:

> *Revision:* To initiate an action from a dialog box, click on a command button. The three command buttons—OK, Cancel, and Help—are located at the bottom of the dialog box or at the box's right border.

Here's a more complicated example of a string of sentences, each competing for the reader's attention because the writer has not subordinated any of the details:

> *Unfocused:* The most recent study of local air pollution was performed by the Metropolitan Air Quality District (MAQD). The study was released on November 15, 1997. (A limited number of copies are available to professional researchers from local MAQD offices.) The MAQD documents provide detailed measures of the level of five airborne pollutants during the past ten years. The level of each of these pollutants has increased dramatically since 1987. In 1997 the daytime level of carbon monoxide in the downtown area exceeded federal standards on 165 days. (Daytime levels are taken at 1 P.M.)

How best to revise this passage depends on the paragraph's function in the document. The author must decide which point is most important: that MAQD recently released a report on air pollution? that levels of five airborne pollutants have increased dramatically since 1987? that in 1997 the daytime level of carbon monoxide in the downtown area exceeded federal standards on 165 days? The choice of the key point will dictate the order of the sentences and the relocation, subordination, or elimination of minor points. The following revision focuses on the findings rather than on the administrative details:

> *Possible revision:* During the past ten years, the levels of five airborne pollutants increased dramatically in Metro City, according to a study released by the Metropolitan Air Quality District (MAQD) on November 15, 1997. In 1997 the midday level of carbon monoxide in the downtown area exceeded federal standards on 165 days.

Short, choppy sentences with insufficient subordination challenge readers to grasp the important ideas and to subsume the minor ones as they go. The opposite problem, sentences overloaded with subordinated detail, may also need revision, especially for the sake of nonnative English speakers and international readers.

> Susan Warner's *The Wide, Wide World* (1850), a novel so sentimental as to be continually awash in tears, is also a novel so stark as to be continually under the shadow of chance, a novel as relentlessly driven by unforeseeable randomness as *Moby-Dick* (1851), its contemporary and in many ways its antithesis, is relentlessly driven by foreseeable destiny.[6]

Say what?

## UNTANGLING NEGATIVES

In general, positively worded statements are easier for readers to understand correctly than are negatively worded statements.[7] The interpretive difficulties caused by the use of *no* or *not* are compounded when a sentence includes negative verbs (fail, disappear, decrease), negative modifiers (poorly, inappropriate, ill-considered), or negative qualifiers (unless, without, absent), and copyeditors should untangle these pretzels. For example:

> *Tangled:* Not all the students, but a majority, failed to turn in the assignment before the deadline.
>
> *Direct:* Less than half the students turned in the assignment before the deadline.
>
> *Or:* More than half the students missed the deadline for turning in the assignment.

---

> *Tangled:* Crime rates will not decline without a citywide effort to reduce poorly lit downtown streets.
>
> *Direct:* To reduce crime, the city should increase lighting on downtown streets.

---

> *Tangled:* You will not be charged your first monthly fee unless you don't cancel within the first 30 days.[8]
>
> *Direct:* To avoid being charged a fee, cancel your service within 30 days.

A negative expression preceding terms joined by *or*, which linguists describe as "disjunction under negation," can produce misunderstandings:

---

6. Wai Chee Dimock, *Residues of Justice: Literature, Law, Philosophy* (Berkeley: University of California Press, 1997), pp. 124–25. The flawless syntax of this sentence, like a perfectly crafted puzzle box, is wondrous to behold. The problem is that all but the most advanced readers may have difficulty parsing it in their first pass.

7. See E. D. Hirsch Jr., *The Philosophy of Composition*, pp. 93, 150.

8. This statement appeared in an offer for a free thirty-day trial subscription to America Online; see *New York Times*, December 7, 1997, business section, p. 9.

I'm not available for lunch or dinner.

[I'm not available for lunch AND I'm not available for dinner *or* I'm not available for one of these meals.]

Context usually suggests the intended meaning, but in law this construction can form the basis for contested interpretations. The linguist Neal Goldfarb describes an instance in which the US Tax Court reversed an IRS decision disallowing a tax deduction for the cost of sex-change surgery on the grounds that it was cosmetic surgery. Cosmetic surgery is defined in the tax code as "any procedure which is directed at improving the patient's appearance and *does not meaningfully promote the proper function of the body or treat illness or disease.*" The appeal to the Tax Court turned on whether, to be excluded from the category of cosmetic surgery, a procedure (a) must *either* promote . . . *or* prevent or treat, or (b) must *both* promote . . . *and* prevent or treat. The court decided in favor of (a) and allowed the deduction.[9] Fortunately, the legal decision was less ambiguous than the legal prose.

The difficulty that English speakers have in processing tangled negatives may lie behind some common solecisms.

The role of this long-playing television series in American culture cannot be understated.

It is impossible to underestimate the importance of Amazon's recent corporate acquisitions.

Unless the irony is intentional, these sentences, of course, say the very opposite of what is meant. A classic example of mis-negation in logic is the statement "No head injury is too trivial to ignore." The sentence is so difficult to analyze that readers often abandon the effort to parse it and simply leap to an interpretation. All head injuries, even trivial ones, should be ignored? No head injury, however trivial, should be ignored?

But accentuating the positive doesn't require eliminating all clusters of negatives. For example, if an author labels an issue "not unimportant," a copyeditor should not automatically substitute "important." There is more than a shade of difference between the two expressions. Negatives can also be used for special emphasis, as in a *New York Times* article concerning women on Wall Street: "It's extremely disheartening to see how far we have not come" (July 26, 2001).

## VARIETY

*Word choice.* Many writers think they should avoid using a word twice in the same sentence or passage and should instead substitute synonyms. This affectation, described as an obsession with "elegant variation" (the irony is *Fowler's*) or "monologophobia and synonymomania" (Theodore Bernstein's *The Careful Writer*), may cause readers to stumble off the well-marked path of an argument and wonder whether the constant changes

---

9. Neal Goldfarb, "Sex-Change Surgery and Universal Grammar," *Language Log,* February 18, 2010, http://languagelog.ldc.upenn.edu/ (the italics here replace Goldfarb's boldface emphasis).

in terminology have some significance. Copyeditors should intervene when this quest for variety in diction has led an author to create a passage that sounds like a transcription from a thesaurus.

> *Overwritten:* Students were asked to sketch a picture of their home. The subjects were given 3 minutes to complete these drawings of their residences. The test compositions were later analyzed independently by four professionally trained scorers. Subsequently, the four evaluators convened to reach a consensus assessment of each subject.
>
> [Only the fear of repeating "home" can explain the choice of "residences." More importantly, renaming the "trained scorers" as "evaluators" doubles the cast, although these refer to the same four people.]
>
> *Clearer:* Students were given 3 minutes to draw their home. The drawings were independently scored by four trained evaluators. After discussing the drawings, the evaluators provided a consensus assessment of each student.

Copyeditors should also intervene when the author's repetition of a key word becomes monotonous. In the following passage, the author packed seven "beginning"s and five "new"s into eighty-three words:

> *Monotonous:* We have just celebrated the Lunar New Year and the beginning of the Year of the Rat. It represents the beginning of a new year, but also the beginning of a new cycle, as the Rat leads the twelve-animal Chinese zodiac. This new beginning in Asia is symbolic perhaps of other noteworthy Asian beginnings. For example, the beginning of a new economic and interest rate cycle in Japan. Also the beginning of a mighty transition for China, involving Hong Kong and Taiwan.

An edited version features four "beginning"s and three "new"s; the word count is sixty-four.

> *Revision:* We have just celebrated the Lunar New Year and the beginning of the Year of the Rat, which also represents the start of a new twelve-year cycle in the Chinese calendar. Two other Asian beginnings are noteworthy: the beginning of a new economic and interest rate cycle in Japan, and the beginning of a mighty transition for China, involving Hong Kong and Taiwan.

Of course, the passage could be rewritten with only one "beginning" and one "new," but the result sounds quite strained.

> *Overwritten:* We have just celebrated the Lunar New Year and the beginning of the Year of the Rat, which inaugurates the twelve-year cycle on which the Chinese calendar is based. Two other Asian commencements are noteworthy: the onset of another economic and interest rate cycle in Japan, and the start of a mighty transition for China, involving Hong Kong and Taiwan.

*Sentence structure.* Good writers also try to provide some variety in the structure of their sentences. A copyeditor can offer suggestions to authors who go to one extreme (every sentence always begins with the subject) or the other (no sentence ever begins with the subject). An unrelenting string of subject-verb-object sentences is readily identifiable by its choppy rhythm.[10] Conversely, the monotonous repetition of sentence structures that delay the subject with participial modifiers, prepositional phrases, and gerund phrases lulls readers into a stupor.

> Entering the last lap of the course, the runner keyed on the previous year's winner ahead of him. Accelerating his pace, he gained steadily on his competitor. Gasping for air and pumping his arms vigorously, he pulled abreast of his rival. In a series of giant strides and through sheer willpower, he surged past the other runner and crossed the finish line first. In a matter of a minutes, he had secured the trophy. But winning the race and the silver cup had never been his primary goal. Defeating his lifelong rival on the course was the sweetest victory.

Not Hemingway.

Still, the postponement of both subject and predicate until the end of a sentence can make effective use of this last position for special emphasis:

> Drawing herself up to her full height and staring him straight in the eye, she belched.

But watch out for sentences that cram too much detail between a subject and a predicate. Readers can lose their way in the forest of intervening modifiers:

> The California Supreme Court refused yesterday to halt preparations for a vote on whether to recall Gray Davis, noting that a trial court's consideration of irregularities in the signature collection process that authorized the election was proceeding. (*New York Times,* July 26, 2003)

Here, eleven words intervene between "consideration" and "was proceeding."

You must also be on the alert when the quest for variety leads an author to write a sentence that cannot be correctly deciphered on first reading:

> *Confusing:* Despite our relatively small sample, extensive observer evaluations, measures of self-perceptions, and the length of the study permitted us to obtain information that cannot be provided by epidemiological investigations.

Only when the reader reaches "permitted" is it clear that "Despite" governs only "our relatively small sample" and that "extensive observer evaluations, measures of self-

---

10. Despite the popular belief that Ernest Hemingway wrote nothing but Dick-and-Jane sentences, even his most spare prose exhibits considerable variety in structure and rhythm:

> He was an old man who fished alone in a skiff in the Gulf Stream and he had gone eighty-four days now without taking a fish. In the first forty days a boy had been with him. But after forty days without a fish the boy's parents had told him that the old man was now definitely and finally *salao,* which is the worst form of unluck, and the boy had gone at their orders in another boat which caught three good fish the first week. (*The Old Man and the Sea* [Toronto: HarperCollins, HarperPerennial Classics, 2013], p. 1)

perceptions, and the length of the study" are the factors that enabled the researchers to obtain valuable information. You might propose:

> *Revision:* Although our sample was relatively small, our use of extensive
> observer evaluations, measures of self-perceptions, and the length of the study
> permitted us to obtain information that cannot be provided by epidemiological
> investigations.

*Sentence length.* A mistake many beginning copyeditors make is to use a word-count approach to sentence length, assuming that any noticeably short sentence is "too short" and that any noticeably long one is "too long." But word count alone is only one measure of the readers' perception of length. A sentence may have many words, but if these are arranged in well-structured phrases and clauses, readers will not complain that the length of the sentence interferes with their understanding of its meaning. Conversely, a short sentence whose meaning is opaque, its structure twisted, may leave readers at sea.

Copyeditors who take the cookie-cutter approach are thus robbing their authors of a valuable tool: the ability to control the readers' attention (even their breathing) by varying the lengths of their sentences to suit the task at hand. For many purposes, indeed, shorter is better. Each period gives the reader a split second to consolidate all the information in one sentence and prepare for the next. But this is not to say that shorter is always better. For when there are too many start-and-stop sentences in a row, some readers will feel that the author is blurting out tidbits of information rather than conveying well-shaped thoughts. Indeed, complicated concepts often require long sentences; to cut a complex idea into two short sentences is to leave the reader with two useless stubs rather than a valid ticket.

Often the disagreeable aspect of a long sentence is a matter less of its length than of its overstuffed shape. In explaining this problem to an author, you can appropriate John Gardner's advice to fiction writers:

> As a rule, if a sentence has three syntactic slots [subject, verb, object], as in
>
>              1       2       3
>      The man walked down the road
>
> —a writer may load one or two of the slots with modifiers, but if the sentence is to have
> focus—that is, if the reader is to be able to make out some clear image, not just a jumble—
> the writer cannot cram all three syntactic slots with details. (*The Art of Fiction* [New York:
> Knopf, 1984], p. 105)

This notion of slots can also be used to explain a guideline for constructing long sentences: although the most important information in a sentence usually belongs in the first slot, when that piece of information is very long, move it to the last slot.

> *Unbalanced:* The effectiveness of administering a ten-day regimen of penicillin
> for the treatment of complications arising from periodontal surgery is their
> current research topic.

*Balanced:* Their current research topic is the effectiveness of administering a ten-day regimen of penicillin for the treatment of complications arising from periodontal surgery.

In sum, the interweaving of shorter and longer sentences is not a matter of mathematics nor of injecting variety for variety's sake. The subject, the intended readership, the rhythm and tone of the entire piece, the architecture of individual sentences and paragraphs, and the ebb and flow of emphasis—all these enter into decisions about sentence length.

## TRANSITIONS

Traditionally, the sentence is described as the core unit of expository prose. The disadvantage of this concept is that a writer may construct lovely individual sentences, but the relationship of one sentence to the next may be unclear. A more useful approach is to view the core unit of composition as the chunk of text running from the last words of one sentence to the beginning of the next:

Lorem ipsum dolor | sit amet. Consecteteur elit, | sedianonummy
| nibh euismod dolor. Ut wisi ad | minim ven iam, quis nostrud
| exerci. Duis autem vel | eum iriure dolor.[11]

This scheme reinforces the importance of making clear connections between one point and the next.

One way to specify the relationship between two consecutive sentences is to use a transitional expression. The following expressions function to add a point, give an example, restate, introduce a result, contrast, concede or qualify, press a point, explain, summarize, or itemize or sequence:

further, in addition, also, moreover
first(ly), second(ly), third(ly), last, finally*
next, later, meanwhile, subsequently
similarly, in the same way, likewise
in contrast, yet, even so, alternatively
but, however, nevertheless, nonetheless, on the contrary
although, while
above all, in particular, indeed
accordingly, so
for example, for instance, in other words, that is
for this reason, for this purpose

11. The use of a placeholder passage beginning with the words *Lorem ipsum* traces back to the 1500s, when an unknown printer scrambled a Latin passage from Cicero to create a type specimen book. Variations of this nonsensical pseudo-Latin text have been common in design layouts since the 1960s and are sometimes used in demonstrations like this one.

as a result, in consequence, therefore, thus
in short, once again, to repeat
of course, surely, certainly, after all
in sum, as we have seen, on the whole, all in all
more important(ly)*
on the other hand*

*Traditionalists have long flagged the *-ly* forms (*firstly*, etc.; *more importantly*) as inferior and have censured the use of *on the other hand* unless paired with *on the one hand.* Today, however, even the more conservative usage guides accept these forms.

A second type of transitional device is repetition. The following sentences are held together by the repetition of key words and synonyms as well as by transitional phrases:

Inconsistencies can damage a writer's credibility. For example, readers are often confused by inconsistencies in hyphenation, such as "drop-down menu" versus "dropdown menu." When hyphenation is inconsistent or haphazard, readers will start to wonder whether the writer's inattentiveness extends to issues of content and accuracy.

Similarly, the repetition of pronouns can provide continuity.

Of course, all copyeditors like to read; no one who finds reading a tiresome chore would take up editorial work. Most copyeditors are also fascinated by language. They are intrigued by new words and unusual expressions. They enjoy debates about grammar and are as interested in an opponent's reasoning as in his or her solution to the problem at hand. Even in their spare time, they are often found playing word games.

## PARAGRAPHING

Expository writers usually rely on medium-length paragraphs (say, 75 to 150 words), broken up by the occasional short paragraph. But conventions about the length of paragraphs vary from field to field, as well as among different types of publications. In newsletters or documents printed in two-column formats, short paragraphs predominate; in scholarly studies long paragraphs are quite common. In writing for the web, paragraphs of two or three sentences predominate, with key ideas "front-loaded" for easy scanning.

A very short paragraph here or there usually requires no editorial intervention. Nor does the occasional very long paragraph—unless the paragraph will seem truly monolithic when poured into a narrow-column format. More important than the mere length of a paragraph is whether the paragraphing facilitates or hinders comprehension. Sometimes the meaning will be clearer if short points are separated into brief paragraphs, and sometimes the meaning will be clearer if a long, complex point is not broken across two paragraphs. When clarity, rather than simple length, is at issue, copyeditors routinely reparagraph.

But if a manuscript is plagued by paragraphs so brief as to suggest breathless thoughtlessness or if the text is beset by clumps of page-long paragraphs, reparagraph-ing every page may be quite time consuming, as well as a waste of your efforts. Ask your editorial coordinator for advice. The usual course in these cases is for the copyeditor to remind the author that paragraphs serve as useful guideposts for readers, to point out several spots that could benefit from either fewer or more paragraph breaks, and to ask the author to reconsider his or her original paragraphing while reviewing the editing.

## CADENCE

For many expository writers and their copyeditors, cadence—the rhythm of sentences and paragraphs—is not of great concern. Technical writers, business writers, researchers, engineers, and the rest of the nonliterary workaday crowd rarely write with an ear tuned to the music of their words. Novelists and essayists, of course, do care about the sound of their prose, as do some literary critics and historians, and some make deliberate use of poetic devices such as assonance, alliteration, consonance, rhyme, rhythm, and onomatopoeia. Regardless of an author's aesthetic aspirations, however, copyeditors working on nonliterary materials should be alert enough to the sound of the text to catch the following types of infelicities: unintended rhymes, tongue-twisting consonant clusters, heavy alliteration, and overly dramatic rhythms.

## TYPOGRAPHICAL DEVICES

Strong writers rely on diction, syntax, and content to convey the desired tone or emphasis in their sentences; less confident writers sometimes rely on typographical devices (italic or bold type, exclamation points, and quotation marks). Copyeditors are expected to reduce the visual clutter.

*Italics and bold.*  In running text, italics and boldface should be used sparingly to set off specific terms and phrases. Most publishers discourage the use of italics or boldface for entire sentences and paragraphs: long passages of wavy italic type are often difficult to read, and large patches of boldface (or frequent small patches of bold type) look unattractive. In addition, when italics and bold are used in the running text as well as in headings, captions, and other display elements, the various typographical treatments compete for the reader's attention.

*Exclamation points.*  Only rarely are exclamation points needed in expository writing. (Novelists, letter writers, and playwrights, of course, are free to revel in them.) And no amount of emphasis or irony in expository prose calls for more than one exclamation point nor for an exclamation point preceded or followed by a question mark.

*Quotation marks.*  Quotation marks may be used for emphasis or irony, but copyeditors should curb authors who overuse this device.

*All caps.*  In running text, there is no call for individual words or phrases to be printed in all caps. ALL CAPS, WITH THEIR RECTANGULAR SHAPES, ARE ESPECIALLY HARD

TO READ; MOREOVER, THEY CREATE THE IMPRESSION THAT A WRITER IS SHOUTING. Lowercase words, with letterforms using ascenders and descenders, aid comprehension and create the impression that a writer is using an indoor voice.

## PLAIN LANGUAGE COMPLIANCE

Readers have long grumbled about unclear writing in documents prepared by legal, financial, business, and government institutions. During the 1970s many US law schools added writing classes to the curriculum to remedy the blight of impenetrable professional prose. In the same decade, consumer-rights legislation began to stipulate *plain language* in contracts, insurance policies, and government regulations. This plain language initiative resulted in the US Plain Writing Act of 2010, which requires all federal agencies to communicate with the public in straightforward language. Various state governments and many private institutions subsequently adopted this goal as well. The Plain Language Action and Information Network (PLAIN), a group of volunteer US federal employees, now works to improve communications from the federal government to the public (see the Selected Bibliography for details about PLAIN's website). The Center for Plain Language, a US-based nonprofit organization, also promotes the use of plain language in both the public and the private sectors and confers annual ClearMark awards for outstanding communication—as well as Work That Failed (WTF) awards for truly awful writing. (The latter award comes with an invitation to revise and resubmit for the more prestigious trophy in the category of "most improved.") The US Plain Language Movement has parallels in Canada, the United Kingdom, and Australia. Some freelance editors specialize in rewriting documents in plain language.

Proponents of plain language emphasize that the goal is not to "dumb down" writing intended to communicate important information; rather, it is to convey this information to a diverse population—readers with different levels of education, English language proficiency, and physical and cognitive abilities—in a way that enables everyone to understand and use the information after a single reading. Not all prose needs to hew to plain language strictures. (One source, for example, recommends limiting sentence length to a maximum of twenty words, which is two words shorter than this sentence.) But tax regulations, health advisories, legal notices, communications about Social Security and Medicare, and other critical information must be simple and direct, especially when bureaucracies address a broad readership. Not surprisingly, the guidelines for plain language reiterate the basic principles of effective writing described in the preceding sections of this chapter, with loud echoes of Strunk and White. All versions of the guidelines emphasize the points summarized in table 23.

Besides repeating long-familiar advice to writers, plain language guidelines describe how to prepare content or to adapt printed text for publication on the web. The *Federal Plain Language Guidelines* cites studies showing that many web readers scan text instead of perusing it word for word, moving their eyes across the top of the webpage and then down the left side in an F pattern as they survey headings and the first few words of sentences and lists. Web users, according to these studies, typically read no more than

TABLE 23. Plain Language Guidelines

*Audiences*
  Identify and prioritize the audience groups
  List the top tasks they must perform
  List what they need to complete these tasks
  Analyze the characteristics of these groups that affect document structure and design

*Content and structure*
  Organize the content logically
  Present the most important information first, specialized information later
  Eliminate digressions, distracting details, and unnecessary exceptions
  Keep paragraphs focused and short (less than 150 words, or three to eight sentences)
  Use transitions to connect ideas
  Break content into brief sections that reflect natural pauses
  Minimize cross-references
  Use short headings with a clear hierarchy of three levels or less
  Make reading easier with lists, tables, illustrations, and examples
  Enforce parallel construction in headings and lists
  Include an introduction and a table of contents for lengthy documents

*Language choices*
  Use verbs rather than nominalizations
  Avoid noun strings
  Prefer the active voice
  Use affirmative rather than negative constructions
  Keep the subject and verb close together
  Break up long sentences
  Use short, familiar words, but avoid slang
  Use key terminology consistently
  Explain technical terms if they must be used
  Avoid most abbreviations
  Omit needless words

*Tone*
  Be direct
  Avoid euphemisms
  Address individuals, not abstract groups
  Use personal pronouns such as *you*

*Document design*
  Use typography to guide the reader's attention
  Avoid an excess of fonts and typographic features
  Use adequate margins
  Separate chunks of information with white space

*Document evaluation*
  Test the draft on sample readers (content specialists, editors, proofreaders, representative
    end users)

*Sources*: Adapted from *Federal Plain Language Guidelines*, Revision 1 (May 2011), Plain Language Action and Information Network (PLAIN), https://www.plainlanguage.gov/; "Top 10 Principles for Plain Language," Open Government at the National Archives, https://www.archives.gov/ (which, curiously, lists *twelve* principles).

20 percent of the text on a given webpage—and less if the page contains more than 110 words! Accordingly, the plain language guidelines for web writing and editing, reproduced in table 24, are adjusted somewhat for this very different environment.[12]

## ACCESSIBILITY

Plain language guidelines have been formulated to prepare documents for broad, diverse audiences. But they seldom directly address the issue of accessibility, that is, the design and production of publications for people with some form of print impairment—a visual impairment, dyslexia, or a motor disability that affects reading. Accessibility is another concern that editors need to be aware of, not just because it is a legal or social mandate in many English-speaking countries but also because it is part of the educational or public service mission (or simply the profit motive) of some traditional publishers.

A simple PDF or a large-print edition meets the needs of some readers with a motor or print impairment. E-book devices offering optional adjustments to typeface, type size, background color, and linespacing can aid others with low vision or dyslexia. Some readers may require a standard embossed braille edition or access to an electronic publication through a special braille device. Many accessible publications use navigable structured production files with text-to-speech (TTS) software: TTS capability aids visually impaired readers by converting digital text to synthetic speech. Additional aids may include a detailed, navigable table of contents, a defined reading order, and alternative-text ("alt-text") descriptions of illustrations and tables in extended captions.

Traditional publishers often accommodate requests for accessible editions by supplying postproduction files to the requester, for example, an educational institution or library for the blind that processes the files to create the desired output. But a publisher's conventional production process can anticipate many accessibility issues by using some level of *semantic tagging* in the files during the initial editorial cycle. (Semantic tagging is markup, or coding, based on meaning rather than on appearance—for example, it differentiates italics used for emphasis, italics for foreign words, and italics for book titles.) Publishers do not ordinarily require copyeditors to supply markup at this granular level, but emerging technologies may eventually affect how publishers process—or ask editors to prepare—files for many forms of output. For example, processing might include the provision of semantic tagging or the creation of alternative-text captions. Some editors may supply such services directly to institutions that prepare accessible publications.

Although for most people *accessibility* simply means "accessible to individuals with disabilities," the editor Iva Cheung, who frequently writes and speaks about both accessibility and plain language issues, defines the term *accessible communication* far more broadly and describes many barriers to the discovery, acquisition, use, and

---

12. Instructions for preparing plain language content for the web are a bit thin in the *Federal Plain Language Guidelines* and at the federal website DigitalGov (https://digital.gov/). For an in-depth analysis of web reading habits and more detailed guidance on writing and editing for a web environment, see *The Yahoo! Style Guide,* listed in the Selected Bibliography.

TABLE 24.  Plain Language Web Writing Tips

*On the Web, people are in a hurry. They skim and scan, looking for fast answers to their questions, so it's important to get to the point—quickly!*

*Help your readers complete their tasks with these Plain Language writing tips:*

| | |
|---|---|
| Audience | Write for your reader. Don't write for the experts, the lawyers, or your management, unless they are your intended audience. |
| Length | ~~Less is more! Be concise.~~ Eliminate ALL unnecessary words. ~~Challenge every word = do you need it?~~ |
| Tone | Use conversational pronouns (you, us, our, we). Write as if you were talking to a colleague or friend. Use contractions (we're *instead of* we are). |
| Voice | Use active voice with strong verbs. Say "We mailed your form on May 1" instead of "Your form was mailed by us on May 1." |
| Word Choice | Use the same words your readers use when they search for your info on the Web. Avoid acronyms and jargon. |
| Simplify | Use simple, descriptive section headings; short paragraphs; and ordinary, familiar words. |
| Links | Never use "click here"—link language should describe what your reader will get if they click that link. Include key words to help search engines. |
| Organization | Put the most important information first, followed by the details. |
| Improve Tasks | Organize content around your customers' tasks, not your organization. Highlight action items (step 1, step 2, etc.). |
| Scannability | Separate content into small chunks. Use lots of white space for easy scanning. In general, write no more than 5–7 lines per paragraph. Use lists and bullets, they are easy to scan. |
| Separate Topics | Present each topic separately. Keep the information on each page to three (or fewer) levels. |
| Context | Don't assume your readers already know the subject or have read related pages. Each page should stand on its own. Put everything in context. |
| Test and Evaluate | Test Web pages with actual customers so you can be sure real people can understand what you write. |
| Train | Encourage all your colleagues (lawyers, accountants, researchers, etc.) to use plain language—because all content is potentially Web content. |

*Source*: Reprinted with original comma splice from DigitalGov, https://www.digitalgov.gov/.

comprehension of documents. Some barriers primarily concern publishers of digital content: for example, limited (or nonexistent) internet access in rural areas, off-brand dissemination platforms, proprietary digital formats, special software requirements, passwords, paywalls, and cost. And other barriers exist not just because of physical and cognitive disabilities but also because of limited literacy, lack of native English proficiency, and cultural differences. In these matters, copyeditors already have a role: to ensure accessibility for diverse readerships, Cheung recommends editing for plain language, translation readiness, inclusiveness, and cultural sensitivity, in addition to facilitating the previously described accessibility strategies when required.[13]

## GLOBAL ENGLISH

According to some estimates, English is the world's most spoken language and the third most common native language, after Mandarin Chinese and Spanish. Nearly a billion people worldwide speak varieties of English as their mother tongue or as a second or foreign language (*ESL* or *EFL*).[14] In technology, commerce, science, and scholarship, English is the lingua franca of globalization—in particular, a simplified form of written English often called *global English* or *international English style.* International technology companies prepare documentation in global English so that the content will be readily comprehensible to nonnative English speakers and suitable for machine-assisted translation into local languages. Other international businesses likewise aim for this precise, logical, and literal style of English in global communications.

Individuals and companies that address global audiences use global English; editors who work in an international environment follow the guidelines for this style. Global English is especially the language of technical writers preparing manuals and instructions that must be completely clear to everyone who reads them. Accordingly, guides such as the *Microsoft Manual of Style* and *The Yahoo! Style Guide* devote many pages to the requirements of global English. (Several books listed in the Selected Bibliography elaborate on these requirements: see John R. Kohl, *The Global English Style Guide,* and Edmond H. Weiss, *The Elements of International English Style.*) No surprise, many of the directives summarized in table 25 simply reiterate the directives for plain language writing long advocated by Fowler, Strunk and White, and other twentieth-century pedagogues. But added to the now familiar advice regarding plain style are dictates explicitly intended to simplify diction and syntax for EFL readers—and especially for machine translation software.

13. Iva Cheung, "Four Levels to Accessible Communications" (blog post), September 17, 2016, *Iva Cheung,* http://www.ivacheung.com/. This post summarizes a paper on accessible publications that Cheung presented at several academic conferences in 2016. Cheung's thoughtful blog is widely read (and her stick-figure cartoons are greatly appreciated) in editorial networks throughout Canada and the US.

14. "English as a second language" is the term commonly used in the US, where English is the primary language; "English as a foreign language" is the preferred term in countries where English is not the native language.

TABLE 25. Guidelines for Global English

*Form*

Write in Standard English free of grammar, punctuation, and spelling errors.

Use conventional capitalization to clearly identify proper names and beginnings of sentences.

To articulate sentence structure clearly, include all optional punctuation, e.g., series commas and commas after short introductory phrases.

*Syntax*

Avoid sentence fragments, even fragments used to introduce a vertical list or add emphasis.

Avoid telegraphic sentences and headings, especially if the text will be machine translated: "Search the document," not "Search document."

Write short sentences (preferably less than twenty-five words).

Use simple subject-verb-object word order.

Avoid joining more than three phrases or clauses with coordinate conjunctions.

Keep adjectives and adverbs close to the words they modify.

Avoid long strings of modifiers and noun stacks.

Use active voice verbs.

Repeat auxiliary verbs in compound predicates to facilitate parsing.

> *Not:* Our business model has changed and expanded in the past ten years.
> *But:* Our business model has changed and has expanded in the past ten years.

Disambiguate verbals (participles, gerunds, and infinitives), for example, by adding optional determiners, creating relative clauses with explicit relative pronouns, or breaking up sentences.

> *Not:* This new product has added value.
> *But:* This new product has an added value.

> *Not:* Calculate limits on your investment based on your annual disposable income.
> *But:* Calculate limits on your investment that are based on your annual disposable income.
> *Or:* Calculate limits on your investment. Base these limits on your annual disposable income.

> *Not:* Editing Macros
> *But:* How to Edit Macros
> *Or:* Macros That Are Used for Editing

Use optional determiners such as *a, an, the, your,* and *this* to mark all nouns clearly.

> *Not:* Be sure to enclose a completed form, self-addressed envelope, and stamp.
> *But:* Be sure to enclose a completed form, a self-addressed envelope, and a stamp.

Supply optional pronouns such as *that* and *who* to clarify grammatical relationships.

> *Not:* Here is a customer you can help. This is the software you need.
> *But:* Here is a customer whom you can help. This is the software that you need.

Use affirmative rather than negative statements.

*Diction*

Use standard vocabulary; avoid slang and neologisms.

Avoid unnecessary technical terms and jargon.

Do not coin words by adding prefixes. They cannot be rendered in non-Latin languages by translation software.

TABLE 25 *(continued)*

Avoid idioms, regionalisms, and colloquial expressions.

Avoid nonliteral expressions, such as ironic statements, puns and wordplay, clichés, metaphors, and other figurative language.

Avoid clipped terms (app, con, vet).

Do not use abbreviations unless they are fully standard; do not use common Latin abbreviations (e.g., i.e.). Spell out state names.

Spell out acronyms.

Avoid non-English words.

Do not use *they* to refer to a singular antecedent: although idiomatic, the construction remains confusing to EFL readers and to machine-translating software.

Simplify alphabetical lists: if the list items are translated, they may have to be reordered.

*Sources:* "Content for a Worldwide Audience," *Microsoft Manual of Style*, 4th ed. (Redmond, Wash.: Microsoft Press, 2012), pp. 33–46; "Write for an International Audience," *The Yahoo! Style Guide* (New York: St. Martin's Griffin, 2010), pp. 80–101; Alexandra Norvet, "What Is Global English?" United Language Group Daily, Sept. 22, 2016, https://daily.unitedlanguagegroup.com/stories/editorials/global-english.

In addition, guidelines for global English communication emphasize the importance of inclusiveness and cultural sensitivity. To wit:

- If applicable, include a disclaimer stating that examples, scenarios, and locations are fictitious.
- Be sensitive to the possible cultural misreading of details in invented scenarios and examples.
- Avoid topics and comments that may seem inappropriate in some cultures: sexual innuendo, jokes about religion, political commentary.
- Avoid culture-specific references that may puzzle or offend some international readers: a New York minute, the unlucky thirteenth floor, a crusade against cancer.
- Diversify invented examples to ensure that they represent many different nationalities and ethnicities: personal names, street and email addresses, phone numbers, URLs, currencies.
- Avoid highly local references unlikely to be understood outside a given city or region: the South Side (of Boston); the Tenderloin (district of San Francisco).
- Do not assume that US standards are worldwide: systems of measurement, keyboard layouts, paper size, character sets, text direction, phone numbers, postal codes, voltages, video standards.
- Use the international (twenty-four-hour) time format: 13:00 hours, not 1:00 p.m.
- Begin calendar weeks on Monday, the first day of the week in much of the world.
- To avoid ambiguity, spell out the names of months using the format *month dd, yyyy:* the order of information in all-number date expressions differs worldwide.

- Refer to months or calendar quarters rather than to seasons: summer and winter are opposite in the Northern and Southern Hemispheres.
- Avoid mentioning real places, except for major world cities.
- If it is necessary to specify actual locations, identify the country or region.
- Do not name countries, regions, cities, or land features in disputed areas.
- Use simple, generic illustrations and colors that are appropriate worldwide: holiday images and gender-mixed social situations may be culturally offensive; almost all hand signals are insulting somewhere; the cultural connotations of colors—for example, white (bridal purity versus mourning and death)—vary.

## EFL AND ESL EDITING

Many scientists and scholars in non-Anglophone countries write in *English as a foreign language* (EFL) for English-language journals and for an international community of peers, often with the help of native-English editors who specialize in preparing EFL writing for publication. In Anglophone countries, nonnative English speakers writing in *English as a second language* (ESL) may likewise turn to editors for refinement of their English prose prior to self-publication or submission to a publisher. Serving the needs of these authors constitutes a significant part of the business of some freelance editors. But EFL-ESL editing is a demanding specialty: it poses unique challenges that can vary greatly with an author's native language and culture.

Some problems in EFL and ESL writing are readily emended: simple errors in English syntax, in the idiomatic use of definite and indefinite articles (the, a, an) and prepositions, in complex verb forms, and in diction—errors such as false cognates and words with unsuitable connotations. But more subtle writing problems may originate in a cultural mismatch between an author's native writing conventions and English-language readers' expectations. For example, an author may use elaborate and confusing (and mixed) metaphors, omit transitions, or make points obliquely. Or an author may recite from others' works extensively without attribution, a practice often discouraged in English-speaking cultures as patch writing (or even plagiarism) but in some cultures considered a demonstration of knowledge.

Key to editing EFL and ESL authors is communication. Editors must manage both the language barrier and possible cultural differences regarding appropriate social behavior in the relationship. Authors may perceive editing as transgressing personal boundaries or disrespecting their expertise. Queries, explanations, and instructions in English must be carefully worded, courteous, and always respectful of an author's knowledge and humanity. Editors should always follow the author's lead in communication style, whether it is perfunctory or chatty, aloof or demonstrative.[15]

15. This discussion is particularly indebted to Katharine O'Moore-Klopf, "Editing for ESL Authors," May 25, 2007, and to the anonymous article "How to Work with ESL Writers," May 12, 2014, both at Copyediting, https://www.copyediting.com/.

## BIAS-FREE LANGUAGE

Copyeditors are expected to query or revise any material—text, diagrams, or photo-graphs—that promotes stereotyping (based on gender, ethnicity, religion, age, or other group designation), that marginalizes groups of people, or that is insensitive to cultural and other differences. To be clear: Authors are free to express their views; publishers are free to publish them—or not; and copyeditors are free to quit if they cannot abide the content of a manuscript. The principle here is not to censor authors who wish to enunci-ate "politically incorrect" views but rather to prevent authors from *unwittingly* offending or excluding groups of people. For example:

> The pioneers crossed the mountains with their women, children, and possessions.

This sentence implies that only men are pioneers and that women and children are of a status roughly equivalent to possessions.

> *Revision:* The pioneers and their children crossed the mountains with their possessions.

> *Or:* The pioneer families crossed the mountains with their possessions.

In the following sentence, in contrast, a possession is accorded the status of a person (Deep Blue is a computer that plays grand master–level chess):

> Deep Blue sacrificed his bishop, but three moves later he could not avoid losing his rook to Kasparov's pawn.

For a computer, surely the pronoun *it* is preferable. Also, using *he* only reinforces the stereotype that competitive chess is "a man's world"—or perhaps that all computers (and computer programmers) are male.

> *Revision:* Deep Blue sacrificed its bishop, but three moves later it could not avoid losing its rook to Kasparov's pawn.

A different kind of occupational stereotype is implied by

> The lives of rock musicians seem to involve a passion for money, women, and fame.

—which assumes that all rock musicians are either heterosexual men or gay women.

> *Revision:* The lives of rock musicians seem to involve a passion for money, sex, and fame.

Sports metaphors can add energy and color, but they may also make some people—for example, those who don't participate in the sports culture of US football and baseball—feel that they are not part of the intended audience:

> As an investor, you need to know your tolerance for risk. On fourth down and two, would you punt or pass?

Every team leader dreams of making the Hail Mary pass or the three-point shot at the buzzer.

An attorney must be able to read opposing counsel's strategy: is the other side likely to call for a hit-and-run play or a suicide squeeze?

Similarly, certain kinds of domestic imagery signal that women, and only women, are the intended audience:

Beyond an understanding of anatomy and physiology, visiting nurses must have good interpersonal skills and not be afraid to let their maternal instincts show.

Some sentences, of course, concern subjects who are all of one sex:

A mother-to-be is encouraged to bring her spouse to the lecture on prenatal genetic testing.

*Her* is the correct pronoun, but *spouse* implies that the only concerned partner a pregnant woman may have is a husband or wife. But some pregnant women are not in intimate relationships, others are in nonmarital relationships (with men or with women), and some married women—for various reasons—rely primarily on a family member or friend for support during their pregnancy.

*Revision:* A mother-to-be is encouraged to bring a spouse, partner, family member, or close friend to the lecture.

In a lighthearted or personal essay, the following hyperbole would be unobjectionable.

Like all the great ideas of our time, this one appeared unbidden one morning, in the bathroom, during the Zen-like satori brought about by the daily ritual of shaving.

Indeed, to raise any objection is to risk being labeled as humorless—the insult most often hurled at people who pose questions about biased language. But notice that this sentence attributes all the great ideas of our time to beardless men. In addition, satori (the state of intuitive enlightenment brought about through the practice of Zen Buddhism) is demoted to a "Zen-like" experience. (For comparison's sake, would one ever refer to baptism as a "Christian-like practice"?) If one wants to be precise, the "like" should modify "satori," not "Zen": "during the satori-like experience." And will those readers who have never experienced the daily ritual of shaving understand what aspect of this experience is satori-like? Is it the scraping of one's cheeks, chin, and throat with a sharp razor blade, the white-noise whirring of an electric razor, or the mindful mindlessness induced by a daily routine?

*Possible revision:* Like all the great ideas of our time, this one appeared unbidden one morning, in the bathroom, during a moment of intuitive clarity brought about by the daily rituals that entail staring at your face in the mirror.

In medical manuals and reference books, in contrast, biased language can have serious consequences:

Jaundice is fairly common in newborns and usually clears up within a week.
After that, if your infant's skin looks yellow or greenish, call your doctor.

The question here is whether this skin-tone indicator is reliable for infants of all ethnicities or whether the author has unintentionally excluded infants of color. A copyeditor should query: "Is 'yellow or greenish' a good indicator for nonwhite infants? If it is not, please supply another indicator."

At other times, biased language introduces illogicalities:

The high school lunchroom is wholly segregated: no one ever shares a table
with any of the Vietnamese students.

What this author seems to want to say is that Vietnamese students and non-Vietnamese students never sit at the same lunch table. Yet surely some of the Vietnamese students eat together, and so it is not true that "no one" shares a table with "any of the Vietnamese students."

*Revision:* The high school lunchroom is wholly segregated: students of other
nationalities never share a table with Vietnamese students.

In the following sentence, changing the Eurocentric "Oriental" (Asia is "the East" only if one is standing in Europe) to "Asian" marks a start:

Ms. Lin's Oriental background makes her an asset to our company.

*Initial revision:* Ms. Lin's Asian background makes her an asset to our company.

But Asia is a vast continent that includes many distinct cultures, and the sentence would also be more informative if it stated the specific skills or attributes that are valuable to the company—for example, Ms. Lin's fluency in Mandarin, her knowledge of Japanese history, her fieldwork in Indonesia, or her personal contacts in the Pakistani business community.

Despite the success of basketball and other competitive events for wheelchair athletes, one still encounters

Though confined to a wheelchair, Granger nonetheless writes at least five articles a year.

The first problem here is that wheelchairs are mobility aids, not prisons; users of wheelchairs are no more "confined" to their chairs than bicyclists are "confined" to their bikes, or motorists "confined" to their cars. Indeed, people who use wheelchairs say that it is when they are without their chairs—not when they are in them—that they feel confined. Second, the "nonetheless" implies that using a wheelchair is an obstacle to being a prolific writer—as though Granger's disability were located in his brain, not his body. Depending on the context, a copyeditor could propose relocating the mention of Granger's disability or, if Granger's health is irrelevant to the theme, deleting the wheelchair entirely.

## DEFAULT ASSUMPTION

Another issue of concern is avoiding what has come to be called "the default assumption." Here, the writer identifies only those people who belong to some special category; people are otherwise assumed to be members of the so-called majority, the default, and they pass unmarked. For example:

> The jury includes five men and two African American women.

If the gender and race or ethnicity of the jurors are important, then the author should state both factors for each of the jurors; if race or ethnicity is not relevant, then the author should not identify any of the jurors by race. Then, too, unless this jury has only seven members, some of the jurors (the women who are not African Americans) are unaccounted for.

The following sentence presents the careful reader with a conundrum:

> The panel includes three professionals, two blue-collar workers, and two women.

Does this panel have five members (three professionals and two blue-collar workers, among whom are three men and two women) or seven members? By identifying some of the panelists by an occupational category and some by gender, the author bungles the count.

The next sentence may seem unremarkable:

> The conference was chaired by a female aerospace engineer.

—until one considers that one would never see its counterpart ("The conference was chaired by a male aerospace engineer") in print. Likewise, all-too-common terms such as "a woman writer" or "a male nurse" seem to suggest that the person's gender is an anomaly in that activity or profession, "like a dog's walking on his hind legs."[16] If gender is irrelevant to the discussion, the adjective should simply be omitted; if it is pertinent, the insinuation of a gender clue elsewhere in the text (e.g., with a strategically placed *she* or *he*) is often preferable to using a gender-marked adjective.

Out of context, this next sentence also appears to demonstrate the default assumption (no mention is made of the physical health or abilities of the other team members).

> The winning design was submitted by a team that includes an architect who is physically disabled.

But one cannot be sure until one has read the full account. If the design is for a new bridge across the Hudson River, then the team members' level of physical ability or disability is irrelevant, and this one architect has been singled out for mention solely

16. When gender is relevant, the noun *woman* may be used attributively ("a woman ironworker") if the isolated adjective *female* seems derogatory because the term is also used for animals; otherwise, *female* is unobjectionable and is preferred in pairings with *male* ("male and female members of Ironworkers Local Union 377"; *Chicago* 5.226). The reference to a (male) dog walking on hind legs comes from Samuel Johnson's infamous remark about a *woman* preacher: "Sir, a woman's preaching is like a dog's walking on his hind legs. It is not done well; but you are surprised to find it done at all" (James Boswell, *The Life of Samuel Johnson*). In some respects, the Age of Enlightenment wasn't.

because of membership in a minority group. But if the design is for a plan to improve access to a library and the architect uses a wheelchair, cane, or braces, the architect's familiarity with the problems faced by people who use mobility aids (rather than the disability itself) may well be relevant.[17]

## BIASED TERMINOLOGY

Copyeditors almost never encounter overt ethnic or racial slurs in manuscripts, but some authors use derivative terms that may strike some readers as insensitive. Controversies abound: Are colloquial verbs like *gyp* and *welsh* (or *welch*) offensive? Do expressions such as *dutch treat, French letter,* and *Siamese twins* (scientists now use *conjoined twins*) promote stereotyping? Or are phrases objectionable only when they attribute negative characteristics to the named group: *Indian giver, French leave, Dutch uncle*? Should editors excise terms such as *niggardly,* even though both the spelling and the etymology of this word differ from those of the racial slur it so unfortunately resembles? Should writers avoid figurative language in which the adjective *black* is used to connote discredit (*black sheep*), illegality (*black market*), or exclusion (*blackball, blacklist*)? What about the metaphoric use of the astronomer's *black hole* to refer to a project that consumes endless financial resources? Or the metaphoric *white knight,* which confers goodness on whiteness? Should they eschew the light or generic use of historically freighted terms, such as *final solution* or *middle passage*?

Proponents and opponents of these kinds of phrases are quick to marshal their arguments. The pro faction appeals to etymology ("*Blackball* refers to the color of the token used to veto a person's entry into an organization, not to the skin color of a person") and utility ("There is no good equivalent expression for *Indian giver*") or accuses opponents of hypersensitivity ("Who really hears *gypsies* in *gyp*?"), overly literal readings ("Using the phrase *black sheep* or *call the kettle black* doesn't mean one is a racist"), and self-righteous humorlessness ("Must every single syllable be ever so politically correct?"). The anti faction notes that some of the phrases are insulting, that the cumulative effect of such "colorful" language is denigrating, and that perhaps it is better to err on the side of caution than to run roughshod over entire nationalities, cultures, and social groups.

A more frequent problem—and a less controversial one—is gender-inflected occupational terms. Many publishers have explicit guidelines on avoiding gender bias and expect their copyeditors to replace gendered terms. For example:

---

17. The difficulties entailed in judging the relevance of a person's physical disability and the prominence to accord it in a piece are illustrated by a review in the *New York Times* of a recital by Evelyn Glennie, a percussionist and composer. The review, extremely enthusiastic about her performance and range, consists of nine long paragraphs. The eighth paragraph reads: "One would be remiss not to mention that Ms. Glennie has been deaf since her teenage years, a point that is not noted in her program biography. In a way, it is beside the point: there is no question of making allowances here, Ms. Glennie's musicianship is extraordinary by any measure"; Allan Kozinn, "From Clay Pots to Cowbells with a Different Drummer," *New York Times,* February 2, 1998, https://www.nytimes.com/1998/02/02/arts /music-review-from-clay-pots-to-cowbells-with-a-different-drummer.html. (The comma after "making allowances here" may have been an oversight, but some writers defend this comma as preferable to a semicolon to emphasize a contrast; see Edward D. Johnson, *The Handbook of Good English,* pp. 122–23.)

| Instead of | Use |
|---|---|
| actress | actor, performer, player, thespian, star |
| blonde | blond |
| businessman | business owner, business manager, business executive, business leader, business professional, businessperson, entrepreneur, employer |
| chairman | presiding officer, convener, coordinator, chair, president |
| congressman | member of Congress, congressional representative |
| craftsman | artisan, craftsperson, craftworker |
| fathers (figurative use) | pioneers, founders, innovators, trailblazers |
| fireman | firefighter |
| housewife | homemaker, householder, woman |
| mailman | mail carrier, postal worker |
| man (noun) | people, human beings, individuals |
| man (verb) | work, staff, operate, serve |
| man-hour | operator-hour, work-hour, staff-hour |
| mankind | humanity, humankind, human beings |
| manmade | manufactured, artificial, synthetic, fabricated |
| manpower | staff, workforce, workers, personnel |
| newsman | reporter, journalist, newscaster |
| ombudsman | ombudsperson, ombuds |
| servicemen | military personnel, soldiers |
| spokesman | representative, spokesperson, press agent, public relations agent |
| statesman | elected official, appointed official, legislator, leader |
| watchman | guard, security guard |
| weatherman | weather reporter, weathercaster |
| workmanlike | skillful, expert |

Some people dislike what they perceive as newfangled forms. For example, the use of *chair* or *chairperson* for *chairman* encountered stiff resistance in US journalism well into the 1990s and still sometimes gets singled out for disapproval. But not all such objections are valid. *M-W Unabridged* points out that *chair* is a standard parliamentary term in use since the second half of the seventeenth century and that the more recent coinage *chairperson,* in use since the early 1970s (almost fifty years longer than *ransomware* and *froyo*), "is common enough that its accepted status cannot be questioned" (s.v. "chairman"). Still, sensitive stylists may find some gender-neutral alternatives contrived, self-conscious, or unnatural in a particular context. (*Garner's* deplores the upstart *chairperson* and casts a vote for the long-established *chair.*) To avoid an undesirable dissonance, writers have recourse to many alternative terms.

For more examples and options, see the books and online guides mentioned in the resources subsection ending this discussion of bias-free language; full details are provided in the Selected Bibliography. No matter what your ideology, some examples in these resources may strike you as hypersensitive, overly fussy, or wrongheaded. But you will also find valuable pointers and provocative ideas about the power (or tyranny) of language.

## THE GENERIC *HE*

The use of *he* as a generic singular pronoun has long been considered standard in formal writing.

> *Generic* he: A senator should meet with his staff at least once a day.

> *Generic* he: An astronaut must prepare himself, physically and mentally, to endure the isolation he will feel as he sees Earth recede in the distance.
> [In both sentences, "he" is supposed to be understood as referring to both men and women; thus the term "generic *he*."]

The practice still has its adherents, but today this group is declining in number and is clearly on the defensive. For the copyeditor, the generic *he* presents two problems. The first is one of policy: when should a copyeditor intervene to eliminate the generic *he*? The second concerns the selection of techniques.

*Policy.* Decisions about removing the generic *he* are relatively easy when a copyeditor is working for a publisher that supplies its authors and editors with written guidelines on bias-free language. The copyeditor can apply the policy to the manuscript, quote the policy in a cover note to the author, and feel confident that the editorial coordinator will support the emendations should the author question them.

When the publisher does not have a formal policy on bias-free language, however, the copyeditor is in a more difficult position. Some copyeditors always eliminate the generic *he* from every manuscript that crosses their desk, trusting that their authors will not raise a fuss. Other copyeditors recast the occasional generic *he* but consult with their editorial coordinator before revising a long manuscript that is replete with generic *he*s and *his*es and *him*s. In these cases, the editorial coordinator will provide on-the-spot suggestions, propose a preedit conversation with the author, or ask the copyeditor to submit a short sample edit for the author's approval.

*Techniques.* Although a writer or a copyeditor can always toss in an "or she," there are many ways to avoid the generic *he* without introducing awkward strings of "he or she" or "his and her." For example:

> Everyone has his problems.

> *Delete the masculine pronoun:* Everyone has problems.

> *Change to the first-person plural:* We all have our problems.

> *Use the plural pronoun* their *after an indefinite pronoun:* Everyone has their problems.

[If your authors scowl at this "betrayal" of pronoun-antecedent agreement, you might show them the discussion of "singular *they*" with indefinite pronouns under "Pronoun-Antecedent Agreement" in chapter 14.]

---

Every student must pay his tuition in full by October 1.

*Change to the third-person plural:* Students must pay their tuition in full by October 1.

*Substitute for the masculine pronoun:* Every student must pay this semester's tuition in full by October 1.

*Change to the second person:* You must pay your tuition in full by October 1.

*Make no reference to people:* October 1 is the deadline for the full payment of tuition.

*Use the passive voice:* Tuition must be paid in full by October 1.

*Or:* All tuition payments must be made by October 1.

---

Ibenz argues that an alcoholic cannot be cured of his disease, that he cannot become a social drinker.

*Change to the third-person plural:* Ibenz argues that alcoholics cannot be cured of their disease and cannot become social drinkers.

*Use an article and repeat a noun:* Ibenz argues that an alcoholic cannot be cured of the disease, that an alcoholic cannot become a social drinker.

*Delete a phrase:* Ibenz argues that an alcoholic cannot be cured and cannot become a social drinker.

*Revise the sentence:* Ibenz argues that alcoholism cannot be cured, that no form of treatment will enable an alcoholic to become a social drinker.

Three methods of avoiding the generic *he* should themselves be avoided:

- Slashed constructions (*he/she* or *s/he*) are too stenographic and casual for formal writing. They are also unpronounceable, and seem to suggest a cavalier attitude toward writing. ("Oh, just slash in some *she*s, would you?")
- Alternating *he* and *she* from paragraph to paragraph, or chapter to chapter, may confuse readers, and the effect may be missed by readers who skim the book or see only an excerpted chapter.
- A note at the beginning of the text stating that "all uses of the generic *he* are intended to be read as 'he or she'" is tokenism at its worst. Despite the note, pages and pages of *he*s and *him*s will leave readers with the impression that men are the true subject of the book and that women are only incidental to the main themes.

An author's use of a nongeneric *he* in an example is perfectly fine unless all the examples in the document use *he* and women are invisible. But a copyeditor should query or revise when an author's examples repeatedly cast women in subordinate roles (female patients and male doctors; female clerks and male managers) or use personal pronouns in stereotypical ways (female nurses and kindergarten teachers; male physicists and pilots).

Special consideration must be given to the choice of pronoun for a transgender person: respect and good manners necessitate using the pronoun preferred by the individual. Likewise, "singular *they*" (*their, them*) should be used if a gender-nonconforming individual requests the epicene pronoun: this exception to conventional pronoun-antecedent agreement rules is now endorsed by several major style manuals, including the *AP Stylebook* and *Chicago*. (For a more detailed discussion of using the epicene pronoun to refer to a gender-nonconforming person, see chapter 14's "Pronoun-Antecedent Agreement.")

## NAMES FOR GROUPS OF PEOPLE

Civility and courtesy suggest that groups, like individuals, be called by the name they prefer:

> My name is William, but please call me Bill.

> An Annie Leibovitz photograph of Caitlyn Jenner, formerly Bruce Jenner, appeared on the cover of *Vanity Fair* with the line "Call me Caitlyn."

Also like individuals, groups may change their preferences over time. As Henry Louis Gates Jr. wrote in 1969: "My grandfather was colored, my father was a Negro, and I am black";[18] today Gates is the director of the Hutchins Center for African and African American Research at Harvard University. In addition, at any given time, members of a group may express different preferences. In recent years, *blacks, Blacks, African Americans, African-Americans,* and *people of color* have each had their partisans.

Different opinions, preferences, and even meanings affect many other group designations as well: Latino/Latina/Latinx, Hispanic, Chicano/Chicana, Mexican American; American Indian, Indian, Native American, Inuit, Native Alaskan, First Nation; Aborigine, Aboriginal, Indigenous, Torres Strait Islander; Caucasian, white, of European descent. The checkboxes on the US Census Bureau's 2010 form fail to accommodate the many, ever-changing group identities and self-naming choices, nor do they make provision for individuals of mixed ancestry.

Some of the most difficult debates in the United States today concern terms for racial and ethnic groups. Researchers now agree that the concept of race has no scientific validity, that it is a carry-over from nineteenth-century pseudoanthropology. But even though *race* has no meaning as a biological term, it does signify a cultural reality: the role of skin color, ethnicity, ancestry, and class in society. Whether the topic is

---

18. This widely cited sentence from Gates's 1969 application to Yale University is quoted in Justin Kaplan and Anne Bernays, *The Language of Names* (New York: Simon & Schuster, 1997), p. 70.

foreign policy, law enforcement, reapportionment, or employment policies, writers may need to use racial and ethnic terms to describe groups of people.

For copyeditors, the best course is to read widely enough to know about historical usage and current conventions, preferences, and controversies. As noted earlier, a copyeditor's job is not to censor authors but to help them avoid inadvertently antagonizing or stereotyping people. If you come upon questionable language that is not addressed by house style or the specified style manual, discuss it with your editorial coordinator. If your coordinator agrees that the wording or content is troublesome, present these concerns to the author, propose substitute language, and ask the author to consider revising the manuscript.

Writers and copyeditors should also be wary of euphemisms that may offend some of the people they are meant to show empathy for. For example, some older people sneer at *senior citizen,* noting that it has no younger counterpart (there are no *junior citizens*) and that the term oddly emphasizes citizenship. (What, they ask, shall we call older people who are not citizens of the country in which they reside?) Similarly, many people who have physical, mental, or sensory disabilities resent such euphemisms as *the physically challenged* or *the differently abled,* and they often prefer terms that emphasize the person (*persons who are disabled* or *people with physical disabilities*) to terms that emphasize the disability (*the disabled, the handicapped, the blind*).[19] Such "people-first" language uses various ways of writing "person with a disability" rather than "a disabled person": "She has a learning disability" *not* "She is learning-disabled"; "He is living with schizophrenia" *not* "He is a schizophrenic."

Although euphemisms should be avoided, negatively formulated descriptions of conditions can prejudice readers' perceptions. Resources for bias-free writing offer many alternatives, for example

| *Instead of* | *Use* |
|---|---|
| birth defect | congenital abnormality |
| brain damage | brain injury |
| handicapped parking | accessible parking |
| retardation | intellectual disability |
| substance abuse problem | substance use disorder |

A final example: Some people object to phrases like *cancer victim* or *afflicted with AIDS,* arguing that these terms deprive people of agency, but others feel that *victim* and *afflicted* are accurate in connoting that these illnesses randomly attack people. To those who propose *cancer patients* or *AIDS patients,* the counterargument is that these terms—compared to *people with cancer* or *people living with AIDS*—emphasize the ill-

---

19. Working along similar lines, some have proposed that "enslaved person" be substituted for "slave" since "slavery was a temporary condition imposed upon people, not part of their essence as human beings." But, the opposition counters, "'slave' is a far more stark and powerful word, expressing more accurately the horror of the owning, buying, and selling of human beings. The term 'enslaved person' sounds like a bureaucratic euphemism"; see Alexander Stille, "The Betrayal of History," *New York Review of Books,* June 11, 1998, p. 15.

ness, not the person who has the illness, and that people's medical status as patients or nonpatients is often irrelevant.

For those of us not now suffering from any infirmity, some of the debates over terminology may seem to be quibbling word games. More than name-calling is at stake, however, for stigmatizing language "leads not only to personal pain, but contributes both directly and indirectly to discrimination in jobs, insurance, and society at large."[20]

## RESOURCES

For detailed advice on bias-free writing, including issues of gender, race, nationality, religion, disability, sexual identity and orientation, and age, see Marilyn Schwartz and others, *Guidelines for Bias-Free Writing;* Rosalie Maggio, *Talking about People; APA* (pp. 71–77); the website Conscious Style Guide; and other resources listed in the Selected Bibliography. You may not agree with the analyses and recommendations presented in these sources, but they will help you become aware of the controversies that swirl around various terms—controversies that almost every copyeditor confronts at one time or another.

## PUBLISHING LAW

In both traditional and indie book publishing, the copyeditor may be the only person other than the author who reads the entire manuscript word by word before publication. For this reason, it falls upon the book copyeditor to alert the editorial coordinator or the self-publishing author to any material in the manuscript that might prompt a lawsuit. Copyeditors are not expected to become experts on legal issues nor to determine definitively if there is a problem, but they should know enough about publishing law to flag material that might present a problem in any of four areas of concern: libel, privacy, obscenity, and copyright. The editorial coordinator or author should review the copyeditor's concerns and forward any troublesome passages to an attorney.

Notice that the preceding paragraph emphasizes book publishing. In magazine publishing and corporate publications departments, several veteran editors and administrators usually read every item that is in production. Many magazines and corporate publishers also routinely send the final drafts of upcoming publications to their in-house legal staff for review. But in book publishing, often only those manuscripts known to be controversial receive a full-dress legal review.

---

20. Kay Redfield Jamison, *An Unquiet Mind: A Memoir of Moods and Madness* (New York: Knopf, 1995), p. 180. Jamison is no Pollyanna: in the next paragraph, she acknowledges that "rigidly rejecting words and phrases that have existed for centuries" is unlikely to transform public attitudes. She also explains that as a clinician and researcher, she values medical terminology but that "as a person and patient, . . . I find the word 'bipolar' strangely and powerfully offensive: it seems to me to obscure and minimize the illness it is supposed to represent. The description 'manic-depressive,' on the other hand, seems to capture both the nature and the seriousness of the disease I have, rather than attempting to paper over the reality of the condition" (pp. 181–82).

If you have any doubt about the legal review procedures for a project, you should consult with the editorial coordinator or client author.

## LIBEL

In the United States, *libel* is defined as the publication of a defamatory false statement about an identifiable living person. Packed into this short definition are four criteria, and a statement is libelous only if it meets *all four:*

1. The statement must be false. A true statement is not libelous.

2. The false statement must be presented as a fact, not as an opinion. An author's expression of a personal opinion, no matter how pejorative, does not constitute libel.

3. The false statement must be defamatory. That is, it must cause—or be reasonably likely to cause—the individual to suffer shame, ridicule, or contempt; a damaged reputation; or loss of employment. Thus all of the following kinds of statements *if untrue* are defamatory:

   > accusations that an individual has committed a criminal act
   > declarations that an individual has a serious illness or disease
   > imputations that the individual is dishonest or incompetent at work
   > mention of an individual's membership in a group held in disrepute
   > mention of an individual's sexual activities

4. The person must be alive and identifiable. Disguising a person's name and changing various details are not always sufficient to make the individual unidentifiable. (Oddly enough, a few novelists have found themselves in court because they invented characters and details that resembled real people, who then sued.) However, if the author has obtained an individual's signed consent to publish material (for example, a series of family letters), the individual cannot later sue for libel.

Defamatory statements about public officials and other public figures are subject to a different standard. (The definition of *public figures* is somewhat vague. The class includes people who wield "pervasive power," who voluntarily enter public controversies, and who have regular and continuing access to the media.) One can print defamatory statements about public officials and other public figures as long as one is acting in good faith and not out of malice; that is, the author must have a legitimate purpose for having published the statement (e.g., the purpose cannot be solely to injure an individual's reputation), the author must not publish a statement he or she knows to be false, and the author must have made a good-faith effort to verify the veracity of the statement.

US libel laws vary from state to state, but all are designed to maximize freedom-of-speech protection. Other countries offer less robust protection to authors and publishers of content alleged to be defamatory. In the US, a plaintiff must prove the *falsity* of a damaging statement and, if the plaintiff is a public figure, must also demonstrate *mal-*

*ice.* In the UK, by contrast, the defendant must prove the *truthfulness* of the statement; in the case of a public figure, absence of malice is not a sufficient defense if the defamatory statement is untrue. Publishers of controversial content intended for international distribution are thus well advised to consult an attorney with expertise in international publishing law.

If you find any statements in a manuscript that might constitute libel, be sure to note those passages for your editorial coordinator and the author.

## INVASION OF PRIVACY

Privacy is an individual's right to not be subjected to undeserved publicity, regardless of whether the published material is true. Thus the issue here is *not* the truth or falsity of the published material, but whether an individual's right to be left alone was intruded upon by a writer or a photographer.

In general, the personal affairs of private individuals who have done nothing newsworthy are protected. Public figures are not accorded the same level of protection, but it is recognized that certain aspects of their personal lives are not newsworthy.

To avoid lawsuits charging invasion of privacy, the careful writer or photographer always obtains a signed consent form (also called a release) from the subject of an interview or any identifiable person in a photograph. The publication of photographs of newsworthy public events, such as political demonstrations and rallies, does not require releases from participants, nor does quoting from their speeches and spontaneous utterances at such events.

Examples of invasion of privacy include

publishing nonnewsworthy facts about a nonpublic figure's personal life without
  that person's permission
publishing an embarrassing photograph simply because it is embarrassing
  (that is, the photograph has no news value) without the subject's permission
using a text or photograph for commercial publicity purposes without the
  subject's permission (commercial misappropriation)

If you spot anything in a manuscript (text or photographs) that raises a privacy issue, bring your concerns to the attention of your editorial coordinator and the author.

## OBSCENITY

*Obscenity* refers to published materials (text or illustrations) that offend current community standards and have no redeeming literary, artistic, political, or scientific value. "Community standards" vary, of course, as do judgments about social value. If you encounter borderline materials or profane or off-color language in a manuscript, ask your editorial coordinator for advice.

Publishers' policies about including or excising "dirty words" in a text vary:

- Print the word in full: always, only when the word occurs in a direct quotation, or only when the word occurs in a direct quotation *and* is relevant rather than merely gratuitous.
- Print the first letter of the word only, followed by hyphens (f----), a 2-em dash (f——), or *word* (the f-word, the f word).
- Use a descriptive euphemism ("a vulgar word for fornication"; "a common expletive").
- Delete the word entirely.

An example: On Labor Day 2000 the presidential candidate George W. Bush, who was standing too close to a hot microphone for his whispered conversation with his running mate, Dick Cheney, referred to the *New York Times* reporter Adam Clymer as a "major-league asshole." Some newspapers quoted Bush's unguarded comment verbatim. Others referred to his "disparaging remark," said he "used an obscenity" or "an expletive," or wrote that he employed "a vulgar euphemism for a rectal aperture."[21]

## COPYRIGHT INFRINGEMENT

The author of a work is often responsible for obtaining written permission to reprint copyrighted material. (Publishers of textbooks and high-profile trade books sometimes assume responsibility for securing clearances and hire a professional permissions editor to perform this work.) In general, works published in the United States before 1978 remain under copyright for ninety-five years after the date of publication; works published after 1978, when the US Copyright Act of 1976 was promulgated, remain under copyright for seventy years after the death of the author; and special rules apply to works created before 1978 but not published until after 1978. (For a detailed layperson's discussion of copyright, including copyright duration, see *Chicago* 4.2–50 or one of the books mentioned in the last paragraph of this chapter.)

Since many authors are not experienced in the ways of copyright, the copyeditor is expected to call to the author's attention any quotations and artwork that may require permission to reprint. On the style sheet, in the "Permissions/credits needed" section (see figure 6, in chapter 2), the copyeditor identifies the following types of materials by manuscript page number or file name and key words:

- Lengthy quotations from published nonfiction works that exceed *fair use,* that is, the limited use of copyrighted material, duly attributed, without formal permission. There are no hard-and-fast rules about what constitutes fair use and no word-count formulas specified in copyright law. Instead, courts apply four criteria in evaluating fair use: (1) the purpose and character of the use, including whether the use is commercial, nonprofit, or educational;

---

21. Both the incident and its media coverage are described in Howard Kurtz, "Bush Gaffe Becomes Big-Time News," *Washington Post,* September 5, 2000, https://www.washingtonpost.com/archive/business/technology/2000/09/05/bush-gaffe-becomes-big-time-news/.

(2) the nature of the copyrighted work used; (3) the amount and substantiality of the portion used; and (4) the effect of the use on the potential market for or value of the copyrighted work. How a court will weigh and interpret these factors in a given case of alleged copyright infringement is difficult to foresee, so most publishers provide simple word-count guidelines for copyeditors to use in flagging quotations for legal evaluation. In the absence of such guidelines (for example, when working with a self-publishing author), apply the following rule of thumb in assessing how much text may probably be used under the fair use principle: up to about fifty words from a short nonfiction article and about four hundred words from a nonfiction book without permission. The copyeditor should add up the *total* number of words quoted from each source throughout the entire manuscript and flag any cases that exceed this guideline.[22]

- Any quotation from a poem, novel, short story, play, or song that is still under copyright—Shakespeare's works are not under copyright; Bob Dylan's are. Reprinting even one or two lines from a creative work may require permission. But brief epigraphs are "probably fair use by virtue of scholarly and artistic tradition. . . . Limited quotation of song lyrics, poetry, and the like in the context of an interior monologue or fictional narrative" also may get a pass under the fair use principle (*Chicago* 4.84, 4.87). Likewise, brief excerpts from creative works that are quoted for purposes of criticism and commentary in a scholarly analysis or a book review are normally allowed as fair use.

- Any quotation from unpublished materials (e.g., correspondence, journals, private manuscripts). Limited quotation from unpublished materials is also permitted under fair use, but access to these materials is often controlled by the author or owner, sometimes in the form of use restrictions. For example, a collection of old family letters on deposit in a university archive may still be owned by family heirs who stipulate that the letters not be made public for a specified period of time. Even in the absence of such stipulations, consideration should always be given to the desire of the author or author's living heirs to control the release of unpublished content to the public.

- Any table, graph, chart, photograph, or illustration that is not the author's own work and is not public domain content from a US government publication.[23] The reproduction of a map, graph, table, or chart that simply presents

---

22. Extensive paraphrasing and even short quotations for purposes other than the presentation of evidence or examples for analysis, commentary, review, or evaluation may not be considered fair use. For this reason, some publishers ask copyeditors to note lengthy passages of paraphrase, and some publishers may require an author to obtain permission for epigraphs and other undiscussed quotations if the original work is still under copyright.

23. Government publications prepared as part of a federal employee's official duties are in the public domain and may be freely used. (This exception does not apply to certain works created by the Department of Commerce or to works created by officers in state and local governments.) However, US government publications may include works copyrighted by a contractor or grantee, copyrighted material assigned to the US government, or copyrighted information from other sources.

nonproprietary factual information without distinctive pictorial embellishment, or "expressive input," is normally considered fair use. Such content may even be beyond copyright protection.

Regardless of whether material is used with permission or under fair use, appropriate attribution is required. Content used with permission requires not only a source citation but also a formal credit line, and the copyeditor may need to advise the author about the wording. If the grantor specifies a wording, it should be followed. (However, *Chicago* 3.32 allows for very minor tweaks to the stipulated wording of credit lines for the sake of editorial consistency within a book, provided the grantor is not adamant about the exact language.) When there is no stipulated wording, credits usually take the form of

Reprinted by permission of ABC.

*Or:* Reproduced by permission of XYZ.

Copyrighted content supplied free and without restrictions is usually credited with the wording

Courtesy of DEF.

As noted earlier, copyeditors are not asked to render judgments or opinions on matters of law, only to flag material that may merit further review.

## CREATIVE COMMONS

Beyond what is permitted under the fair use principle, authors must obtain permission to use or adapt copyrighted materials for their own work. But permissions fees and the negotiation of licensing terms sometimes constitute barriers to creative and intellectual work, especially in the nonprofit sector. Creative Commons (CC) was founded in 2001 as a nonprofit organization dedicated to the free sharing of creative content and knowledge. Copyright owners who want to encourage the reuse of their work make it available for free under one of six basic CC licenses. Appropriate credit must always be given; permission must still be requested from the copyright owner for uses not granted under the license; and some conditions and restrictions may apply, depending on the license used. For example, a CC license may stipulate that any further reuse of the licensed content be licensed under identical terms as those of the first use, that the original work not be altered or abridged, or that the use be noncommercial.

Copyeditors rarely undertake permissions research and clearances, but they should know that even copyrighted content available under a CC license is not simply open range for grazing. This applies especially to web content: it is usually protected by copyright—contrary to a widespread belief among authors that text and images found on the internet are free for the taking—and is sometimes licensed for reuse under CC models. The crowdsourced (and often plagiarized) Wikipedia, for example, makes its content available under a CC BY-SA license, which requires attribution and identical terms in any relicensing. But some public institutions take the idea of "the commons" even further. In February 2017, New York's Metropolitan Museum of Art made nearly four hundred thousand digital images of public domain artworks available for download under a Creative Commons Zero (CC0) license, which allows reuse for any purpose, commercial or noncommercial, free of charge and without permission from the museum. Attribution is the only requirement for use.

## PLAGIARISM

Although plagiarism per se is not a criminal or civil offense, it is illegal when it infringes copyright. But even when plagiarism is not actionable, it is an ethical violation, an appropriation of others' creative or intellectual labor and a betrayal of readers' trust that the content is the author's own work. Most students know that unattributed verbatim copying is reprehensible and that the submission of a purchased term paper is grounds for a failing grade or worse. Scholars, journalists, and other professional writers know these things too, despite occasional scandals involving plagiarism. More common than these highly publicized ethical breaches, however, are the slippery cases in which writers rely too heavily on the research, arguments, interpretations, and words of other writers or endlessly recycle their own work. Such misdeeds—whether the result of naïveté, carelessness, indolence, or deliberate deception—seem far more widespread in an era in which so much content is available at writers' fingertips. Among the many subtle forms plagiarism may take are

> the theft of original wording: an author copies a passage verbatim without quotation marks or attribution
>
> theft by paraphrase: an author copies a passage, making a few superficial changes to the original wording, without attribution
>
> patch writing: an author rearranges phrases and sentences in the unattributed original but relies too heavily on its vocabulary and structure
>
> the misrepresentation of research: an author ransacks an unattributed secondary source to find and cite original sources as though the author has consulted them directly
>
> excessive aggregation: an author compiles information from many unattributed sources without the addition of any original ideas or analysis
>
> missing or misleading bylines: an author omits all mention of co-authors, collaborators, and translators
>
> self-plagiarism: an author reuses his or her own work in identical or nearly identical form without mentioning the previous publication (An author may legitimately build new work on earlier research, citing previously published data and observations, but must offer sufficient new content to justify the claim of originality.)

Some publishers and educational institutions use plagiarism-checking software, such as iThenticate and Turnitin, to screen for egregious abuses. The best of the plagiarism checkers work with citation-management software and screen the content of paywallprotected online professional journals as well as open websites. None comb through the vast universe of undigitized content—all those books and magazines not yet scanned by Google! Some yield too many false positives to be useful.

Even though screening for plagiarism is not a formal part of a copyeditor's duties, copyeditors sometimes, through inadvertence, become the best line of defense against abuses. While quickly checking an oddly worded direct quotation in the cited website, an editor may discover whole passages that the author has copied verbatim, without quotation marks, from the same site. Or the editor may attempt to verify citation details online, only to stumble upon evidence of self-plagiarism. In such unfortunate cases, the copyeditor's responsibility is to inform the editorial coordinator of the problem rather than to confront the author. If the editor is working directly for a self-publishing author, providing advice and instruction will require consummate tact.

## RESOURCES

For a detailed discussion of legal issues of concern to editors, writers, and publishers, see *Chicago,* chapter 4; Tad Crawford and Kay Murray, *The Writer's Legal Guide;* Leonard D. DuBoff and Sarah J. Tugman, *The Law (in Plain English) for Writers;* and Elsa Peterson, *Copyright and Permissions.* If you have the need or desire to plumb the topic, study William S. Strong's *The Copyright Book,* which is authoritative and quite readable—even for nonlawyers.

# Checklist of Editorial Preferences

The checklist on the following pages presents a range of common variants in editorial style in three categories:

1. mechanics

2. formatting

3. documentation

The checklist can be used both as a training tool and as an adjunct to the copyeditor's style sheet. A copyeditor who is about to begin a project for a new publisher can ask the editorial coordinator to complete the checklist according to house style. Freelance copyeditors who work for several publishers can maintain a checklist for each—a convenient way to keep track of variations in house style. The checklist can also be used by an editorial coordinator in preparing a list of do's and don'ts or an informal tipsheet for in-house and freelance copyeditors.

Publisher's name _____

Preferred dictionary _____ , _____ edition

Style manual _____ , _____ edition,

with these exceptions:

## 1. MECHANICS

*Abbreviations: shortened forms, initialisms (pronounced as letters),*
*acronyms (pronounced as words)*

☐  Replace all common Latin abbreviations (etc., i.e., e.g.) with English equivalents.

☐  Restrict use of common Latin abbreviations to parenthetical expressions
   and notes.

☐  Delete periods in all initialisms and acronyms for organizations and sovereignties
   (AFL-CIO, NBA, NATO, UNESCO, and so forth) except U.S. and U.N.

☐  Delete periods in all initialisms and acronyms for organization and sovereignties
   including US and UN.

☐  Use periods in all initialisms and acronyms for organizations and sovereignties
   (A.F.L.-C.I.O., N.B.A., N.A.T.O., U.N.E.S.C.O., U.K., and so forth).

☐  Follow the author's preference.

☐  Use full capitals for all initialisms and acronyms: HMO, NAACP, NAFTA.

☐  Use an initial capital only for an acronym five letters or longer (Nafta, Erisa,
   Basic); use full capitals for all other acronyms (CARE, CORE).

☐  On first mention of a term, introduce its abbreviation in parentheses: Health
   maintenance organizations (HMOs) are preparing . . .

☐  When the initialism or acronym is better known than the spelled-out version,
   introduce the spelled-out version in parentheses on first mention: A sunscreen
   product with an SPF (sun protection factor) rating of 30 blocks nearly 97 percent
   of damaging radiation. Under ERISA (Employee Retirement Income Security Act
   of 1974) employers cannot . . .

☐  Spell out in parentheses only those initialisms and acronyms likely to be
   unfamiliar to readers.

☐  Do not introduce initialisms or acronyms or their spelled-out versions in
   parentheses; if readers cannot deduce the meaning of the acronym from the
   context, spell out the term on each mention.

☐  Do not abbreviate state names in running text.

☐  Use traditional abbreviations (Calif., N.Y., N.J.) in bibliography, notes, and tables.

☐ Use two-letter postal abbreviations (CA, NY, NJ) in bibliography, notes, and tables.

☐ Use two-letter postal abbreviations only in addresses.

☐ Use small caps for A.M., P.M., C.E. or A.D., and B.C.E. or B.C.

☐ Use small caps, no periods, for AM, PM, CE or AD, and BCE or BC.

☐ Use regular caps for A.M., P.M., C.E. or A.D., and B.C.E. or B.C.

☐ Lowercase a.m. and p.m.; use regular caps for C.E. or A.D. and B.C.E. or B.C.

*Capitalization of titles, subtitles, and heads*

☐ Capitalize prepositions of four or more letters; prepositions that are the first or last word of the item; and prepositions that are an inseparable part of the verb (e.g., *Growing Up Absurd*).

☐ Capitalize prepositions of five or more letters; prepositions that are the first or last word of the item; and prepositions that are an inseparable part of the verb.

☐ Capitalize only prepositions that are the first or last word of the item or that are an inseparable part of the verb.

*Contractions*

☐ Spell out all contractions except for the expressions "do's and don'ts" and "aren't I?"

☐ Follow the author's preference.

*Foreign terms, names, quotes*

☐ Use English-style plurals, not the Latin- or Greek-influenced forms: curriculums (*not* curricula), syllabuses (*not* syllabi), memorandums (*not* memoranda).

☐ For French and Spanish words, delete accent marks on capital letters.

☐ For French and Spanish words, keep or add accent marks on capital letters.

☐ For the transliteration of foreign names, use _____ as a reference book.

☐ Do not italicize a quotation in a foreign language; place it in quotation marks.

☐ Mark quotations in foreign languages for special typographic treatment.

*Hyphenation*

☐ Follow _____ [style manual/dictionary] for hyphenation.

☐ Hyphenate compounds in which the last letter of a prefix ending in a vowel is the same as the first letter of the root: intra-arterial, re-elect, anti-intellectual, micro-organism.

☐ Hyphenate compounds in which the last letter of a prefix ending in a vowel is the same as the first letter of the root, *except* if the vowel is an *e*: intra-arterial, anti-intellectual, micro-organism, *but* reelect.

☐ Hyphenate when a closed compound would produce a misleading diphthong or syllable: pre-image, co-op, co-worker.

*Numbers and numerals*

☐ For dates, use January 1, 1990.

☐ For dates, use 1 January 1990.

☐ Follow the author's preference.

☐ For decades, use 1990s.

☐ For decades, use 1990's.

☐ Treat *mid* as a prefix: in the mid-twentieth century; in the mid-'60s.

☐ Treat *mid* as an adjective: in the mid twentieth century; in the mid '60s.

☐ For plurals of numerals, add *'s*: F-111's, AK-47's.

☐ For plurals of numerals, add *s*: F-111s, AK-47s.

☐ Spell out numbers under 101.

☐ Spell out numbers under 10.

☐ Spell out numbers under _____.

☐ Always use numerals with units of measurement: 3 inches, 6 miles.

☐ Follow the author's preference.

☐ Use US units of measurement only (inches, feet, miles, ounces).

☐ Use SI (metric) units of measurement only (meters, liters, grams).

☐ Use US measurements and the SI equivalent in parentheses: 100 yards (91.4 m).

☐ Use SI measurements and the US equivalent in parentheses: 100 kilometers (62 mi).

☐ Follow the author's preference.

☐ Use a comma in four-digit numbers (except dates, addresses, serial numbers, page numbers).

☐ Use a comma only for five-digit and larger numbers (including dates and page numbers).

☐ Follow the author's preference.

☐ Spell out large sums of money: fifty-five million dollars.

☐ For large sums of money, use numerals and a dollar sign: $55 million.

☐ Follow the author's preference.

- ☐ Always spell out *percent*.
- ☐ Spell out *percent* in running text; OK to use % in parenthetical comments.
- ☐ Follow the author's preference.

- ☐ For page ranges, use all digits: pp. 102–105, pp. 215–217.
- ☐ For page ranges, use two digits after the en dash: pp. 102–05, pp. 215–17.
- ☐ For page ranges, show only the digits that change: pp. 102–5, pp. 215–7.
- ☐ For page ranges, follow the elision system described in *Chicago*.

- ☐ Italicize $N$ ( = the size of the data base, e.g., number of subjects in an experiment).
- ☐ Mark N for roman small caps.
- ☐ Mark N as an uppercase roman letter.

*Possessives*

- ☐ For proper names ending in *s*, add *'s* for the possessive: Jones's.
- ☐ For proper names ending in *s*, add only an apostrophe for the possessive: Jones'.
- ☐ Follow the author's preference.

*Punctuation*

- ☐ Use the serial comma.
- ☐ Do not use the serial comma except when necessary to avoid misreading.
- ☐ Follow the author's preference.

*Spelling*

- ☐ For words with variant spellings, always use the first entry in the dictionary that is named at the beginning of this checklist.
- ☐ Change British spellings such as *theatre, colour, organise* to preferred American spellings.
- ☐ For words that have variant spellings, follow the author's preference.

## 2. FORMATTING

*Cross-references*

- ☐ In cross-references, lowercase *chapter*: see chapter 1.
- ☐ Uppercase *chapter*: see Chapter 1.
- ☐ Uppercase *chapter* and spell out the number: Chapter One.

- ☐ Eliminate cross-references to pages or change them to cross-references to chapters.
- ☐ Instruct the typesetter to set page cross-refs as 00 or 000.
- ☐ Instruct the typesetter to set page cross-refs as solid quads (■■■).

*Extracts*

☐ Run in prose quotes of fewer than _____ words or _____ lines.
☐ Run in poetry quotes of fewer than _____ lines.
☐ Set as extracts quotes longer than _____ words or _____ lines.

*Heads*

☐ Do not open a chapter with a 1-level head.
☐ OK to have chapter begin with a 1-level head.

☐ Do not stack a 2-level head directly under a 1-level head.
☐ OK to stack a 2-level head directly under a 1-level head.

☐ For each level of head used in a chapter or section, there must be at least two instances in that chapter or section. A chapter may not have only one 1-level head; a section may not have only one 2-level or 3-level head.

*Lists*

☐ Do not use bulleted lists.
☐ Use numbered lists only when there is need for numbering the items.
☐ When all items in a list consist of a single word, lowercase the items (except for proper nouns and proper adjectives). In all other cases, capitalize the first word of each item.

*URLs*

☐ Use roman type.
☐ Use italic type.
☐ Enclose in angle brackets: <https://www.chicagomanualofstyle.org/>.
☐ Omit any "wrappers," such as angle brackets or curly braces.
☐ Omit any following punctuation normally used as part of the sentence or citation.
☐ Include any following punctuation normally used as part of the sentence or citation.

## 3. DOCUMENTATION

*Bibliography*

☐ Alphabetize names beginning with *Mc* as though spelled *Mac*: MacDonald, McKillan, McStuart, MacWilson, Mayfield.
☐ Alphabetize names beginning with *Mc* as *Mc*: MacDonald, MacWilson, Mayfield, McKillan, McStuart.

☐  If a work has many authors, list the first three and then "and others."
☐  List the first three and then "et al."
☐  List all authors.
☐  Follow the author's preference.

☐  If there is more than one entry by a given author, list the entries in alphabetic order, disregarding any initial *the, a,* or *an.*
☐  List the entries in chronological order.
☐  Follow the author's preference; query any inconsistencies.

☐  Use traditional abbreviations (Calif., N.Y., Mich., Ill.) for state names in bibliography entries.
☐  Use the two-letter postal abbreviations (CA, NY, MI, IL) for state names in bibliography entries.

☐  Follow the bibliographical format in _____.
☐  Follow the author's preference, as long as it is consistent.

☐  To indicate second and third editions: 2d ed., 3d ed.
☐  To indicate second and third editions: 2nd ed., 3rd ed.

☐  To indicate page numbers in a book: p. 1, pp. 1–3.
☐  Use *p.* and *pp.* only if there might be some confusion that the numbers are page numbers.
☐  Follow the author's preference.

*In-text citations*
☐  For joint authors, use "and": Smith and Wilson.
☐  For joint authors, use &: Smith & Wilson.
☐  Follow the author's preference.

☐  If there are many authors, list the first two, followed by "et al."
☐  If there are many authors, list the first two, followed by "and others."
☐  Follow the author's preference.

☐  Arrange multiple in-text citations alphabetically: see Doe, 1978; Jones, 1990; Smith, 1977.
☐  Ask author to arrange multiple citations in order of importance or value to the reader.
☐  Follow the author's preference.

*Footnotes or endnotes*

☐   To indicate page numbers in a book: See p. 1, pp. 1–3.
☐   Use *p.* and *pp.* only if there might be some confusion.
☐   Follow the author's preference.

☐   Use traditional abbreviations for state names (Calif., Wash., Ore., N.Y.) in notes.
☐   Use the two-letter postal abbreviations (CA, WA, OR, NY) in notes.

# Glossary of Copyediting Terms

**AA.** Short for *author's alteration;* used to indicate changes made by an author on a set of proofs. *Compare* **PE.**

**abbreviation.** Shortened form of a word or phrase; a general term that encompasses **acronym, initialism, clipping, contraction,** and other forms combining any of these methods of abridgment.

**acronym.** Abbreviation formed by the first letters of the words in a phrase and pronounced as a word (NASA, FEMA). Often used interchangeably with **initialism,** but some house styles treat these differently.

**acute accent.** Diacritic mark: ´ [á, é, í, ó, ú].

**A-head.** First-level heading within a chapter (or comparable section of a document); also called *1-head. Compare* **B-head.**

**all cap.** FULL CAPITALS.

**alt text.** [Alternative text.] Special markup of tables and illustrations in electronic format to work with text-to-speech (TTS) and other accessibility tools.

**ampersand.** Name of the & character.

**angle brackets.** Name of the < and > characters.

**AP style.** Editorial preferences specified in *The Associated Press Stylebook and Briefing on Media Law.*

**APA style.** Editorial preferences specified in the *Publication Manual of the American Psychological Association.*

**apos.** Short for *apostrophe.*

**art.** Illustration (e.g., drawing, photograph, map, graph); also used to refer to all illustrations in a work. *See also* **line art.**

**art log.** Chart used to inventory and track all art in a manuscript; also called *art inventory.*

**ASCII.** [American Standard Code for Information Interchange; pronounced "ASS-key."] Set of 128 alphanumeric and nonprinting characters (e.g., wordspace, tab, hard return) used in converting word processing files from one format to another. When files are converted into ASCII, all typeface formatting (e.g., italics, bold), diacritics, and other non-ASCII characters are lost.

**asterisk-dagger sequence.** Sequence of symbols used for nonnumbered reference notes: asterisk (*), dagger (†), double-dagger (‡), section mark (§), parallels (||), number sign (#).

**at sign.** Name of the @ character.

**AU.** Short for *author;* used in queries ("AU: Revision OK?").

**author-date system.** System for providing references for works quoted, paraphrased, or cited as evidence in a document, in which the surname of the author and the year of publication of the work are given in the text, along with any specific page numbers. Full bibliographical information is supplied in an alphabetized reference list at the end of the document. Also called *name-year. Compare* **citation-sequence system; reference note system.**

**back matter.** General term for material that comes at the end of a book or book-length document: appendixes, endnotes, glossary, bibliography, index.

**backnote.** *See* **endnote.**

**bad break.** Incorrect division of a word that falls across two lines of type (*bad word break*). Unpleasing division of a paragraph that falls across two pages (*bad page break*). *See also* **orphan; widow.**

**balloons.** Display option for showing **comments** and changes in a Microsoft Word document. *Compare* **review pane.**

**baseline.** Imaginary line on which printed characters sit. For example:

......The. dotted. line. is. the. baseline. for. this. text........

**bastard title.** *See* **half-title page.**

**b/b.** Short for *from baseline to baseline*. The notation *16 pts. b/b* asks for 16 points (of vertical space) between the **baselines** of two successive lines of text. *See also* **leading; linespacing.**

**B-head.** Second-level heading within a chapter (or comparable section of a document); also called *2-head. Compare* **A-head.**

**blind proofing.** Proofreading in which the proofreader is not supplied with an earlier version of the text against which to compare the current version. Also called *cold proofing* or *noncomparison proofing. Compare* **comparison proofing.**

**block quote.** *See* **extract.**

**boilerplate.** Block of text that is reused, without change, in various documents.

**bold.** Short for *boldface.* **These words are boldface.**

**braces.** Name of the { and } characters; also called *curly brackets.*

**brackets.** Name of the [ and ] characters; also called *square brackets.*

**broadside.** Printed page whose top is at the left-hand side of a regular page; readers must turn the document 90 degrees clockwise to read the text. Used to accommodate wide tables and maps. In word processing programs, called *landscape orientation.*

**bubble.** Penciled-in circle or box in which an editor writes a **comment** or instruction on hard copy.

**built-up fraction.** A fraction typeset as separate numbers with a **solidus** (slash) between them: 1/2, 3/4, 7/8. *Compare* **case fraction.**

**bullet.** Heavy, vertically centered dot used as an ornament or as a marker in a vertical list. Bullets are solid (• •; also called *closed* or *filled*) or open (○ ○); square bullets are also solid (▪ ■) or open (□ □).

**bulleted list.** A type of vertical list in which each item is introduced by a bullet or other graphic character (☞ ✓ □). *Compare* **numbered list; unnumbered list.**

**callout.**  (1) *Placement callout,* a notation on hard copy (usually in the left margin) or in a manuscript file (following the publisher's convention) to indicate the placement of an image or table or to signal a cross-reference. (2) *Image callout,* a label identifying an item in an illustration.

**camel cap.**  *See* **intercap.**

**camera-ready copy.**  Text and art positioned in their final printed format, ready to be shot (filmed) by the printer; in this now-outdated production technology, printing plates were made from the film. Also called *CRC.*

**caps.**  Short for *capital letters.*

**caption.**  Heading or title of an illustration—as distinct from the more discursive **legend;** but *caption* is often used to refer to all explanatory text that accompanies a piece of art.

**cardinal number.**  Number used for counting and specifying quantities: one, two, three. *Compare* **ordinal number.**

**case fraction.**  A fraction typeset as one glyph: $\frac{1}{3}$, $\frac{2}{3}$, $\frac{7}{8}$ or ⅓, ⅔, ⅞; also called a *piece fraction. Compare* **built-up fraction.** *See also* **fraction slash.**

**castoff.**  Estimate of the typeset or printed length of a manuscript.

**cedilla.**  Diacritic mark: ˛ [Ç, ç].

**cell.**  Single entry or location in the body of a **table.**

**change bar.**  Very thick vertical rule, as shown here, placed in the outer margin of a technical manual to indicate a paragraph that has been revised since the previous edition. *See also* **redline.**

**character attributes.**  Features that apply to typed characters: boldface, italics, small capitals, subscripts, superscripts.

**Chicago style.**  Editorial preferences specified in *The Chicago Manual of Style.*

**CIP data.**  [Cataloging-in-publication.] Block of publishing information about a book supplied to the publisher, upon request, by the Library of Congress. The CIP block is usually printed on the copyright page.

**circumflex accent.**  Diacritic mark: ˆ [â, ê, î, ô, û].

**citation-sequence system.**  System for providing references for works quoted, paraphrased, or cited as evidence in a document. On first mention, each work is assigned a number, in sequence, which is used in all subsequent references to that work. These numbers appear in the text, usually as superscripts, and complete bibliographical information is supplied in a numbered list at the end of the document. *Compare* **author-date system; reference note system.**

**cleanup.**  (1) *File cleanup,* standardization of formatting and keyboarding, usually with the use of macros, to prepare computer files for editing and the subsequent production process. (2) *Manuscript cleanup,* incorporation of an author's responses to the copyediting into the final hard copy or computer files.

**clear for 10s.**  To align numerals on the last digit (rather than the first digit) in a numbered vertical list. For example:

| *Cleared for 10s* | *Not cleared for 10s* |
|---|---|
| 1. | 1. |
| 2. | 2. |
| 10. | 10. |
| 100. | 100. |

**clipping.** (1) Shortened form of a word usually created by pruning syllables from the front, middle, or back of a longer word: *exam* for *examination*. (2) Abbreviation formed by clipping off the end of a word: Rev., Prof. *Compare* **contraction.**

**close paren.** Name of the ) character.

**close punctuation.** Traditional style of punctuation, characterized by liberal use of marks, especially commas. *Compare* **open punctuation.**

**close up.** To delete unwanted horizontal or vertical space.

**closed compound.** *See* **solid compound.**

**CN.** Standard coding for a chapter number. *See* **markup.**

**CO.** Standard coding for a chapter opening. *See* **markup.**

**coding.** *See* **markup.**

**cold proofing.** *See* **blind proofing.**

**comment.** A remark or **query** for the author; may be shown in **balloons** or the **review pane** in a Microsoft Word document. *See also* **bubble; embedded query; query list; query slip.**

**communications manager.** *See* **editorial coordinator.**

**comparison proofing.** Proofreading in which the proofreader is supplied with an earlier version of the text and compares the typeset copy word for word against the previous iteration. *Compare* **blind proofing.**

**compositor.** Person who "sets" the type, either by hand or by computer, and arranges ("composes") the text in pages; also called *comp* or *typesetter.*

**compound.** Adjective, adverb, conjunction, noun, or preposition composed of two or more words. A compound form may be **open** (written as several words but treated as a unit), **hyphenated** (written as two or more words connected by hyphens), or **solid** (also called *closed*; written as one word). Compound forms are also described as **permanent** (a fixed form listed in a dictionary) or **temporary** (a form determined by a style manual's hyphenation rules and affected by the use and position of the word in a sentence).

**content editing.** *See* **substantive editing.**

**continued line.** Line of text, usually set in italics [*Continued on next page;* Table 14—*Continued*], placed at the foot or top of a page when an element such as a table extends over two or more pages.

**contraction.** Abridgment of a syllable, word, or phrase by omitting some portion (e'er, they'll, Dr., Sr.). *Compare* **clipping.**

**copyediting.** Editing to impose mechanical consistency; correlate parts of a manuscript; correct infelicities of grammar, usage, and diction; query internal inconsistencies and structural or organizational problems; flag content requiring permission; and provide markup or styling of elements. *Compare* **developmental editing; line editing; manuscript editing; stylistic editing.**

**corpus.** [Plural *corpora.*] A collection of written and spoken language used in linguistic study and lexicography.

**CRC.** *See* **camera-ready copy.**

**credit line.** Brief statement of the source of an illustration, often placed at the end of the legend.

**cross-reference.** Phrase that mentions another part of the document or text ("in chapter 5 we discussed," "as table 6 shows"). Also called *x-ref* or *in-text ref. See also* **signposting.**

**CSE style.** Editorial preferences specified in *Scientific Style and Format: The CSE Manual for Authors, Editors, and Publishers.* Called CBE style until 2000, when the Council of Biology Editors (CBE) changed its name to the Council of Science Editors (CSE).

**CT.** Standard coding for a chapter title. *See* **markup.**

**Cupertino.** An erroneous auto-correction on an electronic device. So named after the tendency of an early spell-checker to miscorrect the unhyphenated spelling of *cooperation* to *Cupertino* (Apple's California headquarters).

**curly brackets.** *See* **braces.**

**curly quotes.** *See* **smart quotes.**

**cut-in head.** Head that cuts across the columns of a **table.**

**dagger.** Name for the † character.

**dead copy.** In the production process, a superseded version of copy; manuscript that has been typeset and proofread. *See also* **foul copy.**

**decked heads.** Pair of heads in a **table** consisting of a **spanner** atop two or more single-column heads.

**descriptivist.** Somewhat misleading term applied to a language expert who seeks to document how language is used without prescribing "correct" usage or making value judgments about usage. *Compare* **prescriptivist.**

**designer.** Person responsible for the physical appearance of a book or document, including the typography (typeface, type size, etc.), layout (margins, leading, location of running heads, etc.), and style of the art (drawings, maps, charts, etc.).

**developmental editing.** Editing to develop an idea or proposal into a publishable manuscript, restructure a draft, identify gaps in subject coverage, devise strategies for more effective communication of the content, and create features to enhance the final product and make it more competitive in the marketplace. *Compare* **copyediting; line editing; manuscript editing; stylistic editing.**

**diacritic.** Mark that changes the phonetic value of an alphabetical character. Common diacritic marks include the acute accent (á, é), cedilla (ç), circumflex (â, ô), grave accent (è, ì), tilde (ñ, õ), and umlaut or diaeresis (ö, ü).

**diaeresis.** Mark resembling an **umlaut** but having a different function: it is placed over a vowel to indicate that the vowel is pronounced (naïve, Brontë, coöperate). Omitted in many English names and words except in the pages of the *New Yorker.*

**diction.** Choice of words and phrases.

**dingbat.** Ornamental character in typography: ✍ 📖 🗁 ❧ ▌ ◆.

**display type.** Large, sometimes ornamented or otherwise distinctive type, used to set off, or display, part titles, chapter titles, headings, and the like.

**displayed equation.** Mathematical expression set on its own line. *Compare* **run-in text.**

**displayed list.** *See* **vertical list.**

**DOI.** [Digital Object Identifier.] Permanent, unique alphanumeric identifier assigned to an online document by the International DOI Foundation and the document's publisher.

**dot leaders.** Row of periods between horizontal entries in a table or list; for example:
Annual turnover . . . . . . . . . . 93.4%

**double dagger.** Name of the ‡ character.

**double numeration.** Use of two numerals (separated by a period, hyphen, or other character) in the numbering of pages, figures, tables, or other materials. For example, the pages in chapter 1 of a book might be numbered 1.1, 1.2, 1.3, 1.4, etc.; the pages in chapter 2, 2.1, 2.2, 2.3, 2.4, etc.; in chapter 3, 3.1, 3.2, 3.3, 3.4, etc.

**down style.** Sparse use of capitalization, a style generally favored in book publishing and exemplified in *The Chicago Manual of Style. Compare* **up style.**

**editorial coordinator.** Person who supervises an in-house copyeditor or who assigns work to a freelance copyeditor. In book publishing, often called *managing editor, chief copyeditor, production editor,* or *project editor;* in other industries, may be titled *communications* or *pubs* (short for *publications) manager, editor,* or *specialist.*

**editorial style.** The sum of editorial decisions ensuring consistency in matters of spelling, hyphenation, capitalization, punctuation, treatment of numbers and numerals, treatment of quotations, use of abbreviations, use of italics and bold type, treatment of special elements (headings, lists, tables, charts, graphs), and format of footnotes or endnotes and other documentation.

**EFL.** [English as a foreign language.] The term for nonnative use of English in countries where it is not the native language. *Compare* **ESL.**

**eggcorn.** The erroneous transformation of a stock expression into a new one, often based on an incorrect assumption about the etymology of the original. The linguist Geoffrey Pullum named this type of error, from the mangled saying "Mighty oaks from little eggcorns [acorns] grow." *Compare* **mondegreen.**

**electronic manuscript (EMS) editing.** *See* **on-screen editing.**

**elegant variation.** Misguided stylistic refinement in which a writer substitutes different synonyms simply to avoid repeating a word.

**element.** Specially configured feature of a manuscript other than regular running text: a part or chapter number, title, or subtitle; a heading or subheading; a list, extract, or displayed equation; a table number, title, source line, or footnote; a figure number or figure caption.

**ellipsis.** Name of the . . . character.

**em.** Typesetting measurement whose value depends on the size of the type: in 10-point type, an em space is 10 points wide; in 18-point type, an em space is 18 points wide.

**em dash.** Name of the — character. In manuscripts the em dash is sometimes typed as --.

**embedded query.**  Query placed within the text of the electronic manuscript, usually set off with curly braces or other unique delimiters. *See also* **comment.** *Compare* **balloons; bubble; query list; query slip; review pane.**

**en.**  Half an **em.**

**en dash.**  Name of the – character. An en dash is longer than a hyphen (-) but shorter than an em dash (—). In manuscripts the en dash is often typed as a hyphen.

**end-line hyphen.**  Hyphen that falls at the end of a line of text. A *soft hyphen* is dropped in the final copy if the hyphenated word falls on one line; a *hard hyphen* is always retained no matter where the word falls.

**endnote.**  Reference or explanatory note that appears at the end of a book or document, in a section titled "Notes"; also called *backnote. Chapter endnotes* appear at the end of each chapter of a book (or comparable section of a document). *Compare* **footnote; sidenote.**

**entity.**  Character—especially a character with a **diacritic,** a non-Latin alphabetic character, an ideogram, or a symbol or other glyph—that is not available on a standard **QWERTY** keyboard.

**epigraph.**  Brief quotation conveying the theme of a work or a division of a work, placed in the front matter of a book, on the part title page of a section, or on the opening page of a chapter.

**equal variant.**  Legitimate alternative spelling of a word that occurs with equal or near-equal frequency; usually connected to the headword in a dictionary listing by *or. Compare* **primary variant; secondary variant.**

**ESL.**  [English as a second language.] The term for nonnative use of English in countries (e.g., the US) where it is the primary language. *Compare* **EFL.**

**EX.**  Standard coding for an **extract.** *See* **markup.**

**executive summary.**  Concise front matter section of a business report that summarizes the issue addressed and the report's findings and recommendations.

**extract.**  Quoted passage set off from the running text. Extracts are often set in a smaller type size and on a shorter measure than the running text. Also called *block quote.*

**figure.**  Illustration printed as part of the running text. *Compare* **plate.**

**file cleanup.** *See* **cleanup (1).**

**first ref.**  First appearance of a proper name ("Identify all characters on first ref") or of a source in reference notes ("Give a full citation on first ref").

**flag.**  (1) To call to someone's attention ("Flag all math symbols"). (2) Gummed slip of paper, attached to hard copy, on which a copyeditor writes a query; also called **query slip.**

**flopped.**  Transposed; used to describe an illustration that is inadvertently (or sometimes intentionally) printed as a mirror image of the original.

**flush.**  Positioned at the margin of the text page, either *flush left* or *flush right.*

**flush and hang.**  Style of setting indexes and lists. The first line of each entry or paragraph is set flush left, and the remaining lines of the entry are indented.

**FN.**  Standard coding for a **footnote.** *See* **markup.**

**folio.** Page number in typeset text. A *drop folio* is a page number placed at the bottom of a page. A *blind folio* (also called *suppressed folio*) is not printed, although the page is counted in the numbering of the pages; an *expressed folio* is one that is printed.

**font.** Characters in a given size and style of a **typeface** (10-point Courier roman; 12-point Helvetica italics; 14-point Baskerville roman small caps).

**footer.** *See* **running foot.**

**footnote.** Note placed at the foot of the page. Sometimes incorrectly used to refer to any type of note, regardless of placement. *Compare* **endnote; sidenote.**

**forward slash.** *See* **solidus.**

**foul copy.** In the production process, the previous iteration of a manuscript or proof with corrections indicated thereon; sometimes referred to when checking corrections in the current ("live") version. *See also* **dead copy.**

**FPO.** [For position (*or* placement) only.] Initialism stamped or watermarked on low-resolution images used as placeholders in a layout until the final images are supplied.

**fraction slash.** Name of the character used to construct **case fractions:** ½, ⅓. Not found on a standard **QWERTY** keyboard or in Microsoft Word's Symbol Browser. In Unicode this glyph is U+2044. *Compare* **solidus.**

**front matter.** General term for material that comes at the front of a book, before the first chapter: half-title page, title page, copyright page, dedication, epigraph, table of contents, list of illustrations or tables, foreword, preface, acknowledgments, introduction. Also called *prelims.*

**frontispiece.** Unnumbered illustration facing the title page of a book.

**full caps.** ALL CAPITALS. *Compare* **small caps.**

**full measure.** Width of a **text page** (i.e., the width of a page from margin to margin).

**galleys.** First printed version (*proof*) of a document; so called because these proofs were once printed on long, unnumbered sheets of paper, rather than in page form. Today, galley proofs may be requested for some lengthy, complex books but are likely to take the form of loosely paginated proofs, also called *rough pages,* without final positioning of illustrations or fine-tuning of page makeup. *Compare* **page proofs.**

**garden-path sentence.** Grammatically correct sentence that leads readers astray ("down the garden path") because of incorrect parsing.

**general text.** *See* **running text.**

**ghostwriting.** Writing content to be published under someone else's name.

**global English.** Form of written English optimized for global communication, especially among speakers of regional dialects of English and nonnative English speakers. Sometimes called *international English style.*

**global search.** Search of one or more computer files to locate all instances of a word or words, either to double-check their styling (capitalization, hyphenation, etc.) or to replace them with a specified substitute (*global search and replace* or *global change*).

**GPO style.** Editorial preferences specified in the *GPO Style Manual: An Official Guide to the Form and Style of Federal Government Publishing.* ("GPO," which previously meant "Government Printing Office," now stands for "Government Publishing Office.")

**grammar.** Rules governing the system and structure of a language, usually understood to comprise **syntax** and morphology (the forms of words). *Compare* **usage.**

**grave accent.** Diacritic mark: ` [à, è, ì, ò, ù].

**hair space.** Very thin nonbreaking space sometimes inserted between typeset characters that are touching, as when italic and roman characters crash. *Compare* **thin space.**

**hairline rule.** Lightest (or thinnest) horizontal line available. *See also* **rule.**

**half-title page.** The very first page (p. i) in a printed book, normally showing only the main title and omitting subtitle, author's name, publisher, edition, and other copy. Sometimes called *bastard title.*

**hang.** *See* **flush and hang.**

**hard copy.** Printout of a computer file; by extension, any text that appears on paper.

**hard hyphen.** *See* **end-line hyphen.**

**hard space.** Special word processing character that produces a wordspace but does not permit a line to break at that space. Also called *nonbreaking space.*

**Harvard comma.** *See* **serial comma.**

**head.** Title that indicates the start of a section or subsection of a document or book chapter. Heads are given distinctive typographic treatment (type size and weight; capitalization; set off or run in). *See also* **running head.**

**header.** *See* **running head.**

**headline style.** Capitalization style for heads, display lines, and titles of works in which all words are capitalized except interior articles (a, an, the), coordinating conjunctions, and prepositions. Alternatively, prepositions shorter than four or five letters are lowercased, and longer prepositions are capitalized. Also called *UC/lc. Compare* **sentence style.**

**headnote.** Brief introductory or explanatory material that follows a part, chapter, or section title and precedes the running text.

**homophones.** Words that sound alike or nearly alike but are spelled differently and have different meanings: principle, principal.

**horizontal rule.** Thin horizontal line. *See also* **rule.**

**house style.** Editorial style preferences expressed by a publisher. *See also* **editorial style.**

**humanistic style.** *See* **nontechnical style.**

**hypercorrection.** Replacement of a correct usage, falsely believed to be erroneous, by an incorrect one. *Compare* **incorrection.**

**hyphen.** *See* **end-line hyphen.**

**hyphenated compound.** Term consisting of component words joined by a hyphen: cross-reference. *Compare* **open compound; solid compound.**

**impression.** Print run of a publication.

**incipit notes.** *See* **key phrase endnotes.**

**incorrection.** (1) Replacement of a correct variant, falsely believed to be erroneous, by some other (possibly less satisfactory) correct variant. (2) Replacement of a correct variant by an incorrect one. *Compare* **hypercorrection.**

**indie author.** Independent author. Performs the tasks normally undertaken by a traditional publisher, hires services to do this work, or collaborates with other independent publishing professionals (editors, designers, production specialists, distributors) and commercial publishing platforms to self-publish a work.

**initial cap only.** *See* **sentence style.**

**initialism.** Abbreviation formed by the first letters of the words in a phrase and pronounced as separate letters (NSA, FBI). *Compare* **acronym.**

**intercap.** Capital letter that appears in the middle of a word, as in a company or product name (FedEx, PowerPoint, eBay); also called *midcap* or *camel cap.*

**international English style.** *See* **global English.**

**interrobang.** Fusion of the question mark and exclamation point (‽), once proposed (but never widely adopted) as an addition to the standard list of punctuation marks in English.

**in-text ref.** *See* **cross-reference.**

**ISBN.** [International Standard Book Number.] Thirteen-digit number assigned by a publisher to uniquely identify a book. Before January 2007, ten-digit ISBNs were used.

**ital.** Short for *italics. These words are in italics.*

**jacket copy.** Text that appears on the protective paper wrapper of a clothbound book or on the cover and inward folding flaps of a paperback book.

**justification.** Alignment of left and right margins in typeset text. Most book pages are justified left and right, but some documents are justified only at the left margin (also called *ragged right*).

**kerning.** Fine-tuned adjustments to the spacing between particular characters in a font to improve readability and appearance. *See* **letterspacing.**

**key phrase endnotes.** Reference notes without any note indicators in the text, placed at the end of the document and keyed to the text by page number and a relevant phrase from the text. Sometimes referred to as *incipit notes.*

**kill.** To order the deletion of text or an illustration.

**landscape orientation.** *See* **broadside.**

**leaders.** *See* **dot leaders.**

**leading.** [Pronounced "ledding."] Vertical spacing between the baselines of two successive lines of text, measured in points. The word derives from the lead once used to create space between lines in hot-metal typesetting. *See also* **b/b; linespacing.**

**leading zero.** Zero placed before a decimal point to improve comprehension: 0.25 acres.

**legend.** One or more sentences of explanation that accompany an illustration; often called **caption,** although traditional bookmaking differentiates the terms.

**letterspacing.** Space between the letters of a word. Tight and loose letterspacing are used to enhance the appearance of letters set in display type. *Compare* **wordspacing.**

| | |
|---|---|
| WALLPAPER | normal letterspacing |
| WALLPAPER | tight (kerned) letterspacing |
| WALLPAPER | loose letterspacing |

**levels of edit.** Term used in a 1976 publication by the Jet Propulsion Laboratory to describe a management tool for specifying how much and what kind of **copyediting** to provide for a given manuscript. Other organizations have devised similar schemes. *Compare* **levels of editing.**

**levels of editing.** Degrees of editorial intervention in a manuscript, usually described as a continuum ranging from light through medium to heavy.

**ligature.** Compound typographic character: æ, œ, ff, ffi, fi.

**line art.** Illustration that contains only blacks and whites, no gray tones.

**line editing.** In traditional publishing, revision focusing on literary style at the sentence and paragraph levels. Today often used interchangeably with the term **copyediting.** *Compare* **developmental editing; manuscript editing; stylistic editing.**

**linespacing.** "White space" between successive lines of text; usually called **leading.** *See also* **b/b.**

**lining figures.** Typographical style of numerals in which all digits sit on the baseline: 1 2 3 4 5 6 7 8 9 0. Also called *modern figures. Compare* **old-style figures.**

**macro.** Series of computer keystrokes, commands, and operations that are stored as a unit so that the entire routine plays out when the user invokes the macro.

**managing editor.** *See* **editorial coordinator.**

**manuscript cleanup.** *See* **cleanup (2).**

**manuscript editing.** As defined by *The Chicago Manual of Style,* synonymous with **copyediting** or **line editing** and encompassing tasks that range from simple mechanical corrections to substantial remedial work improving style and clarity, restructuring disorganized passages, tightening baggy prose, and the like. *Compare* **developmental editing; stylistic editing.**

**mark-revisions feature.** A way of showing deletions and insertions in a document on-screen. *See also* **redline; track changes.**

**markup.** Marking of a manuscript (hard copy or computer files) to identify all design elements, i.e., any copy that is not running text: extracts, display equations, part and chapter titles, footnotes, captions, etc. Typical generic markup codes for books include PO (part opening), CO (chapter opening), CT (chapter title), CN (chapter number), FN (footnote), EX (extract). Also called *styling; tagging; typecoding. Compare* **styling (2).**

**measure.** Width of a line of printed text. Running text is set *full measure* (from margin to margin); extracts and lists may be set on a narrower measure.

**mechanical editing.** Editorial interventions in a manuscript made to ensure conformity to an **editorial style.**

**metadata.** Data about data. In publishing, information about an article, book, or other publication—e.g., title, subtitle, author, author biography, contributors, edition, publisher, publication date, ISBN, price, description of content, formats, subject categories, language, and page count. Prepared in a structured digital format by publishers and **indie authors,** with some details supplied by outside sources such as the Library of Congress, metadata auto-fills the product pages and databases of publishers, distributors, vendors, libraries, and content aggregators. Metadata underlies the contemporary system for cataloging, distributing, and selling books and supports online search and discovery.

**midcap.** *See* **intercap.**

**midpoint.** Vertically centered dot, smaller than a bullet: 124 Main Street · Anytown.

**modern figures.** *See* **lining figures.**

**mondegreen.** Misunderstood text of a song or poem, e.g., rendering the line "laid him on the green" as "Lady Mondegreen" in the ballad "The Bonnie Earl O'Murray."

**monospace type.** Printed lettering in which characters are of equal width. This type is monospace. Also called *nonproportional type. Compare* **proportional type.**

**MS.** [Plural *MSS.*] Short for *manuscript.*

**mult.** Short for *multiplication sign* (×), as distinct from a lowercase "x."

**N.** Short for *number;* used in statistical tables to indicate the size of the sample; often set as a small cap.

**name-year.** *See* **author-date.**

**nonbreaking space.** *See* **hard space.**

**noncomparison proofing.** *See* **blind proofing.**

**nondisclosure agreement (NDA).** Contract in which the parties agree not to disclose proprietary and other sensitive information that they share while doing business together.

**nonproportional type.** *See* **monospace type.**

**nontechnical style.** Set of conventions for the treatment of numbers in nontechnical writing. Also called *humanistic style. Compare* **technical style.**

**numbered list.** Vertical list in which each item is introduced by a numeral. *Compare* **bulleted list; unnumbered list.**

**OCR.** [Optical character recognition; optical character reader.] Technology or device that scans printed text, character by character, and translates the character images into character codes, such as ASCII, that can be used in data processing or editing.

**old-style figures.** Typographical style of numerals in which some digits have ascenders or descenders: 1 2 3 4 5 6 7 8 9 0. Sometimes abbreviated *o.s.* or *OS. Compare* **lining figures.**

**online editing.** *See* **on-screen editing.**

**on-screen editing.** Editing that is performed on a document's computer files rather than on hard copy; also called *online editing* or *electronic manuscript (EMS) editing.*

**open compound.** Term consisting of component words separated by a space (e.g., high school). *Compare* **hyphenated compound; solid compound.**

**open paren.** Name of the ( character.

**open punctuation.** Modern punctuation style, characterized by a minimalist approach to the use of marks, especially commas. *Compare* **close punctuation.**

**ordinal number.** Number used for designating position in a numerical sequence: first, second, third. *Compare* **cardinal number.**

**orphan.** First line of a paragraph that is stranded at the bottom of a printed page, separated from the remainder of the paragraph by a page break. Sometimes the last line of any paragraph that contains only the last part of a hyphenated word or the last syllable of the hyphenated word if that syllable is less than four letters long. *Compare* **widow.**

**Oxford comma.** *See* **serial comma.**

**page proofs.** Printed version (*proof*) of a document in page form; also called *pages*. *Compare* **galleys.**

**para-indent.** Width of the indention of the first line of a paragraph, usually specified in picas or em spaces.

**pass.** Read-through of a manuscript by a copyeditor.

**PDF.** [Portable Document Format.] Electronic file format that preserves the font, page layout, and images of the original file independent of a computer's operating system or software.

**PE.** Short for *printer's error;* used to indicate an error made by the **compositor** on a set of proofs. *Compare* **AA.**

**peer en dash.** **En dash** used in place of a hyphen to join equivalently weighted terms in two-word compound adjectives. Recommended in the style manuals for Cambridge (*Butcher's Copy-editing*), Oxford (*New Oxford Style Manual*), the American Chemical Society (*The ACS Style Guide*), the Council of Science Editors (*Scientific Style and Format*), and the American Psychological Association (*Publication Manual of the American Psychological Association*) but not in *Chicago.*

**penalty copy.** Hard-copy manuscript that is difficult to typeset (heavily corrected, replete with math symbols or foreign-language text) for which a **compositor** charges a premium.

**permanent compound.** Term consisting of component words whose form (**open, hyphenated,** or **solid**) is established in the dictionary. *Compare* **temporary compound.**

**pica.** Linear measurement: 1 pica = 12 points. *See* **point.**

**pick up.** To reuse previously printed text or illustrations.

**piece fraction.** *See* **case fraction.**

**plain language.** Style of communication using simple vocabulary, grammar, and sentence structure that is readily accessible to readers. Several English-speaking countries now mandate the use of so-called plain language, or plain English, in government communications with the public; advocates in the Plain Language Movement promote a wider use of plain language.

**plate.** Page of illustrations, usually on special paper, that is printed separately from the regular text and is inserted between text pages during production.

**PO.** Standard coding for a part opening. *See* **markup.**

**point.** Linear measurement:

> 1 point = 0.0138 inches
> 12 points = 1 pica = 0.1656 inches (rule of thumb: 6 picas = 1 inch)
> 72.464 points = 1 inch (rule of thumb: 72 points = 1 inch)

**prelims.** *See* **front matter.**

**prescriptivist.** Somewhat misleading term applied to a language expert who seeks to prescribe "correct" usage or to make value judgments about usage. *Compare* **descriptivist.**

**primary variant.**  Preferred spelling of a word that has variant spellings. *Compare* **equal variant; secondary variant.**

**production editor.**  *See* **editorial coordinator.**

**project editor.**  *See* **editorial coordinator.**

**proofreading.**  Reading typeset copy to correct errors introduced during the typesetting, formatting, or file conversion of the final document and to identify any serious errors not caught during copyediting. *See also* **comparison proofing; blind proofing.**

**proportional type.**  Printed lettering in which characters are of unequal width. *Compare* **monospace type.**

**pull quote.**  Brief, striking excerpt copied, or "pulled," from the main text of a document and treated as a graphic element.

**Q (*or* QY).**  Short for *query;* used in queries ("Q: where is table 3?").

**query.**  Publishing jargon for "question"; used as a verb or a noun. Often called a **comment** in Microsoft Word and other word processors.

**query list.**  Separate sheet of paper interleaved with a hard-copy manuscript and bearing queries keyed to the manuscript by page and paragraph number, query number, or other means.

**query slip.**  Small slip of paper with an adhesive edge that can be attached to the sides of a hard-copy manuscript page; used for writing queries. Sometimes called *query tag, flag,* or *sticky note,* or referred to by the trademarked name *Post-it.*

**query tag.**  *See* **query slip.**

**QWERTY.**  Standard typewriter or computer keyboard layout for the Latin alphabet. The first six letters on the top row of alphabet keys, from left to right, spell *QWERTY.*

**ragged right.**  Sometimes called *rag right.* Text aligned at the left margin but not at the right margin. *See also* **justification.**

**recto.**  Right-hand page of a book, magazine, or brochure. *Compare* **verso.**

**redline.**  On-screen or hard-copy version of a manuscript that indicates which text has been added or deleted since the previous version. In the redline version, the added text is also called *redline,* and the deleted text is called *strikeout.* Here, the redline text is enclosed in braces, and the strikeout text is slashed: I pledge my allegiance to {the} flag.

**redundonym.**  Redundant expression consisting of an **acronym** or **initialism** followed by a word that is part of the abbreviation: ATM machine.

**reference note system.**  System for providing references for works quoted, paraphrased, or cited as evidence in a document, in which sources are placed in notes keyed to the running text by superscript numerals or symbols. The notes appear at the bottom of the page or at the end of the section or document. *Compare* **author-date system; citation-sequence system.**

**register.**  Level of formality in the grammar, usage, and diction of written or spoken communication, as determined by the specific social context and purpose of the communication, e.g., formal, informal, intimate.

**regular running text.**  *See* **running text.**

**review pane.** Split-screen display option for showing **comments** and changes in a Microsoft Word document. *Compare* **balloons; bubble; embedded query.**

**roman.** Type style used most often in printed materials—as distinct from *italic,* GOTHIC, *script.*

**rough pages.** *See* **galleys.**

**rule.** Horizontal or vertical line. The thickness (or weight) of a rule is measured in points or inches.

| | | |
|---|---|---|
| hairline | 1 point | 4 point |

**run-in text.** Text that is not set off on its own line. For example:

*Run-in heads.* Run-in heads are often preceded by a para-indent, set in italics, and followed by a period. The regular text continues on the same line, just as this example shows. (*Run-in* is also used to describe lists and quotations that are embedded in rather than set off from the regular running text.)

**running foot.** One or two lines of copy, such as a chapter title or section title, set at the bottom of each page of a document or book; also called *footer. Compare* **running head.**

**running head.** One or two lines of copy, such as a book title or chapter title, set at the top of each page of a document or book; also called *header. Compare* **running foot.**

**running text.** Portion of a document consisting of sentences and paragraphs, rather than set-off display lines, tables, and other elements; also called *general text* or *regular running text.*

**runover.** Continuation of a lengthy head, displayed equation, line of poetry, and the like onto a second line; also called *turnover* or *turned line.*

**sans serif.** Printed letters that do not have short cross lines (**serifs**) projecting from the main strokes.

This sentence is printed in a sans serif typeface.

**scare quotes.** Quotation marks used to convey that a word or phrase is unusual, dubious, ironic, or overly colloquial; equivalent to *so-called* and therefore rarely used with that expression, except to direct special attention to a part of the whole phrase being held at arm's length: my so-called "safety" net. Sometimes called *shudder quotes* or *sneer quotes.*

**scientific style.** *See* **technical style.**

**secondary variant.** Legitimate alternative spelling of a word that occurs with less frequency than the primary spelling; usually connected to the headword in a dictionary listing by *also. Compare* **equal variant; primary variant.**

**semantic tagging.** Markup of a document based on meaning rather than appearance, for example, to differentiate between italics used for emphasis, for foreign terms, and for book titles.

**sentence style.** Capitalization style for heads, display lines, and titles of works in which all words are lowercased except those that would be capitalized in a sentence (i.e., the first word, proper nouns, proper adjectives, and the word *I*). Also called *initial cap only. Compare* **headline style.**

**serial comma.** Comma preceding *and* or *or* in a list of items (a, b, and c; d, e, f, or g). Also called *Harvard comma* or *Oxford comma.*

**serif.** Short cross line that projects from the main stroke of a printed letter. For example:

These letters have serifs     A C E F M N T W
These letters do not          A C E F M N T W

**set-off list.** *See* **vertical list.**

**short title.** Abbreviated title of a book or article used in a note or in-text citation after the full title has been cited on its first occurrence in the chapter or document.

**shudder quotes.** *See* **scare quotes.**

**SI.** [Système international d'unités.] System of measurement based on the metric system and used by scientists around the world. SI has seven base units: meter (length), kilogram (mass), second (time), ampere (electric current), kelvin (temperature), mole (amount of substance), and candela (luminosity).

**sidebar.** Graphically separate but related text placed alongside the running text in an article, on a webpage, or in a book.

**sidenote.** Note placed in a separate panel alongside the text rather than at the foot of the page or the end of the text or section of text. *Compare* **endnote; footnote.**

**signposting.** Excessive cross-referencing of topics previously discussed and to be discussed ("The court's decision, as we saw in chapters 2 and 3, was controversial but firmly grounded in precedent. We will examine the legacy of this controversy in chapter 5 after we have reviewed the major precedents for the decision").

**singular** *they.* The pronoun *they* (*them, their, theirs, themselves* or *themself*) used as an epicene, or gender-neutral, singular pronoun.

**sink.** Distance from the top of a printed page to the **baseline** of a particular element on that page (e.g., a chapter title).

**slant.** *See* **solidus.**

**slash.** *See* **solidus.**

**small caps.** Capital letters slightly shorter and squatter than **full caps:** B.C.E., B.C., C.E., A.D., A.M., P.M.

**smart quotes.** Name for directional quotation marks (both single and double), the ' and " and the ' and " characters (the single right directional mark doubles as a directional apostrophe). Also called *curly quotes* or *typographer's quotes. Compare* to the ' and " characters, the plain, or straight, quotation marks and apostrophe.

**sneer quotes.** *See* **scare quotes.**

**soft hyphen.** *See* **end-line hyphen.**

**solid compound.** Term consisting of component words spelled as a single word. Also called *closed compound. Compare* **hyphenated compound; open compound.**

**solidus.** Standard character / on the QWERTY keyboard, used in constructing fractions, URLs, and other expressions: 1/2, 1/3, http://, c/o. Also called *forward slash, slant, slash,* and *virgule. Compare* **fraction slash.** *See also* **built-up fraction.**

**spanner.**  Head that extends across two or more columns in a **table.**

**specs.**  Type specifications created by a designer to indicate typeface, point size, vertical and horizontal spacing, margins, and the like.

**spine.**  Backbone of a book that connects the front and back covers. Spine copy usually includes the book title, the author's surname, the publisher's name, and the publisher's logo.

**spousal commas.**  Commas setting off a phrase used as a short appositive of relationship (e.g., "Harvey, my husband, . . ."); sometimes omitted ("my father Ralph") as an exception to the customary practice of setting off nonrestrictive interrupters with commas.

**square brackets.**  *See* **brackets.**

**squib.**  Short parenthetical indicator placed after a table title to identify an element that pertains to the **table** as a whole.

**stacked heads.**  Two or more heads with no text intervening. For example:

**Unpacking the Wondermatic**

*Identifying the Parts*

After you remove the packing straps, slide each component out of its fiberboard sleeve, and write down the serial number of each component. Begin assembling the base . . .

**stet.**  Latin for "let it stand." Used to reinstate text that had been marked for deletion or change.

**sticky note.**  *See* **query slip.**

**straight quotes.**  *See* **smart quotes.**

**strikeout.**  *See* **redline.**

**stub.**  Leftmost column of a **table,** which lists the categories or variables.

**style sheet.**  Form filled in by the copyeditor as a record of editorial choices.

**styling.**  (1) Editorial changes in a manuscript to ensure conformity to an **editorial style;** *see* **mechanical editing.** (2) Formatting of the elements of a manuscript by using the style and template features of a word processor; *compare* **markup.**

**stylistic editing.**  Term used by the organization Editors Canada and some other practitioners to describe line-by-line editing for literary style. *Compare* **line editing.**

**subscript.**  Numeral or character set below the baseline: $H_2O$. *Compare* **superscript.**

**substantive editing.**  Extensive revision of an author's text for literary style and sometimes engagement with content (revision with the latter focus is also called *content editing*).

**superscript.**  Numeral or character set above the baseline: $mc^2$. *Compare* **subscript.**

**suspended compound.**  Set of compound adjectives or nouns in which an element common to all members is not repeated. For example: the fourth-, fifth-, and sixth-graders; steel-plated or -cased equipment; the pre- and posttest scores.

**swung dash.**  In math, a symbol that denotes "approximately" (~1,000 means "approximately 1,000"); in logic, negation (~P means "not P"); over an equals sign, "approximately equal to" ($\cong$1,000 means "approximately equal to 1,000").

**syntax.** Construction of phrases, clauses, and sentences in a language. *See also* **grammar.**

**T of C.** Short for *table of contents.*

**table.** Arrangement of words or numbers in columns and rows. For example:

| | | Alpine County | | Bemine County | |
|---|---|---|---|---|---|
| Spanner head → | | | | | |
| Decked head → | | 1810 | 1820 | 1810 | 1820 |
| Cut-in head → | | Domesticated Animals | | | |
| Stub head → | *Mammals* | | | | |
| | Dogs | 5,212 | 7,022 | 3,272 | 6,265 ← Cell |
| | Cats | 4,242 | 6,888 | 2,212 | 8,122 |
| | *Birds* | | | | |
| | Canaries | 822 | 933 | 544 | 755 |
| | Parrots | 912 | 723 | 454 | 267 |
| | | Wild Animals | | | |
| | *Mammals* | | | | |
| | Lions | 153 | 162 | 83 | 64 |
| | Tigers | 101 | 135 | 27 | 18 |
| | *Birds* | | | | |
| | Condors | 98 | 90 | 33 | 38 |
| | Eagles | 125 | 143 | 88 | 86 |

A *spanner head* ("Alpine County," "Bemine County") applies to two or more columns.
*Decked heads* sit one atop another (here, name of county atop years).
A *cut-in head* ("Domesticated Animals," "Wild Animals") cuts across the columns.
A *stub head* ("Mammals," "Birds") divides the stub into categories.
A *cell* is an entry in the body of a table. (Here, each of the thirty-two cells contains a numeral.)

**tagging.** *See* **markup.**

**tearsheet.** A page "torn" from a printed document for use in the production of a new document.

**technical style.** Set of conventions for the treatment of numbers in technical and scientific writing and in other documents containing many numbers and quantities, including statistical and financial material. Also called *scientific style. Compare* **nontechnical style.**

**temporary compound.** Term consisting of component words whose form (**open, hyphenated,** or **solid**) varies according to grammatical function and position in a sentence. *Compare* **permanent compound.**

**text page.** Area on a printed page in which the body of the text appears. *Compare* **type page.**

**thin space.** Space that is narrower than a regular wordspace but wider than a **hair space,** approximately 1/4 to 1/6 of an em. Sometimes used between personal initials: A. B. Jones.

**tilde.** Diacritic mark: ˜ [ñ, õ].

**TK.** Short for *to come,* a placeholder derived from "to kum," signifying that additional material will be added. (Analog printing has long used deliberate misspellings—"lede" for "lead," "hed" for "head," etc.—to prevent inadvertent typesetting of instructions and prompts to the compositor.)

**track changes.** Feature in Microsoft Word that allows a user to show deletions and insertions in a document; generally described as a *mark-revisions feature. See also* **redline.**

**trade books.** Books intended for general readers, as distinguished from books intended for professionals, scholars, or students.

**trim size.** Dimensions of a page of a book.

**turnover.** *See* **runover.**

**type page.** Area on a printed page defined by the top, bottom, left, and right margins. Includes the running heads and running feet, folios, and sidebars. *Compare* **text page.**

**typecoding.** *See* **markup.**

**typeface.** A named group of **fonts**—consisting of different type sizes and including roman, italic, bold, etc.—in a given design, e.g., Palatino, Times Roman.

**typesetter.** *See* **compositor.**

**typo.** Short for *typographical error;* a misprint.

**typographer's quotes.** *See* **smart quotes.**

**UC.** Short for *uppercase* (capital letters).

**UC/lc.** Short for *uppercase and lowercase;* used to indicate that display text is to be capitalized according to **headline style**—as distinct from text to be set **sentence style.**

**umlaut.** Diacritic mark placed over a vowel to change the pronunciation, especially in German. Usually omitted when words are Englished (*über* becomes the ride-sharing service Uber) but often retained in proper names (Göring) unless a spelling change is used to indicate the pronunciation instead (Goering). *Compare* **diaeresis.**

**Unicode.** International coding system that enables keyboarders to produce over one hundred thousand linguistic, mathematical, and scientific characters.

**unnumbered list.** **Vertical list** in which items carry neither numbering nor bullets. *Compare* **bulleted list; numbered list.**

**up style.** Liberal capitalization of nouns and adjectives, a style favored by some newspapers and magazines. *Compare* **down style.**

**usage.** The way a word or phrase is habitually used by native speakers of a language. *Compare* **grammar.**

**variant spelling.** Legitimate alternative spelling of a word. *See also* **equal variant; primary variant; secondary variant.**

**verso.** Left-hand page of a book, magazine, or brochure. *Compare* **recto.**

**vertical list.**  List that displays items vertically on separate lines below the introductory text; also called *displayed list* or *set-off list*. *See* **bulleted list; numbered list; unnumbered list.**

**vertical rule.**  Thin vertical line. *See also* **rule.**

**vetting.**  Substantive review of a manuscript by an expert in the subject matter; similarly, the checking of a translation by someone who is proficient in both languages.

**virgule.**  *See* **solidus.**

**widow.**  A first line of type on a printed page that runs less than full measure; specifically, the short last line of a paragraph carried over from the preceding page. *Compare* **orphan.**

**wordspacing.**  Amount of space between printed words. *Compare* **letterspacing.**

> *Tight wordspacing:*
> The very big dog and the very fat cat sat on the mat.
> *Normal wordspacing:*
> The very big dog and the very fat cat sat on the mat.
> *Loose wordspacing:*
> The very big dog and the very fat cat sat on the mat.

**XML.**  Short for *extensible markup language.* System for coding the elements in a digital document that reduces or eliminates the need for recoding when the document is produced on a new platform (e.g., print, web, e-reader, computer tablet).

**x-ref.**  Short for **cross-reference.**

# Glossary of Grammar Terms

**absolute participle.** Present or past participle that functions as a preposition or an adverb and therefore does not have a grammatical subject. Examples: <u>Barring</u> an unanticipated delay, the library will reopen in September. <u>Depending</u> on the price, we might increase our order. <u>Granted</u> these exceptions, the new policy takes effect immediately. *Compare* **dangling modifier; gerund; verbal.** *See also* **nominative absolute participle construction.**

**active voice.** Grammatical form in which the doer of the verb is stated. Examples: She fired two shots. He authorized the break-in. TopCo laid off fifty workers. In contrast, in the *passive voice* the recipient of the action conveyed by the verb is stated. Examples: Shots were fired. A break-in was authorized. Fifty workers were laid off.

**adjective.** Word that modifies (i.e., describes, limits, or qualifies) a noun by stating a characteristic or a quantity. Examples: a <u>green</u> pencil; a <u>fair-weather</u> friend; <u>Canadian</u> cheese; <u>three</u> books; a <u>few</u> pointers. *See also* **attributive adjective; compound adjective; coordinate adjective; noncoordinate adjective; predicate adjective; proper adjective.**

**adverb.** Word that modifies (i.e., describes, limits, or qualifies) an adjective, a verb, or another adverb. Adverbs indicate "time, place, manner, or degree"—that is, when, where, or how an action is performed—or specify the extent or degree of an adjective. Examples: She is <u>very</u> smart. We cut the tubes <u>precisely</u>. That is a <u>rather</u> strange view. I am leaving <u>now</u>. Put your books <u>here</u>. *See also* **sentence adverb.**

**adverbial clause.** Dependent clause that functions like an adverb; it may modify a verb, adjective, or adverb. Examples: He is slower <u>than she is</u>. I'll come over <u>when I finish my work</u>.

**adverbial phrase.** Phrase that functions like an adverb; it may modify a verb, adjective, or adverb. Examples: He stood <u>at the corner</u>. I've lived here <u>for fifteen years</u>.

**agreement.** *See* **pronoun-antecedent agreement; subject-verb agreement.**

**antecedent.** Noun or pronoun to which a pronoun refers; also called *referent*. Examples: <u>Jane</u> lost her jacket. <u>Tom, Dick, and Harry</u> had their hands full. <u>We</u> cannot find our books.

**appositive.** Substantive placed after another substantive to name or identify it. Examples: My hometown, <u>New York,</u> is a fine place to visit. His youngest brother, <u>Max,</u> is a plumber. Appositives are usually **nonrestrictive,** but they may be **restrictive:** Their son <u>Joe</u> lives in Fresno, but their son <u>Jim</u> lives at home. *See also* **nonrestrictive modifier; restrictive modifier.**

**article.** Part of speech comprising the words *a, an,* and *the. The* is the *definite article; a* and *an* are *indefinite articles.*

**attributive adjective.** Adjective that precedes the noun it modifies. Examples: a <u>tall</u> tree, an <u>over-the-counter</u> medication. *Compare* **predicate adjective.**

**attributive noun.** Noun that modifies the noun immediately following it. Examples: <u>college</u> textbooks, <u>desk</u> lamp, <u>awards</u> banquet, <u>Veterans</u> Administration.

**back-formation.** Short word extracted from a longer word that was not derived from the simpler word: to burgle, to liaise.

**case.** Form of a noun or pronoun that indicates its grammatical relation to other words in the sentence. *See also* **nominative case; objective case; possessive case.**

**clause.** Group of words that includes a subject and a finite verb. *See also* **dependent clause; independent clause.**

**collecting noun phrase.** Expression of the form "a(n) *x* of *y*," where *x* is a singular noun and *y* is a plural noun. Examples: a bunch of bananas, a set of papers, a flock of geese.

**collective noun.** Noun that denotes two or more people or items. Examples: class, couple, crowd, pair, staff, team.

**comma fault.** *See* **run-on sentence.**

**comma splice.** *See* **run-on sentence.**

**common noun.** Noun denoting a class of objects or an abstraction rather than a particular individual. *Compare* **proper noun.**

**complement.** Word or phrase completing the predicate, such as a direct object, indirect object, subjective complement, or objective complement.

**compound adjective.** Adjective that consists of two or more words. Examples: <u>hand-lettered</u> sign, <u>matter-of-fact</u> approach, refunds <u>smaller than expected</u>.

**compound predicate.** Predicate containing two or more finite verbs governed by the same grammatical subject. Examples: Yesterday I <u>went to the store and then drove home</u>. He says he <u>will look for a job but hasn't yet sent out any résumés</u>. *Compare* **compound sentence.**

**compound preposition.** *See* **preposition.**

**compound sentence.** Sentence containing two independent clauses joined by a conjunction. Examples: I went to the store, but he went home. We are pleased, and they are too. *Compare* **compound predicate.**

**conjunction.** Part of speech comprising the so-called linking words. *Coordinate conjunctions* join words, phrases, or clauses of equal rank: for, and, nor, but, or, yet, so (mnemonic: FANBOYS). *Subordinate conjunctions* join dependent clauses to independent clauses: although, as, because, if, since, so that, unless, while. *Correlative conjunctions* come in pairs: both/and; either/or; neither/nor; not only/but also.

**coordinate adjective.** Adjective that is "of the same rank" as an adjacent adjective; that is, both adjectives apply equally and independently to the noun. Coordinate adjectives are separated by "and" or by a comma. Examples: This is a <u>funny and wise</u> book. She solved a <u>complex, intricate</u> problem. His <u>wise, witty, authoritative</u> speech was well received. *Compare* **noncoordinate adjective.**

**coordinate conjunction.** *See* **conjunction.**

**copula.** Verb that expresses a state of being (rather than an action). Copulative verbs link the subject to another noun, pronoun, or adjective. Examples: We <u>are</u> a party of five. The enemy <u>is</u> us. The ride <u>seems</u> long. The oil <u>smells</u> rancid. It <u>remains</u> true. His opinion <u>has become</u> ours as well.

**correlative conjunction.** *See* **conjunction.**

**count noun.** Noun whose singular form may be preceded by a definite or an indefinite article (the, a, an); its plural form may be preceded by a number or by *some*. Examples: apple, book, cat, desk. *Compare* **noncount noun.**

**dangling modifier.** Also called a *dangler*. Grammatically incorrect construction in which a modifying participial, infinitive, or gerund phrase is not directly followed by its grammatical subject. Examples: <u>Driving down the street,</u> the campanile rang. [Driving down the street, we heard the campanile ring.] <u>Offered the job,</u> it's hard for her to say no. [Offered the job, she found it hard to say no.] <u>To write well,</u> a dictionary is necessary. [To write well, one needs a dictionary.] *See also* **misplaced modifier; squinting modifier.** *Compare* **absolute participle; nominative absolute participle construction.**

**dangling participle.** *See* **dangling modifier.**

**definite article.** *See* **article.**

**dependent clause.** Clause that cannot stand alone as a complete sentence; also called *subordinate clause*. *See also* **adverbial clause; relative clause.** *Compare* **independent clause.**

**direct address.** Speech or dialogue that names the person being spoken to. The name or noun is set off from the rest of the speech by commas. Examples: "Let's eat, grandma" [Compare: "Let's eat grandma"]; "Mom, don't bug me!"; "Can we try, sweetheart, to settle this out of court?"

**direct object.** Noun, pronoun, noun phrase, or noun clause that directly follows a verb and directly "receives" the action conveyed by the verb. In contrast, an *indirect object* follows a preposition or an implied preposition. Examples: He gave the book [direct object] to me [indirect object]. He gave me [indirect object, "to" implied] the book [direct object]. We wrote them [indirect object, "to" implied] a letter [direct object].

**direct question.** Speech or dialogue that asks a question. Examples: "Why did you do that?" I asked her. "Who are you?" she asked me. In contrast, an *indirect question* rephrases the question. Examples: I asked her why she had done it. She asked me who I was.

**direct quotation.** Speech or dialogue directly reproduced and placed in quotation marks. Examples: "I can't wait for summer," I said. She said, "I don't trust you." In contrast, an *indirect quotation* rephrases the words that were spoken. Examples: I said that I couldn't wait for summer. She said she didn't trust him.

**distributive possession.** Noun in the singular form following a plural possessive pronoun. Example: Tom, Dick, and Harry are eating <u>their lunch</u>.

**double genitive.** Idiomatic construction in which the genitive ("possessive") is indicated by the preposition *of* followed by the genitive form of a noun or pronoun. Examples: a friend <u>of Susan's</u>, a classmate <u>of mine</u>. Also called *double possessive*.

**double possessive.** *See* **double genitive.**

**ellipsis (elliptical clause).**  Omission of a word or phrase implied by the syntax or context. Examples: He was the nominee of the Democrats, she of the Republicans. The new machine has eight speeds, the old only three.

**expletive.**  Word or phrase used as a placeholder in a sentence, filling a syntactic role without contributing to meaning. Examples: There is an old folk tale about thrift. There are many reasons to root for the Golden State Warriors. It looks like snow. Not to be confused with the common use of *expletive* to denote a profane or vulgar exclamation. *See also* **impersonal construction.**

**finite verb.**  Verb showing tense (e.g., present, past, future), person (first, second, or third), and number (singular or plural). *Compare* **nonfinite verb.**

**fragment.**  *See* **sentence fragment.**

**fused participle.**  Gerund preceded by a noun or pronoun in the objective case. Examples: We see no likelihood of DotCom accepting the proposed merger. The thought of him receiving a promotion is laughable.

**genitive case.**  *See* **possessive case.**

**gerund.**  Present participle that functions as a noun. Examples: Writing neatly is important. His acting as though he were innocent fooled no one. *Compare* **absolute participle; verbal.**

**historical present tense.**  Use of the present tense to convey actions that occurred in the past.

**hypercorrection.**  Grammatical error committed in the attempt to avoid a grammatical error. Examples: Whom shall I say is calling? He felt badly about the accident. Just between you and I . . .

**impersonal construction.**  Sentence in which "there is," "there are," or "it is" (with the "it" lacking any referent) serves as the subject and main verb. Examples: There is little we can do. There are ten apples on the tree. It is safe to cross now. *See also* **expletive.**

**indefinite article.**  *See* **article.**

**independent clause.**  Clause that can stand as a complete sentence. *Compare* **dependent clause.**

**indirect object.**  *See* **direct object.**

**indirect question.**  *See* **direct question.**

**indirect quotation.**  *See* **direct quotation.**

**infinitive.**  Form of a verb that is always introduced by *to*. Examples: I like to sing. To be here is always a pleasure. To be invited to present this award is an honor. *See also* **verbal.**

**intransitive verb.**  Verb that does not require a **direct object.** Examples: He will go. They have come. I am done. You seem tired. She is lying down. *Compare* **reflexive verb; transitive verb.**

**misplaced modifier.**  Word or phrase positioned so that it appears to modify the wrong word in the sentence. Example: I saw a large animal in a tree with tall and pointed ears. *See also* **dangling modifier; squinting modifier.**

**modal verb.**  Auxiliary verb indicating ability, necessity, obligation, permission, possibility, probability, or willingness: e.g., can, could, may, might, must, need, ought, shall, should, will, would.

**modifier.** Word or phrase that describes, defines, or qualifies another word or phrase. *See also* **adjective; adverb; adverbial clause; adverbial phrase; dangling modifier; misplaced modifier; nonrestrictive modifier; restrictive modifier; squinting modifier.**

**nominative absolute participle construction.** Grammatically independent (absolute) part of a sentence that contains its own subject and a present or past participle and that functions as an adverbial modifier of the main clause. Example: <u>All things considered,</u> the cast performed well. *Compare* **dangling modifier.** *See also* **absolute participle.**

**nominative case.** Form of a noun or pronoun used to indicate that it is the subject of the verb.

**noncoordinate adjective.** Adjective in a series of attributive adjectives that modifies the unit formed by a succeeding adjective and the noun. Examples: She solved a <u>complex</u> calculus problem ["complex" modifies "calculus problem"]. This is a <u>large green</u> clothbound book ["large" modifies "green clothbound book"; "green" modifies "clothbound book"]. Noncoordinate adjectives are not separated by commas. *Compare* **coordinate adjective.**

**noncount noun.** Noun whose singular form may be preceded by a definite article or by *some* but not by an indefinite article (a *or* an). Examples: advice, anguish, evidence, furniture, mail, milk, mud, music, sand, training. The singular of a noncount noun may also stand alone. Examples: <u>Music</u> soothes the soul. <u>Sand</u> is gritty.

**nonfinite verb.** Infinitive (to be, to do, to go), present participle (being, doing, going), or past participle (been, done, gone). *Compare* **finite verb.**

**nonrestrictive modifier.** Clause or phrase that describes its subject but is not essential to the meaning of the sentence. Nonrestrictive modifiers are set off by commas. Examples: Dogs, <u>which are members of the canine family,</u> make good pets. I thank my mother, <u>who always encouraged me to write.</u> In contrast, a **restrictive modifier** is essential to the meaning of the sentence and is not set off by commas. Examples: Dogs <u>that have shiny black coats</u> are my favorites. I thank those teachers <u>who encouraged me</u>—and "So there!" to those <u>who did not.</u>

**object.** Noun, pronoun, or noun clause that follows a transitive verb or a preposition and is the "recipient" of the action. *See also* **direct object.**

**objective case.** Form of a noun or pronoun used to indicate that it is the object of a finite verb or a preposition. Examples: We phoned <u>her</u> yesterday. They waved to <u>us.</u>

**parallel construction.** Principle requiring items in a pair or series to have the same grammatical form. Examples: Our goals are to <u>expand</u> customer services and <u>improve</u> employee morale. The skills needed for this position include <u>proofreading, copyediting,</u> and <u>indexing.</u>

**participial phrase.** Phrase introduced by a present participle (being, going, doing) or a perfect participle (having been, having gone, having done). *See also* **dangling modifier.**

**participle.** *See* **past participle; perfect participle; present participle.**

**particle.** A small function word or affix that has little meaning and does not inflect: for example, prepositions used in phrasal verbs (break <u>down</u>), prefixes (*un-*), and suffixes (*-ness*).

**parts of speech.**  Categorization of words into classes that reflect their function: nouns, pronouns, verbs, adjectives, adverbs, prepositions, conjunctions, interjections. This traditional term confounds what some modern linguists call "word class" (verb, noun, adjective, adverb) and "word function" (predicator, subject, modifier, direct object).

**passive voice.**  *See* **active voice.**

**past participle.**  Verb form that usually ends in *ed* (wanted, noticed), although some verbs have irregular forms (been, gone, said). Past participles are used to form the perfect tenses (I have been, I had been, I will have been) and passive constructions (it was said that; there are thought to be). *Compare* **perfect participle; present participle.** *See also* **absolute participle; dangling modifier.**

**perfect participle.**  Verb form consisting of *having* or *having been* followed by a past participle. Examples: having gone, having been gone. *Compare* **past participle; present participle.** *See also* **dangling modifier.**

**phrasal verb.**  Verb consisting of a verb and a preposition or particle: e.g., hang up (a picture), put out (a fire), fill out (a form), hand in (the homework).

**phrase.**  Group of related words that functions as one part of speech (e.g., adverbial phrase, noun phrase, prepositional phrase, verb phrase).

**possessive case.**  Also called *genitive case.* Form of a noun or pronoun used to indicate possession, origin, or temporal duration. Examples: my house, Chris's book, children's toys, See's candies, a week's worth of errands, six months' vacation.

**predicate.**  Portion of a sentence that makes a statement about the grammatical subject of the sentence. The predicate includes the verb and all its modifiers, objects, and complements. Examples: His four older brothers and their wives are coming tomorrow. We can't think about that nor do anything about it right now. June 21, summer solstice, is the longest day of the year in the Northern Hemisphere.

**predicate adjective.**  Adjective that follows the noun it modifies, coming in the predicate of the sentence. Examples: Iced tea is thirst quenching. He received a bill that was larger than usual. *Compare* **attributive adjective.**

**predicate nominative.**  Noun in the nominative case that is in the predicate of a sentence. Examples: She is the president of the club. He hopes to become an expert in his field. They are a happy couple.

**preposition.**  Word that expresses the physical or temporal relation between a noun or pronoun and other elements in a phrase, clause, or sentence. Examples: above, after, at, before, by, during, for, from, in, of, on, over, to, up, with. *Compound prepositions* consist of two or more words: according to, in place of, instead of, out of, together with, up to, with regard to.

**prepositional phrase.**  Phrase consisting of a preposition and the noun or pronoun that it pertains to. Examples: Before sunrise is the best time to view the skyline. They are requesting a refund instead of a replacement copy. On Friday he appealed to his supervisor for assistance.

**present participle.**  Verb form ending in *ing* (being, doing) that is used to form the progressive tenses: I am singing, I was singing, I have been singing, I had been singing. The present participle may also be used as a noun (I like her singing) and as a modifier (<u>Standing</u> on an empty stage, he looked lost). *Compare* **past participle; perfect participle.** *See also* **absolute participle; dangling modifier; gerund; verbal.**

**pronoun-antecedent agreement.**  Principle by which the form of a pronoun is determined by the number and gender of its antecedent.

**proper adjective.**  Adjectival form of a proper noun. Examples: We purchase only <u>American</u> products. She studied <u>Euclidean</u> geometry.

**proper noun.**  Name of a specific person, group, place, or thing. Examples: Jane Doe, Europeans, Latin America, the Great Wall of China. *Compare* **common noun.**

**quasi-coordinator.**  Phrase that connects terms like a coordinating conjunction but that functions more like a preposition. Examples: accompanied by, added to, along with, as well as, combined with, coupled with, in addition to, no less than, together with, with.

**referent.**  *See* **antecedent.**

**reflexive verb.**  Verb whose **subject** and **direct object** are the same. Examples: I hurt myself. The dog scratched itself. She washed herself. *Compare* **intransitive verb; transitive verb.**

**relative clause.**  Dependent clause introduced by a relative pronoun, adjective, or adverb (e.g., that, what, when, where, which, who, whom, whose, why). Examples: This is the office <u>that she used</u>. Give this report to the journalist <u>who asked for it</u>.

**restrictive modifier.**  Clause or phrase that limits its subject and therefore is essential to the meaning of the sentence. Examples: Editors <u>who have at least five years' seniority</u> will receive a bonus ["who have" limits the set of editors]. Buildings <u>that are scheduled for renovation</u> will close early on Thursday ["that are" limits the set of buildings]. We must vigorously protest <u>when our civil rights are threatened</u> ["when" limits when we must protest]. *Compare* **nonrestrictive modifier.**

**run-on sentence.**  Grammatically incorrect construction consisting of two independent clauses joined by a comma (rather than by a coordinate conjunction or a semicolon). Also called *comma splice* or *comma fault*. Example: The multinational peace force is patrolling the streets, the international food agencies are providing food and medicine.

**sentence adverb.**  Adverb that modifies an entire independent clause. Examples: <u>Surprisingly,</u> inflation has remained flat. No tickets are available, <u>unfortunately</u>.

**sentence fragment.**  Expression punctuated as though it were a complete sentence, even though it lacks either a subject or a finite verb. Fragments are acceptable when used for special effect.

**split infinitive.**  Construction in which one or more words separate *to* from the verb form. Examples: to boldly go, to more than double, to further insist.

**squinting modifier.**  Modifier positioned such that it can be interpreted as modifying either the preceding or the following element in the sentence. Example: Taking a moment to think <u>clearly</u> improves your chances of success. *See also* **dangling modifier; misplaced modifier.**

**subject.**  Person, place, or thing that performs the action (in the active voice) or receives the action (in the passive voice) expressed by a finite verb.

**subject-verb agreement.**  Principle by which the form of a finite verb is determined by its subject: I am, she is, you are.

**subjunctive.**  Set of verb forms used in dependent clauses to express wishes, requests, commands, necessity, uncertainty, and contrary-to-fact or hypothetical conditions. Examples: They asked that the program <u>be</u> canceled. We insist that he <u>be</u> excused. If the commission <u>were</u> to agree to hear the case, the merger might be delayed. It is imperative that construction <u>be</u> halted.

**subordinate clause.**  *See* **dependent clause.**

**subordinate conjunction.**  *See* **conjunction.**

**substantive.**  Any word, phrase, or clause that functions as a noun.

**syllepsis.**  (1) Use of a word that agrees grammatically with only one of two terms by which it is governed (Either he or I am going). (2) Use of a word in the same grammatical relation to two adjacent words, but with different meanings (He lost his hat and his temper).

**syntax.**  The way words are assembled into phrases, clauses, and sentences.

**transitive verb.**  Verb that has a **direct object.** Examples: I trust you. I wrote a letter. She is laying the tile. *Compare* **intransitive verb; reflexive verb.**

**verb.**  Word or group of words that expresses an action or a state of being. *See also* **copula; finite verb; infinitive; intransitive verb; nonfinite verb; reflexive verb; transitive verb.**

**verbal.**  Infinitive or participle of a verb that functions as a noun, adjective, or adverb. Examples: <u>To accept</u> this award gives me great pleasure. There is work <u>to be done</u>. They play <u>to win</u>. <u>Seeing</u> is <u>believing</u>. The <u>opening</u> bars imitate the rhythms of a <u>speeding</u> train. Her long-<u>awaited</u> novel has been published. *Compare* **absolute participle; gerund.**

# Selected Bibliography

The following sources are organized into ten categories: (1) style manuals; (2) dictionaries, thesauruses, and corpora; (3) language, grammar, and usage guides; (4) writing and editing guides; (5) tools for on-screen editing; (6) copyright, permissions, and ethics; (7) design and production; (8) professional organizations, professional training, and certification; (9) other resources; and (10) lagniappe, a miscellaneous category for a few references loved by wordsmiths everywhere.

## 1. STYLE MANUALS

*The ACS Style Guide: Effective Communication of Scientific Information.* 3rd ed. Edited by Anne M. Coghill and Lorrin R. Garson. Washington, D.C.: American Chemical Society, 2006.
> American Chemical Society (ACS) guidance for authors, reviewers, and editors in chemistry and other science, technical, and medical fields.

*AIP Style Manual.* 4th ed. New York: American Institute of Physics, 1990.
> American Institute of Physics (AIP) guidance for authors and editors in physics. See also the AIP Author Resource Center at https://publishing.aip.org/authors.

*AMA Manual of Style: A Guide for Authors and Editors.* 10th ed. Edited by Cheryl Iverson. New York: Oxford University Press, 2007.
> Editorial guidance for medical publishing from the American Medical Association. Also available by subscription at http://www.amamanualofstyle.com/, with updates, an SI calculator, and other tools.

*Apple Style Guide.* Cupertino, Calif.: Apple, 2013. https://help.apple.com/applestyleguide/.
> Guidance for editors and writers preparing documentation for the technology company Apple. Includes general advice about global English and other issues of concern to technical editors. Free downloadable PDF.

*The Associated Press Stylebook and Briefing on Media Law 2018.* New York: Basic Books, 2018.
> Basic reference for journalists, updated annually with new and revised entries. Also available in several e-book formats and by subscription to an online edition, with regular updates, email alerts, and tools, at https://www.apstylebook.com/.

*The Australian Editing Handbook.* 3rd rev. ed. Edited by Elizabeth Flann, Beryl Hill, and Lan Wang. Milton, Queensland: John Wiley & Sons Australia, 2014.
> An industry standard for writers, editors, and students, covering the entire editing process from working with authors and receiving manuscripts to editorial, production, printing, and beyond.

*The Bluebook: A Uniform System of Citation.* 20th ed. Cambridge, Mass.: Harvard Law Review Association, 2015.

The main style guide for legal citation in the United States. Also available by subscription at https://www.legalbluebook.com/.

Butcher, Judith, Caroline Drake, and Maureen Leach. *Butcher's Copy-editing: The Cambridge Handbook for Editors, Copy-editors and Proofreaders.* 4th ed. Cambridge: Cambridge University Press, 2006.

Respected reference for editorial style in the UK.

BuzzFeed Style Guide. https://www.buzzfeed.com/emmyf/buzzfeed-style-guide.

BuzzFeed's free internet style guide for "everything from hard-hitting journalism to fun quizzes," updated regularly to register changes in language and casual usage.

*The Canadian Press Stylebook: A Guide for Writing and Editing.* 18th ed. Edited by James McCarten. Ontario: Canadian Press, 2017.

The style used by journalists at Canada's national news agency, as well as hundreds of newspapers, broadcasters, and websites. Also available by subscription at http://www.thecanadian press.com/writing-guide/stylebook/.

*The Canadian Style: A Guide to Writing and Editing.* Rev. ed. Toronto: Dundurn Press in cooperation with Public Works and Government Services Canada Translation Bureau, 1997.

The Canadian government's English-language style guide. Available in print or online at https://www.btb.termiumplus.gc.ca/tpv2guides/guides/tcdnstyl/index-eng.html?lang=eng.

*The Chicago Manual of Style.* 17th ed. Chicago: University of Chicago Press, 2017.

The authoritative style manual for most US book and journal publishers. Also available by subscription as *The Chicago Manual of Style Online* at https://www.chicagomanualofstyle .org/, along with a discussion forum and other perks; nonsubscribers have free access to the table of contents, a "Citation Quick Guide," "Chicago Style Q&A," and the blog *CMOS Shop Talk,* which includes occasional quizzes on Chicago style and the regular feature "Editor's Corner," previously hosted by the popular "subversive copy editor" Carol Fisher Saller (q.v. in "Lagniappe") and now presided over by Russell David Harper.

*Department of Defense Dictionary of Military and Associated Terms,* November 2018. http:// www.jcs.mil/Portals/36/Documents/Doctrine/pubs/dictionary.pdf.

"Sets forth standard US military and associated terminology to encompass the joint activity of the Armed Forces of the United States." Consists of several hundred pages of alphabetically ordered terminology followed by an extensive appendix of military alphabet soup. Downloadable PDF.

*The Economist Style Guide.* 12th ed. London: Economist Books, 2018.

Style guide for the British weekly magazine for international news, politics, business, finance, science, and technology.

*Editing Canadian English: A Guide for Editors, Writers, and Everyone Who Works with Words.* 3rd ed. Toronto: Editors' Association of Canada, 2015.

Style guide and reference manual for writing and editing in Canadian English for Canadian and North American audiences. Also available by subscription at https://editingcanadianenglish .ca/.

*GPO Style Manual: An Official Guide to the Form and Style of Federal Government Publishing.* 31st ed. Washington, D.C.: US Government Publishing Office, 2016.

Manual for GPO style, used by many US government agencies and some private sector businesses. Available as a free PDF download at https://www.govinfo.gov/content/pkg

/GPO-STYLEMANUAL-2016/pdf/GPO-STYLEMANUAL-2016.pdf or as an at-cost print copy from the online US Government Bookstore, at https://bookstore.gpo.gov/.

*The Gregg Reference Manual.* 11th ed. Edited by William A. Sabin. New York: McGraw-Hill, 2011.

> General handbook for business and other professional writers, with comprehensive sections on grammar and usage as well as guidance on various forms of business communication.

Guardian and Observer Style Guide. https://www.theguardian.com/guardian-observer-style -guide.

> Free online alphabetical list of style preferences for the UK news publications *The Guardian* and *The Observer.*

Hudson, Robert. *The Christian Writer's Manual of Style.* 4th ed. Grand Rapids, Mich.: Zondervan, 2016.

> A standard style manual for the Christian publishing industry, with guidance on many topics not addressed in other references or online.

*Microsoft Manual of Style.* 4th ed. Redmond, Wash.: Microsoft Press, 2012.

> Guidance for authors and editors preparing content about computer technology for a world audience. Includes both general advice and Microsoft-specific style guidelines. Although superseded by the 2018 *Microsoft Writing Style Guide* (listed below), this reference is still useful.

*Microsoft Writing Style Guide.* 2018. https://docs.microsoft.com/en-us/style-guide/welcome/.

> Use at (or download the 1,018-page PDF from) this URL. Supersedes the previous fourth edition, *Microsoft Manual of Style* (2012).

*MLA Handbook.* 8th ed. New York: Modern Language Association, 2016.

> Source for Modern Language Association (MLA) style as of April 2016. Revises previous MLA style for documentation, with new forms for digital sources; supersedes the MLA's 2008 general style guide, the *MLA Style Manual,* now taken out of print. See also the MLA Style Center, at https://style.mla.org/, a free companion to the *MLA Handbook* with writing resources for students, a "quick guide" to citation forms, and a Q&A section.

National Geographic Style Manual. https://sites.google.com/a/ngs.org/ngs-style-manual/.

> A free online guide to preferred National Geographic style and usage, intended as a supplement to other standard references.

*New Oxford Style Manual.* 3rd ed. Oxford: Oxford University Press, 2016.

> A guide for British authors and publishers that combines two old standards: *New Hart's Rules,* on preparing copy for print and electronic publication, and the *New Oxford Dictionary for Writers and Editors,* comprising A-to-Z advice on special treatment of words and names.

*The New York Public Library Writer's Guide to Style and Usage.* Edited by Andrea Sutcliffe. New York: HarperCollins, 1994.

> Aging but still popular general guide for writers of books, magazine features, newsletters, business reports, technical papers, and brochures.

*The New York Times Manual of Style and Usage.* 5th ed. Edited by Allan M. Siegal and William G. Connolly. Revised and updated by Philip B. Corbett, Jill Taylor, Patrick LaForge, and Susan Wessling. New York: Three Rivers Press, 2015.

> The official style guide used by the writers and editors of the New York Times news organization.

*Publication Manual of the American Psychological Association.* 6th ed. Washington, D.C.: American Psychological Association, 2009.

   Style guide used by many writers and editors in the social sciences. Additional resources from the *APA Style Blog,* at https://blog.apastyle.org/.

*The SBL Handbook of Style: For Biblical Studies and Related Disciplines.* 2nd ed. Atlanta: SBL Press, 2014.

   Style guide of the Society of Biblical Literature. A standard resource covering cognate fields (archaeology, ancient Near East, early Islam, etc.) based on but sometimes departing from *The Chicago Manual of Style* (q.v.).

*Science and Technical Writing: A Manual of Style.* 2nd ed. Edited by Philip Rubens. New York: Routledge, 2001.

   A style resource for technical writers. This revised and updated version of the previous (1992) edition covers the techniques and technologies that have revolutionized the communication of scientific and technical information.

*Scientific Style and Format: The CSE Manual for Authors, Editors, and Publishers.* 8th ed. Chicago: University of Chicago Press, 2014.

   Named after its publisher, the Council of Science Editors (CSE); used by writers working in biology, chemistry, physics, medicine, mathematics, earth sciences, and the social sciences. Also available by subscription at https://www.scientificstyleandformat.org/. The searchable online edition offers tools and perks, including the free "Scientific Style and Format Citation Quick Guide."

*Style Manual: For Authors, Editors and Printers.* 6th ed. Milton, Queensland: John Wiley & Sons Australia, 2002.

   An Australian reference standard providing guidance and detailed advice on publishing in both print and electronic formats.

Swanson, Ellen. *Mathematics into Type.* Updated by Arlene O'Sean and Antoinette Schleyer. Providence, R.I.: American Mathematical Society, 1999.

   Guidance for authors typesetting their own manuscripts, as well as for copyeditors, proofreaders, and production staff handling mathematics.

Tarutz, Judith A. *Technical Editing: The Practical Guide for Editors and Writers.* New York: Basic Books, 1992.

   Guidance for the special issues in technical writing and editing, with examples, case studies, and techniques.

*The Times Style and Usage Guide.* Rev. ed. Edited by Tim Austin. London: Times Books, 2003.

   Style guidance for journalists writing for the London *Times.*

Turabian, Kate L. *A Manual for Writers of Research Papers, Theses, and Dissertations.* 9th ed. Revised by Wayne C. Booth et al. Chicago: University of Chicago Press, 2018.

   An old classic favored by students and academic researchers at all levels, now including guidelines for using and citing digital materials, developing information literacy, and formatting and submitting research papers electronically. Updated to conform with the style guidelines of *The Chicago Manual of Style,* 17th ed. (q.v.).

*Words into Type.* 3rd ed. Englewood Cliffs, N.J.: Prentice-Hall, 1974.

   A favorite general reference, despite its age and its outdated information about production processes. The dense and useful content includes an overview of grammar and usage and a long list of prepositional idioms.

*The Yahoo! Style Guide: The Ultimate Sourcebook for Writing, Editing, and Creating Content for the Digital World.* Edited by Chris Barr. New York: St. Martin's Griffin, 2010.

Reference for elements of web style for writers, editors, bloggers, and students, from basics of grammar and punctuation to web-specific writing advice.


## 2. DICTIONARIES, THESAURUSES, AND CORPORA

*American Heritage College Dictionary.* 4th ed. Boston: Houghton Mifflin Harcourt, 2007.

Collegiate edition in the *AHD* suite of dictionaries.

*American Heritage Dictionary of the English Language.* 5th ed. Boston: Houghton Mifflin, 2016.

Unabridged edition in the *AHD* suite of dictionaries. Also available for free at https://www.ahdictionary.com/.

*Australian Oxford Dictionary.* 2nd ed. Oxford: Oxford University Press, 2005.

Authoritative guide to contemporary Australian English, including Australian words and encyclopedic entries on Australian topics.

*Canadian Oxford Dictionary.* 2nd ed. Oxford: Oxford University Press, 2005.

Dictionary covering both world English and Canadian English, with definitions most familiar to Canadians presented first, and including many uniquely Canadian words and senses.

Collins Free Online Dictionary. https://www.collinsdictionary.com/us.

Free online dictionary includes both US and UK spellings.

Corpus of Contemporary American English (COCA). http://corpus.byu.edu/coca/.

Linguistic corpus of some 520 million words from edited text, covering 1990 to the present, with continual additions, organized by genre—spoken (mostly news programs), fiction, magazines, newspapers, and academic writing.

Corpus of Historical American English (COHA). http://corpus.byu.edu/coha/.

Linguistic corpus of some 400 million words from edited text, covering 1810 to the 2000s, organized by genre (though no spoken texts).

*The Describer's Dictionary: A Treasury of Terms and Literary Quotations.* 2nd ed. Edited by David Grambs and Ellen S. Levine. New York: W. W. Norton, 2014.

A combination dictionary-thesaurus using a reverse definition-to-term format to help writers and editors find *le mot juste;* includes illustrative passages by notable authors.

*Descriptionary: A Thematic Dictionary.* 4th ed. Edited by Marc McCutcheon. New York: Checkmark Books, 2010.

Like *The Describer's Dictionary,* a combination of reverse dictionary and thesaurus, with descriptions of terms organized into subject categories and subcategories.

*Diagnostic and Statistical Manual of Mental Disorders: DSM-5.* Washington, D.C.: American Psychiatric Association, 2013.

Authoritative manual used by clinicians and researchers to diagnose and classify mental disorders.

Dickson, Paul. *Labels for Locals: What to Call People from Abilene to Zimbabwe.* Springfield, Mass.: Merriam-Webster, 1997.

Exploration of the lore and history behind the sometimes unusual monikers for people from particular locales, regions, and countries.

*Dorland's Pocket Medical Dictionary.* 29th ed. Philadelphia: Elsevier Saunders, 2013.

A portable resource based on *Dorland's Illustrated Medical Dictionary,* with dependable information about medical terms; with purchase, buyers receive a code for free online access to a specialized spell-checker.

Google Books Ngram Viewer. https://books.google.com/ngrams.

Google's search tool for exploring its linguistic corpora, comprising 155 billion words from 1800 through the first decade of the twenty-first century, compliments of Google Books (Google's repository of scanned titles); allows users to graph the occurrences and collocations of words and phrases in a selected subset of books over a specified period.

*Green's Dictionary of Slang.* https://greensdictofslang.com/.

Free searchable online edition of the three-volume print work (the lifelong project of Jonathon Green) bearing the same title. Largest historical dictionary of English slang, covering 1500 to the present in all the English-speaking countries and regions.

*Merriam-Webster's Collegiate Dictionary.* 11th ed. Springfield, Mass.: Merriam-Webster, 2003.

Collegiate edition in the *M-W* suite of dictionaries; recommended by *The Chicago Manual of Style* and preferred by many book publishers. Now superseded by the regularly updated online edition (print updates ceased in 2011) available free (with ads) at https://www.merriam-webster.com/ or with a subscription to the online *Merriam-Webster Unabridged* (q.v.).

*Merriam-Webster's Collegiate Thesaurus.* 2nd ed. Springfield, Mass.: Merriam-Webster, 2011.

Alphabetically arranged thesaurus; companion volume to *Merriam-Webster's Collegiate Dictionary.* Includes usage examples, idiomatic phrases, and antonyms.

*Merriam-Webster Unabridged.* http://unabridged.merriam-webster.com/.

Retitled, subscription-based online edition of the now-retired 1993 print version, *Webster's Third New International Dictionary of the English Language, Unabridged* (q.v.). Updated twice yearly and undergoing gradual revision.

*Merriam-Webster's Visual Dictionary.* 2nd ed. Springfield, Mass.: Merriam-Webster, 2012.

A reference tool for visual learners and those new to English. Combines terms and definitions with illustrations from many fields and an index for quick searches. Also available at http://www.visualdictionaryonline.com/.

*Mosby's Dictionary of Medicine, Nursing, and Health Professions.* 10th ed. St. Louis: Elsevier, 2017.

A weighty and extensively illustrated medical dictionary used by medical professionals.

*New Oxford American Dictionary.* 3rd ed. New York: Oxford University Press, 2010.

Based on the two-billion-word Oxford English Corpus and the citation files of the *Oxford English Dictionary* (q.v.). Definitions organized by principal contemporary meanings rather than by historical chronology.

One Look Dictionary Search. https://www.onelook.com/.

Portal to many free online dictionaries (including specialized ones), but the authoritativeness of these sources is not always clear.

*Oxford English Dictionary.* 2nd ed. 20 vols. Oxford: Oxford University Press, 1989.

Twenty-volume historical dictionary, with definitions organized chronologically, from earliest to most recent. Available online by subscription, with regular updates and extra features, at http://www.oed.com/.

*Random House Webster's College Thesaurus.* 2nd ed. New York: Random House, 2005.

Alphabetically arranged entries with synonyms, antonyms, and example sentences.

*Random House Webster's Unabridged Dictionary.* 2nd ed. New York: Random House, 2005.

Includes major British, Canadian, and Australian terms; new words section; etymologies; usage notes; encyclopedic entries for people, places, historical events, and cultural works; illustrations and maps; and other features.

*Random House Webster's Word Menu.* Rev. ed. Edited by Stephen Glazier. New York: Random House Reference, 1998.

Billed as an all-in-one dictionary, thesaurus, and almanac, with a reverse dictionary and glossaries.

Rodale, J. I. *The Synonym Finder.* Rev. ed. New York: Warner Books, 1986.

Another popular thesaurus with alphabetically arranged entries.

*Roget's International Thesaurus.* 7th ed. New York: Collins Reference, 2010.

Classic thesaurus arranging words and phrases according to related meanings rather than alphabetically.

*Shorter Oxford English Dictionary.* 6th ed. 2 vols. Oxford: Oxford University Press, 2007.

Abridged edition based on the famous *Oxford English Dictionary* (q.v.) and offering the same lexical quality. Follows changing meanings through history, includes many new words not listed in the twenty-volume 1989 *OED,* and illustrates definitions with contemporary quotations.

*Stedman's Medical Dictionary.* 28th ed. Philadelphia: Lippincott, 2006.

Resource for health care professionals, including medical students, physicians, educators, researchers, and medical editors.

Urban Dictionary. https://www.urbandictionary.com/.

A crowd-sourced dictionary of the trendy and often ephemeral slang ("on fleek"?) that arises in popular culture. Hardly authoritative for copyeditors, but a handy resource for interpreting what the kids are writing.

*Webster's New World College Dictionary.* 5th ed. New York: Macmillan, 2016.

The preferred dictionary of the Associated Press (AP) and the *New York Times.* Available for free (with ads) at http://www.yourdictionary.com/; see also Your Dictionary, below.

*Webster's Third New International Dictionary of the English Language, Unabridged.* Springfield, Mass.: Merriam-Webster, 1993.

This unabridged dictionary is now online under a changed title (see *Merriam-Webster Unabridged*) and is undergoing gradual revision; the print edition is no longer being updated.

Wiktionary. https://www.wiktionary.org/.

A collaboratively produced free multilingual dictionary. Copyeditors may discover definitions for new and nonce words here but should beware of crowd-sourced definitions that haven't been authenticated by lexicographers.

Your Dictionary. http://www.yourdictionary.com/.

Online portal to free (with ads) editions of *Webster's New World College Dictionary, American Heritage Dictionary of the English Language,* and Wiktionary.

## 3. LANGUAGE, GRAMMAR, AND USAGE GUIDES

Bernstein, Theodore. *The Careful Writer: A Modern Guide to English Usage.* 1965. Reprint, New York: Free Press, 1995.

One of the best commonsense usage guides, despite its age, but doesn't cover recent issues.

Bernstein, Theodore. *Miss Thistlebottom's Hobgoblins: The Careful Writer's Guide to the Taboos, Bugbears, and Outmoded Rules of English Usage.* New York: Farrar, Straus & Giroux, 1971.

Corollary to *The Careful Writer* and origin of the character Miss Thistlebottom, a fictional pedant whose spurious rules of usage are wisely repudiated.

Common Errors in English Usage. https://brians.wsu.edu/common-errors/.

Popular student resource created by a now-retired professor of English at Washington State University, Paul Brians. Focuses on deviations from Standard Written English (and "hoards" of homophone errors) as judged by professional writers, editors, teachers, and business executives.

Conscious Style Guide. https://consciousstyleguide.com/.

Resource aggregating links to various media guides that advocate respectful, inclusive language in writing about marginalized communities.

Copperud, Roy H. *American Usage and Style: The Consensus.* New York: Van Nostrand Reinhold, 1980.

A survey of all the other authorities' opinions on contested issues of usage to determine "the consensus" of advice.

The Diversity Style Guide. https://www.diversitystyleguide.com/.

A resource for media professionals developed by the Center for Integration and Improvement of Journalism, Journalism Department, San Francisco State University. Includes terms and phrases related to race and ethnicity; religion; sexual orientation; gender identity; age and generation; drugs and alcohol; and physical, mental, and cognitive disabilities. With links to additional resources.

Evans, Bergen, and Cornelia Evans. *A Dictionary of Contemporary American Usage.* New York: Random House, 1957.

Commonsense guide to usage still valued by many professional editors despite its advanced age and some outdated advice.

Follett, Wilson. *Modern American Usage: A Guide.* Rev. ed. Edited by Erik Wensberg. New York: Hill & Wang, 1998.

One of the most conservative of contemporary usage guides.

Fowler, H. W. *A Dictionary of Modern English Usage.* 2nd ed. Revised by Ernest Gowers. Oxford: Oxford University Press, 1965.

This edition of Fowler's 1926 classic, revised by Gowers, is the urtext most often cited as "Fowler" by prescriptivists. See also the bibliographic entries for the third edition, *The New Fowler's Modern English Usage* (2004), edited by R. W. Burchfield; and for the current, fourth edition, *Fowler's Dictionary of Modern English Usage* (2015), edited by Jeremy Butterfield (in this book cited as *Fowler's*).

*Fowler's Dictionary of Modern English Usage.* 4th ed. Edited by Jeremy Butterfield. Oxford: Oxford University Press, 2015.

The current (fourth) iteration of Fowler's ever-popular *Dictionary of Modern English Usage* (q.v.), recognizing British and American variants and offering somewhat more liberal opinions than the 1965 urtext on which it is based.

Garner, Bryan A. *The Chicago Guide to Grammar, Usage, and Punctuation.* Chicago: University of Chicago Press, 2016.

A student's and writer's reference covering traditional and transformational grammar, syntax and sentence diagramming, usage with reference to corpus linguistics, and conventions of punctuation. An excellent overview of grammar for nonlinguists, combined with moderate prescriptivism.

Garner, Bryan A. *Garner's Modern English Usage.* 4th ed. New York: Oxford University Press, 2016.

Retitled and enlarged edition of *Garner's Modern American Usage,* third edition (2009); blends corpus linguistics and opinion. Moderately prescriptivist, reflecting Garner's judgment of usage appropriate for the conservative environment of formal, academic, and professional prose.

GLAAD (Gay and Lesbian Alliance against Defamation). *Media Reference Guide.* 10th ed., October 2016. https://www.glaad.org/reference.

Media guide for writing about LGBTQ individuals; now available at this site as a free forty-page PDF.

Gordon, Karen Elizabeth. *The Deluxe Transitive Vampire: The Ultimate Handbook of Grammar for the Innocent, the Eager, and the Doomed.* New York: Pantheon, 1993.

Grammar and usage advice with hilariously memorable example sentences and illustrations.

Grammar Girl Quick and Dirty Tips: Complete Archive of Posts and Podcasts. https://www .quickanddirtytips.com/grammar-girl-quick-and-dirty-tips-complete-archive-of-posts -podcasts.

Grammar advice from Mignon Fogarty, a.k.a. Grammar Girl. Useful bite-size chunks of grammar instruction if you can tolerate the annoying pop-up ads.

Greenbaum, Sidney, and Randolph Quirk. *A Student's Grammar of the English Language.* London: Longman, 1990.

A shortened version of the definitive (and expensive) Quirk et al., *A Comprehensive Grammar of the English Language* (q.v.); draws on contemporary linguistics and research in related fields, but suitable for students and nonlinguists.

Hale, Constance, and Jessie Scanlon. *Wired Style: Principles of English Usage in the Digital Age.* Rev. ed. New York: Broadway Books, 1999.

Advice and an A-to-Z list on writing for or about digital media; still useful, despite some datedness owing to the warp-speed evolution of language in this area (e.g., the book anticipates the solid form *email* but capitalizes *Internet* and *Web*).

Herbst, Philip H. *The Color of Words: An Encyclopaedic Dictionary of Ethnic Bias in the United States.* Yarmouth, Maine: Intercultural Press, 1997.

An A-to-Z list, explanation, and historical analysis of US ethnic and racial expressions that convey (or once conveyed) bias or are controversial or confusing.

Huddleston, Rodney, and Geoffrey K. Pullum. *The Cambridge Grammar of the English Language.* Cambridge: Cambridge University Press, 2002.

A comprehensive, advanced (and expensive) descriptive grammar of English, including significant recent developments in linguistic theory.

Huddleston, Rodney, and Geoffrey K. Pullum. *A Student's Introduction to English Grammar.* Cambridge: Cambridge University Press, 2005.

Based on the authors' advanced *Cambridge Grammar of the English Language;* an undergraduate textbook on modern Standard English grammar for university students with little or no background in grammar or linguistics.

Johnson, Edward D. *The Handbook of Good English.* New York: Washington Square Press, 1991.

Revised and updated edition of a guide to modern grammar, punctuation, usage, and style by a longtime book editor working for major publishing houses; includes an alphabetical glossary-index.

Lester, Mark, and Larry Beason. *The McGraw-Hill Handbook of English Grammar and Usage.* 2nd ed. New York: McGraw-Hill Education, 2012.

A simplified approach to correct grammar that "doesn't bog you down in musty grammarian phraseology."

Loberger, Gordon, and Kate Shoup. *Webster's New World English Grammar Handbook.* 2nd ed. Hoboken, N.J.: Wiley, 2009.

Simple guidance for grammar, punctuation, spelling, and usage.

Maggio, Rosalie. *Talking about People: A Guide to Fair and Accurate Language.* Phoenix: Oryx, 1997.

Reference guide offering alternatives for outdated, stereotypical, and damaging language when describing people in terms of their age, gender, employment, economic status, religion, ethnic background, or disability. Needs to be supplemented with more recent resources addressing newly recognized issues.

McLendon, Lisa. *The Perfect English Grammar Workbook: Simple Rules and Quizzes to Master Today's English.* Berkeley, Calif.: Zephyros Press, 2017.

Short, clear, and sensible workbook for students and grammar novices by a linguist and newspaper copyeditor who runs the Bremner Editing Center at the University of Kansas journalism school.

*Merriam-Webster's Dictionary of English Usage.* Repr. ed. Springfield, Mass.: Merriam-Webster, 1994.

One of the best and most comprehensive descriptivist usage guides, despite its age; based on Merriam-Webster's vast linguistic corpus. Summarizes the history of an issue, competing opinions, and usage, and offers commonsense advice.

National Center on Disability and Journalism (NCDJ). "Disability Language Style Guide." http://ncdj.org/style-guide/.

Guidelines (2015) for journalists, communication professionals, and the general public, incorporating both Associated Press and NCDJ recommendations. Also available as a downloadable PDF.

*The New Fowler's Modern English Usage.* 3rd rev. ed. Edited by R. W. Burchfield. Oxford: Clarendon Press, 2004.

Expanded and updated third edition of Henry Fowler's ever-popular *Dictionary of Modern English Usage* (the 1965 urtext, q.v.). Published in 1998 and reissued in 2004 under this slightly different title. Still popular but now superseded by Jeremy Butterfield's 2015 *Fowler's Dictionary,* the current, fourth edition (q.v.).

*The New Webster's Grammar Guide.* Edited by Madeline Semmelmeyer and Donald O. Bolander. New York: Berkley Books, 1991.

A handy mass-market overview.

O'Conner, Patricia T. *Woe Is I: The Grammarphobe's Guide to Better English in Plain English.* 3rd ed. New York: Riverhead Books, 2010.

Entertaining guide to grammar for the grammar-challenged.

Partridge, Eric. *Usage and Abusage: A Guide to Good English.* New ed. Edited by Janet Whitcut. New York: W. W. Norton, 1995.

Revised edition of Partridge's 1942 classic; declares war on bad grammar, "woolliness of expression," and poor choice of vocabulary.

Pinker, Steven. *The Language Instinct: How the Mind Creates Language.* Repr. ed. New York: HarperPerennial, 2007.

Classic work on how language functions, how children learn it, how it changes, how the brain computes it, and how it evolves.

Pinker, Steven. *The Sense of Style: The Thinking Person's Guide to Writing in the 21st Century.* New York: Viking, 2014.

A sort of usage guide for the twenty-first century, by the prominent cognitive scientist, using examples of great and gruesome modern prose and avoiding the scolding tone of the classic manuals.

Pinker, Steven. *Words and Rules: The Ingredients of Language.* Repr. ed. New York: Basic Books, 2015.

Exploration of the nature of language and the human mind through the study of regular and irregular verbs.

Quirk, Randolph, et al. *A Comprehensive Grammar of the English Language.* London: Longman, 1989.

A magisterial (and expensive) grammar for linguists and other specialists.

Schwartz, Marilyn, et al. *Guidelines for Bias-Free Writing.* Bloomington: Indiana University Press, 1995.

Guidance for writing about gender, age, sexual orientation, disabilities and medical conditions, race, ethnicity, citizenship, nationality, and religion. Needs to be supplemented with more recent resources addressing newly recognized issues.

Shertzer, Margaret D. *The Elements of Grammar.* New York: Macmillan, 1986.

Handbook of the basic rules of grammar and usage, including punctuation, capitalization, the parts of the sentence, words often confused, foreign words and phrases, numbers, and signs and symbols.

Strunk, William, Jr., and E. B. White. *The Elements of Style.* 4th ed. Boston: Allyn and Bacon, 2000.

Quirky but perennially popular stylebook combining sage advice with some misguided and outmoded rules. First published by Strunk in 1918, revised by White in 1959, and still in print.

Walsh, Bill. *Lapsing into a Comma: A Curmudgeon's Guide to the Many Things That Can Go Wrong in Print—and How to Avoid Them.* New York: McGraw-Hill, 2000.

Humorous advice from the longtime *Washington Post* celebrity copyeditor, who went on to publish two equally popular works, *The Elephants of Style* and *Yes, I Could Care Less.*

Younging, Gregory. *Elements of Indigenous Style: A Guide for Writing by and about Indigenous Peoples.* Edmonton, Alberta, Canada: Brush Education, 2018.

A guide for Indigenous writers and editors and anyone creating works about Indigenous Peoples, with style principles (e.g., the capitalization of "Indigenous"), advice on culturally appropriate publishing practices, and terminology.

## 4. WRITING AND EDITING GUIDES

Adin, Richard. *The Business of Editing: Effective and Efficient Ways to Think, Work, and Prosper.* Edited by Ruth E. Thaler-Carter and Jack M. Lyon. West Valley City, Utah: Waking Lion Press, 2014.

A collection of essays on the roles, tools, processes, profits, career, and future of freelance editing; useful advice for anyone who makes a living working with words.

Barzun, Jacques. "Behind the Blue Pencil: Censorship or Creeping Creativity?" In *On Writing, Editing, and Publishing,* pp. 103–12. 2nd ed. Chicago: University of Chicago Press, 1986.

Barzun, the cultural historian and essayist, details his grievances against editors in this cautionary sermon against editorial zealotry.

Blake, Gary, and Robert W. Bly. *The Elements of Business Writing.* New York: Macmillan, 1992.

A guide to business communication from interoffice memos to lengthy proposals.

Blake, Gary, and Robert W. Bly. *The Elements of Technical Writing.* New York: Macmillan, 1993.

A guide to writing technical proposals, reports, manuals, letters, memos, and other documents.

Borel, Brooke. *The Chicago Guide to Fact-Checking.* Chicago: University of Chicago Press, 2016.

Description of best practices for fact-checking for various media, including print and online publications, magazines, books, and documentaries.

Cook, Claire Kehrwald. *Line by Line: How to Improve Your Own Writing.* Boston: Houghton Mifflin, 1985.

Information about editing techniques, grammar, and usage for writers at all levels, with hundreds of examples of original and edited sentences.

Cutts, Martin. *Oxford Guide to Plain English.* 4th ed. Oxford: Oxford University Press, 2013.

Guidelines for improving vocabulary, style, grammar, and layout in service of clear, accessible writing, by a leader of the international Plain Language Movement.

Dunham, Steve. *The Editor's Companion: An Indispensible Guide to Editing Books, Magazines, Online Publications, and More.* Blue Ash, Ohio: Writer's Digest Books, 2014.

Advice not just on grammar but also on content, focus, precise language, professional relationships, and workflow; with editing resources and checklists.

Fuller, Barbara. *How to Start a Home-Based Editorial Services Business.* Guilford, Conn.: Globe Pequot Press, 2013.

Description of the steps for setting up a home-based business, from deciding on a menu of services to marketing and developing a fee structure.

Garner, Bryan A. *Legal Writing in Plain English: A Text with Exercises.* 2nd ed. Chicago: University of Chicago Press, 2013.

Advice and practical tools for improving the writing of lawyers, judges, paralegals, law students, and legal scholars.

Germano, William. *Getting It Published: A Guide for Scholars and Anyone Else Serious about Serious Books.* 3rd ed. Chicago: University of Chicago Press, 2016.

Guidance on choosing the best path to publication and navigating the steps, with emphasis on scholarly and other serious content.

Gilead, Suzanne. *Copyediting and Proofreading for Dummies.* Hoboken, N.J.: John Wiley, 2007.

Brief, useful overview of editorial processes for occasional editors and proofreaders; insufficient depth for publishing professionals.

Ginna, Peter, ed. *What Editors Do: The Art, Craft, and Business of Book Editing.* Chicago: University of Chicago Press, 2017.

Essays about the work of editing by leading figures in book publishing, representing both large and small houses and encompassing trade, text, academic, and children's publishing.

Gross, Gerald, ed. *Editors on Editing: What Writers Need to Know about What Editors Do.* 3rd rev. ed. New York: Grove Press, 1993.

Essays on the publishing process, covering the evolution of the American editor; the ethical and moral dimensions of editing; what an editor looks for in a query letter, proposal, or manuscript; line editing; copyediting; the freelance editor; and numerous other topics.

Hacker, Diane, and Nancy Sommers. *A Writer's Reference.* 8th ed. Boston: Bedford St. Martin's, 2015.

One of the most popular all-purpose handbooks for undergraduate writers.

Hale, Constance. *Sin and Syntax: How to Craft Wicked Good Prose.* 2nd ed. New York: Three Rivers Press, 2013.

Witty advice on infusing contemporary communication—email, ads, rap lyrics—with "more spunk than Strunk."

Higham, Nicholas J. *Handbook of Writing for the Mathematical Sciences.* 2nd ed. Philadelphia: Society for Industrial and Applied Mathematics, 1999.

What mathematicians and technical editors must know about mathematical publishing and presentations, from dictionaries through style.

Hirsch, E. D., Jr. *The Philosophy of Composition.* Chicago: University of Chicago Press, 1981.

A theoretical framework for the teaching of composition as a separate discipline in schools.

Johnson-Sheehan, Richard. *Technical Communication Today.* 6th ed. New York: Pearson, 2018.

Recommended by the Society for Technical Communication to editors preparing for STC's certificate testing.

Judd, Karen. *Copyediting: A Practical Guide.* 3rd ed. Fairport, N.Y.: Axzo Press, 2001.

Basic guide to the actual work of copyediting and the world of publishing.

Kohl, John R. *The Global English Style Guide: Writing Clear, Translatable Documentation for a Global Market.* Cary, N.C.: SAS Institute, 2008.

How to communicate technical (and other) information to a global audience that includes nonnative English speakers.

Mackenzie, Janet. *The Editor's Companion.* 2nd ed. Cambridge: Cambridge University Press, 2011.

Australian take on the profession.

Mulvany, Nancy. *Indexing Books.* 2nd ed. Chicago: University of Chicago Press, 2005.

    The definitive treatment of indexing principles and practices for authors and editors.

Norton, Scott. *Developmental Editing: A Handbook for Freelancers, Authors, and Publishers.* Chicago: University of Chicago Press, 2009.

    An approach to developmental editing from shaping the proposal, finding the hook, and building the narrative or argument to executing the plan and establishing a style.

Plain English Campaign. "How to Write in Plain English." www.plainenglish.co.uk/.

    Free UK guidelines for plain language (plain English) writing; the website offers many other free resources as well.

Plain Language Action and Information Network (PLAIN). *Federal Plain Language Guidelines.* https://www.plainlanguage.gov/.

    Official US guidelines for plain language, or plain English, writing.

Plotnik, Arthur. *Spunk and Bite: A Writer's Guide to Bold, Contemporary Style.* Repr. ed. New York: Random House: 2007.

    Title is an irreverent allusion to "Strunk and White" (q.v.), whose staid advice Plotnik overturns.

Thurman, Susan. *The Everything Grammar and Style Book: All You Need to Master the Rules of Great Writing.* 2nd ed. Avon, Mass.: Adams Media, 2008.

    Another helpful handbook for grammarphobes.

Van Buren, Robert, and Mary Fran Buehler. *The Levels of Edit.* 2nd ed. JPL Publication 80-1. Pasadena, Calif.: Jet Propulsion Laboratory, California Institute of Technology, 1980.

    One of the first documents to propose a management and communication tool referred to by JPL and subsequently by many other publication offices as "levels of edit." Available as a free download at https://archive.org/details/nasa_techdoc_19800011701/.

Weiss, Edmond H. *The Elements of International English Style: A Guide to Writing Correspondence, Reports, Technical Documents, and Internet Pages for a Global Audience.* Armonk, N.Y.: M. E. Sharpe, 2005.

    Handbook for writing English-language correspondence and other documents for an international business audience, with special attention to the challenges of intercultural communication and the needs of nonnative English speakers.

Williams, Joseph M. *Style: Toward Clarity and Grace.* Chicago: University of Chicago Press, 1995.

    Guidance by a revered master teacher on the mechanics of writing and on strategies for crafting sentences and paragraphs for concise, focused, organized prose.

## 5. TOOLS FOR ON-SCREEN EDITING

Archive Publications. http://www.archivepub.co.uk/book.html.

    Offers free download of Paul Beverley's vast book of macros, *Computer Tools for Editors* (last update, October 2017), which work with various Windows versions of Word and with Word for Mac 2011. See also the instructional videos on Beverley's YouTube channel.

Copyediting-L. http://www.copyediting-l.info/.

    Offers Diana Stirling's free editing marks (2008) for PDF documents under the Resources tab.

The Editorium. http://www.editorium.com/.

Sells and supports Jack Lyon's software tools for editing in Microsoft Word. Macro packages include Editor's ToolKit Plus, FileCleaner, ListFixer, MegaReplacer, MultiMacro, NoteStripper, RazzmaTag, and WordCounter. Editor's ToolKit Plus 2018, released in March 2018, now runs on both Macintosh and PC.

Hart, Geoff. *Effective Onscreen Editing: New Tools for an Old Profession.* 3rd ed. Pointe-Claire, Quebec: Diaskeuasis Publishing, 2016.

E-book describing basic editing strategies suitable for most word processing applications, with tips and tricks to maximize productivity and effectiveness; uses Microsoft Word (2010 for Windows, 2011 for Macintosh) to illustrate.

Horler, Karin. *Google Docs for Editors.* New York: Editorial Freelancers Association, 2018.

Thirty-page pamphlet, available in print or as a downloadable PDF from Lulu (https://www.lulu.com/). Describes the features and limitations of this free collaborative tool often used for copyediting in the education, corporate, and technical sectors and in indie publishing.

Intelligent Editing. https://www.intelligentediting.com/.

Sells and supports PerfectIt Pro, a suite of customizable tools for electronic manuscript cleanup and consistency checks, for Microsoft Word. Previous versions worked in Microsoft Word 2000 through 2016 on the Windows platform (Windows 2000 through Windows 10). PerfectIt Cloud, a new Macintosh- and PC-compatible version designed to work "on any computer with Office 2016/365 and an internet connection," was released in June 2018. See also the PerfectIt instructional videos on YouTube.

Lyon, Jack M. *Microsoft Word for Publishing Professionals.* West Valley City, Utah: Editorium, 2008.

Provides instructions for using Word 2007 through 2010 for Windows.

Montgomerie, Adrienne. *Editing in Word 2016.* 2nd ed. Self-published, 2018. E-book.

A self-study course for copyeditors using MS Word 2016 (365) on Mac or Windows, with twenty-four video tutorials, twenty-four practice exercises, and a support website. Available at https://www.lulu/com/.

Powers, Hilary. *Making Word 2010 Work for You: An Editorial Guide to the Tools of the Trade.* New York: Editorial Freelancers Association, 2014.

On-demand print edition or e-book available at https://www.lulu.com/. Instructions are for Windows operating systems.

*The Proofreader's Parlour.* https://www.louiseharnbyproofreader.com/blog/.

Offers Louise Harnby's free downloadable PDF (UK-standard) proofreading stamps, along with many blog posts about creating and using stamps for proofreading and editing in Acrobat Pro and the free Acrobat Reader DC.

WordsnSync.com. http://www.wordsnsync.com/.

Sells and supports EditTools 8 for Microsoft Word (Windows only), a suite of nearly forty macros.

## 6. COPYRIGHT, PERMISSIONS, AND ETHICS

"Avoiding Plagiarism, Self-Plagiarism, and Other Questionable Writing Practices: A Guide to Ethical Writing." Rev. ed., 2015. Office of Research Integrity (ORI), US Department of

Health and Human Services. https://ori.hhs.gov/avoiding-plagiarism-self-plagiarism-and-other-questionable-writing-practices-guide-ethical-writing.

Free downloadable module on the responsible conduct of research and ethical writing, courtesy of the ORI.

"Code of Best Practices in Fair Use for Scholarly Research in Communication." 2010. Center for Media and Social Impact (CMSI), School of Communication, American University. http://archive.cmsimpact.org/fair-use/best-practices/code-best-practices-fair-use-scholarly-research-communication.

CMSI is a research center focusing on independent, documentary, entertainment, and public media.

"Copyright Term and the Public Domain in the United States." Copyright Information Center, Cornell University Library. https://copyright.cornell.edu/publicdomain.

Helpful table for assessing the copyright status of works first published in the US.

Crawford, Tad, and Kay Murray. *The Writer's Legal Guide: An Authors Guild Desk Reference.* New York: Allworth Press, 2002.

Survey by two attorneys of the legal and business questions facing anyone who writes professionally.

Creative Commons (CC). https://creativecommons.org/.

Home of the global nonprofit organization that enables sharing and reuse of creative content and knowledge through the provision of free legal tools. Includes CC licenses and facilitates putting work into the public domain at the initiative of rights holders.

DuBoff, Leonard D., and Sarah J. Tugman. *The Law (in Plain English) for Writers.* 5th ed. New York: Allworth Press, 2018.

Information for professional writers but also useful for editors: permissions, Freedom of Information Act (FOIA) requests, contracts, taxes, royalties, copyright ownership, and dispute resolution.

Legal Information Institute. https://www.law.cornell.edu/.

Nonprofit Cornell Law School resource promoting open access to law.

Peterson, Elsa. *Copyright and Permissions: What Every Writer and Editor Should Know.* New York: Editorial Freelancers Association, 2012.

Advice on the essentials of copyright for writers and editors, by a freelance permissions editor and former copyright administrator for the European American Music Distributors Corporation.

Stim, Richard. *Getting Permission: How to License and Clear Copyrighted Materials Online and Off.* 6th ed. Berkeley, Calif.: Nolo, 2016.

Advice for writers and editors concerning when permission is required, whom to ask, and when (and how much) to pay for permissions.

Strong, William S. *The Copyright Book: A Practical Guide.* 6th ed. Cambridge, Mass.: MIT Press, 2014.

Guide for writers, editors, and other creatives covering all aspects of copyright law, including internet issues, open access, peer-to-peer sharing, e-reserves, "orphan works," and decisions under the US Digital Millennium Copyright Act (DMCA). By the author of chapter 4, "Rights, Permissions, and Copyright Administration," in the authoritative *Chicago Manual of Style* (q.v.).

## 7. DESIGN AND PRODUCTION

Bringhurst, Robert. *The Elements of Typographic Style*. Version 4.0. Point Roberts, Wash.: Hartley & Marks, 2015.

Style guide for typography that combines the practical, theoretical, and historical.

Lee, Marshall. *Bookmaking: Editing, Design, Production*. 3rd ed. New York: Norton, 2004.

Introduction to editing, design, and production long regarded as a basic text for students and a comprehensive reference for experienced hands. Now somewhat updated to reflect the major changes in contemporary bookmaking and publishing.

*One Book / Five Ways: The Publishing Procedures of Five University Presses*. Repr. ed. Chicago: University of Chicago Press, 1994.

Detailed description of the publishing processes of five university presses working on the same manuscript, "No Time for Houseplants," in the 1970s. Although the production and editing procedures are outdated, this comparative exercise is still valuable for insights into different editorial approaches and decisions.

Tufte, Edward R. *The Visual Display of Quantitative Information*. 2nd ed. Cheshire, Conn.: Graphics Press, 2001.

Classic book on the design of data graphics, with detailed explanations of how to display data for precise, effective, quick analysis.

## 8. PROFESSIONAL ORGANIZATIONS, PROFESSIONAL TRAINING, AND CERTIFICATION

ACES: The Society for Editing. https://aceseditors.org/.

Founded in 1997 for editors working in news media, formerly known as the American Copy Editors Society, now expanded to include editors in other publishing channels and accordingly rebranded. Offers regional boot camps (intensive training) and an annual national conference. Try Pam Nelson's 78 interactive grammar quizzes under the Resources tab.

American Medical Writers Association (AMWA). https://www.amwa.org/.

Leading professional organization for writers, editors, and other communicators of medical information.

American Society for Indexing (ASI). https://www.asindexing.org/.

Nonprofit organization promoting professional standards in indexing, abstracting, and database construction. Sponsors chapter meetings and regional workshops.

Association of Freelance Editors, Proofreaders and Indexers (AFEPI). http://www.afepi.ie/.

Organization with membership limited to residents of Ireland and Northern Ireland. Provides a directory, email discussion group, newsletter, and other resources.

Association of Health Care Journalists (AHCJ). https://healthjournalism.org/.

Nonprofit organization dedicated to improving the quality, accuracy, and visibility of health care reporting, writing, and editing.

Bay Area Editors' Forum (BAEF). http://www.editorsforum.org/.

Association of in-house and freelance editors from various sectors of publishing. The Editorial Services Guide on the BAEF website defines terms for various editorial tasks.

Board of Editors in the Life Sciences (BELS). https://www.bels.org/.

>   Founded in 1991 to evaluate the proficiency of manuscript editors in the life sciences and to award credentials similar to those obtainable in other professions. Offers professional certification as a Board-Certified Editor (BCE).

Columbia Publishing Course. https://journalism.columbia.edu/columbia-publishing-course.

>   Previously known as the Radcliffe Publishing Course, this six-week summer program in New York prepares students for entry-level work in book, magazine, and digital publishing.

Communication Central. https://www.communication-central.com/.

>   Offers educational programs for communications professionals, including an annual Be a Better Freelancer conference and occasional half-day and one-day workshops in Rochester, N.Y., and elsewhere on request.

Copyediting.com. http://www.copyediting.com/.

>   Until late 2018, offered individual and group training through recorded audio conferences and webinars, and published a bimonthly newsletter, *Copyediting*; a free *Copyediting* blog; and a free *Copyediting Weekly* email. ACES (q.v.) has purchased copyediting.com's entire content (webinars, audio conferences, blog posts, and nearly 30 years of articles from the newsletter) and plans to make it available once again.

Council of Science Editors (CSE). https://www.councilscienceeditors.org/.

>   An international membership organization for editorial professionals publishing in the sciences; before 2000, named the Council of Biology Editors (CBE). Offers the CSE Publication Certificate Program for publishing professionals in the sciences.

Denver Publishing Institute, University of Denver. https://www.du.edu/publishinginstitute/index.html.

>   Four-week immersion course in editing and all things publishing, with guest lecturers from the publishing industry.

Editcetera. http://www.editcetera.com/.

>   San Francisco Bay Area cooperative of freelance publishing professionals (founded in 1971) providing referrals to businesses, institutions, publishers, and independent authors. Also offers workshops and distance learning programs.

Editorial Bootcamp: Professional Training for Editors, Groups, and Publishers. http://www.editorialbootcamp.com/.

>   Live workshops, webinars, recorded classes, self-paced online courses, and private training managed by master editors Laura Poole and Adrienne Montgomerie.

Editorial Freelancers Association (EFA). https://www.the-efa.org/.

>   US-based organization with chapters throughout the country. Useful, publicly accessible information on the website, including the EFA *Code of Fair Practice,* 3rd rev. ed. (2007), a free downloadable PDF; for members, a directory, job board, journal and bimonthly newsletter, and email discussion list. Offers classes, webinars, and online courses.

Editors Canada (formerly Editors' Association of Canada, EAC). https://www.editors.ca/.

>   Canada-based bilingual (English and French) organization. Website provides useful, publicly accessible information on professional editorial standards, professional ethics, and definitions of editorial skills. Organization offers conferences and professional resources and confers professional certification in four categories and a Certified Professional Editor (CPE) accreditation to applicants (including US editors) who pass tests in all four areas.

Emerson College Copyediting Certificate Program. https://www.emerson.edu/professional
-studies/certificate-programs/copyediting.

Certificate program in the Professional Studies curriculum of Boston-based Emerson College.

Freelancers Union. https://www.freelancersunion.org/.

Promotes the interests of independent workers (broadly defined) through advocacy, education, and services.

G. Raymond Chang School of Continuing Education, Ryerson University. https://ce-online
.ryerson.ca/ce/.

Online and distance learning programs in book publishing, copyediting, production, and more offered by the Toronto-based Ryerson University.

Graduate School USA. http://www.graduateschool.edu/content/ep-certificates/editorial.

Certificate of Accomplishment in Editorial Practices. Founded (1921) by the Department of Agriculture, the USDA Graduate School became the independent nonprofit Graduate School USA circa 2010.

Institute of Professional Editors Limited (IPEd). http://iped-editors.org/.

Australia-based organization. Website provides free access to *Australian Standards for Editing Practice,* 2nd ed. (2016), available as a downloadable PDF.

International Association of Business Communicators (IABC). https://www.iabc.com/.

Serves professionals in business communications, including business writing and editing.

International Society of Managing and Technical Editors (ISMTE). https://www.ismte.org/.

Organization for managing editors and technical editors on the staff of scholarly journals worldwide. Combines networking, training, and models for best practices.

New York University School of Professional Studies. https://www.sps.nyu.edu/academics
/noncredit-offerings/certificates.html.

Diploma in Copyediting, Proofreading, and Fact-Checking. Curriculum blends online asynchronous courses and in-person instruction.

Northwest Editors Guild. https://edsguild.org/.

Pacific Northwest organization connecting clients with editors, fostering community, and providing resources for professional development. Free videos and session notes of member meetings available on the website; a one-day Red Pencil Conference, held every two years, is open to all.

Poynter News University and the American Copy Editors Society. https://www.newsu.org/aces/.

Certificate in Editing. Online training program established in 2013 in collaboration with ACES: The Society for Editing (q.v.); also offers webinars and on-demand courses.

Professional Editors' Guild (PEG). https://www.editors.org.za/.

Nonprofit South African group offering a directory, resources, mentoring, and workshops.

Professional Editors Network (PEN). http://www.pensite.org/.

Small organization located in the Minneapolis area. Useful information and resources on website.

Publishers Professional Network (PPN). https://pubpronetwork.org/.

Northern California association providing educational resources and opportunities for staff and freelancers in book publishing and book-related work.

The Publishing Training Centre (PTC) at Book House. https://www.publishingtrainingcentre
.co.uk/.

Online and classroom-based courses in editing, copyright, image research, project management, book production, digital publishing, marketing, and other topics.

*Right Angels and Polo Bears.* http://blog.catchthesun.net/.

Online, video, and webinar instructions by Adrienne Montgomerie in a great range of special skills, such as editing PDFs, using Word macros, and handling numbers.

San Diego Professional Editors Network (SD/PEN). https://sdpen.com/.

Small local organization.

Simon Fraser University Continuing Studies. www.sfu.ca/continuing-studies/programs/editing-certificate/program-at-a-glance.html.

Online Editing Certificate Program. SFU in British Columbia also offers an undergraduate minor in publishing, a master's degree in publishing, and summer publishing workshops.

Society for Editors and Proofreaders (SfEP). https://www.sfep.org.uk/.

Major UK-based professional association providing information about workshops and online training and links to both free and member-only resources; free access to the SfEP blog. Training programs but no certification.

Society for Technical Communication (STC). https://www.stc.org/.

Large professional association. Sponsors publications, annual conferences, an annual salary survey, a job board, mentoring, and networking. Offers webinars, seminars, online courses, and three levels of professional certification: foundation, practitioner, and expert.

UC Berkeley Extension. http://extension.berkeley.edu/spos/edit.html.

Professional Sequence in Editing Certificate, established in 1978 by the University of California, Berkeley.

UC San Diego Extension. http://extension.ucsd.edu/courses-and-programs/copyediting-certificate.

Copyediting Certificate Program, established in the late 1990s by the University of California, San Diego.

University of Chicago Graham School of Continuing Liberal and Professional Studies. https://grahamschool.uchicago.edu/academic-programs/professional-development/editing.

Professional Development in Editing Certificate Program.

University of Washington. https://www.pce.uw.edu/certificates/editing.

Professional and Continuing Education Certificate in Editing Program.

## 9. OTHER RESOURCES

Abbreviations.com. https://www.abbreviations.com/.

Resource for thousands of abbreviations, acronyms, and initialisms organized by category.

Acronym Finder. https://www.acronymfinder.com/.

Comprehensive online dictionary of abbreviations, acronyms, and initialisms.

*AP vs Chicago.* https://apvschicago.com/.

Karen Yin's blog comparing Associated Press and Chicago styles for editors, writers, and others, with regular posts about style changes and questions.

Bartleby.com: Great Books Online. https://www.bartleby.com/.

Internet publisher of literature, reference, and verse for students and researchers, with free, "unlimited access" to out-of-copyright editions of books on the web, including Bartlett's *Familiar Quotations* (1919 edition), *The Oxford Shakespeare,* the King James Version of the Bible, and Gray's *Anatomy* (1918 edition).

British Library. https://www.bl.uk/.

Portal to the vast catalogs of the British Library.

Center for Plain Language. https://centerforplainlanguage.org/.

Website of the nonprofit Center for Plain Language, formed by volunteers from the federal Plain Language Action and Information Network (PLAIN; q.v.) to spread the plain language mission to academics, consultants, health care organizations, and the business community. Annual awards to both successful (ClearMark) and awful (Work That Failed, or WTF) examples of communication.

Copyediting-L. http://www.copyediting-l.info/.

Free email discussion board for editors, available in digest form to minimize the frequent distractions of this highly active list.

*DCBlog.* http://david-crystal.blogspot.com/.

Blog of David Crystal, a UK-based linguist, prolific author, and BBC commentator and consultant.

Editors' Association of Earth (EAE). https://www.facebook.com/groups/EditorsofEarth.

A very large (8,000+) public discussion group on Facebook "for editors . . . from anywhere." Affiliated with other Facebook groups, including the private EAE Backroom, where registered members can chat more freely among themselves about client issues and gripes.

*Encyclopaedia Britannica.* https://www.britannica.com/.

Limited free access (with ads); full access with subscription.

Google Books. https://books.google.com/.

Searchable database of Google's vast repository of scanned books from participating university libraries and publishers. Offers previews or full texts of works online, depending on permissions from copyright owners; buy and borrow options; downloadable PDFs of some public domain content.

Google Scholar. https://scholar.google.com/.

Free database of scholarly literature enabling searches across disciplines and sources: articles, theses, books, abstracts, and court opinions from academic publishers, professional societies, online repositories, universities, and websites. Not as reliable as various dedicated and subscription-based scholarly databases, but a place to start.

Grammargeddon. https://grammargeddon.com/.

Website by Karen S. Conlin and Ray Vallese, including typos found "in the wild," horrible headlines, editing humor, and posts on grammar, usage, and mechanics (GUM).

Hilderley, Sarah. "Accessible Publishing Best Practice Guidelines for Publishers." Accessible Books Consortium. http://www.accessiblebooksconsortium.org/.

Guidelines of the Accessible Books Consortium, a private/public partnership led by the World Intellectual Property Organization (WIPO), which aims to boost the number of books in accessible formats for people who are blind, have low vision, or are otherwise print disabled.

International DOI Foundation. http://www.doi.org/.

The DOI website has a lookup tool that facilitates verification of digital object identifiers, permanent locators used in citations for internet documents, which remain valid regardless of link rot.

Internet Archive. https://archive.org/.

Nonprofit digital library providing free access to its collections of digitized content—websites, software applications and games, music, movies and videos, and public domain books. Digital materials can be uploaded by the public, but most data is collected automatically by IA's web crawlers and stored in its vast archive, the Wayback Machine, where users can search for screenshots of superseded webpages and suppressed content.

KOK Edit. http://www.kokedit.com/.

The website of Katharine O'Moore-Klopf, a.k.a. EditorMom (also the name of her blog), who maintains extensive lists of professional resources at her "Copyeditors' Knowledge Base," including links to education and certification programs, business and editing tools, networking opportunities, tips for finding work, and profession-related reading.

*Language Corner, Columbia Journalism Review.* https://www.cjr.org/language_corner.

Regular feature on language, with articles, reader commentaries, and extensive archives, from *CJR,* a publication of Columbia University's Graduate School of Journalism.

*Language Log.* http://languagelog.ldc.upenn.edu/nll/.

High-level linguistic blog moderated by the University of Pennsylvania phonetician Mark Liberman, with many guest linguists, including John McWhorter, Geoffrey Nunberg, Geoff Pullum, Ben Zimmer, and Arnold Zwicky.

Library of Congress Online Catalog. https://catalog.loc.gov/.

Main access point for the Library of Congress collections.

LibWeb: Library Servers via WWW. http://www.lib-web.org/.

A portal to library catalogs around the world. "Over 8000 pages from libraries in 146 countries."

*Lingua Franca: Language and Writing in Academe.* https://www.chronicle.com/blogs/linguafranca.

A blog column in the *Chronicle of Higher Education,* with guest bloggers on various aspects of language and writing.

MacLeod, Don. *How to Find Out Anything: From Extreme Google Searches to Scouring Government Documents, a Guide to Uncovering Anything about Everyone and Everything.* Upper Saddle River, N.J.: Prentice-Hall, 2012.

Handbook for online detectives searching for anything from CEOs' salaries to police records.

Madam Grammar: Words, Language, Editing. https://madamgrammar.com/.

Website and blog of Lisa McLendon, who runs the Bremner Editing Center at the University of Kansas School of Journalism and Mass Communications.

*Merck Manual Consumer Version.* https://www.merckmanuals.com/.

Brief, basic information about medical conditions, available online for free.

National Geospatial-Intelligence Agency GEOnet Names Server. http://geonames.nga.mil/gns/html/.

NGA database of geographical names to guide the US government and to inform the public.

Perseus Digital Library. http://www.perseus.tufts.edu/hopper/.

Version 4 of the Perseus Project ("Hopper"), hosted by the Department of Classics at Tufts University, comprises digital collections of humanities resources with an emphasis on Greco-Roman classics and English Renaissance texts. Public domain content is available for free download in XML format.

Plain Language Action and Information Network (PLAIN). https://www.plainlanguage.gov/.

Website created by a volunteer group of US federal employees with the goal of "improving communications from the federal government to the public." Includes the *Federal Plain Language Guidelines;* information about the US Plain Language Writing Act, training, and tools; and links to other resources.

Project Gutenberg. http://www.gutenberg.org/.

The oldest digital library, a volunteer effort founded in 1971 to digitize and archive cultural works and to encourage the creation and distribution of e-books. Most of the items in its collection are the full texts of public domain books in long-lasting, open formats that can be used on almost any computer and in other formats (e.g., HTML, PDF, EPUB, and MOBI) as well whenever possible.

Purdue Online Writing Lab. https://owl.english.purdue.edu/owl/.

The Online Writing Lab at Purdue University (Purdue OWL) offers free writing resources, style guidelines (Chicago, APA, MLA, etc.), and instructional materials.

Quote Investigator. http://quoteinvestigator.com/.

Garson O'Toole's investigations to discover the origins of (often misattributed) quotations.

Refdesk.com. https://www.refdesk.com/.

A wormhole (or perhaps a rabbit hole) leading to many websites, information sources, and research tools.

Stebbins, Leslie F. *Finding Reliable Information Online: Adventures of an Information Sleuth.* Lanham, Md.: Rowman and Littlefield, 2015.

Advice for locating credible resources in a digital environment with terabytes of useless and unreliable information and untrustworthy search engine algorithms.

TinEye Reverse Image Search. https://www.tineye.com/.

Image search and recognition site: upload a digital image to find and identify the image if it appears online.

Unicode Consortium. http://www.unicode.org/.

Specifications and data providing the foundation for software internationalization in all major operating systems, search engines, applications, and the World Wide Web.

US Geological Survey: Gazetteer. https://geonames.usgs.gov/domestic/.

URL for the Geographic Names Information System (GNIS), developed by the US Geological Survey as the official repository of US geographical names.

USA.gov. https://www.usa.gov/.

Portal for US government information and services.

Wikipedia. https://www.wikipedia.org/.

A free, collaborative encyclopedia, one of the largest and most popular general reference sites online. A starting point for basic information, but not authoritative: anyone can write or edit an article—anonymously or under a pseudonym—except in limited cases where changes are restricted to prevent disruption or vandalism.

The World Factbook. https://www.cia.gov/library/publications/resources/the-world-factbook /index.html.

> The CIA's annual publication with information on every country—map, flag, geography, history, people, government, economy, communications, transportation, military, and transnational issues.

WorldCat. http://www.worldcat.org/.

> A project of the Online Computer Library Center (OCLC), a nonprofit global library cooperative which maintains the world's largest catalog of library content and services, allowing users to search the collections of participant libraries on the web in order to locate content.

Writers and Editors. http://www.writersandeditors.com/.

> Pat McNees's vast (overwhelming, really) index of resources for writers and editors, with links.

## 10. LAGNIAPPE

The Bulwer-Lytton Fiction Contest. http://www.bulwer-lytton.com/.

> An annual contest inspired by the prose of Edward Bulwer-Lytton, the author of a novel with the memorable opening phrase "It was a dark and stormy night . . ."

Eggcorn Database. http://eggcorns.lascribe.net/.

> Website devoted to collecting unusual English spellings that result from the misapprehension of common expressions; called eggcorns after the saying "Mighty oaks from little eggcorns [acorns] grow."

Houston, Keith. *Shady Characters: The Secret Life of Punctuation, Symbols, and Other Typographical Marks.* New York: W. W. Norton, 2014.

> Essays on historical and esoteric matters of punctuation, typography, and books. See also Houston's blog at https://www.shadycharacters.co.uk/.

Norris, Mary. *Between You and Me: Confessions of a Comma Queen.* New York: Norton, 2015.

> Amusing memoir of editorial culture at the *New Yorker* by a longtime member of the copy department.

Saller, Carol Fisher. *The Subversive Copy Editor: Advice from Chicago (or, How to Negotiate Good Relationships with Your Writers, Your Colleagues, and Yourself).* 2nd ed. Chicago: University of Chicago Press, 2016.

> Practical and humorous wisdom for surviving the occupational hazards of the editing life by maintaining good relations with authors, colleagues, and oneself. See also the entertaining and informative blog of the same title (http://www.subversivecopyeditor.com/blog/), which became "Editor's Corner," a feature of *CMOS Shop Talk,* on the *Chicago Manual of Style* (q.v.) website in 2015; both the archives and the "Editor's Corner" cross-posts are freely available.

Stamper, Kory. *Word by Word: The Secret Life of Dictionaries.* New York: Pantheon, 2017.

> The life of a lexicographer with a sense of humor and a vast vocabulary.

# Index

Page numbers with *t* or *f* refer to tables and figures, respectively. Signs and symbols are indexed under their common names; for a list of these names, see p. 244.

cities
    name forms, 227
    of publication, 279–80
city residents, terms for, 180
clauses
    adverbial, 481
    defined, 93, 482
    dependent, 93, 104–6, 359, 483
    *See also* independent clauses
cleanup. *See* file cleanup; file preparation;
        manuscript cleanup
clearing for 10s, 324, 463–64
ClearMark award, 427
clichés, 133, 410–12
clippings, 146, 228, 463
close paren, 464
close punctuation, 91, 109, 114, 464
close up, hand marking for, 45*f*, 464
closed (solid) compounds, 163, 165, 464, 476
cloud services, 40n
*CMOS Shop Talk* blog, 83
*CN* (chapter number), 464
*CO* (chapter opening), 464
COCA (Corpus of Contemporary American
        English), 77
coding. *See* markup
COHA (Corpus of Historical American English),
        77
cold (blind) proofreading, 35, 462
collecting noun phrases, 342, 482
collective ideas, 342
collective nouns, 341, 343, 373, 482
collegiate dictionaries, 69. *See also specific
        dictionaries*
colloquial terms, quotation marks for, 132
colons, 128–29
    in compound sentences, 98, 99n, 100, 103, 128
    with dependent clauses, 104, 105
    in indexes, 305
    in lists, 323
    with quotations, 128, 218, 219
    with series, 103
    for subtitles, 185
    in tables, 257
    typeface for, 137
    and wordspacing, 137
column heads, in tables, 249*f*, 255–56, 255*t*, 260,
        465
comma splices, 101–2, 122, 487
commas, 115, 117–26
    with abbreviations, 233
    with addresses, 120*t*
    with antithetical elements, 119*t*

in citation-sequence citation system, 290
for clarity, 125
and clutter, 124–25
in compound predicates, 102–3
in compound sentences, 98–99, 100, 101–2
with compound subjects, 348
with coordinate adjectives, 121–22
in dates, 120*t*
with dependent clauses, 104–6
in direct address, 90, 119*t*
and editorial judgment, 109, 125–26
hand marking for, 46*f*
with in-text citations, 275
in indexes, 305
indicating omission, 113, 114
with interdependent clauses, 119*t*
with interrupters, 110–11, 112, 113
with introductory phrases, 32, 108–9
with *Jr., Sr.,* 174
in lists, 128, 323
with nonrestrictive appositives, 107, 136
in numerals, 192, 256
with other punctuation marks, 135–36
principal uses, 118–20*t*
with quotations, 218
with relative clauses, 107
vs. semicolons, 127
with sentence adverb, 32, 108n, 118*t*
serial, 52, 115, 117, 136
with speaker's tag, 94, 97, 116, 120*t*
spousal, 111, 477
with tag questions, 116*t*
with transitional adverbs, 32, 108n, 118*t*
typeface for, 137
when to omit, 122–24
and wordspacing, 137
comments feature, 56–57, 57*f*, 58, 464
common nouns, 153–56, 482
communications manager. *See* editorial
        coordinator's role
comparatives, 387–88
compare and contrast organization, 400
*compare with, compare to,* 392–93
comparison proofing, 464
comparisons, 384–85, 394
*complement, compliment,* 353–54
complements (grammatical term), 482
*compose, comprise,* 354
compositor, 464
compound forms, 163–71
    abbreviations in, 236, 239–40
    adjectives, 130–31, 165–68, 236, 482
    adverbs, 168–69

|  |  |
|---|---|
| Copyeditor: | Juliana Froggatt |
| Proofreaders: | Anne Canright and Barbara Armentrout |
| Designer: | Barbara Haines |
| Compositors: | Barbara Haines and BookMatters, Berkeley |
| Text: | Minion Pro and Benton Gothic |
| Display: | Minion Pro |
| Printer and Binder: | Sheridan Books, Inc. |